FROM HOLLYWOOD

Constance Talmadge as "The Mountain Girl" in Griffith's INTOLERANCE.
Elmer Clifton as "The Rhapsode" in the background

FROM HOLLYWOOD

The Careers of 15 Great American Stars

DeWitt Bodeen

SOUTH BRUNSWICK AND NEW YORK: A. S. BARNES AND COMPANY
LONDON: THE TANTIVY PRESS

© 1976 by A. S. Barnes and Co., Inc.

A. S. Barnes and Co., Inc.
Cranbury, New Jersey 08512

The Tantivy Press
108 New Bond Street
London W1Y OQX, England

Library of Congress Cataloging in Publication Data

Bodeen, DeWitt.
  From Hollywood: the careers of 15 great American
stars.

  CONTENTS: Silents only: Theda Bara. Marguerite
Clark. Geraldine Farrar. Harold Lockwood and May
Allison. Wallace Reid. Anita Stewart. [etc.]
  1. Moving-picture actors and actresses—United States
—Biography. I. Title.
PN1998.A2B62 1975   791.43'028'0922 [B]   73-15158
ISBN 0-498-01346-4

SBN 0-904208-15-X (U.K.)

PRINTED IN THE UNITED STATES OF AMERICA

CONTENTS

ALSO BY DEWITT BODEEN:

Ladies of the Footlights
Romances by Emma
Who Wrote the Movie? (Associate Editor)
"A Glass of Water" (Translation from the French in the book *Camille and Other Well-Made Plays*)
The Films of Cecil B. DeMille (In collaboration with Gene Ringgold)
The Films of Maurice Chevalier (In collaboration with Gene Ringgold)
13 Castle Walk, a novel about Hollywood, then and now

ACKNOWLEDGEMENTS

These screen career stories first appeared in shorter and somewhat different forms in two American film magazines, "Films in Review" and "Screen Facts," and in one English publication, "Focus on Film." They are herewith printed in revised, corrected, and, in some cases, up-dated versions.

I am grateful to Henry Hart and Charles Phillips Reilly, the former and present editors for "Films in Review"; to Alan G. Barbour, editor of "Screen Facts"; and to Allen Eyles, editor of "Focus on Film," for permission to use those pieces as a basis for revising them into their new form and thus to issue them, through the services of Julien Yoseloff, in two volumes.

I am also grateful to librarian Mrs. Mildred Simpson and the entire staff of the Margaret Herrick Library at the Academy of Motion Picture Arts and Sciences in Hollywood for their assistance in my first researching of these pieces; and likewise I wish to acknowledge the help of Miss Brenda Davies and the staff at the library of the British Film Institute in London, who so kindly lent me their resources for double-checking and bringing up-to-date these articles. I also acknowledge gratefully the help of Jacobo Brender, of Caracas.

And, finally, I am most appreciative of the help of Peter Cowie, who, as editor for this book, has been of invaluable aid and encouragement to me.

PHOTO ACKNOWLEDGEMENTS

The author acknowledges his gratitude to the following organisations and individuals for the stills which illustrate this text:

The Academy of Motion Picture Arts and Sciences
(Robert Cushman, still dept.)
The British Film Institute
William C. Brooks (Pebble Beach, CA)
The Cinema Bookshop (London)
The Movie Memorabilia Shop of Hollywood
(Kenneth G. Lawrence)
Barrie Pattison (London)
Gene Ringgold (Hollywood, CA)
Anthony Slide (London)
Edna May Sobie (London)

FROM HOLLYWOOD

1
THEDA BARA

Theda Bara is an outstanding exception to the general rule that publicity-manufactured stars are never *really* accepted by the public.

She was the first movie star to be so foisted on audiences and the exceptionally well-planned publicity campaign for her first picture, *A Fool There Was,* not only made her a top star but lifted the production company that engineered the *coup* to an important position on the Hollywood map. Without Theda Bara the Fox Film Corporation would not have gained the eminence in the motion picture industry it did.

Frank Powell, the director of *A Fool There Was*, is generally credited with creating the name "Theda Bara" for his star, but the background for the personality which that film exploited was the invention of wheeling-dealing press-agents, Johnny Goldfrap and Al Selig.

According to the stories they issued to a still innocent American public, "Theda" was an anagram of "death" and "Bara" was "Arab" spelled backwards, and the bearer of the name had been born on an oasis in the Sahara in the shadow of the Sphinx. She was, Goldfrap and Selig alleged, the daughter of an Arabian princess and Giuseppe Bara, an "illustrious Italian sculptor and painter." Some of the G & S publicity had the princess-mother die soon after giving birth to the child fated to become "a half-Arabian embodiment of wicked delight." In other G & S stories the mother fled the oasis for triumphs on the European stage, leaving the "occult-wise" infant to be raised by her "Garden of Allah" father. All the G & S stories had the father teach her "languages and painting," and had her do "much poetic writing, very little of which has been published." Ultimately, according to G & S, her father sent her to Europe to study acting, and she made her *début* in England "playing classic drama." Subsequently, she "joined Jane Hading's company in Paris, the Grand Guignol Theatre, the Gymnase, and the Théâtre Antoine."

All this was impressive and sufficiently vague for it to go uncontested. Moreover, the film public of the time *wanted* an image representing the worst in women to be dubious, just as it wanted the image of the virtuous *ingénues* to be uplifting — e.g., Mary Pickford ("Our Mary" and "America's Sweetheart") and Lillian Gish ("The Duse of the Silver Screen").

Movie audiences were eager, for a few years, to accept Theda Bara as G & S presented her — as "The Devil's Maidservant," "Purgatory's Ivory Angel,"

13

Theda Bara with her Russian wolfhound

"Serpent of the Nile," "The Vampire," and finally, "The Vamp." Incidentally, Theda Bara is one of the very few film stars whose screen image gave new meaning to a word. Today's dictionaries define "vamp" as "a woman who uses her attractions to win passionate love and to bring her lover to a debased, humiliated, or impoverished condition," and use similar phrases in defining one of the meanings of "vampire."

In her later years Miss Bara confessed that she and her sister Lori used to read the G & S concoctions at breakfast and roar with laughter. "Some of them were so wild," said Miss Bara, "we didn't think they would be printed, or that, if they were printed, they would be believed. But they were printed, all right, and they were believed, too, I suppose. The wildest press stories were the most successful ones. A lot of young ex-newspapermen wrote them. I think for a while I kept a whole publicity staff working nights."

Each G & S morsel the public hungrily devoured caused the next one to be more fantastic. One quoted a bit of ancient abracadabra "written on the stone walls of a tomb near Thebes" which prophesied the advent of Theda Bara to this terrestrial plane: "I, Rhames, priest of Set, tell you this: She shall seem a snake to most men; she shall lead them to sin, and to their destruction. Yet she shall not be so. She shall be good and virtuous, and kind of heart; but she shall not seem so to most men. For she shall not be that which she appears. She shall be called — Theta (the Greek letter was used)."

Needless to say, the real beginnings of Theda Bara had none of this panoply of scarlet and purple dust and hot air. They were, in fact, bourgeois and very respectable.

She was born Theodosia Goodman, in Cincinnati, Ohio, on July 29 of, probably, 1890, although certain Cincinnati ladies insist the year was earlier; some even hint nearer 1880. She never revealed her age, believing, like Louella O. Parsons, that a woman who will tell her real age will tell anything.

Her father was a successful Jewish tailor, and her mother, *née* Pauline Louise Françoise de Coppet, was an intelligent and well-bred Swiss of French descent. She called her daughter Theodosia after the beautiful but tragically destined daughter of Aaron Burr. "Theda" is a diminutive of Theodosia, and the name "Bara" of the movie years derives from the middle name of Mrs. Goodman's Swiss father: François Baranger de Coppet.

There were three children: a son, Marque, the first born; Theodosia; and a younger daughter, Lori.*

As a young girl, Theda was blonde and every night prayed she would grow up to be a tall lady with black hair (the black hair, at least, became a fact). Another of her childhood hopes: to be an actress.

She began acting by reciting in public such oratorical gems as "The Dirty-Faced Brat" and "Which Shall It Be?" Even the school principal, it was said, removed his spectacles on hearing that latter recitation in order to wipe the tears from his eyes.

---

*After Theda's phenomenal success the entire Goodman family took the name of Bara. The brother worked in Newport, Rhode Island, the greater part of his life and to his widow (Alma M. Bara) Theda left a small sum, as did Lori. The latter never married and always signed herself Lori Mary de Coppet Bara. She and Theda were very close, and Lori inherited the major part of Theda's estate. When Lori died, she left half of her $400,000 estate to the Motion Picture Relief Fund in Theda's name, and divided most of the other half among children's hospitals. For two years before her death in August, 1965, Lori lived in Marycrest Manor, a Catholic residence home in Culver City.

Her beginnings as a professional actress are on the vague side. She was using the stage name of Theodosia de Coppet when she was in the cast of Molnar's "The Devil," which Henry W. Savage produced at the Garden Theatre on Broadway in 1908 (she played Mme. Schleswig). Because the play was not copyrighted in the United States, two companies played "The Devil" on Broadway that season: one starred George Arliss; the other, Edwin Stevens. Theodosia de Coppet was in the Stevens production, and played the entire Broadway engagement, but did not go out on the tour.

Hedda Hopper says in "From Under My Hat," her autobiography, that she first met Theda when they were both members of the travelling company of "The Quaker Girl," a popular musical starring DeWolf Hopper. Wrote Mrs. Hopper: "Theodosia played a Frenchwoman, with an accent that wouldn't fool a five-year-old. Oh, brother!"

By that time Theodosia de Coppet had become known in theatrical circles as a very ambitious actress who was adept in *femme fatale* roles, and dabbled in spiritualism. She later avowed that it was her spirit contact who advised her to try her luck in "the shadow world," as the movies were called in certain circles. She didn't have much luck at first.

She was in her twenty-fifth year and was concerned about her future when she encountered Frank Powell, a film director who had learned his craft from Griffith at Biograph and who was one of the directors William Fox had hired to turn out features for his distributing firm (Box Office Attractions, Inc.).

Powell's first picture for Fox was a film adaptation of *A Fool There Was*, a popular play of the time which Porter Emerson Browne had adapted from Kipling's poem, "The Vampire," and he was looking for an actress who could

Theda Bara in CLEOPATRA

personify the deadly female Kipling called "a rag, a bone, and a hank of hair." Powell had seriously considered both Valeska Suratt and Madlaine Traverse for the part, and had almost decided to give it to Virginia Pearson, who had played it on stage, when Theodosia de Coppet fortuitously came into his office looking for work.

Powell was then in the midst of shooting a picture for Pathé, *The Stain,* and he took Theodosia to Lake Ronkonkomo, Long Island, where he was doing location work, and placed her in the background far from the camera. He wanted to observe her reactions to his direction, but didn't want her identified as an extra.

By the time the company returned to Manhattan he had made up his mind and offered her the coveted lead. Fox was as impressed as Powell when he saw the uncut rushes, and ordered a big press build-up for the actress they decided to call Theda Bara.

Miss Bara always denied she had ever been an extra. "I started out as a star," she liked to say, "and remained a star." But Powell's story has the ring of truth, and has generally been accepted ever since Terry Ramsaye included it in his "A Million and One Nights."

Miss Bara also claimed that when playing a vampire was first broached to her, she demurred. I doubt it, for she was then in her mid-twenties, and real success in the theatre had eluded her. *A Fool There Was* offered her a lead role on the screen and a contract that, if she succeeded as a star, could make her wealthy. She also claimed that when she finally decided to accept the role she also determined to apply herself diligently for five years and then retire and live on the loot.

This is exactly what she did.

A Fool There Was established her overnight as an authentic star. Press-agented she may have been, but the public paid to see the commodity that was publicised. *A Fool There Was* is only one of Theda Bara's thirty-nine Fox films to survive intact, and although contemporary audiences laugh at its satanic heroine and her evil power over her victims, the audiences that saw it in 1915 were enthralled.

The Vamp character was imitated at once and the actresses Powell had considered and rejected for the role in *A Fool There Was* — Suratt, Traverse, Pearson — were all signed by Fox as second-string vamps. Louise Glaum, Dorothy Dalton, Olga Petrova, and many another talented actress leapt into the limelight at other studios as hell-bent vamps, and established stars like Clara Kimball Young and Anita Stewart took at least one fling at vamping (the former in *Lola* and the latter in *The Yellow Typhoon*).

Even before *A Fool There Was* had opened, William Fox, anticipating the fabulous grosses, was fretting because he had no vehicle in which his new star could vamp again. In desperation he decided to feature her in a heavy role in a film dramatisation of Tolstoy's *The Kreutzer Sonata*, starring Nance O'Neil.

Of this Miss Bara said later: "When I found myself cast in my second picture in support of an artist, I felt only an ambition to do as well as she did. When the picture was released there were indications that I had done well. Exhibitors wrote me that my name had been the drawing feature. It is a name, therefore, that has some emotional value in a world in which romance is a food all hearts crave."

By the time *Kreutzer Sonata* was ready for release, Fox had been able, via the profits from *A Fool There Was*, to incorporate his own producing company, and was more avid than before to find story properties for the actress whom publicity and the public had made a money-making star.

Miss Bara didn't object to being treated like a workhorse, but she did complain about the restrictions in her contract which affected her personal life. In an effort to keep the public's illusion of her vamp personality inviolate, her contract required that she not be seen in public. She was too weary after a day's work to gad about, but she had moved her parents, brother, and sister to Manhattan and occasionally wanted to get out of the West End Avenue apartment. She fussed when Fox forbade her to take morning walks in Central Park because people had begun to recognise her.

Her vamping days were at their height when Fox decided to film her pictures in California, and she decided to live there. On the way West the party paused in Chicago and a press reception was staged in her suite at the Blackstone Hotel. Louella O. Parsons, then an aspiring Chicago journalist, has described it in her autobiography, "The Gay Illiterate":

"The day was hotter than the proverbial hinges of the proverbial hot spot. We dripped little beads of perspiration in anticipation as we waited in an anteroom in Theda's hotel suite at the Blackstone for the summons to the 'presence.'

"Hollander (the 'Daily News') had just voiced the opinion that it was so hot The Vamp had probably melted into her own eyelash goo when the press agent appeared in our midst and said: Miss Bara will be a moment longer. She is not yet acclimated to this Northern weather!'

"No more were the words out of his mouth than the door of an adjoining room began to open noiselessly and seemingly without the aid of human hands — and there, exposed in unbelievable splendor, sat the Queen of the Sirens, draped to the teeth in magnificent furs.

"'Miss Bara,' declaimed the press agent in the manner of a circus barker, 'was born in the shadow of the Sphinx, you know. It is very, very hot there, and she is cold!'"

Miss Bara later confessed she had hardly been able to sustain the gag and that the instant the last of the press was gone she had torn off the stifling furs and had thrown open all the windows, crying for air.

As her fame mounted, and her bank account grew, she requested, and then demanded, roles other than those of vamps. So Fox grumpily gave her the lead sister role in his screen version of *The Two Orphans* (later played by Lillian Gish in Griffith's *Orphans of the Storm*).

The Two Orphans was a "special," and the name of Theda Bara added to its box-office lure. To assuage the public's disappointment because their vamp had suddenly gone nobly *ingénue*-ish, Fox saw to it that she was billed as "Destiny's Dark Angel" in her follow-up picture, which was called *Sin*.

An examination of Miss Bara's thirty-nine Fox films will reveal how foxy her producer was. Half provided her with parts that were more sympathetic than vampirish. The fact was, after her vampire image had been established and accepted, Miss Bara's audiences read evil meanings into her most innocent actions.

Ironically, when she was allowed to write a story for herself, *The Soul of*

Theda Bara in the title role of CARMEN

Buddha, she conceived a cunning little Oriental vamp who causes all kinds of havoc in men's souls. Miss Bara well knew that her public wanted her to sneer at virtue, array herself in the scantiest of costly attire, and lure heroes and their brothers and fathers and sons to destruction.

What Miss Bara was actually doing has been well stated by Lloyd Morris in his excellent book, "Not So Long Ago": "...Because of her, the 'baby-vamp' became a problem to parents and a nocturnal hazard to collegians. In millions of American homes the fumes of incense came to signify, not the presence of mosquitoes, but the anticipated arrival of a male caller. The undershot 'Bara-look' was either an ominous hint of danger, or a half-explicit promise of pleasure, depending upon the degree of emancipation achieved by the female who practised it. For a while, feminine ambulation was slithery, and feminine posture languorous. An exotic pallor was cultivated by the most robust; necklines dropped alarmingly; and in a sudden wave of black that crossed the land, nubile girlhood appeared to be adopting universal mourning. For Miss Bara made voluptuousness a common American commodity as accessible as chewing gum. And when this had been done, the old order was exposed to successful assault.''

Through a concatenation of irrelevant circumstances, Fox scheduled for her eighth vehicle the Raoul Walsh production of *Carmen*. He hoped to open it *before* the DeMille-Lasky version starring Geraldine Farrar, but both of these *Carmens* were released simultaneously, and both received double-column reviews. Miss Bara's interpretation was praised, but the golden apple went to diva Farrar. Said "Motion Picture News" of Bara's Carmen: "It has all the vampire's fierceness when aroused, but a depth of will power and of mystery that a vampire could never have.''

The very next year (1916) there were two simultaneously released features based upon Shakespeare's *Romeo and Juliet*. Metro's expensive production co-starred Francis X. Bushman and Beverly Bayne, and William Fox, ever the showman, rushed through a big production with Miss Bara as the star-crossed daughter of the Capulets. This time both pictures were praised equally, and Bara's Juliet was called "a signal triumph of versatility." Like the two *Carmens,* the two *Romeo and Juliets* made nothing but money.

J. Gordon Edwards, the grandfather of today's Blake Edwards, directed Miss Bara in *Romeo and Juliet* and twenty-two of her other Fox features. Said Miss Bara: "J. Gordon Edwards was kind and considerate and the nicest director I ever had. Some directors are wonderful. They give you such funny advice on manners and deportment. One time I asked my director about a certain scene. 'Do I repulse the advances of this man or do I lead him on?' I asked. The director was stumped. He hadn't an idea of what to do. Finally he hit upon a lively answer. 'Oh, just keep the audience guessing,' he said.''

Cleopatra, which was released late in 1917, was one of Miss Bara's biggest money-makers. The exteriors were filmed in California, but part of it was shot in the East. It was road-shown in its initial engagements, and a symphony orchestra, supplemented in each city by the best local musicians, travelled with the print.

By 1919 Miss Bara was growing weary and admitting she didn't think much of the pictures she had made. "Always," she cried, "I have been a charlatan, a register of human emotions... When transposed to the movies magnificent tragedies, such as *La gioconda,* become painfully inarticulate attempts.''

But she praised her cameramen. "My cameraman is my artistic speedometer,'' she said. "If he likes a scene, I know it's good; if he shakes his head I sometimes cry a little because I am so tired, but I always do a re-take.''

She was nearing her thirtieth year when she learned that Fox was planning to film a romance called *Kathleen Mavourneen;* she demanded the title role in it, that of a sweet Irish colleen. She got it, and was given a new director, Charles J. Brabin. The mere sight of him fascinated her.

Brabin was a strong, tall man with a hawk-like nose whose virile appearance belied a gentle, artistic nature. Born in Liverpool, he had received a good education before emigrating to the United States, and, on his arrival here, had worked at anything. For a time he was a hotel clerk and a travelling salesman. Somehow, in the mysterious way actors are born, he landed in the cast of George Ade's *The College Widow*, with which he remained for two seasons.

Then, in addition to other acting jobs, he began getting stage-managing ones.

In 1908 he entered movies by playing Abraham Lincoln in an Edison film. A Mr. Plimpton, then manager of Edison production, was impressed by his knowledge and taste, and so made him the Edison stage manager, which then meant that he was in charge of props and the making of sets. Two years later he got a chance to direct, and continued as a film director until his retirement in 1938.

Many of his pictures were distinguished by their pictorial beauty. Among his most important: Universal's *Driven* (1922), the best of the Southern mountaineer films except for *Tol'able David;* Goldwyn's *Six Days,* with Corinne Griffith (1923); First National's *So Big,* with Colleen Moore (1925); Universal's *Stella Maris,* with Mary Philbin (1926); M-G-M's *The Bridge of San Luis Rey* (1929); M-G-M's *Call of the Flesh*, with Ramon Novarro (1930). Also, he had been the first choice as director for *Ben Hur* at M-G-M, but that first attempt at production was ill-fated, and he suffered replacement by Fred Niblo.

Said Miss Bara of Brabin: "His mental brilliance was not the first attractive quality I noticed about him. It was the way he walked. Like an Indian. Or, as if he wore seven-league boots. He stalked in and in two strides crossed the room. It still fascinates me to sit and watch him approach me."

Practically every critic agreed that Miss Bara was miscast in the title role of *Kathleen Mavourneen*, but no critic anticipated that the film would cause riots. Hibernian societies, aroused because a Jewess had been chosen to interpret the heroine typifying the Irish nation, sent their members to stone the outside of theatres in which the picture played, and to throw stink bombs inside them.

None of this concerned Miss Bara in the least.

Brabin then directed her in an adaptation of a Belasco stage hit, *"La belle russe,"* after which she had only one more film to do to complete her long-term Fox contract. This was *Lure of Ambition*, the last serious vamp role she recorded on celluloid. Although Brabin and she had become fast friends, he did not direct her final Fox effort. Edmund Lawrence directed *Lure of Ambition*.

"My health was bad and I needed a rest," Miss Bara explained later. "I had been getting wretched stories and studio life was beginning to get on my nerves. The inefficiency is appalling. Nothing was ever ready and I stopped reporting for work in the morning. We would wait for hours and hours until some carpenter had corrected a mistake in the setting. And all about you there is a grinding and a pounding. The mechanical staff have a way of blaming all the delays on the star, who has no comeback because she can't tell tales on men who can't afford to lose a day's wages. Mr. Fox seldom came to the studio — he was busy at the home office. I only saw him a few times a year. Directors spend a great deal of money on unimportant things and then economize in small ways that prove expensive in the end. It used to hurt me to see money wasted."

At this time Olga Petrova (Muriel Harding) interviewed Miss Bara for the March-April, 1920 issue of "Shadowland." Both women were intelligent, witty, and on the defensive. When Mme. Petrova inquired, "Why did you leave Mr. Fox?" Miss Bara smiled sweetly and asked: "Why did you leave

Theda Bara, between takes in MADAME DUBARRY, with her favourite director, J. Gordon Edwards

Metro?'' Mme. Petrova confessed: "I had expected to find an opulent siren with whom I might discuss the decadence of the times without a blush, but here was a little blue mouse whose gentle ears I hesitated to shock with even an allusion to any one so fantastically sinful as the screen would have us believe Theda Bara's heroines to be. The situation was interesting pathologically.''

Broadway producer A. H. Woods then persuaded Miss Bara to star on the stage for him, and she chose for her return to the footlights a melodrama by George V. Hobart and John Willard titled "The Blue Flame." It was the kind of incredible luridity that road audiences then doted on, and during its out-of-town try-outs every performance was a sell-out. Woods offered Miss Bara every concession, including a private railroad car sumptuously furnished, such as Sarah Bernhardt had enjoyed, if she would remain on the road with the play. But Miss Bara believed she could conquer Broadway in "The Blue Flame." "I chose it because it gave me an opportunity to play the sort of part the public wants to see me play," she later explained.

She was absolutely right, but unfortunately her public did not reside in Manhattan. Some of the reviews of "The Blue Flame" are so honest they're funny. Said Heywood Broun in the "Tribune": "At the end of the third act Miss Bara said that God had been very kind to her. Probably she referred to the fact that at no time during the evening did the earth open and swallow up the authors, the star and all the company. However, it has often been re-marked that the patience of Heaven is infinite. Still, as we remember it, Jonah was eaten by a whale for much less.''

FPA punned in his column in the same paper: ''Perhaps *The Blue Flame* is not a perfect title for Miss Bara's play. Why not: *Tenting on the Old Vamp Ground?''*

''The Blue Flame'' was mercifully extinguished after forty-eight perfor-mances.

Some months later, in 1921, Miss Bara motored to Connecticut with Charles Brabin and married him. ''Neither of us had ever been on time in our lives,'' reminisced Miss Bara. ''So I thought, 'I'll shampoo my hair.' I did. And then bless you if the man wasn't actually punctual. I had to stick up my wet hair under my picture hat, and sneezed throughout the ceremony.''

The Vampire of Vampires was thoroughly content being Mrs. Charles Brabin until, in 1923, while vacationing in a summer house they owned on the Bay of Fundy, the Brabins decided to film Longfellow's ''Evangeline'' in its original locale, despite the fact that Miriam Cooper had starred in a successful film version of ''Evangeline'' for Fox in 1919. Said ''Variety'': ''Theda is said to hold the impression she can show Miriam a few wrinkles about playing the Evangeline role, and incidentally prove to her former employer, Fox, there are some hefty kicks left in the Bara draw, even though indications are not lacking that her power at the box-office has waned.''

The Brabins did not do a film version of ''Evangeline.'' Lewis J. Selznick then announced that Theda Bara would return to the screen under his au-spices in *The Common Law*. But nothing came of that, either.

She *did* return to the screen, however, in 1925 as the star of a film adaptation of Louis J. Anspacher's successful play, *The Unchastened Woman,* which Chadwick Pictures made. It was a domestic comedy drama about a wife who vamps to save her marriage, and it was not successful.

Then Hal Roach persuaded her to make a comedy, *Madame Mystery*, in which The Vamp would be kidded. Miss Bara approached this film with genuine delight, saying: ''Vamping requires no artistry whatever. For me, henceforth, high comedy!''

But *Madame Mystery* turned out to be only hysterical slapstick.

The Brabins were then living in a showplace in the fashionable West Adams district of Los Angeles. They sold it and bought a charming home on Alpine Drive in Beverly Hills, which they filled with tasteful, genuine antiques. When they weren't travelling in Europe, Miss Bara demonstrated very real ability as a cook. Once when a star in a play — probably Tallulah Bankhead in George Kelly's ''Reflected Glory'' — was ordering a dinner that made the audience's mouth water, George Cukor is reported to have whispered to his theatre companion, Ethel Barrymore: ''Ah, pot luck at Theda Bara's!''

But she continued to delude herself with hopes for a success as a star on the legitimate stage, and tried at least two ventures in vaudeville with playlets; appeared in an Oakland California, production of Ernest Vajda's charming sex comedy, ''Fata Morgana''; and played the heroine, Ruby Chepstow, of ''Bella Donna'' on the stage in Beverly Hills. Said Herb Sterne in ''Rob Wagner's Script'': ''Miss Bara has a lovely voice, and a walk that suggests a prowl, which she uses effectively. She manages to imbue the character with the black poppy fragrance it requires. On her entrance she received five minutes of solid audience applause, in which actor John T. Murray, then onstage, joined. It seemed in doubtful taste to flick on the house lights; the actress didn't require the build-up.''

It's difficult to fathom why she went on subjecting herself to this ordeal of stage performances. She certainly didn't need the money, and she had proved herself once; that day was long gone, a memory, and she wanted more than memory. Her husband adored her, and on opening nights he went around asking quietly of critics and reviewers, ''Be kind, please.''

There are rumours of a few other guest appearances in stock in the East, but her name meant nothing to the Depression generation, and she finally gave up, finding she could be very happy as just Mrs. Charles Brabin.

The vamp role continued to be a screen staple, but it had had its fullest bloom in the Bara personality. Fox thought he had a great successor to her in Betty Blythe, and her *Queen of Sheba* was a hit. But he and Miss Blythe had personal differences, and she, rather than sign a contract with him, left Hollywood with her newly married husband, Paul Scardon, to make pictures in England and on the Continent. Fox tried a re-make of *A Fool There Was* with Estelle Taylor in 1922 — unsuccessfully. The *coup de grâce* was given the vamp image by Mae West. In a decade and a half movie audiences had progressed from secret revelry in the wickedness of sex to open amusement over an honest and humourous presentation of it.

Nita Naldi, who had some success playing out-and-out vamp roles in the Bara style, once said of herself and other silent stars, to explain the lure that lay in their ''soulful'' eyes: ''We were all blind as bats. Theda Bara couldn't see a foot ahead of her, and poor Rudy [Valentino] groped his way through many a love scene, and I really mean groped.''

Miss Bara *was* myopic. But she was as careful as George Arliss in knowing exactly where every piece of furniture and props was, and she rehearsed every scene with meticulous care before it was shot. As a result, although she could not see the chalk lines which marked the limits of the camera's vision, she never stepped outside them.

Love deepened between Brabin and her. I have seen birthday cards on which Miss Bara wrote such things as ''To my darling Mouchey-Mou — from your Wiffle Tree.'' He was just as uninhibited in his display of affection. It is one of life's little ironies that the screen's greatest homewrecker enjoyed in real life one of the few really happy marriages known to Hollywood.

Miss Bara once visited Manhattan with the manuscript of a book she had titled ''What Women Never Tell,'' but so far as I know, she did not find a publisher, although I've been told the script was accepted for newspaper syndication. In the early Fifties she sold the rights to her life story to Jerry Wald at Columbia, and it was to have formed the basis for a musical tentatively and variously called *The Vamp* and *The Great Vampire*. But it has never been filmed.

With a wry smile Miss Bara once said of the years when she was the Vamp of Vamps: ''To understand those days you must consider that people believed what they saw on the screen. Nobody had destroyed the grand illusion. Audiences thought the stars were just the way they saw them. Why, women kicked my photographs as they went into the theatres where my pictures were playing, and once on the streets of New York a woman called the police because her child spoke to me."

I remember once when she visited a Hollywood friend of mine for cocktails. Her chauffeur brought her in the Brabin town car, and was instructed to call for her one hour hence. Promptly, at five past the hour she peered at her diamond-studded wristwatch through her diamond-rimmed *lorgnette,* and said, "Theda Bara waits for no man." A taxi was called, and it arrived simultaneously with her chauffeur tardily at the wheel of her town car. Miss Bara brushed past the chauffeur without so much as a glance, got into the cab, and the town car followed the taxi to her home in Beverly Hills.

There were, however, events that waited which could not be so imperiously dismissed.

In February, 1955, she was admitted to the California Lutheran Hospital to be treated for cancer of the abdomen. She soon lapsed into a coma, but did not die until April 7. Charles Brabin survived her for only a little more than two years.

D. W. Griffith once remarked that he was a great admirer of the talents of both Theda Bara and Pearl White, and that neither should have had to abandon her career as soon as she did. "No actress, not even Bernhardt," he declared, "could have saved some of the vehicles handed Miss Bara."

THEDA BARA FILMOGRAPHY

A FOOL THERE WAS (1915). Dramatic tragedy; as "The Vampire." *Dir./Sc:* Frank Powell (from the play by Porter Emerson Browne, which had been inspired by Rudyard Kipling's poem, "The Vampire"). *With* Edward José, May Allison, Clifford Bruce, Mabel Fremyear, Victor Benoit, Runa Hodges. (Refilmed, 1922, by Fox, starring Estelle Taylor in the Bara role). *Prod:* Box Office Attraction Co., subsequently copyrighted by the William Fox Vaudeville Co. (Fox Film Corporation). 6 reels. (Compare listing in May Allison filmography)

KREUTZER SONATA (1915). Russian tragedy, as Esther Rusoff, wicked adultress murdered by the sister she has betrayed. *Dir./Sc:* Herbert Brenon (founded on the theme of Jacob P. Gordon's version of Leo Tolstoy's play). *With* Nance O'Neil, William E. Shay. (Miss Bara was billed as "The Woman of 1000 Faces.") *Prod:* Fox Film Corporation. 5309 ft.

THE CLEMENCEAU CASE (AKA, GB *Infidelity) (1915).* Domestic tragedy; as a wicked wife who is slain by the husband she has wronged. *Dir./Sc.:* Herbert Brenon (from a play by Martha Woodrow, based upon a novel by Alexandre Dumas). *With* William E. Shay, Stuart Holmes, Jane Lee, Mrs. Cecil Raleigh. (Miss Bara's first real star billing, with her name in large letters above the title) *Prod:* Fox Film Corporation. 5900 ft.

THE DEVIL'S DAUGHTER (1915). Dramatic tragedy; as the wicked Cavalina, known as "La Gioconda." *Dir./Sc:* Frank Powell (ad. by Garfield Thompson, from D'Annunzio's play "La gioconda," as translated by Joseph H. Trant). *With* Paul Doucet, Victor Benoit, Robert Wayne, Jane Lee, Doris Haywood, Jane Miller. (Working title: *The Vampire)* Exteriors filmed in Florida. *Prod:* Fox Film Corporation. 4800 ft.

LADY AUDLEY'S SECRET (AKA, GB *Secrets of Society)* (1915). Dramatic tragedy; as the evil Lady Audley, whose secret is the murder she has done. *Dir:* Marshall Farnum. *Sc:* Mary Asquith (from the novel and play by Miss M. E. Braddon). *With* Clifford Bruce, William Riley Hatch, Stephen Gratten, Warner Richmond. (Miss Bara was billed as "The most wickedly beautiful face in the entire world.") *Prod:* Fox Film Corporation. 5000 ft.

THE TWO ORPHANS (1915). Romance of two beautiful orphan sisters in Old France; as Henriette, who protects her blind sister Louise. *Dir./Sc:* Herbert Brenon (from the play by Adolphe D'Ennery). *With* Jean Southern, William E. Shay, Herbert Brenon, Gertrude Berkley, Frank Goldsmith, E. L. Fernandez, Sheridan Block, Mrs. Cecil Raleigh, John Daly Murphy. (Previously filmed at Selig, with Kathlyn Williams in the role of Henriette; and later by D.W. Griffith, as *Orphans of the Storm,* with Lillian Gish as

Henriette.) Working title: *The Hunchback.* Exteriors filmed in Quebec. *Prod:* Fox Film Corporation. 5374 ft.

SIN (1915). Dramatic tragedy; as the Italian peasant girl Cora. *Dir. /Sc:* Herbert Brenon (from a story by Nixola Daniels). *With* William E. Shay, Warner Oland, Mrs. Louise Rial, Henry Leone. (Miss Bara was billed as "Destiny's Dark Angel.") Working title: *The Jewels of the Madonna. Prod:* Fox Film Corporation. 5 reels.

CARMEN (1915) Dramatic tragedy: as the gypsy temptress, Carmen *Dir/Sc:* Raoul A. Walsh (from the novel by Prosper Mérimée). *With* Einar Linden, Carl Harbaugh, James A. Marcus, Elsie McCleod, Fay Tunis, Emil de Varney. (At the same time the Fox-Bara *Carmen* was filmed and released, Cecil B. DeMille directed his version, the movie *début* performance of Geraldine Farrar. Later, Pola Negri was Carmen for Lubitsch, known in America as *Gypsy Love;* and other actresses like Dolores Del Rio, Vivian Romance, Rita Hayworth, and Dorothy Dandridge have scored in their versions of *Carmen*, as have Raquel Meller, 1926, and Imperio Argentina, 1938. *Prod:* Fox Film Corporation. 5 reels.

THE GALLEY SLAVE (1915). Tragedy of revenge; as the wronged wife seeking vengeance. *Dir:* J. Gordon Edwards. *Sc:* Clara Beranger (from Rex Ingram's adaptation of a play by Bartley Campbell). *With* Stuart Holmes, Claire Whitney, Jane Lee. (Miss Bara was billed as "Destiny's Dark Angel.") *Prod:* Fox Film Corporation. 4859 ft.

DESTRUCTION (1916). Melodramatic tragedy; as an evil woman who not only seeks to destroy a father and son, but nearly wrecks an entire town by inciting a strike. *Dir./Sc:* Will S. Davis (ad. from his own story, "Labor"). *With* Joseph Furney, Esther H. Hoier, Warner Oland, J. Herbert Frank, Carleton Macey, Frank Evans, Gaston Bell, J. Walker. (A large advertisement announced: "The most famous vampire in her most daring role brings ruin and disaster to thousands.") *Prod:* Fox Film Corporation. 5 reels.

THE SERPENT (AKA, GB, *Fires of Hate*) (1916). Melodramatic tragedy: as Vania Lazar, a Russian peasant who seeks vengeance on the duke who had wronged her. *Dir:* Raoul A. Walsh. *Sc:* Raoul and George Walsh (from a story by Philip Bartholmae, "The Wolf's Claw"). *With* George Walsh, James. A. Marcus, Lillian Hathaway, Charles Craig, Carl Harbaugh. *Prod:* Fox Film Corporation. 6 reels.

GOLD AND THE WOMAN (1916). Tragedy of revenge; as Theresa Decordova, a woman who has been wronged and forces a venal English colonel to pay. *Dir:* James Vincent. *Sc:* Mary Murillo (from a story by Daniel Roosevelt). *With* H. Cooper Cliffe, Alma Hanlon, Harry Hilliard, Caroline Harris, Ted Griffin, Louis Stern, James Sheehan, Carleton Macey, Frank Whitson, Pauline Barry. (Working title: *Retribution.) Prod:* Fox Film Corporation. 6 reels.

THE ETERNAL SAPHO (AKA, GB, *Bohemia*) (1916). Romantic tragedy; as Moya Wilson, artist's model. *Dir:* Bertram Bracken. *Sc:* Mary Murillo (a modern version of Daudet's "Sapho"). *With* Warner Oland, Frank Norcross, George MacQuarrie, Walker Lewis, Hattie Delano, James Cooley, Einar Linden, Mary Martin, Kittens Reichert. *Prod:* Fox Film Corporation. 5 reels.

EAST LYNNE (1916). Romantic tragedy; as Lady Isabel Carlisle. *Dir:* Bertram Bracken. *Sc:* Mary Murillo (a modern version of Mrs. Henry Wood's novel and play). *With* Claire Whitney, Stuart Holmes, William H. Tooker, Stanhope Wheatcroft. (Later filmed by Fox, with Alma Rubens; and then as an early talkie, with Ann Harding.) *Prod:* Fox Film Corporation. 5600 ft.

UNDER TWO FLAGS (1916). Drama of the French Foreign Legion; as Cigarette. *Dir:* J. Gordon Edwards. *Sc:* George Hall (from the novel by Ouida). *With* Herbert Heyes, Stuart Holmes, Claire Whitney. (Priscilla Dean later starred in a silent version for Universal; it was re-made as a talkie by 20th Century-Fox, with Claudette Colbert as Cigarette.) *Prod:* Fox Film Corporation. 6 reels.

HER DOUBLE LIFE (1916). Melodrama; as Mary Doone, Red Cross nurse, who poses as an English noblewoman. *Dir:* J. Gordon Edwards. *Sc:* Mary Murillo (from her story, "The New Magdalen"). *With* Stuart Holmes, Walter Law, Lucia Moore, Jane Lee. *Prod:* Fox Film Corporation. 6 reels.

ROMEO AND JULIET. (1916). Romantic tragedy; as Juliet, daughter of the Capulets. *Dir:* J. Gordon Edwards. *Sc:* Adrian Johnson (from Shakespeare's play). *With* Harry Hilliard, Glen White, Walter Law, John Webb Dillon, Einar Linden, Edwin Eaton, Edwin Holt, Alice Gale, Victory Bateman, Helen Tracy, Jane & Katherine Lee. (Miss Bara's Juliet was as highly praised as Beverly Bayne's, made and released simultaneously by Metro, in which Francis X. Bushman was the Romeo; in the talking era, the most famous Juliets have been Norma Shearer, with Leslie Howard as her Romeo in George Cukor's M-G-M production; Susan Shentell, with Laurence Harvey as Romeo in the Universal Cine Co. version shot in Italy, directed by Renato Castellani, 1954, Technicolor; and the beautiful colour version, directed by Franco Zeffirelli, 1966, with Olivia Hussey as Juliet and Leonard Whiting as Romeo.) *Prod:* Fox Film Corporation. 7 reels.

THE VIXEN (AKA, GB *The Love Pirate)* (1916). Melodrama; as Elsie Drummond, the wicked sister who nearly ruins her good sister's life. *Dir:* J. Gordon Edwards. *Sc:* Mary Murillo. *With* Mary Martin, A. H. Van Buren, Herbert Heyes, George Clarke, Carl Gerard, George Odell. *Prod:* Fox Film Corporation. 6 reels.

THE DARLING OF PARIS (1917). French medieval romance; as the wild gypsy, Esmeralda. *Dir:* J. Gordon Edwards. *Sc:* Adrian Johnson (from Victor Hugo's "The Hunchback of Notre Dame"). *With* Glen White, Walter Law, Herbert Heyes, Carey Lee, Alice Gale, John Webb Dillon, Louis Dean. (This version is unique in that Quasimodo is a beautiful knight who rescues Esmeralda from the torture rack, not an ugly hunchback.) (In Universal's silent spectacle, 1923, Patsy Ruth Miller was Esmeralda to Lon Chaney's brilliant Quasimodo; in talking versions, Maureen O'Hara was Esmeralda in RKO's 1939 version, with Charles Laughton; and in the 1957 film, made in France, it was Gina Lollobrigida who played the role, with Anthony Quinn.) *Prod:* Fox Film Corporation. 6 reels.

THE TIGER WOMAN (AKA GB, *Behind a Throne)* (1917). Melodramatic tragedy; as a Russian villainess, the Countess Irma, who becomes the ruthless Princess Petrovitch. *Dir:* J. Gordon Edwards. *Sc.:* Adrian Johnson (from a story by James W. Adams). *With* Glen White, Mary Martin, John Webb Dillon, Louis Dean, Emil De Varney, Herbert Heyes, Edwin Hold, Florence Martin, Kate Blanke, Kittens Reichert. (Miss Bara was billed as "The Champion Vampire of the Season.") *Prod:* Fox Film Corporation. 6 reels.

HER GREATEST LOVE (AKA, GB, *Redemption).* (1917). Romantic drama; as Hazel, who chooses to go to Siberia to redeem her soul. *Dir:* J. Gordon Edwards. *Sc:* Adrian Johnson (from Ouida's novel "Moths"). *With* Glen White, Harry Hilliard, Walter Law, Marie Curtis, Alice Gale. *Prod:* Fox Film Corporation. 5 reels.

HEART AND SOUL (1917). Romantic tragedy of the Hawaiian Islands; as Jess. *Dir:* J. Gordon Edwards. *Sc:* Adrian Johnson (from "Jess," a novel by Sir Rider Haggard, with the original African locale changed to the Hawaiian Islands). *With* Harry Hilliard, Glen White, Claire Whitney, Walter Law, Edwin Holt, John Webb Dillon, Alice Gale. *Prod:* Fox Film Corporation. 5 reels.

CAMILLE (1917). Romantic tragedy; as Marguerite Gautier. *Dir:* J. Gordon Edwards. *Sc:* Adrian Johnson (from the novel and play by Alexandre Dumas, *fils).* *With* Albert Roscoe, Walter Law, Glen White, Alice Gale, Claire Whitney. (The ads of the times: "A Masterpiece of Bara Art — A Theda Bara Super Picture.") (Another version by a rival company, starring Helen Hesperia, was released simultaneously; Miss Bara's got top praise. Other *Camilles* of the silents included Sarah Bernhardt, Clara Kimball Young, Nazimova, and Norma Talmadge; in talkies, there have been two French ones, one in 1935 with Yvonne Printemps and the other in 1969 with Danièle Gaubert, *Camille 2000;* but the definitive one is the George Cukor M-G-M production of 1937 with Garbo starring.) *Prod:* Fox Film Corporation. 6 reels.

CLEOPATRA (1917). Historical romance; as Cleopatra, Queen of Egypt. *Dir:* J. Gordon Edwards. *Sc:* Adrian Johnson (from Shakespeare's "Antony and Cleopatra," Sardou's "Cléopâtre," and historical works). *With* Fritz Leiber, Thurston Hall, Albert Roscoe, Genevieve Blinn, Henri de Bries, Dorothy Drake, Dell Duncan, Hector V. Sarno, Herschel Mayall, Art Acord. (Other famous Cleopatras: Claudette Colbert for Cecil B. DeMille; Vivien Leigh in Shaw's *Caesar and Cleopatra;* and Elizabeth Taylor, for 20th Century-Fox.) *Prod:* Fox Film Corporation. 11 reels.

THE ROSE OF BLOOD (1917). Melodrama of revenge; as Lisza Tapenka, a Russian Revolutionist who loves Russia better than the men she loves and kills. *Dir:* J. Gordon Edwards. *Sc:* Bernard McConville (from a story, "The Red Rose," by Richard Ordynski). *With* Richard Ordynski, Charles Clary, Herschel Mayall, Marie Kiernan, Bert Turner, Genevieve Blinn, Joe King, Hector V. Sarno. *Prod:* Fox Film Corporation. 7 reels.

THE FORBIDDEN PATH (1918). Melodrama of artist life in Greenwich Village; as Nellie Lyne, who in her time poses as both the Madonna and for "Sin." *Dir:* J. Gordon Edwards. *Sc:* E. Lloyd Sheldon (from his story, "From the Depths"). *With* Hugh Thompson, Sidney Mason, Walter Law, Florence Martin, Wynne Hope Allen, Alphonse Ethier. *Prod:* Fox Film Corporation. 6 reels.

MADAME DUBARRY (1918). Historical drama of the times of Louis XV and the French Revolution; as the little milliner's assistant, Jeanne Vaubernier, who becomes Madame DuBarry and mistress to the King of France. *Dir:* J. Gordon Edwards. *Sc:* Adrian Johnson (from an Alexandre Dumas novel). *With* Charles Clary, Herschel Mayall, Fred Church, Genevieve Blinn, Willard Louis. (The greatest DuBarry of them all was Pola Negri in Lubitsch's silent, *Passion,* which introduced both Negri and Emil Jannings to the American public; there was the last film Norma Talmadge made, *DuBarry, Woman of Passion;* and in *Madame DuBarry* of 1934 Dolores Del Rio was the most exquisite of them all; Gladys George was also admirable in the role in the

M-G-M 1938 *Marie Antoinette*, with John Barrymore as her King of France.) *Prod:* Fox Film Corporation. 7 reels.

THE SOUL OF BUDDHA (1918). Oriental romantic tragedy; as an alluring priestess in a Javanese temple who breaks her vows for love, and so meets death. *Dir:* J. Gordon Edwards. *Sc:* Adrian Johnson (from a story by Theda Bara). *With* Hugh Thompson, Victor Kennard, Anthony Merlow, Florence Martin, Jack Ridgway, Henry Warwick. *Prod:* Fox Film Corporation. 5 reels.

UNDER THE YOKE (1918). Melodrama of rebellion in the Philippines; as Maria Valverda. *Dir:* J. Gordon Edwards. *Sc:* Adrian Johnson (from a George Scarborough story, "Maria of the Roses"). *With* Albert Roscoe, G. Raymond Nye, E. B. Tilton, Carrie Clark Ward. (Advertised as "A Volcanic Drama of the Philippines — She Scorched Her Soul to Save an American Cavalry Officer.") *Prod:* Fox Film Corporation. 5 reels.

WHEN A WOMAN SINS (1918). Romantic melodrama; as Lillian Marshand, nurse, who becomes Poppaea, heartless dancer and idol of libertines. *Dir:* J. Gordon Edwards. *Sc:* E. Lloyd Sheldon (from a Betta Breuil story, "The Message of the Lilies"). *With* Albert Roscoe, Josef Swickard, Ogden Crane, Alfred Fremont, Jack Rollens. (Advertised as "The Greatest Woman's Story Ever Filmed — The Regeneration of a Modern Vampire"). *Prod:* Fox Film Corporation. 7 reels.

SALOME (1918). Biblical tragedy; as the young step-daughter of Herod who covets the head of John the Baptist. *Dir:* J. Gordon Edwards. *Sc:* Adrian Johnson. *With* G. Raymond Nye, Albert Roscoe, Bertram Grassby, Herbert Heyes, Genevieve Blinn, Vera Doria, Alfred Fremont. (A very stylised *Salome* was made by Nazimova in 1923; a talking version was released by Columbia in 1953, with Rita Hayworth doing the Dance of the Seven Veils.) *Prod:* Fox Film Corp. 8 reels.

THE SHE-DEVIL (1919). Melodramatic romance of Paris and Old Spain; as Lolette, belle of Juanquera. *Dir:* J. Gordon Edwards. *Sc:* George Neje Hopkins (from his original story — known familiarly as "Neje," he is also credited with other writings for Bara; they were close friends, as he was her dress designer). *With* Albert Roscoe, Frederick Bond, George A. McDaniel. (Advertised as "The Story of a Woman Who Raised Havoc with a Dozen Lovers.") *Prod:* Fox Film Corporation. 6 reels.

THE LIGHT (1919). Romantic melodrama of regeneration; as Blanchette Dumond, AKA Madame Lefresne. *Dir:* J. Gordon Edwards. *Sc:* Charles Kenyon and Adrian Johnson (from a story by Luther Reed and Brett Page). *With* Eugene Ormande, Robert Walker, George Renevant, Florence Martin. Exteriors filmed in New Orleans. *Prod:* Fox Film Corporation. 5 reels.

WHEN MEN DESIRE (1919). First World War espionage melodrama; as Marie Lohr.

Dir: J. Gordon Edwards. *Sc:* Adrian Johnson, (from a story, "The Scarlet Altars," by E. Lloyd Sheldon and J. Searle Dawley). *With* Fleming Ward, G. Raymond Nye, Florence Martin, Maude Hill, Edward Elkas. (Advertised as "Womanhood Outraged — the Thrilling Adventures of a Woman Who Tried to be True") *Prod:* Fox Film Corporation. 5 reels.

THE SIREN'S SONG (1919). Romantic melodrama; as a Breton peasant girl, daughter of a lighthouse keeper, Marie Bernais, who becomes a great diva. *Dir:* J. Gordon Edwards. *Sc:* Charles Kenyon. *With* Alfred Fremont, Ruth Handworth, L. C. Shumway, Albert Roscoe, Paul Weigel, Carrie Clark Ward. *Prod:* Fox Film Corporation. 5 reels.

A WOMAN THERE WAS (1919). Romantic melodrama of the South Seas; as the Princess Zara. *Dir:* J. Gordon Edwards. Sc: Adrian Johnson (from a story by George Neje Hopkins, "Creation's Tears"). *With* William B. Davidson, Robert Elliott, Claude Payton, John Ardizoni. *Prod:* Fox Film Corporation. 5 reels.

KATHLEEN MAVOURNEEN (1919). Romance of old Ireland; as an Irish peasant girl, Kathleen Cavanagh. *Dir./Sc.* Charles J. Brabin (from Tom Moore's poem and Dion Boucicault's play). *With* Edward O'Connor, Jennie Dickerson, Raymond McKee, Marc McDermott, Marcia Harris, Henry Hallam, Harry Gripp, Morgan Thorpe. (Advertised as "The Sweetest Irish Love Story Ever Told.") *Prod:* Fox Film Corporation. 6 reels.

LA BELLE RUSSE (1919). Romantic melodrama of Paris and London; as twin sisters, a dual role, the virtuous Fleurette Sackton, and the notorious "La Belle Russe," who poses as Fleurette. *Dir./Sc:* Charles J. Brabin (from a play by David Belasco). *With* Warburton Gamble, Marian Stewart, Robert Lee Keeling, William B. Davidson, Alice Wilson, Robert Vivian. *Prod:* Fox Film Corporation. 6 reels.

THE LURE OF AMBITION (1919). Romantic melodrama; as Olga Dolan. *Dir/Sc:* Edmund Lawrence (from a Julia Burnham story). *With* Thurlow Bergen, William B. Davidson, Fan Mason, Ida Waterman, Amelia Gardner, Robert Paton Gibbs, Dorothy Drake, Peggy Parr, Tammy Young. *Prod:* Fox Film Corporation. 5 reels.

THE UNCHASTENED WOMAN (1925). Domestic drama; as Caroline Knollys, a wife who vamps to save her marriage. *Dir:* James Young. *Sc:* Douglas Doty (from a play by Louis K. Anspacher). *With* Wyndham Standing, John Miljan, Eileen Percy, Dot Farley, Harry Northrup, Maym Kelso, Kate Price, Eric Mayne, Frederic Kovert. *Prod:* Chadwick. 7 reels.

MADAME MYSTERY (1926). Farce comedy; as a secret agent known as "Madame Mystery." *Dir:* Richard Wallace and Stan Laurel. *Sc:* Hal Roach. *With* James Finlayson, Tyler Brooke, "Babe" (Oliver) Hardy, Fred Malatesta. *Prod:* Hal Roach-Pathe. 2 reels.

2
MARGUERITE CLARK

Although she was only a star of the screen for seven years, Marguerite Clark attained a popularity which until 1920 was exceeded only by that of Mary Pickford. Her popularity, however, was as great with sophisticated critics as with the public. Many years after her retirement, H. L. Mencken and George Jean Nathan referred to her in laudatory terms, and continued to do so, privately and in print, until their deaths.

She was only four feet ten inches tall, and during her screen career she never weighed more than ninety pounds; but she had a half-mischievous, half-thoughtful demeanour, and a lilt in her big hazel eyes that captivated both men and women. The essence of her film personality consisted of the wistfulness of Pierrette and the playfulness of Columbine, and is most perfectly exemplified in *Prunella*, which everyone agrees was her best picture, and in *Snow White* and Hans Christian Andersen's *The Seven Swans*.

The negatives of all her Paramount pictures are said to have been consumed in a fire which destroyed Paramount's East Coast vaults, and the negative of her last picture, for First National, is said to have burned in another studio fire. For years it has been avowed that even no prints of her films are in existence. I'm always suspicious of this kind of statement; it would be truer to say that no prints have yet turned up. One, or more, will in time, I'm sure — probably from behind the Iron Curtain, whence other "lost" films have materialised.

I am lucky enough to have seen almost all the Marguerite Clark pictures, and can remember them, especially the very early ones (which were all re-issued in the late teens), better than I remember some of last year's Academy Award contenders. If you have never seen a Marguerite Clark film, Edward Wagenknecht says in his "The Movies in the Age of Innocence," it's like having to confess "you have never seen a silver birch or a daffodil." They had that kind of simple perfect charm.

She was born on February 22, 1883, in Avondale, a suburb of Cincinnati, Ohio. Named for her mother, Helen Marguerite, she was the youngest of the three Clark children: Cora Clark was the eldest; and there was a brother, Clifford, in between, to whom neither sister ever referred in later years when Marguerite was famous. Her mother died on January 21, 1893, when Marguerite was not yet ten, and nearly four years later, on December 29, 1896, her

31

Marguerite Clark

father, A. J. Clark, died after a lingering illness. At one time he had success-fully run a haberdashery store located on a prominent downtown corner in the heart of Cincinnati, but financial reverses and the costs of a long illness sapped his fortune. Marguerite's portion of inheritance (around $4000) went to the completion of her education. She was studying in Brown County's Convent of the Ursulines, where it was discovered that her lyrical singing voice could carry to the furthest reaches of the main auditorium, and that her personality could cross the foot-lights and endear her to every sort of audi-ence.

Cora Clark was twenty-five years old when her father died; she had suc-ceeded her mother in the management of the Clark household, and she was now appointed guardian for her young sister. She decided that Marguerite's vocal and thespian abilities could earn them a good living, and that she herself would manage the career of her sister.

Once Cora had made up her mind that Marguerite should be an actress, the wheels began to turn the hope into a reality. Like Mary Ann Crabtree, mother of the Lotta who had been the darling of American audiences in the Nineteenth century, Cora Clark was content to be the power behind the scenes. In not too many years managers were to cringe at the mere thought of having to deal with her.

Marguerite's name appears only once in a Cincinnati directory — in 1899 — when she was sixteen. That same year Maguerite and Cora left Cincinnati for Baltimore, where the only theatre friends Cora had were located, and there Marguerite Clark made her first professional appearance as a member of the Strakosch Opera Company, managed by Milton Aborn. A year later Cora concluded they had gained all they could from Baltimore and she took Mar-guerite to New York City.*

There Cora got her a position understudying Irene Bentley in a Broadway hit called "The Belle of Bohemia." Marguerite went on several times, and the following year was sufficiently prominent in the original New York casts of "The Burgomaster" and "The New Yorkers" for critics to remark on so much talent being wrapped up in so winsome and diminutive a package.

A year later, after appearing in "The Wild Rose," she attracted the atten-tion of DeWolf Hopper, who engaged her to play the role of Polly in his production of "Mr Pickwick." It made her something of a New York celeb-rity, and, after an appearance in "Babes in Toyland," she was engaged again by Hopper to appear in a revival of his earlier musical triumph, "Wang."

In 1905 she was featured in "Happy Land" and then went on a long, nation-wide tour with the Hopper company. In 1908 she was back on Broad-way with Hopper in "The Pied Piper," and the next year was in "The Beauty Spot," after which she made a national tour as the boy who wouldn't grow up in the title role of Barrie's "Peter Pan." Late in 1909 the Shuberts offered her stardom in "The Wishing Ring."

For the first time she protested. It was a play without music, and, as the star, she would be expected to carry it. "I had never wanted to star," she

---

*I am indebted to Wallace E. Davies, of the University of Pennsylvania at Philadelphia, who discovered some of these revealing facts about Miss Clark's early years while on a visit to Cincinnati, and he published them subsequently in his biographical sketch of her in "Notable American Women."

admitted, "and when Mr. Shubert offered me a contract to star...I became almost hysterical. I could not bear the thought of the responsibility — the feeling that I might look out on empty seats and it would by my fault. It was so much more comfortable just to be a feature *with* a star who had to bear *all* the burden!"

But, apparently, Cora persuaded her that stardom was what she was born to achieve. So much so that in August, 1910 she willingly accepted the starring role in Margaret Mayo's "Baby Mine." Sarah Bernhardt saw her in it and told her she had the enthralling gift, and presented her with a signed photograph of herself as L'Aiglon, inscribed *A ma gentille camarade, Marguerite Clark.*

In 1912-13 she was under the management of Winthrop Ames, and these years mark the peak of her stage career. At one time she was playing thirteen performances a week for Ames — every afternoon and Saturday morning she was the lead in "Snow White"; every evening she was one of the affairs of John Barrymore in Schnitzler's "Anatol," along with Doris Keane, Katherine Emmet, and other eminent ladies of the theatre. She appeared in a comedy-melodrama, "Are You a Crook?," and then played for Ames the title role of "Prunella," by Granville-Barker and Laurence Housman, a performance which is conceded her best on the stage as it was certainly, later, her best in films. In 1914, when she was starring in a revival of "Merely Mary Ann," Adolph Zukor, head of Famous Players, saw her in it, and determined to get her into motion pictures under his sponsorship.

Zukor has said that it was seeing photographs of her in "Prunella" which led him to attend "Merely Mary Ann," and that it was her performance in that play that decided him to get her under personal contract. He asked Daniel Frohman to handle it, but Cora wouldn't talk to Frohman, so Zukor then told his studio manager, Al Kaufman, to seek Miss Clark's signature. After going backstage for seventeen consecutive nights and always being barred by Cora, Kaufman's persistence triumphed, and Cora consented to listen. He offered a three-year contract at $1000 a week. Both Cora and Marguerite were flabbergasted, for Marguerite, despite her stardom and fame, was not earning a stage salary like that. A star didn't make that kind of money in the legitimate theatre. They pretended to demur over the three-year clause. On this Zukor was adamant. "I wanted to build her, like Mary," he said, "as strictly a picture star."

Cora told her sister to sign and later admitted: "I told Marguerite pictures were a fad and in three years would be dead, and that therefore she might as well sign."

Marguerite Clark's first film, *Wildflower,* released in October, 1914, catapulted her to movie fame. Zukor was undoubtedly right in not even listing her stage triumphs in her initial publicity. He didn't want Marguerite Clark to be another famous player, like Bernhardt, Mrs. Fiske, or Lillie Langtry, *consenting* to appear in films, but an actress movie audiences would discover and make a star of at their own instigation. Zukor knew many screen-attending people all over the world had never even seen a stage play, let alone Marguerite Clark in one.

In *Wildflower* she appeared as a piquant child of nature who is attracted by two brothers vacationing in the woods. She elopes with the ne'er-do-well younger one. The elder brother abducts her at the altar, takes her to New

York, where he passes her off to his social family as his own bride. When she realises that the younger brother had committed bigamy in marrying her, she renounces him and falls truly in love with the brother who had saved her from being disgraced.

Her second picture, *The Crucible*, although semi-tragic and full of contemporary social significance in its revealing of conditions in a girl's reformatory, repeated the success of *Wildflower*. The story lines of these two features were basic and uncomplicated, but they presented the star as a beguiling heroine caught up in dramatic situations where her natural innocence is endangered — and audiences everywhere sympathised.

Meanwhile, Mary Pickford — or, more probably, her mother — was urging Zukor to buy a popular novel and stage play called "The Goose Girl." Zukor bid on it, but, regarding it as "one of those plays in which a sweet little girl spends a lot of time in such bucolic pursuits as feeding geese," he let Jesse L. Lasky outbid him, and when Lasky asked for the loan of Marguerite Clark to star in it, Zukor assented. It marked the first major loan by a big studio of one of its top contract stars, and paved the way for the subsequent amalgamation of Famous Players and the Lasky Feature Play Company.

With *The Goose Girl*, critics began to recognise a characteristic which had been evident in the two preceding Clark films, and was to be present in nearly every Clark film thereafter — an attempt at pictorial composition and beauty. Some of this was Cora's doing, for it was she who approved the directors and cameramen on Marguerite's films.

Of Miss Clark's performance in *The Goose Girl,* the "Moving Picture World" spoke in terms exhibitors understood: "She conquers her audience in an instant. You cannot very well determine for yourself whether you liked her better in the guise of the goose girl or in the purple of the queen, but you are sure that no artist could find a better model of either. Petite, dainty, vivacious, gifted, representing a most exquisite type of America's feminine beauty, this little artist takes every heart by storm."

She was always graceful and moved well, as players trained in the theatre did, and still do, on film. Her mannerisms were enchanting — the use of the delicate hands, the throw of the head, and the huge dark eyes that communicated the subtlest of thoughts, making her an entrancing comedienne.

Mary Pickford and Marguerite Clark may have appeared indifferent to one another's stardom, but this was not the case with Cora and Miss Pickford's mother. Zukor, on signing Miss Clark, had voluntarily raised Miss Pickford's salary to $1000 a week, and the following year Mrs. Pickford had that doubled, since the popularity of "America's Sweetheart" obviously warranted it. The studio tried not to schedule the production of Pickford and Clark pictures at the same time in the same studio (Paramount then had studios in New York and Hollywood). According to Zukor, when Mary put on a new costume, she would, at her mother's insistence, "go ducking and weaving and hiding about the set, pretending to be avoiding Cora's inspection." But much of the rivalry was studio induced for publicity purposes. Once established as Paramount's top star, Miss Pickford filmed most of her pictures on the West Coast, while Miss Clark made no more than half a dozen there.

Physically, they were very unalike, although they could easily play the same roles. Miss Clark's personality was brunette; her hair was dark brown

Marguerite Clark in SILKS AND SATINS

with chestnut tints in it. Miss Pickford's image was golden; before she was known by name, she had even been called "Goldilocks" by her public. Miss Clark wore a wig of blonde curls when she played Little Eva in *Uncle Tom's Cabin* (1918), and Miss Pickford donned a dark wig when she did Cho-Cho San in *Madame Butterfly,* and she had done the same earlier at Biograph when she played some Indian and Mexican heroines for Griffith — but one was essentially a brunette and the other a blonde.

Samuel Goldwyn, who at that time was a partner of Jesse Lasky's, says in his "Behind the Screen" that Miss Clark hadn't wanted to go to California to film *The Goose Girl* and *The Pretty Sister of Jose*. "What, Marguerite go all the way out to California!" exclaimed the star's sister when I called at the Clark apartment that first evening.

"An Astor or a Vanderbilt ordered to go out and hoe the potatoes, a Russian nobleman sentenced to Siberia — neither of these could have expressed more profound emotion. Nor was the prejudice of Miss Clark's sister an isolated one. I quote this exclamation, indeed, as significant of an almost universal obstacle I encountered in those early days. Stars did not want to leave New York for California."

Cora Clark never tired of battling for bigger productions and more money for her sister. Marguerite was seldom temperamental on set, but Cora often was. Things were always easier when Cora approved of a director, and Marguerite would thereupon request his services for a following picture. This is one reason why J. Searle Dawley directed so many of her early films (sixteen of them) and Walter Edwards many of her later ones (six).

Miss Clark *was* temperamental during the filming of *The Goose Girl*, however, and Goldwyn describes some of the friction during the shooting of that picture: "From the studio across the continent to my office in New York came constant mutterings of disagreements between Miss Clark and her director, Fred Thompson. Once I wired to DeMille to ask him how the play was coming along, and his answer to the telegram was as follows: 'Don't know much about the play, but geese and photography both look great.'" Cecil B. DeMille, as Director-General for Lasky, did step in on several occasions and personally direct certain scenes on which Thompson, Marguerite and Cora could not agree.

Much later, as Zukor records in his book, "The Public Is Never Wrong," Cora admitted her surprise that Zukor never had his own attorneys present at the conferences to which she and Marguerite brought theirs. At one of these conferences Zukor said to Cora: "Please tell your sister to tell her lawyer to talk more slowly. My mind doesn't work that fast."

Cora's mind worked not only fast but very positively, and when Mary Pickford left Zukor to release through First National and then to become a part of United Artists, Cora saw to it that Marguerite Clark "had the field to herself" at Paramount, as Lasky himself admitted. Her pictures continued to be box-office winners, although not at the top as Miss Pickford's were. Miss Clark, however, made more pictures per year, and thus stayed among the first money-making ten for the time.

Occasionally, Marguerite permitted an interview. "Why should I tell about myself?" she asked. "Isn't it true that the less of a mystery one is, the less interesting one becomes? ...I am working simply and solely to earn my bread and butter, and my ambition is to find a good play. Do you know of one? No. It is a pity. I shall remain in the pictures until I find one. You see how matter-of-fact I am."

Although her screen image was a compound of whimsicality and frail beauty, the real life Marguerite Clark could be cool, often crisp, even prim and business-like, although she never failed to let Cora handle the business. When asked why she had never fallen in love, she replied: "Love is not for the practical...I have no desire to have my heart broken, so I always take care not to leave it around or lose it, and so far it has never even been cracked."

Her practicality pervaded her work, and she was one of the first stage stars to understand, as Duse had instinctively, that screen and stage are different mediums and require different acting styles. "I really much prefer the stage to the pictures," she declared. "I know I am not supposed to say that, but I do." She added that the theatre deals with illusion, and was all the truer because life "is just one illusion after another."

Her diminutive size sometimes irked her. "It isn't all honey," she said in an interview for "Theatre Magazine." "I can't say I've ever longed to be more than six feet tall, and — what shall I say, built in proportion? — but suppose some day I should want to play a *big* part!"

When she entered the third year of her contract, Cora cannily let it be known that Marguerite Clark would soon be returning to the theatre, which elicited the wail Cora hoped for from Marguerite's fans. Eventually she signed another re-negotiated deal with Zukor at Paramount, this time for $5000 a week, thanks to Cora's bargaining. In a statement to the press, Marguerite did not mention the theatre, and instead adopted the following line: "I have spent two years of hard work on the study of the technique of the screen, and I'm not going to let that long period of hard work go for nothing, so I shall continue to appear on the screen. I enjoy my work just as a man enjoys his business. But there is no career in the world — no matter how brilliant — that could be half so enjoyable to me as a quiet home in the country with my friends and my pets."

She also thought it tactical to say she learned to like picture-making. "Wasn't it Barrie," she asked, "who said 'the secret of happiness is not in doing what you like, but in liking what you have to do'? I do *both* — I do what I like and I like what I have to do — and that's all there is to it."

It is true she did not socialise, and she explained her declining of invitations by saying: "There are always so many of them I can't decide which to take, so I let them all go, and have a much better time at home after all.

When she finished her nineteenth picture, *The Amazons*, she burst into tears because it was over. "Oh, what a panic it was to play in that story!" she said. "I had as much genuine wholesome fun out of it as any fan could have, and I hated to see the jollity end."

The pictures she filmed, whether modern romantic comedies like the three based on Mary Roberts Rinehart's adventures of Bab, a sub-deb, or period romances like the Napoleonic *The Fortunes of Fifi*, continued to gain her an ever-increasing circle of admirers; but her most memorable films were those based on escapist fairy stories or pure romantic fantasy. *Snow White* was the big Christmas attraction in all major cinema houses for 1916, and *The Seven Swans* for Christmas of 1917. When Walt Disney, more than a score of years later, compiled his production of *Snow White,* he confessed that he deliberately modeled much of its treatment on the Marguerite Clark film as he remembered it.

Prunella (1918), adapted from her memorable stage production for Winthrop Ames and directed for films by Maurice Tourneur, was not only a popular success but a real artistic screen masterpiece. It was the most exquisite of pantomimes and is one of the few screen representations of a highly stylised form that achieved any degree of universal popularity. It told with becoming simplicity the story of a young girl named Prunella, living in restricted girlhood with her three maiden aunts, who is intrigued when a group of strolling players encamps nearby. Pierrot, the company's star, woos her by moonlight, and persuades her to elope with him. Prunella becomes a famous actress in Paris, but is deserted by the fickle Pierrot. Years later, the last of the aunts is selling the old house, only to find the buyer is a much wiser and older Pierrot. To his twilit garden, Prunella returns, and they are reconciled.

During the First World War, she went on bond-selling tours, and on one of them met the man to whom she gave her heart. He was Lieutenant Harry Palmerson Williams, a socialite pioneer in aircraft manufacture who also had lumber interests in Louisiana. They were married at Greenwich, Connecticut, on August 15, 1918.

Williams was quite willing to let his winsome wife continue her career. Actually, she was six years older than her husband, but she never looked it

Marguerite Clark, centre, with Elsie Lawson and Helen Greene in THE AMAZONS

and he probably never even thought of himself as younger. She shot a few features on the West Coast, and her husband and she rented a big home on Wilshire Boulevard in Los Angeles, while she resumed shooting at Paramount. But, according to Jesse Lasky in "I Blow My Own Horn", Mr. Williams insisted there could be no scenes in which his wife kissed her leading man. "This was the kiss of death for Marguerite Clark's popularity," wrote Lasky. "Every film in those days adhered to the unwritten law of a saccharine clinch at the end. Marguerite's fans expected this as their due and simply couldn't accept their idol as a frigid heroine. Without wasting any time or more dimes at the box-office they got themselves other idols."

Sam Goldwyn offered another reason for the decline in Miss Clark's popularity: ''Mary [Pickford] long outlasted her fair rival. Why was this? Marguerite Clark was beautiful, she was exquisitely graceful, and she brought to the screen a more finished stage technique and a more spacious background than did Miss Pickford. My answer to this question, so often propounded to me, applies not only to Miss Clark, but to all the other actresses who have flashed meteor-like, across the screen horizon. First of all, she did not have Mary Pickford's absorbing passion for work. Secondly, she did not possess the other artiste's capacity for portraying fundamental human emotion. Simple and direct and poignant, Mary goes to the heart much as does a Foster melody. Herein is the real success of a popularity so phenomenally sustained.''

I suspect that Miss Clark, now that she was Mrs. Williams, had reasons of her own for withdrawing. She was in love, and although she admitted to being over thirty, she was actually nearer forty (thirty-seven). She was smart enough to know she couldn't go on much longer playing little girls (she had already graduated to young bride roles). The party *was* over, and she retired happily to reign over her husband's wide-verandaed plantation home in St. Mary's Parish, Louisiana.

But rumours that she had retired because her career was fading must have irked her, for she confessed in an interview: ''And goodness, how it hurt when everyone said I had retired from the screen. I haven't — at least, not completely.'' To prove it, she organised her own production company in 1921 and made one film for First National release, an amusing bedroom farce, *Scrambled Wives*.

It projected her in a grown-up part, was charming, and boasted of a sequence in two-colour Prizma. She *did* kiss her leading man in this picture. But though *Scrambled Wives* was a success, she did not make another picture. She had wanted to prove that her career had not faded, and that she, and she alone, had chosen to fade from it.

When asked by the ''New York Times'' if she contemplated returning to either stage or screen, she replied with a glimmer of her own succinct humour: ''I know enough to go home when the party's over and the guests are gone.''

Huey Long, then Governor of Louisiana, appointed her to that state's Motion Picture Censorship Board, and she probably viewed more movies than most Hollywood stars ever do. In 1925 she was crowned Queen of New Orleans' Mardi Gras. From the village nearest their estate (Patterson) she and her husband each year chose twenty or more boys and girls and sent them to college.

Occasionally, Mrs. Williams gave an interview as Marguerite Clark. After declaring that Mary Pickford ''is and always has been my favourite screen actress,'' and that she was a great admirer of Lillian Gish, she summed up her philosophy with this: ''It is the little things that count after all. The smile, the word of graciousness, the small courtesy here and there, the mite of thoughtfulness, that show what one really thinks. Many of these little things are unconsciously done, and that makes them all the more to the point.''

Her last professional contact with movies was a flurry over the possibility that she might do the title role of Barrie's *Peter Pan,* which she had played once on a national tour. John S. Robertson was first thought of as Paramount's director for it, and he let it be known that his first choice for the part was Gareth Hughes, but that if he couldn't have a boy, he "rather liked the idea of Marguerite Clark" (whom he had already guided through three starring roles). When this remark was repeated to Miss Clark, she, fully aware that she was too old for the part, said she doubted that she would be chosen for the role and added: "If I could do some gorgeous thing like *Peter Pan,* I'd make it my final picture and definitely retire. I want people to remember me at my best." Robertson, who had also had great success with May McAvoy in Barrie's *Sentimental Tommy,* also did his best to get Paramount to cast Miss McAvoy as *Peter Pan,* and nearly succeeded. But then it was Herbert Brenon

Marguerite Clark with Jules Raucourt in Maurice Tourneur's PRUNELLA

who was ultimately chosen to direct *Peter Pan*, and his choice for the title part, with Barrie's approval, was Betty Bronson, then virtually an unknown.

Miss Clark never again mentioned returning to the screen. In 1936 her husband was killed in a plane crash, and she promptly settled his estate, and sold the Wedell-Williams Air Service Corporation, which he had founded, to Eastern Air Lines. Within a very few months, she left Louisiana for good and went to New York City, to live with her sister Cora on Central Park West.

The two sisters seldom missed a change of programme at the Radio City Music Hall, or any stage offering of Broadway consequence. Edward Wagenknecht says he has seen a letter of Marguerite's to an intimate friend in which she states that she never did become really reconciled to widowhood. Her sister and she, as always, however, were very companionable. She might be a widow, but she was a very rich one, and life was not at all dull.

At the time of Paramount's Silver Anniversary, Marguerite Clark came out to Hollywood and appeared, along with Mary Pickford, as an honoured guest of Adolph Zukor. She hadn't made a film in eighteen years, and was very petite, pretty, and plump. Even young players on the lot spotted her, remarked on her charm and vivacity, and wanted to know who she was. They knew instinctively that she was somebody of importance.

It was the last time she was very far away from her home in Manhattan. On September 20, 1940, while shopping in a New York department store, she suffered a cerebral haemorrhage, and died five days later in LeRoy Sanitarium, aged only fifty-seven. Cora, very much alone, survived her for another decade.

MARGUERITE CLARK FILMOGRAPHY

WILDFLOWER (1914). Romance; as Letty Roberts, almost a bigamist. *Dir:* Allan Dwan. *Sc:* Eve Unsell and Allan Dwan (from a story by Mary Germaine). *With* Harold Lockwood, Jack Pickford, James Cooley, E. L. Davenport. *Prod:* Famous Players (Paramount). 5 reels. (Compare listing in Harold Lockwood filmography)

THE CRUCIBLE (1914). Romantic social drama: as Jean, a runaway who finds love. *Dir./Sc:* Edwin S. Porter and Hugh Ford (from a novel by Mark Lee Luther). *With* Harold Lockwood, Justine Johnstone, Helen Hall, Lucy Parker, Barbara Winthrop, Clifford Grey, Blanche Fisher. (Reformatory scenes filmed at New York's Bedford Institute) *Prod:* Famous Players (Paramount). 5 reels. (Compare listing in Harold Lockwood filmography.)

THE GOOSE GIRL (1915). Mythical kingdom romance; as Flavia, a young queen forced to pose as a goose girl. *Dir:* Fred Thompson (with special assistance from Cecil B. DeMille). *Sc:* William C. de Mille (from the novel and play by Harold McGrath). *With* Monroe Salisbury,

Larry Payton, S. N. Dunbar, Sidney Deane, James Neill, Page Peters, Horace B. Carpenter, Ernest Joy, Jane Darwell. Filmed in Southern California. *Prod:* Jesse L. Lasky Feature Play Co. (Paramount). 5 reels.

GRETNA GREEN (1915). Romantic comedy of England's Regency period; as Dolly Erskine, Belle of Harrogate. *Dir./Sc:* Thomas N. Heffron (from a comedy by Grace Livingstone Furniss). *With* Wilmuth Merkyl, Arthur Hoops, Helen Lutrell. *Prod:* Famous Players (Paramount). 4 reels.

THE PRETTY SISTER OF JOSE (1915). Romantic tragedy of Old Spain; as Pepita. *Dir./Sc:* Allan Dwan (based on the story and play by Frances Hodgson Burnett, in which Maude Adams had starred onstage). *With* Jack Pickford, Rupert Julian, Teddy Sampson, Gertrude Norman, Dick Rosson, William Lloyd, Edythe Chapman. (A substitute happy ending was offered exhibitors.) Filmed in the Old Mission country in Southern California. *Prod:* Famous Players (Paramount) 5 reels.

THE SEVEN SISTERS (1915). Romantic Hungarian comedy; as Mici. *Dir:* Sidney Olcott. *Sc:* Edith Ella Furness's version of the popular Hungarian comedy in which Laurette Taylor had starred on Broadway. *With* Conway Tearle, Lola Barclay, Madge Evans, Jean Stewart, Edwin Mordant, George Renevant. (Re-made by M-G-M, 1942, as a musical with Kathryn Grayson — *Seven Sweethearts* — with the locale shifted to Michigan's Dutch settlement at tulip time.) *Prod:* Famous Players (Paramount). 5 reels.

HELENE OF THE NORTH (1915). Romantic drama of the Canadian Northwest; as Helene Dearing. *Dir./Sc:* J. Searle Dawley. *With* Conway Tearle, Elliott Dexter, Frank Losee, Brigham Royce, Kathryn Adams, Ida Darling, Theodore Guise, David Wall. *Prod:* Famous Players (Paramount). 5 reels.

STILL WATERS (1915). Romance of the circus; as Nesta. *Dir:* J. Searle Dawley. *Sc:* Hugh Ford (from a story by Edith Bernard Delano). *With* Robert Broderick, Robert Vaughn, Arthur Evers, Robert Conville, Ottola Nesmith, Phillip Tonge. *Prod:* Famous Players (Paramount). 5 reels.

THE PRINCE AND THE PAUPER (1915). Romantic adventure of Tudor England; in a dual role: as Edward VI, Prince of Wales; and Tom Cantry, the pauper. *Dir:* Edwin S. Porter and Hugh Ford. *Sc:* Hugh Ford (adapted from Mark Twain's novel). *With* William Barrows, William Sorelle, William Frederick, Robert Broderick. *Prod:* Famous Players (Paramount). 5 reels. (Re-made in 1922 and as a talkie in 1937, with Errol Flynn and the Mauch twins.)

MICE AND MEN (1916). Romance of the Old South, in the days of the Mexican War; as Peggy. *Dir:* J. Searle Dawley. *Sc:* Hugh Ford (from the play by Madeline Lucette Ryley). *With* Marshall Neilan, Charles Waldron, Clarence Handysides, Maggie Halloway Fisher, Robert Conville, Helen Dahl. *Prod:* Famous Players (Paramount). 5 reels.

OUT OF THE DRIFTS (1916). Romance of the Swiss Alps on the St. Bernard Pass; as the orphan, Elise. *Dir:* J. Searle Dawley. *Sc:* William Clifford. *With* William Courtleigh Jr. , J. W. Johnston, Albert Gran, Kitty Brown, Robert Conville, Ivan Simpson. *Prod:* Famous Players (Paramount). 5 reels.

MOLLY MAKE-BELIEVE (1916). Romance of a young girl who runs away from a poor farm to find real romance in the big city; as Molly. *Dir:* J. Searle Dawley. *Sc:* Hugh Ford. *With* Mahlon Hamilton, Dick Gray, Helen Dahl, Gertrude Norman, Kate Lester, J. W. Johnston, Edwin Mordant. *Prod:* Famous Players (Paramount). 5 reels.

SILKS AND SATINS (1916). Romance of two generations; in a dual role: the modern Felicité, as well as her ancestor also named Felicité, both of whom wed for love rather than wealth and position. *Dir:* J. Searle Dawley. *Sc:* Hugh Ford. *With* Vernon Steele, Clarence Handysides, W. A. Williams, Thomas Holding. *Prod::* Famous Players (Paramount). 5 reels.

LITTLE LADY EILEEN (1916). Romance of Old Ireland; as Lady Eileen Kavanaugh. *Dir:* J. Searle Dawley. *Sc:* Hugh Ford. *With* Vernon Steele, John L. Shine, J. K. Murray, Harry Lee, Maggie Halloway Fisher, Russell Bassett. *Prod:* Famous Players (Paramount) 5 reels.

MISS GEORGE WASHINGTON (1916). Romantic comedy; as Bernice Somers, who cannot tell the truth. *Dir:* J. Searle Dawley. *Sc:* Lew Allen. *With* Niles Welch, Frank Losee, Herbert Prior, Florence Martin, Joseph Gleason, Maude Turner Gordon, "Billy" Watson. *Prod:* Famous Players (Paramount). 5 reels.

SNOW WHITE (1916). Romantic fairy tale; as Snow White. *Dir:* J. Searle Dawley. *Sc:* Winthrop Ames (ad. from the stage success he produced on Broadway, based on the story by the Brothers Grimm, and starring Miss Clark). *With* Creighton Hale, Dorothy Cumming, Lionel Braham, Alice Washburn. Exteriors filmed in Georgia. Premiered in all big American cities for Christmas, 1916. *Prod:* Famous Players (Paramount). 5 reels.

THE FORTUNES OF FIFI (1917). Romance of the Parisian theatre, in the times of Napoleon; as the actress Fifi. *Dir:* Robert G. Vignola. *Sc:* Eve Unsell (from the novel by Molly Elliot Seawell). *With* John Sainpolis, Kate Lester, William Sorelle, Yvonne Chevalier, Jean Gautier, J. K. Murray. *Prod:* Famous Players (Paramount) 5 reels.

THE VALENTINE GIRL (1917). A romantic drama; as Marion Morgan, known as "The Valentine Girl." *Dir./Sc:* J. Searle Dawley (from a Laura Sawyer story). *With* Richard Barthelmess, Frank Losee, Kathryn Adams, Maggie Halloway Fisher, Adolphe Menjou, Edith Campbell Walker. *Prod:* Famous Players (Paramount). 5 reels.

THE AMAZONS (1917). Comedy of three sisters who are raised with all the freedom of young men, because their father, an English lord, thought of them as "heirs;" as "Lord Tommy," youngest sister and a real tomboy. *Dir:* Joseph Kaufman. *Sc:* Frances Marion (from Sir Arthur Wing Pinero's farcical romance played on Broadway in 1913 by Billie Burke). *With* Elsie Lawson, Helene Greene, Jack Standing, Adolphe Menjou, Edgar Norton, William Hinckley, Andre Bellon, *Prod:* Famous Players (Paramount). 5 reels.

Marguerite Clark in SILKS AND SATINS

BAB'S DIARY (1917). Romantic comedy; as Bab, a sub-deb, caught in the web of her own romantic invention. *Dir:* J. Searle Dawley. *Sc:* Margaret Turnbull (from the "Bab" stories by Mary Roberts Rinehart). *With* Nigel Barrie, Richard Barthelmess, Frank Losee, Guy Coombs, Helene Greene, Isabel O'Madigan, Jack O'Brien *Prod:* Famous Players (Paramount). 5 reels.

BAB'S BURGLAR (1917). Romantic comedy; as Bab, the sub-deb, this time asserting her ideas of female independence. *Dir:* J. Searle Dawley. *Sc:* Margaret Turnbull (from the "Bab" stories by Mary Roberts Rinehart). *With* Richard Barthelmess, Frank Losee, Leone Morgan, Helene Greene, Isabel O'Madigan, William Hinckley, Guy Coombs. *Prod:* Famous Players (Paramount). 5 reels.

BAB'S MATINEE IDOL (AKA, GB *Her Matinee Idol* and *Her Shattered Idol* (1917). Romantic comedy; as Bab, the sub-deb, this time hopelessly enthralled by a handsome actor. *Dir:* J. Searle Dawley. *Sc:* Margaret Turnbull (from the "Bab" stories by Mary Roberts Rinehart). *With* William Hinckley, Nigel Barrie, Frank Losee, Helene Greene, Leone Morgan. *Prod:* Famous Players (Paramount). 4 reels.

THE SEVEN SWANS (1917). Romantic fairy tale; as the Princess Tweedledee, aided by Prince Charming in finding her seven brothers, who have been changed by an evil witch into seven swans. *Dir./Sc:* J. Searle Dawley (from the fairy tale by Hans Christian Andersen). *With* Richard Barthelmess, William Danforth, Augusta Anderson, Edwin Dennison, Jules Raucourt, Daisy Belmore. Premiered in all major American cities for Christmas, 1917. *Prod:* Famous Players (Paramount) 5 reels.

RICH MAN, POOR MAN (1918). Romance; as Betty, a slavey. *Dir./Sc:* J. Searle Dawley (from Maximilian Foster's novel and the subsequent play dramatisation by George Broadhurst). *With* Richard Barthelmess, Frederick Warde, George Backus, J. W. Herbert, Ottola Nesmith, Augusta Anderson. *Prod:* Famous Players (Paramount). 5 reels.

PRUNELLA (1918) Romantic pantomime; as the very proper little innocent named Prunella who runs off to Paris with the fickle Pierrot, and becomes a famous actress. *Dir:* Maurice Tourneur. *Sc:* Charles Maigne (from the play by Granville Barker and Laurence Housman, which Miss Clark had created on Broadway for Winthrop Ames). *With* Jules Raucourt, Harry Leone, Isabel Berwin, Marcia Harris, Nora Cecil. *Prod:* Famous Players (Paramount). 5 reels.

UNCLE TOM'S CABIN (1918) Drama of the Deep South; in a dual role: as little Eva St. Clair; and the inimitable black slave Topsy. *Dir/Sc:* J. Searle Dawley (from the classic American novel by Harriet Beecher Stowe). *With* Frank Losee, J.·W. Johnston, Florence Carpenter, Walter Lewis, Augusta Anderson, Ruby Hoffman, Henry Stanford, Mrs. Priestly Morrison. Exteriors filmed in the Deep South and on the Ohio River. *Prod:* Famous Players (Paramount). 5 reels. (Re-filmed, Universal, '27)

OUT OF A CLEAR SKY (1918) Romantic drama set in the hills of Tennessee at the time of the First World War; as the Belgian refugee, the young Countess Celeste de Bersek et Krymm. *Dir:* Marshall Neilan. *Sc:* (from a novel by Maria Thompson Davies).*With* Thomas Meighan, Bobby Connelly, E. J. Radcliffe, Raymond Bloomer, Robert Dudley, W. P. Lewis, Maggie Halloway Fisher. *Prod:* Famous Players (Paramount). 5 reels.

LITTLE MISS HOOVER (1918). Romantic comedy; as Ann Craddoch, Washington society girl who tries to do her bit in winning the war. *Dir:* John S. Robertson. *Sc:* Adrian Gil-Spear (from the play by Maria Thompson Davies, "The Golden Bird"). *With* Eugene O'Brien, Alfred Hickman, Forrest Baldwin, Hal Reid, Frances Haye. *Prod:* Famous Players (Paramount). 5 reels.

MRS. WIGGS OF THE CABBAGE PATCH (1919) American comedy; as Lovey Mary. *Dir:* Hugh Ford. *Sc:* Eve Unsell (from the play by Alice Hegan Rice and Anne Crawford Flexner). *With* Mary Carr, Vivia Ogden, May McAvoy, Gareth Hughes, Gladys Valerie, Jack MacLean, Lawrence Johnson. (Re-made as an early talkie by Paramount, 1934, with Pauline Lord as Mrs. Wiggs; re-made again, 1942, by Paramount, with Fay Bainter; Bessie Love had made a film, 1926, of *Lovey Mary*, the role Miss Clark played.) *Prod:* Famous Players (Paramount). 5 reels.

THREE MEN AND A GIRL (1919). Romantic comedy; as Sylvia, a modern Goldilocks. *Dir:* Marshall Neilan. *Sc:* Eve Unsell (from the Broadway comedy by Edward Childs Carpenter, "The Three Bears"). *With* Richard Barthelmess, Percy Marmont, Jerome Patrick, Ida Darling, Charles Craig. *Prod:* Famous Players (Paramount.) 5 reels.

LET'S ELOPE (AKA, GB, *The Naughty Wife)* (1919). Marital comedy; as Eloise Farrington. *Dir:* John S. Robertson. *Sc:* Katherine Reed (from Fred Jackson's comedy, "The Naughty Wife"). *With* Frank Mills, Gaston Glass, Helene Greene, Blanche Standing, George Stevens. (Working title: *Three's a Crowd) Prod:* Famous Players (Paramount). 5 reels.

COME OUT OF THE KITCHEN (1919). Comedy romance of the Deep South; as Claudia. *Dir:* John S. Robertson. *Sc:* Clara Beranger (from A. E. Thomas's dramatisation of Alice Duer Miller's story, which had starred Ruth Chatterton. *Prod:* Famous Players (Paramount). 5 reels.

GIRLS (1919). Romantic comedy about three young man-haters who share a New York City apartment; as Pamela Gordon. *Dir:* Walter Edwards. *Sc:* Based upon Clyde Fitch's successful Broadway comedy. *With* Harrison Ford, Helene Chadwick, Mary Warren, Lee Hill, Clarissa Selwyn, Arthur Edmund Carewe. *Prod:* Famous Players (Paramount). 5 reels.

WIDOW BY PROXY (1919). Romantic comedy; as Gloria Grey, who poses as the widow, Dolores. *Dir:* Walter Edwards. *Sc:* Julia Crawford Ivers (from the play by Catherine Chisholm Cushing). *With* Nigel Barrie, Jack Gilbert, Brownie Vernon, Gertrude Norman, Gertrude Claire. *Prod:* Famous Players (Paramount). 5 reels.

LUCK IN PAWN (1919). Romantic comedy; as Annabel Lee. *Dir:* Walter Edwards. *Sc:* Alice Eyton (from the play by Marvin Taylor). *With* Charles Meredith, Leota Lorraine. *Prod:* Famous Players (Paramount). 5 reels.

A GIRL NAMED MARY (1920). Romantic drama; as poor Mary Healey, who finds that she is really the rich Mary Jeffrey. *Dir:* Walter Edwards. *Sc:* Alice Eyton (from a story by Juliet Wilbur Tompkins). *With* Wallace MacDonald, Kathlyn Williams, Aggie Herring, Charles Clary, Lillian Leighton, Pauline Pulliam, *Prod:* Famous Players (Paramount). 5 reels.

ALL-OF-A-SUDDEN PEGGY (1920). English romantic comedy; as Peggy O'Hara. *Dir:* Walter Edwards. *Sc:* Edith Kennedy (from a play by Ernest Denny). *With* Jack Mulhall, Oral Humphrey, Lillian Leighton, Maggie Halloway Fisher, Sylvia Jocelyn. *Prod:* Famous Players (Paramount) 5 reels.

EASY TO GET (1920). Domestic comedy; as Molly Morehouse, who proves to her husband that she may have been easy to get, but she's not so easy to keep. *Dir:* Walter Edwards, *Sc:* Julia Crawford Ivers (from a story by Mann Page). *With* Harrison Ford, Rod La Rocque, Helen Greene. *Prod:* Famous Players (Paramount). 4 reels.

SCRAMBLED WIVES (1921). Domestic farce; as Miss Mary Lucille Smith. *Dir:* Edward H. Griffith. *Sc:* Gardner Hunting (from a play by Adelaide Matthews and Martha M. Stanley). *With* Leon P. (Pierre) Gendron, Ralph Bunke, Florence Martin, Virginia Lee, Alice Mann, Frank Badgley. *Prod:* First National. 6 reels.

3
GERALDINE FARRAR

One of filmdom's little ironies is that the only star from grand opera who really hit it big as a top movie star with a long-lasting career of successive pictures remains Geraldine Farrar — and she did it in *silent* films!

Immediately, the names of Grace Moore and Lawrence Tibbett will be brought up in refutation, but their careers are puzzling, to say the least.

Tibbett established himself immediately as a film personality with *The Rogue Song* (1930), but the three other pictures he made for M-G-M were not in the same category, nor did they do the landslide business of *The Rogue Song*. His two subsequent films (*Metropolitan*, 1935 and *Under Your Spell*, 1936) were even less important, critically and box-officewise.

Grace Moore's two vehicles at M-G-M (*A Lady's Morals* and *The New Moon*, both in 1930) can only be rated as flops as far as establishing her screen image. It was not until four years later, when she made the highly successful *One Night of Love* for Columbia that something more than the "iron butterfly" image was captured by the camera. Yet the four following pictures she made for Columbia, despite all their production value, as well as the version of *Louise* she filmed in 1938, must be rated as illustrative of the law of diminishing returns.

Likewise, the screen careers of Lily Pons, Gladys Swarthout, Rise Stevens, Helen Traubel, Nino Martini, Dorothy Kirsten, Patrice Munsel, and a host of others who tried to establish themselves as film stars can be marked as disappointing, or too much of the one-shot variety, or all too sporadic for establishing them as big stars of the cinema world with a particular niche of their own. Indeed, of the five pictures Miss Swarthout made for Paramount between 1936 and 1939, the best from her standpoint as an actress was a routine programmer, her last, *Ambush* in which she didn't sing a note. Similarly, Jarmila Novotna turned in a very moving performance as the non-singing mother desperately seeking her child in *The Search*, otherwise notable as being Montgomery Clift's most legitimate tearjerker as well as the film that assured his film career.

It must be pointed out, too, that Jeanette MacDonald and Nelson Eddy did not come to Hollywood as established stars of the world of grand opera. Miss MacDonald did sing operatic selections in many of her films, but she was brought to Hollywood, a successful star of Broadway musical comedy, while

Mr. Eddy's career, although it did embrace previous appearances in several operas, was never regarded as one of great grand opera stardom. It was, in fact, his concerts at the Philharmonic in Los Angeles that led to his film *début* in 1933 in *Broadway to Hollywood* and a subsequent M-G-M contract.

But the film career of Geraldine Farrar was different.

She came to Hollywood that first summer of 1915 with a dazzling European background of opera successes, and for nine years she had been indisputably the Metropolitan's most glamourous diva. In her first film role she established herself at once as a great movie personality, and she stayed a big movie star from 1915 to 1920 as the stellar attraction of fourteen silent films.

Geraldine Farrar was born on February 28, 1882, on Mount Vernon Street in Melrose, a suburb of Boston. Her father, Sydney Farrar, was first baseman of the Philadelphia National Baseball Club, and he also managed a small business store between baseball seasons. He was a church singer, and her mother, Henrietta Barnes Farrar, was an accomplished musician who had once dreamed of a career in music for herself. Both Miss Farrar's Norman-English-Irish maternal and paternal families were either musicians in their own right or devotees of music.

As a child, she was playing the piano, first by ear and then studying. Even then, she remarked once to her mother that "The white keys seem like angels and the black ones like devils — and I like the devils best." Aged twelve, at a carnival, she impersonated Jenny Lind, and a thunderstruck audience, expecting to hear her sing "Home, Sweet Home," heard instead an Italian operatic aria, sung in her own self-studied Italian.

She sang in Melrose's Congregational Church, was carefully groomed as a singer in both Boston and New York; for the latter venture her mother, at the advice of Jean de Reszke, borrowed $500 so that she could study with top teachers. In New York she sang for both Nordica and Melba, and Melba advised her to go to Europe for further study. The Farrar home, her father's business, and her own life insurance were mortgaged but it was not enough. An opera lover, Mrs. Bertram Webb, of Salem, Massachusetts, set aside a sum of $30,000 for studies abroad. Accompanied by her mother, Miss Farrar sailed for Paris in 1899 to study there with Trabadello.

But they soon moved on to Berlin, where at Nordica's advice, she studied wuth the eminent Russian-Italian teacher, Graziani. On October 15, 1901, she made her *début* at Berlin's Royal Opera, singing Marguerite in "Faust." She was then nineteen years old.

Lilli Lehmann heard her *début* performance and was so impressed that she took her on as a private pupil, and Miss Farrar then returned to Paris to study the star role of "Manon" with composer Massenet.

For the next five years rumours of the brilliant success of the girl from Melrose echoed across the Atlantic. She sang in Berlin, Paris, Warsaw, Monte Carlo, and Stockholm, where the king gave her the gold cross of the Order of Merit after her performance in "La Traviata."

But, of course, it was her romance with the Kaiser's son, the Crown Prince Frederick Wilhelm, that intrigued the American world. Other American actresses and heiresses might have entranced the nobility or lower royalty, and

were so characterised in the drawings of Charles Dana Gibson, but it remained for Geraldine Farrar, an American girl from the Melrose highlands, to fascinate the Kaiser's son, to gain the respect of both the Kaiser and his Kaiserin, and to have the opera-lovers of Europe worshipping before her own special throne.

Hans Conried, impresario for New York's Metropolitan Opera House, finally got her signature on a Metropolitan contract, although Miss Farrar herself had to clear her temporary leave of absence from her Berlin contract with the Kaiser. On November 26, 1906, she made her *début* at the Metropolitan in Gounod's "Romeo et Juliette," and the American world of music took her as its own top favourite. She went on to further triumphs, and the climax of the first season came with the *première* production of Puccini's "Madama Butterfly" on February 11, 1907, with Puccini himself directing rehearsals, and with Caruso, Scotti, and Louise Homer also singing in the cast. Those were the days of opera's Golden Age in Manhattan, and Miss Farrar, singing in "Madama Butterfly," "Carmen," "Manon," "Tosca," "La Bohème," and many others, was responsible for much of the gold.

Morris Gest, son-in-law of David Belasco, was really responsible for her entry into films in 1915. Europe by then was a battleground for the First World War. Miss Farrar had been on her annual European opera tour in August 1914, when the first flame was ignited at Sarajevo, and had made a hectic flight from the continent. Appearances in European opera houses would thenceforth be closed for the war's duration. She had submitted to a delicate throat operation after her 1915 season at the Met, and her surgeon had advised her not to sing an operatic performance for several months at least.

Morris Gest conceived the idea of her appearing as the star of motion pictures, and he broached the suggestion to Jesse L. Lasky, who attended a matinee performance of hers in "Carmen," and enthusiastically gave Gest the go-ahead.

At that time Miss Farrar had seen only one movie — the Italian *Quo Vadis* at the Cinema Theatre in Paris. Gest took her to the *première* of the film version of Cecil B. DeMille's *Girl of the Golden West*, and she said, "I believe a new and very great art is being born."

She still hesitated, however, at trying that art herself. "They come to the Metropolitan to hear me sing," she protested. "I'm afraid I should be an awful failure if I relied on acting alone." The directors at the Metropolitan were even more affrighted, warning her that "When people can see you in pictures for fifty cents they will not pay six dollars to hear you sing."

But both Lasky and Samuel Goldwyn, then associated with the Lasky Feature Play Co., were now determined to snare her for films. Lasky informed Gest: "You can tell her that for every minute of daylight she is in Southern California, whether she is at the studio or not, I will pay her two dollars — and a royalty and a share of all profits."

For a contract that would last eight weeks this could amount to a munificent sum. Lasky also guaranteed her travelling and living expenses in Hollywood, and her first film would be, he told her, *Carmen*, in which she had already sung both the title role and, earlier, Micaela at the Met.

Miss Farrar signed the contract, and in the summer of 1915 entrained by private car, accompanied by her parents and a few close friends including

Morris Gest and his wife, to conquer the new film capitol of Hollywood.

Cecil B. DeMille, who was to direct her pictures for the Lasky Company, had been far from idle while awaiting her arrival. The production was being carefully planned, and DeMille's older brother William had been assigned the writing of the scenario for *Carmen*

Consternation reigned for a time when it was suddenly realised that although they could film Prosper Mérimée's novel, they could not bring in the character of Micaela, which had been created by the opera librettist. The libretto was fully covered by copyright, and its owners had quoted so fantastic a figure for the rights that Lasky said he thought "it included the Louvre with all its contents."

But DeMille, Director-General, had a solution for that. "Who the hell cares about Micaela?" he asked. "Even Mérimée didn't want her."

There were further protests, but DeMille advised his brother: "You've got smugglers, and a tavern, and soldiers, and a fight between two dames in a cigar factory — and give that the works, too — and the camp in the mountains, and, best of all, the bullfight — STAR the bullfight. All that's in Mérimée, and you're supposed to be a dramatist..."

There was one other decision to be reached. In the eight weeks Miss Farrar would be filming in Hollywood, it was hoped they could produce three pictures, the most ambitious being, of course, *Carmen*. They all knew well that their star was new to the camera, so DeMille proposed as follows: "We have another property, *Maria Rosa*, a Spanish love story, not unlike *Carmen* in its setting. Let's let Miss Farrar cut her motion picture teeth on that, and then make *Carmen*, and she will give you a good performance in it. You can hold up the release of *Maria Rosa*. Release *Carmen* first, as you have announced, and it will have all the values of the experience Miss Farrar will have gained in *Maria Rosa*, which you can bring out afterward."

This was agreed upon, and William de Mille* put aside his script of *Carmen* to concentrate first upon writing the scenario for *Maria Rosa*. Oddly enough, *Maria Rosa* had been a play which had starred Lou Tellegen on Broadway, and although Tellegen had already been brought out to star in a series of films for Lasky, *Maria Rosa* was to be re-written so that the woman would be the lead. William de Mille's work as adaptor was further complicated by the fact that the man whom the heroine actually loves was killed before the play ever began; but he adroitly solved that difficulty, creating an excellent romantic lead for Wallace Reid, building up the heroine's role for Miss Farrar, and building down the Tellegen role for Pedro de Cordoba.

The stage was set for Geraldine Farrar's entrance into Hollywood, and she made it with all the splendid bravura show of the prima donna she was. But also, right from the beginning, she won everybody by her personal magnetism and sincere show of friendliness.

The "Moving Picture World" had declared: "Next to the entry of Belasco into the domain of films, the resolution of this marvelous gifted young woman to employ her talents in the films is the greatest step in advancing the dignity of the motion picture."

*The famous brothers always spelled their names with this slight difference. Socially, the family name was "de Mille" for both, but professionally it was Cecil B. DeMille and William C. deMille. To complicate things, professionally Agnes De Mille, William's talented daughter, spells her name with a slight difference.

Miss Farrar got the full treatment when she arrived at the train station in Pasadena and rode by automobile to Hollywood. The Santa Fe platform and depot were carpeted in red from her private train car to the waiting limousine. Five hundred school children had lined both sides of her pathway, strewing it with rose petals. The mayor and other dignitaries welcomed her officially with fanfare, and there was a procession to the two-story home which had been rented for her stay. The house was banked with flowers, and the maid, cook, and butler, all provided by the studio, were on hand to receive her and her party.

But Miss Farrar no sooner arrived than she asked Lasky to wait a minute while she changed her clothes. She wanted to see the studio, where a special bungalow had been provided for her during the filming days to come.

That was on a Saturday. Monday morning Miss Farrar arrived before anybody else at the Lasky Studios, then on Vine between Selma and Sunset. She was made-up and ready to work. "Where's Mr. DeMille?" she kept asking. "Where's everybody?"

She could never stand to be idle. She was always rarin' to go.

When Lasky arrived a little later, DeMille said, "I want to show you something you'll never forget." He led him through the orchard toward the stage, and the sight that met Lasky's eyes he has noted in his own autobiography: "Every one on our payroll — the cast, carpenters, grips, cowboys, and office staff — was standing bareheaded in a transfixed circle around Miss Farrar's bungalow. The door was open, and she was at the grand piano joyously singing an aria from *Madama Butterfly*."

William de Mille, in his autobiography, likewise wrote: "If an actor or a technician was unaccountably missing from his appointed place, the order was given, 'Go over to Jerry's bungalow and get him;' it was a safe bet that he would be found among the silent listeners outside. I was frequently to be found there myself."

Similarly, Blanche Sweet, then a Lasky star, has told me how she used to leave her bungalow door open when Farrar was on the lot in order to hear the arias the operatic star sang between set-ups.

There was never any show of artistic temperament during her film-making for Lasky. She was a worker, and she was determined to be as celebrated a star in films as she was on the operatic stage.

She asked only that musicians be hired to accompany her scenes while she emoted before the camera, for she responded instinctively to the moods of music — and soon afterward all top movie stars were requiring a three-piece ensemble playing appropriate mood music for their silent camera work, although few responded with the effectiveness of Miss Farrar.

The one question she kept asking was, "Who's to be my Don Jose?" They were waiting for the right moment, however, to give her her first sight of Wallace Reid, for although he had established himself as the Blacksmith in Griffith's *The Birth of a Nation* after playing all kinds of parts in over a hundred programme films, it was feared that Miss Farrar might want some actor better known at the time as her leading man.

Reid attended a banquet given for her in a hotel shortly after her arrival, and, prompted that the moment was at hand, nervously approached her table, where she was again beseeching DeMille and Lasky about the identity of the actor who would be her Don Jose. They pointed Reid out to her, where he had paused to smile in his own quizzical way. She nodded her head approvingly, smiled, and extended her hand. "Good!" she said. "Very, VERY good!"*

"We profited by making *Maria Rosa* first," DeMille was to write later. "I learned more, I think, than our star did. Geraldine, I found, had a talent for screen acting as natural, and so as capable of cultivation, as her vocal talent. As I always do, I tried to help her bring out her own best performance, rather than force upon her arbitrarily my concept of her role. What I learned was more technical."

Without a break, virtually the same company went from completing *Maria Rosa* to beginning *Carmen*. Geraldine Farrar was now simply "Jerry" to everybody. "I love the freedom of pictures!" she was crying enthusiastically to every interviewer.

Of all the vehicles for a female star, *Carmen* ranks along with *Camille* as having been filmed more often than any other. The best movie Carmens, however, have always been those which owed more allegiance to Mérimée than Bizet. Farrar's interpretation became definitive on that score, and most admirers of the "Carmen" story will subscribe to hers, the later Pola Negri-Lubitsch version (*Gypsy Blood*, 1921), Raquel Meller's in 1926, the French version of 1945 with Vivian Romance and Jean Marais, and *Carmen de la Triana* of 1938, starring Imperio Argentina. These were all blood sisters to Farrar's own gypsy girl, and had nothing to do with Bizet or the operatic accoutrements afforded the two American productions of *Loves of Carmen*, starring Dolores Del Rio, 1927, and Rita Hayworth, 1948.

Geraldine Farrar's Carmen was a fiery, earthy, fickle-hearted gypsy wench. DeMille chose Jeanie Macpherson, who was later to write many of his scripts, to play the factory girl with whom Farrar would engage in a fight, the like of which hadn't yet been seen on screen between two women. It became a battle royal between a gypsy whose father was an Irish-American baseball player and a Frasquita whose heritage came from Scottish warriors.

Farrar was delighted, and when she returned to the Met, she re-staged her battle for the opera so that the startled grande-dames in the Diamond Horse-shoe reached simultaneously for their lorgnettes and smelling-salts.

Explaining her approach to a cinematic role, Miss Farrar confessed that at first she had missed the intimate and living relationship between audience and her. She had tried to think of an imaginary audience, but that didn't work for her.

"One must hypnotise oneself into the belief that, for the time being, you ARE the person you are portraying," she said, "and that the other characters playing with you are every whit as real as you are. If you can convince yourself of that, and the actuality of your simulated joys, sorrows, regrets, doubts, madnesses and passions, you will surely convince your audiences."

When shooting ended on *Carmen*, production began immediately on the third feature, *Temptation*, which presented Miss Farrar as a contemporary, struggling opera singer.

The eight weeks of summer shooting came to an end all too soon, and Miss

*Dorothy Reid has said that Miss Farrar was so taken with Reid's presence that when she later learned and had proof of his musical talent, she urged him to come East as her *protégé* and study for grand opera.

Farrar, with her entourage, departed with a contract to return the following summer for more filming. From her star dressing-room at the Metropolitan, she several times intimated when asked about her filming experiences, "I believe *Carmen* is being interpreted for the first time."

If anybody still doubted that an opera star could also be a great silent film star, the New York *première* of *Carmen* erased the smallest reservation. The reviews were sensationally good, and the box-office lines started forming for *Carmen*, both at the movies and at the Met, because her fans wanted to see her on celluloid and alive.

Belasco said of her, "If she lost her singing voice today, she would still be the greatest dramatic actress in America." Lasky went further, saying, "If she lost both voices, singing and speaking, she would still be the greatest motion picture artist I have ever seen."

In a short time, *Carmen* became the biggest money-maker the Lasky Company had yet enjoyed.

On the same day Farrar's *Carmen* was released — November 4, 1915 — another version of *Carmen,* made by Fox, directed by Raoul Walsh, and starring Theda Bara, opened. The two *Carmens* were reviewed simultaneously, and the Bara version suffered in comparison to Farrar's. Strangely, the Fox film, apparently at considerable expense, incorporated the Micaela character, impersonated by Elsie McLeod, but DeMille had been right about a silent Micaela contributing nothing worthwhile to a *Carmen* story line. Farrar's *Carmen* remained vital, free, uncluttered, with none of the posturing of the Bara version.

Temptation followed *Carmen* in release, and the "Motion Picture News" wrote of the Farrar performance: "She stands alone as a pantomimist, whose acting has no bad moments, is astonishingly sustained, and in its total effect is nothing less than dazzling. Miss Farrar needs no subtitles. Her face, her gestures, her whole demeanor are chapters in an open book of emotion, every page of which is turned for you at precisely the right moment as the story unfolds."

Maria Rosa, released several months later, garnered almost as high a regard from the critical faculty as *Carmen* had enjoyed, and both DeMille and Lasky wondered why they'd ever been concerned about the camera and their "Jerry," for that had been a love affair ending in the happiest of marriages.

There was a more personal romance, however, between Farrar and Lou Tellegen, which was to climax in a marriage that would be one of the stormiest.

Tellegen had seen her photograph in Goldwyn's New York office when he signed his own Lasky contract, and inquired about her. Fred Kley, a Lasky executive, was walking across the lot with Tellegen one day when Miss Farrar, in her *Maria Rosa* costume, left her set. Tellegen asked to be introduced, and Kley afterwards said, "I've never seen anything like it before or since. It was just as if a spark came from his eyes and was met by one from hers."

William de Mille noted, on attending what he considered the "first Hollywood party," as hostessed by Miss Farrar, that Tellegen "looked quite unhappy when she was dancing with anyone else, which was most of the time, but he always turned up to ask for the next." Also, at six in the morning when

Geraldine Farrar with Wallace Reid in JOAN THE WOMAN

Mr. and Mrs. de Mille left the party, Miss Farrar had removed her slippers and stockings and was walking across the dewy lawn, accompanied by an earnestly talking Tellegen.

When Miss Farrar departed for the East, Tellegen had accompanied her to the station, and he had run down the length of the platform, holding her hand, as many movie lovers have since done in many movie farewells.

None of this escaped the press, but as late as December of 1915, Miss Farrar was maintaining in a "Photoplay" interview: "Marriage and the artist do not agree. I do not believe a woman can be a great artist until midnight, and then turn a switch and transform herself into a devoted wife and mother. Not that I disapprove of marriage. It is quite all right for the majority of people, but never for an artist, to whom freedom means everything."

Tellegen and she were married in New York on February 8, 1916.

When she came back to Hollywood that summer of 1916 to spend the entire period filming one big DeMille spectacle, *Joan the Woman*, she was still "Our Jerry" to the studio from top man to low, but Tellegen was already asserting himself, jealous of her position in a medium he had failed to conquer, envious of the devotion she inspired in every co-worker. DeMille and Lasky were praying that her performance wouldn't suffer, because their production of the story of Joan of Arc was to be their costliest to date, eventually running up a budget of $302,976.25. With *Joan the Woman*, DeMille himself was later to admit that he fell in love with filming the spectacle.

Farrar worked again like the trouper she was. She bobbed her hair. Frightened of horses, she nevertheless insisted on doing all her own riding until one day a horse ran away with her, and luckily she was rescued by Jack Holt. It was a blazing hot summer, and although everybody else complained of the heat, Farrar, wearing full armour, only said, "I'm too much interested all the time to know what's happening on the outside of me." She threw herself into the massive battle scenes of Les Tourelles, as filmed on the Lasky Ranch, with all the fervour she could muster, and a couple of times was physically knocked unconscious from accidental blows on the head. The crew, adoring her, was so annoyed with one stuntman for having accidentally knocked her out that they tossed him in a blanket.

DeMille had staged that battle like a commanding general on the battlefield, with every director of the Lasky Company being captain of a separate unit of French or English soldiers, riding into the staged conflict at the head of his company. Thus, William de Mille, George Melford, Donald Crisp, and James Young were also bit actors in these scenes.

Geraldine Farrar with Wallace Reid and Theodore Kosloff in DeMille's THE WOMAN GOD FORGOT

Miss Farrar did her own close-ups and medium shots when she was burned at the stake, to the consternation of little Agnes De Mille, then a child allowed to look on during filming and certain that her beloved ''Jerry'' was at least being singed. For the long shots, Gladys Rosson, later to become closely associated with the DeMille production unit, was called away from her desk, taking over at the stake, because DeMille had noted she was about the same size as Farrar.

DeMille shot some scenes in colour in a process perfected by Alvin Wyck-off, registered as the DeMille-Wyckoff colour process.

Joan the Woman was to remain Farrar's personal favourite of all the pictures she made. It was successful, although it did not make the big money *Carmen* had drawn, but the public has always been partial to sinners rather than saints, and there has always been some kind of jinx haunting every film production of the Joan of Arc story.

When Miss Farrar departed for her regular autumn concert tour before the annual season at the Met, she had signed another film contract to make two pictures the following summer for the Lasky Company.

Accordingly, during the summer of 1917, she returned to Hollywood to play Montezuma's daughter in DeMille's drama of the conquest of Aztec Mexico by Cortez, *The Woman God Forgot;* she also played for DeMille a Brittany fishermaid in *The Devil Stone*.

DeMille and Lasky wanted her to return for the fourth summer of film production, but Tellegen upset these plans. He had not registered as a star in Lasky pictures, and had been allowed to direct a couple of features there, about which the company was very unhappy. He asked his wife to intercede on his behalf; she did, but when they still refused to let him direct any more, Miss Farrar was forced to side with her husband in order to keep peace in the family, and unfortunately made no more pictures for the Lasky-DeMille unit.

Lasky, encouraged by the success of Farrar as a film actress, had already tried a similar venture with Enrico Caruso, who had sung many a tenor role to Farrar's soprano. For $200,000, Caruso was launched upon a film career to start with two movies. The first, *My Cousin,* was so poorly received that the second, *The Splendid Romance,* although completed, was shelved, never released in the U.S.A, and the whole venture written off as a loss.

In 1917 Paramount tried to launch a series of pictures starring another celebrated prima donna, Lina Cavalieri, who had already made several films in Italy co-starring with her husband, Lucien Muratore. But Cavalieri, although radiantly beautiful, had none of the fire of Farrar. Nor, as the camera quickly revealed, was she the actress Farrar always was. After four films, her contract was not renewed.*

Meanwhile, Samuel Goldwyn had formed his own company, and Geraldine Farrar signed to star for him on a longterm contract. The summer of 1918 was a far cry, however, from the *camaraderie* and climate of California. The Goldwyn Studio at Fort Lee, New Jersey, was not the Lasky lot in Hollywood. Even the following summer, when Goldwyn moved to Culver City,

*Cavalieri made at least one other picture in 1921 in Italy, and was reported killed in 1944 during an air raid on Florence. A movie, *The Most Beautiful Woman in the World,* filmed in Italy with Robert Z. Leonard directing and starring Gina Lollobrigida, was supposedly based upon Cavalieri's life, but was largely fictitious.

and Miss Farrar was again shooting in Southern California, the wear and tear of also being Mrs. Tellegen was beginning to tell on her. Farrar was still indomitably Farrar, but Tellegen's fits of childish temperament and perpetual sulkiness were devitalising her offscreen.

Just as Goldwyn had let Willard Mack write some of Pauline Frederick's pictures (her worst ones), he signed Tellegen as Miss Farrar's leading man, "doubtless for harmony's sake on the distaff side," as Farrar herself later noted.

Goldwyn has described the Farrar-Tellegen battles on set in his book, "Behind the Screen": "We brought Mr. Tellegen on to play with his wife. He did more than that. He frequently played against her." When they had scenes together, Tellegen tried to hog the camera. Miss Farrar knew it, but she did not protest, even managing to keep a straight face when Tellegen, seeing them take close-ups of his wife, would complain, "You haven't made a single one of me yet."

Goldwyn advised his director to let Tellegen ham it up on the duo shots. "Take him that way," he said, "and then we'll throw away the negatives. The ones we'll keep will be those where Farrar is played up."

Miss Farrar, abetted by her husband, had insisted that Tellegen's name appear on the billboards with hers. When his name was omitted, she went out in her car one night, and with her own hands tore down every offending poster she could find, threatening, when Goldwyn scolded her, to stop work in the middle of the picture she was then making if Tellegen's name was not put up with hers.

"All right," said Goldwyn, "you do that and I am going to show the first part of the picture and then announce on the screen that at this point Madame Farrar would not proceed because the producer did not feature Lou Tellegen's name."

An armistice was declared, but the fire in Farrar's screen work sizzled down in her last Goldwyn feature to a lambent flame.

At the same time Farrar was filming for Goldwyn, he also engaged Mary Garden to make two films, *Thais* and *The Splendid Sinner*, but Miss Garden, although a vivid "singing actress" onstage, was happy about nothing concerning the two pictures except the $125,000 she was being paid for ten weeks' work. Garden had a profound respect for the camera, but after ten weeks of it, she knew it wasn't for her, and said adieu to the medium.

"What a tiring *métier* it is," Miss Garden complained of the films, "beginning and beginning all over again, until you don't know what you're doing."

And how different from Farrar's reaction, for she loved every moment of her work before the camera until Tellegen began spoiling everything for her.

She made seven pictures for Goldwyn, but in mid-winter of 1920, when she was hostessing a formal luncheon for Mr. and Mrs. Fritz Kreisler at her New York home, the butler announced that Mr. Goldwyn was in the music-room, asking to see her on a matter of extreme urgency.

Goldwyn was tentative in his approach. Her recent picture was not drawing well, he said, yet her contract had two years to run, a matter of twenty-four working weeks, with the sum of $250,000 involved. Goldwyn was suggesting that her screen popularity might be restored were she to take a limited vacation from filmwork.

"Don't you think that perhaps it would be better to quit entirely?" was Miss Farrar's counter suggestion. "If you think so, say so, Mr. Goldwyn, and we'll tear up the contract now and here."

He was forced to agree and "without another word and with the most gallant look in the world, she destroyed the contract which meant $250,000."

That same year she contracted to make two films at Pathé, but after the first one, *The Riddle Woman**, asked to be let off making the other. In her opinion, the picture "was spoiled by poor writing, poor camera work, and impossible direction. The excellent actors did their best against studio odds, but I refused to go on with any such further irritations."

It was her last film. She did not long thereafter remain Mrs. Tellegen, divorcing him, while he screamed to the press and anybody else who would listen, humiliating her with a barrage of lawsuits and public accusations. She was a few years older than he, and, as d'Annunzio had done with Duse, he seemed to take a fiendish delight in reminding her and the world of that fact.

When she was awakened one midnight in October 1934 to be informed by a reporter that Tellegen was dead, she replied curtly, "I have nothing to say, and am not interested."

She was horrified later when a friend told her the details of his ugly suicide. Ill, broke, and out-of-work, Lou Tellegen, in a Hollywood which had long ago rejected him, died on October 29, 1934 from self-inflicted wounds made by a pair of scissors. Miss Farrar, stunned, closed her eyes, and said, "May those tormented ashes rest in peace."

As early as 1921, Miss Farrar began being wooed by promoters of a primitive form of talking motion pictures, but she was too busy with opera, concerts, and recordings for Victor to consider the venture seriously. At a bright spring matinee performance on April 22, 1922, at the Metropolitan, she formally retired from her operatic career with a gala performance of Leoncavallo's "Zaza." She was only forty.

Lenore Ulric has told me that Belasco and she sat in Farrar's dressing-room after that occasion, openly weeping while they denounced the talents of her successor, Maria Jeritza. Farrar herself maintained a dignified silence about that lady. Outside the opera house, the "Jerry flappers" were alternately crying hysterically and shouting, "We want Jerry! We want Jerry!" And the posters for the new favourite of the Metropolitan, that blonde "Viennese Thunderbolt" Jeritza, had already been pasted up, for she had inherited, even before the retirement, some of the prize Farrar roles, including that "bone of contention," "Tosca." Farrar made her own farewell speech to her faithful audience, refusing public eulogies and farewell suppers. As she wrote in her book of the leavetaking: "Somehow my motor, sunk in gorgeous blooms, drove to the stage door, and, working my way through the crowds, I was soon carried away — more dead than alive."

The "New York Times" recorded of that farewell performance: "When Miss Farrar in her role of Zaza fell swooning to the floor and the last curtain fell over her, tumult reigned. People jumped to their feet, calling for her, and from every part of the lower floor men and women, girls, youngsters, ran

*Originally, this title was *The Riddle: Woman*. Then the colon was changed to a dash, which soon became a hyphen, and finally all punctuation was omitted, making the title as meaningless as the picture itself.

forward until there was a solid mass of faces looking up at her and cheering as she appeared. A huge banner, 'Hurrah, Farrar — Farrar, Hurrah,' was stretched across the pit.

"Bedlam was the keynote outside of the Met. And 40th Street, between Broadway and Eighth Avenue, was filled. Traffic policemen gave up all attempts to keep a lane through it. Enthusiastic stage-hands had planned to pull her up Broadway by a rope attached to her car, after the fashion set by Jenny Lind. But the rope got tangled up in the wheels.

"Wearing her sparkling tiara on her head — a gift — Miss Farrar waved, and the crowd roared. The car sped north on Broadway, and her career with it."

She enjoyed several seasons on the concert stage and a nationwide tour with a "Carmen" fantasia, featuring the highlights from the opera. She made many appearances during intermissions of the Saturday Metropolitan radio broadcasts, and she wrote her autobiography, "Such Sweet Compulsion," published in 1938.

She lived quietly at her Connecticut farmhouse, and villagers of neighbouring Ridgefield frequently saw her cream-coloured Ford drive into town for shopping sprees.

"Tomorrow can be just as interesting as yesterday," she said on her seventy-seventh birthday, adding a warning against the evils of living at too fast a pace: "So much is pressing in on humans today that they do not have time to stand still long enough to evaluate it. They gulp life and taste nothing. They eat life and have no savour."

An avid movie fan to the last, she regretted only that "my own era was too early for the combination of the present acting and talking features."

On March 11, 1967, she died of a heart attack at her Ridgefield home on New Street. She was eighty-five years old.

GERALDINE FARRAR FILMOGRAPHY

CARMEN (1915). Dramatic tragedy; as Carmen. *Dir:* Cecil B. DeMille. *Sc:* William C. de Mille (from the novel by Prosper Mérimée). *With* Wallace Reid, Pedro de Cordoba, Horace B. Carpenter, Billy Elmer, Jeanie Macpherson, Anita King. (Released simultaneously in Manhattan with Fox production starring Theda Bara; see listing in the Bara filmography.) *Prod:* Lasky Feature Play Co. (Paramount). 5 reels. (Compare listing in Wallace Reid filmography.)

TEMPTATION (1915). Romantic melodrama about the loves of a great diva; as Renée Duprée, opera star. *Dir:* Cecil B. DeMille. *Sc:* Hector Turnbull. *With* Pedro de Cordoba, Theodore Roberts, Raymond Hatton, Elsie Jane Wilson, Sessue Hayakawa. *Prod:* Lasky Feature Play Co. (Paramount). 6 reels.

MARIA ROSA (1916). Romantic melodrama of old Catalonia; as Maria Rosa, a Catalonian peasant wife sworn to avenge her husband's false imprisonment. *Dir:* Cecil B. DeMille. *Sc:* William C. de Mille (from the play by Wallace Gilpatrick and Guido Marburg, translated and adapted from the Spanish play by Angel Guémera). *With* Wallace Reid, Pedro de Cordoba, Ernest Joy, Horace B. Carpenter, Anita King, James Neill. *Prod:* Lasky Feature Play Co. (Paramount). 5 reels. (Re-made in Spain as a talkie, 1965.) (Compare listing in Wallace Reid filmography.)

JOAN THE WOMAN (1917). Historical drama of Joan of Arc. *Dir:* Cecil B. DeMille. *Sc:* Jeanie Macpherson. *With* Wallace Reid, Raymond Hatton, Theodore Roberts, Tully Marshall, Hobart Bosworth, Charles Clary, James Neill, Lawrence Peyton, Horace B. Carpenter, Lillian Leighton, Cleo Ridgely, Marjorie Daw, Stephen Gray, Ernest Joy, Walter Long. (There have been many film versions of the Joan of Arc story, the classic one being the Carl Dreyer interpretation, *The Passion of Joan of Arc,* with Falconetti.) *Prod:* Cardinal Film Co., for Paramount-Artcraft release. 10 reels. (Compare listing in Wallace Reid filmography)

THE WOMAN GOD FORGOT (1917). Romantic melodrama of the conquest of Mexico; as Tezac, Montezuma's daughter. *Dir:* Cecil B. DeMille. *Sc:* Jeanie Macpherson. *With* Wallace Reid, Hobart Bosworth, Theodore Kosloff, Raymond Hatton, Walter Long, Julia Faye, Olga Grey, James Neill. *Prod:* Paramount-Artcraft. 6 reels. (Compare listing in Wallace Reid filmography)

THE DEVIL STONE (1918). Romantic melodrama; as Marcia Namot, a Breton fishermaid who becomes a great lady. *Dir:* Cecil B. DeMille. *Sc:* Jeanie Macpherson (from a story by Beatrice DeMille and Leighton Osmun). *With* Wallace Reid, Tully Marshall, Hobart Bosworth, James Neill, Raymond Hatton, Gustav von Seyffertitz, Ernest Joy, Mabel Van Buren Lillian Leighton, Horace B. Carpenter. *Prod:* Paramount - Artcraft. 6 reels. (Compare listing in Wallace Reid filmography.)

THE TURN OF THE WHEEL (1918). Romantic drama; as Rosalie Dean, a wealthy American in Monte Carlo. *Dir:* Reginald Barker. *Sc:* Ad. from a Tex Charuvate story. *With* Herbert Rawlinson, Percy Marmont, Violet Heming, Hassard Short, Mabel Ballin, Maude Turner Gordon. *Prod:* Goldwyn (Diva Pictures). 5 reels.

THE HELL CAT (AKA GB, *The Wild Cat*) (1918). Western melodrama; as Pancha O'Brien, a hell cat of Wyoming, in love with the sheriff and desired by an outlaw. *Dir:* Reginald Barker. *Sc:* Willard Mack (from his own story). *With* Milton Sills, Thomas Santschi. *Prod:* Goldwyn (Diva Pictures). 6 reels.

SHADOWS (1919). Drama of the Alaskan dance-halls and the Manhattan social whirl; as Cora Lamont who becomes Mrs. Barnes. *Dir:* Reginald Barker. *Sc:* Willard Mack (from his own story). *With* Milton Sills, Thomas Santschi. *Prod:* Goldwyn (Diva Pictures). 5 reels.

THE STRONGER VOW (1919). Spanish melodrama of vengeance and love; as Dolores de Cordova. *Dir:* Reginald Barker. *Sc:* Ad. from a story by Izola Forrester. *With* Milton Sills, Thomas Santschi, Kate Lester, John Davidson, Hassard Short. *Prod:* Goldwyn (Diva Pictures). 6 reels.

THE WORLD AND ITS WOMEN (1919). Romantic drama of the Russian Revolution; as a peasant girl who becomes a great diva in love with a Russian prince. *Dir:* Frank Lloyd. *Sc:* Ad. from a story by Thomas Buchanan. *With* Lou Tellegen, Alec B. Francis, Edward J. Connelly, Naomi Childers, W. Lawson Butt, Arthur Carewe. *Prod:* Goldwyn (Diva Pictures). 7 reels.

FLAME OF THE DESERT (1919). Romantic melodrama of London and Egypt; as Lady Isabel. *Dir:* Reginald Barker. *Sc:* Charles Logue (from his own story). *With* Lou Tellegen, Alec B. Francis, Edythe Chapman, Casson Ferguson, Macy Harlan. *Prod:* Goldwyn (Diva Pictures). 5 reels.

THE WOMAN AND THE PUPPET (1920). Romantic drama of Old Seville; as Concha Perez. *Dir:* Reginald Barker. *Sc:* J. G. Hawks (from the French novel by Pierre Louys). *With* Lou Tellegen, Dorothy Cumming, Bertram Grassby, Macy Harlan, Rose Dione. (Refilmed as a talkie in 1935 by Josef von Sternberg, as *The Devil Is a Woman,* with Marlene Dietrich; re-filmed again in 1960 as *A Woman Like Satan,* starring Brigitte Bardot.) *Prod:* Goldwyn (Diva Pictures). 7 reels.

THE RIDDLE WOMAN (1920). Romantic melodrama; as Lilla Gravert. *Dir:* Edward José. *Sc:* John B. Clymer (from a Broadway play which had starred Bertha Kalich). *With* Montagu Love, Adele Blood, William P. Carleton, Frank Losee, Madge Bellamy. *Prod:* Pathe. 6 reels.

4
HAROLD LOCKWOOD
AND
MAY ALLISON

The movies were very young in 1918, and although the United States was at war and the Spanish influenza epidemic was claiming the lives of Americans at home, the death of Harold Lockwood in Manhattan on Saturday, October, 1918, was a numbing shock.

Only a few movie stars had died and been mourned up to that time. John Bunny had died in 1915 and Arthur Johnson a year later, but Bunny was a mature man and a comedian, not a romantic lead; and it was no secret that Johnson, for all his charm and talent, was a hopeless alcoholic. Lockwood was not addicted to or flawed by any vice, seemed to be bursting with health and vitality, and to have the best years of his life and career ahead of him.

Metro had just released a new Lockwood film, *Pals First,* and it was doing tremendous business in spite of the epidemic that had temporarily closed many movie theatres. He had completed three unreleased Metro features, and was just starting another when he fell ill. He ranked among the topmost stars — Douglas Fairbanks, Wallace Reid, Earle Williams, and Antonio Moreno.

Lockwood had just completed not only three pictures for Metro but also a featurette called *Liberty Bond Jimmy* designed to sell war bonds. And to promote further the fourth "Liberty Loan" drive, he installed himself in the booth of the "Morning Telegraph" in Madison Square Garden and personally sold war bonds in record numbers.

It was this physical contact with his public, and this service to an America-at-war, that exposed him to the virus that took so many lives just before the First World War ended. He was dead within ten days from pneumonia, a sequel to Spanish influenza. The New York and Hollywood branches of Metro shut down on the morning of October 22, the day of his funeral, and every film luminary in the East attended the services in Campbell's Funeral Parlor.

Harold Lockwood was born in Newark, New Jersey, on April 12, 1887. He was the only child of parents who had had no theatrical interests. His father was a trainer and breeder of horses, especially trotters, and young Lockwood spent his boyhood summers on a stock farm in Freehold, New Jersey. Before he was ten, he was a good horseman, and when his family moved to Brooklyn he distinguished himself in swimming, track and football.

While he was still in his teens, his parents moved to Manhattan, much to his delight, for he had already discovered the theatre and become an avid playgoer. Living in Manhattan enabled him to earn a dollar or two as part of some onstage background group. He later said, "These appearances before the footlights, — although I was so far back I couldn't see the lights — carved my future. They decided that the stage was for me!"

His father wanted him to enter a business college, which he obediently did, and later spent a brief time as a drygoods salesman. He hated it and confessed to his father that he wanted to become an actor. To his surprise his father said drily: "It is up to you. Act, if you must, but woe betide you if you are a ham actor. Aim high and go to it!"

For the next seven years he worked as an actor as diligently as he could. In the beginning he was a chorus man in the touring companies of Shubert and Frohman successes. He played better roles with Otis Harlan in "The Broken Idol" and with Edward N. Hoyt in "Mephisto," and became a popular regular not only in musical comedy but in vaudeville and Eastern stock. In later years he referred to his testing time in this way: "I wasn't an instantaneous success on the speaking stage. That's letting myself down about as lightly as I can."

He married an actress, and Alma Lockwood in 1908 bore him a son christened William but later known as Harold Lockwood, Jr.

One morning in the spring of 1911, Lockwood, in one of those "between engagements" periods every actor knows and dreads, was walking down Broadway and encountered Archie MacArthur of "Moving Picture World."

"We chatted," Lockwood said later, "and Mac inquired why I didn't make a try for motion pictures. He was firm in the belief that they were 'coming.' Frankly, I had my doubts at that time, but he kept praising them and even scrawled a note of introduction to Edwin S. Porter, who then controlled the Rex Company. I didn't want to offend him so I took the note he pressed on me and called on Mr. Porter, who engaged me right off. That's how I began in pictures."

From that day in 1911 until he died in 1918, he was never again without an acting engagement. Edwin Porter had sensed at once that he was leading-man timber for the screen, and the camera proved to be Lockwood's best friend. It captured the essence of his extroverted, engaging personality. On the screen he was so much that day's image of the romantic American male that he might have modelled for any of the representations of it painted by Charles Dana Gibson, Harrison Fisher, Coles Phillips, or Howard Chandler Christy.

He was not bragging when he once told an interviewer: "I was especially fortunate in being able to play leads in films from the start." He continued to play leads when he went from Rex to Nestor, then situated at Mariner's Harbor on Staten Island and later in Mauch Chuck, Pennsylvania (later still at Avenue E and 43rd Street in Bayonne, New Jersey, but by that time Lockwood was headquartered in Nestor's California studio).

Dorothy Davenport, who later married Wallace Reid, was frequently Lockwood's leading lady at Nestor, and her mother, Alice Davenport, was a character woman in his films.

In the last months of 1911 Nestor decided to send a nucleus of its Eastern unit to California to set up a Pacific Coast branch. Al Christie was made mentor and guide of the exodus, and he included the two Davenport women in

Harold Lockwood

the company he was taking West. Lockwood went to the station to see them off. He was lonely and unhappy, for he had quarrelled with his wife and was separated from her and his baby son.

"Mother and I felt so sorry for poor Harold," Miss Davenport has said. "He looked so forlorn and miserable we virtually kidnapped him. We deliberately made such a production out of bidding him farewell that he never realised the train was moving until it was too late to get off. By that time he didn't care. He had no luggage, but he borrowed what he needed, and both Al

Christie and Milton Fahrney promised him work as soon as we all got to California. Actors had the hearts of gypsies then. He was one of our tribe and we were all on our way West together!"

Hollywood was then a pastoral village nestling at the foot of the Santa Monica hills. The clean air was redolent of orange and lemon blossoms, and in the spring wild poppies and Indian paintbrush coloured the sloping fields orange and purple. The fences and low roofs of the farmhouses and bungalows were covered with geranium, morning glories, and Cecile Brunner roses. Hollywood wasn't a state of mind *then* — it was a little farming suburb of the thriving but still sleepy Southern California city known as Los Angeles, not too many years removed from its original status as a Spanish-mission trading centre called El Pueblo de Nuestra Señora la Reina de Los Angeles á Porciuncula.

Film directors and producers had been attracted to Southern California several years before Nestor arrived. Its eternal sunshine, and the variety of its natural scenic backgrounds, made it ideal for motion picture production. Colonel William N. Selig had brought his company from Chicago to the West Coast in 1907, and thereafter maintained studios both in the East and on the Pacific Coast. By November, 1909 the prospering Selig Company opened the first large California motion picture studio on North Mission Road in Los Angeles. In 1910 D. W. Griffith began making annual winter pilgrimages to California with his Biograph company.

In the last days of 1911 Al Christie converted Blondeau's Tavern, at what is now the northwest corner of Sunset and Gower, into a studio. Incidentally, it was from Nestor, via amalgamations with other independent companies, that Universal Studios came, one of the few important production and releasing companies still in existence.

Harold Lockwood stayed with Nestor until the spring of 1912, when he moved out to Santa Monica to play for Thomas H. Ince at Broncho, also known as the "101" Ranch, where he stayed nine months, playing leads in Westerns and Civil War dramas. Then, as he said, he "drifted" to the brand new Selig Studios on Alessandro at Edendale, where he remained a year and a half under a contract that stipulated he would be used regularly as leading man.

He played every kind of film for Selig — comedies, dramas, modern and costume romances, action melodramas, sea stories, psychological message stories. The feature films of that day rarely exceeded three reels, and he was often filming more than one picture at a time. Kathlyn Williams and he co-starred in many Selig pictures, and fans everywhere regarded them as an ideal romantic team.

Adolph Zukor, the head of Famous Players, sent a contingent from his New York studio to film two pictures in California that included Mary Pickford as the star and Edwin S. Porter as her director. The two films were *Hearts Adrift* and *Tess of the Storm Country*, and Porter let it be known that he was in the market for a capable leading man for Miss Pickford. Then he remembered Harold Lockwood was on the West Coast, and sent for him. Lockwood secured his release from Selig, and Porter gave him the much-coveted assignment as Mary Pickford's leading man.

Lockwood was so capable in both Pickford vehicles Porter recommended

May Allison

that Zukor hire him as a leading man for Famous Players. Consequently, when Miss Pickford's company returned East early in 1914, Lockwood went back to New York City under a personal contract to Zukor.

During the run of that contract, he graced the casts of twelve Famous Players productions. He played again with Mary Pickford in *Such a Little Queen;* twice — in *The Man from Mexico* and *Are You a Mason?* — he was the romantic juvenile in John Barrymore comedies; and twice — in *Wildflower* and *The Crucible* — he was leading man to Marguerite Clark. Of all the films he played in for Zukor the most important to his career was undoubtedly *David Harum*, which starred William H. Crane in the title role but was more notable because it was the first time Harold Lockwood and May Allison played together as romantic leads.

It remained for Thomas Ricketts*, a director for some of the early Nestor releases, to sense the potential of a Lockwood-Allison co-starring team. Ricketts was then directing for the American Flying "A" Company at Santa Barbara, and he persuaded his employers to hire Lockwood and team him with May Allison.

During the time of his Zukor contract Lockwood reconciled with his estranged wife and he journeyed to Santa Barbara with her and his young son early in the spring of 1915. Thereafter the domestic life of the Lockwoods was revived and shattered almost semi-annually. Lockwood was devoted to his son, and it is probable that his marriage lasted as long as it did only because of his love for the boy and interest in his welfare.

The first feature Lockwood filmed for American was *The Lure of the Mask*, a film adaptation of a popular Harold McGrath novel. Elsie Jane Wilson was his leading lady and even before that picture was finished Lockwood told Tom Ricketts he felt professionally more compatible with May Allison. She was placed under contract and arrived in Santa Barbara for the express purpose of co-starring with Lockwood. She did so fourteen times at American.

May Allison had been born at Rising Farm, Georgia, on June 14, 1895. Her family was well-known in the South, her mother having been a Wise from Virginia (the Wises produced one Governor and the eminent Brigadier-General Henry A. Wise). On the maternal side of her father's family the Hampton name figures, most notably General Wade Hampton.

Miss Allison was educated in Birmingham, Alabama, and at the Centenary Female College in Cleveland, Tennessee, and then attended a girl's finishing school in Philadelphia. She possessed not only an unusual Southern beauty but a good lyric soprano voice. When her father died, she was only sixteen, But she and her mother lost no time in deciding that her looks and voice were the family's most likely assets if only she could become a singing actress on Broadway.

Cinderella stories *do* occur in real life and almost the first producer Miss Allison called on — Henry W. Savage — hired her as a replacement in his production of Walter Browne's modern morality play, "Everywoman." He assigned her to the role of "Vanity" but soon promoted her to the more important role of "Beauty." She then obtained the title role in the second company of "The Quaker Girl," and after a few rehearsals was transferred to the number one company as understudy and alternate to the star, Ina Claire (she got to play the role on several occasions). Thereafter she was *ingénue* lead to DeWolf Hopper in "Miss Caprice"; starred on the New York stage in "Iole," a musical with story and book by Robert W. Chambers; and starred in "Apartment 12-K," a comedy.

---

*Ricketts was born in London in 1853. In England he acted with Henry Irving, and in the United States with Katherine Lewis. He wrote and produced at least one play ("Duvar," 1881), played the male lead in many, and became a director for Charles Frohman. His motion picture career began in 1907. The best known film he directed was *Damaged Goods*, starring Richard Bennett. Toward the end of his life he turned again to acting. The last film in which he appeared was *Son of Frankenstein*. He died in Los Angeles in 1939.

She made her film *début* in 1915 as the *ingénue* in Theda Bara's first starring vehicle, *A Fool There Was*, and almost immediately thereafter was engaged by Adolph Zukor to play the romantic lead in *David Harum*, with Harold Lockwood as her screen lover. She then played the second female lead in *The Governor's Wife*, which starred Edith Wynne Mathison and was a film version of the very successful William C. de Mille play. It was shortly after this that she gratefully boarded the train with her mother and crossed the continent to Santa Barbara, California.

Two blonds don't always make a successful stage or screen team. Miss Allison and Lockwood did. They both had very blue eyes. He was fair-haired, and her hair was golden, and, when they were backlighted, the screen dazzled.

Their American-Mutual features were, from the beginning, just what the public wanted. In some of them Lockwood was rich and Allison poor (*The*

Harold Lockwood with Mary Pickford in HEARTS ADRIFT

Secretary of Frivolous Affairs); in others (*The Secret Wire*) she was a millionaire's daughter and he a hard-working young labourer. There were costume romances too, with Allison a beautiful Southerner and Lockwood a Northerner (*The End of the Road*), and also Westerns (*Thè Buzzard's Shadow*), with him an Army sergeant and her a young widow. But in all, no matter what the *genre* or what their social positions, they were lovers, and a more idealised couple has rarely graced the screen. All their first films together were directed by Thomas Ricketts, and all were shot against picturesque locales.

In "One Reel a Week," a book he co-authored with the late cameraman Arthur Miller, Fred J. Balshofer tells at some length how he acquired the Lockwood-Allison team for the eight co-starring features his Yorke Company made and released through Metro. Balshofer had an interest in the films then being made by Francis X. Bushman with Beverly Bayne, but Bushman's temperamental peccadilloes annoyed Balshofer, and, when Metro acquired Bushman's services, Balshofer sold his interest in Bushman and devoted all his time to promoting the Lockwood-Allison team.

According to Balshofer, it was Owen Moore who had called his attention to the films Lockwood and Allison were making at American. Balshofer journeyed up to Santa Barbara to see the pair, and they signed a contract to co-star for a series, shooting on which would begin on or about April 18, 1916. Lockwood was paid $250 weekly and Miss Allison $200.

The eight features thèy made for Yorke-Metro launched them both into the big time, and big money. In one year their movies surpassed the box-office success of the Bushman-Bayne vehicles. Yorke-Metro, forced to more than double their salaries, concluded it was too costly to continue co-starring them. Each of the Lockwood and Allison names could carry a feature as a solitary star, it was decided, and so the team was broken. Lockwood was signed by Yorke-Metro to a new solo contract, and began immediately to work on his first solo starring feature early in 1917, a comedy fantasy, *The Haunted Pajamas*, with Carmel Myers as his leading lady. Miss Allison held out a little longer before she too signed on a solo basis and began telling the public that co-starred features favour the actor rather than the actress. Lockwood, starring alone, stayed among the top ten box-office actors for the remaining two years of his life.

A few romance-minded gossips tried to intimate that Lockwood and Allison were a romantic team in their real lives. Even today oldtimer Santa Barbarans will tell you that theirs was a real romance — but it is all gossip and hearsay. The truth is that throughout his screen career Lockwood's emotions were drained by his on-again off-again marriage, and during its "bachelor" intervals his widowed mother always came to stay with him. Sometime in 1917 Lockwood and his wife were so quietly divorced — in California — that few knew about it until his death.

Balshofer continued as Lockwood's director, although later on a few others— George Irving, Edwin Carewe, Henry Otto — directed a film or two, but no one actress continued long as his leading lady. Metro even made a point of announcing that Mr. Lockwood would be supported by a top list of players headed by leading ladies like Pauline Curley, Ann Little, Martha Mansfield, Bessie Eyton, and Rubye de Remer.

May Allison with Harold Lockwood in THE HIDDEN CHILDREN

In the first week of October, shooting began in Manhattan on a scenario based upon George Gibbs' popular espionage-aviation novel, "The Yellow Dove." After only a few days of camera work, Lockwood was forced to take to his bed in the suite he occupied at the Hotel Woodward, and production on his film was temporarily halted. It was said, at first, that he was suffering from a severe attack of "la grippe," but it soon became known that it was really Spanish influenza, and within ten days, on October 19, he died of the too-often inevitable pneumonia complications. Three days later, after the large but orderly funeral at Campbell's Funeral Parlor on Broadway at 66th Street, he was buried in Woodlawn Cemetery.

His mother was with him when he died, and Alma Lockwood, his divorced wife, who was living in Los Angeles at the MacDonald Apartments, went into a state of collapse when she learned of her ex-husband's demise. Lockwood's son, only ten at the time, always lamented his father's early death. Alma Lockwood subsequently sailed to Australia for a season of stock, and, on returning to Hollywood, worked briefly as an extra and bit player. Sometime late in 1919 she married a man named Robinson. As Harold Lockwood, Jr. the

May Allison with Rudolph Valentino in THE CHEATER

son was under contract to First National in the late Twenties, but he never clicked, although he was handsome and, it was said, had inherited his father's talent and charm. Both Lockwood Jr. and his mother, Alma Robinson, seem to have vanished long since from the Hollywood scene.

May Allison's career has been longer-lasting. She signed a new and very profitable starring contract with Metro late in 1917, and her solo films were popular. By 1919 her fan mail was the fourth largest of screen actresses (the first three: Mary Pickford, Norma Talmadge, Marguerite Clark).

She may have complained of the inadequacies of her roles as Lockwood's co-star, but she had good reason to lament even more the thinness of her solo starring parts. She hit her happiest stride in comedies based on successful Broadway hits, like *Fair and Warmer* and *The Walk-Offs*. Even in those days, however, a female star found it difficult to maintain a high batting average when she herself had to carry the picture (male stars have always had an easier time because most of their vehicles revolve around action and adventure). In one of Miss Allison's early 1920 releases, *The Cheater,* her supporting cast featured Rudolph Valentino in a small role. Even as *The Cheater* was released, he was working for Rex Ingram and with the release of *The Four Horsemen of the Apocalypse* in 1921, he entered upon one of the cinema's most spectacular, and brief, careers.

Miss Allison had moved to Hollywood when she became, along with Nazimova and Viola Dana, a top star at Metro. She acquired a large, tastefully furnished, well-staffed Beverly Hills mansion, and installed there not only her mother but also her brother and her sister and brother-in-law, with their young baby. Her sister, Mrs. Latham, became her secretary-manager.

In 1921 it became known that she had married secretly, sometime in 1920, at Greenwich, Connecticut. The groom was Robert Ellis, who had been her leading man in two comedies, *In for Thirty Days* and *Peggy Does Her Darndest*.

At the end of 1921, disappointed with the story fare she had been handed at Metro, she did not re-sign and made an independently produced feature with her husband, *The Woman Who Fooled Herself*. Then, at the peak of her fame, she surprised her fans and the entire film colony by temporarily abandoning her career for a round-the-world cruise with her husband and several other friends, including director Robert G. Vignola.

She was away nearly eighteen months, and when she returned to the States she announced that she would resume her career and divorce her husband. Ellis continued in the industry as an actor-director, and is now living in a beach cottage at Malibu. Not until she divorced Robert Ellis did it become known that she had been married previously to Colonel J. L. Stephenson, wealthy mining man. That first marriage and divorce was one of Hollywood's best-kept secrets.

With her announcement, almost at once the fan magazines abounded with stories about "the new May Allison." She had sailed away, a popular, golden-haired Georgia beauty, and had returned, a sophisticate with an exotic hair-do. Her golden hair, once curly, was now parted in the middle and brought straight back over her ears to a large Diana-knot. She wore earrings, elaborately set rings, and the latest Parisian frocks by Lucile.

By 1925 her acting career was booming again, thanks in part to James R.

Harold Lockwood and May Allison in MISTER 44, filmed on the California coast

Quirk's personal interest in her and her future. He was editor of "Photoplay," then the top American film publication, and there was scarcely an issue which did not feature a full-page portrait of "the new May Allison," or a story about her.

She married Quirk in 1926. It was a second marriage for him, and they lived in New York's Buckingham Hotel, a few doors from the "Photoplay" office at 221 W. 57th Street.

Miss Allison's best pictures in these years were two of the four she contracted to do for First National. In *The Greater Glory* she and Anna Q. Nilsson are well-born Viennese sisters and the story chronicles their fates before, during and after the First World War. In *Men of Steel* she is a very modern daughter of a steel magnate intrigued by a brawny steel worker who has risen in the social scale, brilliantly played by the picture's star, Milton Sills. Said "Variety" of Miss Allison in this picture; "She never looked better in her hey-day of popularity, and from this film it would seem that Miss Allison's comeback is already a distinguished and decided success." The picture's exteriors were shot at U.S. Steel's subsidiary in Birmingham, Alabama, and one never-to-be-forgotten sequence has a worker fall into a vat of molten steel; in a subsequent sequence a funeral service is held near the furnace over a cold crucible of the steel in which the worker was consumed.

Unlike most film beauties of that decade, Miss Allison was well-read and could, and did, discuss almost anything with authority and humour. Herb Howe, one of Hollywood's better and frequently very cryptic writers, said she was lovelier in maturity than in youth.

After her 1927 role in Paramount's *The Telephone Girl,* in which she is a woman struggling to keep her past secret, it was predicted that talking movies, then about to revolutionise the industry, would enable her to rise to stardom again. But she never made another film, preferring her non-professional life as Mrs. James Quirk. Her husband died August 1, 1932, aged forty-seven.

By that time movies were all-talking, all-singing, all-dancing, and May Allison was only in her late thirties. Had she wished, she could have resumed her career, for she was still a beauty. Instead, she disappeared completely from both the Manhattan and Hollywood scenes.

She married a fourth time—Carl Osborne, of Chardon, Ohio—and frequently travelled all over the world with him. Nobody in today's Hollywood seems to have contact with her any more. She herself has said of her companions in her movie days: "I don't know who's left."

HAROLD LOCKWOOD FILMOGRAPHY

A WHITE REDMAN (1911). A thriller of the wilderness; as Gene Thomas, a trapper falsely accused of murder who is saved by an Indian he had once rescued from death. *Dir./Sc:* Edwin S. Porter. *Prod:* Rex. 1509 ft.

LOST ILLUSIONS (1811). A marital romance; as a married artist who woos the wife of another man. *Dir./Sc:* Edwin S. Porter. *With* Lois Weber, Phillips Smalley. *Prod:* Rex. 1070 ft.

A TRUE WESTERNER (1911). Western drama; as a young man nearly ruined by gambling fever. *Dir./Sc:* Milton J. Fahrney. *With* Gertrude Claire. *Prod:* Nestor. 850 fit.

THE WHITE MEDICINE MAN (1911). Western Indian drama; as an Indian brave cured by a white doctor. *Dir./.Sc:* Milton J. Fahrney. *Prod:* Nestor. 930 ft.

THE BEST MAN WINS (1911). Western romantic comedy; as an Easterner who wins the girl in a ploughing contest. *Dir./Sc:* Thomas Ricketts. *With* Dorothy Davenport. (This is probably the first moving picture to be filmed in its entirety in Hollywood, as distinguished from Los Angeles.) *Prod:* Nestor. 895 ft.

THE LAW OF THE RANGE. (1911). Western drama; again, as a white man who befriends a half-breed, who subsequently saves

his life. *Dir./Sc:* Milton J. Fahrney. (Advertised as "A Western from the West.") *Prod:* Nestor. 850 ft.

A BRAVE LITTLE WOMAN (1912). Romantic comedy; as a cheating cheater who comes up against a woman smarter than he. *Dir./Sc:* Thomas Ricketts. *With* Dorothy Davenport. *Prod:* Nestor. 595 ft.

THE LOST ADDRESS (1912). Romantic comedy; as a prospective groom named Harry Locke. *Dir./Sc:* Al Christie. *With* Dorothy Davenport, Gordon Sackville. *Prod:* Nestor. 385 ft.

A MATINEE MIX-UP (1912). Romantic comedy; as a jealous husband. *Dir./Sc:* Al Christie. *With* Dorothy Davenport. *Prod:* Nestor. 950 ft.

INBAD. THE COUNT (1912). Romantic comedy; as an American who outwits his titled rival. *Dir./Sc:* Al Christie. *With* Dorothy Davenport. (Advertised as "A Comedy that Counts.") *Prod:* Nestor. 1000 ft

THE FEUDAL DEBT (1912). Kentucky feudal drama; as the lover of the girl whose family is his enemy. *Dir./Sc:* Thomas Ricketts. *With* Dorothy Davenport. *Prod:* Nestor. 950 ft.

OVER A CRACKED BOWL (1912). Domestic drama; as an outsider who patches a newlywed couple's first serious quarrel. *Dir./Sc:* Thomas Ricketts. *With* Betty Keller, D. A. McDonald. *Prod:* Nestor. 1 reel.

THE BACHELOR AND THE BABY (1912). Situation comedy; as a newly-betrothed bachelor who finds a baby in his car. *Dir./Sc:* Thomas Ricketts. *With* Dorothy Davenport, Josephine Ricketts. *Prod:* Nestor. 1 reel.

THE DESERTER (1912) Western Indian drama; as an Army officer who deserts his fort, but returns at the cost of his life to save it from an Indian attack. *Dir./Sc:* Thomas H. Ince. *With* Ethel Grandin, Francis Ford, Winnie Baldwin, Cliff Smith. (Re-made by Ince, 1916, for Triangle, starring Charles Ray.) *Prod:* Ince-Bison-NYMP. 2 reels.

THE CUB REPORTER'S BIG SCOOP (1912). Newspaper comedy; as a reporter who gets a real scoop when he interviews the father of the girl he loves. *Prod:* Nestor. 1 reel.

THE TORN LETTER (1912). Domestic drama; as Scott, a jealous husband. *With* Dorothy Davenport, Henry Otto. *Prod:* Nestor. 950 ft.

A PAIR OF BABY SHOES (1912). Domestic drama; as Richard Darrell, a husband about to part from his wife after the death of their baby. *With* Dorothy Davenport. *Prod:* Nestor. 950 ft.

THE RECKONING (1912). American Civil War drama: as a wounded Yankee soldier who takes refuge in the home of his onetime Confederate sweetheart. *With* Ethel Grandin, Richard Stanton, Ann Little, Leo Maloney. *Prod:* Ince-Broncho. 1 reel.

FOR THE HONOUR OF THE SEVENTH (1912). Western melodrama; as Captain Stanton, a soldier stationed in a Western fort who is accused of cowardice. *With* Ann Little, J. Barney Sherry. *Prod:* Ince-Broncho. 1030 ft.

THE SERGEANT'S BOY (1912). Army drama; as a sergeant who befriends an orphan boy. *With* Nick Cogley, Shorty Hamilton. *Prod:* "101" Bison-NYMP. 1585 ft.

THE ALTAR OF DEATH (1912). Western Indian drama; as a lieutenant loved by an Indian girl who gives her life to save the fort. *Dir./Sc:* Thomas H. Ince and C. Gardner Sullivan. *With* Ann Little. *Prod:* Kay-Bee/NYMP. 2 reels.

THE BALL PLAYER AND THE BANDIT (1912). Western drama; as an Easterner who wins his battles in the West with his fists. *Prod:* Ince-Broncho. 1 reel.

THE PAINTER AND THE PEASANT (1912). Drama; as the Painter. *Prod:* Great Northern. 2 reels.

FOR THE CAUSE (1912). American Civil War drama; as a Confederate soldier who gives his life to save his rival. *With* Ray Myers, Jean Hathaway, Shorty Hamilton, Bud Osborne. *Prod:* Kay-Bee/NYMP. 2 reels.

THE MILLIONAIRE VAGABONDS (1912). Comedy about a group of rich men who become "knights of the road;" as the leader of the rich men. *Dir./Sc:* Lem B. Parker. *With* Eugenie Besserer, George Hernandez, Frank Richardson. *Prod:* Selig. 1020 ft.

HARBOR ISLAND (1912). California romance; as an engineer in charge of a harbour project. *Dir:* Lem B. Parker. *Sc:* Walter Nichols. *With* Kathyln Williams, Henry Otto, Frank Richardson, Anna Dodge, Hobart Bosworth, George Hernandez, Frank Clarke, Robert Greene. *Prod:* Selig. 1008 ft.

THE LIPTON CUP: INTRODUCING SIR THOMAS LIPTON (1913). Drama of a sailing boat race; as a ship-builder who builds the yacht that wins the Lipton cup. *Dir./Sc:* Lem B. Parker. *With* Kathlyn Williams, Henry Otto, Robert Greene, Baby Lillian Wade, Sir Thomas Lipton. *Prod:* Selig. 1006 ft.

A LITTLE CHILD SHALL LEAD THEM (1913). Marital drama; as the husband whose marriage is saved by his child. *Dir:* Lem B. Parker. *Sc:* M. B. Gardner. *With* Kathlyn Williams, Baby Lillian Wade, Henry Otto, Daisy Prideaux. *Prod:* Selig. 1 reel.

THE GOVERNOR'S DAUGHTER (1913). Melodrama; as a man unjustly convicted. *Dir:* Lem B. Parker. *Sc:* Maibelle Heikes Justice. *With* Kathlyn Williams, Eugenie Besserer, Henry Otto, Lem B. Parker. *Prod:* Selig. (Working title: *Executive Clemency.*) 1 reel.

HER ONLY SON (1913). Social drama; as Jack Temple, a young man from the country who goes to the city, and is nearly ruined. *Dir:* Lem B. Parker. *Sc:* Malcolm Douglas. *With* Herbert Rawlinson, Henry Otto, Ormi Hawley, William Hutchinson. *Prod:* Selig. 1 reel.

TWO MEN AND A WOMAN (1913) A triangle of two men and one woman; as Conrad, a rich banker married to the woman. *Dir./Sc:* Lem B. Parker (from his own story). *With* Kathlyn Williams, Henry Otto. *Prod:* Selig. 1133 ft.

THE SPANISH PARROT-GIRL (1913). Romantic adventure; as Richard Avery, a rich American traveling in Spain. *Dir:* Lem B. Parker. *Sc:* Mabel Heikes Justice. *With* Eugenie Besserer, Al E. Garcia, George Hernandez, Henry Otto, Amy Trask. *Prod:* Selig. 1000 ft.

DIVERGING PATHS (1913). Marital drama; as Jed, the happily wed husband in this study of the contrasting marriages of two sisters. *Dir:* Lem B. Parker. *Sc:* Malcolm Douglas. *With* Eugenie Besserer, Henry Otto, Amy Trask, Goldie Colwell, Al. W. Filson. *Prod:* Selig. 1012 ft.

LOVE BEFORE TEN (1913). Comedy of elopement; as Jack Mason, the groom. *Dir:* Lem B. Parker. *Sc:* William A. Corey. *With* Eugenie Besserer, Roy Clarke, Baby Lillian Wade. *Prod:* Selig. 1009 ft.

MARGARITA AND THE MISSION FUNDS (1913). Romance of Old Mexico; as Stewart Hopewell, an American captain in the Mexican service. *Dir:* Lem B. Parker. *Sc:* William A. Corey. *With* Margarita Loveridge, Henry Otto, Al. E. Garcia, Goldie Colwell, George Hernandez, William Hutchinson. *Prod:* Selig. 1017 ft.

THE HOYDEN'S AWAKENING (1913). Marital drama; as the lover of a rich man's daughter. *Dir:* Lem B. Parker. *Sc:* C. A. Frambers. *With* Amy Trask, Henry Otto, Lillian Hayward, Goldie Colwell, William Hutchinson, Robert E. Greene, Wallace Brownlow, Daisy Prideaux, Sidney Franklyn. *Prod:* Selig. 1004 ft.

WITH LOVE'S EYES (1913). Romantic drama; as Charles, blinded in a fire, who falls in love with an actress disfigured in the same conflagration. *Dir:* Lem B. Parker. *Sc:* Emmett C. Hall. *With* Kathlyn Williams, Al. E. Garcia, Al W. Filson, Henry Otto, Lillian Hayward. *Prod:* Selig. 1 reel.

THE TIE OF THE BLOOD (1913). Love story of a modern Indian; as "Deer Foot," a Cherokee brave. *Dir:* Lem B. Parker. *Sc:* Hampton Del Ruth. *With* Amy Trask, Al E. Garcia, Henry Otto, Al. W. Filson. Filmed at the Indian school in Carlisle, Pennsylvania. *Prod:* Selig. 1012 ft.

THE BURGLAR WHO ROBBED DEATH (AKA *When a Burglar Robbed Death*) (1913). Drama; as a doctor disgraced because of drink who has turned burglar. *Dir:* Lem B. Parker. *Sc:* Lanier Bartlett. *With* Kathlyn Williams, Baby Lillian Wade, Al. E. Garcia, Dorothy Arnold, Jessie Wyckoff, Daisy Prideaux, Lillian Clark. *Prod:* Selig. 1018 ft.

THEIR STEPMOTHER (1913). Domestic drama; as a widower with two small daughters who falls in love. *Dir:* E. A. Martin. *Sc:* Hettie Gray Baker. *With* Kathlyn Williams, Utahna La Reno, Jessie Wyckoff, Baby Lillian Wade. *Prod:* Selig. 1020 ft.

A WELDED FRIENDSHIP (1913). An Alaskan romance; as Paul Trevor. *Dir:* Lem B. Parker. *Sc:* J. G. Nattinger. *With* Kathlyn Williams, Henry Otto, Al W. Filson, Ferdinand

Galvez, Baby Lillian Wade. *Prod:* Selig. 808 ft.

LIEUTENANT JONES (1913). Drama of regeneration; as Jones, a lieutenant whom the Indians help rehabilitate. *Dir:* Lem B. Parker. *Sc:* F. Sample. *With* Kathlyn Williams, Al. E. Garcia, Eugenie Besserer, Robert Chandler. *Prod:* Selig. 1027 ft.

THE STOLEN MELODY (1913). Romantic drama; as Henry Richard, a music publisher who loves the daughter of a composer whose music has been stolen. *Dir:* Lem B. Parker. *Sc:* Malcolm Douglas. *With* Kathlyn Williams, Al E. Garcia, Al W. Filson. *Prod:* Selig. 1027 ft.

WOMAN — PAST AND PRESENT (1913). Comedy drama of two generations of suffragettes; as the despised hero who ends up loved. *Dir./Sc:* Lem B. Parker. *With* Kathlyn Williams, Eugenie Besserer, Al E. Garcia. *Prod:* Selig. 1242 ft.

THE FIGHTING LIEUTENANT (1913). A Mexican romance; as a cavalry lieutenant stationed on the Mexican border who loves a beautiful señorita. *Dir./Sc:* E. A. Martin. *With* Eugenie Besserer, Adele Lane, Al E. Garcia, George Hernandez, William Hutchinson. *Prod:* Selig. 904 ft.

A MANSION OF MISERY (1913). Romantic drama; as Wilbur Notre, an Annapolis cadet who waits to wed the woman he loves. *Dir./Sc:* Lem B. Parker. *With* Kathlyn Williams, Al E. Garcia, Henry Otto. *Prod:* Selig. 1042 ft.

THE FLIGHT OF THE CROW (1913). Romantic adventure; as a man who disguises himself as a hobo. *Dir:* E. A. Martin. *Sc:* Arthur Preston Hankins. *With* Kathlyn Williams, William Hutchinson, Henry Otto. *Prod:* Selig. 2143 ft.

THE CHILD OF THE SEA (1913). Romantic drama; as an assistant lighthouse keeper. *Dir:* Lem B. Parker. *Sc:* Edward McWade. *With* Kathlyn Williams, Herbert Rawlinson, Al W. Filson, William Hutchinson, Lillian Hayward, Baby Lillian Wade. *Prod:* Selig. 1985 ft.

THE YOUNG MRS. EAMES (1913). Romantic drama; as Gerald Leighton, a man who falls in love with the daughter of the woman who loves him. *Dir:* Francis J. Grandin. *Sc:* Kathlyn Williams. *With* Kathlyn Williams, Hobart Bosworth, Ethyl Davis. *Prod:* Selig. 1281 ft.

THE BRIDGE OF SHADOWS (1913). Romantic drama; as Edward Warren, a man accused of embezzlement, who is acquitted, but the shadow persists in hounding him. *Dir:* Fred W. Huntly. *Sc:* W. E. Wing. *With* Mabel Van Buren, William Brown, Al W. Filson, Camille Astor, George Ketcham, Lea Errol, Al Hatch. *Prod:* Selig. 2416 ft.

THE DANGLING NOOSE (1913). Romantic drama; as Bill, a Westerner who loves a girl also loved by an Indian. *Dir:* Edward J. LeSaint.*Sc:* W. E. Wing. *With* Stella Razetto, Guy Oliver, Al W. Filson, Joe King, Scott Dunlap. *Prod:* Selig. 990 ft.

THE LOVE OF PENELOPE (1913). Romantic drama; as Robbin Abbot, a selfish lover who breaks off his engagement when the girl he loves is crippled in an accident. *Dir:* Francis J. Grandin. *Sc:* Maibelle Heikes Justice. *With* Kathlyn Williams, Hobart Bosworth, William Brown. *Prod:* Selig. 1037 ft.

PHANTOMS (1913). Backstage romance; as a young man who weds an actress. *Dir:* Colin Campbell. *Sc:* W. E. Wing. *With* Eugenie Besserer, Wheeler Oakman, Lillian Hayward, Gertie Ryan, Frank Clarke. *Prod:* Selig. 2250 ft.

THE HOPELESS DAWN (AKA *A Mind in the Shadow*) (1913). Romantic tragedy; as one of two fishermen brothers who both love and fight to the death over a heartless coquette. *Dir./Sc:* Colin Campbell. *With* Bessie Eyton, Wheeler Oakman, Gertie Ryan. *Prod:* Selig. 1091 ft.

THE TIDE OF DESTINY (1913). Romantic drama; as Frank Stafford, a struggling writer who loves a rich girl. *Dir:* Lem B. Parker. *Sc:* Ruth E. Morris. *With* Kathlyn Williams, William Brown, Anna Dodge, Baby Lillian Wade. *Prod:* Selig. 1000 ft.

NORTHERN HEARTS (1913;. Canadian melodrama; as Sergeant Jim McGrath, a Mounted Policemen forced to track down his best friend. *Sc:* E. N. Wells. *Prod:* Selig. 1234 ft.

UNTIL THE SEA — (1913) Romantic drama of the sea; as Jim Hall, a fisherman supposedly lost at sea who returns to find his brother wed to the girl they have both loved. *Dir./Sc:* Colin Campbell. *Prod:* Selig. 1234 ft.

MESSAGE FROM ACROSS THE SEA (1914). Romantic drama; as John Lund, the son of a Norwegian fisherman. *Sc:* H. W. Hill. *With* Mabel Van Buren, Henry Otto. *Prod:* Selig. 1043 ft.

THE CONSPIRATORS (1914). Espionage melodrama; as Webster, a reporter who rescues a girl operative for the United States Secret Service. *Sc:* Robert Gage. *Prod:* Selig. 981 ft.

TONY AND MALONEY (1914). Comedy; as Maloney, an Irish policemen. *Sc:* Edgar Hungerford. *Prod:* Selig. 643 ft.

HEARTS ADRIFT (1914) Romantic tragedy; as a castaway, Jack Graham. *Dir:* Edwin S. Porter. *Sc:* Mary Pickford (from a story, "As the Sparks Fly Upward," by Cyrus Townsend Brady). *With* Mary Pickford. Filmed on the California coast. *Prod:* Famous Players (Paramount). 4 reels.

THROUGH THE CENTURIES (1914). Romantic comedy; as Raymond Truxton, an archeologist in Egypt. *Dir:* Fred W. Huntly. *Sc:* L. J. Withers. *With* Mabel Van Buren, Henry Otto. *Prod:* Selig. 1095 ft.

MEMORIES (1914). Romantic drama; as Clyde Lawrence, an impoverished young man who loves a professor's daughter. *Dir:* Edward J. LeSaint. *Sc:* Gladys P. Pullen. *With* Stella Razetto, Guy Oliver, Lillian Hayward, Al W. Filson, Lea Errol, Eugenie Besserer. *Prod:* Selig. 1089 ft.

TESTED BY FIRE (1914). Forest fire melodrama; as Hal Arnold, a forest ranger. *Sc:* Lanier Bartleet. *Prod:* Selig. 1030 ft.

THE ATTIC ABOVE (1914). Drama of vengeance; as Bates, a bank teller seeking vengeance on the bank president who had him convicted of thievery. *Sc:* E. Mason Hopper. *With* Henry Otto, Horace B. Carpenter, Mrs. A. D. Blake, Utanah La Reno. *Prod:* Selig. 1072 ft.

SMUGGLER'S SISTER (AKA *Duty*) (1914). Melodrama of smuggling; as a smuggler protected by his sister, who is loved by a revenue officer. *Dir:* Colin Campbell. *Sc:* Bessie Eyton. *With* Bessie Eyton, Wheeler Oakman. *Prod:* Selig. 761 ft.

ELIZABETH'S PRAYER (1914). Marital drama; as Henry Ashton, a husband and father who falls in love with an unscrupulous actress. *Dir:* Fred W. Huntly. *Sc:* Bertha E. DeLecuona. *With* Mabel Van Buren, Henry Otto, Baby Lillian Wade, Eugenie Besserer. *Prod:* Selig. 1028 ft.

TESS OF THE STORM COUNTRY (AKA *Tessibel of the Storm Country*) (1914). Human drama among the fisher folk; as Frederick Graves, a divinity student. *Dir./Sc:* Edwin S. Porter (from the novel by Grace Miller White). *With* Mary Pickford, Lorraine Thompson, Olive Fuller Golden (Mrs. Harry Carey), Louise Dunlap, Richard Garrick, David Hartford, W. R. Walters, Jack Henry, H. R. Macy, Eugene Walter, H. L. Griffith. Filmed on the California coast. (A completely new version of *Tess* was re-filmed by Mary Pickford later, in 1922; it was filmed again as a talkie by Fox, with Janet Gaynor and Charles Farrell, in 1932; and again by Fox in 1961, with Millie Perkins.) *Prod:* Famous Players (Paramount). 4 reels.

WHILE WIFEY IS AWAY (1914). Comedy; as Dodd, a young husband whose wife goes to the country and he tries to arrange an evening with his poker-playing pals whilst she's away.

Dir: Fred W. Huntly. *Sc:* Edwin R. Coffin. *With* Mabel Van Buren, Henry Otto, George Hernandez, Philo McCullough, Count Alberti, Lillian Hayward, Lea Errol, J. W. Wade. *Prod:* Selig. 842 ft.

THE MIDNIGHT CALL (1914). Melodrama; as Dr. Brontë, a doctor who is able to rescue an heiress held prisoner for two years. *Dir:* Fred W. Huntly. *Sc:* James Oliver Curwood. *With* Mabel Van Buren, Lillian Hayward, Henry Otto, George Hernandez, Gordon Sackville. *Prod:* Selig. 933 ft.

WHEN THIEVES FALL OUT (1914). Romance; as a gentleman burglar who falls in love with his victim. *Dir:* Fred W. Huntly. *Sc:* E. Lynn Summers. *With* Mabel Van Buren, Henry Otto, Charles Whittaker, Al W. Filson, Helen Kendricks, Lea Errol. *Prod:* Selig. 1014 ft.

THE SQUATTERS (1914). Drama of struggle between squatters and millionaire owners; as a young business man who rescues the daughter of a millionaire, the pawn in the struggle. *Dir:* Fred W. Huntly. *Sc:* John M. Kiskadden. *With* Mabel Van Buren, Wheeler Oakman, Frank Clarke, George Hernandez, Philo McCullough, Margaret Allen. *Prod:* Selig. 1000 ft.

THE SCALES OF JUSTICE (1914). Drama; as Walter Elliott, whose lies involve the heroine in a web of circumstantial evidence. *Dir/Sc:* Thomas N. Heffron (from the play by John Reinhart). *With* Paul McAllister, Jane Fearnley, Hal Clarendon, Mark Price, Mary Blackburn, Beatrice Moreland, Daniel Jarrett, Katherine Lee. (Advertised by Daniel Frohman as "A Terrific Arraignment of Circumstantial Evidence.") *Prod:* Famous Players (Paramount). 4 reels.

UNWELCOME MRS. HATCH (1914). A mother love drama; as the betrothed of a wealthy girl whose banished mother returns to be the seamstress on her daughter's wedding gown. *Dir./Sc:* Allan Dwan (from a play by Mrs. Burton Harrison). *With* Henrietta Crosman, Walter Craven, Lorraine Huling, Minna Gale, Paul Trevor, Gertrude Norman. *Prod:* Famous Players (Paramount). 4 reels.

SUCH A LITTLE QUEEN (1914). Romantic drama; as Robert Trainor, an American, who aids the romance of the pretty young Queen of Herzegovina and the handsome King of Bosnia. *Dir./Sc:* Hugh Ford (from the play by Channing Pollack, in which Elsie Ferguson had starred on Broadway). *With* Mary Pickford, Carlyle Blackwell, Arthur Hoops, Russell Bassett. (Re-filmed by Realart, 1921, starring Constance Binney.) *Prod:* Famous Players (Paramount). 5 reels.

THE COUNTY CHAIRMAN (1914). Homespun American comedy drama; as Tilford Wheeler, political rival of his sweetheart's father. *Dir./Sc:* Allan Dwan (from the comedy by George Ade). *With* Maclyn Arbuckle, William P. Sweatman, William Lloyd, Daisy Robinson, Helen Aubrey, Mabel Wilbur, Amy Simmons, Wellington A. Playter. (Re-filmed as a talkie by Fox, 1935.) *Prod:* Famous Players (Paramount). 4 reels.

WILDFLOWER (1914). Romance; as Arnold Boyd, who falls in love with and rescues the innocent girl with whom his brother enters into a bigamous marriage. *Dir:* Allan Dawn. *Sc:* Eve Unsell and Allan Dwan (from a story by Mary Germaine). *With* Marguerite Clark, Jack Pickford, James Cooley, E. L. Davenport. *Prod:* Famous Players (Paramount). 5 reels. (Compare listing in Marguerite Clark filmography.)

THE MAN FROM MEXICO (1914). Comedy; as Danton, suitor to the *ingénue* lead. *Dir:* Thomas N. Heffron. *Sc:* Eve Unsell (from the comedy by H. A. DuSouchet). *With* John Barrymore, Wellington A. Playter, Pauline Neff, Anton Ascher, Fred Annerly, Winona Winters. (Re-filmed by Paramount, 1926, as *Let's Get Married*, with Richard Dix.) *Prod:* Famous Players (Paramount). 5 reels. (Compare listing in John Barrymore filmography.)

THE CONSPIRACY (1914). Drama; as Jack Howell, a reporter in search of a story. *Dir:* Allan Dwan. *Sc:* John Emerson and Allan Dwan (from a play by Robert Baker and John Emerson, as produced by Charles Frohman). *With* John Emerson, Lois Meredith, Iva Shepherd, Hal Byrne, Edward Durand. (Re-filmed as a talkie, 1930, RKO-Radio.) *Prod:* Famous Players (Paramount). 5 reels.

THE CRUCIBLE (1914). Romantic social drama; as Craig an artist, who shelters a reformatory school runaway and falls in love with her. *Dir./Sc:* Edwin S. Porter and Hugh Ford (from a novel by Mark Lee Luther). *With* Marguerite Clark, Justine Johnstone, Helen Hall, Lucy Parker, Barbara Winthrop, Clifford Grey, Blanche Fisher. *Prod:* Famous Players (Paramount). 5 reels. (Compare listing in Marguerite Clark filmography.)

DAVID HARUM (1915). Homespun American romance; as John Lennox, a poor but honest clerk who loves the country schoolteacher. *Dir./Sc:* Allan Dwan (from a story and play by Edward Noyes Wescott). *With* William H. Crane, May Allison, Kate Meeks, Hal Clarendon, Guy Nichols. (Re-filmed as a talkie by Fox, 1934, starring Will Rogers.) *Prod:* Famous Players (Paramount). 5 reels. (Compare listing in May Allison filmography.)

THE LOVE ROUTE (1915). Western romance of the railroad vs. ranch people; as a railroad engineer, John Ashley. *Dir:* Allan Dwan. *Sc:* Edward Peple. *With* Winifred Kingston, Jack Pickford, Donald Crisp, Juanita Hansen. *Prod:* Famous Players (Paramount). 4 reels.

ARE YOU A MASON? (1915). Farce; as the juvenile romantic lead. *Dir:* Thomas N. Heffron. *Sc:* (Leo Ditrichstein play ad. from German play by Lauf and Kraatz). *With* John Barrymore, Helen Freeman, Charles Dixon, Ida Waterman, Alfred Hickman, Charles Butler, Dodson Mitchell, Jean Acker, Lorraine Huling, Kitty Baldwin. (Re-filmed as a British farce and released in the USA 1934, with Sonnie Hale.) *Prod:* Famous Players (Paramount). 5 reels. (Compare listing in John Barrymore filmography.)

THE LURE OF THE MASK (1915). Romantic adventure; as Jack Hilliard, American, who falls in love with a masked prima donna. *Dir:* Thomas Ricketts. *Sc:* Mary O'Connor (from the novel by Harold McGrath). *With* Elsie Jane Wilson, Irving Cummings, Lucy Paton, Hal Clements. *Prod:* American-Mutual. 5 reels.

JIM, THE PENMAN (1915). Drama; as Louis Percival, whose whole life is changed by a forged letter. *Dir./Sc:* Hugh Ford (from the play by Charles J. Young). *With* John Mason, Russell Bassett, Frederick Perry, William Roselle, Marguerite Leslie. (Re-filmed, 1921, by First National) *Prod:* Famous Players (Paramount). 5 reels.

THE SECRETARY OF FRIVOLOUS AFFAIRS (1915). Romance; as a rich woman's son who falls in love with his mother's social secretary. *Dir./Sc:* Thomas Ricketts (from a novel by May Futrelle). *With* May Allison, Hal Clements, Carol Holloway, Wallace MacDonald, William Enfe, Carl von Schiller, Josephine Ditt, Lucy Payton. *Prod:* American-Mutual. 4 reels. (Compare listings in May Allison filmography.)

THE GREAT QUESTION (1915). Romance of Gotham society and the Far West. *Dir./Sc:* Thomas Ricketts. *With* May Allison, Harry Von Meter, Eugenie Forde, William Stowell. *Prod:* American-Mutual. 4 reels. (Compare listing in May Allison filmography.)

THE HOUSE OF A THOUSAND SCANDALS (AKA, GB, *House of Scandal*) (1915). Romance; as the owner of a rich estate who falls in love with a poor farm girl. *Dir./Sc:* Thomas Ricketts (from a story by Theodosia Harris). *With* May Allison, Josephine Ditt, William Enfe, Hal Clements, Bessie Banks, Perry Nanks. *Prod:* American-Mutual. 4 reels. (Compare listing in May Allison filmography.)

PARDONED (1915). Romantic drama; in a dual role: as the Governor's son and the man who impersonates him. *Dir./Sc:* Thomas Ricketts. *With* May Allison, Eugenie Forde, Charles Bartlett, Harry Von Meter, William Stowell. *Prod:* American-Mutual. 4 reels. (Compare listing in May Allison filmography.)

THE END OF THE ROAD (1915). Romantic melodrama; as Paul Harvard. *Dir./Sc:* Thomas Ricketts (from a play by Grattan Donnelly). *With* May Allison, William Stowell, William Enfe, Helene Rosson, Lizette Thorne, Harry Von Meter, Hal Clements, Beatrice Van, Nan Christie, William Carroll. *Prod:* American-Mutual. 4 reels. (Compare listing in May Allison filmography.)

THE BUZZARD'S SHADOW (1915). Desert Army camp drama; as Sergeant Barnes. *Dir./Sc:* Thomas Ricketts. *With* May Allison, William Stowell, Dick La Reno, Betty Harte, Virginia Fordyce, Harry Von Meter. *Prod:* American -Mutual. 4 reels. (Compare listing in May Allison filmography.)

THE TRAGIC CIRCLE (1915). A dramatic moral lesson about the folly of suicide; as a novelist. *Dir./Sc:* Thomas Ricketts. *With* May Allison. *Prod:* American-Mutual. 2 reels. (Compare listing in May Allison filmography.)

THE OTHER SIDE OF THE DOOR (1916). Late Nineteenth century romance; as a man accused of murder. *Dir:* Thomas Ricketts. *Sc:* Clifford Howard (from a novel by Lucia Chamberlain). *With* May Allison, William Stowell, Harry Von Meter, Dick La Reno, Josephine Humphreys, Roy Stewart, Walter Spencer. *Prod:* American-Mutual. 5 reels. (Compare listing in May Allison filmography.)

THE SECRET WIRE (1916). Romantic melodrama; as a telephone lineman. *Dir./Sc:* Thomas Ricketts. *With* May Allison, William Stowell, Harry Von Meter. *Prod:* American-Mutual. 4 reels. (Compare listing in May Allison filmography.)

THE GAMBLE (1916). A drama of the American wheatfields; as a farmer who neglects his wife for his farm. *Dir./Sc:* Thomas Ricketts. *With* May Allison, William Stowell, Harry Von Meter. *Prod:* American-Mutual. 4 reels. (Compare listing in May Allison filmography.)

THE MAN IN THE SOMBRERO (1916). Romantic comedy; as the son of a rich hatter who poses for a sombrero advertisement, and so wins a pretty wife. *Dir./Sc:* Thomas Ricketts. *With* May Allison, Willam Stowell, Harry Von Meter. *Prod:* American-Mutual. 4 reels. (Compare listing in May Allison filmography)

THE BROKEN CROSS (1916). Romance; as a disinherited son. *Dir./Sc:* Thomas Ricketts. *With* May Allison, Queenie Rosson, Rose Donnelly, Harry Von Meter. *Prod:* American-Mutual. 2 reels. (Compare listing in May Allison filmography.)

LILLO OF THE SULU SEAS (1916). Romantic adventure; as a young American sent to the South Seas to learn about pearls. *Dir./Sc:* Thomas Ricketts. *With* May Allison, William Stowell, Perry Banks, Harry Von Meter. *Prod:* American-Mutual. 2 reels. (Compare listing in May Allison filmography.)

LIFE'S BLIND ALLEY (1916). Romantic tragedy; as the owner of an isolated ranch who falls in love with an Easterner's daughter. *Dir./Sc:* Thomas Ricketts. *With* May Allison, Robert Klein, Nell Franzen, Perry Banks, Warren Ellsworth, William Tedmarch, Carl Morrison, Pete Morrison. *Prod:* American-Mutual. 5 reels. (Compare listing in May Allison filmography.)

THE COMEBACK (1916). Logging drama and romance; as a wayward son who goes to his father's logging camp and reforms. *Dir./Sc:* Fred. J. Balshofer. With May Allison, George Henry, Lester Cuneo. Mitchell Lewis, Howard Truesdell, Bert Starkey, Clarissa Selwynne. Filmed in the Dead River country of upper Maine. *Prod:* Metro. 5 reels. (Compare listing in May Allison filmography.)

THE MASKED RIDER (1916). Southern melodrama; as a revenue officer who masquerades as a parson and then as a masked rider in white buckskin. *Dir./Sc:* Fred J. Balshofer. *With* May Allison, H. W. Willis, John MacDonald, Harry Berkhart, Clarissa Selwynne, Harry Linkey, Lester Cuneo. Filmed in the Blue Ridge Mountains of North Carolina. *Prod:* Metro. 5 reels. (Compare listing in May Allison filmography.)

THE RIVER OF ROMANCE (1916). Romantic comedy; as an heir to millions who goes to work running a river launch, and takes the name "Sam." *Dir:* Henry Otto. *Sc:* Henry Otto and E. J. Rath (from Rath's novel, "Sam"). *With* May Allison, Lester Cuneo, Bert Busky, Lee Walker, Mathilde Brundage, Lillian Halperin. Filmed among the Thousand Islands in the St. Lawrence River. *Prod:* Metro. 5 reels. (Compare listing in May Allison filmography.)

MISTER 44 (1916). Western romantic comedy; as a Westerner who falls in love with an Eastern girl. *Dir:* Henry Otto. *Sc:* Charles A. Taylor (from Henry Otto's adaptation of an E. J. Rath story). *With* May Allison, Lester Cuneo, Franklin Hall, Henry Otto, Aileen Allen, Belle Hutchinson, Lee Arms. Filmed at Lake Tahoe, California. *Prod:* Metro. 5 reels. (Compare listing in May Allison filmography.)

BIG TREMAINE (1916). Southern romance; as David Tremaine, Virginia gentleman who is branded a thief by his brother. *Dir./Sc:* Henry Otto (from a novel by Marie Van Vorst, "David Tremaine"). *With* May Allison, Lester Cuneo, Albert Ellis, Lillian Hayward, William Enfe, Andrew Arbuckle, Josephine Rice, William DeVaull, Virginia Southern. Filmed in Imperial Valley, California. *Prod:* Metro. 5 reels. (Compare listing in May Allison filmography.)

PIDGIN ISLAND (1917). Romantic melod-

rama; as a government agent tracking down a smuggler's ring. *Dir:* Fred J. Balshofer. *Sc:* Balshofer and Richard V. Spencer (from the Harold McGrath novel). *With* May Allison, Pomeroy Cannon, Lester Cuneo, Fred Wilson, Lillian Hayward. Filmed in Monterey and Big Sur, California. *Prod:* Metro. 5 reels. (Compare listing in May Allison filmography.)

THE PROMISE (1917). Logging camp romance; as Bill Carmody, college champion halfback who goes to work as a logger. *Dir:* Fred J. Balshofer. *Sc:* Richard V. Spencer (from the James B. Hendryx novel). *With* May Allison, Lester Cuneo, Paul Willis, Lillian Hayward, W. H. Bainbridge, George Fisher, Leota Lorraine, Gibson Gowland, John Steppling. Filmed in Oregon. *Prod:* Metro. 5 reels. (Compare listing in May Allison filmography.)

A BATTLE OF WITS (1917). A border-action melodrama; as the hero. (Obviously made about 1912, and released by Big U five years later with no other credits than Lockwood's, to cash in on his popularity.)

THE HIDDEN CHILDREN (1917). Pre-Revolutionary War romance; as a man seeking his real parents. *Dir./Sc:* Oscar Apfel (from the novel by Robert W. Chambers). *With* May Allison, Lillian West, Henry Herbert, George MacDaniel, Lester Cuneo, A. B. Ellis, Howard Davies, Lillian Hayward, Clara Lucas, Daniel Davis, Charles Cummings. *Prod:* Metro. 5 reels. (The last of the Lockwood-Allison co-starring films) (Compare listing in May Allison filmography.)

THE HAUNTED PAJAMAS (AKA, GB, *The Girl in the Black Pyjamas*) (1917). Romantic fantasy about a pair of silk pyjamas that change anybody donning them into somebody else; as Richard Hudson. *Dir./Sc:* Fred J. Balshofer (from a story by Francis Perry Elliott). *With* Carmel Myers, Lester Cuneo, Edward Sedgwick, Paul Willis, Goro Kino, Harry DeRoy, William DeVaull. *Prod:* Metro. 5 reels.

THE HIDDEN SPRING (1917). Adventure romance; as a young man who comes to a small town dominated by a tyrant. *Dir./Sc.* by Fred J. Balshofer (from a Clarence Buddington Kelland story). *With* Vera Sisson, Herbert Standing, Lester Cuneo, H. F. Crane, Arthur Millette, Billie West. *Prod:* Metro. 5 reels.

UNDER HANDICAP (1917). Western romance; as a young man who goes West to make good, and does. *Dir:* Fred J. Balshofer. *Sc:* Balshofer and Richard V. Spencer (from the novel by Jackson Gregory). *With* Ann Little, W. H. Bainbridge, Lester Cuneo, William Clifford. *Prod:* Metro. 8 reels.

PARADISE GARDENS (1917). Romantic comedy; as a young man who has been raised in isolated wealth with no knowledge of the other sex. *Dir:* Fred J. Balshofer. *Sc:* Balshofer and Richard V. Spencer (from the novel by George Gibbs). *With* Vera Sisson, Virginia Rappé, William Clifford, Lester Cuneo, Catherine Henry, Olive Bruce, Harry DeRoy. *Prod:* Metro. 5 reels.

THE SQUARE DECEIVER (1917). Romantic comedy; as a millionaire who poses as a chauffeur to deceive fortune-hunting ladies and their mothers. *Dir:* Fred J. Balshofer. *Sc:* Balshofer and Richard V. Spencer (from the novel, "Love Me for Myself Alone," by Francis Perry Elliott). *With* Pauline Curley, William Clifford, Dora Mills Adams, Kathryn Hutchinson, Betty Marvin, Dick L'Estrange. *Prod:* Metro. 5 reels.

THE AVENGING TRAIL (1917). Romance of the Northwest; as a logger who comes to town, and stays to become the sheriff. *Dir:* Fred J. Balshofer. *Sc:* Balshofer and Mary Murillo (from the novel, "Gaston Olaf," by Henry Oyen). *With* Sally Crute, Walter P. Lewis, Louis R. Wolheim, William Clifford, Joseph Dailey. *Prod:* Metro. 5 reels.

BROADWAY BILL (1918). Romance of Broadway and the northwoods; as the rich William Clayton, known to Manhattan as the happy-go-lucky "Broadway Bill." *Dir./Sc:* Fred J. Balshofer. *With* Martha Mansfield, Cornish Beck, Raymond Hadley, Stanton Heck, Bert Starkey, Tom Burke, William Clifford. *Prod:* Metro. 5 reels.

THE LANDLOPER (1918). Romantic adventure; as a millionaire who poses as a hobo and finds love and happiness. *Dir:* George Irving. *Sc:* John B. Clymer (from Fred J. Balshofer's adaptation of a Holman Day novel). *With* Pauline Curley, William Clifford, Stanton Heck, Gertrude Maloney, Bert Starkey. *Prod:* Metro. 5 reels.

LEND ME YOUR NAME (1918). Romantic comedy; in a dual role: as a titled earl who changes places with a burglar, neither knowing that they are really twin brothers. *Dir:* Fred J. Balshofer. *Sc:* Balshofer and John Clymer (from the novel by Francis Perry Elliott). *With* Pauline Curley, Bessie Eyton, Bert Starkey, Stanton Heck, Peggy Prevost, Harry Derody. *Prod:* Metro. 5 reels.

PALS FIRST (1918). Romance of the South; as Danny Rowland, the long-lost heir to a Southern plantation. *Dir:* Edwin Carewe. *Sc:* Lee Wilson Dodd (from the novel by Francis Perry Elliott). *With* Rubye de Remer, James Lackaye, Frank De Vernon, Richard R. Neill, Anthony Byrd, Pauline Dempsey, Walter P. Lewis, Rollo Lloyd. *Prod:* Metro. 6 reels. (Re-filmed, 1931, by M-G-M as a musical with Lawrence Tibbett and Esther Ralston; also filmed at First National, 1926.)

LIBERTY BOND JIMMY (1918). A short screen sermon devised as Lockwood's contribution to the fourth Liberty Loan Drive. *Dir:* Edwin Carewe. *Sc:* Finis Fox. *With* Frank Currier, Louis Stern. *Prod:* Metro. 1 reel.

THE GREAT ROMANCE (1918). Mythical kingdom romance; as a Columbia University graduate who travels abroad and finds that he is the legitimate heir to a small kingdom. *Dir:* Henry Otto. *Sc:* Finis Fox. With Rubye de Remer, Joseph Granby, Frank Currier, Helen Lindroth, Franklyn Hanna, Clare Grenville. *Prod:* Metro. 6 reels.

SHADOWS OF SUSPICION (1919). Espionage melodrama; as Cyril Hammersley, an Englishman who is a secret agent for the British Secret Service. *Dir:* Edwin Carewe. *Sc:* Finis Fox (from the novel by George Gibbs). *With* Naomi Childers, Helen Lindroth, Kenneth Keating, William Bailey, Bigelow Cooper, Capt. Leslie Peacock. *Prod:* Metro. 5 reels.

A MAN OF HONOUR (AKA, GB, *Paradise Island*) (1919). South Seas drama; as a man known as "Smith," who is manager of a tropical island. *Dir./Sc:* Fred J. Balshofer (from the story, "A King in Khaki," by Henry Ketchell Webster). *With* Bessie Eyton, Stanton Heck, William Clifford, Bert Starkey, Gordon MacGregor, Pomeroy Cannon. *Prod:* Metro. 5 reels.

MAY ALLISON FILMOGRAPHY

A FOOL THERE WAS (1915). As sister to the wife of the hero; when she is hurt in an autombile accident, the hero's wife does not accompany her husband on board ship, and he thus meets "The Vampire" and is ruined by her. (Compare listing in Theda Bara filmography.)

DAVID HARUM (1915). As Mary Blake. (Compare listing in preceding Harold Lockwood filmography.)

THE GOVERNOR'S LADY (1915). Domestic drama; as Katherine Strickland, the ambitious young daughter of a senator, determined to so captivate the new governor that he will divorce his wife and wed her. *Dir:* George Melford. *Sc:* William C. de Mille (from the play by Alice Bradley and Cecil B. DeMille, as produced by David Belasco). *With* Edith Wynn Mathison, James Neill, Theodore Roberts, Tom Forman, (Re-filmed, Fox, 1923.) *Prod:* Famous Players (Paramount). 4 reels.

THE SECRETARY OF FRIVOLOUS AF-FAIRS (1915). As a social secretary to a woman with whose son she falls in love. (Compare listing in preeeeding Harold Lockwood filmography.)

THE GREAT QUESTION (1915). As the girl with whom the hero falls in love. (Compare listing in preceding Harold Lockwood filmography.)

THE HOUSE OF A THOUSAND SCAN-DALS (AKA, GB, *House of Scandal*) (1915). As a poor farm girl who falls in love with the owner of a rich estate. (Compare listing in preceding Harold Lockwood filmography.)

PARDONED (1915). As the *fiancée* of the governor's son, who is being impersonated by the hero. (Compare listing in preceding Harold Lockwood filmography.)

THE END OF THE ROAD (1915). As Grace Wilson, a beautiful Southerner, who falls in love with a Yankee in trouble. (Compare listing in preceding Harold Lockwood filmography.)

THE BUZZARD'S SHADOW (1915). As Alice Corbett, a young widow acting as camp cook for a frontier post in the Great Southwest. (Compare listing in preceding Harold Lockwood filmography.)

THE TRAGIC CIRCLE (1915). As the woman who loves the novelist hero. (Compare listing in preceding Harold Lockwood filmography.)

THE OTHER SIDE OF THE DOOR (1916). As a girl in late Nineteeth century California who helps vindicate her sweetheart, a man falsely accused of murder. (Compare listing in preceding Harold Lockwood filmography.)

THE SECRET WIRE (1916). As a millionaire's daughter, kidnapped and rescued by a telephone lineman. (Compare listing in preceding Harold Lockwood filmography.)

THE GAMBLE (1916). As a girl of the great American wheatfields who is left destitute, but pitied by a young farmer, who marries her. (Compare listing in preceding Harold Lockwood filmography.)

THE MAN IN THE SOMBRERO (1916). As a girl who falls in love with a man in an advertisement who wears a sombrero. (Compare listing in preceding Harold Lockwood filmography.)

THE BROKEN CROSS (1916). As a fisher girl who falls in love with a disinherited son. (Compare listing in preceding Harold Lockwood filmography.)

LILLO OF THE SULU SEAS (1916). As the daughter of an oyster gatherer who falls in love with a young man sent to the South Seas to learn about pearl-fishing. (Compare listing in preceding Harold Lockwood filmography.)

LIFE'S BLIND ALLEY (1916). As the daughter of a rich Easterner who falls in love with a young Westerner who has saved her father's life. (Compare listing in preceding Harold Lockwood filmography.)

THE COME-BACK (1916). As the belle of the hills, who falls in love with and helps reform a wayward son. (Compare listing in preceding Harold Lockwood filmography.)

THE MASKED RIDER (1916). As a girl of the Blue Ridge Mountains who falls in love with a revenue officer. (Compare listing in preceding Harold Lockwood filmography.)

THE RIVER OF ROMANCE (1916). As a New York society girl who falls in love with a young man running a river launch on the St. Lawrence River. (Compare listing in preceding Harold Lockwood filmography.)

MISTER 44 (1916). As Sadie Hicks, a shirt factory working girl who longs to meet a real he-man and slips a note in the pocket of a shirt, size 44, sent West in a shipment. (Compare listing in preceding Harold Lockwood filmography.)

BIG TREMAINE (1916). As the banker's daughter who loves the hero, a Southern gentleman falsely branded as a thief. (Compare listing in preceeding Harold Lockwood filmography.)

PIDGIN ISLAND (1917). As the daughter of the head of a smuggling ring being smashed by the hero, a government agent. (Compare listing in preceding Harold Lockwood filmography.)

THE PROMISE (1917). As Ethel Manton, a girl in a lumber camp who falls in love with a disowned son working there. (Compare listing in preceding Harold Lockwood filmography.)

THE HIDDEN CHILDREN (1917). As a girl of the pre-American Revolution days seeking her real mother and father, who had placed her for safety with foster parents during the Iroquois raids. (Compare listing in preceding Harold Lockwood filmography.)

SOCIAL HYPOCRITES (1918). Society melodrama; as Leonore, a young girl who clears her father and herself of a false accusation of cheating at cards. *Dir:* Albert Capellani. *Sc:* June Mathis and Capellani (from the play, "Bridge," by Alice Ramsey). *With* Frank Currier, Joseph Kilgour, Stella Hammerstein, Henry Kolker, Ethel Winthrop, Maggie Breyer. *Prod:* Metro. 6 reels.

The WINNING OF BEATRICE (1918).

Romantic comedy; as Beatrice Buckley, left penniless, who becomes a successful candymaker. *Dir:* Harry L. Franklin. *Sc:* June Mathis and Katherine Kavanaugh (from a story by May Tully). *With* Hale Hamilton, Frank Currier, Stephen Grattan, John Davidson, Peggy Parr, Baby Ivy Ward. *Prod:* Metro. 5 reels.

A SUCCESSFUL ADVENTURE (1918). Romance; as Virginia Houston, who works as a maid in order to obtain a legacy. *Dir:* Harry L. Franklin. *Sc:* June Mathis and Katherine Kavanaugh (from a story by June Mathis). *With* Frank Currier, Edward Connelly, Pauline Dempsey, Harry Hilliard. *Prod:* Metro. 5 reels.

THE RETURN OF MARY (1918). Drama; as Mary, who had been kidnapped as a child and is returned to the president of a railroad empire as his missing daughter. *Dir:* Wilfred Lucas. *Sc:* George D. Bucker (from a play by Hale Hamilton). *With* Clarence Burton, Claire McDowell, Darrell Foss, Frank Brownlee, Joseph Belmont. *Prod:* Metro. 5 reels.

THE TESTING OF MILDRED VANE (1918). Drama; as Mildred Vane, whose father subjects her to a series of tests to determine if her moral fibre is what her mother's had been. *Dir:* Wilfred Lucas. *Sc:* George D. Baker (from the story by Charles T. Dazey). *With* Darrell Foss, George Field, Nigel de Brulier, Fred Goodwins. *Prod:* Metro. 5 reels.

HER INSPIRATION (1918). Romantic comedy; as Kate, a Broadway actress who goes down to the Kentucky hills to absorb local colour for a role she is going to play. *Dir:* Robert Thornby. *Sc:* George D. Baker and Tom J. Geraghty. *With* Herbert Heyes, Charles Edler, Allen D. Sears, Jack Branmall. *Prod:* Metro. 5 reels.

IN FOR THIRTY DAYS (1919). Romantic comedy; as a reckless hoyden sent to jail for thirty days for reckless driving. *Dir:* Webster Cullison. *Sc:* George D. Baker and Tom J. Geraghty (from a story by Luther Reed). *With* Robert Ellis, Jay Dwiggins, Bull Montana, Maym Kelso, Rex Cherryman, George Berrell. *Prod:* Metro. 5 reels.

PEGGY DOES HER DARNDEST (1919). Romantic comedy; as Peggy, a tomboy whose hobby is detective work. *Dir./Sc:* George D. Ellis (from a "Red Book" story by Royal Brown). *With* Robert Ellis, Rosemary Theby, Frank Currier, Augustus Phillips, Wilton Taylor, Dick Rosson, Sylvia Ashton, Ernest Morrison. *Prod:* Metro. 5 reels.

THE ISLAND OF INTRIGUE (1919). Romantic melodrama; as a girl on a holiday who is kidnapped, but rescued by the hero. *Dir:* Henry Otto. *Sc:* June Mathis and A. S. LeVino (from a novel by Isabelle Ostrander).

With Jack Mower, Frederick Vroom, Lucille Ward, Gordon Marr, Lillian West, Hector V. Sarno, Tom Kennedy, Chance Ward, Edward Alexander. *Prod:* Metro. 5 reels.

CASTLES IN THE AIR (1919). Romantic comedy; as a theatre usherette wooed by a number of men. *Dir./Sc:* George D. Baker (from a "Saturday Evening Post" story by Kate Jordan). *With* Ben Wilson, Clarence Burton, Walter I. Percival, Irene Rich. *Prod:* Metro. 5 reels.

ALMOST MARRIED (1919). Romantic comedy; as Adrienne LeBlanc, a singer in a Swiss Alps café, who comes to Manhattan seeking an American who had wooed her. *Dir:* Charles Swickard. *Sc:* Luther A. Reed and June Mathis (from an E. V. Durling story). *With* Frank Currier, Harry Rattenbury, James Wharton, Hugh Fay. *Prod:* Metro. 5 reels.

THE UPLIFTERS (1919). Romantic social comedy; as a stenographer interested in socialism, who finds that the uplifting socialists are only using her. *Dir:* Herbert Blaché. *Sc:* George D. Baker (from a "Saturday Evening Post" story by Wallace Irwin). *With* Pell Trenton, Alfred Hollingsworth, Kathleen Kerrigan, Caroline Rankin, Howard Gaye, Lois Wood. *Prod:* Metro. 5 reels.

FAIR AND WARMER (1919). Romantic bedroom farce; as Laura Bartlett, newlywed, who finds that her husband believes that the way to insure marital happiness is to keep his wife guessing, so she starts keeping him guessing. *Dir:* Henry Otto. *Sc:* June Mathis and A.P. Younger (from the play by Avery Hopwood). *With* Pell Trenton, Eugene Pallette, Christine Mayo, William Buckley, Effie Conley. *Prod:* Metro. 6 reels.

THE WALK-OFFS (1920). A comedy of divorce; as Kathleen Rutherford whose way of solving a problem is to walk away from it. *Dir:* Herbert Blaché. *Sc:* June Mathis and A. P. Younger (from the play by Frederic and Fanny Hatton). *With* Emory Johnson, Effie Conley, Darrell Foss, Joseph Kilgour, Richard Morris, Estelle Evans, Kathleen Kerrigan, Yvonne Davis. *Prod:* Metro. 7 reels.

THE CHEATER (1920). Social drama; as Lilly Meany, also known as Vashti Dethic, who pretends to a healing through faith. *Dir:* Henry Otto. *Sc:* Lois Zellner (from the play "Judah" by Henry Arthur Jones. *With* King Baggott, Frank Currier, Harry Von Meter, Rudolph Valentino. *Prod:* Metro. 5 reels.

HELD IN TRUST (1920). Romantic melodrama; as a shopgirl who resembles an invalid heiress who has just died, and agrees to impersonate her. *Dir:* John E. Ince. *Sc:* Sarah Y. Mason (from the "Red Book" novel by George Kibbe Turner). *With* Darrell Foss, Walter Long, John H. Elliott, Lawrence

Grant. *Prod:* Metro. 6 reels.

ARE ALL MEN ALIKE? (1920). Romance; as Teddy Hayden, an emancipated young painter in Greenwich Village. *Dir:* Philip E. Rosen. *Sc:* A. P. Younger (from the novel, "The Waffle Iron," by Arthur Stringer). *With* Wallace MacDonald, Lester Cuneo, Ruth Stonehouse, Emanuel Turner, Winifred Greenwood. *Prod:* Metro. 6 reels.

MARRIAGE OF WILLIAM ASHE (1921). Marital romance; as convent-bred Lady Kittv Bristol who weds England's home Secretary. *Dir:* Edward Sloman. *Sc:* Ruth Ann Baldwin (from the novel by Mrs. Humphrey Ward and play by Margaret Mayo). *With* Wyndham Standing, Frank Elliott, Zeffie Tilbury, Robert Boulder, Lydia Yeamans Titus, Clarissa Selwynne. (A version had been filmed in England by Hepworth, 1916, with Alma Taylor.) *Prod:* Metro. 6 reels.

EXTRAVAGANCE (1921). Domestic drama; as Nancy Vane, an extravagant wife, who nearly ruins her marriage. *Dir:* Philip Rosen. *Sc:* Edward T. Lowe Jr. (from the story, "More Stately Mansions," by Ben Ames Williams). *With* Theodore Von Eltz, Robert Edeson. *Prod:* Metro. 6 reels.

THE LAST CARD (1921). Melodrama; as Elsie Kirkwood, who clears her husband of a murder charge. *Dir:* Bayard Veiller. *Sc:* Molly Parro (from Mary O'Hara's adaptation of "Dated," a story by Maxwell Smith). *With* Albert Roscoe, Stanley Goethals, Frank Elliott, Irene Hunt, Dana Todd, Wilton Taylor. *Prod:* Metro. 6 reels.

BIG GAME (1921). Romantic melodrama; as Eleanor Winthrop, who has to choose between her Boston-bred husband and a French-Canadian guide. *Dir:* Dallas Fitzgerald. *Sc:* Edward T. Lowe Jr. (from a play by Willard Robertson and Kilbourne Gordon). *With* Forrest Stanley, Edward Cecil, Zeffie Tilbury, William Elmer, Sidney D'Albrook. *Prod:* Metro. 5 reels.

THE WOMAN WHO FOOLED HERSELF (1922). Romantic melodrama; as Eva Lee, cabaret entertainer, who goes to South America as the pawn of a group of crooked financiers. *Dir:/Sc:* Charles A. Logue. *With* Robert Ellis, Frank Currier, Bessie Wharton, Robert Schable, Louis Dean. *Prod:* Associated Exhibitors. 6 reels.

THE BROAD ROAD (1923). Melodrama; as Mary Ellen Haley, a city girl brought to a lumber camp, where the hero and villain fight for her affections. *Dir:/Sc:* Edmund Mortimer (from a story by Hapsburg Liebe.) *With* Richard C. Travers, Ben Hendricks Jr., D. J Flanagan, Mary Foy, Charles McDonald, L.

Emile La Croix, Roy Kelly, Alicia Cottens. *Prod:* First National. 6 reels.

FLAPPER WIVES (AKA, GB, *Perilous Love*) (1924). Jazz-age drama; as Claudia Bigelow, involved with faith healers and other charlatans. *Dir:* Jane Murfin and Justin McCloskey. *Sc:* Jane Murfin and Lawrence Trimble (from a play, "The Flaming Sign," by Jane Murfin & Jane Cowl). *With* Rockcliffe Fellowes, Vera Reynolds, Harry Mestayer, Edward Everett Horton, William V. Mong, Evelyn Selbie, Tom O'Brien, Eddie Phillips, Stanley Goethals, Robert Dudley, J. C. Lawler, "Brawn," son of "Strongheart". (Working title: *The Sign.*) *Prod:* Lewis J. Selznick. 7 reels.

YOUTH FOR SALE (1924). Jazz-age drama; as Molly Malloy, a flapper who nearly loses her eyesight when she drinks wood alcohol. *Dir:* William Christy Cabanné. *Sc:* Raymond S. Harris. *With* Richard Bennett, Sigrid Holmquist, Charles Emmett Mack, Dorothy Allen, Alice Chapin, Tom Blake, Charles Beyer. *Prod:* C. C. Burr. 6 reels.

I WANT MY MAN (1925). Romantic drama; as Lael, a mercenary flapper who nearly ruins a marriage. *Dir:* Lambert Hillyer. *Sc:* Joseph Poland and Earle Snell (from Earl Hudson's adaptation of *The Interpreter's House,* a novel by Struthers Burt). *With* Milton Sills, Doris Kenyon, Phyllis Haver, Paul Nicholson, Kate Bruce, Theresa Maxwell Conover, Louis Stern. *Prod:* First National 7 reels.

WRECKAGE (1925). Melodrama; as Rene, partners with a crooked nobleman in gem smuggling, involved in a big shipwreck. *Dir:* Scott Dunlap. *Sc:* Agnes Parsons (from the novel, "Salvage," by Izola Forrester). *With* Holmes Herbert, John Miljan, Rosemary Theby, Grant Demarest. *Prod:* Banner. 6 reels.

THE GREATER GLORY (1926). Drama; as Corinne, the younger of two sisters in Vienna before and after the First World War. *Dir:* Curt Rehfeld. *Sc:* June Mathis (from the novel, "Viennese Medley," by Edith O'Shaughnessy). *With* Conway Tearle, Anna Q. Nilsson, Ian Keith, Lucy Beaumont, Jean Hersholt, Nigel de Brulier, Bridgetta Clark, John Sainpolis, Marcia Manon, Edward Earle, Virginia Southern, Isabel Keith, Kathleen Chambers, Hale Hamilton, Cora Macey, Carrie Daumery, Boris Karloff, George Billings, Bess Flowers, Marcelle Corday. *Prod:* First National. 11 reels.

MEN OF STEEL (1926). Romantic drama of the steel mills; as Clare Pitt, a steel king's daughter intrigued by a steelworker who has fought his way up. *Dir:* George Archainbaud. *Sc:* Milton Sills (from the story, "United States Flavor," by R.G. Kirk). *With* Milton

Sills, Doris Kenyon, Victor McLaglen, Frank Currier, George Fawcett, John Kolb, Harry Lee, Henry West, Taylor Graves. *Prod:* First National. 10 reels.

MISMATES (1926). Mother-love drama; as Belle, a flapper who befriends a mother deprived of her child. *Dir:* Charles Brabin. *Sc:* Sada Cowan (from a play by Myron C. Fagan). *With* Doris Kenyon, Warner Baxter, Philo McCullough, Charles Murray, Maude Turner Gordon, John Kolb, Cyril Ring, Nancy Kelly. *Prod:* First National. 7 reels.

THE CITY (1926). Drama; as Elinor Voorhees, a sophisticated woman of the city. *Dir:* R. William Neill. *Sc:* Gertrude Orr (from the play by Clyde Fitch). *With* Nancy Nash, Robert Frazer, George Irving, Lillian Elliott, Walter McGrail, Richard Walling, Melbourne MacDowell, Bodil Rosing, Fred Walton. *Prod:* Fox. 6 reels.

HER INDISCRETION (1927). No information available except that it was a Jans Production, and that Miss Allison was supported by Mahlon Hamilton.

ONE INCREASING PURPOSE (1927). Post First World War drama in England; as Linda Travers Paris, an errant wife. *Dir:* Harry Beaumont. *Sc:* Bradley King (from the novel by A. S. M. Hutchinson). *With* Edmund Lowe, Lila Lee, Holmes Herbert, Huntley Gordon, Lawford Davidson, Emily Fitzroy, George Irving, Josef Swickard, Jane Novak, Nicholas Sousannin, Frank Elliott, Tom Maguire, Pat Somerset. *Prod:* Fox. 8 reels.

THE TELEPHONE GIRL (1927). Melodrama; as Grace Robinson, caught in the maze of a gubernatorial campaign, with her reputation and happiness in the hands of a telephone girl, who knows the truth about her past. *Dir:* Herbert Brenon. *Sc:* Elizabeth Meehan (from the play, "The Woman," by William C. de Mille). *With* Madge Bellamy, Holbrook Blinn, Warner Baxter, Hale Hamilton, Lawrence Gray. Filmed previously as a silent in 1915 under its original title, *The Woman;* subsequently filmed as a talkie in 1931, re-titled *The Secret Call. Prod:* Paramount. 6 reels.

5
WALLACE REID

The number of handsome men at any one time is never large. Nor is the number of men who know innately how to charm. Needless to add, the number of handsome men who also possess innate charm is miniscule.

Wallace Reid, however, was one. And as though such unusual gifts from the gods were not enough, he was given another: he was placed in the forefront of an industry which, for the first time in human history, made a handsome and charming man adored throughout the world.

At the pinnacle of his fame, it was said in Hollywood that "Wally Reid has· everything." He did—a beautiful, talented wife; two lovely children; international acclaim; a big beautiful home that was a showplace; $3000 a week fifty-two weeks a year; and an addiction to morphine.

William Wallace Reid was born on April 15, 1891, in St. Louis. His father, James Halleck Reid, had been a reporter on the Cincinnati "Times Star," and, as Hal Reid, became a successful playwright *(Human Hearts, The Night Before Christmas, The Confession,* and many others). He also became a motion picture actor and director. One of the Reid progenitors had been a lieutenant-colonel in Washington's army.

Wallace Reid's mother, Bertha Belle Westbrooke, was a St. Louis society girl interested in the theatre when she met Hal Reid. After their marriage they toured the United States as a man-and-wife acting team. Some of her ancestors were Virginia landowners in the early days of the Old Dominion. She named her only son William Wallace after the Scottish hero in Sir Walter Scott's "Scottish Chiefs."

The first time Wally Reid saw his mother onstage was when she was acting in an old-time melodrama called "The Phoenix." He was about four, and started his own acting career not long afterward in the role of a small girl in a play starring his parents called "Slaves of Gold." He also played with them, in a young boy's role, in one of his father's best-known dramas, "Human Hearts."

His parents separated while he was still very young and his mother whisked him away from the theatre so he would not get stage-struck. The boy saw little of his father, who was on tour most of the time, either as an actor or as author-director of a new play. In a few years his parents divorced.

The slim, sentimental biography of Wallace Reid which his mother wrote and published shortly after his death makes it plain that he was surrounded during his formative years by an adoring mother and female relatives. That they didn't make him a victim of "smother love" was due to the same kind of independence that imbued his Revolutionary ancestor, and to an insatiable curiosity about everything, which led him, in his teens, to start a lifelong love affair with books.

"The only real rival I ever had after marriage," says Dorothy Reid, "was our library. Thanks to Wally, I acquired a literary education I never got in my youth. Whenever he sat down with a book in the rocking-chair he favoured, he would lose himself so completely in what he was reading that when he came to later, he would seem a bit surprised to find he'd rocked himself into the adjoining room — about forty feet from his starting point."

He was also interested in music. Says Mrs. Reid: "Wally played not only the violin but every stringed instrument entirely by ear until I taught him to read music. And he sang so well that Geraldine Farrar urged him to go back to New York and study for opera. At the time of World War One he formed the 'Blue Bungalow Band' and took it on camp tours. During the months I was carrying our son, he was determined to learn how to play every wind instrument there is and there were times when our house so wailed with the notes of a saxophone that I said, 'Our poor child's going to be born tone deaf or hate music!'"

In boyhood Reid also painted in oils — he was self-taught — and the landscapes he executed still grace the homes of his widow and children. Later, at the height of his fame, he would often, during the waits while cameras were being set up, make line-drawings of the crew and fellow actors. And in addition to these artistic talents Reid was a magnificent swimmer, good with the boxing gloves, could operate any kind of camera, drive a car like a professional racer, and even repair or rebuild a motor.

When he completed his elementary schooling, his mother let it be known that she had her heart set on his going to Princeton and sent him to Perkiomen Academy, a prep school at Pennsburg, Pennsylvania. While there, he attended a series of medical lectures in Allentown with the idea of becoming a doctor, but his interest in medicine lasted only long enough to prove that "a little knowledge is a dangerous thing," for the little medicine he learned probably contributed to his tragic undoing.

Although Reid graduated from Perkiomen, he did not go to Princeton. For a few months he wrote a column on motoring for the Newark "Morning Star," and then struck out on his own for Wyoming, where he worked in a hotel, on a ranch, and on a Government survey for the Shoshone Dam Project.

On his return to the East, he assisted his father in the writing of a play, "The Confession," on which he took no credit. But it was seeing Theodore Roberts performing in the lead of this play that got him stage-struck. Roberts remained a friend and frequent counsellor throughout most of his life.

His first grown-up acting job was as a college boy in the try-out of "Unto the Fourth Generation," starring Robert Edeson. He acquitted himself so well that he received other acting offers, and when his mother tried one final time to interest him in Princeton, he told her he had a small part in a vaudeville sketch his father had written and was starring in, "The Girl and the Ranger," and was going on tour in it.

Wallace Reid

When the tour ended in Chicago, Hal Reid was hired as a scenario writer at the Selig Studio and his son Wally "got into pictures more from curiosity than anything else, although I landed my first job because I could swim. It was with the Selig Company in Chicago. I saved the heroine from the icy waters of Lake Michigan, and then from a burning building, in the same picture, *The Phoenix*."

This was a film version of the play in which he had first seen his mother act.

Reid was at Selig when Tom Mix was also getting his film start there. Reid did all the water stuff, and Mix the horse stunts. Of those years Reid later wrote: "... I stayed at Selig's till November, 1910, learning the camera, use of crepe hair (I was utility man and *always* wore variegated whiskers), and how to write scenarios. At that time I had no idea of sticking to the work, so returned to New York that winter and went to work as an assistant editor of 'Motor Magazine.' But when springtime came along 'the office' began to be a nightmare, so I went over and knocked at the Vitagraph gates and said: 'Please let me in.' They did, and here I am, and glad to be a photoplayer."

Vitagraph let him in because his father had sent him there with a script of his play, "The Confession," in a film version of which Hal Reid hoped to star with his son. Vitagraph bought the film rights, but delayed making it because of its controversial subject — a priest's insistence on keeping a confession inviolate. The picture was eventually made, but by that time both Wallace Reid and his father had aligned themselves with another studio.

Before they switched studios, however, Hal Reid had acted in, written, and directed many films for Vitagraph, and his handsome son had been in more than a few of them.

"I began my screen career doing character parts, not as a juvenile," Reid always said. He also began it filling in at Vitagraph as a cameraman (he had learned how to operate a motion picture camera at Selig's). And he picked up extra money playing mood music on the violin or viola for Vitagraph stars as background for their camera emoting.*

He also succeeded in selling scenarios to Vitagraph and in directing some of the pictures in which he appeared.

But his talents as an actor were Vitagraph's chief interest and he was soon graduated from small unbilled roles to supporting parts in John Bunny comedies, and then to leads opposite every top female star Vitagraph had. Nevertheless, when Hal Reid was offered his own company at the eastern Reliance's studio, Wally went with him, and played both bits and leads in films his father directed. He also wrote several of the pictures in which he acted.

Meanwhile, the movie industry was moving west, and Wallace Reid went west as assistant cameraman to director Otis Turner. But almost immediately he was put to work as an actor. A Nestor Western starring Dorothy Davenport was ready to go before the cameras and no leading man had been cast. Reid was conscripted.

The picture's name was *His Only Son,* Mrs. Reid told me recently, "And the cowboys, among them Hoot Gibson, were waiting eagerly to show up this good-looking young greenhorn from the East. They gave him a very frisky horse to ride, and then stood aside, expecting him to be thrown. But Wally galloped away as if he were saddle born. They never tried any other tricks — he had proved himself one of them."

The number of pictures Wallace Reid wrote, directed and played in during the next two years is staggering. Most of them were two-reelers; none was more than four.

---

*Although Geraldine Farrar's use of a small orchestra for mood music on the Lasky sets in 1915 made it mandatory thereafter for silent stars to have musicians on hand, it is usually conceded that the first use of on-set mood music began at Vitagraph in 1910 when Dick Rosson picked up a violin and played a soulful melody in order to aid Florence Reed to express emotion for the camera.

"Everybody took a crack at writing in those days," Mrs. Reid says. "A writer got $25 for every scenario reel. At Universal films were never longer than two reels, but Wally and I often did two films a week. Most of us never even saw the pictures we made. We simply shot them in California, cut off the scene numbers, and shipped the negative East, where it was printed, edited and sub-titled. Half the time the Eastern office fastened a new main title on the picture, so there was no way of our identifying it when it was released. By that time we'd made about a dozen more anyway, and the pictures playing at the movie houses seemed ancient history." There is great similarity in the plots of these pictures, most of which are simple variations on the same theme. At least two are extended re-makes of earlier scripts Reid had himself written.

Not a few film historians believe, and write, that Wallace Reid played in a few pictures at Vitagraph and then got a break with Griffith in *The Birth of a Nation,* which led to stardom for Lasky. Nothing could be more erroneous. I have tracked down over a hundred of Reid's acting credits prior to *The Birth's* release, and there are a few more I have been unable to trace by title. By the time Reid gained international recognition as a film star he was well-grounded in every phase of the art, both before and behind the camera.

"I have never ceased to marvel," wrote James R. Quirk, publisher of "Photoplay," "how the camera caught that lovable quality in the man and reflected it on the screen. Handsome, accomplished, successful, there wasn't an ounce of personal conceit in him, and the amount of work he could and did perform would be inconceivable to most men."

Soon after his arrival in Hollywood Reid had gone to work for the American Company in Santa Barbara, but after about six months there he left, along with Allan Dwan and Pauline Bush (later Mrs. Dwan), and signed with Universal. A month later Carl Laemmle began his long leadership of that company.

Wally Reid worked as writer, director and actor for Universal and always regarded this period of his career as his happiest, because it was at this time that he fell in love with and married Dorothy Davenport, the leading lady in most of his Universal films. They were soon announced as an acting team, and "Moving Picture World" observed that "In Dorothy Davenport he has a delightful little leading woman, for Dorothy is a great favourite with a discerning public, and her work is always conscientious and carefully thought out."

This should not have been surprising, for, as Wally proudly told all interviewers: "My wife comes from one of America's best and oldest theatrical families, one that is aligned in marriage to the Rankins, Drews, and Barrymores." Her grandfather, E. L. Davenport, was one of the great actors of his time, and one of her aunts was Fanny Davenport, who thrilled American audiences by her performances in most of the roles created in France by Sarah Bernhardt. Her father was Harry Davenport, an extremely versatile actor both on stage and in films, and her mother was Alice Shepard, leading lady to her father in the theatre and in later years much loved by the original Keystone company as "Mother Davenport."

Before their first co-starring pictures could be released, Wallace Reid and Dorothy Davenport were married at Christ Episcopal Church in Los Angeles on October 13, 1913, with Phil Dunham as best man and Ruth Roland as the bride's attendant. One newspaper headline read: UNIVERSAL FILM DIRECTOR MARRIES LEADING WOMAN.

They were married after their day's work at the studio, then at Gower and Sunset on the site of the present CBS building, and they returned the following morning to continue with the picture they were then shooting (*The Lightning Bolt*). Said "Moving Picture World": "The young couple are held in the highest esteem by their professional associates, and their reception at the Hollywood studios Tuesday morning attested to their popularity. There was the popping of guns and cheers as the couple were heralded down the street, until the locality presented the aspect of an insurrecto proceeding."

Says Mrs. Reid today: "Months after our marriage, our own small unit went up into the Sierras to film several scripts, all of which had a mountain background. This location jaunt gave Wally and me a belated honeymoon — and for free, which was important then. Later on, it seemed that Wally always got jobs on pictures to be shot at the studio, while I got the sleeper-jump locations. That meant getting up at dawn, taking the red electric car downtown, racing from Hill to Main on foot, and catching another Pacific Electric car out to Long Beach, or some place like that, where I had to be ready to start shooting by eight o'clock."

In May 1914 Reid left Universal for Mutual and its two important subsidiaries, Majestic and the new western Reliance. He made the change because of D. W. Griffith's interest in him as an actor.

When Griffith first summoned him, Reid and his wife drove to the studio together, and she waited for him in the car.

"Wally came out boiling mad," Dorothy Reid now reminisces. "Griffith was in one of his playful moods, and joked and shadow-boxed on set, barely noticing Wally's presence. Wally thought he'd hardly been given even a courteous reception by the 'great master,' and he was sure he could charge the whole incident to time wasted. But Griffith did send for him again, and Wally started to work in a great many features supervised by Mr. Griffith."

Everybody knew Griffith was planning to film *The Clansman* (later re-titled *The Birth of a Nation*), and every actor in Hollywood was trying to get into the cast, for it was already an axiom that Griffith was a star-maker and that any actor who played in a Griffith special would get better treatment from other studios.

Says Mrs. Reid of this turn in their fortunes: "Wally thought the gods were smiling on him when Griffith called him in one day and told him that although Henry B. Walthall had been cast to play the principal male lead of the Little Colonel, he had been taken ill with a kidney ailment, and it wasn't likely he'd be well enough in time, so Wally was to get the role. He was even fitted for costumes and uniforms and made tests — and then just as he was about to start work, word came that Walthall had recovered sufficiently to assume the part.

"Griffith tried to assuage Wally's disappointment by telling him he had him in mind for another role in the picture, one which would undoubtedly make him star material. When Wally found out that what Griffith had in mind was the small but dramatic bit of Jeff, the blacksmith, he was incensed to the point of mayhem—a reaction the wily Mr. Griffith had counted on. It worked—and how! Every poor guy Wally threw out of that blacksmith's shop was D. W. Griffith."

Wallace Reid as Peter Ibbetson in FOREVER

"But in this instance, as it turned out, Griffith had been right, Jeff, the blacksmith, did engineer Wally into stardom. Incidentally, Mr. Griffith also used Wally for the Christ figure in some of the allegorical tableaux at the close of the film. It was bitterly cold when those scenes where shot, and Wally, almost naked and tied to the cross, was freezing. They kept dosing him with shots of brandy to keep his blood circulating, and when he was finally taken down he was stoned."

In his autobiography, "I Blow My Own Horn," Jesse L. Lasky recounts the "larcenous inspiration" Cecil B. DeMille and he had after attending the opening of the Griffith epic at Clune's Auditorium in Los Angeles: "A young man who played a bit part as a blacksmith had a perfect physique, large expressive eyes, and flawless features. He was over six feet tall and weighed in the neighborhood of 180 pounds. Seeing him was just like finding a 180-pound diamond, for within a year we would be reaping gratifying profits from eight pictures featuring his brawn and irresistible appeal, and the tonnage of his fan mail would be making our distaff stars jealous. We signed him and kept him under contract to the day of his tragic death eight years later at the height of unprecedented popularity."

The contract was signed on June 26, 1915, and Lasky, who always praised Reid highly, told the press how Reid "had inherited his father's gift for story-telling, had a keen sense of humor, a good singing voice, played the saxophone and piano, and was altogether the most magnetic, charming, personable, handsome young man I've ever met. And the most co-operative.''

The first Reid film released under the Lasky banner was *The Chorus Lady*, in which he was leading man to Cleo Ridgely. But before that picture was shot, he had spent the summer of 1915 being leading man to Geraldine Farrar in two of the three pictures she made that year for Lasky, with Cecil B. DeMille directing. He played Don Jose in *Carmen* and was her romantic interest in *Maria Rosa*. Farrar would have no other actor as her leading man when she returned to Hollywood the two following summers (1916 and 1917), and Reid played opposite her in *Joan the Woman, The Woman God Forgot,* and *The Devil Stone.*

In addition he supported Mae Murray in her first film, *To Have and To Hold* and Miss Murray in her life-story, ''The Self-Enchanted,'' says Reid made her film *debut* bearable by telling her not to be frightened when director George Melford shouted at her. Reid's popularity grew with every film, and he was soon a star in his own right.

In 1917 Dorothy Reid bore him a son, whom they named William Wallace Reid Jr., and a couple of years later an adopted daughter, Betty Ann, joined the family.

In her autobiography, ''The Gay Illiterate,'' Louella O. Parsons says of the Reid of this time: ''Wallace Reid, one of the most attractive and lovable men who ever lived, drove the Hollywood streets as if he were on the last lap of the chariot race in *Ben Hur*—only Wally's chariot was a low-slung robin's egg blue car with a horn that played 'Yankee Doodle Dandy.'''

It was inevitable that Reid's love of cars should lead to his playing an auto racer on the screen. The first such film released in 1919 was *The Roaring Road,* from a Byron Morgan story. It went over so well that Morgan was kept busy writing yarns about imaginary racing heroes named ''Speed'' Carr, or ''Toodles'' Walden, or ''Dusty'' Rhodes, all designed for Wally Reid to play on the screen.

Lasky wrote of these pictures:''...the audiences couldn't get enough of him behind a steering wheel. We virtually turned these road-racing items out on an assembly line, and every one was a money-maker. But that didn't type Wally. He was believable in almost any role we gave him.''

Reid secretly plotted to race under a pseudonym at the big Indianapolis Speedway races, and was ready to depart for Indiana, presumably as a spectator only, when the studio chanced to learn what he had in mind, and brought legal pressure denying him permission to race. Reid was disappointed and more than a little indignant, but then shrugged and went off to view the races, while his wife breathed a sigh of relief. ''He had talked about it, but I didn't even dream he was thinking of so dangerous a stunt,'' she says.

Reid was also a versatile ballroom dancer and he and his wife won many dancing cups, especially for the tango and the hesitation waltz. Non-professional dancing contests were then the rage and were held every weekend at the Sunset Inn, the Vernon Country Club, and Nat Goodwin's on the pier. Paramount soon capitalised on this skill of Reid's and put him into *Dancin' Fool*, with Bebe Daniels as his partner.

''Wally is some stepper,'' said a ''Motion Picture Classic'' columnist of a

Sunset Inn dancing contest. "Let me tell you that boy *can* dance. And when he wasn't dancing, he was borrowing the musicians' instruments. First, he substituted at the drums, then took a turn at the saxophone, and last played the violin with one arm around his wife's neck. And he jazzes better than any of the professionals do."

Although Wallace Reid was never able to persuade Paramount to let him direct, he did go to bat with some success for James Cruze, who had acted in many of his films, and Cruze's first directorial efforts were for a series of Wally Reid vehicles. Cruze came back later to direct others, and was the director on Reid's last film, *Thirty Days*.

By Christmas of 1920 the Reids were installed in the handsome, California-style home they had built on an acre of land between Sweetzer and De-Longpre that had a 400-foot backing, which is now frontage on Sunset Boulevard. It's reputed to have been filmdom's first home with a private swimming pool. It also had a music room with a pipe organ, a playroom with a billiard table, and a library with books and a movie projector, which Reid operated himself for weekend showings of current films lent him by the various films exchanges. The basement housed not only the organ's pipes but a small, well-equipped chemistry laboratory. And last, but far from least, the garages had a pit to enable Wally to repair and reassemble the cars he loved.

In this new house that year there were three Christmas trees—a huge one for the grown-ups, and two smaller ones for each of the children.

And that was the last merry Christmas Wallace Reid had in that house—or any other.

Sometime in 1919, the special train chartered to take the company on location to the High Sierras for Reid's *The Valley of the Giants* was wrecked, and Reid, although injured by the falling debris, helped get the women out and was one of the last to receive medical attention. A bad gash on his head healed quickly enough, but he was subject to blinding headaches. His back, at the base of the spine, had also been damaged and there was a sciatic nerve impingement. In order to ease the pain and enable him to continue acting before the camera, a doctor gave him morphine.

After completing the picture, he was in bed for three months at home, and a medical source continued giving him morphine—beyond the time when there could be any normal withdrawal.

"I blame no one person," says Dorothy Reid today. "What happened to Wally had happened to many a soldier released from hospitals after World War One, and happened to patients—both men and women—released from hospitalisation, cured perhaps of their ailments and injuries, but made into hopeless addicts through the then abysmal ignorance of the medical profession.

"I don't mean to minimise a terrible tragic situation, but I want to get one thing straight: my husband did not get morphine through any underworld connection. His source was neither illicit nor illegal—it didn't have to be. Wally could charm any doctor into giving him the tablets he wanted. He knew just enough about medicine to convince doctors that he knew exactly how many grams he could safely take every day.

"Nor were there ever any great financial outputs for the narcotic. That I know, for I kept the family books, and would have been the first to know had there been any large payments to any peddler, some of whom may have tried to ensnare Wally in the hope of blackmailing him. But they never succeeded. He got what he wanted—and on his own. He took the morphine orally, and there were never any disfiguring needle scars on his body.

"It was worse, in a way, with Wally, because he had always been the picture of health, and he was confident that he knew enough about medicine to believe that addiction wouldn't happen to him.

"But it did. And when he found he couldn't put a stop or even a check to the morphine, he began to use liquor as a cover-up for what he was really doing. Before that, he had only drunk for relaxation and fun. Drinking now made things even tougher for him. There were times when he behaved badly in public. Today most people recognise morphine and alcohol as two forces which work dangerously and destructively against another. Yet cases like Wally's still happen—unfortunately."

In spite of what he was doing, Reid turned in some of his best screen

Wallace Reid with Bebe Daniels in DeMille's THE AFFAIRS OF ANATOL

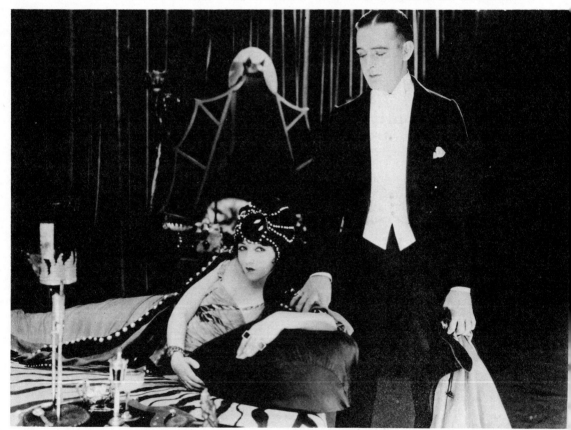

performances at this time, including his role of Peter Ibbetson opposite Elsie Ferguson's Duchess of Towers in *Forever*.

"Wally *became* a good actor," says Mrs. Reid. "In the beginning, his popularity was based on his good looks and engaging personality, but when he was offered a challenge, as he was with *Forever*, he rose to the occasion."

In view of his actual situation, one of the interviews Reid gave at this time is plaintive indeed. Said he to Herb Howe: "They would laugh at you if you told them I ever had a serious thought, but just between you and me, I'd like to do something worthwhile some day—give something to the world beside my face."

But there was the physical battle with morphine to be won first. Time after time he said to his wife: "Nothing can lick us. We're going to win. I'll shake this thing." But the agony of total withdrawal and abstinence drove him back to morphine—and alcohol with it.

What he was doing could not be kept secret, and he stopped seeing many of his friends, some of whom did not know until his death that more than alcoholism was destroying him. The studio several times suggested that he take a rest, and Lasky once proposed that he and his wife take a trip around the world. But he insisted on working, and continued to delude himself that he could conquer the addiction, and that when he was freed from morphine he wouldn't have to drink.

In the beginning of 1922, when he played a prize-fighting hero in *The World's Champion*, he still looked well and in the pink, but toward the end of 1922, in *The Dictator,* he was looking tired. His last four pictures reveal the rapidity of his physical disintegration: In *Nice People* he looks thin and withdrawn; in *The Ghost Breaker* there is a *sad* aspect in his strained face; in *Clarence* he often looks really ill; and in *Thirty Days,* his last picture, he looks ghastly. At one point during the making of *Thirty Days* he collapsed.

When that picture was finished and the studio indicated it would not risk putting him in another, Reid decided to enter the Banksia Place Sanitarium and cure himself once and for all. Before he went, he told Cecil B. DeMille: "I'll either come out cured or I won't come out."

Paramount, which had a $2,000,000 investment in Reid, did not know how to inform the public about his plight. Mrs. Reid herself solved that problem. She summoned the press to her home and, as calmly as she could, gave the facts. The press treated her like the lady she was, and is. The first newspaper accounts were honest and wholly sympathetic, not lurid and sensational as some of the later ones were. The public was likewise sympathetic. As a matter of fact, when *Thirty Days* opened in December 1922, audiences applauded when the name of Wallace Reid flashed on the screen.

Reid never knew that the public knew. The "Los Angeles Examiner," on its own volition, ran off a copy of its regular edition for delivery to him from which the story about his struggle had been deleted.

Early in January, 1923, he seemed to be improving and had regained ten pounds. "Wally is winning his fight!" Mrs. Reid told the press.

But the sudden total withdrawal of morphine had changed his metabolism, and he caught influenza. After a few days of critical illness, he began lapsing into a coma. His wife kept a vigil at his bedside. Once he opened his eyes and the ghost of his world-famous smile appeared on his sunken cheeks, and he said, "Tell them, mama, we're going to make it."

On Thursday, January 18, 1923, shortly after one in the afternoon, he again recovered consciousness for a moment. His last muttered words were "God...I...please."

"Hypostatic congestion of the lungs and renal suppression" were given as the causes of his death. He was only thirty-one.

Reid was buried in Forest Lawn. Shooting stopped at the studio, and the flag was flown at half-mast. His tragedy was not exploited by the press immediately after his death. The "Los Angeles Times" said in an editorial that "the sympathy his illness engendered was denoted by the applause which first rippled and then rolled in a frenzy of enthusiastic hand-clapping in the theatre showing *Thirty Days*," and the "Examiner's" editorial was equally on Reid's side: "He occupied a place unique in the flickering world of the cinema, a niche he had hollowed out in the wall of movie fame by hard sincere work. He was 'game' in life — and he died 'game.'" Said Will Hays at the time Reid entered the sanitarium: "I hope he comes back. I have nothing but sympathy for him. I have always greatly admired him on the screen, and I want to see him come back." Mary Pickford tearfully told the press: "His death is a very great tragedy. I know he would have lived down every mistake he made."

Not long after his death, Mrs. Reid, accompanied by Adela Rogers St. Johns, attended a conference in Washington on narcotics in order to contribute what she could from her intimate knowledge of her husband's tragedy. When she returned to Hollywood, she accepted an offer from Thomas H. Ince to make an anti-narcotics film, *Human Wreckage,* in which she also acted, and for the exploitation of which she toured the country, trying to awaken the public to the problems that the addict faces. She made another exploitation film for Ince, *Broken Laws,* and produced and wrote pictures on other problems of the day for other companies. In the early Thirties she began her long association as writer and assistant to director-producer Arthur Lubin. She occasionally still works as a freelance writer, and since her voice is unusually good, she has done a great deal of recording for the blind. She lives in a modest, charming bungalow only two blocks from the lot in North Hollywood, where Wally Reid and she helped Carl Laemmle turn the first spades of earth for Universal's new studios.

William Wallace Reid Jr. is married and has a son and daughter. Like his father, he has a love of automobiles and in his youth made several films, one of which, an auto racing story, was written for him by Byron Morgan, who had written so many of his father's most popular successes. He is an architect, with offices in Santa Monica, and at one time recently he was in South Vietnam helping to build air bases, but he has now returned to Southern California.

Betty Ann Reid lived with her mother, and was a real estate saleswoman for many years. She had married at an early age, divorced, and had a daughter who is now married and has two small sons. A few years ago Betty Ann died.

Dorothy Reid has never re-married. "I had over nine wonderful years of the best with Wally," she says. "I wouldn't trade anything for them. Wally died very young — but he gave freely of the gifts of his youth. Most of all, he loved people, and the public responded in kind. He was much loved. He had so many talents — the gods were overly kind, but they also made him vulnerable, his own worst enemy, to compensate for their lavishness. He knew too much — and not enough."

WALLACE REID FILMOGRAPHY

THE PHOENIX (1910). Melodrama; as a young reporter who rescues the heroine from both watery and fiery graves. *Sc:* (from the popular American melodrama). *With* Milton Nobles, Dolly Nobles. *Prod:* Selig. 1 reel.

THE REPORTER (1911). Comedy; as the assistant to a reporter assigned to write a feature, "How It Feels to Be a Burglar." *With* Fred Woltan, Sam Pickens, Karl King, Barbara Swager. *Prod:* Selig. 1 reel.

THE LEADING LADY (1911). Farce comedy; as an actor who has his problems with a temperamental cook who has been persuaded to become an actress. *Dir:* Ned Finley. *With* John Bunny, Van Dyke Brooke. *Prod:* Vitagraph. 1 reel.

JEAN INTERVENES (1912). Domestic drama with a canine star; as Billy Hallock, jealous of his sweetheart's collie dog. *With* Hal Reid, Florence Turner, Edith Halleran, Jean (the Vitagraph dog). *Prod:* Vitagraph. 806 ft.

CHUMPS (1912). Subtitled "A Fairy Story for Overgrown-ups"; as a flying trapeze artist named "George, the Denouement." *With* Leah Baird, William Shea, John Bunny, Marshall P. Wilder. *Prod:* Vitagraph. 1007 ft.

INDIAN ROMEO AND JULIET (1912). Indian romantic tragedy; as Oniatore, a Huron brave, in love with Ethona, a Mohican, his deadliest tribal enemy. *Dir:* Larry Trimble. *Sc:* Hal Reid (based upon Shakespeare's tragedy). *With* Florence Turner, Harry T. Morey, Hal Reid, Mrs. Adelaide Ober, Harold Wilson. *Prod:* Vitagraph. 1010 ft.

THE TELEPHONE GIRL (1912). Melodrama; as Jack Watson, a fireman who rescues his sweetheart when she is trapped remaining at her switchboard during a fire. *With* Edith Storey. *Prod:* Vitagraph. 925 ft.

THE SEVENTH SON (1912). Civil War drama; as one of the seven sons of the Widow Beechem who is killed in battle. *Dir./Sc:* Hal Reid. *With* Mary Maurice, Earle Williams, James Morrison, William R. Dunn, Robert Gaillord, Tefft Johnson, Ralph Ince (as Lincoln). *Prod:* Vitagraph. 767 ft.

THE ILLUMINATION (1912). Religious drama; as a middle-aged character whose life is affected by the spiritual light emanating from the Christus. *With* Tom Powers, Helen Gardner, Rosemary Theby, Harry Northrup, Rose Tapley. *Prod:* Vitagraph.

BROTHERS (1912). Drama; as a wounded renegade who seeks sanctuary in a church where his brother is a priest. *Dir:* George Field. *Prod:* Champion. 1 reel.

THE VICTORIA CROSS (Subtitled "The Charge of the Light Brigade") (1912). Historical drama; as a young lieutenant in the famed Light Brigade. *Dir./Sc:* Hal Reid. *With* Edith Storey, Tefft Johnson, Julia Swayne Gordon (as Florence Nightingale), Rose Tapley (as Queen Victoria). *Prod:* Vitagraph. 1018 ft.

THE HIEROGLYPHIC (1912). Crook melodrama; as a man-about-town *With* Zena Keefe, Tom Powers, Harry Northrup. *Prod:* Vitagraph. 990 ft.

AT SCROGGINSE'S CORNER (1912). Farce; as one of the young men. *With* John Bunny, Helen(e) Costello, Edith Halleran, Robert Gaillord, Julia Swayne Gordon, Leo Delaney, Harold Wilson, James Morrison. *Prod:* Vitagrpah. 1 reel.

DIAMOND CUT DIAMOND (1912). Farce; as a young clerk who enters into a scheme to confound Bunny's wife. *With* John Bunny, Flora Finch, Dick Rosson, Miss Ray Ford, Mrs. Costello, Jack Standing. *Prod:* Vitagraph. 1007 ft.

THE GAMBLERS (1912). Drama; as one of the young gamblers. *Sc:* From the play by Charles Klein. *With* Zena Keefe, Earle Williams, Julia Swayne Gordon, Leah Baird. *Prod:* Vitagraph. 1000 ft.

CURFEW SHALL NOT RING TONIGHT (1912). Civil War melodrama; as the lover soldier saved by the heroine. *Dir./Sc:* Hal Reid (from the popular poem). *Prod:* Reliance. 995 ft.

KAINTUCK (1912). Outdoor drama; as a young mountaineer jealous of a city artist who paints his sweetheart. *Dir:* Hal Reid. *Sc:* Wallace Reid (who was also the star). *With* Gertrude Robinson, Robert Tabor, Virginia

Westbrooke. *Prod:* Reliance. 985 ft.

BEFORE THE WHITE MAN CAME (1912). Indian romantic tragedy; as Waheta, a warrior. *Dir:* Otis Turner. *Sc:* Wallace Reid (who was also the star). *With* Gertrude Robinson. *Prod:* Reliance. 985 ft.

A MAN'S DUTY (1912). Civil War drama; as a captured Union soldier brought before his own father, a Confederate officer. *Dir:* Hal Reid. *With* Hector Dion, Charles Herman, George Seigman, Sue Balfour, E. P. Sullivan. *Prod:* Reliance. 966 ft.

AT CRIPPLE CREEK (1912). Western melodrama; as Joe Mayfield, U. S. deputy marshal. *Dir./Sc:* Hal Reid (from his own play). *With* Sue Balfour, Gertrude Robinson. *Prod:* Reliance. 1750 ft.

HIS ONLY SON (1912). Western drama; as a young Easterner who falls into bad company out West, but is proved innocent by the ranch-owner's daughter. *Dir:* Milton H. Fahrney. *With* Dorothy Davenport, Jack Conway, Victoria Forde (Mix), Hoot Gibson. (Reid's first picture to be filmed in Hollywood) *Prod:* Nestor-Universal. 1 reel.

MAKING GOOD (1912). Romance; as a young man who rescues the heroine at Brighton Beach and eventually wins her as his wife. *With* Jane Fernley. *Prod:* Imp-Universal. 1 reel.

THE SECRET SERVICE MAN (1912). Espionage melodrama; as an enemy spy. *With* Rodman Law. *Prod:* Reliance. 998 ft.

INDIAN RAIDERS (1912). Western; as a Westerner who fights it out for the girl. *Prod:* Bison-Universal. 1 reel.

EVERY INCH A MAN (1912). Crime melodrama; as Robert, son of a rancher, who helps two detectives run down a criminal. *Dir:* William Humphrey. *With* Hal Reid, Rose Tapley, Robert Gaillord, Morris McGee, Frank Mason. *Prod:* Vitagraph. 928 ft.

THE TRIBAL LAW (1912). Indian romantic melodrama; as an Apache brave who marries a Hopi Indian girl, and flees with her to Mexico. *Dir:* Otis Turner. *With* Margarita Fischer, Charles Inslee. *Prod:* Bison-Universal. 1950 ft.

LOVE AND THE LAW (1913). Western; as Sheriff John, who has to chose between love and justice when he captures the thieving brother of the girl he loves. *Dir:* Wallace Reid. *With* Lillian Christy, Edward Coxen. *Prod:* American. 1 reel.

A ROSE OF OLD MEXICO (1913). Costume melodrana; as Paquita's father, who accidentally kills himself with a gun, and his disowned daughter is suspected of murdering him. *Dir:* Wallace Reid. *With* Lillian Christy, Edward Coxen. Chet Withey. *Prod:* American. 1 reel.

THE WAYS OF FATE (1913). Romantic melodrama; as Jim Conway, in pursuit of his father's killer, who is detoured by romance. *Dir:* Wallace Reid. *With* Vivian Rich. *Prod:* American. 1 reel.

THE PICTURE OF DORIAN GRAY (1913). Drama; as the ill-fated Dorian Gray. *Dir:* Phillips Smalley. *Sc:* (from the novel by Oscar Wilde). *With* Lois Weber, Phillips Smalley. (Filmed as a talkie, 1945, M-G-M, with Hurd Hatfield; subsequently filmed, 1972, abroad, with Helmet Berger). *Prod:* NYMP.

WHEN JIM RETURNED (1913). Western romantic comedy; as Jim, who returns from college to the old ranch. *Dir:* Wallace Reid. *With* Vivian Rich, Eugene Pallette. *Prod:* American. 1 reel.

THE TATTOED ARM (1913). Western mining melodrama; as Ben Hart, a mining expert. *Dir:* Wallace Reid. *With* Vivian Rich, Eugene Pallette. *Prod:* American. 1 reel.

THE DEERSLAYER (1913). Indian drama; as Chingachgook, the friendly Delaware chief who guides a party of frontiersmen to safety. *Dir./Sc:* Hal Reid (from the novel by James Fenimore Cooper). *With* Florence Turner, Hal Reid, Harry T. Morey, Ethel Dunn, Edward Thomas, Evelyn Dominicus, William F. Cooper. *Prod:* Vitagraph. 2092 ft.

YOUTH AND JEALOUSY (1913). Western romance; as Bill Higgins, a jealous cowboy. *Dir:* Wallace Reid. *With* Vivian Rich. *Prod:* American. 1 reel.

THE KISS (1913). Romance; as Ralph Walters, a city artist who falls in love with a trapper's daughter. *Dir:* Wallace Reid. *Prod:* American. 1 reel.

HER INNOCENT MARRIAGE (1913). Drama; as Bob Evans. *Dir:* Wallace Reid. *With* Vivian Rich, George Field. *Prod:* American. 1 reel.

HIS MOTHER'S SON (1913). Drama; as a dissolute son who reforms. *Dir:* W. Christy Cabanné. *Prod:* Reliance. 1 reel.

A MODERN SNARE (1913). Western; as the new sheriff, who has to fight the prejudicial discrediting of the old one. *Dir:* Wallace Reid. *With* Vivian Rich, George Field. *Prod:* American. 1 reel.

WHEN LUCK CHANGES (1913) . Western romance; as Cal, a young prospector, staked by a gambler's wife, who strikes it rich. *Dir:* Wallace Reid. *With* Vivian Rich. *Prod:* American. 1 reel.

VIA CABARET (1913). Drama; as Harry Reeder, who falls in love with and marries a cabaret entertainer. *Dir:* Wallace Reid. *With* Vivian Rich, George Field. *Prod:* American. 1 reel.

THE SPIRIT OF THE FLAG (1913). Drama of the Philippines; as a doctor who falls in love with a teacher and, together, they teach the islanders the meaning of freedom. *Dir:* Allan Dwan. *Sc.:* Wallace Reid. *With* Pauline Bush. *Prod:* Bison-Universal. 1950 ft.

HEARTS AND HORSES (1913). Western romance; as Bill Walters who, although jealous of his sweetheart's affection for her pony, goes out to capture it when it is stolen. *Dir:* Wallace Reid. *With* Vivian Rich. *Prod:* American. 1 reel.

IN LOVE AND WAR (AKA *The Call to Arms*) (1913). Civil War drama; as a one-armed journalist who becomes a great hero. *Dir./Sc:* Allan Dwan. *With* Pauline Bush, Marshall Neilan. *Prod:* Bison-Universal. 1880 ft.

WOMEN AND WAR (1913). Civil War romantic drama; as a Virginia soldier. *Dir:* Allan Dwan. *Sc:* Wallace Reid. With Pauline Bush, Jessalyn Van Trump, Marshall Neilan. *Prod:* Bison-Universal. 2 reels.

DEAD MAN'S SHOES (1913). Drama; as a hobo who sees a man named Tom killed, and assumes his identity. *Dir:* Wallace Reid. *With* Vivian Rich, George Field. *Prod:* American. 1 reel.

PRIDE OF LONESOME (1913). Western romance; as Ed Daton, a cowboy, who befriends and falls in love with a waif. *Dir:* Wallace Reid. *Prod:* American. 1 reel.

THE POWDER FLASH OF DEATH (1913). Drama of three friends, separated by the Civil War, who die on the same battlefield; as the Union soldier. *Dir./Sc:* Allan Dwan. *With* Marshall Neilan, Hardee Kirkland. *Prod:* Bison-Universal. 1880 ft.

A FOREIGN SPY (1913). Espionage drama; as an engineer who loves the daughter of an Army man. *Dir:* Wallace Reid. *With* Vivian Rich. *Prod:* American. 1 reel.

THE PICKET GUARD (1913). Civil War drama; as a sentry on the Potomac whose life is reviewed in flashbacks before he is mortally wounded. *Dir:* Allan Dwan. *Sc:* Arthur Rosson (from a poem by Ethelin Eliot Beer). *With* Pauline Bush, Marshall Neilan, Jessalyn Van Trump, David Kirkland. *Prod:* Broncho-Universal. 1830 ft.

MENTAL SUICIDE (1913). Drama; as a young contractor who accepts a bribe and becomes unwittingly responsible for his sweetheart's death. *Dir:* Allan Dwan. *Sc:* Wallace Reid. *With* Pauline Bush, Jessalyn Van Trump. *Prod:* Powers-Universal. 1 reel.

MAN'S DUTY (1913). Western; as Bill. *Dir:* Allan Dwan. *Sc:* M. de la Parelle. *With:* Marshall Neilan, Jessalyn Van Trump, Pauline Bush.

THE ANIMAL (1913). Drama of father love; as "Reid," a strong but simple brute who learns to love his baby son. *Dir./Sc:* Allan Dwan. *With* Pauline Bush, Marshall Neilan. (One of Reid's favourite roles.) *Prod:* Rex-Universal. 1 reel.

THE HARVEST OF FLAME (1913). Melodrama; as the inspector of an overall factory who rescues the heroine when she is trapped in a disastrous fire. *Dir./Sc:* Wallace Reid. *With* Pauline Bush, Marshall Neilan. *Prod:* Rex-Universal. 1500 ft.

THE MYSTERY OF THE YELLOW ASTER MINE (1913). Western drama; as "Reid," the miner-hero. *Dir:* Frank Borzage. *With* Pauline Bush, Arthur Rosson. *Prod:* Bison-Universal. 1540 ft.

THE GRATITUDE OF WANDA (1913). Indian melodrama; as "Wally," a rancher, who befriends an Indian girl, and she later brings help when he is besieged. *With* Pauline Bush, Arthur Rosson, Jessalyn Van Trump. *Prod:* Bison-Universal. 1155 ft.

THE WALL OF MONEY (1913). Drama; as a young man out of college who persuades his miserly father to install modern safety devices in the factory. *Dir:* Allan Dwan. *Sc:* Marshall Neilan. *With* Pauline Bush, Marshall Neilan, Jessalyn Van Trump, James McQuarrie. *Prod:* Rex-Universal. 1790 ft.

THE MENACE (1913). Civil War romance; as Captain Bruce Douglas, of the South. *Dir./Sc:* Allan Dwan. *With:* Pauline Bush, Marshall Neilan, Jessalyn Van Trump, David Kirkland. *Prod:* Universal. 1 reel.

THE HEART OF A CRACKSMAN (1913). Crook drama; as a gentleman crook. *Dir:* Willis Lobards. *Sc:* Wallace Reid. *With* Cleo Madison, James Neill, Edward Brady, Marcia Moore. *Prod:* Powers-Universal. 895 ft.

THE CRACKSMAN'S REFORMATION (1913). Crook drama; as a gentleman crook. *Sc:* Wallace Reid. *With* Dorothy Davenport, Edward Brady. *Prod:* Powers-Universal. 1 reel.

CROSS PURPOSES (1913). Romance; as "Wally," who doesn't want to wed his parents' choice of a bride. *With* Cleo Madison. *Prod:* Powers-Universal. 836 ft.

THE FIRES OF FATE (1913). Melodrama; as "Wally," who rescues the girl he loves from a tenement fire. *With* Dorothy Davenport, Edward Brady. *Prod:* Rex-Universal. 1 reel.

RETRIBUTION (1913). Western mine melodrama; as "Reid," who is rescued by the girl he had aided when he is trapped in a mine explosion. *Dir:* Wallace Reid. *With* Dorothy Davenport, Edward Brady, Phil Dunham. *Prod:* Nestor-Universal. 865 ft.

A CRACKSMAN SANTA CLAUS (1913). Crook drama; as a gentleman cracksman. *Sc:* Wallace Reid. *With* Dorothy Davenport. *Prod:* Powers-Universal. 1038 ft.

THE LIGHTNING BOLT (1913). Northwest melodrama; as "Reid," a mounted policeman. *Dir:* Wallace Reid. *With* Dorothy Davenport, Edward Brady, Phil Dunham. *Prod:* Nestor-Universal. 885 ft.

A HOPI LEGEND (AKA *A Pueblo Romance*) (1913). A condensed re-make of *Before the White Man Came*, 1912; as Waheta, a warrior. *Dir./Sc:* Wallace Reid. *With* Dorothy Davenport, Edward Brady, Phil Dunham. *Prod:* Nestor-Universal. 920 ft.

WHO SO DIGGETH A PIT (1914). Melodrama; as "Wally," who saves the girl he loves when she is charged with murder. *With* Lurline Lyons, James Neill, Edward Brady. *Prod:* Powers-Universal. 955 ft.

THE INTRUDER (1914). Romance of the redwoods; as a woodsman. *Dir:* Wallace Reid. *With* Dorothy Davenport, Edward Brady, Phil Dunham. *Prod:* Nestor-Universal. 940 ft.

THE COUNTESS BETTY'S MINE (1914). Romantic mine melodrama; as "Wallace," superintendent of a mine inherited by a titled English girl. *Dir:* Wallace Reid. *With* Dorothy Davenport, Edward Brady, Phil Dunham. *Prod:* Nestor-Universal. 920 ft.

THE WHEEL OF LIFE (1914). Western drama of revenge; as a prospector who revenges the deaths of his wife and child. *Dir:* Wallace Reid. *With* Dorothy Davenport, Edward Brady. *Prod:* Nestor-Universal. 980 ft.

FIRES OF CONSCIENCE (1914). Desert drama; as a prospector. *Dir:* Wallace Reid. *With* Dorothy Davenport, Gertrude Robinson, *Prod:* Nestor-Universal. 1004 ft.

THE GREATER DEVOTION (1914). Morality drama of early California; as "Devotion," whom "Love" chooses rather than "Wealth." *Dir:* Wallace Reid. *With* Dorothy Davenport, Fred Gamble, Edward Brady, Phil Dunham. *Prod:* Nestor-Universal. 915 ft.

A FLASH IN THE DARK (1914). Melodrama; as a miner blinded in a mine explosion who senses that his sweetheart is being wooed away from him. *Dir:* Wallace Reid. *With* Dorothy Davenport, Edward Brady. *Prod:* Nestor-Universal. 955 ft.

BREED OF THE MOUNTAINS (1914). Romance of the redwoods; as Joe, a woodsman who finds a forsaken baby on his doorstep and goes looking for a proper mother and wife. *Dir:* Wallace Reid. *With* Dorothy Davenport, Edward Brady, Lucile Wilson. *Prod:* Nestor-Universal. 1 reel.

REGENERATION (1914). Romance; as a painter who chooses a prostitute for his model of the Madonna. *With* Helen Taft, Edward Brady. *Prod:* Powers-Universal. 610 ft.

THE HEART OF THE HILLS (1914). Romance; as a woodsman who turns moonshiner to get money to aid his crippled brother, and then falls in love with a female revenue officer. *Dir./Sc:* Wallace Reid. *With* Dorothy Davenport, Phil Dunham, Edward Brady, Lucile Wilson. *Prod:* Rex-Universal. 1 reel.

THE WAY OF A WOMAN (1914). Canadian Northwest romance; as Pierre, a Canadian woodsman, who kidnaps the girl he loves. *Dir:* Wallace Reid. *With* Dorothy Davenport. *Prod:* Rex-Universal. 1 reel.

THE VOICE OF THE VIOLA (1914). Romance of the redwoods; as "Wallace," a woodsman who courts his fiddling brother's sweetheart when she is blinded. *Dir:* Wallace Reid. *With* Dorothy Davenport, William Gettinger, Edward Brady, Phil Dunham. *Prod:* Nestor-Universal. 1007 ft.

THE SPIDER AND HER WEB (1914). Drama; as a young victim to the lure of a gambling casino queen. *Dir:* Phillips Smalley. *With* Lois Weber, Dorothy Davenport, Phillips Smalley, Billy Wolbert, Rupert Julian. *Prod:* Rex-Universal. 1987 ft.

THE MOUNTAINEER (1914). A re-make of the 1912 *Kaintuck;* again as a jealous young mountaineer. *Dir./Sc:* Wallace Reid. *With* Dorothy Davenport, Phil Dunham, Lucile Wilson, Edward Brady. *Prod:* Rex-Universal. 927 ft.

CUPID INCOGNITO (1914). Western mine romance; as a wealthy young man who protects the mining interests of an heiress. *Dir:* Wallace Reid. *With* Dorothy Davenport, Phil Dunham, John G. Blystone, Billy Wolbert, Edna Maison. *Prod:* Nestor-Universal. 997 ft.

A GYPSY ROMANCE (1914). Romantic drama; as the newly-elected king of a gypsy tribe who fights for the bride he desires. *Dir:* Wallace Reid. *With* Dorothy Davenport, Edward Brady, William Gettinger, Phil Dunham. *Prod:* Nestor-Universal. 987 ft.

THE SKELETON (1914). Domestic comedy; as a young husband. *Dir:* Wallace Reid. *With* Dorothy Davenport, Phil Dunham, Billy Wolbert. *Prod:* Nestor-Universal. 1 reel.

THE FRUIT OF EVIL (AKA, *The Sins of the Fathers*) (1914). Dramatic tragedy; as the son of a broken marriage who does not meet his sister until they are grown and fall in love without knowing they are brother and sister. *Dir./Sc:* Wallace Reid. *With* Dorothy Davenport, Edward Brady, Gladys Montague, Antrim Short, Gertrude Short. *Prod:* Nestor-Universal. 985 ft.

THE TEST (1914). Social problem drama; as a poor husband whose marriage is breaking up who robs a rich husband also facing matrimonial disaster. *Dir:* Wallace Reid. *With* Dorothy Davenport, Frank Lloyd, Tom Santschi, Edward Brady, Antrim Short, Gertrude Short, Gladys Montague. *Prod:* Nestor-Universal. 1 reel.

WOMEN AND ROSES (1914). Romantic drama; as a man with three women in his life — wife, mother, mistress. *Dir./Sc:* Wallace Reid (suggested by a line from a Robert Browning poem: "And which of these roses three is the dearest to me?") *With* Dorothy Davenport, Lillian Brockwell, Vera Sisson. *Prod:* Nestor-Universal. 996 ft.

THE QUACK (1914). Courtroom melodrama; as Wallace Rosslyn, successful attorney, whose sweetheart testifies against his father, a wealthy quack. *Dir:* Wallace Reid. *With* Dorothy Davenport, Billy Wolbert, Phil Dunham, Robert Chandler, Lucile Bolton. *Prod:* Nestor-Universal. 990 ft.

THE SIREN (1914). Drama; as the older brother of a young man who commits suicide over a woman, and he avenges his brother's death. *Dir:* Wallace Reid. *With* Dorothy Davenport, Lillian Brockwell, David Kirkland, Page Peters, Lucille Bolton, Billy Wolbert. *Prod:* Nestor-Universal. 1023 ft.

THE MAN WITHIN (1914). Western drama; as an outlaw who forces the girl he loves to turn him in so that she may claim the reward. *Dir:* Wallace Reid. *With* Dorothy Davenport, Phil Dunham, William Gettinger, Clarence Burton. *Prod:* Nestor-Universal. 981 ft.

THE SPARK OF MANHOOD (1914). Drama; as a ne'er-do-well who proves himself a hero. *Dir:* Wallace Reid. *With* Dorothy Davenport. *Prod:* Powers-Universal. 1 reel.

PASSING OF THE BEAST (1914). Drama of the Northwest; as a Canadian woodsman jealous of the friendship his wife shares with a Mounted Policeman. *Dir:* Dorothy Davenport, Joe King, John G. Blystone, William Gettinger, Phil Dunham, Helen Keller. *Prod:* Nestor-Universal. 947 ft.

LOVE'S WESTERN FLIGHT (AKA, GB, *Children of Fate*) (1914). Drama; as "Wally", rancher who marries a widow, but her husband turns up very much alive and starts blackmailing her. *Dir:* Wallace Reid. *With* Dorothy Davenport, Joe King, Phil Dunham. *Prod:* Nestor-Universal. 965 ft.

A WIFE ON A WAGER (AKA, GB, *A Wife for a Wager*) (1914). Romance; as Wally Bristow, an Easterner, who wins a Western girl on a wager. *Dir:* Wallace Reid. *With* Dorothy Davenport. *Prod:* Nestor-Universal. 1008 ft.

'CROSS THE MEXICAN LINE (1914). Romantic drama of the Mexican War; as Lt. Wallace, loved by two women, an American and a Mexican. *Dir:* Wallace Reid. *With* Dorothy Davenport, William Gettinger, Phil Dunham, Helen Keller. *Prod:* Nestor-Universal. 1008 ft.

THE DEN OF THIEVES (1914). Drama; as David, in love with a girl whose downfall her own mother is plotting. *Dir:* Wallace Reid. *With* Dorothy Davenport, Lillian Brockwell, David Kirkland, Billy Wolbert, Phil Dunham. *Prod:* Nestor-Universal. 978 ft.

THE EXPOSURE (1914). Newspaper drama; as a reporter exposing graft. *With* Irene Hunt. *Prod:* Mutual-Reliance. 1996 ft.

ARMS AND THE GRINGO (AKA, GB, *The Rifle Smugglers*) (1914). Romantic drama of the Mexican border; as the gringo lover of a vivacious señorita. *Dir:* W. Christy Cabanné. *Sc:* Anna Tupper Wilkes. *With* Dorothy Gish, F. A. Lowery, Fred Kelsey, Howard Gaye. *Prod:* Mutual-Majestic. 2034 ft.

DOWN BY THE SOUNDING SEA (1914). Romantic sea drama; as John Ward, a shipwreck castaway, found by two young lovers. *Dir:* W. Christy Cabanné. *With* Robert Harron, Mae Gaston. *Prod:* Mutual-Majestic. 970 ft.

MOONSHINE MOLLY (1914). Romantic drama of the Kentucky Hills; as Lawson Keene. *Dir:* W. Christy Cabanné. *With* Mae Marsh, Robert Harron, Fred Burns, Eagle Eye. *Prod:* Mutual-Majestic. 1963 ft.

THE CITY BEAUTIFUL (1914). Romance of early film-making in Los Angeles; as a country boy who gets a good studio job as a property boy. *Dir:* W. Christy Cabanné. *With* Dorothy Gish. *Prod:* Mutual-Majestic. 1 reel.

THE SECOND MRS. ROEBUCK (1914). Marital drama; as Samuel Roebuck, who takes a second wife. *Dir:* W. Christy Cabanné & John O'Brien. *Sc:* (from a W. Carey Wonderly "Smart Set" story). *With* Blanche Sweet, Mary Alden, Raoul Walsh. *Prod:* Mutual-Majestic. 1979 ft.

FOR THOSE UNBORN (1914). Romantic

drama; as the Western lover of an Eastern girl who has come West to die. *Dir:* W. Christy Cabanné. *With* Blanche Sweet, Robert Harron, Irene Hunt. *Prod:* Mutual-Majestic. 2 reels.

SIERRA JIM'S REFORMATION (1914). Western; as Tim, who is aided by Sierra Jim (Walsh), an outlaw. *Dir:* John O'Brien. *With* Gertrude McLynn, Raoul Walsh, Eagle Eye, Dark Cloud, Fred Burns. *Prod:* Mutual-Reliance. 991 ft.

DOWN THE HILL TO CREDITVILLE (1914). Domestic comedy; as a $15-a-week clerk who takes on an extravagant bride. *Dir:* Donald Crisp. *With* Dorothy Gish. *Prod:* Mutual-Majestic. 992 ft.

HER AWAKENING (1914). Drama; as the lover of a girl who is almost robbed of her rightful inheritance and life. *Dir:* W. Christy Cabanné. With Blanche Sweet, Ralph Lewis. *Prod:* Mutual-Majestic. 2 reels.

FOR HER FATHER'S SINS (1914). Social problem drama; as the lover of a girl out to reform her father's business morale. *Dir:* John O'Brien. Sc: Anita Loos. *With* Blanche Sweet, Billie West. *Prod:* Mutual-Majestic. 1710 ft.

A MOTHER'S INFLUENCE (AKA, *His Mother's Last Word*) (1914). Drama; as a rich man's son who, when he is disinherited, plots to rob his father's house. *Dir:* John O'Brien. *With* Billie West. *Prod:* Mutual-Majestic. 1 reel.

THE NIGGARD (1914). Drama; as a young man, accused of being a tightwad, who spends every cent he owns on a good time. *Dir:* Donald Crisp. *With* Billie West, Cora Drew. *Prod:* Mutual-Majestic. 1009 ft.

THE ODALISQUE (1914). Society drama; as a villain who tries to seduce the heroine into a life of shame. *Sc:* (from a LeRoy Scott magazine story). *With* Blanche Sweet, Henry B. Walthall, Miriam Cooper, Robert Harron. *Prod:* Mutual-Majestic. 2 reels.

THE LITTLE COUNTRY MOUSE (1914). Society gambling drama; as a young lieutenant who saves the heroine from high society gamblers. *With* Blanche Sweet, Mary Alden, Raoul Walsh. *Prod:* Mutual-Majestic. 989 ft.

ANOTHER CHANCE (1914). Drama; as a man without a job. *Dir:* Donald Crisp. *With* William Lowery, Mary Alden, Donald Crisp. *Prod:* Mutual-Majestic. 1 reel.

AT DAWN (1914). Drama; as an American ne'er-do-well in the Philippines. *Dir:* Donald Crisp. *With* George Seigmann, Billie West, William Lowery. *Prod:* Mutual-Reliance. 1005 ft.

OVER THE LEDGE (AKA, *On the Ledge*) (1914). Drama; as a brother who is reunited with his sister because of a runaway kite caught on a high ledge. *Dir:* Fred A. Kelsey. *With* Irene Hunt. *Prod:* Mutual-Reliance. 1 reel.

BABY'S RIDE (1914). Comedy; as the father of a child who runs away. *Dir:* George Beranger. *With* Loretta Blake. *Prod:* Mutual-Majestic. 1002 ft.

THE AVENGING CONSCIENCE (1914) Subtitled "Thou Shalt Not Kill," it was an anthology drama of three Edgar Allan Poe short stories; in a bit role. *Dir./Sc:* D. W. Griffith (from three Poe stories — "The Tell-Tale Heart," "The Pit and the Pendulum," and a love story based upon the poem, "Annabel Lee". *With* Blanche Sweet, Henry B. Walthall, Spottiswoode Aitken, George Seigmann, Ralph Lewis. *Prod:* Mutual. 4 reels.

THE CRAVEN (1915). Tragedy; as George, a strong but timid young blacksmith. *Dir:* W. Christy Cabanné. *With* Signe Auen (Seena Owen), William Hinckley, A. D. Sears. *Prod:* Mutual-Reliance. 1 reel.

THE THREE BROTHERS (1915). Drama; as the middle brother of three French Canadians who all love the same girl. *Dir:* W. Christy Cabanné. *With* A. D. Sears, William Hinckley, Claire Anderson, Josephine Crowell. *Prod:* Mutual-Reliance. 1861 ft.

THE BIRTH OF A NATION (1915). A drama of the Civil War; as Jeff, the blacksmith, and also as the Christus in the epilogue. *Dir:* D. W. Griffith. *Sc:* D. W. Griffith and Frank E. Woods (from the novel, "The Clansman," by Thomas E. Dixon). Premiered at Clune's Auditorium in Los Angles, as *The Clansman*, on Feb. 8, 1915; then, retitled *The Birth of a Nation*, premiered at the Liberty Theatre in New York City, on March 3, 1915. *With* Henry B. Walthall, Lillian Gish, Mae Marsh, Miriam Cooper, Josephine Crowell, Walter Long, Mary Alden, Ralph Lewis, George Seigmann, Joseph Henabery, Raoul Walsh, Robert Harron, Elmer Clifton, Spottiswoode Aitken, André Beranger, Maxfield Stanley, Jennie Lee, Donald Crisp, Howard Gaye, Sam De Grasse, Elmo Lincoln, Olga Grey, Eugene Pallette. *Prod:* Epoch. 12 reels.

THE LOST HOUSE (1915). Melodrama; as Ford, a reporter, who rescues a Kentucky heiress from a house where she has been held prisoner. *Dir:* W. Christy Cabanné. Sc: (from a story by Richard Harding Davis). *With* Lillian Gish, A. D. Sears, E. A. Turner, Elmer Clifton. *Prod:* Mutual-Majestic. 3 reels.

STATION CONTENT (1915). Railroad drama; as a railroad man. *Dir:* Fred A. Kelsey. *With* Catherine Henry. Re-filmed by Triangle,

1918, starring Gloria Swanson. *Prod:* Mutual-Reliance. 2 reels.

ENOCH ARDEN (AKA, GB, *As Fate Ordained*; subsequently re-issued, U.S.A., *The Fatal Wedding*). (1915). Drama; as Walter Fenn, who weds the heroine when Enoch Arden is believed lost at sea. *Dir:* W. Christy Cabanné. *Sc:* D. W. Griffith (who also supervised; adapted from Lord Alfred Tennyson's poem). *With* Lillian Gish, Alfred Paget, Mildred Harris, D. W. Griffith. *Prod:* Mutual-Majestic. 4 reels.

A YANKEE FROM THE WEST (1915). Romantic drama; as a battling Yankee known as "Hell-in-the-Mud." *Dir:* George Seigmann. *With* Signe Auen (Seena Owen), Tom Wilson, Josephine Crowell, Chris Lynton, Bill Brown, George Seigmann, Al Fillson. *Prod:* Mutual-Majestic. 2 reels.

SHERIFF FOR AN HOUR (1915). Comedy. *With* Arthur Mackley. *Prod:* Mutual. 992 ft.

THE CHORUS LADY (1915). Manhattan drama; as Danny Mallory, detective in love with the chorus lady. *Dir:* Frank Reicher. *Sc:* Marion Fairfax (from the play by James Forbes). *With* Cleo Ridgely, Marjorie Daw, Richard Grey, Mrs. Lewis McCord. *Prod:* Lasky-Paramount. 5 reels. (Re-made, PDC, with Albert Roscoe and Margaret Livingston.)

OLD HEIDELBERG (1915). Romance; as Karl Heinrich, the prince who finds his only happiness as a student at Heidelberg. *Dir:/Sc:* John Emerson (an updated dramatisation of the novel, "Karl Heinrich," by W. Meyer-Forest and a play by Richard Mansfield). Production supervised by D. W. Griffith. Technical director on military details: Erich von Stroheim. *With* Dorothy Gish, Erich von Stroheim, Karl Forman, Raymond Wells, Madge Hunt, Erik von Ritzau, Kate Toncray, Harold Goodwin, Francis Carpenter. Re-filmed by Ernst Lubitsch at M-G-M, 1927, starring Ramon Novarro and Norma Shearer; re-made as a musical by M-G-M, 1954, with Edmund Purdom and Ann Blyth (with Mario Lanza singing for Purdom). *Prod:* Triangle/Fine Arts. 5 reels.

CARMEN (1915). Dramatic tragedy; as Don Jose. *Dir:* Cecil B. DeMille. *Sc:* William C. de Mille (from the novel by Prosper Mérimée) *With* Geraldine Farrar, Pedro de Cordoba, William Elmer, Horace B. Carpenter, Jeanie Macpherson, Anita King, Milton A. Brown. *Prod:* Lasky-Paramount. 5 reels. (Compare listing in Geraldine Farrar filmography.)

THE GOLDEN CHANCE (1915). Romantic drama; as Roger Manning, a wealthy young man. *Dir:* Cecil B. DeMille. *Sc:* DeMille and Jeanie Macpherson. *With* Cleo Ridgely, Edythe Chapman, Horace B. Carpenter,

Raymond Hatton, Ernest Joy. Re-filmed by DeMille, 1921, as *Forbidden Fruit*. *Prod:* Lasky-Paramount. 5 reels.

TO HAVE AND TO HOLD (1916). Costume drama; as Captain Ralph Percy who wins a bride from the court of King James I. *Dir:* George Melford. *Sc:* Margaret Turnbull (from the novel by Mary Johnson). *With* Mae Murray, Tom Forman, Ronald Bradbury, Raymond Hatton, James Neill, Lucien Littlefield, Robert Fleming, Camille Astor. Re-filmed by Paramount, 1922, with Bert Lytell and Betty Compson. *Prod:* Lasky-Paramount. 5 reels.

THE LOVE MASK (1916). Western romance; as Dan Derring, blacksmith-sheriff. *Dir:* Frank Reicher. *Sc:* Cecil B. DeMille and Jeanie Macpherson. *With* Cleo Ridgely, Earle Foxe, Robert Fleming, Dorothy Abril. Working title: *Under the Mask*. *Prod:* Lasky-Paramount. 5 reels.

MARIA ROSA (1916). Romantic drama of Old Catalonia; as Andreas, lover of Maria Rosa, unjustly condemned to prison. *Dir:* Cecil B. DeMille. *Sc:* William C. de Mille (from the play by Wallace Gilpatrick and Guido Marburg, translated and adapted from the original play by Angel Guimera). *With* Geraldine Farrar, Pedro de Cordoba, Ernest Joy, Anita King, Horace B. Carpenter, James Neill. *Prod:* Lasky-Paramount. 5 reels. (Compare listing in Geraldine Farrar filmography.)

THE SELFISH WOMAN (1916). Domestic drama; as Tom Morley, almost ruined by his money-mad wife. *Dir:* E. Mason Hopper. *Sc:* Hector Turnbull. *With* Cleo Ridgely, Edythe Chapman, Charles Arling, Joe King, Jane Wolff, William Elmer, Horace B. Carpenter, Robert Fleming, Milton A. Brown. *Prod:* Lasky-Paramount. 5 reels.

THE HOUSE WITH THE GOLDEN WINDOWS (1916). Modern allegory; as Tom Wells. *Dir:* George Melford. *Sc:* Charles Server (from a story by E. V. Jefferson). *With* Cleo Ridgely, Robert Fleming, James Neill, Billy Jacobs, Mabel Van Buren, Marjorie Daw. *Prod:* Lasky-Paramount. 4 reels.

THE YELLOW PAWN (1916). Romantic drama; as a young painter known as "The King." *Dir:* George Melford. *Sc:* Margaret Turnbull (from a story, "A Close Call," by Frederic Arnold Kummer). *With* Cleo Ridgely, William Conklin, Tom Forman, Olive Golden, Clarence Geldart, George Webb, George Kuwa. *Prod:* Lasky-Paramount. 4 reels.

JOAN THE WOMAN (1917) Historical drama about Joan of Arc; as the English soldier, Eric Trent, who betrayed Joan, and as the Eric Trent of the First World War who redeems his sin. *Dir:* Cecil B. DeMille. *Sc:* Jeanie Macpherson. *With* Geraldine Farrar, Raymond

Hatton, Theodore Roberts, Tully Marshall, Hobart Bosworth, Charles Clary, James Neill, Lawrence Peyton, Horace B. Carpenter, Lillian Leighton, Cleo Ridgely, Marjorie Daw, Stephen Gray, Ernest Joy, Walter Long. *Prod:* Cardinal Film Co., for Paramount-Artcraft release. 10 reels. (Compare listing in Geraldine Farrar filmography)

THE GOLDEN FETTER (1917). Western romance; as a mining engineer who thwarts the villains robbing the heroine of her mine. *Dir:* Edward J. LeSaint. *Sc:* Charles Maigne (from a story by Charles T. Jackson. *With* Anita King, Tully Marshall, Guy Oliver, Walter Long, Mrs. Lewis McCord, Clarence Geldart, Lawrence Peyton , Lucien Littlefield. *Prod:* Lasky-Paramount. 5 reels.

THE PRISON WITHOUT WALLS (1917). Prison reform drama; as Huntington Babbs, a prison reform expert who gets himself imprisoned in order to learn its evils. *Dir:* E. Mason Hopper. *Sc:* Beulah Marie Dix (from a story by Robert E. MacAlarney). *With* Myrtle Stedman, William Conklin, Marcia Manon, William Elmer. *Prod:* Morosco-Paramount. 5 reels.

THE WORLD APART (1917). Western romance; as Bob Fulton, mine superintendent. *Dir:* William Desmond Taylor. *Sc:* Julia Crawford Ivers (from a story·by George Middleton). *With* Myrtle Stedman, John Burton, Eugene Pallette, Florence Carpenter, Henry A. Barrows. *Prod:* Morosco-Paramount. 5 reels.

BIG TIMBER (1917). Logging camp romance; as Jack Fife, a logger. *Dir:* William Desmond Taylor. *Sc:* Gardner Hunting (from a novel by Bertrand W. Sinclair). *With* Kathlyn Williams, Joe King, Alfred Paget, Helen Bray. *Prod:* Morosco-Paramount 5 reels.

THE SQUAW MAN'S SON (1917). Anglo-Western romance; as young Lord Effington, known as "Hal," who falls in love with an Indian girl. *Dir:* Edward J. LeSaint. *Sc:* Charles Maigne (sequel to Edwin M. Royle's highly successful play and movie, *The Squaw Man)*. *With* Anita King, Dorothy Davenport, Lucien Littlefield, Clarence Geldart, Donald Bowles, Frank Lanning, Ernest Joy, Mabel Van Buren, Raymond Hatton. *Prod:* Lasky-Paramount. 5 reels.

THE HOSTAGE (1917). Satirical romance about war; as Lt. Kemper, a Lowlander held hostage by Mountaineers. *Dir:* Robert Thornby. *Sc:* Beulah Marie Dix. *With* Dorothy Abril, Gertrude Short, Clarence Geldart, Guy Oliver, Marcia Manon, Noah Beery, George Spaulding, Lillian Leighton, Lucien Littlefield. *Prod:* Lasky-Paramount. 5 reels.

THE WOMAN GOD FORGOT (1917). Historical romantic drama of the conquest of Mexico; as Captain Alvarado, of the invading army of Cortez, who falls in love with Montezuma's daughter. *Dir:* Cecil B. DeMille. *Sc:* Jeanie Macpherson. *With* Geraldine Farrar, Hobart Bosworth, Raymond Hatton, Theodore Kosloff, Walter Long, Olga Grey, Julia Faye, James Neill. *Prod:* Paramount-Artcraft. 6 reels. (Compare listing in Geraldine Farrar filmography.)

NAN OF MUSIC MOUNTAIN (1917). Railroad drama; as a special deputy assigned to clean out an outlaw gang. *Dir:* George Melford. *Sc:* Beulah Marie Dix (from a serial by Frank H. Spearman published in "Everybody's Magazine"). *With* Ann Little, Theodore Roberts, James Cruze, Charles Ogle, Raymond Hatton, Hart (Jack) Hoxie, Ernest Joy, Guy Oliver, James P. Mason, Henry Woodward, Horace B. Carpenter. Lasky-Paramount. 5 reels.

THE DEVIL STONE (1917). Romantic melodrama; as Guy Sterling. *Dir:* Cecil B. DeMille. *Sc:* Jeanie Macpherson (from a story by Beatrice DeMille and Leighton Osmun). *With* Geraldine Farrar, Tully Marshall, Hobart Bosworth, James Neill, Raymond Hatton, Gustav von Seyffertitz, Ernest Joy, Mabel Van Buren, Lillian Leighton, Horace B. Carpenter. *Prod:* Paramount-Artcraft. 6 reels. (Compare listing in Geraldine Farrar filmography)

RIMROCK JONES (1918). Mining drama; as Rimrock Jones. *Dir:* Donald Crisp. *Sc:* Harvey F. Thew and Frank X. Finnegan (from a story by Dane Coolidge). *With* Ann Little, Charles Ogle, Paul Hurst, Guy Oliver, Fred Huntley, Edna Mae Cooper, Toto Ducrow, Gustav von Seyffertitz, Ernest Joy. *Prod:* Lasky-Paramount. 5 reels.

THE THING WE LOVE (1918). Patriotic drama; as Rodney Sheridan. *Dir:* Lou Tellegen. *Sc:* Harvey F. Thew (from a story by H. B. and M. G. Daniel). *With* Kathlyn Williams, Tully Marshall, Maym Kelso, Charles Ogle, William Elmer. *Prod:* Lasky-Paramount. 4 reels.

THE HOUSE OF SILENCE (1918). Mystery melodrama; as a French detective, Marcel Levington. *Dir:* Donald Crisp. *Sc:* Margaret Turnbull (from a novel by Elwyn Barron). *With* Ann Little, Adele Farrington, Winter Hall, Ernest Joy, Henry A. Barrows, *Prod:* Lasky-Paramount. 5 reels.

BELIEVE ME, XANTIPPE (1918). Romantic comedy; as George MacFarland, who bets $20,000 that he can commit a crime and not be caught within a year. *Dir:* Donald Crisp. *Sc:* Olga Printzlau (from a play by Frederick Ballard). *With* Ann Little, Ernest Joy, Henry Woodward, James Farley, Noah Beery, Charles Ogle, James Cruze, Winifred Greenwood, Clarence Geldart. *Prod:* Lasky-Paramount. 5 reels.

THE FIREFLY OF FRANCE (1918). First World War espionage drama; as Devereux Bayne, aviator. *Dir:* Donald Crisp. *Sc:* Margaret Turnbull (from a story by Marion Polk Angelotti). *With* Ann Little, Charles Ogle, Raymond Hatton, Winter Hall, Ernest Joy, William Elmer, Clarence Geldart, Henry Woodward, Jane Wolff. *Prod:* Lasky-Paramount. 5 reels.

LESS THAN KIN (1918). Romantic melodrama; in a dual role: as Hobart Lee, a wealthy American, who dies; and Lewis Vickers, who impersonates him. *Dir:* Donald Crisp. *Sc:* (from a story by Alice Duer Miller). *With* Ann Little, Raymond Hatton, Gustav von Seyffertitz, Noah Beery, James Neill, Charles Ogle, Jane Wolff, James Cruze, Guy Oliver, Jack Herbert, *Prod:* Lasky-Paramount. 5 reels.

THE SOURCE (1918). Patriotic drama of regeneration in a lumber camp; as Van Twiller Yard. *Dir:* Donald Crisp. *Sc:* Monte Katterjohn (from a story by Clarence Buddington Kelland). *With* Ann Little, Theodore Roberts, James Cruze, Noah Beery, Raymond Hatton, Charles West, Charles Ogle, Nina Byron. *Prod:* Lasky-Paramount. 5 reels.

THE MAN FROM FUNERAL RANGE (1918). Melodrama; as Harry Webb, who comes back twenty years after serving time to trap a killer. *Dir:* Walter Edwards. *Sc:* Monte Katterjohn (from a play, "Broken Threads," by W. E. Wilkes). *With* Ann Little, Willis Marks, George McDaniel, Tully Marshall, Lottie Pickford, Phil Ainsworth. *Prod:* Lasky-Paramount. 5 reels.

TOO MANY MILLIONS (1918). Comedy drama; as Walsingham Van Doren, unsuccessful book salesman, who inherits forty million dollars. *Dir:* James Cruze. *Sc:* Gardner Hunting (from a play, "Someone and Somebody," by Porter Emerson Browne). *With* Ora Carewe, Tully Marshall, Charles Ogle, James Neill, Winifred Greenwood, Noah Beery, Percy Williams, Richard Wayne. *Prod:* Lasky-Paramount. 5 reels.

THE DUB (1919). Crook melodrama; as John Craig, whom a gang of crooks try to use. *Dir:* James Cruze. *Sc:* Will M. Ritchey (from a story by Edgar Franklin). *With* Nina Byron, Charles Ogle, Ralph Lewis, Raymond Hatton, Winter Hall, Guy Oliver, William Elmer. *Prod:* Lasky-Paramount. 5 reels.

ALIAS MIKE MORAN (1919). Patriotic melodrama about a draft dodger who assumes the identity of an ex-convict; as Larry Young, who becomes Mike Moran. *Dir:* James Cruze. *Sc:* Will M. Ritchey (from a story by Frederick Orin Bartlett). *With* Ann Little, Emory Johnson, Charles Ogle, Edythe Chapman, William Elmer, Winter Hall, Jean Calhoun, Guy Oliver. *Prod:* Lasky-Paramount. 5 reels.

THE ROARING ROAD (1919). Automobile racing comedy drama; as "Toodles" Walden, who wins the girl and the 400-mile Santa Monica Road Race. *Dir:* James Cruze. *Sc:* Marion Fairfax (from a story by Byron Morgan). *With* Ann Little, Theodore Roberts, Guy Oliver, Clarence Geldart. *Prod:* Lasky-Paramount. 5 reels.

YOU'RE FIRED (1919). Romantic comedy; as Billy Deering, who has to hold a job for a month before he can claim the girl he loves. *Dir:* James Cruze. *Sc:* Clara Genevieve Kennedy (from a short story, "The Halberdier of the Little Rheinschloss," by O. Henry). *With* Wanda Hawley, Henry Woodward, Theodore Roberts, Lillian Mason, Herbert Pryor, Raymond Hatton, William Lesta. *Prod:* Lasky-Paramount. 5 reels.

THE LOVE BURGLAR (1919). Romantic melodrama; as David Strong, who enters the underworld to bring out his errant brother. *Dir:* James Cruze. *Sc:* Walter Woods (from a play, "One of Us," by Jack Lait). *With* Anna Q. Nilsson, Raymond Hatton, Wallace Beery, Wilton Taylor, Edmund Burns, Alice Taafe (Terry), Richard Wayne, Henry Woodward. *Prod:* Lasky-Paramount. 5 reels.

THE VALLEY OF THE GIANTS (1919). Romantic drama of the California redwoods; as Bryce Cardigan. *Dir:* James Cruze. *Sc:* Marion Fairfax (from a novel by Peter B. Kyne). *With* Grace Darmond, William Brunton, Charles Ogle, Ralph Lewis, Alice Taafe (Terry), Kay Laurel, Hart (Jack) Hoxie, Noah Beery, Guy Oliver, William H. Brown. (Refilmed by First National, 1927, with Milton Sills and Doris Kenyon; again, as a talkie by Warner Bros., 1938, with Wayne Morris and Claire Trevor). *Prod:* Paramount-Artcraft. 5 reels.

THE LOTTERY MAN (1919). Romantic comedy; as Jack Wright, who raffles himself off as a $50,000 bridegroom. *Dir:* James Cruze. *Sc:* Elmer Harris (from a Broadway play by Rida Johnson Young). *With* Wanda Hawley, Harrison Ford, Wilton Taylor, Clarence Geldart, Fanny Midgely, Sylvia Ashton, Carolyn Rankin, Virgina Flotz, Winifred Greenwood, Marcia Manon, Fred Huntley. *Prod:* Paramount-Artcraft. 5 reels.

HAWTHORNE OF THE U.S.A. (AKA, GB, *Hawthorne, the Adventurer*) (1919). Romantic mythical kingdom comedy; as Hawthorne. *Dir:* James Cruze. *Sc:* Walter Woods (from the play by James B. Fagan, in which Douglas Fairbanks had starred on Broadway). *With* Lila Lee, Harrison Ford, Tully Marshall, Charles Ogle, Guy Oliver, Edwin Stevens, Clarence Burton, Theodore Roberts, Ruth Rennick, Robert Brower. *Prod:* Paramount-Artcraft. 5 reels.

DOUBLE SPEED (1920). Automobile racing comedy drama; as "Speed" Carr, cross-country racer. *Dir:* Sam Wood. *Sc:* Clara Genevieve Kennedy (from a story, "Speed Carr," by J. Stewart Woodhouse). *With* Wanda Hawley, Theodore Roberts, Tully Marshall, Lucien Littlefield, Guy Oliver. *Prod:* Paramount-Artcraft. 4 reels.

EXCUSE MY DUST (1920). Automobile racing comedy drama; as "Toodles" Walden, racer. *Dir:* Sam Wood. *Sc:* Will M. Ritchey (from a "SatEvePost" story, "The Bear Trap," by Byron Morgan). *With* Ann Little, Tully Marshall, Theodore Roberts, Walter Long, Byron Morgan, Will M. Ritchey, William Wallace Reid, Jr., Guy Oliver, Otto Browner. *Prod:* Paramount-Artcraft. 5 reels.

THE DANCIN' FOOL (1920). Romantic comedy; as Sylvester Tibble, a clerk who becomes a favourite ballroom dancer. *Dir:* Sam Wood. *Sc:* Clara Genevieve Kennedy (from a story by Henry Payson Dowst). *With* Bebe Daniels, Raymond Hatton, Lillian Leighton, Tully Marshall, Ernest Joy. *Prod:* Paramount-Artcraft. 5 reels. (Compare listing in Bebe Daniels filmography.)

SICK ABED (1920). Romantic comedy; as Reggy Jay, wealthy hypochondriac who falls in love with his nurse. *Dir:* Sam Wood. *Sc:* Clara Genevieve Kennedy (from a play by Ethel Watts Mumford). *With* Bebe Daniels, Winifred Greenwood, Tully Marshall, Clarence Geldart, Lucien Littlefield. *Prod:* Paramount-Artcraft. 5 reels. (Compare listing in Bebe Daniels filmography.) (Subsequently, Reid toured in this onstage on the Pacific Coast, with Kathleen Clifford as the heroine.)

WHAT'S YOUR HURRY? (1920). Automobile racing comedy drama; as "Dusty" Rhodes, racer, who, with a caravan of motor lorries, saves a dam from breaking. *Dir:* Sam Wood. *Sc:* Byron Morgan (from his story, "The Hippopotamus Parade"). *With* Lois Wilson, Charles Ogle, Clarence Burton, Ernest Butterworth, Jack Young. *Prod:* Paramount-Artcraft. 5 reels.

ALWAYS AUDACIOUS (1920). Romantic melodrama; in a dual role: as Perry Dayton, shanghaied millionaire, and "Slim" Attucks, who impersonates him. *Dir:* James Cruze. *Sc:* Tom J. Geraghty (from a story, "Toujours de l'Audace," by Ben Ames Williams). *With* Margaret Loomis, Clarence Geldart, J. M. Dumont, Rhea Haines, Carmen Phillips, Guy Oliver, Fanny Midgely. *Prod:* Paramount-Artcraft. 5 reels.

THE CHARM SCHOOL (1921). Romantic comedy; as Austin Bevans, who inherits a girls' school. *Dir:* James Cruze. *Sc:* Tom J. Geraghty (from a story and play by Alice Duer Miller). *With* Lila Lee, Adele Farrington, Beulah Bainse, Edwin Stevens, Grace Morse,

Lincoln Stedman, Kate Toncray, Snitz Edwards, Tina Marshall. (In 1929 this formed a story basis for a musical re-make, *Sweetie*, with Nancy Carroll, a switch from boy to girl lead; re-filmed, 1936, as *Collegiate*, returning it to a male lead, with Jack Oakie, Frances Langford and Betty Grable.) *Prod:* Paramount-Artcraft. 5 reels.

THE LOVE SPECIAL (1921). Romantic railroad drama; as Jim Glover, civil engineer. *Dir:* Frank Urson. *Sc:* Eugene B. Lewis (from a story, "The Daughter of a Magnate," by Frank H. Spearman). *With* Agnes Ayres, Theodore Roberts, Lloyd Whitlock, Sylvia Ashton, William Gaden, Clarence Burton, Snitz Edwards, Ernest Butterworth, Zelma Maja. *Prod:* Paramount-Artcraft. 5 reels.

TOO MUCH SPEED (1921). Romantic automobile drama; as "Dusty" Rhodes, racer and inventer. *Dir:* Frank Urson. *Sc:* Byron Morgan (from his "SatEvePost" story). *With* Agnes Ayres, Theodore Roberts, Jack Richardson, Lucien Littlefield, Guy Oliver, Henry Johnson, Jack Herbert. *Prod:* Paramount-Artcraft. 5 reels.

THE HELL DIGGERS (AKA, GB, *The Gold Dredgers*) (1921). Automobile drama; as Teddy Darman, who has invented a dredge which will re-soil land that has been mined. *Dir:* Frank Urson. *Sc:* Byron Morgan. *With* Lois Wilson, Alexander Brown, Frank Leigh, Lucien Littlefield, Clarence Geldart, Bud Post. *Prod:* Paramount. 5 reels.

THE AFFAIRS OF ANATOL (AKA, GB, *A Prodigal Knight*). (1921). Romantic comedy drama; as Anatol DeWitt Spencer, who learns about love. *Dir:* Cecil B. DeMille. *Sc:* Jeanie Macpherson, Beulah Marie Dix, Lorna Moon and Elmer Harris (suggested by the comedy, *Anatol,* by Arthur Schnitzler, and the paraphrase thereof by Granville Barker). *With* Gloria Swanson, Elliott Dexter, Bebe Daniels, Monte Blue, Wanda Hawley, Theodore Roberts, Agnes Ayres, Theodore Kosloff, Polly Moran, Raymond Hatton, Julia Faye, Charles Ogle, Winter Hall, Guy Oliver, Ruth Miller, Lucien Littlefield, Zelma Maja, Shannon Day, Elinor Glyn, William Boyd, Maude Wayne, Fred Huntley, Lady Gilbert Parker. *Prod:* Famous Players-Lasky (released as a DeMille Paramount-Special). 9 reels. Working title: *Five Kisses.* (Compare listing in Bebe Daniels filmography.)

DON'T TELL EVERYTHING (1921). Romantic comedy; as Cullen Dale. *Dir:* Sam Wood. *Sc:* Albert Shelby LeVino (from a story by Lorna Moon, a left-over Anatolian sequence). *With* Gloria Swanson, Elliott Dexter, Dorothy Cumming. Paramount. 5 reels.

RENT FREE (1922). Romantic comedy; as Buell Arnister, Jr. *Dir:* Howard Higgin. *Sc:* Elmer Rice (from a story by Izola Forrester and Mann Page). *With* Lila Lee, Henry A. Barrows, Gertrude Short, Lillian Leighton, Clarence Geldart, Claire McDowell, Lucien Littlefield. Paramount. 5 reels.

THE WORLD'S CHAMPION (1922). Romantic drama; as William Burroughs, Englishman, who comes to America and becomes a champion boxer. *Dir:* Philip E. Rosen *Sc:* J. E. Nash and Albert Shelby LeVino (from a play, "The Champion," by Thomas Louden and Augustus E. Thomas). *With* Lois Wilson, Lionel Belmore, Henry Miller Jr., Helen Dunbar, Leslie Casey, W. J. Ferguson, Guy Oliver. Paramount. 5 reels.

FOREVER (1922). Period romance; as Peter Ibbetson. *Dir:* George Fitzmaurice. *Sc:* Ouida Bergere (from the novel, "Peter Ibbetson," by George Du Maurier and the play therefrom by Jules Nathan Raphael). *With* Elsie Ferguson, Montagu Love, George Fawcett, Dolores Cassinelli, Paul McAllister, Elliott Dexter, Barbara Dean, Charles Eaton, Jerome Patrick, (Re-made as a talkie, *Peter Ibbetson,* 1935, starring Gary Cooper and Ann Harding.) Working title: *The Great Romance. Prod:* Paramount. 7 reels. (Compare listing in Elsie Ferguson filmography.)

ACROSS THE CONTINENT (1922). Romantic automobile racing comedy; as Jimmy Dent, trancontinental race-driver. *Dir:* Philip E. Rosen. *Sc:* Byron Morgan. *With* Mary MacLaren, Theodore Roberts, Betty Francisco, Walter Long, Lucien Littlefield, Jack Herbert, Guy Oliver, Sidney D'Albrook. *Prod:* Paramount. 6 reels.

THE DICTATOR (1922). Romantic drama in South America; as Brooke Travers, who wins a revolution and a beautiful girl. *Dir:* James Cruze. *Sc:* Walter Woods (from the play by Richard Harding Davis). (Previously filmed, 1915, by John Barrymore.) *With* Lila Lee, Theodore Kosloff, Kalla Pasha, Sidney Bracey, Fred Butler, Walter Long, Alan Hale. *Prod:* Paramount. 6 reels. (Compare listing in John Barrymore filmography.)

NICE PEOPLE (1922). Romantic comedy drama of the jazz age; as Captain Billy Wade, a Westerner who comes East and is shocked by the cavortings among "nice people." *Dir:* William C. de Mille. *Sc:* Clara Beranger (from the play by Rachel Crothers). *With* Bebe Daniels. Conrad Nagel, Julia Faye, Claire McDowell,

Edward Martindel, Eve Southern, Bertram Johns, William Boyd, Ethel Wales. *Prod:* Paramount. 7 reels. (Compare listing in Bebe Daniels filmography.)

THE GHOST BREAKER (1922). Romantic adventure comedy; as Warren Jarvis, who helps a Spanish señorita rid her castle of robbers posing as ghosts. *Dir:* Alfred Green. *Sc:* Jack Cunningham (from the play by Paul Dickey and Charles W. Goddard). *With* Lila Lee, Walter Hiers, Arthur Edmund Carewe, J. Farrell MacDonald, Frances Raymond, Snitz Edwards. (Previously filmed, 1915, with H. B. Warner; re-filmed as the basis for a talkie comedy, 1940, with Bob Hope). *Prod:* Paramount. 5 reels.

CLARENCE (1922). Romantic character comedy; as Clarence Smith. *Dir:* William C. de Mille. *Sc:* Clara Beranger (from the Booth Tarkington play which had starred Alfred Lunt on Broadway). *With* Agnes Ayres, May McAvoy, Kathlyn Williams, Edward Martindel, Robert Agnew, Adolphe Menjou, Bertram Johns, Dorothy Gordon, Maym Kelso. (Remade as a talkie, 1937, by Paramount.) *Prod:* Paramount. 7 reels. (Compare listing in May McAvoy filmography.)

THIRTY DAYS (1922). Farce; as John Ford. *Dir:* James Cruze. *Sc:* Walter Woods (from a play by Augustus E. Thomas and Clayton Hamilton). *With* Wanda Hawley, Charles Ogle, Cyril Chadwick, Herschel Mayall, Helen Dunbar, Carmen Phillips, Kalla Pasha, Robert Brower. *Prod:* Paramount. 5 reels.

(Wallace Reid appears in a cameo bit as himself in the exploitation two-reeler, *A Trip to Paramountown,* 1922, which, made under the supervision of Jerome Beatty, included all the Paramount contract players and directors then working in Hollywood. Jack Cunningham wrote the continuity for it, and Rob Wagner wrote the subtitles. The distinguished Karl Brown was cameraman, and Vernon Keays was assistant director, and Walter Reed was technical director. Footage of Reid was shot for James Cruze's *Hollywood,* but was deleted because Reid looked very ill in it, was, in fact, dying. Reid also made a number of War Bond shorts during the War, urging the purchase of Liberty Bonds.)

6
ANITA STEWART

Although Anita Stewart never made a talking picture, she never relinquished the thought that she should make one. Even in the last year of her life.

She had been one of the most reliable players of the movies' early years, and was Vitagraph's leading actress from 1912, when she made her first big success in *The Wood Violet,* until 1917. She continued to be top box-office until 1922, even during 1918, when no Anita Stewart picture was released.

Then, despite three high-budgeted films for Hearst's Cosmopolitan Productions, she suddenly was no longer in demand, and descended to doing a dozen unimportant quickies. Her career was definitely over before the advent of sound. But by that time she was a wealthy woman.

She was born in Brooklyn on February 7, 1895, or, at least, that was the year given in her earliest publicity. As time passed, the year of her birth grew closer to 1900, and finally was placed boldly within this century. This was ridiculous, for it was well known that she had started as an extra at Vitagraph in 1911 and was then a high school student.

Both of her parents, William and Martha Stewart, were of English-Irish descent, and she was christened Anna Marie. A sister, Lucille Lee, was five years older than she, and a brother, George, several years younger.

Her father, a moderately successful Brooklyn business man, owned a pleasant home, and his wife interested her daughters in singing lessons. It was by singing in the choir of an Episcopal church in Brooklyn that Lucille Lee Stewart met Ralph Ince.

He was then regarded as "Vitagraph's handyman" and wrote, directed and acted in many of the films Vitagraph was then producing in its Brooklyn studio. Born in 1887, he was five years younger than his famous brother (Thomas Harper Ince), and, like him, as well as like John, oldest of the Ince brothers, had been a child actor on the stage. Their parents were actors and their father later became a well-known theatrical agent in New York City. Tom and Ralph were always close, and the former often employed Ralph, both as director and actor.

Ralph Ince married Lucille Lee Stewart. He at once put her on Vitagraph's list of regular players, and not long after he did so he telephoned her one day and said: "Send Anna down to me after school. I haven't enough youngsters for a picture we're starting."

Anna was then a student at Brooklyn's Erasmus High School. She was also studying music and had done a little modeling "for high class pictorial lithographs." She was soon spending more time at Vitagraph, working as an extra and bit player, than she was at Erasmus High. In later years, she made a point of acknowledging that "all I am I owe to my brother-in-law."

By September 30, 1912, the date on which *Her Choice,* in which she received her first billing, was released, she was under contract at Vitagraph and was making $25 a week. For the public responded to her. Said "Photoplay" a few years later: "What is the Anita Stewart charm? Isn't it, mainly, an elusive sort of virginity, an expression of complete girlhood unsullied by the knowing complacency of maturity? There is no one on our screens who can be at once so ardent and so pure, and this is a rare quality in an age in which babies hear sex-talk."

In the autumn of 1912, Anna accompanied Ralph and her sister to Saratoga, where he was supposed to film Rosemary Theby in *The Wood Violet.* But the studio sent him word that it had concluded Miss Theby was too old for the part. Ince replaced her with Anna Marie, and *The Wood Violet* became a showcase for her fresh, young, American beauty. The picture was at once very popular, and it opened the doors to stardom for her.

In addition to projecting "purity," Miss Stewart also had a "patrician quality" that audiences liked. Indeed, the critics were soon praising her versatility—her impersonations of a child of nature puzzled by urban society (*The Wood Violet, 'Midst Woodland Shadows, The Goddess*); of a modern sophisticate *(The Web, The Girl from Prosperity)*; of addiction to gambling, alcohol or narcotics (*The Prince of Evil, The Painted World, The Sins of the Mothers*); of a woman-of-the-world who discovers that the young man she loves is the son she had deserted (*He Never Knew*); and of innocence and charm as Ann Rutledge in *Lincoln, the Lover* (in which Ralph Ince played Lincoln).

She owed her professional name of Anita Stewart to a printer's error. Her first billings were as "Anna M. Stewart" or "Anna Stewart," or even "Stuart." But in July 1913, for *The Song Bird of the North,* her given name name was mistakenly listed as "Anita." She approved it, and so did Vitagraph when fan mail addressed to "Anita Stewart" flooded in. There were a few lapses in subsequent billings to "Anna," but the name Anita Stewart was soon known throughout the world.

The feature that made her a hot star was *A Million Bid,* wherein she played the beautiful daughter of a socially ambitious mother who makes her marry a millionaire she does not love. It was based on a play ("Agnes") that had been written by Mrs. Sidney Drew, a handsome matronly actress who co-starred with her husband in very popular two-reel marital comedies for Vitagraph. Mrs. Drew had not been able to sell "Agnes" to the Broadway producers, but the film Ralph Ince made of it became one of Vitagraph's biggest moneymakers.

After *A Million Bid,* Miss Stewart had her pick of Vitagraph's story properties and was soon Vitagraph's most profitable acting property. Her $25 a week was raised to $100.

The depiction of catastrophes on the screen was then a novelty that paid off at the box-office and Vitagraph went to extensive lengths to stage them for the

Sincerely
Anita Stewart

Anita Stewart

climaxes of Anita Stewart pictures. A realistic shipwreck was one of the features of *A Million Bid*; the *dénouement* of *The Wreck* was a wreck of a real train; an automobile collided with a train in Miss Stewart's *The Shadow of the Past;* a runaway train was the feature of *Four Thirteen;* and the most spectacular wreck of all climaxed *The Juggernaut* (1915), which was advertised as "The Colossus of Modern Railroad Dramas" and had a speeding train go off a high trestle.

Late in 1914, Vitagraph began teaming her with handsome Earle Williams, and in 1915 co-starred them in a serial, *The Goddess,* which was largely shot in the North Carolina mountains. The story was naïve — a girl raised in idyllic circumstances on a deserted island is brought back to civilisation to reform the world, and, instead, becomes a pawn of its corruption — but *The Goddess* proved to be almost as popular as the Pearl White serials, and Vitagraph publicity hinted of a real-life romance between Williams and Miss Stewart. She, however, did not go along with the ruse and stated flatly: "Yes, I like to act with Mr. Williams, who is very nice. But I am not engaged to him and have no intention of becoming so. I don't think I could ever marry an actor. Too much attention makes actors conceited and selfish." Years later, when Williams was dying from pneumonia, he asked to see Anita Stewart, and she was his last visitor before he lapsed into a coma.

There *was* a young man at Vitagraph who was very much in love with her and who did everything he could to make her change her mind about becoming engaged. S. Rankin Drew, son of Mr. and Mrs. Sidney Drew and a promising young actor, was her leading man in both *The Suspect* and *The Girl Philippa,* and directed both of them, as well as another Stewart vehicle in which he did not appear — *The Daring of Diana.* He made no secret of his infatuation, and pressed her continually to become his bride. She admitted she was attracted, but told him she didn't love him. Disappointed, he enlisted in the Lafayette Escadrille and was soon in France, where his plane crashed in combat. Before he died, he sent her the wings he had won, along with a farewell letter, which began with a poem: "Off to fly in the sky/Perhaps to die..." and ended, "I love you."

Sometime in the latter part of 1917 she secretly married Rudolph Cameron (*né* Brennan). Cameron was her leading man in *The More Excellent Way, Clover's Rebellion,* and *The Message of the Mouse,* all released sometime during 1917. Obviously, she had changed her mind about the wisdom of marrying an actor.

Miss Stewart's infatuation with and secret marriage to Cameron were not her only concerns at that time. Her sister was harrying Ralph Ince to do for her what he had done for Anita, and, with Ince busy, Anita Stewart pictures were being directed by men with whom Miss Stewart was considerably less simpatico. She was very conscious of her nose, which, unless photographed correctly, could mar her appearance. When Wilfred North, for example, was directing her in *Clover's Rebellion*, she was constantly pleading: "Please, please be careful of my nose."

More important: a Massachusetts movie exhibitor who wanted to become a movie producer, Louis B. Mayer, was offering her a contract that gave her what she was then getting from Vitagraph ($1000 a week plus ten per cent of the profits of her films, with a guarantee of $127,000 a year) but also provided that she would have her own company — Anita Stewart Productions, Inc. — and hence be in a position to decide what stories she would film, what directors she would use, etc.

She had met Mayer through a dwarfed newspaper vendor named Toby, who was her greatest fan. Toby was also impressed by Mayer's aura of success, and when he learned that Mayer was incorporating for film production, he arranged for Mayer to meet the actress.

Miss Stewart's contract with Vitagraph, however, did not expire until

January 31, 1918, and in the spring and summer of 1917 she began to be "ill." When, on September 15, 1917, Mayer announced that he had signed her to a long term contract, Vitagraph took legal steps to prevent her from acting for him or anyone else. Her lawyers countered with charges that Vitagraph had not shown her proper financial statements; had forced her to do stories which weren't right for her, with directors who hadn't appreciated her abilities; and had been uninterested in the effects of all this on her health.

Vitagraph won the case, and the company's victory is a precedent that still figures in the enforcement of actor-studio contracts today. The New York courts ruled that every day lost because of the legal battle would extend the contract a day. Miss Stewart resignedly returned to Vitagraph to film two final pictures for them, and Vitagraph instituted a suit against Mayer for $250,000 "for alleged conspiracy to induce Anita Stewart to break her contract."

Miss Stewart was not at all happy, even though one of the films she was required to make for Vitagraph was an adaptation of the Arthur Wing Pinero comedy in which Billie Burke had played on Broadway, *The Mind-the-Paint Girl.* During her absence, Vitagraph had begun building up one of its promising contract beauties, Corinne Griffith and was publicising her as "The Orchid Lady." In rapid time, Miss Griffith had supplanted Miss Stewart as Vitagraph's top star, and was getting the velvet glove treatment.

Ouida Bergere seized the occasion to try to interest Miss Stewart in forgetting any obligations she might think she had toward Mayer and signing with Jesse L. Lasky after her two films for Vitagraph were completed. Lasky and Adolph Zukor, ever since Mary Pickford had left Paramount, had been hunting for a Pickford successor, and they offered Anita Stewart a million dollar contract to star for them. But she felt obligated to Mayer, and declined. They then offered the contract to Mary Miles Minter, and Miss Minter's mother, Mrs. Shelby, pushed her daughter into it, with much resultant unhappiness and tragedy. Had Miss Stewart gone with Lasky and even played in some of the stories bought for Miss Minter, she might have rivalled Mary Pickford as Box-Office Queen of Hollywood.

Mayer was finally able to settle out of court with Vitagraph. For $70,000 he took over the two uncompleted pictures the court had made Miss Stewart do in order to finish her Vitagraph contract (*The Mind-the-Paint Girl* and *Human Desire*), and in August, 1918, Miss Stewart started filming, for Mayer, Owen Johnson's popular novel, "Virtuous Wives," the rights to which had cost Mayer $15,000. George Loane Tucker did the adaptation, and directed. The picture was filmed in studio space Mayer rented from Vitagraph!

Virtuous Wives, advertised as "a truthful story of married life in New York society," was accorded a big press campaign, but Miss Stewart didn't care for the story and hadn't been happy making it. Much of her discontent derived from Mrs. DeWolf (Hedda) Hopper, who played the second lead, a venal society matron. Mrs. Hopper had been approved for the role by director Tucker, but was told Miss Stewart herself would also have to approve her. For her Tucker interview, Mrs. Hopper had worn her fashionable best, but when she journeyed over to Brooklyn to be interviewed by Miss Stewart, she deliberately wore her tackiest outfit. Miss Stewart smiled winningly when she saw her, and said: "You're perfect — what I dreamed of for the part. What a shame to bring you all the way over here!"

ANITA STEWART
in "VIRTUOUS WIVES"

Anita Stewart, with Conway Tearle and Hedda Hopper in VIRTUOUS WIVES

Then, as soon as her contract, which guaranteed her $5000, was signed, Mrs. Hopper rushed to Lucile, Inc. and blew it all on clothes that Lady Duff-Gordon, who *was* Lucile, Inc., personally designed. On the first day Hedda Hopper worked, on location at a Long Island mansion, and appeared wearing a flowing Lucile tea gown of lilac and mauve chiffon, Miss Stewart protested — and rightly. The second woman does not out-dress the star.

Despite what Hedda Hopper has written in "From under My Hat," Miss Stewart was not long resentful. Mrs. Hopper says Miss Stewart's wardrobe had been "run up by loving hands at home," and does not mention that Miss Stewart had her own exclusive modiste, and had she been malicious, could have held up production and had Lady Duff-Gordon, or any other couturier, design a special star's wardrobe for three times the sum the extravagant Hedda had spent.

It's true that the ladies did not speak during the making of *Virtuous Wives*.

Anita Stewart never bothered to seek out Hedda Hopper, and when Miss Stewart clowned between takes on the set, Mrs. Hopper observed coldly: "Would you look at the dignity of our star!" It was Hedda Hopper who kept the so-called feud alive until, twenty-five years later, a public relations man persuaded them, at a "Pickfair" party, to bury the hatchet — and not in each other's necks.

After *Virtuous Wives*, Mayer moved to Hollywood, and so did Anita Stewart Productions, Inc. Rudolph Cameron was a member of its board of directors and entitled to one-eighth of its profits.

The day Miss Stewart arrived in Hollywood, it was raining, and it is never wise to be introduced to Southern California during a forty-day-and-night deluge. She was also distressed to learn that the studio in which she would work had no glass stages and that she would not have the flattering advantages of reflected natural sunlight.

Her husband and she took up residence in an attractive Laughlin Park estate. Their house later became the home of George Loane Tucker, Fred Stone, and then Charles Chaplin (when he was married to Mildred Harris). It was next door to the Cecil B. DeMille home, and DeMille subsequently acquired it and turned it into his home-office, connecting it by means of a covered pergola to his own residence. Today it is the headquarters of the Cecil B. DeMille Estate.

Few of the fifteen pictures Miss Stewart did for Mayer had much beside her presence to recommend them. They were given superior production values; the casts were star-studded; the directors were the best money could buy — Lois Weber, Marshall Neilan, John M. Stahl, Edwin Carewe, Fred Niblo, *et al.* But the stories were shabby, even for their time, and Mayer had to talk Miss Stewart who had good taste, into filming most of them. She liked that hardy theatrical perennial called *In Old Kentucky,* and she also approved of *Sowing the Wind* and *The Yellow Typhoon.* The last gave her a dual role: two sisters, one brunette and virtuous; the other a blonde scheming adventuress.

For *In Old Kentucky* and another of her films, *A Midnight Romance*, Miss Stewart wrote theme songs which were featured in the promotion of those productions.

During the final year of her contract with Mayer, he became interested in Mildred Harris and began promoting her as his premiere star. In 1922, when Miss Stewart's contract expired, Mayer wanted to renew it, but she did not. "I have often wondered," she said some years later, "if I wouldn't have been better off had I remained in dear old Brooklyn with Vitagraph."

Her final year with Mayer was also the last year she and Cameron lived together. They separated in 1923, and divorced five years later.

William Randolph Hearst had always admired Miss Stewart as an actress — it was largely Hearst money that had made *The Goddess* possible — and after her contract with Mayer ended, she made three films for his Cosmopolitan Productions.

The Love Piker was ineffectual, but *The Great White Way,* adapted from an H. C. Witmer story, *Cain and Mabel,* was a big special filmed in New York City that featured nearly every celebrity in the theatre or under contract to Hearst's syndicated newspaper empire.

Miss Stewart's third Cosmopolitan film turned out to be the only really good feature she filmed away from the Vitagraph lot: *Never the Twain Shall Meet*. It was adapted from a Peter B. Kyne novel and was beautifully directed by Maurice Tourneur. It was, essentially, a return for her to *The Wood Violet* formula. She played a South Seas half-breed who falls in love with a wealthy San Francisco black sheep, reforms him from alcoholism, but wilts unhappily when exposed to civilisation, and so returns to her South Sea Isle. *Never the Twain Shall Meet* became Miss Stewart's favourite of all the pictures she made.

When Vitagraph was briefly re-activated, Miss Stewart made an unimportant outdoor melodrama, *Baree, Son of Kazan*, for it. The new Vitagraph did not long survive.

Miss Stewart made a dozen pictures after *Never the Twain Shall Meet*, including a ten-chapter serial for Mascot called *Isle of Sunken Gold*, but only one of these final pictures was of consequence: the film adaptation of Martha Ostenso's prize-winning novel, *Wild Geese*.

She might have made one other picture of quality. Peter B. Kyne, who had at first opposed her being cast for *Never the Twain Shall Meet*, was so delighted by her performance in it that he brought her the galleys of his subsequent novel, "Tide of Empire," and she took the property to Louis B. Mayer. He told her he wasn't interested in the story, but the moment she left his office he started negotiations for its purchase, and filmed it with Renée Adorée.

On July 24, 1929, after a well-publicised courtship, Miss Stewart married George Peabody Converse, a New York sportsman and a grandson of a president of the United States Steel Corporation. They at first travelled extensively, and she made personal appearance tours, both in the United States and Europe. On one of these she sang a medley of songs by Irving Berlin, who was one of her admirers. I remember her singing in a vaudeville tour "Broken Hearted," and putting it over with all the blue wistfulness of an Aileen Stanley. She occasionally appeared on radio — sometimes to sing. She wrote a novel, a melodramatic story with a backstage setting called "The Devil's Toy". The Converses maintained a home on Hanover Drive in Beverly Hills, and were happy. Once in a while there would be an announcement that she was contemplating making a return to films in a musical; it's regrettable nothing came of any of her plans for a comeback, because she had proved she could sing and dance most charmingly. There were those who said she would never do for talking features, because she still spoke with a trace of a Brooklyn accent. A Brooklyn accent hasn't impeded the ascent to talkie fame of many another personality, and if she had had to lose it, she could have.

During the Second World War, when Converse had to be on duty in Washington, Miss Stewart did not join him because she was caring for her brother, George, who had become an invalid and could not be moved. He had been an actor, and a good one. Starting at Vitagraph, he had played more than a few leads in Hollywood, and was much liked in the young set. Unfortunately, he got into a dispute with his brother-in-law, Ralph Ince, when both were drinking, and it climaxed in a savagely brutal fight, in which George Stewart was permanently injured and forced to be bedridden. His sister Anita took him over as her personal charge, and saw to it that he was cared for until his death in 1946.

Forced to live apart from her husband, Miss Stewart later told Louella O. Parsons, led to a legal separation, and, in 1946, to divorce.

Miss Stewart continued to reside in Beverly Hills, and after her brother's death, her sister, Lucille Lee Stewart, who had had several husbands after her divorce from Ralph Ince, came to live with her. Miss Stewart became president of the Film Welfare League and personally supplemented some of its benefactions. She took up painting as a hobby, and her canvases attracted considerable attention.

On May 4, 1961, she died in her sleep in her Beverly Hills home, from a heart ailment. Her sister was her chief heir, and is still alive.

ANITA STEWART FILMOGRAPHY

HER CHOICE (1912). Problem drama of two nieces, one of whom is chosen as an heiress; as one of the nieces. *Dir./Sc:* Ralph Ince. (Miss Stewart received her initial billing as "Anna M. Stewart.") *Prod:* Vitagraph. 932 ft.

THE GODMOTHER (1912). Comedy; as one of several schoolgirls chaperoned by a "Charley's Aunt." *Dir:* Ralph Ince. *Sc:* Mrs. Beta Breuil. *With* Marshall P. Wilder, Hughie Mack, H. L. Barry, R. Richmond, E. Thomas, Lucy Lee (Lucille Lee Stewart), Rosemary Theby. *Prod:* Vitagraph. 816 ft.

THE WOOD VIOLET (1912). Romantic idyll; a woodland girl who falls in love with a man from the city. *Dir./Sc:* Ralph Ince. *With* E. K. Lincoln, L. Roger Lytton. *Prod:* Vitagraph. 1 reel.

SONG OF THE SHELL (1912). Romance; as a social worker. *Dir./Sc:* Ralph Ince. *With* Earle Williams. *Prod:* Vitagraph. 954 ft.

THE CLASSMATES FROLIC (1913). Comedy; as a schoolgirl. *Dir./Sc:* Ralph Ince *With* Flora Finch, Rosemary Theby, Lucille Lee Stewart, Lillian Walker, Edith Storey, William Shea, Charles Edwards. *Prod:* Vitagraph. 426 ft.

LOVE LAUGHS AT BLACKSMITHS or LOVE FINDS A WAY (1913). Romance; as Bess, a determined girl in love. *Dir:* Ralph Ince. *With* Flora Finch, Frank Bennett, Frank Currier. *Prod:* Vitagraph. 754 ft.

THE WEB (1913). Melodrama; as Agatha, a girl who traps a murderer in order to free her lover. *Dir.* Ralph Ince. *With* Rosemary Theby, James Morrison, Courtenay Foote, Ned Finley. *Prod:* Vitagraph. 1990 ft.

A FIGHTING CHANCE (1913). Romance; as a secretary who patches up the broken marriage of her boss. *Dir:* Ralph Ince. *Sc:* James Oliver Curwood. *Prod:* Vitagraph. 1 reel.

TWO'S COMPANY, THREE'S A CROWD (1913). Romantic farce; as Sadie, a stenographer wooed by two men. *Dir:* Ralph Ince. *With* E. K. Lincoln, James Lackaye. *Prod:* Vitagraph. 754 ft.

A REGIMENT OF TWO (1913). Marital farce; as one of two wives who cure their husbands of prevaricating. *Dir:* Ralph Ince. *With* Sidney Drew, Rose E. Tapley, Edith Storey, E. K. Lincoln, Ralph Ince. *Prod:* Vitagraph. 2040 ft.

THE FORGOTTEN LATCHKEY (1913). Romantic comedy; as Mrs. Burton, who spends a night with her husband in a taxi. *Dir:* Ralph Ince. *With* Harry T. Morey, Florence Ashebrooke, George Randolph, James Lackaye. *Prod:* Vitagraph. 994 ft.

THE SONG BIRD OF THE NORTH (1913). Romance of the Civil War; as Elida Rumsey, who sings at recruiting centers and at hospitals, and so finds the man she loves. *Dir:* Ralph Ince (based on a factual incident). *With* Ralph Ince. (In this film, thanks to a printer's error, she was first billed as "Anita Stewart.") *Prod:* Vitagraph. 1030 ft.

SWEET DECEPTION (1913). Romance; as Mrs. Grace Bradley, who rediscovers romance with her husband. *Dir:* Ralph Ince. *Sc:* Mrs. Sidney Drew. *With* Mary Maurice, Sidney Drew. *Prod:* Vitagrpah. 1007 ft.

THE MOULDING (1913). Romantic drama; as Meg Jones, an untutored girl who learns how to hold her husband's love. *Dir:* Ralph Ince. *Sc:* Leah Baird. *With* Gladden James, Rose E. Tapley. *Prod:* Vitagraph. 1013 ft.

THE PRINCE OF EVIL (1913). Drama; as Georgia Rivers, who gambles recklessly and nearly destroys herself. *Dir:* Ralph Ince. *With* Edith Storey, L. Rogers Lytton, E. K. Lincoln, Harry Northrup. *Prod:* Vitagraph. 2020 ft.

THE TIGER (1913). Melodrama; as Gladys Bardon, whose murder is avenged by a tiger who hates her bestial husband. *Dir:* Frederic Thomson. *Sc:* Marguerite Bertsch. (Supervised by Ralph Ince). *With* Charles Kent, Paul Bourgeois. *Prod:* Vitagraph. 1026 ft.

THE LOST MILLIONAIRE (1913). Romance; as Josephine Blake, a Tennessee mountain girl who falls in love with an amnesiac who is really a millionaire. *Dir:* Ralph Ince. *With* E. K. Lincoln, Charles Kent, Tefft Johnson, Mary Maurice. *Prod:* Vitagraph. 2020 ft.

THE TREASURE OF DESERT ISLAND (ISLE) (1913). Romantic drama; as Jean, a beachcomber's daughter. *Dir:* Ralph Ince. *With* E. K. Lincoln, Charles Kent, George Stevens. *Prod:* Vitagraph. 1020 ft.

HIS LAST FIGHT (1913). Drama; as a young heiress wife, whose life is saved by a stranger who loves her. *Dir:* Ralph Ince. *With* Gladden James, Ralph Ince. *Prod:* Vitagraph. 967 ft.

WHY I AM HERE (1913). Flashback prison drama; as a stenographer. *Dir:* Ralph Ince. *Sc:* James Oliver Curwood. *With* Sidney Drew, Charles Eldridge. *Prod:* Vitagraph. 784 ft.

THE WRECK (1913). Railroad drama, with a spectacularly staged wreck; as the young Mrs. Genevieve Carlyle. *Dir:* Ralph Ince. *Sc:* Marguerite Bertsch. *With* Harry T. Morey, E. K. Lincoln, Donald Hall, Gladden James. *Prod:* Vitagraph, 3 reels.

THE SWAN GIRL (1913). Romance; as "The Swan Girl," a poor country girl loved by a rich young man. *Dir./Sc:* Ralph Ince. *With* E. K. Lincoln, Charles Kent. *Prod:* Vitagraph. 1017 ft.

HIS SECOND WIFE (1913). Romance; as Alice, a young schoolteacher. *Dir:/Sc:* Eliza G. Harral. *With* E. K. Lincoln. *Prod:* Vitagraph. 826 ft.

DIANA'S DRESS REFORM (1914). Comedy; as Diana, who starts a new fashion because she can't hook up a ball gown. *Dir:* Ralph Ince. *Sc:* Dean Willets. *With* E. K. Lincoln, Charles Wellesley, Josie Sadler. *Prod:* Vitagraph. 958 ft.

THE RIGHT AND THE WRONG OF IT (1914). Marital drama; as Elsie Maynard, a wife who leaves her husband and then is re-won by him. *Dir:* Ralph Ince. *Sc:* B. C. Flanders. *With* E. K. Lincoln, Lucille Lee Stewart,

Harry T. Morey. *Prod:* Vitagraph. 1026 ft.

THE LUCKY ELOPEMENT (1914). Romantic melodrama; as Madeline, a girl who elopes with her lover and they capture a couple of crooks. *Dir:* Ralph Ince. *Sc:* C. Shea. *With* Charles Wellesley, Ralph Ince, Tod Talford, George Stewart. *Prod:* Vitagraph. 1000 ft.

LINCOLN, THE LOVER (1914). Historical romance; as Ann Rutledge. *Dir./Sc:* Ralph Ince (from a story by Catherine Van Dyke). *With* E. K. Lincoln, Ralph Ince, Logan Paul, Johnny Hines. *Prod:* Vitagraph. 1059 ft.

AGNES, or A MILLION BID (1914). Romantic melodrama; as Agnes Belgradin, whose true romance is nearly ruined by a mercenary mother. *Dir./Sc:* Ralph Ince (adapted from an unproduced play by George Cameron [Mrs. Sidney Drew]). *With* E. K. Lincoln, Julia Swayne Gordon, Charles Kent, Harry T. Morey, Gladden James. *Prod:* Vitagraph. 5 reels.

BACK TO BROADWAY (1914). Romance; as "Bessie, the Manicure," who falls in love with a financier. *Dir./Sc:* Ralph Ince (from a story by George R. Chester). *With* E. K. Lincoln, Mert Haley. *Prod:* Vitagraph. 1993 ft.

THE GIRL FROM PROSPERITY (1914). Romantic comedy; as Bessie Williams, who makes her over-confident sweetheart a success. *Dir:* Ralph Ince. *With* Billy Quirk. *Prod:* Vitagraph. 1850 ft.

HE NEVER KNEW (1914). Romantic drama; as Grace Devereux (AKA Mme Renée) who falls in love with her own son. *Dir:* Ralph Ince. *Sc:* Marguerite Bertsch (from a story by Bessie Boniel). *With* James Morrison, Rose E. Tapley, Julia Swayne Gordon. *Prod:* Vitagraph. 2 reels.

WIFE WANTED (AKA, *Too Much Uncle*) (1914). Comedy; as Grace, who poses as the wife of her husband's best friend. *Dir:* Ralph Ince. *Sc:* Marguertie Bertsch (from a story by Joseph Allen). *With* Albert Roccardi, Ralph Ince, Billy Quirk, Lucille Lee Stewart, James Lackaye. *Prod:* Vitagraph. 2122 ft.

THE SHADOW OF THE PAST (AKA, GB, *Shadows of the Past*) (1914). Political melodrama, climaxing in a big auto-train crash; as Antoinette, a secretary. *Dir:* Ralph Ince. *Sc:* Marguerite Bertsch. *With* Harry T. Morey, Rose E. Tapley, L. Rogers Lytton, Julia Swayne Gordon. (Re-released in 1919.) *Prod:* Vitagraph. 3 reels.

UNCLE BILL (1914). Farce; as Vivien Trent, who gets involved in a farcical gubernatorial campaign. *Dir:* Ralph Ince. *Sc:* Marguerite Bertsch. *With* Constance Talmadge, Julia Swayne Gordon, Donald Hall, William Humphrey, Billy Quirk, Albert Roccardi, Jack

Brown, Anders Randolph. *Prod:* Vitagraph. 3 reels. (Compare listing in Constance Talmadge filmography.)

THE PAINTED WORLD (1914). Backstage melodrama, advertised as "A Vivid Page from the Book of Broadway"; as Yvette Muree, an actress. *Dir:* Ralph Ince. *Sc:* Marguerite Bertsch (from a Jacques Futrelle story). *With* Julia Swayne Gordon, E. K. Lincoln, Charles Kent, Harry Northrup, Janice Cummings, R. A. Roberts. *Prod:* Vitagraph. 3 reels.

FOUR THIRTEEN (1914). Melodrama, ciimaxed with a runaway train; as Elaine Hall, the daughter of a Manhattan jeweler. *Dir:* Ralph Ince. *Sc:* Donald I. Buchanan. *With* Julia Swayne Gordon, Harry T. Morey, Anders Randolph, Harry Northrup, Paul Scardon. *Prod:* Vitagraph. 3 reels.

'MIDST WOODLAND SHADOWS (1914). Romance; as a girl of the forest. *Dir./Sc:* Ralph Ince. *With* Earle Williams, Herbert Frank, Frank Currier. *Prod:* Vitagraph. 887 ft.

TWO WOMEN (1915). Romantic drama; as Enid Arden, an innocent girl of nature who marries a divorced man and then has to battle his ex-wife, who wants him back. *Dir:* Ralph Ince. *Sc:* James Oliver Curwood. *With* Earle Williams, Julia Swayne Gordon, Harry Northrup. (Re-released in 1919.) *Prod:* Vitagraph. 5 reels.

THE SINS OF THE MOTHERS (1915). Gambling melodrama; as Trix Raymond, who has inherited her mother's vice—gambling—and is destroyed by it. *Dir:* Ralph Ince. *Sc:* Elaine Sterne (a prize-winning "Evening Sun" original scenario). *With* Earle Williams, Julia

Anita Stewart in THE PAINTED WORLD

Swayne Gordon, Lucille Lee Stewart, Mary Maurice, Paul Scardon. (Re-released in 1919) *Prod:* Vitagraph. 5 reels.

THE RIGHT GIRL (1915). Romantic comedy; as a young wife involved in a marital mix-up. *Dir./Sc:* Ralph Ince. *With* Earle Williams, William Dunn. *Prod:* Vitagraph. 1026 ft.

FROM HEADQUARTERS (1915). Melodrama; as Rose Peters, daughter of a police detective involved in a crime. *Dir:* Ralph Ince. *Sc:* David Sonnenblick. *With* Earle Williams, Anders Randolph. (Re-released in 1919) *Prod:* Vitagraph. 5 reels.

THE JUGGERNAUT (1915). Melodrama, climaxed by a train's going off a high trestle; in a dual role: as Viola Hardin, and then as Louise, her daughter. *Dir:* Ralph Ince. *Sc:* Ralph Ince & Donald I. Buchanan. *With* Earle Williams, Julia Swayne Gordon, William Dunn, Frank Currier, Eulalie Jensen, Paul Scardon, Jack Brawn. (Re-released in 1919). *Prod:* Vitagraph. 5 reels.

HIS PHANTOM SWEETHEART (1915). Romantic melodrama; as a dream princess who becomes a nemesis. *Dir:* Ralph Ince. *Sc:* Earle Williams. *With* Earle Williams. *Prod:* Vitagrph. 773 ft.

THE-SORT-OF-GIRL-WHO-CAME-FROM-HEAVEN (1915). Romantic comedy, as an actress who's a flirt. *Dir:* Ralph Ince. *Sc:* Arthur Applin. *With* Earle Williams. *Prod:* Vitagraph. 1077 ft.

THE GODDESS (1915). A romantic fifteen-episode serial; as Celestia, raised on a deserted isle, who escapes to civilisation, believing she has been sent to reform the world. *Dir:* Ralph Ince. *Sc:* Gouverneur Morris and Charles W. Goddard. *With* Earle Williams, Paul Scardon, William Dangman, Ned Finley. *Prod:* Vitagraph. First episode—3 reels; remaining 14 episodes, 2 reels each.

THE AWAKENING (1915). Romance; as Jo, a girl of the slums, loved by a doctor. *Dir:* Ralph Ince. *Sc:* James Oliver Curwood. *With* Earle Williams, William Dangman, Dorothy Leeds. *Prod:* Vitagraph. 2083 ft.

COUNT 'EM (AKA, GB, *The Counts*) (1915). Romantic comedy; as Gladys Barnes, who hankers for nobility. *Dir./Sc:* Ralph Ince. *With* Earle Williams, William Roccardi, Hughie Mack, William Dangman, Frank Brule, James Dent, Donald MacBride, Arthur Robinson. *Prod:* Vitagraph. 1 reel.

MY LADY'S SLIPPER (1916). Costume romance; as the Countess de Villars, rescued during the French Revolution by an American naval lieutenant. *Dir./Sc:* Ralph Ince (from a story by Cyrus Townsend Brady). *With* Earle Williams, Julia Swayne Gordon, Joseph Kil-gour, Harry Northrup, William Shea, George Stevens, George O'Donnell. *Prod:* Vitagraph. 5 reels.

THE SUSPECT (19156). Romantic drama; as Sophie Karrenina, leader of a band of nihilists, out to avenge her father's death by the Tsarist government. *Dir:* S. Rankin Drew. *Sc:* (Ad. from a play, "The Silver Shell," by H. J. W. Bam). *With* Anders Randolph, S. Rankin Drew, Julia Swayne Gordon, Bobby Connelly, Edward Elkas, Frank Wupperman (Morgan), George Cooper, Albert Rabock, Anna Brody.*Prod:* Vitagraph. 6 reels.

THE DARING OF DIANA (1916). Melodrama; as Diana, girl reporter. *Dir:* S. Rankin Drew. *Sc:* Charles L. Gaskill. *With* Anders Randolph, Julia Swayne Gordon, Francis (Frank) Morgan, Donald MacBride, Charles Wellesley, Joseph Donohue. *Prod:* Vitagraph. 5 reels.

THE COMBAT (1916). Marital melodrama; as Muriel Fleming, pampered society girl, who unwittingly becomes a bigamist. *Dir:* Ralph Ince. *Sc:* Edward J. Montayne. *With* John Robertson, Richard Turner, Virginia Norden, Winthrop Mendell *Prod:* Vitagraph. 5 reels.

THE GIRL PHILIPPA (1917). Romantic espionage melodrama; as Philippa, a cashier in an English restaurant who turns out to be a princess incognito. *Dir./Sc:* S. Rankin Drew (from a novel by Robert W. Chambers). *With* Anders Randolph, Francis (Frank) Morgan, S. Rankin Drew. *Prod:* Vitagraph. 7 reels.

THE GLORY OF YOLANDA (1917). Romantic drama; as Yolanda, a Russian peasant who becomes a ballerina. *Dir:* Marguerite Bertsch. *Sc:* Maibelle Heikes Justice. *With* John Ardizonia, Denton Vane, Evart Overton, Bernard Siegel. *Prod:* Vitagraph. 5 reels.

THE MORE EXCELLENT WAY (1917). Romance; as Chrissy Desselden, who marries her guardian. *Dir:* Perry M. Vekroff. *Sc:* (Ad. from a story by Cyrus Townsend Brady). *With* Charles Richman, Rudolph Cameron, Gordon Gray, Josephine Earle, Katherine Lewis, Charles A. Stevenson. *Prod:* Vitagraph.5 reels.

CLOVER'S REBELLION (1917). Romance; as Clover Dean, Southern heiress, who chooses marriage with a penniless doctor. *Dir:* Wilfred North. *Sc:* A. Van Buren Powell (from a novel by James Oliver Curwood). *With* Rudolph Cameron, Brinsley Shaw, Eulalie Jensen, Charles A. Stevenson, Julia Swayne Gordon, H. Weaver, William Dunn. *Prod:* Vitagraph. 5 reels.

THE MESSAGE OF THE MOUSE (1917). Espionage melodrama; as Wayne Winthrop. *Dir:* J. Stuart Blackton. *Sc:* George Randolph Chester and Lillian Christy Chester. *With*

Rudolph Cameron, Julia Swayne Gordon, Robert Gaillord, Franklyn Hanno, L. Rogers Lytton. (Miss Stewart was billed as "America's Daintiest Actress.") *Prod:* Vitagraph. 6 reels.

VIRTUOUS WIVES (1919). Marital drama; as Amy Forrester, a flirtatious wife who nearly loses the love of her husband. *Dir./Sc:* George Loane Tucker (from the novel by Owen Johnson). *With* Conway Tearle, Edwin Arden, William (Stage) Boyd, Mrs. DeWolf (Hedda) Hopper, Virginia Norden, Philip Leigh, Harold Gwynn, Katherine Lewis, Lucille Clayton, Gwen Williams. The first film presented by Louis B. Mayer for the Anita Stewart Productions, Inc. *Prod:* First National. 6 reels.

A MIDNIGHT ROMANCE (1919). Romance; as Marie, a chambermaid who marries into society. *Dir:* Lois Weber. *Sc:* Marion Orth. *With* Jack Holt, Edward Tilton, Elinor Hancock, Juanita Hansen, Helen Yoder, Montague Dumont. *Prod:* First National. 6 reels.

MARY REGAN (1919). Romantic melodrama; as Mary Regan, daughter of a notorious thief, who tries to live down her father's past. *Dir./Sc:* Lois Weber (from a story by Leroy Scott). *With* Frank Mayo, Carl Miller, J. Barney Sherry, Brinsley Shaw, George Hernandez, L. W. Steers, Hedda Nova. *Prod:* First National. 6 reels.

HER KINGDOM OF DREAMS (1919). Romance; as Judith Rutledge, a secretary who outwits a scheming adventuress. *Dir:* Marshall Neilan. *Sc:* Agnes Louise Provost. *With* Mahlon Hamilton, Thomas Santschi, Anna Q. Nilsson, Kathlyn Williams, Edwin Stevens, Tully Marshall, Thomas Jefferson, Robert McKim, Wesley Barry, Thomas Holding, Spottiswoode Aitken, Ralph Graves, Frank Currier. Working title (favoured by Mayer): *The Way of the World. Prod:* Vitagraph. 5 reels.

THE MIND-THE-PAINT GIRL (1919). Backstage romance; as Lily Upjohn, afterwards Lily Parradell, star of the Pandora Theatre. *Dir:* Wilfred North. *Sc:* (Ad. from the play by Sir Arthur Wing Pinero, in which Billie Burke had starred). *With* Conway Tearle, Vernon Steele, Templar Saxe, Evart Overton, Denton Vane, Arthur Donaldson, Virginia Norden, George Stewart, Katherine Lewis, Gladys Valerie. *Prod:* First National. 5 reels.

IN OLD KENTUCKY (1919). Horse-race melodramatic romance; as Madge Brierly, Kentucky orphan, who rides the hero's horse to victory. *Dir:* Marshall Neilan. *Sc:* Thomas J. Geraghty (from a play by Charles T. Dazey). *With* Mahlon Hamilton, Edward Coxen, Charles Arling, Edward Connolly, Adele Far-

rington, Marcia Manon, Frank Duffy, John Currie. (Re-made by Warner Bros., 1927, starring Helene Costello; re-filmed as a talkie, Fox 1935, with Will Rogers.) *Prod:* First National. 6 reels.

THE FIGHTING SHEPHERDESS (AKA, GB, *Vindication*) (1920). Romantic melodrama; as Kate Prentice. *Dir:* Edward José. *Sc:* Frank T. Dazy (from a novel by Caroline Lockhart). *With* Wallace MacDonald, Noah Beery, Walter Long, John Hall, Gibson Gowland, Calvert Carter, Billie DeVail, Maud Wayne, Ben Lewis, Will Jeffries. *Prod:* First National. 6 reels.

THE YELLOW TYPHOON (1920). Espionage melodrama; in a dual role: as sisters, Hilda and Berta Nordstorm, one brunette and virtuous, the other blonde and wicked. *Dir:* Edward José. *Sc:* Monte Katterjohn (from a novel by Harold McGrath). *With* Ward Crane, Donald MacDonald, Joseph Kilgour, George Fisher, Edward Brady. *Prod:* First National. 6 reels.

HARRIET AND THE PIPER (1920). Social drama; as Harriet Field, who lives indiscreetly in Greenwich Village, for which she nearly ruins her subsequent happiness. *Dir:* Bertram Bracken. *Sc:* Monte Katterjohn (from a novel by Kathleen Norris). *With* Charles Richman, Ward Crane, Irving Cummings, Myrtle Stedman, Margaret Landis, Byron Munson, Barbara La Marr (Deely), Loyola O'Connor. *Prod:* First National. 5 reels.

HUMAN DESIRE (1920). Romance; as Bernice, a waif who adores children. *Dir:* Wilfred North. *Sc:* (Ad. from a novel by Violet Irwin). *With* Conway Tearle, Eulalie Jensen, Naomi Childers, Templar Saxe, Vernon Steele. *Prod:* First National. 5 reels.

SOWING THE WIND (1921). Melodrama; as Rosamund Athelstane, who seeks the identity of her longlost mother — and finds her in a Chinatown opium den. *Dir:* John M. Stahl. *Sc:* Franklyn Hall (from a play by Sydney Grundy). *With* Myrtle Stedman, Josef Swickard. James Morrison, Ralph Lewis, William V. Mong. *Prod:* First National. 6900 ft.

PLAYTHINGS OF DESTINY (1921). Romantic melodrama; as Julie Arnold, victimised by romance. *Dir:* Edwin Carewe. *Sc:* Anthony Paul Kelly (from a story by Jane Murfin and Larry Trimble). *With* Herbert Rawlinson, Walter McGrail, Grace Morse, Richard Headrick, William V. Mong. Working title: *The Tornado. Prod:* First National. 7 reels.

HER MAD BARGAIN (1921). Romantic melodrama; as Alice Lambert. *Dir:* Edwin

Carewe. *Sc:* Josephine Quirk (from a novel, "The Prince of Happiness," by Florence Auer. *With* Walter McGrail, Gertrude Astor, Arthur Edmund Carewe, Helen Raymond, Alice Farrington, Margaret McWade, Ernest Butterworth. *Prod:* First National. 6 reels.

A QUESTION OF HONOUR (1922). Melodrama of the West; as Anne Wilmot, a society girl who falls in love with an engineer building a dam. *Dir:* Edwin Carewe. *Sc:* Josephine Quirk (from a novel by Ruth Cross). *With* Edward Hearn, Arthur Stewart Hall, Walt Whitman, Bert Sprotte, Frank Beal, Adele Farrington, Mary Land, Edward Brady, Doc Bytel. Exteriors filmed in California's Feather River country. *Prod:* First National. 7 reels.

THE INVISIBLE FEAR (1922). Melodrama; as Sylvia Langdon, haunted by the fear that she has murdered a man. *Dir:* Edwin Carewe. *Sc:* Madge Tyrone (from a story by Hampton del Ruth). *With* Walter McGrail, Allan Forrest, Hamilton Moore, Estelle Evans, George Evans, George Kuwa, Edward Hunt, Ogden Crane. *Prod:* First National. 6 reels.

THE WOMAN HE MARRIED (1922). Romantic drama; as Natalie Lane, artist's model. *Dir:* Fred Niblo. *Sc:* Bess Meredyth (from a story by Herbert Bashford). *With* Darrel Foss, Donald MacDonald, William Conklin, Shannon Day, Charlotte Pierce, Charles Belcher, Frank Tokunga. *Prod:* First National. 5 reels.

ROSE O' THE SEA (1922). Romance; as Rose Eton, who rises from salesgirl to bride of a millionaire. *Dir:* Fred Niblo. *Sc:* Bess Meredyth (from a story by the Countess Barcynsky). *With* Rudolph Cameron, Hallam Coolley, Kate Lester, Thomas Holding, Margaret Landis, John P. Lockney, Charles Belcher. *Prod:* First National. 7 reels.

THE LOVE PIKER (1923). Romance; as Hope Warner. *Dir:* E. Mason Hopper. *Sc:* Frances Marion (from a story by Frank R. Adams). *With* Robert Frazer, William Norris, Carl Gerrard, Arthur Hoyt, Betty Francisco, Maym Kelso. *Prod:* Cosmopolitan-Goldwyn. 7 reels.

THE GREAT WHITE WAY (1924). Manhattan romance of an actress and a prizefighter; as Mabel Vandegrift. *Dir:* E. Mason Hopper. *Sc:* Larry Doyle (ad. by Luther Reed from a story, "Cain and Mabel," by H. C. Witwer). *With* Oscar Shaw, T. Roy Barnes, Tom Lewis, Dore Davidson, Olin Howland, Arthur Brisbane, Tex Richard, Ned Wayburn, Irvin S. Cobb, H. C. Witwer, Harry Hershfield, Damon Runyon, "Bugs" Baer, George McManus, Nell Brinkley, Hal Coffman, J. W. McGurk, Winsor McKay, Billy De Beck. (Re-made by Warner

Bros. as a talkie, *Cain and Mabel,* with Marion Davies and Clark Gable.) *Prod:* Cosmopolitan-Metro-Goldwyn. 10 reels.

THE BOOMERANG (1925). Romantic comedy; as Virginia Zelva, a nurse. *Dir:* Louis Gasnier. *Sc:* John Goodrich (from the play by Winchell Smith and Victor Mapes). *With* Bert Lytell, Donald Keith, Mary McAllister, Ned Sparks, Arthur Edmund Carewe, Philo McCullough, Winter Hall. (Re-made by Paramount, 1920, as a talkie, *The Love Doctor,* with Richard Dix and June Collyer, in the Stewart role). *Prod:* Schulberg-Preferred. 7 reels.

BAREE, SON OF KAZAN (1925). Melodrama of the Great Northwest; as Nepeese, a beautiful half-breed protected by a half-wild dog. *Dir:* David Smith. *Sc:* (Ad. from the novel by James Oliver Curwood). *With* Donald Keith, Joe Ricksen, Jack Curtis. (Previously filmed by Vitagraph, 1917, with Nell Shipman). *Prod:* Vitagraph. 6800 ft.

NEVER THE TWAIN SHALL MEET (1925). Romance of the South Seas; as Tamea, South Seas half-breed, queen of her own island. *Dir:* Maurice Tourneur. *Sc:* Eugene Mullin (from the novel by Peter B. Kyne). *With* Bert Lytell, Huntley Gordon, Justine Johnstone, George Seigmann, Lionel Belmore, William Norris, Emily Fitzroy, Princess Marie de Bourbon, Florence Turner, Ernest Butterworth, Ben Deeley. Exteriors filmed in Tahiti and other South Sea Islands. Miss Stewart's favourite of all her films. (Re-made as an M-G-M talkie; with Conchita Montenegro and Leslie Howard). *Prod:* Cosmopolitan-Metro-Goldwyn. 8,143 ft.

THE PRINCE OF PILSEN (1926). Mythical kingdom romantic comedy; as Nellie Wagner, whose father is mistaken for the Prince of Pilsen because of all the lodge regalia he wears. *Dir:* Paul Powell. *Sc:* Anthony Coldeway (from the musical comedy by Frank Pixley and Gustave Luders). *With* George Sidney, Allan Forrest, Otis Harlan, Myrtle Stedman, Rose E. Tapley, William von Brincken, William von Hardenburg. *Prod:* PDC. 7 reels.

RUSTLING FOR CUPID (1926). Romantic Western; as Sybil Hamilton, schoolteacher, who falls in love with a cowboy. *Dir:* Irving Cummings. *Sc:* L. G. Ritz (from the story by Peter B. Kyne). *With* George O'Brien, Russell Simpson, Edith Yorke, Herbert Prior, Frank McGlynn Jr., Sid Johnson. *Prod:* Fox. 5 reels.

WHISPERING WIRES (1926). Murder mystery; as Doris Stockbridge whose life is in danger. *Dir:* Albert Ray. *Sc:* L. G. Rigby (from the play by Kate L. McLaurin and the story by Henry Leverage). *With* Edmund Burns, Charles Clary, Mack Swain, Heinie Conklin,

Otto Matiesen, Scott Welsh, Arthur Housman, Maym Kelso, Frank Campeau, Cecille Evans, Charles Sellon. *Prod:* Fox. 6 reels.

LODGE IN THE WILDERNESS (1926). Lumber camp melodrama; as Virginia Coulson. *Dir:* Henry McCarthy. *Sc:* (suggested by the novel by Gilbert Parker). *With* Edmund Burns, Duane Thompson, Larry Steers. *Prod:* Tiffany. 6 reels.

MORGANSON'S FINISH (1926). Alaskan melodrama; as Barbara Wesley, heiress. *Dir:* Fred Windermere. *Sc:* (suggested by a Jack London story). *With* Johnnie Walker, Mahlon Hamilton, Victor Potel. *Prod:* Tiffany. 7 reels.

ISLE OF SUNKEN GOLD (1927). A ten-episode serial filmed in the Hawaiian Islands; as an island princess of European parentage. *Dir:* Harry Webb. With Duke Kahanamoku, Bruce Gordon, Evangeline Russell, Snowball McHenry. *Prod:* Mascot. Twenty reels; two to each episode.

WILD GEESE (1927). Drama of the Minnesota farmlands; as Lind Archer, schoolteacher. *Dir:* Phil Stone. *Sc:* L. P. Younger (from the prize-winning novel by Martha Ostenso). *With* Belle Bennett, Russell Simpson, Eve Southern, Donald Keith, Jason Robards, Wesley Barry, Bodil Rosing. *Prod:* Tiffany. 7 reels.

NAME THE WOMAN (1928). Courtroom murder drama; as Florence Marshall, mystery witness. *Dir:* Erle C. Kenton. *Sc:* Peter Milne (ad. by Elmer Harris from his own novel, "Bridge"). *With* Huntley Gordon, Gaston Glass, Chappell Dossett, Julanne Johnston, Jed Prouty. *Prod:* Columbia. 6 reels.

THE ROMANCE OF A ROGUE (1928). Romantic melodrama; as Charmain, who fights her husband's desire for revenge when he is released from prison. *Dir:* King Baggot. *Sc:* Adrian Johnson (from a novel by Ruby M. Ayres). *With* H. B. Warner, Albert Fisher, Charles Gerrard, Fred Esmelton, Billy Franey. *Prod:* Quality. 6 reels.

SISTERS OF EVE (1928). Mystery drama; as Beatrice Franklin, whose sister's millionaire husband disappears on their honeymoon. *Dir:* Scott Pembroke. *Sc:* Arthur Hoerl (from a novel, "The Tempting of Tavernake," by E. Phillips Oppenheim). *With* Creighton Hale, Betty Blythe, Francis Ford, Harold Nelson, Charles King. *Prod:* Rayart. 6 reels.

(Anita Stewart made cameo appearances as herself in such features as HOLLYWOOD, Paramount, 1923; MARY OF THE MOVIES, Columbia, 1923; SOULS FOR SALE, Goldwyn, 1923, GO STRAIGHT, B. P. Schulberg, 1925.)

(I am greatly indebted to Edward Eagan, personal manager for Anita Stewart throughout her film career and later associated with her husband (George Converse) for many of the anecodotes in Miss Stewart's career-story as well as for some of the facts in the preceding filmography.)

7
CONSTANCE TALMADGE

Although Constance and Norma Talmadge were sisters, they could not have been less alike, both in what they projected from the silent screen and in their personal temperaments.

Comedienne Constance had a vivacity which invigorated audiences, and a sense of realism which caused her to marvel that audiences could be so easily beguiled. The same clear-eyed realism made her wonder that men could also be conquered so effortlessly. Irving Berlin called her "a virtuous vamp." Anita Loos has said she was "one of the few genuine *femmes fatales* I have ever known."

Constance Talmadge was born in Brooklyn on April 19, 1899.* Her mother, Margaret, of Spanish descent, had grown up in Brooklyn, and there, in the last bloom of a youth that had not been the most ecstatic, she caught the fancy of Connecticut-born Frederick Talmadge, whose Presbyterian ancestors were British. After he fathered three daughters by Peg, as his ambitious and driving wife was always called, he took off and settled for the drifter's life of odd jobs and cheap bars.

Peg Talmadge had good reason to be aggressive: her beginnings had been not only humble but starkly impoverished. However, though she had learned to make every penny count, poverty had not embittered or demeaned her, and she retained throughout her life a dry gutsy humour that made her popular in Hollywood, where the mothers of stars are rightly regarded as the scourge of God. Indeed, Anita Loos has always freely acknowledged that many of the wisecracks of both Lorelei Lee and Dorothy in "Gentlemen Prefer Blondes" "are direct quotes from Peg Talmadge," who well knew that "kissing your hand may make you feel very, very good but diamond and sapphire bracelets last forever." Peg determined very early that the Talmadge girls were going to be given things that last.

Her daughters developed, or she guided them, into quite different personalities. Velvet-eyed Norma was moody; Natalie was orderly and correct

---

*The year 1900 is sometimes given erroneously. Constance was often thought to be the middle Talmadge sister, a mistake her mother tried to correct in her book about her daughters, "The Talmadge Sisters" (1924); "Natalie, who is the second youngest of the girls instead of the youngest, as so many people believe, was really the least troublesome of the three."

— the "just-so-girl," Peg called her; and Constance, nicknamed "Dutch" because of her fair hair and pink cheeks, was carefree. Mrs. Talmadge often wondered how Constance "came by her shock-proof courage. It is not a matter of heredity, unless she is a throw-back." Constance herself was aware of this lucky trait and called it "my main asset."

Mrs. Talmadge decided very early that show business offered her daughters the most accessible opportunities and while they still attended Brooklyn's Public School No. 9, encouraged them to stage "shows" in the basement of their home for neighbourhood children on Saturdays. They continued to do so after they entered Brooklyn's Erasmus High School. Natalie collected the penny admissions; Norma handled the emotional parts of the home-written melodramas; and Constance supplied the comedy and acrobatics (handsprings, improvised trapeze work). She billed herself as Constanzia de Talmadgio.

Said Mrs. Talmadge in her book: "Constance was saved, I think, from a great deal of emotionalism by the fact that she released so much energy in her tomboy outdoor playing. For a prolonged period she cared for the company of boys, not merely because they were boys, but because they could throw a good ball, or turn a jolly handspring, and she could equal them in their daring stunts. She rarely played with girls other than her sisters.

"'Why don't you play with so-and-so?' I often asked her.

"'She's afraid to risk her life,' would be the contemptuous answer."

Peg Talmadge, by dint of hard work and scrimping, managed to make a comfortable and lively home for the girls, and they *all* saved for the weekly treat of Friday night at the movies. It's significant that Constance's favourite stars were Maurice Costello and John Bunny, the first because he pleased her romantic fancies, the second because he tickled her funny bone.

Costello and Bunny were Vitagraph stars, and the Vitagraph studio was situated in Brooklyn. When, in 1910, the miracle happened and Norma actually became a Vitagraph player, Constance insatiably questioned her about each day's remarkable events. But after a while, according to Peg, "reflected glory failed to suffice Constance. She was much too curious, too healthy and too restive, to thrive long upon vicarious tales. She wanted to see for herself, hear for herself, so in time I permitted her to go to the studio."

Norma had been given a part to play, and proper billing, from the start and had never had to be an extra. But Constance, regarded merely as "Norma's little tomboy sister," began at Vitagraph as an extra in an Anita Stewart production at $5 a day.

One morning Constance was amusing a group of extras with an impromptu burlesque of Vitagraph's top comedienne, Flora Finch, when Ralph Ince and Anita Stewart passed by on their way to a set. They paused to watch, and could not help laughing. When Ince yelled an amiable "Stick around," Constance replied unhesitatingly, "I certainly will." She was already convinced of something she repeated throughout her career: "A movie studio is the funniest place in the world and screen actors are the funniest people I've ever seen. I adore them!"

Shortly thereafter, Ince had her placed on Vitagraph's contract list and in

no time at all she was called "The Vitagraph's Tomboy" and cast in one comedy after another. She performed effortlessly, and surprised everyone when, because all contract dramatic actresses were busy, she, Constance, was tossed an emotional role and proved she had a grasp of dramatic requirements. Twice, in *The Moonstone of Fez* and *The Mysterious Lodger,* she essayed dramatic leads opposite her childhood idol, Maurice Costello, and acquitted herself nobly. She was also used as a pretty model for artist Antonio Moreno in the dramatic romance called *In the Latin Quarter.*

She was in her mid-teens and audiences responded to her vivacity and zest for life. Nevertheless, Vitagraph didn't quite know what to do with her, and if it hadn't been for their ambitious mother both Constance and Norma might have become lost in the Vitagraph shuffle. Many gifted actresses got bogged down in Vitagraph programmers and progressed no further.

Mrs. Talmadge obtained contracts for Norma and Constance at a brand new California studio, National Pictures, and on August 2, 1915, entrained for Hollywood with all three daughters. Constance was given an unimportant bit in Norma's first starring vehicle in Hollywood (*Captivating Mary Carstairs),* and leads opposite "Smiling Billy" Parsons in several two-reel comedies.

But National Pictures lacked adequate resources and the Talmadges were saved from having to crawl back to Vitagraph by D. W. Griffith, who, late in 1915, placed Norma and Constance under contract for his Fine Arts-Triangle productions.

Norma was awed by Griffith, who supervised the films she made at Fine Arts and wrote her first picture (under one of his pseudonyms: Granville Warwick). But he never actually directed a Norma Talmadge film.

Constance was not awed by Griffith and whenever she saw him, on the lot or off, hailed him and talked to him. Wrote her mother later: "Part of Constance's value to Mr. Griffith lay in the fact that she amused him, just as she had amused Mr. Ince and the others back in the Vitagraph days...She made him laugh largely because of her absolute disregard of his importance, in contrast to the awe and respect and head-bowing accorded him by all the others. They rarely approached him if they could help, it, save on matters of the utmost importance, while Constance, to Norma's frequent horror, would rush up to him with everything, anything, be it trivial or be it great. After a while they became such good friends — this leggy girl and the great man — that he would often send for her when he had a few spare moments and say: 'Just sent for you, Constance, because I want to laugh.'

"'Well, here I am, Your Majesty may begin at once,' was her stock reply. She would make a salaam of mock humility, and the very sight of her seemed to set him up immediately."

Griffith's regard for the talents of Constance Talmadge endured. I got to know him in the last years of his life and on several occasions he said that of all the actresses he had directed, his two favourites, because of their unique and malleable talents, were Clarine Seymour and Constance Talmadge. Although he always held Lillian Gish in the highest respect, he frequently declared that for all her fragility she had "a masculine mind" and "thought like a man."

So did Constance Talmadge, but in a far less immediate way. Nor did she ever awe Mr. Griffith, as Lillian Gish frequently did with her swift changes from applied techniques to sheer brilliance. That Griffith sensed there was more to Constance Talmadge than superficial clowning is proven, I think, by the fact he used her so perfectly in *Intolerance*.

He had already filmed much of one episode of *Intolerance*, first as a feature in itself (*The Mother and the Law*), and he was planning to use it as the modern episode in one of four stories that would portray the theme of "Love's Struggle Throughout the Ages." In the most spectacular of the four, the story of the Fall of Babylon, he decided to use Constance in the part of The Mountain Girl.

When he told her, she pretended to be offended and said her suit must have been so badly made he thought her dowdy. But the truth was, as her mother wrote later, "...she was so elated, so proud and pleased and excited, that she threw both arms about him in a strangling grip and simply hugged and hugged him! They had a long talk then, Mr. Griffith and the funny girl, and she promised him, with tears in her laughing eyes, that she would do her very, very best, and would study every day and practise every angle of the part." And she had to do things she did not especially like — eat raw onions, and drive horses while standing in a chariot. Griffith once said she had no knowledge of the word "fear".

Griffith also gave her the coquettish Marguerite de Valois part in the medieval story in *Intolerance*, which has the St. Bartholomew's massacre for background. This part was originally more extensive than it seems in the prints of *Intolerance* that circulate today, wherein Marguerite de Valois is seen only in one close-up as she arrives in Paris for her betrothal ceremonies.

Because Griffith knew Constance would be acclaimed for her performance as The Mountain Girl, he credited the Marguerite role, on the original prints of *Intolerance*, to a fictitious "Georgia Pearce." Although this billing was later dropped and the role was credited to Constance Talmadge, the "Georgia Pearce" credit resulted in a ludicrous error that has persisted down to the present day, to wit, that Constance Talmadge starred in a serial, set in medieval France, entitled *Georgia Pearce!*

Intolerance was released in the fall of 1916 and made Constance Talmadge a star, which created a problem for Fine Arts-Triangle, for, like Vitagraph, it didn't really know what to do with her. The best of the four features she made after *Intolerance* was *The Matrimaniac*, in which she was leading lady to Douglas Fairbanks. It owed its verve not only to its players but to the scenario by Anita Loos, who sensed at once the kind of screen image that Constance Talmadge could most easily project.

In 1919 the Babylonian sequence of *Intolerance* was issued as a separate feature and called *The Fall of Babylon*. For this Griffith shot new footage of Constance so the film would have a happy ending (The Mountain Girl and the Rhapsode go off into exile together). It should be noted that Constance's acting style had changed in the three years since the original footage in *Intolerance* was shot.

When the Fine Arts contracts of the Talmadge sisters expired, their indomitable mother again assumed command. They returned to the East where, Mrs. Talmadge had reason to hope, Joseph M. Schenck would set up a production company of her own for Norma, and one for Constance as well.

Schenck and his brother (Nicholas) were the sons of Russian-Jewish immigrants who had risen, via an amusement park across the Hudson River, to part ownership of a chain of movie houses still in existence (Loew's). Joseph Schenck had long wanted to be a film producer, and his ambitions became a reality when he married Norma Talmadge. He not only established a producing company for her, as Peg Talmadge was sure he would, but formed a second company for films starring Constance Talmadge. Everywhere that Norma went Constance was sure to go, was the way the sisters themselves, as well as their mother, wanted it. Never for one moment was there any jealousy between any of the Talmadges. They moved as a unit from East Coast to West, back and forth, and frequently all lived in one big house. Hollywood has never known a more "all for one and one for all" family. And men who married the Talmadge girls, like Joe Schenck, and later Buster Keaton, who married Natalie, became merely adjuncts, or were divorced, or both.

Schenck arranged with Lewis J. Selznick to release the Talmadge sisters' films through his company (Select), and in the June 23, 1917 issue of "Moving Picture World," Selznick announced his acquisition of the eighteen-year-old star, Constance Talmadge, and concluded with this: "For weeks I had daily reports upon Miss Constance from her director (Charles Giblyn), and looking them over I find not one unfavourable comment. Mr. Giblyn's favourite word for her is 'plastic.' He says that mentally and physically she is able to adapt any attitude with the greatest ease, one of the most important of all characteristics in a screen artist. So I decided I was right in my original intention to

Constance Talmadge as "The Mountain Girl" and Elmer Clifton as "The Rhapsode" in Griffith's INTOLERANCE

star Miss Constance Talmadge, and she will appear in a series of productions which will be released on my open booking plan.''

The first scenario Constance filmed for her own company was a rather sober little comedy called *The Lesson*. Neither Schenck nor Selznick thought it quite right for the re-launching of her career and hence the initial Constance Talmadge-Select release was *Scandal*, which set the pattern for many of Constance's subsequent pictures: vivacious, spoiled and terribly rich, she is tamed by the man who loves her. In fact, all sixteen of the feature-length comedies Constance filmed for Select owe more than a minimum of their plot substance to *Taming of the Shrew*.

Nevertheless, they were highly successful, especially the ones adapted from popular marital farces that had brightened the theatre when Grace George, Marie Tempest, Margaret Illington, Laura Hope Crews, Margaret Lawrence and other stage comediennes starred in them. Walter Edwards directed nine; Harrison Ford was leading man in ten consecutively, and subsequently played opposite her in two more; Kenneth Harlan was her *vis-à-vis* in seven.

Constance had become an expert *farceuse*, but Peg Talmadge began to worry that custom would stale the far from infinite variety of her youngest daughter's stories. So, when Schenck moved Norma's company over to Associated First National release, his mother-in-law persuaded him to do the same for Constance.

Free of Selznick influence on what was produced, Schenck called in Anita Loos, who had married actor-director-writer John Emerson. He had liked the breezy comedies Miss Loos had written for Douglas Fairbanks at Fine Arts, and he remembered the part she had written for Constance in *The Matrimaniac*. ''I'd like to turn 'Dutch' over to you,'' he told Emerson, ''and have Anita do for her the sort of thing she did for Fairbanks. Have her write Constance into some films that will satisfy Peg, and get that woman off my neck.''

The Loos-Emerson combo was responsible for Constance's next six pictures, and for six others (*Learning to Love*, their last, was one of the best). Four of their Talmadge films were adaptations of well-known Broadway comedies; two were adaptations from other sources; six were original scenarios expressly fashioned for Constance. They were all so fantastically successful, according to Miss Loos, that Schenck gratefully summoned the Emersons to his office and said: ''Look, folks, when I put 'Dutch' into your hands, it was only to satisfy Peg. I never expected to make money on the deal. But the pictures have turned out to be gold mines, so I want you two to have a little bonus.'' And he presented them with a check for $50,000!

Miss Loos has lamented in her partial autobiography, ''A Girl Like I,'' that the movies made by the Talmadge sisters are today lost, which is not altogether correct. Recently, the Schenck estate is rumoured to have sold outright all the Constance and Norma Talmadge features in their vaults to Raymond Rohauer! What he will do with them remains to be seen. Perhaps, in another way, Miss Loos is right.

John Hampton, manager of the Silent Movie Theatre on Fairfax Avenue in Los Angeles, has acquired prints of two 1920 Constance Talmadge features — *In Search of a Sinner* and *Two Weeks*. He has said: ''Most of the old films are gone, not just in fires in labs — the Rothacker Chicago Lab fire took most of the old First National negatives — but willful destruction, partly as a fire prevention measure (old nitrate film stock is chemically unstable), but more often, when old films were commercially worthless, to make vault space for new releases.''

The Loos-Emerson scenarios were all masterfully constructed around the battle of the sexes. Any one of them, with smart dialogue and updated treatment and played by someone like Constance Talmadge, would seem doubly attractive today, when comedy is all too often a psychedelic black.

My own personal favourite of the Emerson-Loos originals that Constance Talmadge brought to the screen is *Woman's Place,* a most delightful comedy of a young lady who becomes the rival of the man she loves in a mayoral contest in a little Ohio city. She gets the male vote, but loses to her beloved rival because the women don't trust her and vote for him. She really wins, however, because she becomes his bride. Women's Lib today wouldn't buy that one, but it's psychologically sound, and plays charmingly.

In 1920 Mrs. Talmadge and her daughters sailed to Europe in the royal suite of the ''Berengaria.'' Anita Loos and John Emerson met them in Paris. Dorothy Gish and her mother accompanied them ''on a tour of Europe's capitals.''

Constance says she and the younger Gish sister first met when they were apprentice players for Griffith at Fine Arts. They came to be known as ''The Two Inseperables.'' When D. W. Griffith was in England to film a propaganda story he had devised, *Hearts of the World,* he told his star, Lillian Gish, that he had fashioned the role of the The Little Disturber for Constance Talmadge. Miss Gish persuaded him to give the part to her sister Dorothy. This made absolutely no difference to the close friendship between Constance Talmadge and Dorothy Gish. In a double interview, they once said that if they ever got married, they'd marry at the same time to keep up each other's courage. And on Sunday afternoon, December 26, 1920, at Greenwich, Connecticut, a Justice of the Peace married Constance Talmadge to John Pialoglou, a handsome young Greek importer and exporter of tobacco of New York City who was also ''an exceptional ballroom dancer;'' and then married Dorothy Gish to actor James Rennie, who had been Dorothy's leading man in two films. Mr. and Mrs. Pialoglou drove off to Alantic City on a honeymoon; Mr. and Mrs. Rennie hastened back to Manhattan, where the groom gave a Sunday night performance in ''Spanish Love.''

Years later, Dorothy told me: ''Yes, Constance was always getting engaged — but never to less than two men at the same time. She blithely accepted suitors and their engagement rings the way debutantes of the day collected frat pins. She could go from a *thé dansant* at the Ritz to a dancing party at the Plaza, and end up engaged at least twice. If she liked an admirer and he said, 'Let's get engaged,' she always agreed brightly, 'Okay, let's.'''

To name a few of the more ardent swains of Constance Talmadge: Jack Pickford, Irving Berlin, Buster Collier, John Charles Thomas, Kenneth Harlan, Michael Arlen, William Rhinelander Stewart Jr., Richard Barthelmess, Robert Vignola, the ballroom dancer known as Maurice, and Irving Thalberg. On two separate occasions during the early Twenties she almost became Mrs. Thalberg.

Constance Talmadge with her sister, Norma

Constance Talmadge separated from Pialoglou after only a few months and the Talmadge matriarchy again moved its home base to Hollywood shortly after Buster Keaton married Natalie Talmadge, in May, 1921. Norma and Joe Schenck owned a mansion on the West Coast, and Natalie and Keaton, along with Peg and Constance, rented a three-story house on Hollywood's Westmoreland Place, in the ballroom of which Constance learned to ride a bicycle! She also tore around town in a roadster, broke a lot of hearts, and wistfully complained that in Hollywood "there are only two big nights a week."

In his "Behind the Screen," Samuel Goldwyn tells of seeing the Talmadge sisters at various social events and how Norma, after dancing once or twice, would sit quietly apart watching "her little sister" be the belle of the ball.

In 1922, the year in which her divorce became final, Constance was beginning to say being a movie star was a bore. She was much more knowledgeable about herself than her conduct led the average observer to suppose, and she was fond of saying: "Some day people will wake up to what a joke I am"

In December 1920 she had told a writer for "Moving Picture World": "I enjoy making people laugh, because this type of work comes easiest and most naturally to me. I am not a highly emotional type. My sister could cry real tears over two cushions stuffed into a long dress and with a white lace cape made to look like a dead baby, and she would do it so convincingly 900 people out front would weep with her. That is real art, but my kind of talent would lead to bouncing that padded baby up and down on my knee with absurd grimaces that would make the same 900 people roar with laughter. In my way I take my work quite as seriously as my sister does hers — I would be just as in earnest about making it seem real. That, I think, is the secret of being funny on the speaking stage, as well as on the screen. One has to be serious in one's levity."

And on a later occasion: "I try to handle a comedy role in much the way a cartoonist handles his pencils. If he is drawing a picture of the late Theodore Roosevelt, he emphasises Teddy's eye-glasses and teeth, and leaves the ears and nostrils and the lines of the face, barely suggested. One must leave a great deal to the imagination of the audience."

Her mother was one of the few human beings who knew there was more to Constance than a belle of the ball, or a screen comedienne. Wrote Mrs. Talmadge: "Constance has made a sort of mask for herself. She wears it almost all the time; partly because it fits well; partly because it protects her and amuses others. It is a laughing mask. I, her mother, have rarely seen it slip, and the few times I have are not mine to record. I will say only this: underneath the mask, Constance is still as she was when a little girl — ardent for fair play, eagerly partisan of the injured and weak, contemptuous only of the cowardly and petty."

There was more to this than maternal bias and publicity pap. One day while the Talmadges still lived in Manhattan, the four of them, swathed in mink, were being driven in their limousine through Central Park when Mrs. Talmadge suddenly ordered the chauffeur to back up and stop opposite a threadbare derelict sitting on a bench. "If you girls care to know who that tramp is," Peg said, "he's your father." It was Constance who got out of the limousine and went up to him and with the same natural nonchalance she would have accorded D. W. Griffith or studio night watchmen, said: "Hello, Fred, how'd you like to meet your family?"

The result: Peg Talmadge put Fred in a hotel and made Schenck give him a job at the studio. But work and Fred were such strangers that he spent most of his time in Third Avenue saloons, and visited the Talmadge women only in order to collect the weekly allowance they accorded him. Anita Loos says he went to California when the Talmadges moved there in 1921, and died four years later. Peg wrote Miss Loos that "There were hundreds of set pieces, and a Hawaiian orchestra played 'Aloha.' The girls went down to see Fred at the undertakers two and three times a day — they were wrecks, he looked about thirty-five."

On February 27, 1926, in California, Constance Talmadge took a second husband: Captain Alastair MacIntosh, "a Scottish sportsman." They went to London to live. Within a year, "bored to death," she divorced Captain

MacIntosh, returned to Hollywood, and did two very charming comedies: *Venus of Venice* and *Breakfast at Sunrise*.

Joseph Schenck had terminated the Talmadges' contracts with First National and now set up a potentially profitable releasing unit for them at United Artists, which released Norma's last four films.

But Constance's career in movies was virtually over.

Schenck hired F. Scott Fitzgerald to write a "modern" college story for her that was to be called. *Lipstick*. Fitzgerald was drinking, and deliberately quarrelled with her. He was paid off, and the idea on which *Lipstick* was to have been based was abandoned. A proposed costume comedy, *Pompadour* (which had also once been announced for sister Norma), was shelved because Herbert Wilcox's *Mme. Pompadour,* with Dorothy Gish, had just been released in England.

The only Constance Talmadge picture United Artists released was a silent romantic comedy called *Venus,* which she made on the Riviera. UA held it up till 1929, by which time sound films had defeated the silents in the battle for American screens. Constance did finally consent to making a sound test, and passed it with flying colours — but she didn't like the medium.

On May 9, 1929, Constance became the bride of Townsend Netcher and announced that she would never make another film. She never did. She was a very rich woman, and later became the principal inheritor of fortunes larger than her own.

Wrote Anita Loos of this marriage which lasted a couple of years, not counting time out for several separations: "After divorcing MacIntosh, Dutch took as her third husband a Chicago playboy and millionaire whose first and last claim to fame was that he had annexed Dutch, just as his brother had earned headlines for having married one of the playful Dolly sisters. Dutch enjoyed her husband's way of life until his persistent jealousy began to spoil her fun and she once more sought relief in divorce."

Norma Talmadge tried the talkies in 1930, first with a Manhattan backstage-gangster melodrama, *New York Nights,* and then disastrously with a heavy costumer, *Dubarry, Woman of Passion.*. Whereupon Constance is supposed to have cabled her: "Leave them while you're looking good and thank God for the trust funds Momma set up." Norma took her sister's advice and bade adieu to a long and very successful screen career.

In 1939 Constance Talmadge married a fourth time; the fourth was Walter Michael Giblin, then a vice-president of Blyth & Co., New York stock brokers. Anita Loos says this marriage worked because Giblin understood his wife was in fact what Irving Berlin had called her — "a virtuous vamp."

When Giblin went overseas for OSS during the Second World War, Constance took a Red Cross course with the intention of following him abroad, but was prevented from doing so by the prohibition of wives being with husbands who were in service. So she worked as a practical nurse in Manhattan hospitals throughout the war. Afterwards she became a volunteer at Memorial Hospital, which specialises in cancer. Few of the frightened patients arriving there knew that the Mrs. Giblin who took their names, made arrangements, and talked so encouragingly, had been one of Hollywood's brightest comediennes.

She visited Hollywood only occasionally, for business unconnected with

EXPERIMENTAL MARRIAGE: left to right, director Robert G. Vignola explains a scene to actors Harrison Ford, Constance Talmadge, and Raymond Hatton

films. On one such visit, however, a telephone interviewer asked if she contemplated "a comeback." There was a noticeable silence at her end of the wire. Finally, she said, "Why on earth would I ever do a thing like that?"

On May 1, 1964, Walter Giblin died, and Constance buried him in Hollywood, near Norma, who died in 1957, and Peg, who had died a few years before Norma, from cancer.

For a time, Constance Talmadge continued to live in Manhattan, but shortly after Natalie died, Constance moved from the East to take up residence in a suite at the Beverly Wilshire Hotel in Beverly Hills. She made no public appearances, and saw only very close friends. She was said to regard her fifteen-year career in silent movies as something that happened to someone she knew a long time ago.

On November 23, 1973, Constance Talmadge, aged seventy-three, died at California Hospital in Los Angeles, following a long illness. Her lengthy obituary in "The Times" of London noted that she was the wisest of the Talmadge sisters, and concluded: "Her retirement was due to the advent of sound, and not to any failure to keep abreast of the times, for she had taken to playing the sophisticated 'vamp' type of woman-of-the-world which the young Joan Crawford was soon to establish as a part of the American scene."

CONSTANCE TALMADGE FILMOGRAPHY

BUDDY'S FIRST CALL (1914). Comedy; as a mischievous kid sister. *Dir:* Tefft Johnson. *Sc:* F. Marion Brandon. *With* Paul Kelly. *Prod:* Vitagraph. 930 ft.

OUR FAIRY PLAY (1914). Comedy about amateur theatricals; as an ambitious would-be actress. *Dir:* Lee Beggs. *Sc:* Charles Brown. *With* Billy Quirk, Josie Sadler, Charles Brown, James Lackaye, Hughie Mack, Richard Leslie. *Prod:* Vitagraph. 1994 ft.

THE MOONSTONE OF FEZ (1914). Mystery drama; as Winifred Osborne, whose mother disappears completely after she purchases a valuable jewel from an Algerian beggar. *Dir:* Maurice Costello and Robert Gaillord. *Sc:* Robert W. Ritchie. *With* Maurice Costello. *Prod:* Vitagraph. 2002 ft.

BUDDY'S DOWNFALL (1914). Comedy; as a city flirt who makes a fool of a country boy. *Dir:* Tefft Johnson. *Sc:* Paul Kelly. *With* Paul Kelly, Mary Anderson, Rose E. Tapley, Adele De Garde. *Prod:* Vitagraph. 1072 ft.

UNCLE BILL (1914). Farce; as Gladys, a sister-in-law who gets involved in domestic and political mix-ups. *Dir:* Ralph Ince. *Sc:* Marguerite Bertsch. *With:* Anita Stewart, Julia Swayne Gordon, Donald Hall, William Humphrey, Billy Quirk, Albert Roccardi, Jack Brawn, Anders Randolph. *Prod:* Vitagraph. 3 reels.

THE MYSTERIOUS LODGER (1914). Romantic mystery; as Lucy Lane. *Dir:* Maurice Costello and Robert Gaillord. *Sc:* Rita Humphreys. *With* Maurice Costello. *Prod:* Vitagraph. 1002 ft.

THE PEACEMAKER (1914). Romantic comedy; as Kitty Grey, the pretty catalyst for two lovers quarrelling. *Dir:* Van Dyke Brooke. *Sc:* A. Tremayne. *With* Norma Talmadge, Antonio Moreno, Van Dyke Brooke, Gary McGarry. *Prod:* Vitagraph. 1018 ft. (Compare listing in Antonio Moreno filmography.)

(During this period — 1914-15, inclusive, Vitagraph co-starred Constance Talmadge with Billy Quirk in a series of one-reel comedies, all directed by Lee Beggs, in which she was usually know simply as "Connie," and usually he as "Billy." These comedies include FATHER'S TIMEPIECE, THE EVOLUTION OF PERCIVAL, IN BRIDAL ATTIRE, THE EGYPTIAN MUMMY, THE MAID FROM SWEDEN, FORCING DAD'S CONSENT, all released in 1914; the series continued in 1915 with BILLY'S WAGER, THE GREEN CAT, THE YOUNG MAN WHO FIGGERED, BURGLARIOUS BILLY, A STUDY IN TRAMPS, THE MASTER OF HIS HOUSE, THE BOARDING HOUSE FEUD, THE VANISHING VAULT, SPADES ARE TRUMPS, BERTIE'S STRATAGEM, BILLY THE BEAR TAMER.)

IN THE LATIN QUARTER (1915). Romantic drama; as Marion, the model. *Dir:* Lionel Belmore. *Sc:* Florence Bolles. *With* Antonio Moreno, Edith Storey, S. Rankin Drew, William Dunn. *Prod:* Vitagraph. 2 reels. (Compare listing in Antonio Moreno filmography.)

A KEYBOARD STRATEGY (1915). Romantic comedy; as Mrs. Walter Gibson. *Dir:* Courtlandt Van Deusen. *Sc:* J. H. Bacon. *With* Lillian Walker, Evart Overton, J. H. Lewis, Mary Maurice. *Prod:* Vitagraph. 1061 ft.

THE LADY OF SHALOTT (1915). Comedy paraphrase of Tennyson's poem; as the Lady. *Dir:* C. J. Williams. *Sc:* Cecilie B. Peterson. *With* Flora Finch, Kate Price, William Shea, Jay Dwiggins. *Prod:* Vitagraph. 1083 ft.

CAPTIVATING MARY CARSTAIRS (1915). Romantic comedy; in only a small un-named role. *Dir:* Bruce M. Mitchell. *With* Norma Talmadge, Allan Forrest, Bruce M. Mitchell, Jack Livingston. This was the first film the Talmadges made in Hollywood. *Prod:* National. 5 reels.

(Constance Talmadge was then leading lady to "Smiling" Billy Parsons in at least three one-reel comedies, the first released by National, the other two by MinA. Titles for these three are CAN YOU BEAT IT? BEACHED AND BLEACHED, THE LITTLE PURITAN, all released in 1915. D. W. Griffith then came to the Tamadges' rescue, and Constance and Norma Talmadge were put under contract to him at Triangle.)

THE MISSING LINKS (1915). Detective mystery; as the daughter of a village merchant who helps solve a murder by the clue of missing cuff-links. *Dir:* Lloyd Ingraham. *Sup:* D. W. Griffith. *Sc:* Granville Warwick (D. W. Griffith). *With* Norma Talmadge, Robert Harron, Thomas Jefferson, Elmer Clifton, William Higby, Hal Wilson, Loyola O'Connor, Elinor Stone, Robert Lawler. *Prod:* Triangle/Fine Arts. 5 reels.

THE SHE-DEVIL (1916). Melodrama; as an American girl who is tortured and nearly driven insane by a Parisian gypsy whom her lover has spurned. *With* Gladys Brockwell. *Prod:* Mutual-Reliance. 2 reels.

INTOLERANCE (1916). Dramatic spectacle;

as "The Mountain Girl" in the Babylonian sequence and, briefly, as Marguerite de Valois in the St. Bartholomew's Massacre story. *Dir:/Sc:* D. W. Griffith. In "The Babylonian Story," in which Miss Talmadge plays the Mountain Girl, there also appear the following players: Elmer Clifton, Alfred Paget, Seena Owen, Carl Stockdale, Tully Marshall, George Seigmann, André Beranger, James Curley, Kate Bruce, Mildred Harris, Pauline Starke, Alma Rubens, Ruth Darling, Margaret Mooney, Grace Wilson, Lotta Clifton, Ah Singh, Ranji Singh, Ed Burns, James Burns, Charles Eagle Eye, William Dark Cloud, Charles von Cortland, Jack Cosgrove, Elmo Lincoln, Lawrence Lawlor, George Fawcett, Loyola O'Connor, Howard Scott, Winifred Westover, Carmel Myers, Monte Blue, Tod Browning, Jewel Carmen, Natalie Talmadge, Eve Southern, Ethel Terry, Daisy Robinson, Anna Mae Walthall, Francis Carpenter, Frank Campeau, Donald Crisp, Nigel de Brulier, Wilfred Lucas, Owen Moore, Tammany Young, William Brown, Chandler House, Gino Corrado, Russell Hicks, J. P. McCarthy, Ruth St. Denis and the Denishawn Dancers. In "The Medieval (or St. Bartholomew's Night) Story," in which Miss Talmadge is billed as Georgia Pearce and plays Marguerite de Valois, there also appear these players: Margery Wilson, Eugene Pallette, Spottiswoode Aitken, Ruth Handforth, A. D. Sears, Frank Bennett, Maxfield Stanley, Josephine Crowell, W. E. Lawrence, Morris Levy, Joseph Henabery, Howard Gaye, Martin Landry, Arthur Meyer, Frank Brown Lee, Louis Romaine. When the Babylonian sequence was issued in 1919 as a separate feature (*The Fall of Babylon*), Griffith shot some additional footage which permitted "The Mountain Girl" and her lover, "The Rhapsode," (Elmer Clifton) to survive and go off into exile together. Said "Variety" of Miss Talmadge's performance in this "re-issue": "Three years after *Intolerance* it is still the finest thing she has done. The part made her a star, and she has never exceeded that performance." *Prod:* Wark Producing Co. 13 reels.

THE MICROSCOPE MYSTERY (1916). Murder mystery; as Jessie Barton who, with her sweetheart, solves a murder by means of a microscope. *Dir:* Paul Powell. *Sup:* D. W. Griffith. *Sc:* (Ad. from a story, "Bugs," by George Randolph Chester). *With* Wilfred Lucas, F. A. Turner, Winifred Westover, Pomeroy Cannon, Fred Warren, James T. O'Shea, Kate Bruce, Monte Blue. *Prod:* Triangle/Fine Arts.

THE MATRIMANIAC (1916). Romantic comedy; as Marna Lewis. *Dir:* Paul Powell. *Sup:* D. W. Griffith. *Sc:* Anita Loos (from a story by Octavus Roy Cohen and J. V Giesy). *With* Douglas Fairbanks, Winifred Westover, Fred Warren, William Higby, Clyde Hopkins. *Prod:* Triangle/Fine Arts. 5 reels. (Compare listing in Douglas Fairbanks filmography.)

A GIRL OF THE TIMBER CLAIMS (1917). Mountaineer drama; as Jessie West, who leads Pacific timber folk against land grabbers. *Dir:* Paul Powell. *Sup:* D. W. Griffith. *Sc:* (Ad. from a story, "The Girl Homesteader," by Mary H. O'Connor). *With* A. D. Sears, Clyde Hopkins, Beau Byrd, Bennie Schumann, F. A. Turner, Charles Lee, Joseph Singleton, Mrs. Margaret (Peg) Talmadge. *Prod:* Triangle/Fine Arts. 5 reels.

BETSY'S BURGLAR (1917). Romantic comedy drama; as Betsy, a maid-of-all-work in a boarding house. *Dir:* Paul Powell. *Sup:* D. W. Griffith. *Sc:* (Ad. from a story by Frank E. Woods). *With* Kenneth Harlan, Josephine Crowell, Kate Burns, Hal Wilson, Monte Blue, Clyde Hopkins, Elmo Lincoln, Joseph Singleton. *Prod:* Triangle/Fine Arts. 5 reels.

SCANDAL (1917). Romantic comedy; as Beatrix, impulsive and indiscreet, who is nearly ruined by scandal, but gains a husband instead. *Dir:* Charles Giblyn. *Sc:* Bess Meredyth and Charles Giblyn (from a story by Cosmo Hamilton). *With* Harry C. Brown, J. Herbert Frank, Aimee Dalmores, Gladden James, W. P. Carleton, Mattie Ferguson, Ida Darling. *Prod:* Select. 5 reels.

THE HONEYMOON (1917). Romantic comedy; as Susan, who gets divorced on her honeymoon, but is reconciled. *Dir:* Charles Giblyn. *Sc:* (Ad. from a story by E. Lloyd Sheldon), *With* Earle Foxe, Maude Turner Gordon, Russell Bassett, Harriss Gordon, Lillian Cook, Julia Burns, Sam Colt. Filmed at Niagara Falls. *Prod:* Select. 5 reels.

THE STUDIO GIRL (1918). Romantic comedy; as Celia Laird, a New England girl who falls in love with a Manhattan artist. *Dir:* Charles Giblyn, *Sc:* Paul West (from a play, "The Runaway," which was an adaptation of a French farce, "La Gamine," by Pierre Veber and Henri de Gorsse). *With* Earle Foxe, Russell Bassett, Isabel O'Madigan, Johnny Hines, Gertrude Norman, Grace Barton. Working title: *The Cliff's*. *Prod:* Select. 5 reels.

THE SHUTTLE (1918). Romantic comedy drama; as Betty Vandepoel. *Dir:* Rollin Sturgeon. *Sc:* Harvey Thew and Margaret Turnbull (from a novel by Frances Hodgson Burnett). *With* Albert Roscoe, Edith Johnson, E. B. Tilton, Helen Dunbar, George McDaniel, Thomas Persse, Edward Peil, Casson Ferguson. *Prod:* Select. 5 reels.

UP THE ROAD WITH SALLIE (1918). Romantic comedy; as Sallie Cabot. *Dir:* William Desmond Taylor. *Sc:* Julia Crawford Ivers (from a novel by Frances Sterrett). *With* Norman Kerry, Kate Toncray, Thomas Persse, Karl Formes, M. B. Paanakker. *Prod:* Select. 5 reels.

THE LESSON (1918). Romantic drama; as Helen Drayton, who carves out a career for herself in spite of marital woes. *Dir:* Charles Giblyn. *Sc:* Virginia Terhune Van De Water. *With* Tom Moore, Walter Hiers, Herbert Heyes, Dorothy Green. This was the first feature Miss Talmadge filmed for Lewis J. Selznick and Joseph Schenck for release by Select, but it was released as her sixth. *Prod:* Select. 5 reels.

GOODNIGHT, PAUL (1918). Romantic farce; as Mrs. Richard, who poses as the wife of her husband's partner. *Dir:* Walter Edwards. *Sc:* Julia Crawford Ivers (from a comedy by Roland Oliver and Charles Dickson). *With* Harrison Ford, Norman Kerry, John Steppling, Beatrice Van, Rosita Marstini. *Prod:* Select. 5 reels.

A PAIR OF SILK STOCKINGS (1918). Romantic farce; as Molly Thornhill. *Dir:* Walter Edwards. *Sc:* Edith M. Kennedy (from a comedy by Cyril Harcourt). *With* Harrison Ford, Wanda Hawley, Sylvia Ashton, Vera Doria, Florence Carpenter, Thomas Persse, Louis Willoughby, Helen Haskell, L. W. Steers, Robert Gordon. *Prod:* Select. 5 reels.

MRS. LEFFINGWELL'S BOOTS (1918). Romantic farce; as Mrs. Leffingwell, whose purchase of a pair of dancing slippers leads to nothing but misunderstandings. *Dir:* Walter Edwards. *Sc:* Edith M. Kennedy (from a comedy by Augustus Thomas which had starred Margaret Illington on Broadway). *With* Harrison Ford, Fred Goodwins, Vera Doria, Mercedes Temple, Herbert Prior, Julia Faye. *Prod:* Select. 5 reels.

SAUCE FOR THE GOOSE (1918). Described as "A Farcical Dissertation on Woman's Rights"; as Kitty Constable, who pretends to philander in order to cure her husband. *Dir:* Walter Edwards. *Sc:* Julia Crawford Ivers (from the comedy by Geraldine Bonner and Hutcheson Boyd, in which Grace George starred on Broadway). *With* Harrison Ford, Harland Tucker, Vera Doria, Edna Mae Cooper, Louis Willoughby, Jane Keckley. *Prod:* Select. 5 reels.

A LADY'S NAME (1918). Romantic comedy; as Mabel Vere, a novelist who advertises for a husband. *Dir:* Walter Edwards. *Sc:* Julia Crawford Ivers (from the comedy by Cyril Harcourt in which Marie Tempest had starred). *With* Harrison Ford, Emory Johnson, Vera Doria, James Farley, Fred Huntley, John Sterling, Truman Van Dyke, Lillian Leighton, Emma Gerdes, ZaSu Pitts. *Prod:* Select. 5 reels.

WHO CARES? (1919). Romantic comedy; as Joan Ludlow who marries on the rebound and then realises she loves the man she has married. *Dir:* Walter Edwards. *Sc:* Julia Crawford Ivers (from a story by Cosmo Hamilton). *With*

Constance Talmadge as "The Mountain Girl" in Griffith's INTOLERANCE

Harrison Ford, Donald MacDonald, California Truman, Spottiswoode Aitken, Beverly Randolph, Claire Anderson, Gerard Alexander, J. Morris Foster, J. Park Jones, Dorothy Haggar, Tom Bates. *Prod:* Select. 5 reels.

ROMANCE AND ARABELLA (1919). Romantic comedy; as Arabella Cadenhouse, a widow, who determines that her next husband will not be a stick-in-the-mud. *Dir:* Walter Edwards. *Sc:* Edith M. Kennedy (from a comedy by William J. Hurlburt). *With* Harrison Ford, Gertrude Claire, Monte Blue, Arthur Edmund Carewe, Antrim Short, James Neill. *Prod:* Select. 5 reels.

EXPERIMENTAL MARRIAGE (AKA, GB, *Saturday to Monday*). (1919). Romantic comedy; as Suzanne Ercoll. *Dir:* Robert G. Vignola. *Sc:* Alice Eyton (from a comedy, "Saturday to Monday," by William J. Hurlburt). *With* Harrison Ford, Walter Hiers, Vera Sisson, Edythe Chapman, Raymond Hatton, Maym Kelso. In reviewing this film, "Bioscope" claimed that Constance Talmadge has "a distinction of style which recalls the best work of Miss Irene Vanbrugh." *Prod:* Select. 5 reels.

THE VEILED ADVENTURE (1919). Romantic comedy; as Geraldine Barker, who is engaged to one man, but marries another. *Dir:* Walter Edwards, *Sc:* Julia Crawford Ivers. *With* Harrison Ford, Stanhope Wheatcroft, Vera Doria, Rosita Marstini, T. D. Crittenden, Eddie Sutherland, Margaret Loomis, Vera Sisson. Working title: *The Grey Chiffon Veil. Prod:* Select. 5 reels.

HAPPINESS A LA MODE (1919). Romantic comedy; as Barbara Townsend, who gets a divorce and then re-wins her husband. *Dir:* Walter Edwards. *Sc:* Alice Eyton (from a story by Edwina Le Vin). *With* Harrison Ford, Betty Schade, Myrtle Richelle, Paul Weigel, Thomas Persse, A. Fremont. *Prod:* Select. 5 reels.

A TEMPERAMENTAL WIFE (1919). Romantic comedy; as Billie Billings, who weds and separates from the Senator from Nevada, but he wins her back. *Dir:* John Emerson. *Sc:* Anita Loos and John Emerson. *With* Wyndham Standing, Ben Hendricks, Eulalie Jensen, Armand Kaliz. *Prod:* First National. 6 reels.

A VIRTUOUS VAMP (1919). Romantic comedy; as Gwendolyn Armitage, who concludes that flirting and a successful business career don't mix. *Dir:* David Kirkland. *Sc:* Anita Loos and John Emerson (from a play, "The Bachelor," by Clyde Fitch). *With* Conway Tearle, Gilda Grey, Harda Belle Daube, Ned Sparks, Jack Kane, Wallace McCutcheon. *Prod:* First National. 5 reels.

TWO WEEKS (1920). Romantic comedy; as Lillums, a chorus girl. *Dir:* Sidney Franklin. *Sc:* Anita Loos and John Emerson (from a play, "At the Barn," by Anthony Wharton). *With* Conway Tearle, Reginald Mason, George Fawcett, Templar Saxe, William Fredericks, Tom Cameron. *Prod:* First National. 6 reels.

IN SEARCH OF A SINNER (1920). Romantic comedy; as Georgianna Chadbourne, who's in search of a sinner for a husband so she can reform him. *Dir* David Kirkland. *Sc:* John Emerson and Anita Loos (from a story by Charlotte Thompson). *With* Rockcliffe Fellowes, Corliss Giles, William Roselle, Marjorie Milton, Evelyn C. Carrington, Lillian Worth, Arnold Lucy, Charles Whittaker, Ned Sparks. *Prod:* First National. 5 reels.

THE LOVE EXPERT (1920). Romantic comedy; as Babs, who marries off the three women tying down the young man she wants to marry. *Dir:* David Kirkland. *Sc:* John Emerson and Anita Loos. *With* Arnold Lucy, John Halliday, Natalie Talmadge, Fannie Bourke, Mrs. Nellie P. Spaulding, Marion Sitgreave, David Kirkland. *Prod:* First National. 5 reels.

THE PERFECT WOMAN (1920). Romantic comedy; as Mary Blake, who vamps a millionaire misogynist into falling in love with her. *Dir:* David Kirkland. *Sc:* John Emerson and Anita Loos. *With* Charles Meredith, Joseph Burke, Elizabeth Garrison, Ned Sparks. *Prod:* First National. 5 reels.

GOOD REFERENCES (1920). Romantic comedy; as Mary Wayne, who poses as Nell Norcross, secretary. *Dir:* R. William Neill. *Sc:* Dorothy Farnum (from a story by E. J. Rath). *With* Vincent Coleman, Ned Sparks, Mrs. Betts (Betz), Arnold Lucy, Dorothy Walters, George Fawcett. *Prod:* First National. 5 reels.

DANGEROUS BUSINESS (1921). Romantic comedy; as Nancy Flavelle, an indiscreet flirt. *Dir:* R. William Neill. *Sc:* Anita Loos and John Emerson (from a prize-winning scenario, "The Chessboard," by Madeleine Buckley). *With* Kenneth Harlan, Jack Raymond, George Fawcett, Nina Cassavant, Matilda Brundage, Florida Kingsley. *Prod:* First National. 5 reels.

MAMA'S AFFAIR (1921). Romantic comedy drama; as Eve Orrin, driven to a nervous breakdown by a possessive hypochondriac mother. *Dir:* Victor Fleming. *Sc:* John Emerson and Anita Loos (from a play by Rachel B. Butler). *With* Effie Shannon, Kenneth Harlan, George LeGuere, Katherine Kaelred, Gertrude Le Brandt. *Prod:* First National. 6 reels.

LESSONS IN LOVE (1921). Romantic comedy; as Leila Calthorpe, who poses as her own maid, "Perkins." *Dir:* Chet Withey. *Sc:* Grant Carpenter (from a play, "The Man from Toronto," by Douglas Murray). *With* Kenneth Harlan, Flora Finch, Florence Short, James Harrison, George Fawcett, Frank Webster, Louise Lee. Exteriors filmed in Miami. *Prod:* First National. 5 reels.

WEDDING BELLS (1921). Romantic comedy; as Rosalie Wayne. *Dir:* Chet Withey. *Sc:* Zelda Crosby (from a comedy by Salisbury Field). *With* Harrison Ford, Emily Chichester, Ida Darling, William Roselle, Polly Van, Dallas Welford, Frank Honda. *Prod:* First National. 6 reels.

WOMAN'S PLACE (1921). Romantic comedy of politics; as Josephine Gerson, who runs for mayor in an Ohio city against the man she loves. *Dir:* Victor Fleming. *Sc:* John Emerson and Anita Loos. *With* Kenneth Harlan, Hassard Short, Florence Short, Ina Rorke. *Prod:* First National. 6 reels.

POLLY OF THE FOLLIES (1922). Romantic backstage comedy; as Polly Meacham, a slavey in a small-town drugstore, who becomes a hit in Ziegfeld's Midnight Frolics. *Dir:* Joseph Plunkett (John Emerson). *Sc:* Anita Loos and John Emerson. *With* Kenneth Harlan, Billie Dove, James Gleason, Horace Knight, Thomas Carr, Harry Fisher, Frank

Lawlor, George Fawcett, Ina Borke, Mildred Arden, Paul Doucet, Theresa Maxwell Conover, Bernard Randall, John Daly Murphy. *Prod:* First National. 7 reels.

THE PRIMITIVE LOVER (1922). Romantic comedy; as Phyllis Tomley, a divorcee who is wooed by both her ex-husband and a one-time suitor. *Dir:* Sidney Franklin. *Sc:* Frances Marion (from a play, *"The Divorcee,"* by Edgar Selwyn). *With* Harrison Ford, Kenneth Harlan, Joe Roberts, Charles Pina, Chief Big Tree, Matilda Brundage, George Pierce, Clyde Benson. *Prod:* First National. 7 reels.

EAST IS WEST (1922). Romantic comedy; as Ming Toy. *Dir:* Sidney Franklin. *Sc:* Frances Marion (from the play by John Hymer and Samuel Shipman, in which Fay Bainter had starred on Broadway).*With* Nigel Barrie, Warner Oland, Edmund Burns, Frank Lanning, Winter Hall, Lillian Lawrence. (Remade as an early talkie by Universal with Lupe Velez.) *Prod:* First National. 8 reels.

DULCY (1923). Comedy; as Dulcy Smith, who turns out to be not as dumb as everybody had thought. *Dir:* Sidney Franklin. *Sc:* John Emerson and Anita Loos (from the George S. Kaufman and Marc Connelly comedy in which Lynn Fontanne had starred on Broadway). *With* Jack Mulhall, Johnny Harron, Claude GIllingwater, May Wilson, Anne Cornwall, André Beranger, Gilbert Douglas, Frederick Esmelton, Milla Davenport. (Re-made at M-G-M, with Marion Davies and again with Ann Southern.) *Prod:* First National. 7 reels.

THE DANGEROUS MAID (1923). Costume comedy drama; as Barbara Winslow, Seventeeth century Englishwoman. *Dir:* Victor Heerman. *Sc:* C. Gardner Sullivan (from a novel, "Barbara Winslow — Rebel", by Elizabeth Ellis). *With* Conway Tearle, Morgan Wallace, Charles Gerard, Marjorie Drew, Kate Price, Tully Marshall, Lou Morrison, Phil Dunham, Otto Matiesen, Wilson Hummel, Thomas Ricketts, Ann May, Ray Hallor, Lincoln Plummer. *Prod:* First National. 7,445 ft.

THE GOLDFISH (1924). Romantic comedy; as Jennie Wetherby. *Dir:* Jerome Storm. *Sc:* C. Gardner Sullivan (from the Gladys Unger comedy in which Marjorie Rambeau had starred on Broadway). *With* Jack Mulhall, Jean Hersholt, William Conklin, ZaSu Pitts, Frank

Elliott, Edward Connelly, Leo White, *Prod:* First National. 7 reels.

IN HOLLYWOOD WITH POTASH AND PERLMUTTER (1924). Comedy about Hollywood; in an extended cameo role, as herself playing a gold-digger vamping her way into a star part. *Dir:* Al Green. *Sc:* Frances Marion (from the play by Montague Glass and Jules Eckert Goodman). *With* Alexander Carr, George Sidney, Vera Gordon, Betty Blythe, Belle Bennett, Anders Randolph, Peggy Shaw, Charles Meredith, Lillian Hackett, David Butler, Sidney Franklin, Joseph W. Girard, Louis Payne, Cyril Ring, Norma Talmadge. Both Talmadge sisters were unbilled guest appearances. *Prod:* Goldwyn-First-National. 7 reels.

HER NIGHT OF ROMANCE (1924). Romantic comedy; as Dorothy Adams, a millionaire heiress who poses as a penniless spinster. *Dir:* Sidney Franklin. *Sc:* Hans Kraly. *With* Ronald Colman, Albert Gran, Jean Hersholt, Robert Rendel, Sidney Bracy, Templar Saxe, Emily Fitzroy. Working title: *Heart Trouble. Prod:* First National. 7 reels.

LEARNING TO LOVE (1925). Romantic comedy; as Patricia Stanhope, an heiress flirt, who falls in love with her guardian. *Dir:* Sidney Franklin. *Sc:* John Emerson and Anita Loos. *With* Antonio Moreno, Emily Fitzroy, Johnny Harron, Ray Hallor, Alf Goulding, Wallace McDonald, Edythe Chapman, Byron Munson, Edgar Norton, Percy Williams. *Prod:* First National. 7 reels. (Compare listing in Antonio Moreno filmography.)

BREAKFAST AT SUNRISE (1927). Romantic comedy; as Madeleine, who marries a poor young man out of pique and falls in love with him. *Dir:* Mal St. Clair. *Sc:* Fred de Gresac (from an adaptation by Gladys Unger of a play, "Le Déjeuner au soleil," by André Birabeau). *With* Bryant Washburn, Alice White, Paulette Du Val, Marie Dressler, Albert Gran, Burr McIntosh, David Mir, Don Alvarado, Nelly Bly Baker. *Prod:* First National. 7 reels.

VENUS (1929). Romantic comedy about a princess who falls in love with a sea captain; as the Princess Beatrice Doriani. *Dir:* Louis Mercanton. *Sc:* Adrien Gaillard (from a novel by Jean Vignaud). *With* André Roanne, Jean Murat, Max Maxudian, Baron Fils, Jean Mercanton. Filmed on the French Riviera. *Prod:* United Artists. 8 reels.

8
JOHN BARRYMORE
AND
DOLORES COSTELLO

Cinematically, John Barrymore was a comedian of rare wit and charm. He could play burlesque, farce, or any comedy of humours and manners with an ease and perfection that amounted to pure genius. Any actor knows that the most difficult dramatic *genre* to master is, and has always been, comedy. John Barrymore was Comedy's King, the true Master of the Revels.

Ironically, because he was also blessed with a physical beauty which would have done credit to Lord Byron, he is remembered by many film fans as the pasteboard hero of a series of costume romances that any actor with a profile and an Adonis-like body could have played. He himself once characterised these "Great Lover" performances as "male impersonations of Lilyan Tashman." Not more than half a dozen of his screen performances in serious drama remain memorable. But the comedies attest his brilliance; they are the perfectly matched pearls in his cinematic crown.

Born John Sidney Blythe in Philadelphia on February 14, 1882, with St. Valentine's as his natal day, he was cast from the beginning as a timeless Harlequin, a vagabond knave with a jest on his lips and mirth in every glance. His grandmother, Mrs. John Drew, was a matchless comedienne; his mother, Georgianna Drew, and his uncle, John Drew, wrote their names in the annals of American Comedy. His father, an Englishman who had been born Herbert Blythe, had studied for law at Oxford, where he was also amateur lightweight boxing champion of England. Choosing acting as a career, he adopted the name of Maurice Barrymore, made his American *début* in Dion Boucicault's comedy "The Shaughraun," and was playing Laertes to Edwin Booth's Hamlet when he met Georgianna Drew. They fell in love at once, and were married.

They became the parents of three children — Lionel, Ethel, and John — and the Barrymores were soon carrying on the tradition of the Drews: they had become the American theatre's royal family. John, the youngest, resisted becoming an actor; both he and Lionel wanted to be artists. Lionel could have been top drawer. Of his own talents, John remarked succinctly, "I might have been, but wasn't." Nor was he the journalist he briefly strived to become.

"We became actors," Ethel Barrymore once said of herself and her brothers, "not because we wanted to go on the stage but because it was the thing we could do best."

John Barrymore first appeared onstage in Philadelphia and then in Chicago. Of the latter engagement in Sudermann's "Magda," Amy Leslie, Chicago critic, had written: "The part of Max was essayed by a young actor who calls himself Mr. John Barrymore. He walked about the stage as if he had been all dressed up and forgotten." Then, aged twenty-one John Barrymore made his New York *début* as an actor in a Clyde Fitch comedy, "Glad of It." The play did not last long, but William Collier saw young Barrymore in it, thought he had the makings of a comedian, and engaged him for a role in Richard Harding Davis's "The Dictator." Barrymore went on tour, managed to live through the San Francisco fire and earthquake, and continued on tour with Collier. It marked the real beginning of John Barrymore, comedian extraordinary, although Collier made no secret that teaching his protege the facts of comedy proved almost the end of him.

Other engagements followed, and finally on September 4, 1909, Barrymore made his *début* as a Broadway star in his own right in Winchell Smith's romantic comedy, "The Fortune Hunter," and became the darling of Manhattan theatregoers. The following year, on September 1, John Barrymore also took his first bride, Katherine Corri Harris, a beautiful stagestruck socialite. She was just nineteen; he was twenty-eight.

During his last years, he once characterised this union as "the first of my three and one-half marriages — all of them bus accidents." Yet he encouraged Katherine Harris Barrymore, as she was billed, and she played opposite him both in the theatre and in two of his early films.

In 1913, Adolph Zukor induced John Barrymore to make his screen *début* for Famous Players (later, Paramount). Out of curiosity, but mostly because the money was good and somehow John Barrymore always needed more money, he consented.

J. Searle Dawley, veteran screen director, once recalled: "John Barrymore, the Great Profile, in his first time to appear on the silver screen, was under my direction at the Famous Players Studio on 26th Street, New York City. It was a great event, but at that time nobody seemed to know it or realise that one of the greatest clowns and tragedians of the stage and screen was entering our new art. The title of the picture was a comedy, *An American Citizen,* adapted from the play of that name in which Nat Goodwin had starred on the stage.

"The fourth day after I had been using Barrymore, Mr. Zukor came to me and asked what I thought of the young actor Barrymore. I remember my reply well — 'Mr. Zukor, he is the best actor I've ever had the privilege to handle.'

"'You think we ought to put him under contract?'

"'If you don't, you're losing a great opportunity.'

"'Zukor signed him up, and they cast him to play slapstick comedy; they wanted to make a Charlie Chaplin out of him.

"Barrymore was always the bad boy of the theatre and screen. His sense of humour would always get the best of him, and his sense of freedom made him want to wander. He was a wild spirit that must have no bounds.

"I recall one time when he decided to wander away while making a picture at the studio. It took three days and a small force of searchers to find him. Where? In a Bowery saloon, peacefully sleeping under the table, happy in the arms of oblivion. Still kidding, he was induced to return to work, and from

GRAND HOTEL: The only time Garbo ever asked a still photographer to take a picture of her on set was for this shot of her with Barrymore, whom she greatly admired

then on until the picture was finished, John Barrymore's address was Dressing Room 2, Famous Players Studio.

"It was shortly after this event that Barrymore left the picture art forever — so he thought — and I think Mr. Zukor heaved a sigh of relief."

From 1914-19 Barrymore made eleven feature films for Famous Players. Most of them were screen versions of hit stage comedies that had starred Nat C. Goodwin, Leo Ditrichstein, or William Collier, but the camera caught the essential spirit of John Barrymore, comedian, and translated it to the screen. His pictures were enormously successful, and the romantic figure of Barrymore, debonair and moustached, resembled in a way that of the French comedian, Max Linder. Of these early comedies, only one, *The Incorrigible Dukane*, has ever turned up to my knowledge in a film history retrospective (at Eastman House). It's unfortunate that the others seem to be numbered among the so-called "lost films," because they all had an audacity that was to be treasured.

In between these Famous Players escapades filmed during the day while he was appearing nightly on Broadway, Barrymore in 1917 filmed *Raffles, the Amateur Cracksman* for an independent company. To this silent screen adventure of a gentleman crook he brought a droll insouciance, an easy sophistication remarkable for the time. His graceful pantomime imparted an elegance to the role that Ronald Colman and David Niven subsequently conveyed in dialogue versions of *Raffles*.

He may have given his producers a bad time, but he had developed a healthy respect for the cinematic medium, declaring once in a happy moment: "The film determines an actor's qualities. Mental impressions can be conveyed by the screen more quickly than vocally. The moving picture is not a business; it is an art."

The theatre, however, remained his dazzling magnet. Like every proven comedian, he was tempted to try his talents as a serious actor. His good friend, playwright Edward Sheldon, with whom he travelled in Italy, encouraged him in so doing. "In fact," Barrymore acknowledged of Sheldon, "I'm not sure that he didn't make me a serious actor."

It was Sheldon who brought him the John Galsworthy play "Justice," and laid the foundation for its Broadway production in 1916. Overnight, Barrymore was hailed by New York as a dramatic star. And it was Sheldon also who subsequently brought him the play version of "Peter Ibbetson," in which Barrymore played the title role, with Constance Collier the Duchess of Towers, while at Barrymore's insistence his brother Lionel returned to the theatre to play the villainous Colonel Ibbetson.

It was inevitable that he exhibit his newly-recognised gifts for drama on the screen. To quote again from director J. Searle Dawley: "It was while John Barrymore, the now-assured star, was playing the subway circuit in his Broadway success 'Peter Ibbetson' that we again met. I went backstage to see him in his dressing-room after the show. We had quite a talk, and then the subject of motion pictures came up.

"'No, Dawley, I'm through with that, I'm no good in pictures and never will be.'

"That's where I went to bat with him. I begged him to make another try at it, not as a clown but as something really seriously worthwhile. 'Go see Zukor,' I said.

"Barrymore's eyes twinkled as he replied, 'He'd throw me out of the place. I was a bad boy then, but I'm off the stuff for life — I swear I am!'

"That old delightful twinkle was in his eyes, however, and I had me doubts. But finally I got him to say that he'd give Zukor a buzz.

"Well, that buzz ended in a contract and his screen comeback in *Dr. Jekyll and Mr. Hyde*, a smashing big hit, and he was on his way up and up. In fact, he never did stop climbing and clowning, and even in the end his clowning made him famous and funny again. The great art of Barrymore was that he knew how to laugh at himself and at life — and the public loved him for it."

Today it is all too obvious that *Dr. Jekyll and Mr. Hyde* closely approximates his own dual-natured life. Born with Gemini rising, it was sadly inevitable that all the goodness, truth and beauty of his creative self should be dimmed and destroyed by the self-indulgent, repulsive ugliness of the alcoholic Mr. Hyde he too frequently became.

Barrymore had starred on stage in Arthur Hopkins's production of Tolstoy's "Redemption", and he had again joined forces with brother Lionel to appear for Hopkins in a memorable production of the Italian tragedy, "The Jest." In fact, he was still starring in "The Jest" nightly and rehearsing for the forthcoming "Richard III" with a private coach, Margaret Carrington, when he filmed *Dr. Jekyll and Mr. Hyde* at the Paramount New York Studios.

He was the lion of the hour — but a very weary one, for, once divorced from his first wife, he had now fallen in love again, this time with a married woman, Mrs. Leonard Thomas, born Blanche Oelrichs, and known in artistic circles as a poet-playwright named Michael Strange. Barrymore spent two months at a White Plains rest-farm. When he reappeared that summer, he looked marvellous, seventeen pounds heavier, and ready to roar again. Meanwhile, Mr. Thomas had divorced his wife in Paris, and on August 5, 1920, Barrymore, aged thirty-eight, and Michael Strange, aged twenty-nine, were married. Seven months later she bore him a daughter christened Diana.

Soon thereafter, Ethel and John Barrymore were the stars of Michael Strange's verse-drama, with music, "Clair de Lune," adapted from Victor Hugo's "The Man Who Laughs." It was, unfortunately, the critics who laughed at "Clair de Lune." and the play did not last long. Barrymore railed against the gentlemen of the press for their treatment of his wife's play, and then went off on location to Florida to film *The Lotus Eater,* with Marshall Neilan directing and Colleen Moore as his leading lady.

The Lotus Eater remains a beautiful and idealistic but very curious film. The only movie it even faintly resembles in my memory is Vitagraph's 1915 serial, *The Goddess,* which had starred Anita Stewart and Earle Williams. Both show how wicked and venal contemporary life has become, with the only hope for man's surcease and happiness being an escape from it all to some remote island paradise.

After *The Lotus Eater,* Barrymore travelled abroad with his wife. Rumours of their bombastic, and frequently bizarre, quarrels in every capital sparked across the Atlantic. Michael Strange left Barrymore in Paris to return to the States, and he agreed to do a film version of *Sherlock Holmes,* with exteriors shot in England and Switzerland.

Roland Young was his Dr. Watson. Amusingly, Barrymore subsequently confessed that Young had seemed so modest and self-effacing that he had decided to help him so that he wouldn't be lost in the shuffle before the camera. Said Barrymore: "When I saw the completed film, I was flabbergasted, stunned, and almost became an atheist on the spot. That quiet, agreeable bastard had stolen, not one, but every damned scene! This consummate artist and myself have been close friends for years, but I wouldn't think of trusting him on any stage."

Barrymore returned to the States puzzled, lonely and angry because his wife had insisted upon a temporary separation and had sailed off for Europe with her friend, Cynthia Mosley. He sought refuge with his sister and one day she gave him a copy of "Hamlet" to read.

The great idea was born. Now was the time to do it! He again sought out

Margaret Carrington, who had coached him for "Richard III," and they conferred with producer Arthur Hopkins and scene designer Robert Edmund Jones (who later married Mrs. Carrington).

John Barrymore's "Hamlet" was his greatest stage appearance, and his was one of the finest Hamlets of this century. He broke all existing records in New York up to that time, playing the role 101 consecutive performances; he played a return engagement in Manhattan and toured it in several Eastern cities; he then played it in London and was enthusiastically acclaimed by the English public and press. His presentation of "Hamlet" remains one of the notable occasions of an American actor being favourably received by the English critics and public for his performance in an English classic.

Just before he appeared in "Hamlet" in Manhattan and London, Barrymore journeyed to Hollywood to film *Beau Brummel* for Warner Bros. His wife and he had reconciled at the time, but gossip, false and true, quickly rent their newly patched domesticity, and they parted once again. Barrymore was soon enjoying a secret romance off camera with his seventeen-year-old leading lady in *Beau Brummel*, Mary Astor. In later years, both were frank about this interlude, Miss Astor especially in her autobiography, "My Story." It was a love that was to flare and flame again and again until Barrymore met the girl who was to become his third wife.

Viewed at this date, *Beau Brummel* is curiously static, but in its day it was greatly admired. It still presents Barrymore at the peak of his romantic beauty, and the last episode, with him as the aged, exiled and dying Beau, at least affords him a chance at a believable and sympathetic character study.

In May 1925, Barrymore and Michael Strange agreed to a final and amicable separation, and soon thereafter Barrymore entrained for Hollywood again to fulfil a new Warner Bros. contract. For each picture he filmed on a seven weeks shooting schedule, he was to receive $76,250, with $7,625 paid him for every week the production ran over. He had complete story approval, and the studio agreed to pay travelling expenses for himself, his English valet Blaney, and his pet monkey Clementine, once known as "Iris" when Barrymore had "borrowed" her from Gladys Cooper in London. Warner Bros. also provided him with a four-room suite at the Ambassador Hotel on Wilshire Boulevard, and they paid for his meals there and for an automobile and chauffeur. Even today in 1973, this is a better than usual contract between artist and production company.

Barrymore had asked for Mary Astor as his leading lady again, but she was busy filming several features for First National. His first vehicle on his new contract was to be a screen version of Herman Melville's novel, "Moby Dick," retitled *The Sea Beast*. There is no heroine in Melville's novel, but the very competent scenarist Bess Meredyth had introduced a romantic interest into her screenplay that did not cloud the conflict between Captain Ahab and the White Whale named Moby Dick. The essential question now became — what actress would play that heroine? Barrymore resisted the casting-office's idea that a pretty rising starlet, Priscilla Bonner, play the role. For days he sat in a projection room with director Millard Webb viewing tests of every available young actress, known and unknown, for the role of Esther.

During one recess, Barrymore paced the small balcony outside Jack Warner's office at the old Warner Bros. Studio on Sunset Boulevard, arguing for a postponement of the picture's starting date so that Mary Astor would be free to play opposite him. A taxicab drove up, and three women got out — one middle-aged, with two young girls, a brunette and a blonde. Barrymore grabbed Warner's arm.

"Quick, man — who is she? There's Esther!"

"The dark-haired one?"

"No, the blonde! She's the most preposterously lovely creature in all the world!"

The blonde was nineteen-year-old Dolores Costello; the brunette was her sister Helene; they were accompanied by their mother, Mrs. Maurice Costello. And, by a stroke of luck, the Costello girls were already under contract to Warner Bros.! Helene was making out fairly well, but the studio hadn't really known what to do with Dolores. Needless to say, Barrymore was properly introduced, and at his insistence Dolores Costello was given the role of Esther opposite him in *The Sea Beast.*

It was not really the first time they had met. Maurice Costello, their father, one of filmdom's first romantic stars, under contract to Brooklyn's Vitagraph Studio, had owned a charming country estate on Long Island. Sometime in 1914, when he was beginning his film career for Famous Players and was wooing his first wife, Katherine Harris, Barrymore had been a guest at the Costello's Long Island home. Even then, the Costello sisters were already professional movie actresses. Since 1911, they had been playing kid roles at Vitagraph, usually in their father's pictures, sometimes together, sometimes alone, and sometimes one of them even dressed as a boy wearing a Buster Brown suit to play brother to her own sister. They were used to actors on and off set, and were not to be easily impressed. Dolores was then nine; Helene, twelve. They thought Barrymore romantic and amusing, but Gentleman Jim Corbett and Pearl White, also frequent visitors in their father's home, were far more exciting.

But now in 1925, Dolores, not yet twenty, found John Barrymore, aged forty-three, the proper god for her idolatry. As sister Helene wrote in later years: "They fell in love with the sudden violence of an earthquake."

Their love posed some problems. Wary of actors and especially one who, more than double her daughter's age, was twice married and not yet divorced from his estranged wife, Mrs. Costello chaperoned them constantly. But Barrymore, in love again, was at his most charming, and Mrs. Costello relaxed her vigilance. From the beginning, however, Maurice Costello had distrusted Barrymore. His resistance to the Barrymore charm brought about a breakdown in the domestic relations between him and his wife, and they were eventually divorced in 1927.

Dolores and Helene Costello had not only been child actresses at Vitagraph long before John Barrymore faced a camera, but they had posed for the top magazine illustrators in Manhattan. Dolores, who was born in Pittsburgh on September 17, 1905, had modelled for James Montgomery Flagg's illustrations to Adela Rogers St. Johns' popular magazine serial, "The Skyrocket". Flagg had chosen her because the movie star heroine of "The Skyrocket" had been described not only as blonde but as "very slender, with no bones showing anywhere." Dolores had also played bits at the Paramount Long Island Studio, and she had a small role in a film Allan Dwan directed in

Florida, in which her father had appeared (*Glimpses of the Moon,* starring Bebe Daniels); she also played the role of Norah, the maid, in another Dwan feature for Paramount in 1923, *Lawful Larceny.* When the Costello sisters were playing dancing leads on the stage in the "George White Scandals of 1924," a talent scout saw them in Chicago and persuaded Warner Bros. to put them under contract.

In Hollywood, Helene had fared better in the beginning. She had quickly graduated to leading ladies in Westerns. Dolores had played a small unbilled role in a Marie Prevost flapper film, *Bobbed Hair,* and Warners had thereafter lent her for a lead in an Edmund Lowe Fox feature, *Greater than a Crown.* But she was regarded by her home studio as so much deadwood.

Now, however, Warner Bros. was giving her the deluxe star treatment. Instead of being thought cold and "just another blonde okay for maids and background," she was being termed "luscious," "sultry," "the exquisite Dolores."

Barrymore himself coached her for her role with him in *The Sea Beast.* It was not a lengthy part, but she was the only woman of any importance in the film. The minute she finished shooting on *The Sea Beast,* her studio, having no immediate assignment for her, lent her to Paramount to play the heroine in *Mannequin*, a tinselly "Liberty Magazine" prize story by Fannie Hurst, directed by James Cruze.

Ironically, *The Sea Beast* and *Mannequin* were premiered almost simultaneously, and fans and critics could see for themselves how exquisite Dolores Costello could be both in costume drama and modern melodrama. The love scenes in *The Sea Beast* were photographed by Byron Haskins with a true lyric beauty, and Barrymore and Costello at once became the new love duet of the day. He was again the proud, handsome, stalwart lion; she was like the loveliest of all April mornings.

The Sea Beast was breaking box-office records, and Warner Bros. wished they had not already signed Mary Astor to play opposite Barrymore in his next, *Don Juan.* Miss Astor, hopeful that her romance with him might be renewed off camera as well as on, had heard rumours of the blossoming new love, but it was not until she went on set and saw that a chair for Miss Costello had been placed next to Barrymore's that she sadly realised how her lovely secret romance had become just another idyll for yesterday. On the set, between takes, she nerved herself to ask if it were all over, and he said with his sad, twisted smile, "I'm just a son of a bitch."

Don Juan, if only a pretty but hack romance, nevertheless proved a milestone in film history. It opened in New York at the Warner Theatre on August 5, 1926, and was the first feature for which a recorded musical score with sound effects was synchronised with the action. It was shown with a selection of the first Vitaphone talking and singing short subjects, and audience reception of the programme far surpassed that of the critics in approval. Two things were indicated: the end of the silent film; the definite future of the talking picture.

While Barrymore was occupied with *Don Juan,* Dolores Costello was busy making three programme features — *Bride of the Storm, The Third Degree,* and *The Little Irish Girl.* They were scheduled to be reunited on the screen in a lavish version of *Manon Lescaut,* which would appropriately be re-titled

John Barrymore with Dolores Costello in THE SEA BEAST (English title, MOBY DICK)

When a Man Loves. The male lead, the Chevalier des Grieux, is secondary to that of the heroine, the lovely materialistic tease Manon, and Barrymore's approval of it as a vehicle for him indicates how completely fascinated he was by Dolores Costello. Ethel Barrymore witnessed a rough-cut and was heart-sick, seeing how her brother had literally given the picture to the girl he loved. Miss Barrymore, a thorough professional, seldom gave anything to a fellow player other than his proper cue, and it dismayed her to see her brother, a film star in his own right with the memories still bright of his own stage "Hamlet," behave so unprofessionally. Critics were likewise taken aback when they reviewed *When a Man Loves,* and delegated most of their praise to Miss Costello, praising her blonde beauty and noting that she was also a skilful film actress. Warner Bros. assented by awarding her full stardom.

Barrymore then revealed the method in his generous show of madness. Instead of re-signing with Warners, he signed for three films at United Artists, and to Joseph Schenck's horror he tried to inveigle Miss Costello away from her new stardom to join him as co-star. Warner Bros. and the Motion Picture Association quickly reminded him that he could face severe punitive damages, and so Miss Costello remained at Warners and he was stuck at United Artists, where he was not getting the cash he had before and few of the star benefits that Warners had so generously accorded him. He began to feel how

John Barrymore with Dolores Costello in WHEN A MAN LOVES (English title, HIS LADY)

expensive it was to live like a movie star when you have to foot the bills yourself.

He made the three films he had contracted for at United Artists; all three were costume romances — *The Beloved Rogue, Tempest,* and *Eternal Love*. None of them advanced his career. The public was interested only in talkies. At Warners, Dolores Costello was studying for her talking *début*. After *A Million Bid, Old San Francisco, The Heart of Maryland,* and *The College Widow*, Miss Costello had become the hottest property on the lot, and when she made two part-talkies, *Tenderloin* and *Glorious Betsy*, both of which were great box-office hits, the studio regarded her as their top feminine star.

Barrymore, meanwhile, had secured his freedom from Michael Strange, and on November 24, 1928, Dolores Costello and he were married. After a honeymoon, he signed again with Warner Bros., glad to get away from the percentage deals he had dealt with at United Artists. He and his wife both appeared in *The Show of Shows,* Warners' contribution to the revue film, then very much in vogue at every major studio. Miss Costello, billed as the "Belle of the Box-Office," appeared with her sister Helene in a musical number, "My Sister," which featured all the available sister teams then working as actresses in Hollywood. Barrymore was the real star of *The Show of Shows;* he introduced his own number and appeared as the Duke of Gloucester (later, Richard III) in the soliloquy from Shakespeare's *Henry VI, Part 3.* It was a stunning talkie *début* for him, and remains the highlight of a feature that is otherwise more than a little ersatz.

Barrymore's first full talkie, *General Crack,* was better than most of the costumers he had made for Warner Bros. Weekly "Variety," in fact, called it his "most interesting production since *Beau Brummel.*" His leading ladies were Marian Nixon, Armida, and Jacqueline Logan. The public was hopeful that he and his bride might be reunited on the screen, but most of Dolores's time was taken up with her appearance with George O'Brien in the big spectacle, *Noah's Ark,* which had a reincarnation theme and took place both in Old Testament times and Europe prior to the First World War.

Shortly thereafter, she withdrew from the screen, and on April 8, 1930, she gave birth to a daughter, christened Dolores Ethel Mae. Warner Bros. had several programme films starring her, which they released in this 1929/30 period, hopeful that she might be induced later to co-star for them with her husband.

John Barrymore, as his second starring talking feature, made a popular old British farce, *The Man from Blankley's.* It was the kind of comedy he had first appeared in with great success for Famous Players, but although it was highly amusing and extremely well acted by its cast, it was a box-office flop in the United States. Regrettably, Barrymore returned to the costume shows his public demanded of him.

On June 4, 1932, Dolores Costello Barrymore gave birth to a son, who was named John II. Hollywood was treated to the spectacle of their onetime bad boy turning into a devoted husband and proud father. Cynics speculated. Those who knew Barrymore's long addiction to alcohol wondered how long he could hold off the return of Mr. Hyde.

Barrymore completed the three films he owed Warner Bros. on his five picture deal — a talkie re-make of *Moby Dick*, with Joan Bennett playing the heroine originally created for and by Dolores Costello; *Svengali,* in which a pretty newcomer, Marian Marsh, played Trilby; and Miss Marsh, who bore a faint resemblance to Dolores Costello, appeared with Barrymore again in *The Mad Genius,* which boasted a ballet background and a thinly disguised Diaghileff-Nijinsky conflict. Unfortunately, the film was only very thin drama.

Between 1932-34 John Barrymore filmed the talking features that mark his best screen performances. It was amazing, because all the while he was making them, he was destroying himself with drink, and he was thereby ruining any happiness he had hoped to find in his third marriage. His co-workers frequently covered up for him; he made friends easily, and every professional or labourer working on a Barrymore picture plainly adored him. Only those very close to Barrymore ever called him "Jack." To most of his co-workers he was "Mr. Barrymore," and once, when an over-friendly one kept calling him "Jack," Barrymore cocked a quizzical brow and said, "Why so formal? Just call me 'kid.'" He never went beyond such a reproof to any member of his crew. His manners, when he was sober, were exemplary. He allowed those of lesser talent their needed bouts of temperament, but he did not indulge himself. At least, in public.

Brilliance glowed from every member of the star-studded cast of M-G-M's 1932 release of *Grand Hotel.* Viewed today, that picture is unlike anything else from the M-G-M lot; it more closely resembles the top product from Ufa in its heyday. John Barrymore, as the elegant Baron reduced to robbing the fading *première* ballerina Grusinskaya played by Garbo, was brilliant, and his love scenes with her still shine. When they finished playing a particular scene together, she, the shy, silent Swede, impulsively grabbed and kissed him, crying, "You have no idea what it means to me to play opposite so perfect an artist!" And she later stated publicly: "I admired him greatly. Barrymore was one of the very few who had that divine madness without which a great artist cannot work or live."

Later that same year, Barrymore went over to RKO to appear under George Cukor's direction in the film that introduced Katharine Hepburn to the cinema, *A Bill of Divorcement.* He played her father, long confined to a mental institution, who regains his sanity and returns to his family just after his wife has divorced him and is about to re-marry. Seen today, only Billie Burke's scenes as the unhappy wife do not hold up. Barrymore's scenes with young Hepburn are electric, and he manages to infuse his characterisation with an extraordinary pity and terror. The subject was close to home. Nobody ever mentioned it in his presence, but his own father, Maurice Barrymore, dissipated his talents and ended his days in a complete escape into a world of fantasy. It was a fearful cloud out of the past from which Barrymore was never free, and that fear is evident in his portrayal in *A Bill of Divorcement.*

In 1933, Barrymore offered three portrayals in rapid succession — two brilliantly comedic and the other intensely dramatic. In RKO's *Topaze,* immaculately directed by Harry d'Arrast, Barrymore gave a highly amusing performance of a shy, eccentric French professor tricked into participating in a huge swindle who manages to turn the tables on the political crooks who would have done him in. He followed this picture with a performance in

M-G-M's *Reunion in Vienna* that was in dazzling contrast, for he played a showy former archduke now reduced to driving a taxi, whose life is centred on spending one more night with his former mistress, now wed to a successful doctor. Barrymore and Diana Wynyard played together in high style, and brought much of the same skilful bantering comedy to the film version that the Lunts had imparted to Robert E. Sherwood's comedy on stage. Finally, in midsummer of 1933, M-G-M released another star-filled production, *Dinner at Eight,* directed by George Cukor, in which Barrymore played Larry Renault, a fading matinee idol, fighting alcoholism and clutching for one more moment of romance. There were moments when Larry Renault's dilemma bordered closely on Barrymore's own, but it remains a sympathetic and stunning performance.

It was in December of 1933 that Universal released William Wyler's production of Elmer Rice's *Counsellor at Law,* in which I must agree with others that Barrymore gave his finest performance in screen drama. It might have been just another attempt at a *Grand Hotel* set in a top attorney's office, but Barrymore made the role of George Simon, Manhattan's most brilliant counsellor at law, multi-dimensional and highly sympathetic. He was aided not only by his director's and writer's assistance but by a perfect supporting cast headed by Bebe Daniels, whose work as Regina Gordon, his secretary, remains her best assay into drama. I am amazed that Universal does not reissue this; it is far superior to any of their current product. which they probably wouldn't want shown up. Even the women's fashions, which date most films, are out of today's dress design magazines.

Counsellor at Law is also significant in any recounting of Barrymore's career because it was when he went back to the studio to film a single day's re-take that he experienced his first serious loss of memory. The scene was shot at night, and was in itself simple. Barrymore was not intoxicated, but he was mentally exhausted, and after fifty-six unsuccessful takes, director Wyler postponed the scene until the following morning when Barrymore reappeared on the sound stage and played the scene through perfectly in one take. He was more exhausted than he had been the previous night, because on returning home from his failure at the studio, he had been summoned to John Gilbert's home nearby to console a monumentally drunk and suicide-minded man.

Barrymore had temporarily proved to himself and others that he himself was not at the end of his tether, but in December 1933 he made a Technicolor test for a long-projected production of "Hamlet." Over and over again he blew the lines from the soliloquy in Act One, Scene Five, which contains the phrase, "Yea, from the table of my memory..." He could not remember anything further, and driven by fears that he too was to be claimed by the illness that had haunted his father, he abandoned all thoughts of making a screen version of "Hamlet." The 492 feet of this Technicolor test, however, repose in the vaults of the Museum of Modern Art in New York.

In the spring of 1934 Columbia released *Twentieth Century,* a comedy containing one of Barrymore's zaniest performances. That he was able to perform at all is due to director Howard Hawks's skill, patience, and sympathetic handling of him and to the challenge his leading lady Carole Lombard presented when she thought at first that he didn't think much of her as an actress. A wonderful professional rapport grew between them.

After that, there is a two years' break in his career on the screen. His marriage to Dolores Costello ended in a bitterly sad separation, and he eventually fled to take refuge in a sanitarium in New York. It was there that he encountered a Hunter College student named Elaine Jacobs, who eventually became his fourth and final wife. He also helped her, re-christened Elaine Barrie, to achieve some success in films and radio as an actress.

In 1936, Barrymore returned to Hollywood to play Mercutio in George Cukor's M-G-M production of *Romeo and Juliet;* his performance has great style and is mockingly picaresque.

It was in 1936 also that Dolores Costello Barrymore returned to films, more beautiful than ever, in David O. Selznick's first for his own company after leaving M-G-M; her portrayal of Dearest (mother to Freddie Bartholomew) in *Little Lord Fauntleroy* revealed her as a mature actress of great charm and warmth. She made several follow-up appearances, but nothing of note until 1942, when she played Isabel Amberson in Orson Welles's production of *The Magnificent Ambersons,* a role she was born to play. It remains poignant and very real, her best screen performance.

Barrymore was driven during the last years of his life by a desperate psychological and financial need to work. Acting was all he knew, as his sister had said of them all when they were young, and he took acting jobs in films and considered himself fortunate to get them, because he could no longer re-member lines and was often forced to resort to an idiot or cue board to get through a scene. Radio was the perfect medium for him during this period because he could read his speeches. He returned to the theatre, however, for a play, "My Dear Children," which was painful to witness when one remem-bered his former brilliance behind the proscenium; it was only a mediocre script, but it attracted audiences and was a better than modest success because of Barrymore's clowning and nightly improvisations, gruelling and vulgar though they were.

There are moments in a few of his last pictures when, in spite of all his handicaps, the old Barrymore skill and charm shine again. This was true in the MacDonald-Eddy operetta *Maytime,* in which he was a romantic and prop-erly villainous menace; in *True Confession,* wherein he again played with Carole Lombard, this time in a role that was a carbon copy of his own existence — a wacky but amiable psychopathic drunk; as King Louis XV, a resplenddnt vignette in Norma Shearer's *Marie Antoinette;* as an ex-college professor who has become a drunken philosopher in Garson Kanin's 1939 sleeper, *The Great Man Votes;* and finally, also in 1939, in the elegant *Midnight,* a star-studded and wonderfully bright comedy.

The flame of his great talent flared, and then became only a lambent flicker as he foolishly jested in public at his own great achievements. On May 19, 1942, during the rehearsal for an NBC radio appearance, he collapsed, and was taken to the Hollywood Presbyterian Hospital, suffering from chronic liver and kidney ailments and a hypostatic pneumonia which had weakened his heart. For ten days he lingered, although months before when he knew his time was short, he had said cryptically, "I'm ready." On the night of May 29, he died.

Lionel Barrymore was at his brother's bedside when death came. Ethel Barrymore was in Boston playing "The Corn Is Green"; bravely she played her matinee and evening performances the following day, a Saturday.

Dolores Costello was herself ill, and did not attend her onetime husband's funeral. After *The Magnificent Ambersons,* Miss Costello only appeared once again on the screen, lending her beauty to a brief role in *This Is the Army* in 1943 for Warner Bros. On December 1, 1939, she had become the wife of Dr. John Vruwink, an eminent child specialist, but after eleven years of marriage they separated and divorced. She lives today apart from the film colony on a farm she owns in San Diego County, and takes no part in a dwindling and faded Hollywood society in which she had once reigned as its greatest beauty. Her daughter by Barrymore has never been interested in an acting career; her son, John Barrymore Jr., started well, but was somehow detoured, and is now more often in the headlines because of his conduct rather than his talent.

At the time of her divorce from her second husband, Dolores Costello spoke to the press lovingly of John Barrymore. "When I think of him," she said, "it is with great compassion... He came to me just before he died, and told me he was sorry."

JOHN BARRYMORE FILMOGRAPHY

AN AMERICAN CITIZEN (1914). Comedy romance; as Beresford Kruger, an American who marries and becomes a British subject in order to inherit a fortune, then falls in love with his English bride. *Dir./Sc:* J. Searle Dawley (from a play by Madeleine Lucette Ryley). *With* Evelyn Moore, Ernest Truex, Wellington A. Playter. *Prod:* Famous Players (Paramount). 4 reels.

THE MAN FROM MEXICO (1914). Farce; as Fitzhew, who has to spend thirty days in jail and tries to make his wife believe he's gone on a business trip to Mexico. *Dir:* Thomas N. Heffron. *Sc:* Eve Unsell (from the comedy by H. A. DuSouchet, adapted from the French of Gondinet and Bisson). *With* Pauline Neff, Harold Lockwood, Wellington A. Playter. *Prod:* Famous Players (Paramount). 5 reels. (Re-made by Paramount, 1926, as *Let's Get Married,* with Richard Dix in the Barrymore role.) (Compare listing in Harold Lockwood filmography.)

ARE YOU A MASON? (1915) Farce; as Frank Perry, an eccentric alcoholic who explains his drunken idiosyncrasies to his wife as part of his Masonic initiation rites. *Dir./Sc:* Thomas N. Heffron (from the German play by Lauf and Kraatz adapted by Leo Ditrichstein as a stage vehicle for him). *With* Helen Freeman, Harold Lockwood, Charles Dixon, Ida Waterman, Alfred Hickman, Charles Butler, Dodson Mitchell, Jean Acker, Lorraine Huling, Kitty Baldwin. (Re-filmed as a British farce and re-leased in the USA, 1934, with Sonnie Hale.) *Prod:* Famous Players (Paramount). 5 reels.

(Compare listing in Harold Lockwood filmography.)

THE DICTATOR (1915). Romantic farce filmed in Cuba; as Brooke Travers, who flees to Central America to avoid being indicted on a false charge, and in Porto Banos poses as the new dictator. *Dir:* Oscar Eagle. *Sc:* (from a play by Richard Harding Davis). *With* Charlotte Ives, Ruby Hoffman, Ivan Simpson, Walter Craven, Mario Majerino. *Prod:* Famous Players (Paramount). 5 reels. (Barrymore had toured in the play with William Collier. In the Paramount re-make, 1922, Wallace Reid played the Barrymore role.)

THE INCORRIGIBLE DUKANE (1915). Romantic comedy; as James Dukane, ne'er-do-well who redeems himself, saves the honour and fortune of his father, and wins the girl he loves. *Dir:* James Durkin. *Sc:* (from a play by George C. Shedd). *With* W. T. Carleton, Helen Weir, Stewart Baird, William MacDonald. *Prod:* Famous Players (Paramount). 4 reels. (He was billed as "The Inimitable John Barrymore.")

NEARLY A KING (1916). Mythical kingdom romance; in a dual role: as both Jack Merriwell and the Prince of Bulwana, whom Merriwell impersonates, falling in love with the Princess of Zonia, the girl the prince is supposed to wed. *Dir:* Frederick Thompson. *Sc:* William H. Clifford. *With* Katherine Harris (Mrs. Barrymore), Russell Bassett. *Prod:* Famous Players (Paramount). 5 reels.

THE LOST BRIDEGROOM (1916). Romantic comedy; as Bertie Joyce who, beaten up whilst coming home from his bachelor party, suffers amnesia and becomes involved with a gang of crooks. *Dir:* James Kirkwood. *Sc:* Williard Mack. *With* Katherine Harris, Ida Darling, Edwin Sturgis, H. Kirkland, Jack Dillon. *Prod:* Famous Players (Paramount). 5 reels.

THE RED WIDOW (1916). Romantic comedy; as Cicero Hannibal Butts, corset salesman, who gets to Russia with another woman whilst he's on his honeymoon. *Dir:* James Durkin. *Sc:* Channing Pollock and Rennold Wolk (from their play). *With* Flora Zabelle, Lillian Tucker, John Hendricks, George E. Mack. *Prod:* Famous Players (Paramount). 4 reels.

RAFFLES, THE AMATEUR CRACKSMAN (1917). Romantic crook melodrama; as Raffles, a gentleman who gallantly steals both jewels and hearts. *Dir:* George Irving. *Sc:* Anthony B. Kelly (from the novel, "The Amateur Cracksman," by E. W. Hornung and the play by Hornung & Eugene W. Presbrey). *With* Frank Morgan, Evelyn Brent, Christine Mayo, Nita Allen, Mathilda Brundage, Frederick Perry, H. Cooper Cliffe, Mike Donlin. *Prod:* Lawrence Weber Photodrama Co. 7 reels. Subsequent film performances of the role of Raffles were enacted by House Peters (Universal-Jewel, 1925); Ronald Colman (Goldwyn, 1930); David Niven (Goldwyn, 1939); Rafael Bertrand (Mexican prod., c 1960, entitled *El Raffles Mexicano*).

ON THE QUIET (1918). Romantic farce; as Robert Ridgway, who is expelled from Yale for general wildness, then falls in love and must prove that he has reformed before he can be wed. *Dir:* Chester Withey. *Sc:* Charles E. Whittaker (from the play by Augustus Thomas. *With* Lois Meredith, J. W. Johnston. *Prod:* Famous Players (Paramount). 5 reels.

DR. JEKYLL AND MR. HYDE (1920). Romantic psychological melodrama; in a dual role: as both the virtuous Dr. Jekyll and the evil Mr. Hyde. *Dir:* John S. Robertson. *Sc:* Clara Beranger (from the story, "The Strange Case of Dr. Jekyll and Mr. Hyde" by Robert Louis Stevenson and the play version created for Richard Mansfield). *With* Martha Mansfield, Brandon Hurst, Charles Lane, J. Malcolm Dunn, Cecil Clovelly, Nita Naldi, George Stevens. *Prod:* Paramount. 7 reels. Other portrayers of this famous dual role have been Sheldon Lewis (also in 1920, for Louis B. Mayer and the Pioneer Film Co.); Fredric March (Paramount, 1932); Spencer Tracy (M-G-M, 1941); Paul Massie (Hammer, 1961), G.B.: *The Two Faces of Dr. Jekyll; US: House of Fright;* Ralph Bates (Hammer, 1971, *Dr. Jekyll and Sister Hyde*).

THE LOTUS EATER (1921). Romantic idyll;

in a dual role: as both Jacques Leroi and his father, each of whom, disillusioned by the world as it is, seeks refuge on an isle in the Pacific, and there at least the son finds happiness and love. *Dir:* Marshall Neilan. *Sc:* Marion Fairfax (from a story by Albert Payson Terhune). *With* Colleen Moore, Anna Q. Nilsson, Ida Waterman, Frank Currier. *Prod:* First National. 7 reels. Filmed on a Florida island.

SHERLOCK HOLMES (AKA, GB, *Moriarty*) (1922). Detective melodrama filmed in London, Switzerland, New York; as Sherlock Holmes, matching his wits with his arch enemy, Moriarty. *Dir:* Albert Parker. *Sc:* Marion Fairfax, Earle Brown (from the play by William Gillette and stories by Sir Arthur Conan Doyle). *With* Roland Young, Carol Dempster, Hedda Hopper, Peggy Bayfield, Gustav von Seyffertitz, Anders Randolph, Robert Schable, William Powell, Reginald Denny, David Torrence, Lumsden Hare, Louis Wolheim. *Prod:* Major Edward J. Bowes for Goldwyn Dist. Co. 9 reels. Many actors have played Sherlock Holmes on the screen, the best known of whom are William Gillette (Essanay, 1916); Clive Brook (Paramount, 1929 and Fox, 1932); Raymond Massey (First Divison, 1931); Arthur Wontner, in England, during the Thirties; Reginald Owen (Fox, 1933); Basil Rathbone (20th Century-Fox, 1939 and Universal, twelve films between 1942-46); Peter Cushing (Hammer, 1959); Robert Stephens (United Artists, 1970).

BEAU BRUMMEL (1924). Costume drama; as George Bryan Brummel, dandy, showing his rise and fall, his hopeless love and death in exile. *Dir:* Harry Beaumont. *Sc:* Dorothy Farnum (from the play by Clyde Fitch). *With* Mary Astor, Willard Louis, Irene Rich, Alec B. Francis, Carmel Myers, Richard Tucker, André Beranger. *Prod:* Warner Bros. 10 reels. Stewart Granger played Brummel in the M-G-M 1954 re-make with Elizabeth Taylor. Vitagraph released a version in 1913 with James Young, who also wrote and directed, in the lead, co-starring with his wife, Clara Kimball Young.

THE SEA BEAST (1926). Period sea drama; as Captain Ahab Ceeley, who fights a lifelong battle with his bitterest enemy, the white whale known as Moby Dick. *Dir:* Millard Webb. *Sc:* Bess Meredyth (from the novel, "Moby Dick," by Herman Melville). *With* Dolores Costello, George O'Hara, Sam Baker, Sojin, Mathilde Comont, Mike Donlin. Warner Bros. 10 reels. Barrymore played Captain Ahab again in Warner Bros. talkie 1930 version, *Moby Dick.* Gregory Peck played the role in 1956. (Compare listing in Dolores Costello filmography.)

DON JUAN (1926). Costume romance; dual role: as both the elder Don Juan and his daredevil son who gets involved in every kind of escapade in the court of the Borgias. *Dir:*

Alan Crosland. *Sc:* Bess Meredyth (from the narrative poem by Lord Byron). *With* Mary Astor, Warner Oland, Estelle Taylor, Willard Louis , Montagu Love, Helene Costello, Jane Winton, Myrna Loy, John Roche, June Marlowe, Phyllis Haver, Nigel de Brulier, Hedda Hopper, Philippe De Lacy. *Prod:* Warner Bros. 10 reels. Sound effects and orchestral score. This is the only film version of this Don Juan story. Many impersonations of Don Juan have been seen on the screen, including those of Douglas Fairbanks and Errol Flynn.

WHEN A MAN LOVES (AKA, GB, *His Lady*). (1927). Costume romance; as the Chevalier des Grieux, in love with Manon Lescaut. *Dir:* Alan Crosland. *Sc:* Bess Meredyth (from the novel, "Manon Lescaut," by the Abbé Prevost). *With* Dolores Costello, Sam De Grasse, Holmes Herbert, Warner Oland, Charles Clary, Eugenie Besserer, Rose Dione, Stuart Holmes, Bertram Grassby, Thomas Santschi. *Prod:* Warner Bros. 10 reels. Sound effects and orchestral score. Other actors playing the Chevalier des Grieux role include Wladimir Gaidarow (German, Ufa, 1926); Vittorio De Sica (Italian, 1941); Michel Auclair (French, 1950); Sami Frey (French, 1968.) (Compare listing in Dolores Costello filmography.)

TEMPEST (1928). Romance of the Russian Revolution; as Sgt. Ivan Markov, a peasant who rises in the ranks of the Tsar's army and attracts the scorn and then the love of a princess. *Dir:* Sam Taylor. *Sc:* C. Gardner Sullivan (from a story by Erich von Stroheim). *With* Camilla Horn, Louis Wolheim, George Fawcett, Ulrich Haupt, Michael Visaroff. *Prod:* United Artists. 10 reels. Musical score by Dr. Hugo Riesenfeld.

THE BELOVED ROGUE (1928). Romance of Paris at the time of Louis XI; as Francois Villon, poet and daredevil rogue. *Dir:* Alan Crosland. *Sc:* Paul Bern. *With* Conrad Veidt, Marceline Day, W. Lawson Butt, Henry Victor, Slim Summerville, Mack Swain, Nigel de Brulier, Jane Winton, Lucy Beaumont, Otto Matiesen, Rose Dione, Bertram Grassby. *Prod:* United Artists. 10 reels. Sound and orchestral score. Other film Villons include William Farnum (Fox, 1920, *If I Were King*); Dennis King (Paramount, 1930, *The Vagabond King*); Ronald Colman (Paramount, 1938, *If I Were King*); Oreste (Paramount, 1956, *The Vagabond King*.)

ETERNAL LOVE)1929). Costume romance in the Tyrolean Alps during the Franco-Austrian War of 1812; as Marcus Poltram, who is separated from the girl he loves, but they meet in death during an avalanche. *Dir:* Ernst Lubitsch. *Sc:* Hans Kraly (from the story, "Der König der Bernina," by J. C. Heer). With Camilla Horn, Victor Varconi, Hobart Bosworth, Bodil Rosing, Mona Rico, Evelyn

Selbie. *Prod:* United Artists. 9 reels. Musical synchronisation and score by Dr. Hugo Riesenfeld.

THE SHOW OF SHOWS (1929). Variety revue; as the Duke of Gloucester, later Richard III, in the soliloquy from Shakespeare's "Henry VI, Part 3." *Dir:* John Adolfi. *With* E. J. Radcliffe and Anthony Bushell. Barrymore also introduced his own number. *Prod:* Warner Bros. 124m (entire film). Mostly in colour. Barrymore's *début* in talking films. Laurence Olivier played Richard III in the English-made 1956 Shakespearean tragedy of that name.

GENERAL CRACK (1929). Costume drama; in a dual role: as both the Duke of Kurland and Prince Christian, known as "General Crack," who becomes involved in the Emperor of Austria's struggle to possess the crown of the Holy Roman Empire. *Dir:* Alan Crosland. *Sc:* J. Grubb Alexander, adapted by Walter Anthony (from the novel by George Preedy). *With* Lowell Sherman, Marian Nixon, Armida, Hobart Bosworth, Jacqueline Logan, Otto Matiesen, Andre De Segurola, Philippe De Lacy, Douglas Gerrard, Julanne Johnston, *Prod:* Warner Bros. 10 reels. Barrymore's first full-length feature talking role.

THE MAN FROM BLANKLEY'S (1930). Period farce; as Lord Strathpeffer, gentleman inebriate. *Dir:* Alfred E. Green. *Sc:* Harvey Thew, Joseph Jackson (from the play by E. Anstey). *With* Loretta Young, William Austin, Albert Gran, Emily Fitzroy, Dick Henderson, Edgar Norton, Dale Fuller, Louise Carver, *Prod:* Warner Bros. 8 reels. Robert Warwick had played Barrymore's role in a 1920 Paramount version, *The Fourteenth Man*. Re-made, 1934, as *Guest of Honor*, with Henry Kendall in the Barrymore role.

MOBY DICK (1930). Period sea drama; as Captain Ahab. *Dir:* Lloyd Bacon. *Sc:* J. Grubb Alexander (from the novel by Herman Melville). *With* Joan Bennett, Lloyd Hughes, May Boley, Walter Long, Tom O'Brien, Nigel de Brulier, Noble Johnson, William Walling, Virginia Sale, Jack Curtis, John Ince, *Prod:* Warner Bros. 7 reels. (Compare listing in Barrymore filmography on *The Sea Beast*, 1926.)

SVENGALI (1931). Romantic drama; as Svengali, who hypnotises the unmusical model Trilby into becoming a great opera star. *Dir:* Archie Mayo. *Sc:* J. Grubb Alexander (from the novel, *Trilby*, by George Du Maurier). *With* Marian Marsh, Bramwell Fletcher, Donald Crisp, Lumsden Hare, Carmel Myers, Luis Alberni, Ferike Boros, Adrienne d'Ambricourt, Yola d'Avril, Paul Porcasi. *Prod:* Warner Bros. 9 reels. Other actors who have played Svengali include Wilton Lackaye to Clara Kimball Young's Trilby (World, 1915); Arthur Edmund Carewe to Andrée

Lafayette's Trilby (First National, 1923); Donald Wolfit to Hildegarde Neff's Trilby (Renown, 1955—British.)

THE MAD GENIUS (1931). Romantic drama of the ballet; as Tsarakov, a ballet master who teaches a boy to become a leading dancer and then goes insane with jealousy when he cannot possess him completely. *Dir:* Michael Curtiz. *Sc:* J. Grubb Alexander and Harvey Thew (from the play "The Idol," by Martin Brown). *With* Donald Cook, Marian Marsh, Carmel Myers, Charles Butterworth, Luis Alberni, Boris Karloff, Frankie Darro. *Prod:* Warner Bros. 8 reels.

ARSENE LUPIN (1932). Detective-crook melodrama; as the Duke of Chermerace, known to the police as "Arsene Lupin," who outwits France's greatest detective (played by Lionel Barrymore) and steals the Mona Lisa from the Louvre. *Dir:* Jack Conway. *Sc:* Carey Wilson, with dialogue by Bayard Veiller and Lenore Coffee (from the French play and novel, "Arsene Lupin, Super-Sleuth" by Maurice LeBlanc and Francis de Croisset). *With* Lionel Barrymore, Karen Morley, John Miljan, Tully Marshall, Henry Armetta. *Prod:* M-G-M. 64m. In *Arsene Lupin Returns* M-G-M, 1938) Lupin was taken over by Melvyn Douglas; in *Enter Arsene Lupin* (Universal, 1944) Lupin was played by Charles Korvin; In Vitagraph's 1917 *Arsene Lupin*, Earle Williams was the star, while Robert Lamoureux had the title role in the French film, *Les Aventures de Arsène Lupin* (1956).

GRAND HOTEL (1932). Character melodrama; as the Baron who has fallen upon bad times and is forced to steal from a fading ballerina, with whom he falls in love. *Dir:* Edmund Goulding. *Sc:* Vicki Baum (her novel and play, with American version of her play by William A. Drake). (Goulding always averred the screenplay, uncredited, was actually written by Frances Marion.) *With* Greta Garbo, Lionel Barrymore, Joan Crawford. Wallace Beery, Lewis Stone, Jean Hersholt, Robert McWade, Rafaela Ottiano. *Prod:* M-G-M. 112m. In 1945 M-G-M released *Weekend at the Waldorf*, an Americanised, updated version of *Grand Hotel*, with Walter Pidgeon as a weary war correspondent, a role supposedly approximating Barrymore's Baron, and with Ginger Rogers as a very tired actress. In 1961 a German version of *Grand Hotel* appeared in Europe under the title, *Menschen im Hotel*, with O. W. Fischer in the Barrymore role, and Michèle Morgan playing the Garbo ballerina. (Compare listing in Garbo filmography.)

STATE'S ATTORNEY (AKA, GB, *Cardigan's Last Case*) (1932). Courtroom drama; as Tom Cardigan, wealthy criminal lawyer, who falls in love with a girl he has had acquitted. *Dir:* George Archainbaud. *Sc:* Gene Fowler and Rowland Brown (from a story by

Louis Stevens). With Helen Twelvetrees, William (Stage) Boyd, Jill Esmond, Mary Duncan, Oscar Apfel, Raoul Roulien, Ralph Ince, Leon Waycoff (Ames). *Prod:* RKO Radio 79m. Re-made by RKO, 1937, as *Criminal Lawyer*, with Lee Tracy in the Barrymore role.

A BILL OF DIVORCEMENT (1932). Domestic problem drama; as Hilary, who returns home cured after years of insanity, only to find that his wife has divorced him and is about to re-marry. *Dir:* George Cukor. *Sc:* Howard Estabrook, Harry Wagstaff Gribble (from a play by Clemence Dane). With Katharine Hepburn (her film *début*), Billie Burke, David Manners, Bramwell Fletcher, Henry Stephenson, Paul Cavanagh, Elizabeth Patterson. *Prod:* RKO Radio 75m. Malcolm Keen had played Barrymore's role in the British 1922 version with Constance Binney: Adolphe Menjou played the part in an RKO Radio 1940 re-make with Maureen O'Hara.

RASPUTIN AND THE EMPRESS (AKA, GB, *Rasputin, the Mad Monk*) (1932). Historical drama; as Prince Chegodieff, who murders the mad monk called Rasputin, *Dir:* Richard Boleslavsky. *Sc:* Charles MacArthur (story by Ben Hecht). *With* Ethel Barrymore, Lionel Barrymore, Diana Wynyard, Ralph Morgan, C. Henry Gordon, Edward Arnold. *Prod:* M-G-M 133m. There have been many filmings of the Rasputin story (from the Peerless-World version, 1917, called *Rasputin, the Black Monk* to the British 1966 release, *Rasputin, the Mad Monk*), but none of them boldly used the Barrymore and Wynyard characters, for which M-G-M has since been sued, and lost the case.

TOPAZE (1933). High character comedy; as Topaze, an eccentric French professor who outwits crooks. *Dir:* Harry d'Abbadie d'Arrast. *Sc:* Benn W. Levy (from the play by Marcel Pagnol). *With* Myrna Loy, Albert Conti, Luis Alberni, Reginald Mason, Jobyna Howland, Jackie Searle, Frank Reicher. *Prod:* RKO Radio. 80m. Three French actors have played Topaze in films: Louis Jouvet (1935); Arnaudy (1936); Fernandel (1952). Peter Sellers played the role and directed *Mr. Topaze* (1961) in a British version. (US: *I Love Money.*)

REUNION IN VIENNA (1933). High romantic comedy; as Rudolf, once an archduke, now a Viennese taxi-driver, who aspires to spend one more night with his ex-mistress, now the wife of a prominent doctor. *Dir:* Sidney Franklin. *Sc:* Ernest Vajda and Claudine West (from the play by Robert E. Sherwood). *With* Diana Wynyard, Frank Morgan, Henry Travers, May Robson, Eduardo Ciannelli, Una Merkel, Bodil Rosing, *Prod:* M-G-M. 97m.

DINNER AT EIGHT (1933). Character comedy drama; as Larry Renault, former matinee idol, who has become an alcoholic, but makes one final effort to find success and true romance. *Dir:* George Cukor. *Sc:* Frances Marion and Herman J. Mankiewicz (additional dialogue: Donald Ogden Stewart) (from the play by George S. Kaufman and Edna Ferber). *With* Lionel Barrymore, Billie Burke, Marie Dressler, Jean Harlow, Wallace Beery, Lee Tracy, Edmund Lowe, Madge Evans, Phillips Holmes, Jean Hersholt, Karen Morley, Louise Closser Hale, May Robson, *Prod:* M-G-M. 110m.

NIGHT FLIGHT (1933). Aviation drama; as Riviene, the ruthless managing director of the Trans-Andean Mail Service who cares only for the success of his company. *Dir:* Clarence Brown. *Sc:* Oliver H.P. Garrett (the 1931 Prix Femina novel by Antoine de Saint-Exupéry). *With* Lionel Barrymore, Clark Gable, Helen Hayes, Robert Montgomery, Myrna Loy, William Gargan, C. Henry Gordon, Leslie Fenton, Harry Beresford, Frank Conroy, Ralf Harolde. *Prod:* M-G-M. 89m.

COUNSELLOR AT LAW (1933). Behind the scenes courtroom drama; as George Simon, top Manhattan criminal lawyer. *Dir:* William Wyler. *Sc:* Elmer Rice (from his own play). *With* Bebe Daniels, Onslow Stevens, Doris Kenyon, Melvyn Douglas, Isabel Jewell, Thelma Todd, John Qualen, Clara Langner. *Prod:* Universal. 78m.

LONG LOST FATHER (1934) Father-daughter drama; as Carl Bellairs, manager of a stylish London restaurant, who saves his daughter from a charge of theft. *Dir:* Ernest B. Schoedsack. *Sc:* Dwight Taylor (from a novel by G. B. Stern). *With* Helen Chandler, Donald Cook, Alan Mowbray, Claude King, Reginald Sharland, Ferdinand Gottschalk, Phyllis Barry, Tempe Piggot. *Prod:* RKO Radio. 63m.

TWENTIETH CENTURY (1934). Riotous farce comedy aboard a fast deluxe train between Chicago and New York; as Oscar Jaffe, producer, who has to get his now famous star's signature on a contract before the Limited reaches its destination. *Dir:* Howard Hawks. *Sc:* Charles MacArthur and Ben Hecht (from their play). *With* Carole Lombard, Walter Connolly, Roscoe Karns, Charles Levison, Etienne Girardot, Dale Fuller, Ralph Forbes, Edgar Kennedy, Ed Gargan, Snowflake, Herman Bing. *Prod:* Columbia. 84m.

ROMEO AND JULIET (1936). Classic romantic tragedy; as Mercutio, whose death provokes the tragedy that takes the lives of the lovers. *Dir:* George Cukor. *Sc:* Talbot Jennings (from the tragedy by William Shakespeare). *With* Norma Shearer, Leslie Howard, Edna May Oliver, Basil Rathbone, C. Aubrey Smith, Andy Devine, Ralph Forbes, Reginald Denny, Maurice Murphy, Conway Tearle, Henry Kolker, Robert Warwick, Virginia

Hammond, Violet Kemble-Cooper. *Prod:* M-G-M. 126m. In the 1968 Zeffirelli production, John McEnery was Mercutio; others have included Aldo Zollo (Rank, 1954); David Blair danced it in a 1966 release, with Fonteyn and Nureyev; Carlos Estranda played the role in a 1968 Italo-Spanish version.

MAYTIME (1937). Romantic operetta; as Nicolai, the heroine's protector and mentor who, obsessed by jealousy, kills her lover. *Dir:* Robert Z. Leonard. *Sc:* Noel Langley (from the play by Rida Johnson Young, with music by Sigmund Romberg and additional music by Herbert Stothart). *With* Jeanette MacDonald, Nelson Eddy, Tom Brown, Lynn Carver, Herman Bing, Rafaela Ottiano, Charles Judels, Paul Porcasi, Sig Rumann, Walter Kingsford, Edgar Norton, Guy Bates Post. *Prod:* M-G-M. 132M. In a 1923 Preferred release of a silent version, there was no character of Nicolai; the nearest to it is a villain known as Monte, played by Robert McKim. (Compare listing in Jeanette MacDonald filmography.)

BULLDOG DRUMMOND COMES BACK (1937). Detective melodrama; as Colonel Nielson, of Scotland Yard, who in a series of disguises aids his friend Capt. Hugh "Bulldog" Drummond in thwarting a kidnap for revenge case. *Dir:* Louis King. *Sc:* Edward T. Lowe (from the novel, "Female of the Species," by H. C. (Sapper) McNeile). *With* John Howard, Louise Campbell, Reginald Denny, E. E. Clive Frank Puglia, Nydia Westman, Lucien Littlefield, John Sutton. *Prod:* Paramount. 6 reels.

NIGHT CLUB SCANDAL (1937). Murder melodrama; as Dr. Ernest Tindal, who murders his faithless wife, then carefully sets the stage to point suspicion toward another man as well as to provide an alibi for himself. *Dir:* Ralph Murphy. *Sc:* Lillie Hayward (from the play, "Riddle Me This," by Daniel N. Rubin). *With* Lynne Overman, Charles Bickford, Louise Campbell, Elizabeth Patterson, Harvey Stephens, J. Carrol Naish, Evelyn Brent, Cecil Cunningham. *Prod:* Paramount. 72m. Working title: *City Hall Scandal.* Previously made by Paramount, 1932, as *Guilty as Hell,* with Henry Stephenson in the Barrymore role.

TRUE CONFESSION (1937). Comedy; as Charley, an amiable psychopathic drunk. *Dir:* Wesley Ruggles. *Sc:* Claude Binyon (from a French play, "Mon Crime," by Louis Verneuil and Georges Berr). *With* Carole Lombard, Fred MacMurray, Una Merkel, Porter Hall, Edgar Kennedy, Richard Carle, John T. Murray, Lynne Overman, Fritz Feld, Hattie McDaniel. *Prod:* Paramount. 85 m. Re-made by Paramount, 1947, as *Cross My Heart,* with Michael Chekhov in the Barrymore role.

BULLDOG DRUMMOND'S REVENGE (1938). Detective melodrama; as Colonel Nielson, who joins forces with Bulldog Drummond to chase munition plans thieves to Paris. *Dir:* Louis King. *Sc:* Edward T. Lowe (from the novel, "The Return of Bulldog Drummond," by H. C. (Sapper) McNeile). *With* John Howard, Louise Campbell, Nydia Westman, Lucien Littlefield, John Sutton, Ethel Clayton, *Prod:* Paramount. 55m. Working title: *Bulldog Drummond's Nephew.*

ROMANCE IN THE DARK (1938). Musical romance; as Jason, impresario of a Budapest theatre who steals his favourite singer's girl friends. *Dir:* H. C. Potter. *Sc:* Frank Partos and Anne Morrison Chapin (from the play, "The Yellow Nightingale," by Hermann Bahr). *With* Gladys Swarthout, John Boles, Claire Dodd, Fritz Feld, Curt Bois. *Prod:* Paramount. 77m.

BULLDOG DRUMMOND'S PERIL (1938). Detective melodrama; as Colonel Nielson, Scotland Yard operative, who helps Bulldog Drummond uncover the criminals who have stolen a secret formula for making synthetic gems. *Dir:* James Hogan. *Sc:* Stuart Palmer (from the novel, "The Third Round," by H. C. (Sapper) McNeile). *With* John Howard, Louise Campbell, E. E. Clive, Porter Hall, Elizabeth Patterson, Nydia Westman, Halliwell Hobbes, Zeffie Tilbury, David Clyde, Clyde Cook, John Sutton. *Prod:* Paramount. 66m. This marked the third and final time Barrymore played Colonel Nielson to John Howard's Bulldog Drummond. There have been many filmings of the adventures of Bulldog Drummond: Colonel (sometimes known as "Inspector") Nielson was played by Sir Guy Standing to Ray Milland's Drummond in *Bulldog Drummond Escapes* (Paramount, 1936); by H. B. Warner to John Howard's Drummond in *Bulldog Drummond in Africa, Bulldog Drummond's Bride,* and *Bulldog Drummond's Secret Police* (Paramount, 1938 and 1939). In the UA-20th Century production, 1934, *Bulldog Drummond Strikes Back,* C. Aubrey Smith was Colonel Nielsen to Ronald Colman's Drummond.

MARIE ANTOINETTE (1938). Historical drama; as Louis XV of France, grandfather of the unfortunate Louis XVI, husband to Marie Antoinette. *Dir:* W. S. Van Dyke. *Sc:* Claudine West, Donald Ogden Stewart, Ernest Vajda (from the biography by Stefan Zweig). *With* Norma Shearer, Tyrone Power, Robert Morley, Anita Louise, Joseph Schildkraut, Gladys George, Henry Stephenson, Cora Witherspoon, Barnett Parker, Reginald Gardiner, Henry Daniell, Albert van Dekker, Alma Kruger, Joseph Calleia. *Prod:* M-G-M. 160m. Louis XV has often been enacted in films, but never with the elegant sardonicism Barrymore gave the role. William Farnum played Louis XV in *DuBarry, Woman of Passion* (UA, 1930); Emil Jannings had played the role in *Passion* (Ufa-First National, 1920; Reginald

Owen was Louis XV in *Madame DuBarry* (Warner Bros., 1934); Stuart Holmes had played King Louis in Barrymore's own film, *When a Man Loves* (Warner Bros., 1927).

SPAWN OF THE NORTH (1938). Melodrama adventure set in Alaska; as "Windy" Turlon, a small town editor, who likes his booze and provides the comedy in this battle between licensed fisherman and pirates who steal the salmon catches. *Dir:* Henry Hathaway. *Sc:* Jules Furthman, Talbot Jennings (from a story by Barrett Willoughby). *With* George Raft, Henry Fonda, Dorothy Lamour, Louise Platt, Akim Tamiroff, Lynne Overman, Fuzzy Knight, Vladimir Sokoloff, Duncan Renaldo. *Prod:* Paramount. 105m. Re-made as *Alaska Seas,* but without the Barrymore character.

HOLD THAT CO-ED (AKA, GB, *Hold That Girl*) (1938). College musical comedy; as the slightly screwy Governor who wins a senatorial election by building a worn-out college into a winning one. *Dir:* George Marshall. *Sc:* Karl Tunberg, Don Ettlinger, Jack Yellen (from an original story by Tunberg and Ettlinger). *with* George Murphy, Marjorie Weaver, Joan Davis, Jack Haley, George Barbier, Ruth Terry, Donald Meek, Johnny Downs, Paul Hurst, Guinn Williams. *Prod:* 20th Century-Fox. 80m.

THE GREAT MAN VOTES (1939). Political comedy; as Vance, a drunken ex-college professor who finds himself in the unique position of being able to swing an election. *Dir:* Garson Kanin. *Sc:* John Twist (from a story by Gordon Malherbe Hillman). *With* Peter Holden, Virginia Weidler, Katherine Alexander, Donald MacBride, Bennie Bartlett, Brandon Tynan, Elisabeth Risdon, Granville Bates, Luis Alberni, J. M. Kerrigan, William Demarest. *Prod:* RKO Radio.70m.

MIDNIGHT (1939). Sophisticated comedy; as George Flammarion, who hires Claudette Colbert, posing as a countess, to distract his wife's lover. *Dir:* Mitchell Leisen. *Sc:* Charles Brackett, Billy Wilder (from a story by Edwin Justus Mayer and Franz Schulz). *With* Claudette Colbert, Don Ameche, Francis Lederer, Mary Astor, Elaine Barrie, Hedda Hopper, Rex O'Malley, Monty Woolley, Armand Kaliz. *Prod:* Paramount. 92m. Re-made by Paramount, 1945, with Patric Knowles in the Barrymore role, *Masquerade in Mexico.*

THE GREAT PROFILE (1940). Farce comedy; as Garrick, a theatrical producer whose adventures approximate those of Barrymore when he was hitting the headlines during the tour of "My Dear Children." *Dir:* Walter Lang. *Sc:* Milton Sperling, Hilary Lynn. *With* Mary Beth Hughes, Gregory Ratoff, John Payne, Anne Baxter, Lionel Atwill, Edward Brophy, Willie Fung. *Prod:* 20th Century-Fox. 79m.

THE INVISIBLE WOMAN (1941). Trick adventure; as Professor Bibbs, a crafty old scientist capable of making people invisible. *Dir:* Edward Sutherland. *Sc:* Robert Lees, Fred Rinaldo, Gertrude Purcell (from a story by Joe May and Kurt Siodmak). *With* Virginia Bruce, John Howard, Charles Ruggles, Oscar Homolka, Donald MacBride, Edward Brophy, Shemp Howard, Margaret Hamilton, Anne Nagel, Kathryn Adams, Maria Montez, Kay Leslie. *Prod:* Universal. 70m.

WORLD PREMIERE (1941). Comedy; as Duncan DeGrasse, a producer who goes to Washington, D.C. on a junket to premiere his newest film. *Dir:* Ted Tetzlaff. *Sc:* Earl Felton, (from a story by Felton and Gordon Kahn). *With* Frances Farmer, Eugene Pallette, Virginia Dale, Ricardo Cortez, Sig Rumann, Don Castle, William Wright, Fritz Feld, Cliff Nazarrio. *Prod:* Paramount. 71m.

PLAYMATES (1941). Musical comedy; as himself, a onetime Shakespearean actor who is hired to coach Kay Kyser for an appearance in a Shakespearean festival. *Dir:* David Butler. *Sc:* James V. Kern, with added dialogue by Artie Phillips (from a story by Kern, David Butler, M. M. Musselman). *With* Kay Kyser, Lupe Velez, Ginny Simms, May Robson, Patsy Kelly, Peter Lind Hayes, George Cleveland, Alice Fleming. *Prod:* RKO Radio. 96m.

DOLORES COSTELLO FILMOGRAPHY

Dolores Costello began her film career as a child actress with her sister Helen (or Helene, as she became) at the Eastern Vitagraph Studios. Whenever there was a child's role in a Maurice Costello picture, one of the Costello girls played it, usually Helene who, being older but more diminutive, acted more frequently. On December 13, 1912, a contingent known as the Vitagraph Globe Trotters sailed from San Francisco on a round-the-world cruise aboard the "Tanyo Maru." They were to be gone until the following summer, and they were to make a series of films en route and at selected stop-over ports. Mr. and Mrs. Maurice Costello and their daughters, Dolores and Helene, were members of the troupe, as were James Young and his beautiful wife Clara Kimball Young. When the company returned to New York, there were a few more acting roles at Vitagraph for the Costello sisters, but Mrs. Costello then wisely withdrew them to place them in separate private schools. The appearances in Vitagraph films by the Costello girls were almost never publicised, but film reviewers of the time noted them: the reviewer for "Dramatic Mirror," in reviewing *Wanted, a Grandmother*, in which Maurice Costello co-starred with Florence Turner, observed that the film also presented "the pleasing and bewitching little Dolores." Those Vitagraph features known to include Dolores Costello in an important role are as follows:

THE MEETING OF THE WAYS (1911)
HIS SISTER'S CHILDREN (1911)
A JUVENILE LOVE AFFAIR (1912)
WANTED, A GRANDMOTHER (1912)
VULTURES AND DOVES (1912)
IDA'S CHRISTMAS (1912)
A REFORMED SANTA CLAUS (1912)
THE HINDOO CHARM (1913)
SOME STEAMER SCOOPING (1914)
ETTA OF THE FOOTLIGHTS (1914)
THE EVIL MEN DO (1914)
TOO MUCH BURGLAR (1914)

THE GLIMPSES OF THE MOON (1923). Romantic society drama; in an uncredited supporting role. *Dir:* Allan Dwan. *Sc:* E. Lloyd Sheldon, Edfrid Bingham (from the novel by Edith Wharton). *With* Bebe Daniels, Nita Naldi, David Powell, Maurice Costello, Rubye de Remer, Charles Gerard, William Quirk, Pearl Sindelar. *Prod:* Paramount. 7 reels. Exteriors filmed in Florida. (Compare listing in Bebe Daniels filmography.)

LAWFUL LARCENY (1923). Domestic melodrama of gambling and deception; as Nora, a maid. *Dir:* Allan Dwan. *Sc:* John Lynch. (from the play by Samuel Shipman). With Hope Hampton, Conrad Nagel, Nita Naldi, Lew Cody, Russell Griffin, Yvonne Hughes, Gilda Gray, Florence O'Denishawn, Alice Maison. *Prod:* Paramount. 6 reels. Refilmed as a talkie, RKO, 1930, *Dir:* Lowell Sherman and starring Bebe Daniels with Sherman.

GREATER THAN A CROWN (1925). Romantic melodrama of royal intrigue; as Isabel Francis, who is really the Princess of Lividia, a mythical kingdom. *Dir:* R. William Neill. *Sc:* Wyndham Gittens (from the novel, "The Lady from Longacre," by Victor Bridges). *With* Edmund Lowe, Margaret Livingston, Ben Hendricks, Paul Panzer, Anthony Merlo, Robert Klein. *Prod:* Fox. 5 reels. Filmed by Fox, 1922, as *The Lady from Longacre*, starring Mary Thurman.

BOBBED HAIR (1925). Comedy melodrama of the flapper era; in an uncredited supporting role. *Dir:* Alan Crosland. *Sc:* Lewis Milestone (from a book by Alexander Woollcott, Louis Bromfield, and others). *With* Marie Prevost, Kenneth Harlan, Louise Fazenda, John Roche, Emily Fitzroy, Reed Howes, Pat Hartigan, Walter Long, Francis McDonald, Tom Ricketts, Otto Hoffman, Kate Toncray. *Prod:* Warner Bros. 6 reels.

THE SEA BEAST (1926). Period sea drama; as Esther Wiscasset. (See preceding Barrymore filmography for full details.)

MANNEQUIN (1926). Manhattan melodrama; as Joan Herrick, mannequin, accused of murder, and brought into her own father's court. *Dir:* James Cruze. *Sc:* Frances Agnew; adapted by Walter Woods (from Fannie Hurst's "Liberty Magazine" story). *With* Alice Joyce, Warner Baxter, ZaSu Pitts, Walter Pidgeon. *Prod:* Paramount. 6981 ft.

BRIDE OF THE STORM (1926) Seacoast melodrama; as Faith Fitzhugh, an orphan raised by three generations of Vrooms in a lighthouse, who attracts a young ensign. *Dir:* J. Stuart Blackton. *Sc:* Marion Constance (Blackton) (from a story, "Maryland, My Maryland," by James Francis Dwyer). *With* John Harron, Otto Matiesen, Sheldon Lewis, Tyrone Power Sr., Julia Swayne Gordon. *Prod:* Warner Bros. 70m.

THE LITTLE IRISH GIRL (1926). Crook melodrama; as Dot Walker, a come-on girl for a gang. *Dir:* Roy Del Ruth. *Sc:* Darryl Francis Zanuck (from the story, "The Grifters," by G. D. Lancaster). With John Harron, Matthew Betz, Lee Moran, Gertrude Claire, Henry Barrows, Dot Farley, Joseph Dowling. *Prod:* Warner Bros. 67m.

THE THIRD DEGREE (1927). Romantic melodrama; as Annie Daly, carnival star, who marries a rich young man and gets involved in a murder. *Dir:* Michael Curtiz. *Sc:* C. Graham Baker (from the play by Charles Klein). *With* Louise Dresser, Rockcliffe Fellowes, Jason Robards, Kate Price, Tom Santschi, David Torrence, Myrna Loy. *Prod:* Warner Bros. 80m. Alice Joyce had appeared in the Costello role in a 1919 Vitagraph production as had Ethel Clayton for Lubin, 1913.

WHEN A MAN LOVES (AKA, GB, *His Lady*) (1927). Costume romance; as Manon Lescaut, torn between her love of luxury and for the Chevalier des Grieux. (See listing in John Barrymore filmography for full details.) Other famous film Manons have been Lya de Putti (German, Ufa, 1926); Alida Valli (Italian, 1941); Cecile Aubrey (French, 1950); Catherine Deneuve (French, 1968).

A MILLION BID (1927). Romantic melodrama; as Dorothy Gordon, put on the marriage auction block by her money-mad mother. *Dir:* Michael Curtiz. *Sc:* Robert Dillon (story by George Cameron, from Mrs. Sidney Drew's play, "Agnes"). *With* Warner Oland, Malcolm McGregor, Betty Blythe, William Demarest, Douglas Gerrard, *Prod:* Warner Bros. 7 reels. Anita Stewart had created the Costello role (then named Agnes Belgradin) for Vitagraph, 1913. (See listing in Anita Stewart filmography.)

OLD SAN FRANCISCO (1927). Period melodrama; as Dolores Vasquez, daughter of an old Spanish California family, loved by an Irishman, desired by a Chinese, saved by the 1906 earthquake and fire. *Dir:* Alan Crosland. *Sc:* Anthony Coldeway (from a story by Darryl Francis Zanuck). *With* Charles Emmett Mack, Warner Oland, Josef Swickard, John Miljan, William Demarest, Anders Randolph, Sojin, Anna May Wong, Rose Dione, W. Lawson Butt, Otto Matiesen, Walter McGrail, Martha Mattox, Tom Santschi. *Prod:* Warner Bros. 9 reels.

THE HEART OF MARYLAND (1927). Period romance; as Maryland Calvert, proud Confederate heroine who loves a Union soldier and saves his life by swinging on the clapper of the bell that would summon guards to apprehend him. *Dir:* Lloyd Bacon. *Sc:* C. Graham Baker (from the play by David Belasco). *With* Jason Robards, Carroll Nye, Charles Edward Bull, Erville Alderson, Warner Richmond, Myrna Loy, Francis Ford. *Prod:* Warner Bros. 6 reels. Mrs. Leslie Carter had played Maryland for Metro, 1915, recreating her original stage role; and Catherine Calvert had played it for Vitagraph, 1921.

THE COLLEGE WIDOW (1927). Romantic college comedy; as Jane Witherspoon, college president's daughter, who recruits a prize football team, each player thinking he is her chosen favourite. *Dir:* Archie L. Mayo. *Sc:* Paul Schofield and Peter Milne (from a play by George Ade.) *With* William Collier Jr., Anders Randolph, Charles Hill Mailes, Douglas Gerrard, Sumner Getchell, Guinn "Big Boy" Williams. *Prod:* Warner Bros. 67m. Ethel Clayton had played the Costello role in 1915 for Lubin; in 1936 Patrica Ellis played it in the re-titled version, *Freshman Love.*

TENDERLOIN (1928). Crook melodrama; as Rose Shannon, cabaret dancer, who falls in love with a crook trying to go straight and is implicated with him in a big bank robbery. *Dir:* Michael Curtiz. *Sc:* E. T. Lowe, Jr. (from the story by Melville Crosman) dialogue by Lowe and Joseph Jackson, the latter also titlewriter). *With* Conrad Nagel, Mitchell Lewis, Georgie Stone, Dan Wolheim, Pat Hartigan, Fred Kelsey, G. Raymond Nye. *Prod:* Warner Bros. 85m. (15m in spoken dialogue). (Miss Costello's talking picture *début.*)

GLORIOUS BETSY (1928). Period romance; as Betsy Patterson, who falls in love with a French tutor who turns out to be Napoleon's brother Jerome Bonaparte incognito. *Dir:* Alan Crosland. *Sc:* Anthony Coldeway (from the play by Rida Johnson Young). *With* Conrad Nagel, John Miljan, Marc McDermott, Betty Blythe, Pasquale Amato, Michael Vavitch, André De Segurola, Clarissa Selwynne. *Prod:* Warner Bros. 7 reels. Part talkie (featured a Southern melody and "La Marseil-

Dolores Costello with George O'Brien in NOAH'S ARK

laise''). Re-made, 1936, as *Hearts Divided* with Marion Davies in the Costello role.

THE REDEEMING SIN (1929). Romantic melodrama; as Fleurette, flower of the French underworld, who loves the young doctor she has sworn to kill because she thinks he let her brother die. *Dir:* Howard Bretherton. *Sc:* Harvey Gates, with dialogue by Joseph Jackson (from a story by L. V. Jefferson). *With* Conrad Nagel, Georgie Stone, Philippe De Lacy, Lionel Belmore, Warner Richmond, Nina Quartero. *Prod:* Warner Bros. 75m. (32m. of sound). Previously filmed by Vitagraph, 1925, with Nazimova in the Costello role.

NOAH'S ARK (1929). Reincarnation drama, with Biblical and pre-World War One settings; a double role: as Miriam, the Old Testament heroine, spared in the Great Flood; and Mary, a touring actress, caught in a train wreck on the Orient Express and nearly drowned. *Dir:* Michael Curtiz. *Sc:* Anthony Coldeway, with dialogue by De Leon Anthony (story by Darryl Francis Zanuck). *With* George O'Brien, Noah Beery, Louise Fazenda, Guinn Williams, Paul McAllister, Nigel de Brulier, Anders Randolph, Armand Kaliz, Myrna Loy, William V. Mong. *Prod:* Warner Bros. Ten reels, of which two had dialogue.

GLAD RAG DOLL (1929). Comedy romance; as Annabel Lee, who likes dancing and pretty clothes. *Dir:* Michael Curtiz. *Sc:* C. Graham Baker (from a story by Harvey Gates). *With* Ralph Graves, Audrey Ferris, Albert Gran, Maude Turner Gordon, Arthur Rankin, Dale Fuller, Claude Gillingwater, Douglas Gerrard,

André Beranger, Lee Moran, Tom Kennedy, Louise Beavers. *Prod:* Warner Bros: 70m. Miss Costello's first all-talkie film.

MADONNA OF AVENUE A (1929). Mother-daughter drama; as Maria, educated at an exclusive boarding school, although her mother operates a saloon on Avenue A. *Dir:* Michael Curtiz. *Sc:* Ray Doyle, with dialogue by Francis Powers (from a story by Mark Canfield). *With* Louise Dresser, Grant Withers, Douglas Gerrard, Otto Hoffman, Lee Moran. *Prod:* Warner Bros. 71m., 60% of which is dialogue.

THE SHOW OF SHOWS (1929). In a song and dance number, "My Sister," introduced by Richard Barthelmess, with her own sister Helene. The number was staged by Larry Ceballos, and had music by Ray Perkins, with lyrics by Perkins and J. K. Breenan. The Costello sisters headlined a group featuring other actresses who were real-life sisters. Loretta Young and Sally Blane, Sally O'Neil and Molly O'Day, Lola Vendrill and Armida, Viola Dana and Shirley Mason, Harriet Lake and Marion Byron, Alice and Marceline Day, Adamae and Alberta Vaughn. *Prod:* Warner Bros. 124m. (Entire film, all-talking, singing and dancing, 86% in colour.)

HEARTS IN EXILE (1929). Romantic melodrama, of old Russia; as Vera Zuanova, fishmonger's daughter, who rises in the world. *Dir:* Michael Curtiz. *Sc:* Harvey Gates (from a play by John Oxenham). *With* Grant Withers, James Kirkwood, George Fawcett, David Torrence, Olive Tell, Rose Dione. *Prod:* Warner Bros: 82m., all-talkie, with songs. Clara Kimball Young had played the same role in a 1915 World release (re-issued two years later as *Hearts Afire*).

SECOND CHOICE (1930). Romance; as Vallery Grove, who is loved and sought by two men. *Dir:* Howard Bretherton. *Sc:* Joseph Jackson (from a story by Elizabeth Alexander). *With* Chester Morris, Jack Mulhall, Edna Murphy, Charlotte Merriam, Ethlynne Claire. *Prod:* Warner Bros. 67m.

EXPENSIVE WOMEN (1931). Romantic drama; as Constance Newton, a girl of whims who goes from one man to another and almost loses the man she really loves. *Dir:* Hobart Henley. *Sc:* Harvey Thew and Raymond Griffith (from a story, "Passionate Sonata," by Wilson Collison). *With* Warren William, Anthony Bushell, Joe Donahue, H. B. Warner, Polly Walters, William House. *Prod:* First National. 62m.

LITTLE LORD FAUNTLEROY (1936). Period juvenile drama; as "Dearest," widow, whose son becomes heir to an English earldom. *Dir:* John Cromwell. *Sc:* Hugh Walpole (from a novel by Frances Hodgson Burnett). *With* Freddie Bartholomew, C. Aubrey Smith,

Guy Kibbee, Mickey Rooney, Eric Alden, Jackie Searle, Henry Stephenson, Reginald Barlow, Ivan Simpson, E. E. Clive, Una O'Connor, Jessie Ralph, Gilbert Emery, Mary MacLaren. *Prod:* David O. Selznick, released by United Artists. 98m. In 1921, for United Artists, Mary Pickford had played both "Dearest" and young Ceddie, her son, in a silent version.

YOURS FOR THE ASKING (1936). Gambling romance; as Lucielle Sutton, impoverished society beauty, who becomes partners with a gangster in a gambling establishment. *Dir:* Alexander Hall. *Sc:* Eve Greene, Harlan Ware, Philip MacDonald (from a story by William R. Lipman and William H. Wright). *With* George Raft, Ida Lupino, Reginald Owen, James Gleason, Edgar Kennedy, Lynne Overman, Skeets Gallagher, Betty Blythe, Olive Tell. *Prod:* Paramount. 68m.

THE BELOVED BRAT (AKA, GB, *A Dangerous Age*) (1938). Juvenile delinquency drama; as Miss Cosgrove, who understands the problems of a neglected and unhappy girl and is largely responsible for her regeneration. *Dir:* Arthur Lubin. *Sc:* Lawrence Kimble (from a story, "Girls on Probation," by Jean Negulesco). *With* Bonita Granville, Donald Crisp, Donald Briggs, Natalie Moorehead, Lucille Webster Gleason.*Prod:* Warner Bros. 63m. Working title: *Too Much of Everything*.

BREAKING THE ICE (1938). Drama of the Pennsylvania Mennonites; as Martha Martin, widowed mother of a boy who makes a hit at a Philadelphia ice rink. *Dir:* Edward Cline. *Sc:* Mary McCall Jr., Manuel Seff, Bernard Schubert (from a story by Fritz Falkenstein and N. Brewster Morse). *With* Bobby Breen, Charlie, Ruggles, Robert Barrat, Dorothy Peterson, John King, Billy Gilbert, Charlie Murray, Margaret Hamilton, Jonathan Hale. *Prod:* Sol Lesser, released by RKO. 80m.

THE KING OF THE TURF (1939). Racetrack drama; as Mrs. Barnes, whose son by a first marriage becomes a jockey. *Dir:* Alfred E. Green. *Sc:* George Bruce. *With* Adolphe Menjou, Roger Daniel, Walter Abel, Alan Dinehart, William Demarest, Harold Huber, William Bakewell. *Prod:* United Artists. 88m.

WHISPERING ENEMIES (1939). Drama of rivalries, as Laura Crandall, head of a cosmetic firm, who fights a whispering campaign conducted by a commercial rival. *Dir:* Lewis D. Collins. *Sc:* Gordon Rigby, Tom Kilpatrick (from a story by John Rawlins and Harold Tarshis). *With* Jack Holt, Addison Richards, Joseph Crehan, Pert Kelton. *Prod:* Columbia. 62m.

OUTSIDE THESE WALLS (1939). Prison-newspaper melodrama; as Margaret Bronson, newspaper owner, who uses prison politics to gain her way to a governor's race. *Dir:* Raymond McCarey. *Sc:* Harold Buchman (from a story by Ferdinand Reyher). *With*

Michael Whalen, Virginia Weidler, Don Beddoe, Mary Forbes, Robert Emmett Keane, Pierre Watkin, Kathleen Lockhart, *Prod:* 20th Century-Fox. 60m.

THE MAGNIFICENT AMBERSONS (1942). Story of the decline of an American family; as Isabel Amberson, widowed mother of George Minafer, who possesses her life and finally gets his come-uppance. *Dir./Sc:* Orson Welles (from the novel by Booth Tarkington). *With* Joseph Cotten, Tim Holt, Anne Baxter, Agnes Moorehead, Ray Collins, Richard Bennett, Erskine Sanford, Don Dillaway, *Prod:* RKO. 88m. Alice Calhoun had played Isabel Amberson in a 1925 Vitagraph silent version of Tarkington's novel, called *Pampered Youth*.

THIS IS THE ARMY (1943). War musical; as Mrs. Davidson, who sees both her husband and son in the service. *Dir:* Michael Curtiz. *Sc:* Casey Robinson and Claude Binyon (from the stage show by Irving Berlin). *With* George Murphy, Joan Leslie, Ronald Reagan, George Tobias, Alan Hale, Charles Butterworth, Una Merkel, Stanley Ridges, Rosemary De Camp, Ruth Donnelly, Dorothy Peterson, Frances Langford, Gertrude Niesen, Kate Smith, Joe Louis, Irving Berlin. *Prod:* Warner Bros. 118m.

9
ALICE BRADY

Although Alice Brady is most widely remembered for the zany Malaprop she so often portrayed on the screen, she was a versatile and perceptive actress and gave, as Lavinia Mannon in the Theatre Guild's stage production of Eugene O'Neill's "Mourning Becomes Electra," one of the great performances of the American theatre.

That she subsequently became identified more with comedy than tragedy was due, in the opinion of those who knew her best, to the tragedies in her own life. Carefree actors sometimes yearn to play Hamlet; Pagliaccis have a deeper need to appear other than as they are.

She was born in New York City on November 2, 1892, and was the only child of theatrical producer William A. Brady and his first wife, Rose Marie René. Her mother, a French-born dancer, retired from show business when she married Brady and died when the daughter she had named Alice was only four years old. A year later, Brady married actress Grace George, whom he made a star.

The relationship between stepmother-actress Grace George and stepdaughter-actress Alice Brady was one of understanding and affection. "Mom" was how Alice Brady addressed her stepmother. Her father was usually, fondly, "Dad," or, when she was deliberately putting on the dog, *"Faw-ther."* The love that father and daughter shared is the purest and most enduring light shining through Alice Brady's life.

San Francisco-born Bill Brady, Irish, gruff, and outspoken, had begun life as a "butcher boy," selling candies, peanuts and fruit on railroad trains. Before entering theatrical production, he had become the biggest prize-fight promoter in the sporting world and had handled the careers of James J. Corbett and Jim Jeffries. As a stage producer, he was one of Broadway's "great," and is most fondly remembered because he built and managed one of New York's best intimate theatres — The Playhouse.

Alice Brady was educated at the Sacred Heart Convent in Fort Lee, New Jersey, and at St. Elizabeth's Convent in Madison, New Jersey. She was gifted from childhood with a charming lyric-soprano voice, tremendous vitality, and a quick wit. She also had the theatre in her blood, this slim, dark-haired, black-eyed daughter of a French dancer and Irish producer.

She didn't dare admit it to her father, who thought the theatre not good enough for her, and told him she wanted to study for opera. He agreed to her enrolling in Boston's Conservatory of Music, and she studied there for the grand opera stage under the tutelage of Theodora Irvine.

Her gift of mimicry was so astute that after hearing an aria on a phonograph she could sing it in exactly the same style, complete with every nuance and shading. In her early teens, *en route* to Europe with her parents, she astounded the audience at a shipboard concert with a faultless rendition of an aria from "Faust." Her father was flabbergasted but proud, even though one sharp-eared music critic said she sang like a first-class tenor. She didn't tell the critic, or anybody until much later, that she had simply memorised Caruso's recording of the aria, and had sung it parrot-like.

In 1909, when she was not yet seventeen, she made her stage *début* in Boston by performing under a stage name in Robert Mantell's production of "As You Like It" (salary: $8 a week). She also appeared under an assumed name as a member of the chorus of "The Mikado." In January, 1911, a knowledgeable critic discovered that the singer billed as "Marie Rose" (a variation of her mother's name) in "The Balkan Princess," an operetta trying out in New Haven, was none other than Bill Brady's teenage daughter Alice.

Before her father could learn of it from someone else, she phoned him from New Haven and told him bluntly: "I've been acting under an assumed name. If you'll okay what I've done and promise to give me a chance in New York after I make good here, I'll remain anonymous. Otherwise, I'll spread your name on billboards all over Boston."

Irish-tempered Bill Brady acceded to her appearing as Olga in "The Balkan Princess" because there was nothing else he could do gracefully, and he gruffly indicated she might as well be billed under her own name. When the operetta opened in New York on February 9, 1911, the programme credited the role of Olga to Alice Brady.

On opening night, her father exclaimed to everybody: "By God, she has it in her — blood will tell!" But privately he scolded her for not continuing her operatic studies. She flashed him her typical Brady grin and murmured: "But I couldn't wait, Faw-ther."

He thereupon set three conditions: 1) she must not use his name in her efforts to succeed; 2) she must not ask his advice about plays or roles; 3) she must make good within one year, or quit.

She accepted the conditions, and when "The Balkan Princess" ended its run, secured a job on her own as a regular member of the Gilbert and Sullivan Repertory Company, singing a season with it at Broadway's Casino and then going on tour.

When her father acknowledged that she had proved worthy of being called "actress," she thanked him and added: "I'd like to be starred in one of your new plays." She also made it plain that she didn't want to be confined to singing roles. When Brady reminded her that she hadn't thought much of his productions, even though most of them had been unqualified successes, she didn't deny it. Instead, she asked to play one of the March girls in the stage dramatisation he was planning to produce of "Little Women."

In October, 1912, she made her non-singing *début* as Meg in "Little Women," and received good notices. Subsequently, she had leads on Broadway in such plays as "The Family Cupboard" and "The Things That Count."

Alice Brady

When DeWolf Hopper toured with Gilbert and Sullivan repertory, she and John Charles Thomas sang all the romantic leads. Hedda Hopper was travelling with her husband's company that year and relates in her autobiography, ''From Under My Hat,'' how unforgettable Thomas and Miss Brady were — ''...their voices had such freshness and vibrancy, all you could think about was wood violets and spring.''

To quote Miss Hopper further, however: ''With her tremendous vitality,

Alice was the despair of Wolfie. She would come flying into the theatre fifteen minutes before curtain time. Some of the Gilbert and Sullivan roles are extremely tricky to sing. For instance, Mabel, in *Pirates of Penzance*, makes her entrance at the top of a long, winding staircase. A brilliant trill is followed by a difficult cadenza as she descends to the stage. Many a night Alice would give us cold chills by irresponsibly forgetting the words and music, just standing on the stairway and giggling cheerfully. How well Wolfie knew that the Gilbert and Sullivan devotee is infuriated by any tampering with the beloved operas!''

With the permission of her husband, Miss Hopper one day cornered Miss Brady and told her solemnly that if she misbehaved again, she would be hissed, and Hedda herself would start the hissing. Miss Brady apparently didn't believe her, or forgot, because several performances later she once more fumbled the lyrics. It was the last time she ever did it, because Hedda hissed loudly, and the audience joined in like a bed of disapproving rattle-snakes.

"Of course she had never meant to throw the opera off,'' Hedda excused her; "she was simply high-spirited, young, and thoughtless.''

The truth was that she was also bored with the limitations of singing roles in the theatre and accepted only one subsequent singing engagement (a brief tour of Gilbert and Sullivan repertory).

Miss Brady had a slight vocal impediment which was easy to disguise in a singing role, and she worked hard to make it unnoticeable in speaking roles, in which she spoke rapidly but with faultless enunciation. "I have scarcely any r's and no s's,'' she admitted to one interviewer, "but it's not so noticeable now, is it?''

She was an avid theatre-goer and studied all sorts of performances in plays, vaudeville and motion pictures. Again, it is Hedda Hopper who tells of accompanying her to one vaudeville performance. Miss Brady was near-sighted, wouldn't wear glasses, but carried a lorgnette. During a monkey act she sat on the edge of her seat peering in rapture through her lorgnette.

"'Good Lord, Alice!' said Miss Hopper. 'What can you see in them? I think they're disgusting!'

"'Be quiet!' she commanded me. 'I might have to play one of them some day.'''

When her father entered film production, some of his movies were among the best released by the World Company, and, after two short-lived plays, "Sylvia Runs Away'' and "What Is Love?'', Miss Brady cornered him in his office and said with characteristic candour, "I want to go into films. I would like to start with you, but if you won't give me a job, I'll get one with some other company.''

She starred for him first in *As Ye Sow*, released by World late in 1914. But it was her second Brady-World picture, *The Boss*, in which she co-starred with Holbrook Blinn (making his film *début*), that established her on the screen.

In 1915 she opened on Broadway in an Owen Davis play, "Sinners,'' which five years later she made into a starring film. For the next eight years she was often simultaneously appearing in a play on Broadway and working before the camera. Most of her silent films were shot in New York studios.

Said "Moving Picture World'' (October 6, 1917): "...Alice Brady has shown herself to be a remarkably versatile performer on the screen. Although still a very young girl, her range of roles covers many mature parts, as well as joyous impersonations of youth. Her work on the screen has made a place for itself in the motion picture industry, and Alice Brady pictures are a standard commodity of high value in the film mart.''

Until 1918 she starred for World in films produced by her father. ''I worked much harder than I would have done under any other manager, and Dad certainly can't be accused of having shown partiality. Still, I knew that it was often said of me that I could never have won so much prestige had I not been Brady's daughter — and I resented it. I wondered if I really did amount to anything in myself, or was it true I had won a measure of success just because I was the daughter of William A. Brady. I decided to strike out for myself, and show them.''

So she moved out of his home, took a Manhattan apartment of her own, and signed with Select Films. In 1918 she also returned to the theatre in one of her longest-running hits, a romance called ''Forever After.''

Almost all her silent movies had entailed heavy dramatic roles and although she admitted that she had liked playing Mimi at World in *La Vie de Bohème* and Jane Eyre at Select in a modernisation of the Brontë novel entitled *Woman and Wife,* she fretted about not being given comedy.

''I am naturally buoyant and happy,'' she said, ''yet I am always cast for melodrama — just why I don't know.''

She never thought of herself as a beauty. ''The celluloid world,'' she said, ''I find hard and heartless. It doesn't want people who 'keep' their ages, or who do not 'show' their ages. It wants those without ages...because of my silly, irregular features I have to work a great deal harder.''

''Alice had her own method for keeping trim,'' wrote Hedda Hopper. ''At lunch time, instead of eating, she would invite a playwright to come in and read her his new play, or she'd sample a song writer's new tune; or, if she happened to be decorating a new apartment, which she did every whipstitch, she'd have fabrics brought in, select colours for her room, decide on antiques, do any and every thing to keep herself occupied so the thought of food couldn't enter her mind.

''When she was fast becoming a skeleton, she became worried. She lost her appetite completely, and her stomach had shrunk so she had trouble retaining anything. An expert doctor told her: 'Miss Brady, I treated starving children in Belgium during the war. But yours is the worst case of starvation I have ever seen. What are you doing to yourself?'''

In *His Bridal Night,* the last picture she made for Select, she finally got a chance to play romantic comedy. It was also the first of several pictures in which she had as her leading man James Crane.

Miss Brady fell head-over-heels in love with him. Her friends warned her he was absolutely unreliable and the last man in the world she should consider marrying, but because she was in love, she closed her ears.

She married Crane on Tuesday, May 20, 1919; the ceremony was performed by Crane's father, the well-known clergyman-writer, in the study of the Reverend Mr. Crane's Manhattan home. When her father returned from Europe, at his request, they went through a religious ceremony in the rectory of the Church of the Ascension on Broadway at 107th Street on Saturday,

Alice Brady with Carole Lombard and Alan Mowbray in MY MAN
GODFREY

June 21, 1919.

Jimmy Crane was handsome, debonair, and a good actor. He was also a bad
drinker and was guilty of inhumanly cruel behaviour when intoxicated. Miss
Brady separated from him before their child was born, and eventually divorced him on grounds of cruelty.

He degenerated into hopeless alcoholism, and did not last long. Miss Brady
never re-married.

Hedda Hopper says that when she ran into Miss Brady shortly after the
divorce and said, "I'm sorry," Miss Brady "looked at me with a straight,
steady gaze from those beautiful eyes and said slowly, 'Hedda, for almost a
year I knew perfect happiness. That's more than most women ever get.' It was
the first time I'd heard that line. Many times since I've heard it on stage and
screen. But to me forever it comes straight from the heart of Alice Brady."

After leaving Select, Miss Brady contracted with Paramount, which released the first of her vehicles for them through a subsidiary (Realart). Few of those Paramount films, if one excepts two comedies — *The New York Idea* and *Anna Ascends* — were worthy of her.

Anna Ascends she had done as a successful play on Broadway, and it was during that engagement she learned she was pregnant — and for a brief time was divinely happy.

Then everything went wrong. One day, *en route* to the theatre from her Long Island home, she was painfully injured in an automobile accident, in which her chauffeur was killed. As a result of the accident, her baby, a boy, was born prematurely.

She was also disenchanted with the films she was making for Paramount release. "I want to do character roles on the screen," she said, "but the managers want me merely to go through the usual polite experiences in pretty frocks. I'm beginning to think the screen is afraid of acting." Although she owed Paramount two pictures on her contract, they were cancelled by mutual agreement, and she resolved to return to the stage.

And it was at this juncture that she realised her prematurely-born son, Donald Crane, would "ever and ever be ill." She gave up her Long Island home, put the boy in a private school and began a lonely devotion to the living theatre that is still memorable.

Her performances distinguished many Broadway productions during the Twenties — "The Bride of the Lamb," "Sour Grapes," "The Witch," "Lady Alone," "The Thief," "Bless You, Sister" — but this phase of her career left her unimpressed. "I did so many — well — lush ladies," she said. "Women good enough, but also faintly bad. It was the style then, on the stage. The style hasn't changed much. I recall my Faw-ther dropping in to see one of these plays and coming back to my dressing-room after the performance. 'Alice,' he said, 'do you know you had practically nothing on in the second act?'"

Although she often scolded her father for his slick, well-mounted, successful stage productions, she was the first to praise him when he produced Elmer Rice's Pulitzer prize-winning "Street Scene." She once wanted Brady to present her in vaudeville in Eugene O'Neill's "Ile," but he rebelled. Nor would he let her take him to see O'Neill's "The Hairy Ape."

"Parents are so provincial and reactionary," she remarked affectionately.

Late in 1927, the Theatre Guild wanted Miss Brady to play Nina Leeds in Eugene O'Neill's marathonic "Strange Interlude," still one of the most taxing feminine roles ever written. According to George Freedley, Miss Brady was playing stock at Elitch's Gardens in Denver when the manuscript arrived in two, thick, heavy bundles. She didn't even read it, but on the advice of her manager returned the play to the Guild. Lynn Fontanne was then selected to play the role and created it on Broadway.

Late in 1928, Miss Brady herself was back on Broadway in a sensational comedy, "A Most Immoral Lady." The Theatre Guild then starred her in two distinguished failures: "Karl and Anna" and The Game of Love and Death." She was also the star of "Love, Honor and Betray" (with Clark Gable), "Brass Ankle," and a revival of "Ladies of the Jury."

She then undertook an O'Neill role far more demanding than that of Nina

Leeds and on October 26, 1931, opened in "Mourning Becomes Electra." She played Lavinia, with Nazimova as her Clytemnestra-mother. That performance is still memorable, and in itself entitles Alice Brady to be included among the great American actresses.

She was always very fond of her younger half-brother, Bill Brady Jr., the son of her father and Grace George, and proud that he had distinguished himself as a stage producer. Among his productions was Robert E. Sherwood's "The Road to Rome," and in 1932 she appeared in a summer revival of it at Red Bank, New Jersey. Her father was so impressed with her talent as a comedienne that he engaged her to co-star with Grace George in an adaptation of a French comedy called "Mademoiselle."

It proved to be a success in which stepmother and stepdaughter divided honours equally, and it brought Miss Brady a flood of Hollywood offers. But not until six years later did she confess: "When I did my first stage comedy in *Mademoiselle* I hadn't the foggiest notion of how to be funny. I didn't know what on earth to do. I just thought I'd flap my hands about even more than normally and 'talk silly.' I did — and I've lived off of it for six years. But I never have any idea of what I'm doing, or why."

She signed with M-G-M and resumed the film career she had abruptly forsaken ten years previously. She was not the star of her first talkie, *When Ladies Meet,* but few will deny that she stole the acting honours from those billed above her — and they included Ann Harding, Myrna Loy, and Robert Montgomery.

For the rest of Miss Brady's career, comedy was the *leit motif* of almost every role, although frequently there was heart-drama mingled with the comedy, as in *Broadway to Hollywood, Stage Mother,* and *Miss Fane's Baby Is Stolen.* She made the zany Mrs. Malaprop she played not only as nutty as Gracie Allen and as whimsical as Billie Burke but distinctively her own.

She had no illusions about her personal appearance, and said of her face: "It skids, that's the trouble with it. It needs chains. Just when I'm trying to be serious on the screen the thing skids, and I'm doing a tragic scene with a comic face. Look at it. I've often seen those little blonde babes around here giving me the once over. I'm sure they wonder how a face like that fits into pictures."

Similarly, a well-meaning woman once asked her why she always wore black. "Because I love red so much," Miss Brady replied cryptically. "What I meant," she explained later, "was that if once I started wearing red, there'd be no stopping me."

In 1934 she took time out from her new screen career to star in a Pacific Coast stage production of S. N. Behrman's "Biography," which Ina Claire had created on Broadway. She was brilliant in it, but when she finished the engagement, she surprised everyone by announcing that she would never again return to the theatre. "I have had the heights," she said, "and I have known the depths. Now all I want is the peaceful in-between."

She bought a house in Beverly Hills, and settled down. Of her theatrical past there were no mementos — no clippings, reviews or letters, no photos, no pressbooks.

She decorated her house in red and white, and allowed her dogs, of which she never had less than five, to chew and soil whatever they could reach. But she was careful to hang her Matisse in the white dining-room and her George Bellows in the crimson living-room in such a way that no dog could reach them.

"I sometimes find animals kinder and more understanding," she confided to a friend. "Human beings build walls around themselves — and call it personality. But most of the time it's a sham. Animals — dogs, for instance — are much realer. I literally lead a dog's life." She even became president of the Tailwaggers' Foundation.

She was an unusually self-sufficient woman, largely, her closest friends thought, because of the tragedies in her personal life — her broken marriage, the irremediable defects in her only child. Her religion, Roman Catholic, was one of the sources of her psychological strength. It certainly helped when her half-brother, Bill Brady Jr., burned himself to death by falling asleep with a lighted cigarette.

"I am perfectly happy alone in this house for days," she said, "and never once want to go out that front door. Sleeping, playing with my dogs, and reading detective novels. But after awhile I get a terrific desire for companionship and want people around me — in clumps. Not one, but dozens."

At such times she telephoned everybody she knew and staged a Brady cocktail production that usually lasted on into the night.

At one of her parties — she drank only champagne, which she called "fizz" — she was asked if she was happy. She gave the questioner an amused look and replied: "Of course not. No one but an idiot is really happy. But I'm content with my dog's life."

The motto she most often quoted was: "Never stand up when you can sit down; never sit down when you can lie down; never just lie down if you can lie down and sleep."

When she went out, she wore expensive furs, jangled armloads of bracelets, and often was accompanied by a coterie of handsome young men, because there was always safety in numbers.

She had no patience with acting schools or with actors who studied acting, and believed acting could be learned only *by* acting in a play for an audience, and that when an actor was between engagements he should study a foreign language, or take singing or dancing lessons, or learn to play the piano or some other musical instrument, or even learn how to use a typewriter, since sometime in his acting career he'd be called on to do these things onstage or in front of the camera.

Although her Beverly Hills home was strewn with detective novels, she did read other things. Once, while playing a long run in Chicago, she had reviewed books for the Chicago "Post." She could read and speak French, Italian, Spanish, German, and even Latin. During one rehearsal on a movie stage, she had trouble saying a line. "There's something faulty in its construction," she insisted, and sat down with a pencil to parse the sentence. Triumphantly, she changed it slightly, proving her point, and, glancing at the director, asked with a grin: "Ain't that better?" Sometimes the comedy roles she played were so fragmentary and one-dimensional she was hard pushed to flesh out the image that made audiences laugh as soon as they took one look at her.

Director Henry King, who considers her one of the great dramatic actresses of our day, says that when he had 20th Century-Fox approach her for the role

Alice Brady with Tyrone Power in IN OLD CHICAGO

of Mrs. O'Leary in *In Old Chicago,* she was reluctant to test for it, but after reading the screenplay she "dashed to the studio and made a test plenty fast." She wanted to get away from comedy as much as she had once wanted to do it.

She was filled with foreboding, however, for Hollywood memories were still green about what happened when ZaSu Pitts had essayed a tragic role in *All Quiet on the Western Front,* one of the first important talkie dramas. Preview audiences had gone into gales of laughter at the mere sight of her, and her scenes had had to be re-shot with Beryl Mercer.

In the first ten minutes of *In Old Chicago,* her husband dies, she buries him, and continues on with her three sons to lusty, young, brawling Chicago. Favouring her portrayal of all this was the alteration in her appearance produced by period clothes and a lightening of her hair colour. But the face was still the Brady face. "My very appearance may be a signal for loud guffaws," Miss Brady warned King.

Audiences did not laugh, and Miss Brady won an Academy Award for the best supporting performance by an actress in 1937. She did not receive it in person, because on the night of the ceremony she was laid up with a broken ankle sustained during the filming of *Goodbye Broadway*. She was proud of her Oscar and later gave a party for herself.

But she had little cause to celebrate. She had cancer, and kept her suffering to herself. She was receiving medical treatment, but continued accepting film roles. In her last one, in John Ford's *Young Mr. Lincoln,* when she is on the witness stand testifying for her young son accused of murder, there is one of the profoundest manifestations of humanity's frightened bafflement before an inexplicable universe ever recorded by the camera.

She became tell-tale thin, and her father learned the truth. He hurried to the Coast, and, bursting into tears when he saw her, took her back to New York.

"The last time I saw her," Louella O. Parsons subsequently wrote, "she was so emaciated I had to turn away so she couldn't see the tears in my eyes. I knew she was seldom free from pain, and her effort to prove to me that she was in perfect health was pathetic." Indeed, Miss Brady even exclaimed to Miss Parsons, "Don't you dare print that I have been sick. Look at me. I never felt better."

Nothing *was* printed until, on Monday morning, October 30, 1939, when the newspapers announced that late on the preceding Saturday, October 28, Alice Brady had died in New York City's LeRoy Sanitarium.

She is buried in Sleepy Hollow Cemetery, Tarrytown, New York.

ALICE BRADY FILMOGRAPHY

AS YE SOW (1914). Marital drama; as Dora Mason, a much beleaguered heroine. *Dir:* Frank Hall Crane. *Sc:* (from a play by the Rev. John M. Snyder). *with* Douglas MacLean, Walter Fischter, Beverly West, Johnny Hines, Edmund Mortimer, George Moss, Charles Dungan, Lydia Knott. *Prod:* World. 4500 ft.

THE BOSS (1915). Drama; as Emily Griswold, who marries a man she detests in order to protect her father. *Dir:* Emile Chautard. *Sc:* (from a play by Edward Sheldon). *With* Holbrook Blinn, Charles Abbe, William Marion, Fred C. Truesdale. *Prod:* World. 5 reels.

THE CUP OF CHANCE (1915). Melodrama; in a dual role: as mother and daughter, both notoriously amoral. *Dir:* Joseph Levering. *Sc:* Clarence J. Harria. *With* George W. Howard, Gladia Acaro, George Reinhart, James Levering, Fritz Orlamond, Elaine Evans. *Prod:* Knickerbocker-World. 3000 ft.

THE LURE OF WOMAN (1915). Melodrama on a remote army post; as Katie O'Day. *Sc:* (from a play, "The Renegade," by Paul Armstrong). *With* George Ralph, June Elvidge. *Prod:* World. 5 reels.

THE RACK (1916). Marital drama of the prob-

lems of three couples; as the well-meaning but innocent Mrs. Gordon. *Dir:* Emile Chautard. *Sc:* Thompson Buchanan. *with* Milton Sills, Chester Barnett, June Elvidge, Doris Kenyon. *Prod:* World. 5 reels.

THE BALLET GIRL (1916). Backstage drama; in a dual role: as mother and daughter, known as Jenny Pearl, both dancers, *Dir:* George Irving. *Sc:* (from a novel, "Carnival," by Compton MacKenzie). *With* Holbrook Blinn, Robert Frazer, Alec B. Francis, Julia Stuart, Laura McClure, Fred Radcliffe, Robert Kegeris, George Ralph. *Prod:* World. 5 reels.

THE WOMAN IN 47 (1916). Romantic drama; as Viola, an impassioned Italian girl, who follows her lover to America. *Dir:* George Irving. *Sc:* Frederick Chapin. *With* William Raymond, John Warwick, George D. Melville, Eric Blind, Lillian Concord, Tom McGrath, Bert Rooney, Jack Sherrill. *Prod:* World. 5 reels.

THEN I'LL COME BACK TO YOU (1916). Romantic drama; as a well-bred girl who learns to love the fighting engineer who had first repelled her. *Dir:* George Irving. *Sc:* Frances Marion (from a novel by Larry Evans). *With* Jack

Sherrill, Eric Blind, Leo Gordon, George Kline, Marie Edith Walls. *Prod:* World. 5 reels.

TANGLED FATES (1916). Romantic drama of New England, Manhattan, and Alaska; as an elder sister who takes the blame for her younger sister's indiscretion. *Dir:* Travers Vale. *Sc:* Frances Marion (from a story by William Anthony McGuire, known as both "Grub Stake" and "Grubstakers"). *With* Arthur Ashley, Helen Weir, George Morgan. *Prod:* World. 5 reels.

LA VIE DE BOHEME (AKA, GB, *La Bohème*). (1916). Period romance; as Mimi, *Dir:* Albert Capellani. *Sc:* Frances Marion (from the stories by Henri Murger). *With* Paul Capellani, Chester Barnett, Zena Keefe, Leslie Stowe, June Elvidge. (Re-made by King Vidor for M-G-M-, 1926, with Lillian Gish and John Gilbert; it was a British talkie in 1935, *Mimi,* with Gertrude Lawrence and Douglas Fairbanks Jr.) *Prod:* World. 5 reels.

MISS PETTICOATS (1916). Romantic drama; as a girl who works in a New England woolen mill and is known as "Miss Petticoats." *Dir./Sc:* Harley Knoles (from a novel by Dwight Tilton). *With* Arthur Ashley, Isobel Berwin, Robert Elliott, John(ny) Hines, Edward M. Kimball, Lila Chester. *Prod:* World. 5 reels.

THE GILDED CAGE (AKA, GB, *The Heart of a Princess)* (1916). Romantic mythical kingdom drama; as Honoré, Royal Princess and then Queen of Balkany. *Dir:* Harley Knoles. *Sc:* Frances Marion (from a story, "Her Majesty," by J. I. C. Clarke). *With* Irving Cummings, Alec B. Francis, Gerda Holmes, Montagu Love, Arthur Ashley, Sidney D'Albrook Clara Whipple. *Prod:* World. 5 reels.

BOUGHT AND PAID FOR (1916). Marital drama; as Virgina Blaine, working girl, who weds a wealthy alcoholic. *Dir:* Harley Knoles. *Sc:* Frances Marion (from the play by George Broadhurst). *With* Montagu Love, Josephine Drake, Frank Conlon. (Re-made by Paramount, 1922, with Agnes Ayres and Jack Holt). *Prod:* World. 5 reels.

A WOMAN ALONE (1917). Romantic drama; as the wife of a railroad station attendant, who is tempted by a rich idler from the city. *Dir:* Harry Davenport. *Sc:* Frances Marion (from a story, "Loneliness," by Willard Mack). *With* Edward T. Langford, Edward M. Kimball, Justine Cutting, Arthur Ashley, J. Clarence Harvey, Walter Greene. *Prod:* World. 5 reels.

THE HUNGRY HEART (AKA, GB, *Frou-Frou*) (1917). Marital drama; as Gilberte Brigarde, the foolish toy wife, who abandons her husband and child for a worthless love. *Dir:* Emile Chautard. *Sc:* Frances Marion

(from the French play, "Frou-Frou," a favourite of Sarah Bernhardt's, by Henri Meilhac and Ludovic Halevy). *With* Edward T. Langford, George MacQuarrie, Gerda Holmes, Alec B. Francis, John Dudley, Edna Whistler, Charles Harley, Josephine Earle, Mrs. H. J. Brundage. (Re-made as a talkie by M-G-M, 1938, as *The Toy Wife. Prod:* World. 5 reels.

THE DANCER'S PERIL (1917). Romantic melodrama of the Russian Imperial Court and the Paris Montmartre; in a dual role: as mother and daughter, both dancers. *Dir:* Travers Vale. *Sc:* (from a story, "The Snowbird," by Harriet Morris). *With* Montagu Love, Philip Hunt, Cecil Fletcher, Louis Grisel, John(ny) Hines, Sidney D'Albrook, Jack Drumier, Auguste Burmeister, Alexis Kosloff and the Russian Imperial Ballet. *Prod:* World. 5 reels.

DARKEST RUSSIA (1917). A melodrama of Jewish persecution in Imperial Russia; as a Jewish girl who, with her brother, is threatened with exile to Siberia. *Dir:* Travers Vale. *Sc:* Frances Marion (from a play by J. Gratten Donnelly and Sidney R. Ellis). *With* John Bowers, J. Herbert Frank, Norbert Wicki, Boris Korlin (Karloff?), Jack Drumier, Herbert Barrington, Kate Lester, Lillian Cook, Frank DeVernon. *Prod:* World. 5 reels.

MATERNITY (1917). Psychological drama of the fear of childbirth; as Ellen Franklin. *Dir:* John O'Brien. *Sc:* Shannon Fife (from Fife's story, "The Cry of the Unborn"). *With* John Bowers, Marie Chambers, David Powell, Herbert Barrington, Florence Crane, Stanhope Wheatcroft, Charles Duncan, Louis Grisel, Julia Stuart, Madge Evans, John Dudley. *Prod:* World. 5 reels.

THE DIVORCE GAME (1917). Marital drama; as Fifi, American wife who loves her noble French husband, but they plot to divorce in order to gain her family's money. *Dir:* Travers Vale. *Sc:* Frances Marion (from the French play, "Mlle. Fifi," by Leo Ditrichstein). *With* John Bowers, Arthur Ashley, Kate Lester, Joseph Herbert, Jack Drumier, Maire Lavafre. *Prod:* World. 5 reels.

A SELF-MADE WIDOW (1917). Romantic comedy drama; as Sylvia, who poses as the widow of Fitzhugh Castleton, but Castleton turns up, very much alive. *Dir:* Travers Vale. *Sc:* (from a comedy, "The Romance of a Self-Made Widow," by Henry Albert Phillips). *With* John Bowers, Curtis Cooksey, Justine Cutting, Richard Clarke, Henrietta Simpson, Herbert Barrington, Lila Chester. *Prod:* World. 5 reels.

BETSY ROSS (1917). Biographical romantic drama; as Betsy Griscam, Quaker wife, who, when she is widowed, becomes Betsy Ross, and subsequently designs and makes the first American flag. *Dir:* Travers Vale and George

Cowl. *Sc:* Henry Du Souchet. *With* John Bowers, Lillian Cook, Victor Kennard, Eugenie Woodard, Kate Lester, Frank Mayo, George MacQuarrie, Justine Cutting, Robert Forsyth, Robert Cummings, Richard Clarke. *Prod:* World. 5 reels.

A MAID OF BELGIUM (AKA, GB, *A Maid of Flanders*) (1917). Propaganda drama; as Adorée, a Belgian raped by a German, who loses her memory. *Dir:* George Archainbaud. *Sc:* Adrian Gil-Spear. *With* George MacQuarrie, Louise de Rigney, Richard Clarke, Lotta Burnell, Anthony Merlo, *Prod:* World. 5 reels.

HER SILENT SACRIFICE (1918). Romantic drama; as Arlette, a maid of Brittany. *Dir:* Edward José. *Sc:* Eve Unsell (from a play, "The Red Mouse," by Henry J. W. Dam). *With* Henry Clive, R. Peyton Gibbs, Edmund Pardo, Blanche Craig, Arda LaCroix . *Prod:* Select. 5 reels.

WOMAN AND WIFE (1918). Gothic romance; as Jane Eyre, in a modernised version. *Dir:* Edward José. *Sc:* (from Charlotte Brontë's novel). *With* Elliott Dexter, Helene Greene, Helen Lindroth, Victor Beloit, Madge Evans, Leonora Morgan. ("Jane Eyre" has been filmed many times: in 1915 Kineto released a version, *The Castle of Thornfield,* with an Italian cast; also in 1915 Biograph released a version; in '14 Whitman had released its *Jane Eyre;* in 1921 Hugo Ballin released his production with his wife, Mabel Ballin, in the name role; in 1934 Monogram released a talking version starring Virginia Bruce; in 1944 20th Century-Fox released the Robert Stevenson version with Joan Fontaine and Orson Welles; and in 1970 the Omnibus version was made for television, and theatrical release with Susannah York and George C. Scott). *Prod:* Select. 5 reels.

THE KNIFE (1918). A dramatic shocker; as Kate Tarleton, who loses her reason when she is abducted into white slavery; for revenge her surgeon-sweetheart innoculates the culprits with a virulent syphillitic culture. *Dir:* Robert G. Vignola. *Sc:* Charles Maigne (from a play by Eugene Walter). *With* Frank Morgan, Crauford Kent, Helen Lackaye, Paul Doucet, Alice Hollister, Johnnie Walker, Frank Evans, *Prod:* Select. 5 reels.

THE SPURS OF SYBIL (1918). Romantic drama; as a wealthy girl, Sybil, who spurns her wealth to make her living for one year in Manhattan, and finds romance. *Dir:* Travers Vale. *Sc:* Louise Winter. With John Bowers, John Davidson, Isett Munro, Justine Cutting, Eugenie Woodward, Herbert Barrington, Richard Clarke. *Prod:* World. 5 reels.

AT THE MERCY OF MEN (1918). A dramatic shocker; as a Russian girl who has been raped by three Tsarist guardsmen, and finds that the man she loves and marries subse-

quently is one of them. *Dir:* Charles Miller. *Sc:* Paul West. *With* Frank Morgan, Jack W. Johnson, Robert Walker, Helen Lindroth, William T. Carleton, Tula Belle. (The assault scene was considered so shocking that after the initial showing it was deleted.) *Prod:* Select. 5 reels.

THE TRAP (1918). Romantic drama; as Doris Shaw, who finds love in Manhattan in spite of the lies told about her past. *Dir:* George Archainbaud. *Sc:* Robert F. Hill. *With* Frank Mayo, Curtis Cooksey, Crauford Kent, Robert Cummings. *Prod:* World. 5 reels.

THE WHIRLPOOL (1918). Gambling melodrama; as Isabel Corbyn, known as Bella Cavello in her stepfather's gambling salon. *Dir:* Alan Crosland. *Sc:* Eve Unsell (from a novel by Victoria Morton). *With* Holmes E. Herbert, J. H. Gilmore, William Davison, Robert Walker, Warren CooK, W. E. Williams. *Prod:* Select. 5 reels.

THE DEATH DANCE (1918). Melodrama of Manhattan cabaret life; as Flora, a dancer in danger. *Dir:* J. Searle Dawley. *Sc:* Paul West. *With* Holmes E. Herbert, Mahlon Hamilton, Helen Montrose, Robert Cain, Charles Slattery , Nadia Gary. *Prod:* Select. 5 reels.

THE ORDEAL OF ROSETTA (1918). Romantic drama of revenge: in a dual role: as the virtuous Rosetta Gelardi and her vengeance-minded twin, Lola. *Dir:* Emile Chautard. *Sc:* Paul West (from a story by Edmund Goulding). *With* Crauford Kent, Ormi Hawley, Edmund Burns, Maude Turner Gordon, Henry Leone, Hazel Washburn. *Prod:* Select. 5 reels.

THE BETTER HALF (1918). Romantic drama; in a dual role: as twin sisters, Louise and Beatrix Thorley, who love the same man. *Dir:* John S. Robertson. *Sc:* Louis Sherwin (from a novel, "Michael Thwaite's Wife," by Miriam Michelson). *With* David Powell, Crauford Kent, William T. Carleton, Isabel O'Madigan, Richard Allen. *Prod:* Select. 5 reels.

IN THE HOLLOW OF HER HAND (1918). Drama; as Hetty Castleton, who kills a man when he tries to compromise her. *Dir./Sc:* Charles Maigne (from the novel by George Barr McCutcheon). *With* Percy Marmont, Myrtle Stedman, Louise Clark, A. J. Herbert, Harold Entwhistle. *Prod:* Select. 5 reels.

HER GREAT CHANCE (1918). Romantic drama; as Lola Gray, a salesgirl, who loves a millionaire's son, but not until he is disgraced and disowned does she consent to marry him. *Dir./Sc:* Charles Maigne (from the novel by Fannie Hurst). *With* David Powell, Nellie Parker-Spaulding, Gloria Goodwin, Gertrude Barry, Hardee Kirkland, Ormi Hawley, Jefferson de Angelis. *Prod:* Select. 5 reels.

THE INDESTRUCTIBLE WIFE (1919).
Comedy romance; as Charlotte Ordway, who
marries a man who can't keep up with her.
Dir./Sc: Charles Maigne (from a comedy by
Frederic and Fanny Hatton). *With* Percy
Marmont, Saxon Kling, Sue Balfour, George
Backus, Roy Adams, W. A. Williams, Anne
Cornwall, Leonore Hughes, Thomas Donnell.
Prod: Select. 5 reels.

THE WORLD TO LIVE IN (AKA, GB, *The
World We Live In*) (1919). Romantic comedy;
as Rita Charles, private secretary, much
sought after by men. *Dir:* Charles Maigne. *Sc:*
Margaret Turnbull (from a story by W. Carey
Wonderly). *With* William T. Carleton Jr., Earl
Metcalfe, Virginia Hammond, Robert Scha-
ble, Zyllah Shannon, Anne Cornwall. *Prod:*
Select. 5 reels.

MARIE, LTD. (1919). Romantic comedy; as
Drina, daughter of a famous milliner, is much
sought after by the men who buy her mother's
creations. *Dir:* Kenneth Webb. *Sc:* Jane Mur-
fin (from a story by Louise Winters). *With*
Frank Losee, Leslie Austen, Mrs. Gertrude
Hillman, Josephine Whittell, Gladys Valerie.
Prod: Select. 5 reels.

THE REDHEAD (1919). Romantic drama; as
Dazil Mellows, cabaret dancer, who marries a
millionaire's son, and his family fires him from
his free-loading job. *Dir./Sc:* Charles Maigne
(from a story by Henry Payson Dawst). *With*
Conrad Nagel, Robert Schable, Charles A.
Stevenson, Charles Eldridge, May Brettone.
Prod: Select. 5 reels.

HIS BRIDAL NIGHT (1919). Romantic com-
edy; in a dual role: twin sisters, Vi and Tiny
Playfair, one a coquette and the other shy. *Dir:*
Kenneth Webb. *Sc:* Katherine Stuart (from a
story by Lawrence Irving Rising). *With* James
Crane, Edward Earle, Daniel Pennell, Daisy
Belmore, Mrs. Stuart (May) Robson. *Prod:*
Select. 5 reels.

THE FEAR MARKET (1920). Drama; as a
society girl who discovers that her own father
is the power behind a notorious scandal sheet.
Dir: Kenneth Webb. *Sc:* Clara Beranger (from
a play by Amelie Rives Troubetsky). *With*
Frank Losee, Harry Mortimer, Richard Hat-
teras, Edith Stockton, Bradley Barker, Nora
Reed, Fred Burton, Alfred Hickman, Sara
Riola. *Prod:* Realart (Paramount). 5 reels.

SINNERS (1920). Romantic drama of a small-
town girl who goes to New York; as Mary
Horton. *Dir:* Kenneth Webb. *Sc:* Eve Unsell
(from the play by Owen Davis, in which Miss
Brady had starred on Broadway). *With* James
L. Crane, Lorraine Frost, Agnes Everett, Augusta Anderson, Nora Reed, William T. Carleton, Frank Losee, Crauford Kent, Robert
Schable. *Prod:* Realart (Paramount). 5 reels.

A DARK LANTERN (1920). Romantic

melodrama; as Katherine Dereham, society
girl, torn between two loves. *Dir:* John S.
Robertson. *Sc:* Burns Mantle (from a story by
Elizabeth Robbins). *With* James L. Crane, Re-
ginald Denny (in a villainous role), Brandon
Hurst, Marie Burke, David Monterno, Caro-
lyn Irwin, Russell McDermott. *Prod:* Realart
(Paramount). 5 reels.

THE NEW YORK IDEA (1920). Society
comedy of divorce; as Cynthia Karslake. *Dir:*
Herbert Blaché. *Sc:* Mary Murillo (from the
play by Langdon Mitchell, in which Mrs, Fiske
had starred). *With* Lowell Sherman, Hedda
Hopper, George Howell, Lionel Pape, Mar-
garet Linden, Edward Davis, Julia Hurley,
Marie Burke, Emily Fitzroy, Robert Vivian,
Edgar Norton, George Stevens. *Prod:* Realart
(Paramount). 5 reels.

OUT OF THE CHORUS (1921). Romantic
drama; as Florence Maddis, chorus girl, who
marries a rich young man. *Dir:* Herbert
Blaché. *Sc:* Collidge Streeter (from a story by
H. Chandler and W. Lamb). *With* Vernon
Steele, Charles Gerrard, Emily Fitzroy, Edith
Stockton, Richard Carlyle, Constance Berry,
Ben Probst. *Prod:* Realart (Paramount) 5 reels.

THE LAND OF HOPE (1921). Romantic
drama; as Marya Nisko, a Polish immigrant.
Dir: E. H. Griffith. *Sc:* Fred Myton (from a
story by Robert Milton and Frederic and
Fanny Hatton). *With* Jason Robards, Ben
Hendricks, Jr., Schuyler Ladd, Lawrence
Wheat, Martha McGraw, Betty Carsdale, Fuller Mellish. *Prod:* Realart (Paramount). 5
reels.

LITTLE ITALY (1921). Romantic comedy
drama; as Rosa Mascani, Italian emigrant. *Dir:*
George Terwilliger. *Sc:* Peter Milne (from a
play by Frederic and Fanny Hatton). *With*
Norman Kerry, George Fawcett, Jack Ridgway, Gertrude Norman, Luis Alberni, Marguerite Forrest. *Prod:* Realart (Paramount). 5
reels.

DAWN OF THE EAST (1921). Melodrama; as
the Countess Natalya, Russian refugee, who is
blackmailed because she is a bigamist. *Dir:* E.
H. Griffith. *Sc:* E. Lloyd Sheldon. *With* Ken-
neth Harlan, Michio Ito, America Chidester,
Betty Carpenter, Harriet Ross, Sam Kim,
Frank Honda, H. Takemi, Patricia Reyes.
Prod: Realart (Paramount). 5 reels.

HUSH MONEY (1921). Drama; as Evelyn
Murray, a rich girl, who runs over a newsboy.
Dir./Sc: Charles Maigne (from a story by
Samuel Merwin). *With* George Fawcett,
Lawrence Wheat, Harry Benham, Jerrry De-
vine. *Prod:* Realart (Paramount). 5 reels.

MISSING MILLIONS (1922). Romantic
crook drama; as Mary Dawson. *Dir:* Joseph
Henabery. *Sc:* Albert Shelby LeVino (from
two Jack Boyle stories — "A Problem in

Grand Larceny'' and ''An Answer in Grand Larceny''). *With* David Powell, Frank Losee, Riley Hatch, John B. Cooke, William B. Mack, George LeGuere, Alice May, Cooper Cliffe, Sidney Dean, Beverly Travers, Sidney Herbert. *Prod:* Paramount. 6 reels.

ANNA ASCENDS (1922). Romantic comedy melodrama; as Anna Ayyob, a Syrian immigrant. *Dir:* Victor Fleming. *Sc:* Margaret Turnbull (from the play by Harry Chapman Ford, in which Miss Brady had starred on Broadway). *With* Robert Ellis, David Powell, Nita Naldi, Charles Gerrard, Edward Durand, Florence Dixon, Grace Griswold, Fred Burton. *Prod:* Paramount. 6 reels.

THE LEOPARDESS (1923). Romantic melodrama; as Tiare, untamed half-caste of the South Seas. *Dir:* Henry Kolker. *Sc:* J. Clarkson Miller (from a story by Katherine Newlin Burt). *With* Montagu Love, Edward T. Langford, Charles Kent. *Prod:* Paramount. 6 reels.

THE SNOW BRIDE (1923). Romantic melodrama; as Annette Leroux, daughter of a hotel keeper in the Canadian sub-Arctic. *Dir:* Henry Kolker. *Sc:* Sonya Levien (from her story, co-written with Julie Herne). *With* Maurice B. Flynn, Mario Majeroni, Nick Thompson, Jack Baston, Stephen Gratton, W. M. Cavanaugh, Margaret Morgan. *Prod:* Paramount. 5 reels.

WHEN LADIES MEET (1933). Comedy; as Bridget Drake (her talkie debut, in which she received fourth billing, and stole the show). *Dir:* Harry Beaumont. *Sc:* John Meehan and Leon Gordon (from a play by Rachel Crothers). *With* Ann Harding, Myrna Loy, Robert Montgomery, Frank Morgan, Louis Alberni, Martin Burton. (Re-filmed by M-G-M, 1941, with Joan Crawford, Greer Garson, Herbert Marshall, and with Spring Byington in Miss Brady's role). *Prod:* M-G-M. 9 reels.

BROADWAY TO HOLLYWOOD (1933) Backstage saga, with songs and dances; as Lulu Hackett, hoofer, who becomes a big name. *Dir:/Sc:* Williard Mack (co-written with Edgar Allan Woolf). *With* Frank Morgan, Madge Evans, Russell Hardie, Jackie Cooper, Eddie Quillan, Mickey Rooney, Ted Alexander, Edward Brophy, Ruth Channing, Jean Howard, Jimoz Durante, Fay Templeton, May Robson, Claire DuBrey, Muriel Evans, Claude Kaye, Nelson Eddy, Una Merkel, Albertina Rasch Dancers. *Prod:* M-G-M. 10 reels.

BEAUTY FOR SALE (AKA, GB, *Beauty*) (1933). Beauty salon drama; as Letty, a skittish blonde wife. *Dir:* Richard Boleslawski. *Sc:* Zelda Sears and Eve Greene (from a novel, ''Beauty,'' by Faith Baldwin). *With* Madge Evans, Una Merkel, Hedda Hopper, Florine McKinney, Isabel Jewell, Louise Carter, John

Roche, Charles Grapewin. *Prod:* M-G-M. 9 reels.

STAGE MOTHER (1933). Backstage drama; as Kitty Lorraine, a twice-wedded actress, who dedicates herself to her daughter's career. *Dir:* Charles Brabin. *Sc:* John Meehan and Bradford Ropes (from a novel by Ropes). *With* Maureen O'Sullivan, Franchot Tone, Phillips Holmes, Ted Healy, Russell Hardie, C. Henry Gordon, Alan Edwards, Ben Alexander. *Prod:* M-G-M. 81m.

SHOULD LADIES BEHAVE? (1933). Comedy; as Laura, an addle-pated wife. *Dir:* Harry Beaumont. *Sc:* Bella and Samuel Spewack (from a play, ''The Vinegar Tree,'' by Paul Osborn). *With* Lionel Barrymore, Conway Tearle, Katherine Alexander, Mary Carlisle, William Janney, Halliwell Hobbes. *Prod:* M-G-M-. 9 reels.

MISS FANE'S BABY IS STOLEN (AKA, GB, *Kidnapped*) (1934) Melodrama; as Molly Prentiss, farmwife, who outwits some kidnappers. *Dir:* Alexander Hall. *Sc:* Adela Rogers St. Johns (from an adaptation by Jane Storm of a novel by Rupert Hughes). *With* Dorothy Wieck, Baby LeRoy, William Frawley, George Barbier, Alan Hale, Jack LaRue, Dorothy Burgess, Irving Bacon, George ''Spanky'' McFarland, Cullen Johnson, Carmencita Johnson, Kay Lou Barnes. *Prod:* Paramount. 7 reels.

THE GAY DIVORCEE (1934). Romantic musical; as Aunt Hortense. *Dir:* Mark Sandrich. *Sc:* George Marion Jr., Dorothy Yost, Edward Kaufman (from the musical play, ''The Gay Divorce'' by Dwight Taylor, with lyrics and music by Cole Porter). *With* Fred Astaire, Ginger Rogers, Edward Everett Horton, Erik Rhodes, Eric Blore, Betty Grable. *Prod:* RKO. Radio. 13 reels.

LET 'EM HAVE IT (AKA, GB, *False Faces*) (1935). Gangster melodrama; as Aunt Ethel. *Dir:* Sam Wood. *Sc:* J. M. March and Elmer Harris (with additional dialogue by Al Boasberg). *With* Virginia Bruce, Bruce Cabot, Richard Arlen, Harvey Stephens, Eric Linden, Gordon Jones, J. Farrell MacDonald, Paul Stanton, Hale Hamilton, Dorothy Appleby, Barbara Spencer, Matthew Betz, Harry Woods. *Prod:* Reliance-UA. 12 reels.

THE GOLD DIGGERS OF 1935. (1935) Romantical musical; as Mrs. Prentiss. *Dir:* Busby Berkeley. *Sc:* Manuel Seff and Peter Milne (from a story by Milne and Robert Lord). *With* Dick Powell, Gloria Stuart, Adolphe Menjou, Glenda Farrell, Grant Mitchell, Dorothy Dare, Frank McHugh, Hugh Herbert, Winifred Shaw, Joe Cawthorn, Ramon & Rosita, Matty King. *Prod:* Warner Bros. First National. 10 reels.

LADY TUBBS (AKA, GB, *The Gay Lady*).

(1935). Character comedy; as Henrietta ("Mom") Tubbs, who inherits a title. *Dir:* Alan Crosland. *Sc:* Barry Trivers (from a novel by Homer Croy). *With* Douglass Montgomery, Anita Louise, Alan Mowbray, Minor Watson, Russell Hicks, Hedda Hooper, June Clayworth, Lumsden Hare, Harry Tyler, Walter Brennan, Rafael Storm. *Prod:* Universal. 7 reels.

METROPOLITAN (1935). Musical drama; as Ghita Galin, temperamental opera star. *Dir:* Richard Boleslawski. *Sc:* Bess Meredyth and George Marion Jr. (From a story by Miss Meredyth). *With* Lawrence Tibbett, Virginia Bruce, Cesar Romero, Thurston Hall, Luis Alberni, George Marion, Sr., Ruth Donnelly, Franklyn Ardell, Jessie Ralph, Jane Darwell, Walter Brennan, Christian Rub. *Prod:* 20th Century-Fox. 6,685 ft.

THE HARVESTER (1936). Farm comedy drama; as Mrs. Biddle, an ambitious mid-West mother. *Dir:* Joseph Santley. *Sc:* Gertrude Orr and Homer Croy (from an adaptation by Robert Lee Johnson and Elizabeth Meehan of a novel by Gene Stratton Porter). *With* Russell Hardie, Ann Rutherford, Frank Craven, Cora Sue Collins, Emma Dunn, Eddie Nugent, Joyce Compton, Roy Atwell, Spencer Charters, Russell Simpson. *Prod:* Republic. 8 reels. (Filmed as a silent by FBO, 1927.)

MY MAN GODFREY (1936). Screwball romantic comedy; as Angelica Bullock. *Dir:* Gregory LaCava. *Sc:* Morrie Ryskind and Eric Hatch (from a novel by Hatch, "1011 Fifth"). *With* William Powell, Carole Lombard, Gail Patrick, Jean Dixon, Eugene Pallette, Alan Mowbray, Mischa Auer, Robert Light, Pat Flaherty, Franklin Pangborn, Grady Sutton, Edward Gargan, James Flavin, Robert Perry. (Re-made by Ross Hunter, 1957, with David Niven and June Allyson, and with Jessie Royce Landis in Miss Brady's role.) *Prod:* Universal. 10 reels.

GO WEST YOUNG MAN (1936). Romantic comedy; as Mrs. Struthers. *Dir:* Henry Hathaway. *Sc:* Mae West (from the play, "Personal Appearance," by Lawrence Riley.). *With* Mae West, Warren Williams, Randolph Scott, Lyle Talbot, Isabel Jewell, Elizabeth Patterson, Margaret Perry, Jack LaRue, Etienne Girardot, Maynard Holmes, Alice Andell. *Prod:* Paramount. 9 reels.

MIND YOUR OWN BUSINESS (1936). Comedy; as Melba Shanks. *Dir:* Norman McLeod. *Sc:* Dore Schary (from a story by John Francis Larkin). *with* Charlie Ruggles, Lyle Talbot, Benny Baker, Jack LaRue, Frankie Darro, Robert Baldwin, Lloyd Crane, Horace Stewart, William Demarest, Gene Lockhart, Theodore von Eltz. *Prod:* Paramount. 8 reels.

THREE SMART GIRLS (1937). Romantic comedy; with music; as Mrs. Lyons, mother of a fortune hunter. *Dir:* Henry Koster. *Sc:* Adele Comandini and Austin Parker (from a story by Miss Comandini). *With* Deanna Durbin, Nan Grey, Barbara Reed, Charles Winninger, Binnie Barnes, Mischa Auer, Ernest Cossart, Ray Milland, Hobart Cavanaugh, John King, Lucile Watson, Nella Walker. *Prod:* Universal. 9 reels.

CALL IT A DAY (1937). Romantic comedy; as the gabby Muriel West. *Dir:* Archie Mayo. *Sc:* Casey Robinson (from a play by Dodie Smith). *With* Olivia de Havilland, Ian Hunter, Frieda Inescort, Anita Louise, Roland Young, Bonita Granville, Marcia Ralston, Peggy Wood, Walter Woolf King, Peter Willes, Una O'Connor, Beryl Mercer, Elsa Buchanan, Mary Field. *Prod:* Warner Bros. 10 reels.

MAMA STEPS OUT (1937). Domestic comedy; as Ada Cuppy, who drags her family all over Europe in search of culture. *Dir:* George B. Seitz. *Sc:* Anita Loos (from a play, "Ada Beats the Drum," by John Kirkpatrick). *With* Guy Kibbee, Betty Furness, Stanley Morner (Dennis Morgan), Gene Lockhart, Edward Norris, Gregory Gaye, Ivan Lebedeff, Heather Thatcher, Frank Puglia, Adrienne d'Ambricourt. Working title: *Burnt Fingers*. *Prod:* M-G-M. 8 reels.

MR. DODD TAKES THE AIR (1937). Comedy, with music; as Mme. Morro. *Dir:* Alfred E. Green. *Sc:* William Wister Haines and Elaine Ryan (from a story by Clarence Buddington Kelland). *With* Kenny Baker, Jane Wyman, Henry O'Neill, Frank McHugh, Ferris Taylor, Gertrude Michael, John Eldredge, Harry Davenport, Linda Perry. *Prod:* Warner Bros. 88m.

100 MEN AND A GIRL (1937). Romantic comedy, with music; as Mrs. Frost. *Dir:* Henry Koster. *Sc:* Bruce Manning, Charles Kenyon and James Mulhauser (from a story by Hans Kraly). *With* Deanna Durbin, Adolphe Menjou, Leopold Stokowski, Eugene Pallette, Mischa Auer, Billy Gilbert, Alma Kruger, Jack Smart, Jed Prouty, Jameson Thomas, Howard Hickman, Frank Jenks, Christian Rub, Gerald Oliver Smith, Jack Mulhall. *Prod:* Universal. 9 reels.

MERRY-GO-ROUND of 1938 (1937). Musical romance of show business; as Aunt Hortense, eccentric society leader. *Dir:* Irving Cummings. *Sc:* Monte Brice and A. Dorian Otvos (from a story by Brice and Henry Meyers). *With* Bert Lahr, Jimmy Savo, Billy House, Mischa Auer, Joy Hodges, Louise Fazenda, John King, Barbara Read, Dave Apollon, Richard Carle, Hattie McDaniel. *Prod:* Universal. 10 reels.

IN OLD CHICAGO (1937). Period drama, culminating with the great fire which destroyed most of the city; as Molly O'Leary,

Irish widow, whose cow started the fire by kicking over a lantern. *Dir:* Henry King. *Sc:* Lamar Trotti and Sonya Levien (from a story, "We, the O'Learys," by Niven Busch). *With* Tyrone Power, Alice Faye, Don Ameche, Andy Devine, Brian Donlevy, Phyllis Brooks, Tom Brown, Sidney Blackmer, Berton Churchill, June Storey, Paul Hurst. For her performance, Miss Brady won an Academy Award as Best Supporting Actress. *Prod:* 20th Century-Fox. 10,002 ft.

THE JOY OF LIVING (1938). Romantic comedy; as Minerva, pixillated mother of the heroine. *Dir:* Tay Garnett. *Sc:* Gene Towne, Graham Baker and Allan Scott (from a story by Dorothy and Herbert Fields). *With* Irene Dunne, Douglas Fairbanks Jr., Guy Kibbee, Jean Dixon, Eric Blore, Lucille Ball, Warren Hymer, Billy Gilbert, Frank Milan, Franklin Pangborn, John Qualen. *Prod:* RKO Radio. 10 reels.

GOODBYE, BROADWAY (1938). Backstage character comedy; as Molly Malloy, the femme half of a Broadway song-and-dance team. *Dir:* Ray McCarey. *Sc:* Roy Chanslor and A. Dorian Otvos (from the play, "The Shannons of Broadway," by James Gleason). *With* Charles Winninger, Tom Brown, Dorothea Kent, Frank Jenks, Jed Prouty, Willie Best, Donald Meek, Henry Roquemore, Del Henderson, Tommy Riggs. (Previously filmed in 1929 with James and Lucille Webster Gleason.) *Prod:* Universal 8 reels.

ZENOBIA (1939). Comedy; as Mrs. Carter, small-town social dictator. *Dir:* Gordon Douglas. *Sc:* Corey Ford (from the a story by Walter DeLeon and Arnold Belgard). *With* Oliver Hardy, Harry Langdon, Billie Burke, James Ellison, Jean Parker, June Lang, Olin Howland, J. Farrell MacDonald, Stephin Fetchit, Hattie McDaniel, Phillip Hurlie, Hobart Cavanaugh, Clem Bevans, Chester Conklin, Tommy Mack, Robert Dudley, the Hall Johnson Choir, Zenobia (an elephant). *Prod:* United Artists. 8 reels.

YOUNG MR. LINCOLN (1939). Historical drama; as Abigail Clay, whose son is successfully defended in court on a murder charge by young Abe Lincoln. *Dir:* John Ford. *Sc:* Lamar Trotti. *With* Henry Fonda, Marjorie Weaver, Arleen Whelan, Eddie Collins, Pauline Moore, Richard Cromwell, Donald Meek, Judith Dickens, Eddie Quillan, Spencer Charters, Ward Bond, Francis Ford, Fred Kohler Jr., Russell Simpson, Jack Kelly, Dickie Jones, Milburn Stone. *Prod:* 20th Century-Fox. 9,050 ft.

(There is a cameo bit of Miss Brady as herself in an exploitation two-reeler of 1922, *A Trip to Paramountown.*)

10
LON CHANEY

Too many think of Lon Chaney only as a master of the macabre, an actor who excelled in horror. He is thought of quite rightly as "The Man of a Thousand Faces," and even he was reportedly amused by the old anecdote about an onlooker cautioning somebody in the act of crushing a spider underfoot, "Don't step on it — it may be Lon Chaney!"

The best pictures Chaney made go much deeper than the obviously bizarre. They are romances, love stories in the purest sense of the word. His big starring features, the ones most fondly remembered, are variations of "La belle et la bête."

Since the days of the ancient Greeks, when Aphrodite gave her love to the mis-shapen Hephaestos, audiences have found any tale about Beauty and the Beast strangely attractive, one with which they can empathise. A woman's beauty is magnified when she is adored and protected by a supremely ugly and/or deformed man. She may be drawn to him through pity which, if not akin to love, is at least nourishing of an erotic affection. Such a union represents the ideally romantic mating: the strong but ugly male who gives of all that he possesses, even unto his own life; and the radiantly beautiful female who takes of all that is given and frequently does not even bestow gratitude in return.

This was the framework for the stories of *The Hunchback of Notre Dame; The Phantom of the Opera; Laugh, Clown, Laugh; The Tower of Lies; He Who Gets Slapped;* and on back to such primitive Universal offerings as *Remember Mary Magdalen* and *The Sea Urchin.* Chaney was at his best when he loved and sacrificed in silence and most often in vain, when a forced or painted smile hid a broken heart. He was the Frog Prince who never had a chance to turn into the handsome lover; he was Pagliacci or Cyrano de Bergerac, who loved and were betrayed by love.

It is an element obvious even in certain phases of his early personal history.

He was born Alonso Chaney on April 1, 1883, in Colorado Springs, Colorado, the second of four children born to deaf and dumb parents, Frank H. and Emma Chaney. His father, who worked profitably as a barber, had emigrated from Ireland, and had been deaf and mute since the age of three. Chaney's mother had never heard or spoken; her own mother, Emma Kennedy, who had given birth to four impaired children, was known importantly

as one of the original founders of Colorado's State Institution for the Deaf and Dumb. Emma Chaney's children, however, heard everything and spoke from infancy loudly and clearly; they suffered no impairment of this kind.

When Chaney was only nine years old and a fourth-grade student in Colorado Springs' public school, his mother was hopelessly stricken with inflammatory rheumatism, and remained bedridden throughout the rest of her life. It was her son Lon who left school to tend her faithfully during the first three years of her invalidism. It was he who filled his eyes and mind with both the unusual and everyday happenings of Colorado Springs, and later interpreted their essence in pantomime so that she too might see and relish his experiences. Small wonder that he became and remained a master of the pantomimic art. He learned out of necessity at an early age how to touch the heart through expression and gesture alone.

In the summertime he worked as a tourist guide on Pike's Peak, and later, through the offices of his elder brother John, who was employed at Colorado Springs' Opera House, he found work backstage as property boy, scene painter, and stagehand. By the time he had been granted brief stage appearances in crowd scenes and then allowed to speak fragments of lines in leading mobs, he was admittedly and hopelessly stagestruck.

His father, however, was of the opinion that one son in the theatre was quite enough; Frank Chaney pulled a few strings, and Lon, scarcely in his midteens, was sent off to Denver, where he became an apprentice paper-hanger and carpet-layer. In later years he remarked: "It's one trade I really know. I can hang paper and lay carpets as well as any man...Say, the old Antler's Hotel in Colorado Springs is one of my jobs and there still is paper on those walls that I hung."

But he couldn't get the theatre out of his blood; he had had a taste of the footlights; he had watched great actors like Richard Mansfield transform themselves through the magic of make-up into Beau Brummel one night and Ivan the Terrible the next. It was a life he himself yearned to live.

When his brother John decided to form a company of his own and embark upon a one-night stand tour of the Southwest, he called Lon home and, together, they wrote an original play, "The Little Tycoon." Aged seventeen Lon went out on the road as an actor playing in the drama of which he was co-author; he also played singing and dancing roles in a modest *mélange* of Gilbert and Sullivan operettas which were added to the repertory. Thus he was not only playwright and player, but also song-and-dance man, transportation agent, scene shifter, and stage manager as well. To the end of his days he carried his life-membership card in the stage employee's union, and when asked, would open his wallet and proudly display it and all the other trade union cards in which he kept up his membership.

The inevitable happened and the little travelling company went broke. John Chaney sold out his interest to the leading tenor, and returned to Colorado Springs; but by this time Lon was a pro and continued on the road with the Columbia Musical Comedy Repertory Company. He now sustained all his previous duties plus an added one: wardrobe *mistress!* He was paid $12 weekly, out of which he somehow managed to save $4. Of his work at this time, he said: "Though I played in musical comedy for years, I know nothing of music and couldn't sing a note, but a comedian has much liberty in this line and can always get by with reciting his songs and adding a little dancing to the number. The only dramatic role I ever played was Gaspard in 'Chimes of Normandy'.''

Chaney was only 19 when, in Oklahoma City, he fell in love with a singer he'd hired for the show, Cleva Creighton. They were finally married in the spring of 1905, and the following year Chaney's only child, a son, was born. The boy was named Creighton Chaney; he too became an actor and years later, after his father's death, changed his name to Lon Chaney Jr.

The Chaneys went to Chicago where, through an actor friend Lee Moran, Lon Chaney got a job in a show called "The Red Kimono." He and his young wife were anxious to get to the warmer climate of the Pacific Coast with their baby. Gradually they made it, and John Chaney, by this time stage manager of the Lyceum Theatre in Los Angeles, found a job for his brother as a song-and-dance comedian. Chaney then joined the company of Kolb and Dill, German comedians who enjoyed a great vogue on the Coast, and played a season with them in San Francisco.

It was there that his young wife came into her own as a singer in the theatre and she was also the hit of many a midnight cabaret show. Her popularity topped Chaney's. For the first time he wasn't pre-eminently Lon Chaney, actor; he was more often to be pointed out as the homely husband of beautiful Cleva Creighton.

She had many insecurities. Worst of all, she was not an amiable drinker, and she began to drink too much. Their quarrels were frequent. On one occasion, at least, Chaney accused her of infidelity. Dramatically, she attempted to take her life by swallowing poison. She did not die, but after a long hospital siege, she found that the poison she had taken had ruined her vocal cords forever. Her husband had gained control of their baby son when she had been committed as a psychological alcoholic, and they both disappeared from her life. The desperate letters she wrote remained unanswered, and eventually in 1914 he divorced her. Chaney could be a hard man. He had a strict ethical code, and when it was violated, he became ruthlessly cold.

There had been a girl in the chorus at San Francisco's Princess Theatre when Chaney was playing there with the Ferris Hartman Opera Company; her name was Hazel Hastings, and she was married to the legless man who ran a cigar counter. Chaney and she fell in love, and when they were each free, they married, and until he was grown, young Creighton Chaney did not even know that Hazel Hastings Chaney was not his real mother. Chaney and his second wife were a devoted couple, and he frequently declared that her love and steadfast faith helped him become one of the top actors of his time.

Chaney once stated that he got into films because the musical he was playing in got stranded in Santa Ana, then a sleepy little rural centre about forty miles south of Los Angeles in Orange County. Almost penniless, he spent what little he had on carfare into Los Angeles and thence out to Universal City, where his old friend from Chicago, Lee Moran, again opened the door, this time paving the way for Chaney's initial film work. This was in 1912, but it was not until 1913 that Chaney began to get credit for his work as an actor. He learned his craft by playing extra and bits in countless comedies and western action dramas. At that time the regular feature film rarely exceeded three reels in length, and was more often one or two. By 1913, at least at Universal, players and sometimes directors were beginning to be credited; it took longer for writers, cameramen, film editors, and the entire coterie of craftsmen who contribute to the making of a film. But Chaney received definite billing, and sole billing at that, for an Imp comedy released through Universal in August, 1913, called *Poor Jake's Demise*.

He became a regular on the Universal lot, and while never under actual contract during those early years, he was on the weekly payroll list. In those days a great many unit companies filmed at Universal and released regularly through the company's distributing office. Chaney worked for almost all of those units — Powers, Joker, Victor, Gold Seal, Rex, 101 Bison, Nestor, Bluebird, Red Feather, Jewel. As his importance as an actor grew, his versatility became recognised, for he played leading man, hero, villain, character man, comic, or monster with equal ease. He often worked with film people who were just getting a good start, and they became, like him, the best. Together, they all learned this new business of film-making. Names like Allan Dwan, Joseph de Grasse, Allen Holubar, Ida May Park, Jeanie Macpherson, Robert Z. Leonard, Bess Meredyth, Dorothy Phillips — directors, writers, actors — these were only some of his studio associates during these beginning years.

For more than five years Chaney remained exclusively on the Universal lot. He was not entirely content. Considering the amount of work he did without complaint, he was certainly underpaid; but most of the films in which he appeared were only routine feature fare. He was already a master of the art of make-up, and it must have galled him when players like Murdoch MacQuarrie and King Baggott were elevated to starring roles and given demanding parts with fascinating protean characters (in one picture Baggott was billed as playing nine different characterisations), while he usually got no more than the one-dimensional cardboard stock characters. But he kept his silence, for the work was regular and he had constant domestic obligations to meet.

Even then, few at the studio really knew him; he was always agreeable; he did his job and was patient; he was never temperamental. For a while at Universal he and Jean Hersholt shared a dressing-room, but although there was a mutual respect between them, they were not really close friends. Chaney was actually friendlier with the members of his crew, both skilled and unskilled, and many such a labourer has tales to tell of Chaney's personal unsolicited help and kindness, given when he knew it was needed. But for most of his fellow workers, Chaney from the beginning followed one maxim: "Between pictures, there is no Lon Chaney." His own life, his privacy, he determined, would always be his alone.

In 1915, Universal gave him a chance to direct several programme features; he also wrote several scripts — but he pursued neither field to any great length. He knew that he excelled as an actor, and he was basically too much of a perfectionist not to want to excel. Besides, his wife kept assuring him that some day the chance to rise to the top of the acting profession would be his. By no means did his talent as an actor, however, go unrecognised. In the April 25, 1914, issue of his own studio's exhibitor's organ, "Universal Weekly," the reviewer for a 101 Bison feature, *The Tragedy of Whispering Creek,* noted: "And then there is Mr. Chaney in the role of the Greaser. Mr. Chaney has used his own idea in working out the character, a pervert, in this play and what he has given us is startling to an unusual degree. True, he paints a horrible picture for us — one that is apt to cause a feeling of revulsion. But that is as it should be. In fact Mr. Chaney has created a new character — one that will live long — that will be copied as a newer standard by others.''

Chaney gained billing in over seventy-five films before, in 1917, he finally had a good part in a major feature that was not only critically rewarding but also a big audience box-office attraction. His characterisations had changed so completely from picture to picture that many fans were not quite sure who Lon Chaney really was. After *Hell Morgan's Girl*, he did not lack for recognition, at least of a surface kind. Directed by Joseph de Grasse from a Harvey Gates story scenarised by Ida May Park (Mrs. de Grasse), *Hell Morgan's Girl* presented Chaney in the role of Sleter Noble, a tough but sexy politician gang leader of San Francisco's Barbary Coast. Sleter is intrigued by Lola (Dorothy Phillips), a dancehall entertainer known as Hell Morgan's Girl, because her father Hell Morgan (Alfred Allen) runs the honky tonk gambling saloon where she is queen. Into the dive one night wanders Roger Curwell (William Stowell), an alcoholic socialite, and when Lola is drawn almost at once to help and then to love Roger, and Sleter Noble sees the girl he had hoped to win for himself falling for this handsome ne'er-do-well, his passions are twisted into hate, and a burning desire for revenge begins to rule his life. The story is climaxed dramatically with the 1906 fire and earthquake, which destroyed a good part of San Francisco. Sleter Noble loses his life in the roaring holocaust, but Lon Chaney's career as an important star in special features was born.

He had already played leads with Dorothy Phillips in Universal-released films, and after their success in *Hell Morgan's Girl*, they and William Stowell were cast in a series of features, every one of which rang the bell of success at the box-office. Also in 1917 a version of Ibsen's play, *A Doll's House,* brought all three of them critical and audience recognition; in fact, in the very next year, the highly acclaimed and beautiful Elsie Ferguson made a version of *A Doll's House* with Maurice Tourneur directing for Paramount-Artcraft. Bigger budgeted and more promising, it somehow did not come off with the genuine success accorded the Universal programme feature.

With every top actor, there are certain titles that are signposts at crossroads in his career. *Hell Morgan's Girl* pointed the way, but Chaney had to go off the Universal lot for the first time in order to play a role that not only clearly indicated his star potential, but restored in him conclusively his own self-confidence as a player. After five years at Universal, he had unwittingly fallen into a rut. Other players stormed, were accused of being impossible and temperamental, had the good fortune to meet a sponsor, and became stars. Chaney, a far more accomplished actor, had become almost non-assertive. Even on camera he had learned that it was wiser not to steal the picture from the star. Being always competent was at least better than being incompetent or, even worse, seeing a good performance land on the cutting-room floor because his histrionics dared outshine those of the principal player.

It was, oddly enough, a star, William S. Hart, who gave him a new perspective on his craft. Hart had seen Chaney as the villain in several Universal westerns and also in *Hell Morgan's Girl*. When he was casting a new film which he had written for Paramount-Artcraft, *Riddle Gawne,* he asked that

Lon Chancy in PHANTOM OF THE OPERA

Lon Chaney be sent for and considered for the role of the villain, Hame Bozzam. Both director Lambert Hillyer and the studio casting man interviewed Chaney; it was their shared opinion that he had a strong face, but was too short to play opposite Hart.

Hart was still curious and asked that Chaney be sent for again, saying he would wait at the studio until the actor came and met him personally. In his autobiography, "My Life East and West," Hart describes his first meeting with Chaney: "The actor came back and I saw him. There were quite a few inches difference in our height. We were alone in the room. He turned away regretfully, saying 'I didn't think you were as tall as you are. They told me I wouldn't do, that I was too short.'

"'Inches never made an actor,' I replied. 'You're an actor. You get the part.'"

Hart goes on to reveal how in the first scene he played before the camera with Chaney, he was dissatisfied. Something was wrong; Chaney was holding back; the conflict didn't measure up, and naturally the scene didn't come off. After several takes, Hart took Chaney aside, and told him: "That scene is all wrong, Lon. There is no question about your ability to play it. You can play anything. You just haven't got the idea. Do you mind if we change parts and rehearse the scene over? I will play your part and you play mine. I want to show you just what I mean."

Chaney could hardly believe what was happening. He was playing a gunman, and so was Hart, but the star was insisting that their work together should be "diamond cut diamond." He openly admitted to both Lambert Hillyer and Hart: "I can't realise it; boys, I'm up in the air — it's the first time I've ever been allowed to *play* a scene when the star was in it."

That scene, when they finally shot it, was, in Hart's words, "a pippin." It also made Chaney determine that in the future he would always play a scene to the best of his ability, no matter who the actor was in it with him.

He went back to Universal, played in some more programme features, but never again deliberately soft-pedalled a scene, even when the star was as noted for her temperamental displays as Mae Murray (*Danger – Go Slow*). The most important thing that happened to Chaney at this time was his meeting and working with Tod Browning as director. It was for a Priscilla Dean crook melodrama, *The Wicked Darling*. There was an instant *simpatico* between Chaney and Browning, and the subsequent Chaney features which Browning directed at Universal and later at M-G-M were to be among the best and most popular either made.

At this point, however, Universal was not willing to give Chaney either the roles or the money he believed his work merited. He had gained a place on the company's stock player list, but the studio let him go, believing it cheaper to hire him by the picture if they so wished. He was told he was "just another player," and was entirely expendable.

Hazel Hastings Chaney never once lost faith in her husband's ability during this trying crisis in his career. She encouraged him to seek roles at other studios. He did so, however unimportantly, with a Lone Wolf spy melodrama, *False Faces,* for Thomas H. Ince, and a western thriller, *A Man's Country,* for Robertson-Cole, in which he made life hell for beautiful Alma Rubens, who wanted to change her dancehall ways.

At this point Universal sent for him to return and play a role for the studio in *Paid in Advance*, a feature directed by Allen Holubar and co-starring Dorothy Phillips and Priscilla Dean. Grudgingly, Universal met the terms Chaney asked. It was long before the day of agents, and Chaney quoted his own terms, and made his own deals. He was a thorough professional, and he had forced respect for his talents from the studio that had created and then sought to belittle him.

But Universal had no intention of putting him under contract at his own terms after *Paid in Advance,* good as he was and profitably as that Klondike melodrama paid off at the box-office.

He had reached another crossroads, and again the picture that signalled a new phase of his career was off his "home" lot. It was *The Miracle Man,* directed by George Loane Tucker.

Chaney was signed to play the role of a bogus cripple known as "The Frog." He was one of a gang of crooks who sees in the honest spiritual manifestations of a blind miracle worker a chance for quick money; but instead, with the others, "The Frog" is regenerated. Thomas Meighan, Betty Compson, Elinor Fair, and Chaney played the leads in *The Miracle Man,* and the picture brought stardom to all of them.

Somewhat later, to Maude S. Cheatham, in an interview for the March 1920 issue of "Motion Picture Classic," Chaney gave one of his few authorised and revealing interviews. Miss Cheatham noted of Chaney in *The Miracle Man:* "All through the horror of the early scenes, where as an underworld derelict preying upon the sympathies of the slum sight-seekers with his faked paralysis, to his inspiring regeneration, not one false note was struck, and it remains as a unique study in sharp contrasts."

Said Chaney to her: "I'll confess that, with all my knowledge of make-up — and I have been character actor both in musical comedy and on the screen during my entire professional career — I had some difficulty in deciding just what to use for 'The Frog.' In the first place, I planned to be a cripple, have a withered hand, a hump on my back, but when I discovered that I had to unfold *twice* before the camera, these three infirmities were, of course impossible.

"Finally, after several sleepless nights and a number of experiments, I decided on — paralysis! I let my beard grow, and altogether I worked out a convincing make-up, horrible as it was.

"We spent twelve weeks making *The Miracle Man,* and it was a wonderful experience, for Mr. Tucker was certainly inspired, and he inspired us until we were all living our parts every minute of the time. He works very quietly, directing every scene himself, and he went through those underworld scenes relentlessly, with set jaw and cold eyes, while in the emotional moments he cried as hard as the rest of us."

The Miracle Man brought Chaney real success critically as well as audience-wise, and it also brought him the unending respect of every worker in his own profession. In the next eighteen months he was constantly busy; the best of his pictures during this period were the two he made directed by Maurice Tourneur — a version of Conrad's *Victory,* in which he played the despicable Ricardo, and a dramatisation of Robert Louis Stevenson's *Treasure Island,* in which he enacted two entirely different roles: the blood-thirsty pirate Merry and the blind man named Pew. Late in 1920, *The Penalty,* the first film he made for Samuel Goldwyn, was released; in it he played Blizzard, the legless ruler of San Francisco's underworld who lives to avenge himself on the respected surgeon who had crippled him.

Tod Browning wanted him for a crook drama, *Outside the Law,* which he was directing at Universal with Priscilla Dean, and once again Universal was

4159-143

Lon Chaney descends the great staircase in PHANTOM OF THE OPERA

forced to meet Chaney's rising financial terms. They could only console themselves that he was worth every penny of the salary he demanded, and got. This time he was unique in another dual role, playing both "Black Mike" Sylva, arch criminal of San Francisco's underworld, and the enigmatic but ruthless Chinese named Ah Wing. In the film's exciting *dénouement,* it is Ah Wing who shoots and kills Sylva, and the scene was much commented on in its day, for it involved a highly effective use of trick photography in which Chaney playing one character murders himself playing another. *Outside the Law* remains one of the best crook melodramas of the silent era, and it stands as the third important signpost in Chaney's illustrious career, for it not only gave him two electrifying parts to play, but also served to cement the professional rapport between Tod Browning, director, and Lon Chaney, actor.

During the next two years, Chaney continued to dazzle his audiences with one vivid characterisation after another: there were four more for Goldwyn, two for the old Metro company, several independent features, one more for Universal, and a pair for First National, the better one being his appearance as Fagin in the Frank Lloyd version of *Oliver Twist*, starring Jackie Coogan in the title role.

In 1923 Universal consummated a two-picture deal with Chaney. They had determined to make a twelve-reel Super-Jewel screen version of Victor Hugo's "Notre-Dame de Paris," more commonly known to English readers as *The Hunchback of Notre Dame,* and it was obvious that only one actor could play the role of Quasimodo. This characterisation marks the fourth real milestone in Chaney's distinguished career, for with it he was for the first time the undisputed star of a special big-budgeted film, and it brought him into close professional association with Irving Thalberg, then working as a production executive for Carl Laemmle at Universal and soon to be responsible for the best films emerging from M-G-M. From the beginning, Thalberg had only the highest regard for Chaney's work, and the Chaney productions he sponsored at Universal and subsequently at M-G-M were always to reflect faultless taste and careful thought, and to provide their star with superlative acting roles.

While the massive sets were being constructed and all the pre-production work on *The Hunchback* was being completed, Chaney agreed to film a Universal-Jewel presentation directed by Lambert Hillyer, who had guided him through *Riddle Gawne* with William S. Hart. The picture was *The Shock,* and again he played a crippled leader of the San Francisco underworld who finds regeneration and peace in his love for a beautiful innocent young girl, sensitively played by Virginia Valli. Once more the big 1906 fire and earthquake brought the filmic drama to an exciting climax, but *The Shock* has become one of the overlooked, almost forgotten features of the time, because only a summer intervened between its release and that of the truly spectacular *Hunchback of Notre Dame*.

Chaney's Quasimodo remains a definitive performance, although *The Hunchback of Notre Dame* has twice been re-made in talking films, once by Charles Laughton and subsequently in Paris by Anthony Quinn. Chaney's Quasimodo stands as the only one that is emotionally stirring and truly tragic; his Quasimodo was the ugly beast who adored and protected the beautiful gypsy girl Esmeralda, and although his make-up was grotesque and repulsive, no one could miss the innocent beauty and childlike devotion flooding this unfortunate monster's heart. His performance was not just an acting *tour de force;* it was much more than that — a believable interpretation of a very human being.

Chaney is the only actor who went directly to the pages of Hugo's novel for his interpretation of the role of Quasimodo. All other actors playing the part have been gimmicky, but Chaney's was basically simple and true; there was in it the catharsis that always distinguishes genuine tragedy.

The ugly hump that disfigured his shoulders and back consisted of forty pounds of rubber, and he added another thirty pounds of weight to his own with a breastplate and leather harness. When Charles Laughton did his version of Quasimodo for RKO's *Hunchback of Notre Dame,* he used a *papier mâché* hump that only weighed two pounds, for he knew he could never achieve what Chaney had with so excessive a handicap. Said Laughton: "Chaney not only was a great actor; he was a magnificent dancer. The famous ballet stars, like Nijinsky, could express every emotion and every shade of meaning in the movements of their bodies. Chaney had that gift. When he realised that he had lost the girl, his body expressed it — it was as though a bolt of lightning had shattered his physical self. Extraordinary, really!"

Chaney's performance of Quasimodo stunned the entire world into a universal acclaim for his talent. The next year, when Thalberg took over the production reins at M-G-M, one of the first things he did was to sign Chaney to a long-term starring contract at the Culver City lot. Chaney's first starring vehicle there was directed by the brilliant Swedish actor-director Victor Seastrom: *He Who Gets Slapped,* based on the Andreyev play. Norma Shearer and John Gilbert were the lovers, and Chaney scored a genuine artistic triumph as the once-great scientist who, on being betrayed by his wife and best friend, renounces his personal identity to seek refuge as the clown known simply as "He," who every night under the circus tent delights a packed audience with the sadistic treatment he so unprotestingly accepts. The picture was an artistic triumph and established Chaney as a top M-G-M star, even though the company was then about to announce that they had "More Stars Than There Are In the Heavens!"

In the late summer of 1925, the talents of Browning and Chaney merged again to present for M-G-M what was probably their best joint endeavor — *The Unholy Three,* a crime drama of three master criminals, which gave Chaney a chance to offer a vivid characterisation as Echo, the Ventriloquist, and also an opportunity to don a grey wig, be-ribboned bonnet and bombazine skirts to play a bizarre but believable fence for the criminal world referred to in the picture as both Mrs. O'Grady and Grandma O'Grady, but identified on the programme cast-list as "The Little Lady Who Sells Parrots."

The Unholy Three met with great public and critical response, and that, coupled with the gratifying response *The Hunchback of Notre Dame* had met, forced Universal to admit too late what they had let slip through their fingers in allowing Chaney to sign with a rival studio. The powers-that-be there thus negotiated with Thalberg for a loan-out on a single-picture basis. Chaney, when he learned that the projected special was to be a big ten-reel version of Gaston Leroux's novel *The Phantom of the Opera,* was not unwilling; and when he returned to the studio to play Erik, the Phantom, he did so, knowing that his position was satisfyingly unique, that without him Universal would never even have tried to film *The Phantom of the Opera.* He had become not "just another player," as he had been told he was when the front-office rejected his request for bigger money and roles; he was a star who could not be replaced, whose presence in this particular film was mandatory.

The Phantom of the Opera had its problems during production, but none of them emanated from Chaney. Again, he had the perfect role, the kind in which he had proved himself a master — a disfigured genius who lives for vengeance and so trains and brings a beauteous singer to stardom in order to achieve his end. The studio constructed the interior of the Paris Opera, as well as a maze of elaborate sets representing the Paris underground domain. No expense was spared, and the deluxe production paid off munificently for both the studio and, of course, for Chaney himself. Who can forget the big moments of this classic horror romance? — the fall of the crystal chandelier; that terrifying moment when Mary Philbin, as Christine, tears off the Phantom's mask, revealing for the first time his horrible ugliness; the love scene on the Opera rooftop where the lovers steal away for a rendezvous, while the Phantom hovers over them, his red-lined cloak whipping ominously in the night wind; the climactic chase through the streets and sewers when all Paris seeks to trap the maddened Phantom.

After *The Phantom of the Opera,* Chaney returned to M-G-M, the acknowledged giant among the male stars of the lot. He had much in common with the goddess of the studio, Greta Garbo: they were dedicated; they worked hard; they shunned publicity, demanding that their personal lives be their own; and they were idolised. Chaney and Garbo used to pass one another as they walked to their separate stages and dressing-rooms; they smiled in amusement at one another, but never spoke. They were kindred spirits and did not have to exchange words. Twice announcements were made about Chaney and Garbo co-starring: once in a feature that Tod Browning would direct from a story he had devised tentatively called *Alonso, the Armless,* but when that was filmed in 1927 it was called *The Unknown,* and a rising young star in her own right, Joan Crawford, played the role. There was a sea story, too, called *The Ordeal,* announced in mid-1926 to co-star Chaney with Garbo, with Marcel de Sano directing; but de Sano withdrew because "when he found Greta Garbo was in the cast and would be expected to fall in love with Lon, he thought that was too terribly incongruous, and refused to direct it." The following year it was again announced for Chaney and Garbo, with John Griffith Wray to direct, but nothing came of that either. Finally filmed, it was called *The Ship from Shanghai* (1930), and had neither Chaney nor Garbo in it, but Louis Wolheim and Kay Johnson in the leads, and there was no love interest between them.

Chaney continued to be the mystery man of M-G-M. He let no one know much about him. He lived unostentatiously in Beverly Hills, and only on very rare occasions did he don black tie and attend a *première* with his wife. The studio, in an effort to be co-operative, once offered him a valet; he was amused by their generosity, but declined the offer. His hobby was amateur film-making, and scarcely anybody at M-G-M recognised him in the quiet, average-sized, ordinarily dressed cameraman wearing a cap who took candid shots of the dignitaries from all parts of the globe who nearly every day visited the studio. If he was seen in the company of anybody at all, it was usually his chauffeur, John Jeske. When a picture had finished shooting, he disappeared somewhere up in the high Sierras with all his fishing gear, his camera equipment, and a bagful of books. He and his wife often entertained at home, but their guests were not film people. He chose to be withdrawn, uncommunicative, and, sometimes, even dour.

Thalberg soon had another production ready for Chaney, one to be directed again by Victor Seastrom: *The Tower of Lies,* adapted from Selma Lagerlöf's Swedish novel, "The Emperor of Portugallia." Norma Shearer played Chaney's daughter, and the farmboy who loved her was William Haines. It was a moody intense psychological drama, with beautiful pastoral backgrounds, and Chaney played a simple, hard-working peasant whose tormented loneliness and frustrated desires finally drive him into a world of complete fantasy. There are many who consider it his greatest artistic triumph, and it may very well be exactly that. It is a picture that has demanded, and is finally getting revival.

In the next four years, Chaney starred in thirteen more features for M-G-M. Supervised by Thalberg and allowed every production advantage, they presented their star in a variety of roles designed to exhibit to the fullest his many-faceted skill as an actor. Seven of them were directed by Tod Browning, and Chaney portrayed a London criminal who poses as a bishop (*The Blackbird*); a vengeance-seeking, ruthless one-eyed ruler of Singapore's underworld (*The Road to Mandalay*); the armless knife-throwing star of a European circus (*The Unknown*); dual roles as a hypnotist and modern vampire (*London after Midnight*); a bitter gangster who finally lets himself be won by Betty Compson as the one woman who loves him, and when she embraces him in gratitude, he snarls, "Listen! I ain't going to buy you nothing. I'm just going to marry you" (*The Big City*); a onetime vaudeville performer who follows the man who had ruined his happiness to Africa and there sets about destroying him (*West of Zanzibar*); a sympathetic trapper of wild animals who adores his daughter and when his evil ex-wife traps him, he looses a savage gorilla upon her (*Where East Is East*).

In my opinion, however, his best performance during these years was in a ten-reel special M-G-M made to glorify the American Marine Corps, directed by George W. Hill, and titled *Tell It to the Marines*. Chaney played the tough Sergeant O'Hara without any trace of make-up whatsoever, and it became a memorable characterisation replete with guts, sympathy, and virile humour. Because of it, he was made an honorary member of the Marine Corps and an honour guard officer for life. *Tell It to the Marines* also gave William Haines his best role as a racetrack heel forced to become a Marine and made into a man by his hard-boiled sergeant. This is still another feature which I hope will be resuscitated and revived.

Chaney's own particular favourite of all the roles he played was released in June of 1928, *Laugh, Clown, Laugh*, a film of the David Belasco-Tom Cushing play. It bordered perilously upon bathos, but, because of Chaney's consummate art and director Herbert Brenon's skill, it never once slipped into that trap. Chaney played a circus clown who fathers an orphan girl, falls hopelessly in love with her, and then realising that she loves and is loved by a wealthy young nobleman of her own generation, he releases her by "accidentally" falling to his death in the perilous stunt nightly climaxing his circus act.

The three features Chaney filmed in 1929 all boasted special sound effects, but no talking sequences. Chaney, like Garbo and Chaplin, held out as long as he could from making a talking picture. He felt that the prime illusion of the cinema was contained in the pantomimic art, and he knew he was a master of that. But after his final silent release, *Thunder*, a railroad drama in which he played a fearless and grumpy engineer, he realised that he must resign himself to the inevitable and make his *début* in a talking film.

Thalberg permitted him to take his time in selecting a vehicle. Hollywood buzzed with the rumour that Chaney would not make a talkie because he suffered from a throat affliction that had affected his vocal cords. During the filming of *Thunder*, a piece of artifical snow had lodged in his throat and was causing a constant irritation. Actually, the delay in announcing his first talking picture was caused because Chaney, with Thalberg's help, was negotiating a new and highly profitable contract at M-G-M. When it was approved and signed, he agreed to make his talking feature *début* in a new version of his big silent success, *The Unholy Three*. He wanted Betty Compson to appear with him, but she was already committed to a highly profitable renaissance of her own career in talkies at two other studios, and so she suggested that he give the role of Rosie, which Mae Busch had created, to her own good friend Lila Lee, who had already proved her worth in talking films. Chaney was agreeable, and he also did not object to Jack Conway's directing the film, nor did he dispute the screenplay's being revised into dramatic continuity and dialogue sequences by the proficient father-son team of J. C. and Elliott Nugent.

He concentrated entirely on his own role. If he had gained the catch-phrase of "The Man of a Thousand Faces," he was determined that he would also aptly be known as "The Man of a Thousand Voices." He played his original dual role, but also affected several other disguises and used five distinct character voices in promoting the part. Wanting the public to rest assured that he had dubbed no other actor's voice to fit his lip movements, he had the studio's attorney draw up an affidavit to that effect. It was notarised; he signed it, and it was featured in all publicity.

The talking version of *The Unholy Three* was enthusiastically received when it was premiered in midsummer of 1930. Meanwhile, ironically, Chaney

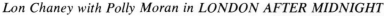

Lon Chaney with Polly Moran in LONDON AFTER MIDNIGHT

was plagued with a recurring throat illness. Hollywood rumour once more became hard fact.

Following the completion of *The Unholy Three* Chaney journeyed to New York, where he consulted throat specialists. His trouble was more than tonsillitis, because he had recently undergone a tonsillectomy, or any throat irritation caused by a fleck of artificial snow. The specialists determined among themselves that he was suffering from a bronchial cancer that could be terminal. He was not told, nor did his public, of course, know that his days were numbered. Several possible vehicles were announced as follow-up productions for him by Thalberg. Chaney went to his cabin in the high Sierras, hoping that a long rest would restore his health, but struck by pneumonia and then found to be suffering from anaemia, he was forced to return to Los Angeles and St. Vincent's Hospital there, where he underwent a series of blood transfusions.

He responded to treatment, although his voice was completely gone and ironically for a star who had just made his *début* as a talking actor, he could only pantomime his needs and thoughts. In the early hours of August 26, 1930, he died of a haemorrhage of the throat.

At the funeral services, Sam and Jack Feinberg, set musicans who had played mood music for him on the sets of all his silent features since *The Hunchback of Notre Dame,* played a selection of the songs he had loved, reducing the very few who had known him and all those who had worked with him to a state of helpless tears.

With him, died a cinematic era and in him perished a master of the pantomimic art. Re-makes have been attempted of some of his great hits, but none has risen again to greatness without him. In 1957, Universal released a film, *Man of a Thousand Faces,* based upon Chaney's life, but it was mainly a synthetic feature distinguished only by a remarkably effective performance by James Cagney as Lon Chaney. When Cagney had been announced for the part, many thought it one more patent example of miscasting, but Cagney, a true artist in his own right, caught the vital essence that was Chaney and translated it into film.

Chaney's only son Creighton entered films as an actor in 1933, and did not fare well until sometime after the death of his father when he became known professionally as Lon Chaney Jr., and he then played in a great many horror films. But his fame never touched that of his father; he filmed very little after 1959, and died July 14, 1973.

In the forty-seven years of his busy life, Lon Chaney carved a very special niche for himself in the world of the moving picture. No other character actor so captured the fancy of film fans and critics as this ugly Colorado boy who became a genius of pantomime, a master of make-up, a consummate and very unique actor who brought a strangely satisfying and wilder beauty into millions of starved lives. He was a true poet, and he worked with film rather than words. Because of that, the "beast" himself finally became utterly beautiful.

LON CHANEY FILMOGRAPHY

POOR JAKE'S DEMISE (1913). Farce; in his first official billing, and the only player listed by name. *Dir:* probably Allan Curtis. *Prod:* Imp/Universal. 1 reel.

THE SEA URCHIN (1913). Sea romance; as Ben, a hunchbacked fisherman who relinquishes his love to another. *With* Jeanie Macpherson and Robert Z. Leonard. *Prod:* Powers/Universal.

THE TRAP (1913). Social drama; as a ne'er-do-well who steals from his brother. *With* Cleo Madison. *Prod:* Powers/Universal.

ALMOST AN ACTRESS (1913). Slapstick comedy, with a movie-making background; as the Cameraman. *Dir:* probably Allan Curtis. *With* Louise Fazenda, Max Asher, Edward Holland, Lee Morris (Moran?), Silvion de Jardins. *Prod:* Joker/Universal. 1 reel.

BACK TO LIFE (1913). Morality melodrama; as The Rival. *Dir:* Allan Dwan. *Sc:* (Story by M. de la Parelle). *With* J. Warren Kerrigan, William Worthington, Pauline Bush, Jessalyn Van Trump. *Prod:* Victor/Universal. 2 reels.

RED MARGARET — MOONSHINER (1913). Moonshine outlaw melodrama: as Lon, lover of Red Margaret. *Dir:* Allan Dwan. *Sc:* Jeanie Macpherson. *With* Pauline Bush, Murdoch J. MacQuarrie; James Neill. *Prod:* Gold Seal/Uinversal. 2 reels.

AN ELEPHANT ON HIS HANDS (1913). Comedy; as Eddie, who does not like animals, but inherits an elephant. *Dir:* probably Al Christie. Nestor-universal. 1 reel.

BLOODHOUNDS OF THE NORTH (1913). Northwest Mounted Police melodrama; as one of two Mounties. *Dir:* Allan Dwan. *Sc:* Arthur Rosson. *With* Pauline Bush, William Lloyd, James Neill, Murdoch J. MacQuarrie. *Prod:* Gold Seal/Universal. 2 reels.

THE LIE (1914). Social drama of a Scottish family; as Young MacGregor. *Dir:* Allan Dwan. *Sc:* Jeanie Macpherson. *With* Murdoch MacQuarrie, Pauline Bush, William Lloyd, Dick and Arthur Rosson, Fred McKay, James Neill. *Prod:* Gold Seal/Universal. 2 reels.

THE HONOUR OF THE MOUNTED (1914). Northwest Mounted Police melodrama; as Jacques Laquox, a French-Canadian. *Dir:3* Allan Dwan. *Sc:* A. H. Rosson. *With* Pauline Bush, Murdoch MacQuarrie, James Neill. *Prod:* Gold Seal/Universal. 2 reels.

REMEMBER MARY MAGDALEN (1914).

Social drama; as The Half-Wit who is accidentally killed when he defends the woman of easy virtue from the wrath of the townspeople. *Dir/Sc:* Allan Dwan. *With* Pauline Bush, Murdoch MacQuarrie. *Prod:* Victor/Universal. 2 reels.

DISCORD AND HARMONY (1914). Costume romance; as The Sculptor. *Dir:* Allan Dwan. *Sc:* Arthur H. Rosson (based on an incident in the life of Beethoven). *With* Pauline Bush, Murdoch MacQuarrie, Allan Forrest, James Neill, *Prod:* Gold Seal/Universal. 3 reels.

THE MENACE TO CARLOTTA (1914). Social underworld drama; as Giovanni Bartholdi, unscrupulous Italian, who nearly allows the girl he loves to be compromised. *Dir:* Allan Dwan. *Sc:* Lon Chaney. *With* W. C. Dowlan, Pauline Bush, Murdoch MacQuarrie, John Burton. *Prod:* Rex/Universal. 2 reels.

THE EMBEZZLER (1914). Blackmailing and embezzling melodrama; as J. Rogers Dixon, blackmailer. *Dir/Sc:* Allan Dwan. *With* Murdoch MacQuarrie, Pauline Bush, W. C. Dowlan, William Lloyd, Richard Rosson. *Prod:* Gold Seal/Universal. 2 reels.

THE LAMB, THE WOMAN, THE WOLF (1914). Triangle melodrama; as The Wolf. *Dir:/Sc:* Allan Dwan. *With* Pauline Bush, Murdoch MacQuarrie. *Prod:* 101 - Bison / Universal. 3 reels.

THE END OF THE FEUD (1914). Melodrama of the feud between the Dawsons and the Putnams; as Wood Dawson. *Dir:* Allan Dwan. *Sc:* Richard Rosson. *With* Murdoch MacQuarrie, Pauline Bush, William Lloyd, W. C. Dowlan. *Prod:* Rex/Universal. 2 reels.

THE TRAGEDY OF WHISPERING CREEK (1914). Western melodrama; as The Greaser. *Dir:* Allan Dwan. *Sc:* Lon Chaney (from a story by Elliott J. Clawson). *With* Murdoch MacQuarrie, Pauline Bush, W. C. Dowlan, George Cooper, Mary Ruby, William Lloyd, John Burton, Doc Cane. 101-Bison/Universal. 2 reels.

THE UNLAWFUL TRADE (1914). Moonshine melodrama; as The Cross Blood, who sells out to the revenue officers. *Dir:* Allan Dwan. *Sc:* George Cooper. *With* Pauline Bush, William Lloyd, George Cooper, W. C. Dowlan, Murdoch MacQuarrie. *Prod:* Rex / Universal. 2 reels.

THE FORBIDDEN ROOM (1914). Murder melodrama; as John Morris, interested in hypnotism, who is murdered. *Dir:* Allan Dwan. *Sc:* Bess Meredyth. *With* Pauline Bush, Murdoch MacQuarrie, W. C. Dowlan, John Burton. *Prod:* 101-Bison/Universal. 3 reels. Working title: *The Web of Circumstance*.

THE OLD COBBLER (1914). Mining camp melodrama; as Wild Bill, a Two-Gun Man. *Dir:* Murdoch MacQuarrie. *With* Murdoch Mac-Quarrie, Richard Rosson, Agnes Vernon. *Prod:* 101-Bison/Universal. 2 reels.

THE HOPES OF BLIND ALLEY (1914). Character drama; as The Rascally Dealer. *Dir./Sc:* Allan Dwan. *With* Pauline Bush, Murdoch MacQuarrie, George Cooper, W. C. Dowlan. 101-Bison/Universal. 3 reels.

A RANCH ROMANCE (1914). Western melodrama; as the villainous Raphael Praz, who kidnaps the heroine. *With* Murdoch MacQuarrie, Agnes Vernon, Seymour Hastings, E. Keller. *Prod:* Nestor/Universal. 2 reels.

HER GRAVE MISTAKE (1914). Western romance; as the villainous Nuñez, a Mexican spy. *With* Murdoch MacQuarrie, Agnes Vernon, Seymour Hastings. *Prod:* Nestor/Universal. 2 reels.

BY THE SUN'S RAYS (1914). Western melodrama; as a discarded suitor who finds vengeance in warning bandits by means of flashing a mirror. *With* Murdoch MacQuarrie, Agnes Vernon, Edward Lyons. *Prod:* Nestor/Universal. 2 reels.

A MINER'S ROMANCE (1914). Western romance; as the villain, John Burns. *With* Murdoch MacQuarrie, Agnes Vernon, Seymour Hastings. *Prod:* Nestor/Universal. 2 reels.

THE ADVENTURES OF FRANCOIS VILLON (1914). French period melodrama of the court of Louis XI, released in four parts; in the first part, *The Oubliette,* as the Chevalier Bertrand de la Poyne; and in the second part, *The Higher Law,* as Sir Stephen. (He is not in Parts Three and Four). *Dir:* Charles Giblyn. *Sc:* H. G. Stafford (from a "Century Magazine" story by George Bronson Howard). *With* Murdoch MacQuarrie, Pauline Bush, Harry F. Crane, Chet Withey. *Prod:* 101-Bison/Universal. Twelve reels complete (three reels in each episode).

HER BOUNTY (1914). A factory romance; as Fred Howard, unhappy junior partner. *Dir:* Joseph de Grasse. *Sc:* Ida May Park. *With* Pauline Bush, Joe King, Beatrice Van. *Prod:* Rex/Universal. 1 Reel.

RICHELIEU (1914). Romantic melodrama of the French court; as Baradas, a traitor, who ends on the guillotine. *Dir./Sc:* Allan Dwan (from story by E. Bulwer Lytton).*With* Murdoch MacQuarrie, Pauline Bush, W. C. Dow-

lan, Edna Maison, James Neill, Edythe Chapman, Richard Rosson, William Lloyd. Universal Special. 6 reels.

THE PIPES OF PAN (1914). Society triangle; as Arthur Farrell, who tries to seduce his best friend's wife. *With* Joe King, Pauline Bush, Carmen Phillips. *Prod:* Rex/Universal. 2 reels.

VIRTUE ITS OWN REWARD (1914). A factory romance; as Duncan Bronson, despised manager of a factory department. *Dir:* Joseph de Grasse. *Sc:* H. G. Stafford (from a story by John Barton Oxford). *With* Pauline Bush, Gertrude Bambrick, Tom Forman. *Prod:* Rex/Universal. 2 reels.

THE SMALLTOWN GIRL (1914). Drama of a girl's seduction; as The Procurer. *Dir:* Allan Dwan. *Sc:* Beatrice Van. *With* William Lloyd, Pauline Bush, Richard Rosson, Rupert Julian, Murdoch MacQuarrie. *Prod:* 101 Bison / Universal. 3 reels.

HER LIFE'S STORY (1914). Costume drama of Old Spain; as Don Valesquez, Spanish nobleman. *Sc:* James Dayton (from a poem, "The Cross," by Miriam Bode Rasmus). *With* Pauline Bush, Laura Oakley, Ray Gallagher, Beatrice Van, Felix Walsh. Rex/Universal. 2 reels.

LIGHTS AND SHADOWS (1914). Backstage drama; as Bentley, a seducer. *With* Pauline Bush (in dual role of mother and daughter). Rex/Universal. 2 reels.

THE LION, THE LAMB, THE MAN (1914). Kentucky mountain triangle, with flashback to the Stone Age; as the craftier of two brothers both in love with the same girl. *Dir:* Joseph de Grasse. *With* Pauline Bush, Millard K. Wilson. *Prod:* Rex/Universal. 2 reels.

A NIGHT OF THRILLS. (1914). Farce about a haunted house; as one of the house's visitors. *Prod:* Rex/Universal. 2 reels.

HER ESCAPE (1914). Gangster melodrama; as an underworld mob leader. *Dir:* Joseph de Grasse. *Sc:* Lon Chaney. *With* Pauline Bush, W. C. Dowlan, Richard Rosson. *Prod:* Rex/Universal. 2 reels.

THE SIN OF OLGA BRANDT (1915). Social drama; as Stephen Leslie, attorney. *Dir:* Joseph de Grasse. *With* Pauline Bush, W. C. Dowlan. *Prod:* Rex/Universal. 2 reels.

THE STAR OF THE SEA (1915). Drama of the sea; as Tomasco, an Italian fisherman. *Dir:* Joseph de Grasse. *Sc:* Phil Walsh. *With* Pauline Bush, Laura Oakley, W. C. Dowlan. *Prod:* Rex/Universal. 2 reels.

THE MEASURE OF A MAN (1915). Triangle drama set in the Northwest; as a Mountie, Lt. Jim Stuart. *Dir:* Joseph de Grasse. *With*

Pauline Bush, W. C. Dowlan. *Prod:* Rex/Universal. 2 reels.

THE THREADS OF FATE (1915). Psychological drama; as The Count. *Dir:* Joseph de Grasse. *With* Pauline Bush, W. C. Dowlan. Rex/Universal. 2 reels.

WHEN THE GODS PLAYED A BADGER GAME (AKA *The Girl Who Couldn't Go Wrong*) (1915). Backstage drama; as The Property Man. *Dir:* Joseph de Grasse. *With* Pauline Bush. *Prod:* Rex/Universal. 2 reels.

SUCH IS LIFE (1915). Backstage drama; as Tod Wilkes, employed in a burlesque show. *Dir:* Joseph de Grasse. *With* Pauline Bush, W. C. Dowlan, Olive Golden. *Prod:* Rex/Universal. 2 reels.

WHERE THE FOREST ENDS (1915). Drama of city life; as Paul Rouchelle, artist. *Dir:* Joseph de Grasse. *With* Pauline Bush, W. C. Dowlan, Joseph de Grasse. *Prod:* Rex/Universal. 2 reels.

OUTSIDE THE GATES (1915). Romantic fantasy of Old Spain; as Perez, a peddler. *Dir:* Joseph de Grasse. *With* Pauline Bush, W. C. Dowlan. *Prod:* Rex / Universal. 2 reels.

ALL FOR PEGGY (1915). Horse-racing melodrama; as The Stable Groom, father to the heroine. *Dir:* Joseph de Grasse. *Sc:* Ida May Park. *With* Pauline Bush, W. C. Dowlan. *Prod:* Rex/Universal. 1 reel.

THE DESERT BREED (1915). Desert Western; as a lost prospector named Fred. *Dir:* Joseph de Grasse. *Sc:* Tom Forman. *With* Pauline Bush, W. C. Dowlan. *Prod:* Rex/Universal. 2 reels.

MAID OF THE MIST (1915). Romance; as a jealous Postmaster. *Dir:* Joseph de Grasse. *Sc:* James Drayton. *With* Pauline Bush, Ray Gallagher. *Prod:* Rex/Universal. 1 reel.

THE GIRL OF THE NIGHT (1915). Regeneration crime drama; as a reformed crook. *Dir:* Joseph de Grasse. *Sc:* Ida May Park. *With* Pauline Bush, Hilda Slomen. *Prod:* Rex/Universal. 2 reels.

THE STOOL PIGEON (1915). International crook drama; Chaney does not act in this. *Dir:* Lon Chaney. *Sc:* L. G. Stafford. *With* J. Warren Kerrigan, Vera Sisson, George Periolat. *Prod:* Victor/Universal. 2 reels. (This is the first of six films Chaney directed for Universal release in 1915).

THE GRIND (AKA, GB, *On the Verge of Sin*) (1915). The lives and loves of three sisters; as an old man who compromises one of the sisters. *Dir:* Joseph de Grasse. *Sc:* Ida May Park. With Pauline Bush, Queenie Rosson, Helen Rosson. *prod:* Rex/Universal. 3 reels.

HER CHANCE (1915). Gangster romance; as Jerry, an honest gangster. *Dir:* Joseph de Grasse *Sc:* Ida May Park. *With* J. Warren Kerrigan, Vera Sisson. *Prod:* Victor/Universal. 2 reels.

FOR CASH (1915). Romance of a mountain girl and an artist; Chaney does not act in this. *Dir:* Lon Chaney. *Sc:* W. M. Caldwell. *With* J. Warren Kerrigan, Vera Sisson. *Prod:* Victor/Universal. 2 reels.

AN IDYLL OF THE HILLS (1915). Mountaineer feud drama; as one of the mountaineers. *with* Pauline Bush, Millard K. Wilson. *Prod:* Rex Universal. 2 reels.

THE STRONGER MIND (1915). Regeneration crook drama; as the real crook. *Dir:* Joseph de Grasse. *With* Murdoch MacQuarrie, Pauline Bush. *Prod:* United Release. 2 reels.

THE OYSTER DREDGER (1915). Social drama; Chaney does not act in this. *Dir./Sc:* Lon Chaney. *With* J. Warren Kerrigan, Vera Sisson. *Prod:* Victor/Universal. 2 reels.

THE VIOLIN MAKER (1915). Marital drama; as an Italian violin maker. *Dir:* Lon Chaney. *Sc:* Milton M. Moore. *With* Gretchen Lederer. *Prod:* Victor/Universal. 1 reel.

STEADY COMPANY (1915). Factory workers' romance; as the factory man. *Dir:* Joseph de Grasse. *Sc:* Ida May Park (from a story by Julius G. Furthman). *With* Pauline Bush. *Prod:* Rex/Universal. 1 reel.

THE TRUST (1915). Drama; as The Burglar, who reconciles an estranged couple. *Dir:* Lon Chaney. *Sc:* Katherine M. Kingsherry. *With* Vera Sisson, William Quinn. *Prod:* Victor/Universal. 1 reel.

BOUND ON THE WHEEL (1915). Marital drama; as an alcoholic husband. *Dir:* Joseph de Grasse. *Sc:* Ida May Park (from a story by Julius G. Furthman). *With* Elsie Jane Wilson, Lydia Yeamans Titus, Arthur Shirley. *Prod:* Rex/Universal. 3 reels.

MOUNTAIN JUSTICE (1915). Marital drama; as a mountaineer. *Dir:* Joseph de Grasse. *Sc:* Ida May Park (from a story by Julius G. Furthman). *With* Elsie Jane Wilson, Arthur Shirley, Grace Thompson. *Prod:* Rex/Universal. 2 reels.

QUITS (1915). Western melodrama; as "Frenchy." *Dir:* Joseph de Grasse. *Sc:* Ida May Park (from a story, *The Sheriff of Long Butte,* by Julius G. Furthman). *With* Arthur Shirley. *Prod:* Rex/Universal. 1 reel

THE CHIMNEY'S SECRET (1915). Bank robbery drama; as the cashier, who is the robber. *Dir./Sc:* Lon Chaney (from a story by Milton Moore). *With* Gretchen Lederer. *Prod:*

Victor/Universal. 1 reel.

THE PINE'S REVENGE (1915). Forest ranger melodrama; as one of three men who love the same girl. *Dir:* Joseph de Grasse. *Sc:* Nell Shipman (from her story, *The King's Keeper*). *With* Cleo Madison, Arthur Shirley, Millard K. Wilson. *Prod:* Gold Seal/Universal. 2 reels.

THE FASCINATION OF THE FLEUR DE LIS (1915). Royal romance; as the Duke of Safoulrug. *Dir:* Joseph de Grasse. *Sc:* Bess Meredyth. *With* Cleo Madison, Arthur Shirley, Millard K. Wilson. *Prod:* Rex/Universal. 3 reels.

ALAS AND ALACK (1915). Marital drama; as a husband whose wife loves another. *Dir:* Joseph de Grasse. *Sc:* Ida May Park. *With* Cleo Madison, Arthur Shirley. *Prod:* Rex/Universal. 1 reel.

A MOTHER'S ATONEMENT (1915). Drama; as The Tempter. *Dir:* Joseph de Grasse. *Sc:* Ida May Park. *With* Cleo Madison (in a dual role), Wyndham Standing, Arthur Shirley, Millard K. Wilson. *Prod:* Rex/Universal. 3 reels.

LON OF LONE MOUNTAIN (1915). Mountaineer drama; as Lon Moore, who protects a helpless girl. *Dir:* Joseph de Grasse. *Sc:* Ida May Park. *With* Marcia Moore, Arthur Shirley, George Burrell. *Prod:* Rex/Universal. 1 reel.

THE MILLIONAIRE PAUPERS (1915). Romance; as a meddlesome villain who tries to separate the lovers. *Dir:* Joseph de Grasse. *Sc:* Ida May Park. *With* Grace Thompson, Gretchen Lederer, Arthur Shirley, Marcia Moore, Milliard K. Wilson. *Prod:* Rex/Universal. 3 reels.

FATHER AND THE BOYS (1915). Comedy; as Tuck Bartholomew. *Dir:* Joseph de Grasse. *Sc:* Ida May Park (from a story by George Abe). *With* Digby Bell, Doc Crane, Louise Carbasse (a beautiful Australian who was subsequently known briefly as Louise Welch, then finally as Louise Lovely), Yona Landowska, Harry Ham, Hayward Mack, Bud Chase, Tom Chatterton, Harry Davenport. *Prod:* Broadway/Universal. 5 reels.

UNDER A SHADOW (1915). Marital drama, of mistaken identity; as an insanely jealous husband. *Dir:* Joseph de Grasse. *Sc:* F. McGrew Willis (from his story, "A Secret Service Affair"). *With* Gretchen Lederer, Arthur Shirley, Milliard K. Wilson. *Prod:* Rex/Universal. 2 reels.

STRONGER THAN DEATH (1915). Love story; as the lover. *Dir:* Joseph de Grasse. *Sc:* Bess Meredyth. *With* Louise Carbasse (Lovely), Arthur Shirley, Millard K. Wilson. *Prod:* Rex/Universal. 2 reels.

DOLLY'S SCOOP (1916). Newspapaer drama; as Dan Fisher. *Dir:* Jospeh de Grasse. *Sc:* Ida May Park (from a story by Hugh Weir). *With* Louise Welch (Lovely), Howard Mack, Millard K. Wilson, Marjorie Ellison, Mae Gaston. *Prod:* Rex/Universal 2 reels.

THE GRIP OF JEALOUSY (1916). Slavery days in the Old South; as Silas Lacey, a rich planter. *Dir:* Joseph de Grasse. *Sc:* Ida May Park (from her story, "Love Thine Enemy"). *With* Louise Lovely, Jay Belasco, Hayward Mack, Marcia Moore, Grace Thompson. *Prod:* Bluebird/Universal. 5 reels.

TANGLED HEARTS (1916). Dangers of close friendship vs. marital love; as a society husband. *Dir:* Joseph de Grasse. *Sc:* Ida May Park. *With* Louise Lovely, Agnes Vernon, Marjorie Ellison, Hayward Mack, Jay Belasco. *Prod:* Bluebird/Universal. 5 reels.

THE GILDED SPIDER (1916). Drama of vengeance; as Giovanni, half-crazed Sicilian. *Dir:* Joseph de Grasse. *Sc:* Ida May Park (from her story, "The Full Cup"). *With* Louise Lovely (in a dual role, as mother and daughter), Jay Belasco, Lule Warrenton, Gilmore Hammond, Marjorie Ellison, Hayward Mack. *Prod:* Bluebird/Universal. 5 reels.

BOBBIE OF THE BALLET (1916). Backstage romance; as Hook Hoover, a villain. *Dir:* Joseph de Grasse. *Sc:* Ida May Park (from a story by Grant Carpenter). *With* Louise Lovely, Jay Belasco, Jean Hathaway, Gretchen Lederer, Gilmore Hammond, Lule Warrenton. *Prod:* Bluebird/Universal. 5 reels.

GRASP OF GREED (1916). Romance on a desert isle; as a castaway named Jimmie. *Dir:* Joseph de Grasse. *Sc:* Ida May Park (from a novel, "Mr. Meeson's Will," by H. Rider Haggard). *With* Louise Lovely, Jay Belasco, Gretchen Lederer. *Prod:* Bluebird/Universal. 5 reels.

THE MARK OF CAIN (1916). Crook melodrama; as Dick Temple, who goes to prison for his father's crime. *Dir:* Joseph de Grasse. *Sc:* Stuart Paton. *With* Dorothy Phillips, Frank Whitson, Gilmore Hammond, Gretchen Lederer, Lydia Yeamans Titus, Mark Fenton. *Prod:* Red Feather/Universal. 5 reels.

IF MY COUNTRY SHOULD CALL (1916). Drama of patriotism, with a background of the American-Mexican War; as Dr. George Ardrath. *Dir:* Joseph de Grasse. *Sc:* Ida May Park (from a story by Virginia Terhune Van de Water). *With* Dorothy Phillips, Helen Leslie, Adele Farrington, Frank Whitson, Jack Nelson, Gretchen Lederer. *Prod:* Red Feather/Universal. 5 reels.

PLACE BEYOND THE WINDS (1916). Romance of the forests; as Jerry Jo, a crippled half-breed. *Dir:* Joseph de Grasse. *Sc:* Ida May Park (from a story by Harriet T. Comstock). *With* Dorothy Phillips, Jack Mulhall, Joseph de Grasse. *Prod:* Red Feather/Universal. 5 reels.

FELIX ON THE JOB (1916). Farce; as Tod, whose house's roof is being wrecked rather than re-shingled. *Dir:* Joseph de Grasse. *Sc:* Harry Wiele. *With* George Felix, Eva Loring, Lydia Yeamans Titus. *Prod:* Victor/ Universal. 1 reel.

ACCUSING EVIDENCE (1916). Northwest Mounted Police melodrama; as Lon, a Mountie. *Dir:* Allan Dwan. *With* Pauline Bush. *Prod:* Big Universal. 1 reel. (Possibly a cut-down re-issue of *Bloodhounds of the North,* 1913.)

THE PRICE OF SILENCE (1916). Society blackmail drama; as Dr. Edmund Stafford. *Dir:* Joseph de Grasse. *Sc:* Ida May Park (from a story by W. Carey Wonderly). *With* Dorothy Phillips, Viola Smith, Frank Whitson, Evelyn Selbie, Jay Belasco, Jack Mulhall. *Prod:* Bluebird/Universal. 5 reels.

THE PIPER'S PRICE (1917). Domestic drama; as Billy Kilmartin, who loves his divorced wife. *Dir:* Joseph de Grasse. *Sc:* Ida May Park (from a story by Mrs. Wilson Woodrow). *With* Dorothy Phillips, William Stowell, Maud George, Claire Du Brey. *Prod:* Bluebird/ Universal. 5 reels.

HELL MORGAN'S GIRL (1917). Melodrama of San Francisco's Barbary Coast; as Sleter Noble, politician and gang-leader killed in the 1906 earthquake and fire which climax the film. *Dir:* Joseph de Grasse. *Sc:* Ida May Park (from a story by Harvey Gates). *With* Dorothy Phillips, William Stowell, Joseph Girard, Alfred Allen. *Prod:* Bluebird Special/ Universal. 5 reels.

THE MASK OF LOVE (1917). Crime melodrama; as Marino, a hardened character of the underworld. *Dir:* Joseph de Grasse. *With* Pauline Bush. *Prod:* Laemmle Big U/Universal. 1 reel.

THE GIRL IN THE CHECKERED COAT (1917). Crook melodrama; as the villain, Hector Maitland. *Dir:* Joseph de Grasse. *Sc:* Ida May Park (from a story by E. Magnus Ingleton). *With* Dorothy Phillips (dual role), William Stowell, Mrs. A. E. Whiting. *Prod:* Bluebird/Universal. 5 reels.

THE FLASHLIGHT (1917). Mystery romance; in a dual role: as twin brothers, one known as Henry Norton, the other as Porter Brixton. *Dir./Sc:* Ida May Park (from a story by Albert M. Treynore.) *With* Dorothy Phillips, William Stowell, Alfred Allen, George Burrell. *Prod:* Bluebird/Universal. 5 reels.

A DOLL'S HOUSE (1917). Marital drama; as Nils Krogstad. *Dir:* Joseph de Grasse. *Sc:* Ida May Park (from the play by Henrik Ibsen). *With* Dorothy Phillips, William Stowell, Sydney Dean, Miriam Shelley, Helen Wright. (In the 1918 Artcraft-Elsie Ferguson version, Chaney's role was played by Alex K. Shannon; in the 1922 United Artists-Nazimova version, his role was played by Wedgwood Nowell. In 1973 two different versions were released, one starring Clare Bloom as Nora; the other starring Jane Fonda. Patrick Garland directed the first, with Denholm Elliott as Krogstad; Joseph Losey directed the second, with Edward Fox as Krogstad.) *Prod:* Bluebird / Universal. 5 reels.

FIRES OF REBELLION (1917). Modern melodrama; as The City Tempter. *Dir./Sc:* Ida May Park. *With* Dorothy Phillips, William Stowell, Richard La Reno, Edward Brady, Golda Madden, Belle Bennett. *Prod:* Bluebird/Universal. 5 reels.

THE RESCUE (1917). Domestic drama of a woman who re-weds her divorced husband; as Thomas Holland, a sympathetic role. *Dir./Sc:* Ida May Park (from a story by Hugh Kahler). *With* Dorothy Phillips, William Stowell, Gretchen Lederer, Molly Malone, Claire Du Brey, Gertrude Astor. *Prod:* Bluebird/ Universal. 5 reels.

TRIUMPH (1917). Backstage story; as Paul Niehoff, drama critic. *Dir:* Joseph de Grasse. *Sc:* Fred Myton (from a story by Samuel Hopkins Adams). *With* Dorothy Phillips, William Stowell, Claire Du Brey, William J. Dyer. *Prod:* Bluebird/Universal. 5 reels.

PAY ME (AKA, *Vengeance of the West*) (1917). *Dir:* Joseph de Grasse. *Sc:* Bess Meredyth. *With* Dorothy Phillips, Evelyn Selbie, William Stowell, Claire Du Brey, William Clifford. *Prod:* Universal Jewel. 5 reels.

THE EMPTY GUN (1917). Western melodrama; in the lead role. *Dir:* Joseph de Grasse. *Sc:* J. Grubb Alexander and Fred Myton, *With* Claire McDowell, Sam De Grasse. *Prod:* Gold Seal/Universal. 3 reels.

BONDAGE (1917). Manhattan drama; as The Seducer. *Dir:/Sc:* Ida May Park. (from a story by Edna Kenton). *With* Dorothy Phillips, William Stowell, J. B. MacLaughlin, Gertrude Astor. *Prod:* Bluebird/Universal. 5 reels.

ANYTHING ONCE (1917). American action comedy; as a greedy man known as Waughnt More. *Dir:* Joseph de Grasse. *Sc:* William Parker (from a story by Izola Forrester and Mann Page). With Franklyn Farnum, Claire Du Brey, Marjory Lawrence, Sam De Grasse. *Prod:* Bluebird/Universal. 5 reels.

THE SCARLET CAR (1917). Comedy melodrama about a bank robbery; as Forbes, the bank's cashier. *Dir:* Joseph de Grasse. *Sc:* William Parker (from a novel by Richard Harding Davis). *With* Franklyn Farnum, Edith Johnson, Al Filson, Sam De Grasse. *Prod:* Bluebird/Universal. 5 reels.

BROADWAY LOVE (1918). Backstage and New York Tenderloin drama; as Elmer Watkins, unsuccessful country lover of the heroine. *Dir:/Sc:* Ida May Park (from a story by W. Carey Wonderley). *With* Dorothy Phillips, Juanita Hansen, Gladys Tennyson, William Stowell, Harry Van Meter. *Prod:* Bluebird/Universal. 5 reels.

THE KAISER, THE BEAST OF BERLIN (1918). First World War propaganda melodrama; as Admiral Von Tirpitz. *Dir:* Rupert Julian. *Sc:* Julian and E. J. Clausas. *With* Rupert Julian, Nigel de Brulier, Harry Van Meter, Joseph Girard, Henry Barrows, Henry Holden, Elmo Lincoln, Ruth Clifford, Billy Carpenter, Ruby Lafayette, Gretchen Lederer, Zoe Rae. *Prod:* Renown Pictures/Universal. 7 reels.

FAST COMPANY (1918). Light comedy; as Dan McCarthy. *Dir:* Lynn F. Reynolds. *Sc:* Eugene Lewis and Waldemar Young (from a story by John McDermott). *With* Franklyn Farnum, Katherine Griffith, Fred Montague, Juanita Hansen, Edward Cecil. *Prod:* Bluebird/Universal. 5 reels.

THE GRAND PASSION (1918). Western melodrama; as Paul Argos. *Dir:/Sc:* Ida May Park (from a novel, "The Boss of Powderville," by Thomas Addison). *With* Dorothy Phillips, William Stowell, Jack Mulhall, Evelyn Selbie, Bert Appling. *Prod:* Universal Jewel. 6 reels.

A BROADWAY SCANDAL (1918). Manhattan melodrama; as "Kink" Colby. *Dir:* Joseph de Grasse. *Sc:* Harvey Gates (from his story, "My Parisian Sweetheart"). *With* Carmel Myers, Edwin August, Andrew Robson. Bluebird/Universal. 5 reels.

RIDDLE GAWNE (1918). Western melodrama of revenge; as the villainous gunfighter, Hame Bozzam. *Dir:* Lambert Hillyer, *Sc:* Charles Alden Selter (from a story by William S. Hart). *With* William S. Hart, Katherine MacDonald, Gretchen Lederer, Gertrude Short, Leon Kent, Milton Ross, Edwin B. Tilton. *Prod:* Paramount-Artcraft. 5 reels.

THAT DEVIL, "BAT'EESE" (1918). Northwest French-Canandian melodrama: as Louis Courteau, French-Canadian villain. *Dir:* William Wolbert. *Sc:* Bess Meredyth. *With* Monroe Salisbury, Ada Gleason, Lamar Johnstone, Andrew Robson. *Prod:* Bluebird/ Universal. 5 reels.

THE TALK OF THE TOWN (1918). Manhattan society comedy-melodrama: as Jack Lan-

chome, idler playboy. *Dir:* Allen Holubar. *Sc:* (from a story, "Discipline of Ginevra," by Harold Vickers). *With* Dorothy Phillips, William Stowell, George Fawcett, Clarissa Selwynne, Norman Kerry, Charles Hill Mailes. *Prod:* Bluebird/Universal. 6 reels.

DANGER — GO SLOW (1918). Romantic crook comedy; as "Bud," editor of a small-town paper. *Dir:* Robert Z. Leonard, *Sc:* Leonard and Mae Murray. *With* Mae Murray, Jack Mulhall, Joseph Girard, Lydia Knott. *Prod:* Universal Special. 6 reels.

THE WICKED DARLING (1919). Romantic melodrama; as "Stoop," who loves the jewel thief heroine. *Dir:* Tod Browning. *Sc:* Harvey Gates (from a story by Evelyn Campbell). *With* Priscilla Dean, Wellington Playter, Spottiswoode Aitken, Gertrude Astor. *Prod:* Universal. 6 reels. (This was the first of ten feature films Browning directed with Chaney prominently featured or starred.)

FALSE FACES (1919). A "Lone Wolf" counter-espionage drama on the high seas; as Karl Eckstrom, German spy. *Dir./Sc:* Irvin S. Willat (from a novel by Louis Joseph Vance). *With* Henry B. Walthall. Mary Anderson, Thornton Edwards, William Bowman, Milton Ross. *Prod:* Thomas H. Ince/Paramount. 6 reels.

A MAN'S COUNTRY (1919). Western melodrama; as "Three Card" Duncan, a gambler. *Dir:* Henry Koker. *Sc:* John Lynch. *With* Alma Rubens, Albert Roscoe, Joseph S. Dowling. *Prod:* Robertson-Cole. 5 reels.

PAID IN ADVANCE (1919). Klondike melodrama; as the villain, "Bat'eese" Le Blanc. *Di./Sc:* Allen Holubar (from a James Oliver Curwood story, "The Girl Who Dared"). *With* Dorothy Phillips, William Stowell, Priscilla Dean, Joseph Girard. *Prod:* Universal Jewel Special. 6 reels.

THE MIRACLE MAN (1919). Crook regeneration drama; as a phony cripple, "Frog". *Dir:/Sc:* George Loane Tucker (as dramatised by George M. Cohan from a Frank Packard story). *With* Thomas Meighan, Betty Compson, J. M. Dumont, W. Lawson Butt, Elinor Fair, F. A. Turner, Lucille Hutton, Joseph S. Dowling. *Prod:* Paramount-Artcraft. 8 reels. (In the 1932 Paramount talking version starring Sylvia Sidney with Chester Morris, Chaney's role was played by John Wray.) (Compare listing in Betty Compson filmography.)

WHEN BEARCAT WENT DRY (1919). Mountaineer romance; as a mountaineer, Kindard Powers. *Dir:/Sc:* Oliver Sellers (from a novel by Charles Neville Buck). *With* Vangie Valentine, Walt Whitman, Bernard Durning, Winter Hall, Edward Brady, Millard K. Wilson. *Prod:* Charles R. McCauley Photoplays/ World Release. 6 reels.

VICTORY (1919). Psychological romantic drama on a South Seas island; as the villainous Ricardo. *Dir:* Maurice Tourneur. *Sc:* Stephen Fox (from the novel by Joseph Conrad). *With* Jack Holt, Seena Owen, Wallace Beery, Bull Montana, George Nicholls. *Prod:* Paramount-Artcraft. 8 reels. (In a 1930 talking version, *Dangerous Paradise,* Chaney's role was played by Francis McDonald; in the 1940 version, by Jerome Cowan.)

DAREDEVIL JACK (1920). Fifteen chapter serial; as a villain in one of the later chapters. *Dir:* W. S. Van Dyke. *Sc:* Frederic Chapin and Harry Hoyt (from a story by Jack Cunningham). *With* Jack Dempsey, Josie Sedgwick, Herschel Mayall, Frank Lanning. *Prod:* Pathé. 33 reels (first chapter had 3 reels; all others, 2).

TREASURE ISLAND (1920). Pirate adventure drama; in a dual role: as the blind pirate "Pew" and as "Merry." *Dir:* Maurice Tourneur. *Sc:* Stephen Fox and Jules Furthman (from the novel by Robert Louis Stevenson). *With* Shirley Mason, Josie Melville, Charles Ogle, Bull Montana, Charles Hill Mailes, Al Filson, Harry Holden, Sydney Dean, Wilton Taylor, Joseph Singleton. *Prod:* Paramount-Artcraft. 6 reels. (Chaney's roles were played by William V. Mong (Pew) and by James Burke ("Merry") in the 1934 M-G-M version; and by John Laurie ("Pew") and by Ralph Truman ("Merry") in the 1950 RKO Radio version.)

THE GIFT SUPREME (1920). Melodrama; as a drug addict,. Merney Stagg. *Dir./Sc:* Oliver Sellers (from a novel by George Allan England). *With* Bernard Durning, Seena Owen, Melbourne McDowell, Eugenie Besserer, Tully Marshall, Jack Curtis, Dick Morris, Claire McDowell. *Prod:* Charles R. McCauley Photoplays/Selznick release for Republic/Inter-Ocean. 6 reels.

NOMADS OF THE NORTH (1920). Canadian northwoods romance; as Raoul Challoner. *Dir:* David M. Hartford. *Sc:* Hartford and James Oliver Curwood (from Curwood's novel). *With* Lewis Stone, Betty Blythe, Francis McDonald, Melbourne McDowell, Spottiswoode Aitken. *Prod:* First National. 6 reels.

THE PENALTY (1920). Revenge melodrama set in San Francisco's underworld; as "Blizzard," a legless criminal. *Dir:* Wallace Worsley. *Sc:* Charles Kenyon and Phillip Lonergan (from a novel by Gouverneur Morris). *With* Claire Adams, Kenneth Harlan, Charles Clary, Ethel Grey Terry, Edouard Trabaol, Milton Rose, James Mason. *Prod:* Goldwyn. 7 reels.

OUTSIDE THE LAW (1921). Crook melodrama set in San Francisco's Chinatown; in a dual role: as the gangster Mike Silva; and as a Chinaman, Ah Wing, who slays Silva. *Dir:* Tod Browning. *Sc:* Lucien Hubbard (from a story

by Tod Browning). *With* Priscilla Dean, Ralph Lewis, Wheeler Oakman, E. A. Warren, Stanley Goethals, Melbourne McDowell, Wilton Taylor. *Prod:* Universal Jewel. 8 reels. (Remade by Tod Browning, 1930, with Edward G. Robinson as a gangster, Cobra Collins, equivalent to the Chaney role; there was no equivalent to the Chinese role Chaney had played.)

FOR THOSE WE LOVE (1921). Gambling drama; as a sympathetic character, Trix Ulner. *Dir./Sc:* Arthur Rosson (from a story by Perley Poore Sheehan). *With* Betty Compson, Richard Rosson, Harry Duffield, Camille Astor, Bert Woodruff, Walter Morosco, George Cooper, Frank Campeau. *Prod:* Goldwyn. 6 reels.(Compare listing in Betty Compson filmography)

BITS OF LIFE (1921) Four-episode feature; as an oriental villain in the Chinese melodrama sequence. *Dir:* Marshall Neilan (with assistance from James Flood and William Scully). *Sc:* Lucita Squier (from stories by Hugh Wiley, Walter Turnbull, Thomas McMorrow, Marshall Neilan. *With* Anna May Wong; in the other three other three sequences are Wesley Barry, John Bowers, Teddy Sampson, Dorothy Mackaill, Edythe Chapman, Frederick Burton, Noah Beery, James Bradbury Jr., Rockcliffe Fellowes, Tammany Young, Harriet Hammond, James Neill. *Prod:* First National. 6 reels.

ACE OF HEARTS (1921). Melodrama; as the villainous Farralone. *Dir:* Wallace Worsley. *Sc:* Ruth Wightman (from a story by Gouverneur Morris). *With* Leatrice Joy, John Bowers, Hardee Kirkland, Edwin N. Wallack, Ray Laidlaw, Raymond Hatton. *Prod:* Goldwyn. 6 reels.

THE TRAP (1922). Canadian Northwest melodrama; as Gaspard. *Dir:* Robert T. Thornby. *Sc:* George C. Hull. *With* Alan Hale, Dagmar Godowsky, Stanley Goethals, Irene Rich, Spottiswoode Aitken, Herbert Standing, Frank Campeau. *Prod:* Universal Jewel. 6 reels.

VOICES OF THE CITY (1922). Melodrama of the San Francisco underworld; as O'Rourke, a crooked hotel proprietor. *Dir:* Wallace Worsley. *Sc:* Arthur F. Statler (from a story, "The Night Rose," by LeRoy Scott). *With* Leatrice Joy, John Bowers, Cullen Landis, Richard Tucker, Mary Warren, Edythe Chapman, Betty Schade, Maurice B. "Lefty" Flynn, Milton Ross. *Prod:* Goldwyn. 6 reels.

FLESH AND BLOOD (1922). Crime melodrama; as the vengeance-minded David Webster. *Dir:* Irving Cummings. *Sc:* Louis Duryea Lighton. *With* Edith Roberts, Jack Mulhall, Ralph Lewis, Noah Beery, DeWitt Jennings, Togo Yamamoto, Kate Price, Wilfred Lucas. *Prod:* Cummings-State Rights. 6 reels.

THE LIGHT IN THE DARK (1922). City romance; as Tony Pantelli, a thief with a heart of gold. *Dir:* Clarence Brown. *Sc:* Brown and William Dudley Pelley. *With* Hope Hampton, E. K. Lincoln, Theresa Maxwell Conover, Dorothy Walters, Charles Mussett, Edgar Norton, Dore Davidson. *Prod:* First National. 7 reels.

SHADOWS (1922). Romantic drama; as a Chinaman, Yen Sin. *Dir:* Tom Forman. *Sc:* Eve Unsell, Hope Loring (from a story, "Ching, Ching Chinaman," by Wilbur Daniel Steele). *With* Marguerite de la Motte, Harrison Ford, John Sainpolis, Walter Long, Buddy Messenger, Priscilla Bonner. *Prod:* Preferred/ B. P. Schulberg. 7 reels.

OLIVER TWIST (1922). Period social drama: as Fagin. *Dir:* Frank Lloyd. *Sc:* Lloyd Henry Weil and Elizabeth Meehan (from the novel by Charles Dickens). *With* Jackie Coogan, Gladys Brockwell, George Seigmann, Aggie Herring, Lewis Sargent, James Marcus, Joseph Hazelton, Eddie Boland, Taylor Graves, Edouard Trebaol, Lionel Belmore, Carl Stockdale, Esther Ralston. *Prod:* Sol L. Lesser/First National. 8 reels. (Other actors who have played Fagin include Irving Pichel in the 1933 version; Alec Guinness in the 1948 one; and Ron Moody in the musical version, *Oliver!*).

QUINCY ADAMS SAWYER (1922). American rural romantic drama; as Obadiah Strout. *Dir:* Clarence Badger. *Sc:* Bernard McConville (from the novel by Charles Felton Pidgin). *With* Blanche Sweet, John Bowers, Barbara La Marr, Elmo Lincoln, Louise Fazenda, Joseph S. Dowling, Claire McDowell, Edward Lester, June Elvidge, Vic Potel, Gale Henry, Hank Mann, Kate Lester. *Prod:* Metro. 8 reels. (Compare listing in Blanche Sweet filmography.)

A BLIND BARGAIN (1922). Horror film; in a dual role: as Dr. Lamb, a mad scientist; and the ape-like hunchback. *Dir:* Wallace Worsley. *Sc:* J. G. Hawks (from a story, "The Octave of Claudius," by Barry Pain). *With* Raymond McKee, Jacqueline Logan, Fontaine La Rue, Virginia True Boardman, Aggie Herring. *Prod:* Goldwyn. 5 reels.

ALL THE BROTHERS WERE VALIANT (1923). Melodramatic sea adventure; as the half-crazed brother, Mark Shore. *Dir:* Irvin S. Willat. *Sc:* Julien Josephson (from a novel by Ben Ames Williams). *With* Malcolm McGregor, Billie Dove, William H. Orlamond. Robert McKim. (Ernest Torrence played Chaney's role in the 1928 version, *Across to Singapore*; Stewart Granger played it in the 1953 re-make.) *Prod:* Metro. 7 reels.

WHILE PARIS SLEEPS (1923). Horror melodrama; as Henri Santados, a lunatic waxworks attendant. *Dir:* Maurice Tourneur. *Sc:* (from a story, "The Glory of Love", by Pan). *With* John Gilbert, Mildred Manning, Hardee Kirkland, Jack F. MacDonald, J. Farrell MacDonald. *Prod:* W. W. Hodkinson. 6 reels.

THE SHOCK (1923). Melodrama of the San Francisco underworld, climaxing with the 1906 fire and earthquake; as Ailse Dilling, a crippled criminal. *Dir:* Lambert Hillyer. *Sc:* Charles Kenyon (from a story by William Dudley Pelley). *With* Virginia Valli, Jack Mower, Henry Barrows, Christine Mayo, Walter Long. *Prod:* Universal Jewel. 7 reels.

THE HUNCHBACK OF NOTRE DAME (1923). Romantic horror story of medieval France; as Quasimodo. *Prod:* Irving Thalberg. *Dir:* Wallace Worsley. *Sc:* Edward T. Lowe Jr. (adapted by Perley Poore Sheehan from the novel by Victor Hugo). *With* Patsy Ruth Miller, Norman Kerry, Kate Lester, Winifred Bryson, Nigel de Brulier, Brandon Hurst, Ernest Torrence, Tully Marshall, Harry Van Meter, Raymond Hatton, Eulalie Jensen, Gladys Brockwell, Nick de Ruiz, Edwin Wallack, John Cossar, W. Ray Meyers, William Parks Sr. (Charles Laughton played Quasimodo in the 1939 RKO version; Anthony Quinn, in the 1957 version filmed in France; there was no Quasimodo in the Theda Bara Fox version, *The Darling of Paris*.) *Prod:* Universal Super Jewel. 12 reels.

THE NEXT CORNER (1924). Marital drama; as Juan Serafin, a seducer from Spain. *Dir:* Sam Wood. *Sc:* Monte Katterjohn (from a novel and play by Kate Jordan). *With* Dorothy Mackaill, Conway Tearle, Ricardo Cortez, Louise Dresser, Dorothy Cumming. *Prod:* Paramount. 7 reels.

HE WHO GETS SLAPPED (1924). Psychological drama; as "He." *Dir:* Victor Seastrom. *Sc:* Seastrom and Carey Wilson (from the play by Leonid Andreyev). *With* Norma Shearer, John Gilbert, Tully Marshall, Marc McDermott, Ford Sterling, Harvey Clarke, Clyde Cook, Paulette DuVal, Ruth King, Brandon Hurst, George Davis. *Prod:* Produced by Louis B. Mayer for Metro-Goldwyn. 7 reels.

THE MONSTER (1925). Horror melodrama; as Dr. Ziska, a mad scientist. *Dir:* Roland West. *Sc:* Willard Mack and Albert G. Kenyon (from the play by Crane Wilbur). *With* Gertrude Olmstead, Hallam Cooley, Johnny Arthur, Charles Sellon, Walter James, Ethel Wales. *Prod:* Metro-Goldwyn. 6 reels.

THE UNHOLY THREE (1925). Crook melodrama; as Echo, the Ventriloquist, who masquerades as Mrs. O'Grady, a little lady who sells parrots. *Dir:* Tod Browning. *Sc:* Waldemar Young (from a novel by Clarence Aaron Robbins). *With* Mae Busch, Matt Moore, Walter Perry, Percy Williams, John Merkyl, Marjorie Morton, Violet Crane, Vic-

Lon Chaney in THE MONSTER

tor McLaglen, Harry Earles, Matthew Betz, Edward Connelly, *Prod:* M-G-M. 7 reels.

THE PHANTOM OF THE OPERA (1925). Romantic melodrama set in 19th century Paris; as Erik, the Phantom. *Dir:* Rupert Julian. with Edward Sedgwick directing added sequences. *Sc:* Elliott J. Clawson (from the novel by Gaston Leroux). *With* Mary Philbin, Norman Kerry, Snitz Edwards, Gibson Gowland, John Sainpolis, George B. Williams, Cesare Gravina, Edith Yorke, Alexander Bevani, Virginia Pearson, Arthur Edmund Carewe. *Prod:* Universal Jewel. 10 reels. (Claude Rains portrayed the Phantom in the 1943 version, and Herbert Lom in the 1962 British release.)

THE TOWER OF LIES (1925). Psychological Swedish drama; as Jan, a peasant. *Dir:* Victor Seastrom. *Sc:* Agnes Christine Johnston and Max Marcin (from the novel, "The Emperor of Portugallia," by Selma Lagerlöf). *With* Norma Shearer, Ian Keith, William Haines, Claire McDowell, David Torrence. *Prod:* M-G-M. 7 reels.

THE BLACKBIRD (1926). Murder melodrama; as the man who poses as brothers: the Cockney crook known as "The Blackbird" and the crippled Bishop of Limehouse. *Dir:* Tod Browning. *Sc:* Waldemar Young (from a story by Tod Browning). *With* Renée Adorée, Owen Moore, Doris Lloyd, Polly Moran. *Prod:* M-G-M. 7 reels.

THE ROAD TO MANDALAY (1926). Melodrama of the Singapore underworld; as a one-eyed criminal known as "Singapore Joe." *Dir:* Tod Browning. *Sc:* Elliott Clawson (from a story by Browning and Hermann J. Mankiewicz). *With* Lois Moran, Owen Moore, Henry B. Walthall, Sojin. *Prod:* M-G-M. 7 reels.

TELL IT TO THE MARINES (1927). Drama of the making of a no-good racetrack tout into a

Marine; as The Sergeant, *Dir:* George W. Hill. *Sc:* E. Richard Sayer. *With* William Haines, Eleanor Boardman, Eddie Gribbon, Carmel Myers, Warner Oland, Mitchell Lewis, Frank Currier. *Prod:* M-G-M. 10 reels.

MR. WU (1927). Oriental revenge drama; in a dual role: as Mr. Wu and as his Honourable Father. *Dir:* William Nigh. *Sc:* Lorna Moon (from the play by Harry Maurice Vernon and Harold Owen.) *With* Renée Adorée, Louise Dresser, Ralph Forbes, Holmes Herbert, Gertrude Olmstead, Anna May Wong, Claude King, Sonny Lou, Mrs. Wong Wing. (Previously filmed in England by Stoll, 1920, with Matheson Lang.) *Prod:* M-G-M. 8 reels.

THE UNKNOWN (1927). Revenge romance, played against a European variety background; as Alonso. *Dir:* Tod Browning. *Sc:* Waldemar Young (from a story, *Alonso, the Armless,* by Tod Browning). With Joan Crawford, Norman Kerry, John George, Nick de Ruiz, Frank Lanning. *Prod:* M-G-M. 7 reels.

MOCKERY (1927). Russian Revolution melodrama; as Sergei, a serf. *Dir:* Benjamin Christensen. *Sc:* Bradley King (from a story by Christensen). *With* Barbara Bedford, Ricardo Cortez, Mack Swain, Emily Fitzroy, Charles Puffy. *Prod:* M-G-M. 7 reels.

LONDON AFTER MIDNIGHT (1927). Horror melodrama; in a dual role: as Scotland Yard Inspector Blake and a Human Vampire. *Dir:* Tod Browning. *Sc:* Waldemar Young (from a story by Browning). *With* Henry B. Walthall, Marceline Day, Conrad Nagel, Polly Moran, Edna Tichenor, Claude King. *Prod:* M-G-M. 7 reels.

THE BIG CITY (1928). Crook drama; as a gangster, Chuck Collins. *Dir:* Tod Browning. *Sc:* Waldemar Young (from a story by Browning). *With* Betty Compson, James Murray, Marceline Day, Matthew Betz, John George, Virginia Pearson. *Prod:* M-G-M. 8 reels. (Compare listing in Betty Compson filmography.)

LAUGH, CLOWN, LAUGH (1928). Romantic psychological drama; as Tito, the clown. *Dir:* Herbert Brenon. *Sc:* Elizabeth Meehan (from the play by David Belasco and Tom Cushing). *With* Loretta Young, Bernard Seigel, Nils Asther, Cissy Fitzgerald, Gwen Lee. *Prod:* M-G-M. 8 reels.

WHILE THE CITY SLEEPS (1928). Melodrama; as Dan Callahan, a tough plainclothes detective. *Dir:* Jack Conway. *Sc:* A. P. Younger. *With* Anita Page, Carroll Nye, Wheeler Oakman, Mae Busch, Polly Moran, Lydia Yeamans Titus. *Prod:* M-G-M. 9 reels.

WEST OF ZANZIBAR (1929). Revenge melodrama; as "Phroso," called "Dead Legs." *Dir:* Tod Browning. *Sc:* Elliott Clawson (from a story by Chester De Vonde and Kilbourn Gordon). *With* Lionel Barrymore, Warner Baxter, Mary Nolan. *Prod:* M-G-M. 9 reels.

WHERE EAST IS EAST (1929). Revenge melodrama; as "Tiger," a catcher of wild animals. *Dir:* Tod Browning. *Sc:* Waldemar Young (adapted by Richard Schayer from a story by Tod Browning and Harold Sinclair Drago). *With* Estelle Taylor, Lupe Velez, Lloyd Hughes. *Prod:* M-G-M. 9 reels.

THUNDER (1929). Railroad drama; as Engineer Grumpy Anderson. *Dir:* William Nigh. *Sc:* Byron Morgan and Ann Price (from a story by Morgan). *With* Phyllis Haver, James Murray, George Duryea, Frances Morris, Wally Albright Jr. *Prod:* M-G-M. 9 reels.

THE UNHOLY THREE (1930). Chaney's only talking film was this re-make of his 1925 silent success; in his original role of Echo, the Ventriloquist, who masquerades as Mrs. O'Grady; he simulates five distinct character voices. *Dir:* Jack Conway. *Continuity/ dialogue:* J. C. Nugent and Elliott Nugent (from a novel by Clarence Aaron Robbins). *With* Lila Lee, Elliott Nugent, Harry Earles, John Miljan, Ivan Linow, Clarence Burton, Crauford Kent. *Prod:* M-G-M. 8 reels.

11
BETTY COMPSON

Betty Compson says, "No one could have started with less that I did," and that a doggedness inherited from her mother's "peasant ancestors" enabled her to achieve movie stardom and make two comebacks. Golden-chestnut hair, unusually bright blue eyes, shapely legs, and at least two of Hollywood's most talented directors, also helped.

Her career began in 1915 in Al Christie comedies and might never have gone anywhere had George Loane Tucker, the director, not happened to see her in one. He gave her a starring role in *The Miracle Man,* and, ultimately falling in love with her, taught her the things about film-making and life that enabled her to escape the bounds of ignorance and acquire self-confidence. A fine sense of wit and humour she always had, and they came to her rescue more than once.

She was born March 18, 1897, at Beaver City, Utah. "There's a reason for everything," Miss Compson says, "and I was born in Beaver City because the town my parents were living in — Frisco, Utah — didn't have a doctor. So two or three days before my advent, Mother drove behind a team of mules to Beaver City, and I was born there in a log hut. Ten days later she drove home with me."

Miss Compson's maternal grandmother, Anita Matilda Larsen, had run away on her wedding day with visiting Mormon missionaries, and had sailed with them from Norway to America. They journeyed from New York by steamboat and train to Kansas City, and from there to Utah in a covered wagon. Her first husband was a Mormon, but Brigham Young granted her a divorce from him (cost: $10). Her second was a Catholic — a cavalry lieutenant stationed at Utah's Fort Douglas who had studied at Heidelberg and served in the Prussian Army. George Rauscher was twenty-one and she thirty-one when they married. They had a daughter, Mary Elizabeth, and Rauscher soon resigned his commission to work for the Horn silver mine in Frisco, Utah.

Recalls Miss Compson: "When Mother (Mary Elizabeth Rauscher) was sixteen and was sitting on the porch of the family farmhouse, she saw a man ride by on horseback, and exclaimed: 'That's the man I'm going to marry!' It took her eight years to do so — but she did it!

"He was Virgil K. Compson, a graduate of Cornell University who had come to Utah as a mining engineer. The Compsons, English by descent, immigrated before the Revolution, and the Compson house in Seneca Falls, New York, is still something of a landmark historically.''

Within a few months of Miss Compons's birth, her father left for the gold fields of Alaska, probably against his wife's wishes, for he did not write, and she believed he'd deserted her. She supported herself and baby daughter by working as a domestic. After several years of this, letters arrived from her husband, informing her he had prospered, and was returning. He did so — with $25,000.

The stock market got it almost at once, and he moved his family to Salt Lake City, where, with what little he had saved, he opened a corner grocery store. Whatever dreams he may have had of making another fortune behind a counter did not long bemuse him. He contracted tuberculosis, that disease which so often in those days afflicted the broken-spirited. He died in 1912.

Mrs. Compson got a job in the linen room of the Utah Hotel, and her fifteen-year-old daughter continued to attend high school. At night the adolescent girl played the violin in the orchestra of the Mission Theatre, which supplied background music when the feature picture was on, and she accompanied the visiting vaudeville performers in their acts. She made $15 a week.

"I got my big break when one of the acts disappeared," Miss Compson says. "Bad liquor will do that to an act. Anyway, the manager asked me to do a violin solo. I didn't have the clothing needed, but remembering the gypsy costume worn by Nonette, the touring violinist known to the West, I put together one like it."

Nearly every Scandinavian knows how to fiddle competently, and Betty Compson was no exception. But she played better than competently — her father had paid for lessons before his illness — and her solo, an act called "The Vagabond Violinist, " was received so well that she lined up with three young men and went to San Francisco in the hope of getting bookings. Her mother quit the Utah Hotel and accompanied her "to see that no wrong was done her Nell." The act got no bookings, and the boys went to work in cafés. Eventually, Miss Compson wangled fifteen weeks on a tank circuit for her solo gypsy-violinist act.

When she returned to San Francisco, the season was dead and she and her mother took jobs as domestics with an old San Francisco family, the John J. Havisides. Mrs. Compson was housekeeper-cook; Betty, not quite sixteen, waitress and nursemaid. Their combined salaries were $60 a month.

Unfortunately, her employer's young brother, Olsen Haviside, soon developed bright eyes for the pretty teenage maid. "He wanted to marry me," says Miss Compson, "and he would've been a good catch. But I knew I was going to be an actress, and marriage and a career don't mix. I told him as much after a Saturday matinee movie at which the feature was Griffith's *Oil* and *Water,* with Blanche Sweet. It was about a dancer who married into a social family and found that 'oil and water don't mix.' Olsen was persistent, and Mother solved the problem by getting us jobs as servants in a summer resort at Inverness, on California's Tomales Bay, run by three spinsters."

By the end of the season they had saved enough to return to Salt Lake City, where Miss Compson got a $25-a-week job with a Pantages tabloid show, "The Wrong Bird," performing her violin specialty. After which she toured our Northwest and Canada in a variety skit called "The Shadow Girl."

Most Sincerely
Betty Compson

Edward Mayer Monroe N.Y.

While playing in Edmonton, Alberta, she encountered an actor she'd known in Salt Lake City named Robert Bradbury. He was on his way to becoming a successful stage and movie director, and told her she ought to be in pictures. He sent a telegram about her to a friend, Al MacQuarrie, who was then working for Al Christie.

When her act played Los Angeles, Miss Compson made a film test for Christie and went on to finish the vaudeville tour. He wired her in Salt Lake City, offering her $40 a week to be a Christie Comedies leading lady.

It was Christie who named her Betty. She had been christened Eleanor Luicime — the latter was the idea of the doctor who had delivered her in the log hut in Beaver City — and she had always been called "Lou." Christie thought "Luicime" sounded like a vegetable and that exhibitors wouldn't be able to spell it. For a reason he never explained, "Betty" popped into his head when he was trying to find something that would go with the sound of Compson.

Several weeks after arriving in Hollywood, Miss Compson had sent for her mother and was getting up at dawn six days a week and journeying from Hollywood to Universal City, where Chrisite filmed his first series of comedies for Nestor (Universal released). Said "Motion Picture News" of the first comedy, *Wanted – a Leading Lady:* "We hope Betty Compson, the leading lady, retains her job, for she's very pretty."

Christie's comedies were successful and by the time the fifth one, *Some Chaperone,* came out, "Motion Picture News" was saying: "Betty Compson grows more fascinating with each succeeding picture." By the summer of 1916 she had made twenty-nine comedies, and her salary had risen to $50 a week.

Al Christie then formed his own releasing company, and Betty Compson went with him. He billed her as "The Prettiest Girl in Pictures" when the first of his own company's comedies, *His Baby,* was released (September, 1916).

She did forty-three more two-reelers for Christie before he fired her, in the spring of 1918, because she refused to make a personal appearance.

In her words, "The panic was on," for she had worked for Christie for several months on half-salary and was up to her neck in back rent and unpaid bills. Even so, when Mack Sennett offered to hire her, she declined.

"Before I was fired, Sennett had offered me $150 a week to leave Christie," Miss Compson says, "and I was tempted. But on a hunch, I asked him: 'Mack, is all that money for acting alone — or does it include homework, too?' Sennett admitted with a twinkle that 'homework' was involved. 'In that case,' I said, 'the bid's not high enough.'"

She finally landed a job as leading lady in a Pathe serial, *The Terror of the Range,* and then made westerns and melodramas for that studio, Robertson-Cole, Universal, and World. She worked six days a week from dawn to dusk, and often stayed on for night shots.

The pay was slight, but she was becoming known to the Hollywood regulars and was friends with other ambitious players of the time, including Rudolph Valentino, Bebe Daniels, Gloria Swanson, Ethel Clayton, John Gilbert, Phyllis Haver, Marie Prevost, ZaSu Pitts.

Valentino, who was then working as a dancer at a popular suburban roadhouse called Watts Tavern, complained to her one day: "You're getting along fine, Betty. But me — I'm nothing more than a gigolo. A gigolo in Watts, which makes it worse." ZaSu Pitts, fresh from the California seaside village of Santa Cruz, had been turned over to Betty Compson to be made up for a film test. "She was nervous and excited," Miss Compson recalls, "but babbling at a great rate and absolutely confident that she would make it. Nothing could stop her. She was going to film picture after picture, make piles of money, and then buy herself a big red racing auto and drive around in it. My heart sank for her, but I tried to be hopeful.

"The next time I saw ZaSu, some months later, she was at the wheel of a new shining roadster — a red one. King Vidor was using her constantly in the films he directed, and she'd just made a big hit in a Mary Pickford movie. That gave me new hope. I cut out a Harrison Fisher magazine cover of a beautiful girl in gorgeous clothes sitting in an Ascot box with an elegantly garbed dowager. 'That's going to come true for you and me,' I told my mother. And it did! Which proves that if you really believe something, it'll be so."

But it didn't come true for Miss Compson until after she had faced one disappointment after another. "I'd always admired James Cruze," she says. "Back in Salt Lake City I had enjoyed playing for all his movies. He was acting, then, usually with his first wife — Marguerite Snow — and I used to buy the movie magazines which had his latest photos. You had to buy them then at box-offices. He had become an established director, and he did everything to get me the job of leading lady to Wally Reid in *The Valley of the Giants*, but the front-office assigned it to Grace Darmond. There was something psychic about Cruze. Later on, I nicknamed him 'the Great Dane,' not so much because he was of Danish descent as because he seemed to sense everything before it actually happened.

"'Don't be that way,' he said when I burst into tears on hearing I'd missed out being Wally Reid's leading lady. 'You're going to be back here at Lasky's one day soon, not as a leading lady but as a star. And not at $1000 a week, but $2500. You wait and see!' After that, I was turned down by both DeMilles, Jesse Lasky, and D. W. Griffith. The last, however, promised that if something came along, he'd give me a chance."

Early on the evening of December 23, 1918, she arrived home after a day's work on location at Oxnard, sixty miles from Hollywood, and was told by her mother that director George Loane Tucker had phoned and wanted to see her that evening about a picture he was going to make. There were still remnants of make-up in her hairline and Oxnard mud on her skirt. Her mother urged her to clean up and change, but Miss Compson had an intuitive feeling. "I think he wants the real me," she told her mother, and added: "He'll sure get it tonight."

Tucker, Miss Compson recently told me, "was the son of George Loane, a Southern gentleman by profession, and the actress Ethel Tucker. He took his mother's name as his own surname as a tribute to her, when he left the University of Chicago, where he had been working his way through, to go on the stage. He had developed into a stage director of some reputation before Carl Laemmle hired him. I first heard of him when Stuart Paton, director of the serial, *The Terror of the Range*, said in the course of a casual conversation between scenes: 'I'd give anything in the world to be able to direct half as well as he.'

"While Tucker was working for Laemmle, he made a picture in his spare time called *Traffic in Souls* that cost thousands and made millions. It was a dirty story of white slavery, but Tucker handled it so well that the public wasn't offended."

Tucker never saw the released version of *Traffic in Souls*. He had been

Betty Compson and Joseph E. Dowling in THE MIRACLE MAN

making one-reelers for IMP when he directed it and it was referred to as "Tucker's Folly" until Laemmle got behind it and exploited it. By then Tucker was directing in England for the London Film Company and had married the actress, Elizabeth Risdon. His first wife, by whom he had a son, had died in childbirth, and Miss Risdon became his second wife. After the success of *Traffic in Souls*, Tucker could write his own ticket in Hollywood. He was a quiet, introspective, sensitive man who didn't in the least resemble the sort of Hollywood director who is "always on".

Thomas Meighan, a friend of George M. Cohan's, brought Tucker the play Cohan had fashioned from Frank L. Packard's novel, "The Miracle Man." Tucker had made a treatment of it and had tried to get Gloria Swanson for the part of Rose. Meighan wanted Edna Purviance, and they were thinking of compromising on Dorothy Green, a New York actress, when Tucker suddenly thought Betty Compson, whom he had chanced to see in a Christie comedy, would be just right for it.

Says Miss Compson of their first meeting: "I took a trolley to the Los Angeles Athletic Club and was feeling pretty cynical about the motion picture business. I remember there was a big Christmas tree in the lobby, and the mere sight of it made me a little bitter — which was fine for the part of Rose. When we concluded our talk, I called a cab to impress Tucker, and when he left me and entered the smoking-room, I ducked out and caught a streetcar home. I had been there only a moment when the phone rang and Tucker said: "I'm going to give you the finest Christmas present you ever received. I'm going to let you play the role of Rose in *Miracle Man*." She received $125 a week for doing so, and it made her a star. It also made stars of Meighan, Lon Chaney, and Elinor Fair.

After it was released, Tucker and Miss Compson happened to pass the theatre in which it was playing. Looking at the people waiting in line to buy tickets, Tucker said: "They think they're being inspired by a religious picture, and they are, but at the same time they're seeing one of the sexiest pictures ever produced. Pick it apart, and you'll see."

Miss Compson says Tucker taught her almost everything she knows — "the best of literature, music, all the arts, everything!"

He began directing her in another picture, *Ladies Must Love,* and agreed to supervise the production by her own company of three pictures financed by Samuel Goldwyn. She was to receive half the profits as well as a salary.

"I fell in love with Tucker," Miss Compson does not hesitate to say. "But it did me no good — he was married."

Cancer, not his wife, who was then acting on the London stage, prevented the love between Pygmalion Tucker and Galatea Compson from resulting in marriage. He collapsed while directing the final portions of *Ladies Must Love,* and was operated on at once. A second operation made him realise what his malady was, and that he was dying.

He did not want Miss Compson to see how wasted his appearance had suddenly become, but *he* wanted to see *her*. So screens were put around his bed and mirrors were rigged so that he could see her without her seeing him.

It was in such a situation that he advised her about the films being produced by her own company, and negotiated a new starring contract for her with Paramount. "I want everything set for you before I leave," he told her.

Shortly before he died, he asked to be taken home, to the house he had bought in fashionable Laughlin Park. And he sent for his wife, his mother, and his son by his first wife.

Elizabeth Risdon tried to console the grief-stricken Miss Compson. "I understand — you love him," Miss Risdon told her, and added kindly: "Poor Betty! You're too young to have to go through this."

On the day Miss Compson signed the Paramount contract that Tucker had negotiated for her before dying, she was posing for publicity shots with Jesse Lasky outside his bungalow office when James Cruze happened by. He surveyed the scene with a grin and said to her: "I told you you'd be a Paramount star. What're you getting? $2500 a week?"

She *was* and, in her own words, had succeeded in "climbing onto the golden wagon at just the right time." For the next two years, in such films as *The Little Minister, The Rustle of Silk, To Have and to Hold,* and *Kick In,* she was one of Lasky's brightest stars.

But some of her pictures were mediocre, as the box-office returns on them revealed . She explains this by saying she was unfortunate in having four of her first Paramount films directed by Penrhyn Stanlaws, "who was a charming man and a very fine commercial artist, but he knew absolutely nothing about movie directing and cut his directorial teeth on my films. He got a job as director for Lasky because he was giving painting lessons to Mrs. Lasky. A Stanlaws film was lovely to look at, but dramatically it got nowhere. I was like any other young actress promoted to stardom — I needed a director who knew what he was doing."

And so, when two years of her contract were up, Paramount's New York office sent out word not to renew it if it meant raising her salary to a weekly $3000. Lasky offered to keep her on the star list without the usual salary increase, but she declined. "There is nothing soft about Compson," observed Adela Rogers St. Johns. Adds Miss Compson today: "It wasn't not getting a raise that upset me. It was the thought that my work hadn't been good enough for Lasky to want to pay a little more to keep me."

During her two years of stardom at Paramount she had been enjoying a romance with Walter Morosco, the handsome son of play-and-film producer Oliver Morosco, and when, after her departure from Paramount, she contracted to make several features in London at the then fabulous weekly salary of 1000 pounds, he wanted to accompany her so they could be married there. But she wasn't certain she was ready for marriage, and departed alone for London. She left her prized Cunningham roadster with Morosco for him to use in her absence.

Her first London film, *Woman to Woman,* was a big 1922 hit throughout Europe, and when Lewis J. Selznick put it into every Paramount theatre in the United States in 1924, it earned a tremendous profit. Alfred Hitchcock had collaborated on its script and was assistant director during its production. He was also both assistant director and art director for another of her English movies, *The White Shadow.* He admired her, and years later, when she was no longer a star, he gave her a supporting role as a good-time girl in *Mr. and Mrs. Smith.*

By 1924, she decided she was not only homesick but was ready to marry Walter Morosco. She was about to cable him to that effect when, happening to pick up a newspaper in her Savoy Hotel suite, she read that he and Corinne Griffith were planning marriage.

"I was heartbroken," she says, "but I also couldn't help wondering if I'd ever get my Cunningham roadster back. I did."

After she returned to Hollywood, Jesse Lasky obtained for her, from Paramount no less, the only woman's role in a special they were filming with Richard Dix and Lewis Stone called *The Stranger,* based on a John Galsworthy story, "The First and the Last."

"I was the one who felt like a stranger," Miss Compson says. "Hollywood had changed. I'd come home, and yet I'd not come home at all; it was a different place."

Without much enthusiasm, she signed with an independent producer, at $3500 a week, to make *Miami,* on location in Florida. While she was doing so, *Woman to Woman* was released in the United States, and its success caused Lasky to wire her to come back to Paramount and make *The Enemy Sex.*

Director James Cruze, he said, wanted her as the star for the film version of Owen Johnson's sexsational novel, "The Salamander."

Cruze was in the process of getting divorced from Marguerite Snow and as soon as the final papers were issued, he asked Miss Compson to marry him. "I held off a little, at first," she says. "I certainly didn't want to marry on the rebound, and I felt 'the Great Dane' and I had much to learn about each other. But he was persistent. 'What do you say — do you want the job?' he kept asking. And one day I surprised us both by saying yes, I'd take it. He didn't have a diamond ring conveniently in his pocket, of course, so he jerked a piece of string from a tobacco sack and tied that around my finger. We were married on October 25, 1925."

Miss Compson's early years had made her aware of the value of money, and studio executives, grudgingly paying her what she demanded, called her "the Hetty Green of Hollywood." From childhood I've had the fear of poverty," Miss Compson says. "I forced myself to do without until I could afford to buy that $11,000 custom-built Cunningham for cash."

Cruze, on the other hand, bought everything that attracted his eye, whether he could afford it, or even use it — and always more on credit than for cash. He was well-read and loved beautiful things around him, but was not always discriminating. He was a sensitive, talented, burly man who also loved to entertain. His home at Flintridge, in the foothills beyond Glendale, was a big, rambling, California-Spanish dwelling with a gardened patio, tennis court and swimming-pool. The last was bordered with tiles on which small covered wagons were embossed, in honour of *The Covered Wagon,* which Cruze had directed.

Gown designer Howard Greer described a weekend at the Cruzes in his autobiography, "Designing Male": "Saturday nights at Jimmy's were carnivals. Anyone and everyone he might have met the week before was warmly asked to appear. Stars mingled with extras, novelists with publicity men, millionaires with paupers. In the patio a long table was laden with gin bottles and soda, and in the kitchen three servants took short orders for food or prepared banquets for as many as 150 unexpected guests...Betty Compson was hostess and a more gracious or beautiful gal Hollywood will never see."

When H. L. Mencken was brought to the Cruzes by some of the weekend regulars — Jim Tully, Wilson Mizner, Laurence Stallings, Michael Arlen, Johnny Weissmuller, Frank Condon, and Roscoe Arbuckle — Cruze, aware that Mencken loved beer, went to considerable trouble in those Prohibition days to round up two barrels of it. On another occasion, Cruze looked over his guests and, deciding they lacked class, called Central Casting and told them to send out some top dress extras.

The Cruzes had their personal difficulties. "One thing we always did," Miss Compson says, "was to make peace before the lights went out. We never went to bed mad. It's a great rule."

In 1925 she again quit Paramount and began making single-picture deals at Fox, First National and Columbia. But the pictures she was given bored her and she decided "to let Jim support me in ease and comfort. In a short time, I got fat."

She was Mrs. James Cruze for seven years and when they parted, "too many parties and too many pals" were blamed for the failure of their marriage. They separated, went back together, separated again, and let several years pass before they divorced. They were both uncompromising individualists. "It had never been a peaceful marriage," Adela Rogers St. Johns observed.

"I want my own life," Miss Compson declared, and added: "Jim's a brutal man in some ways. I don't know where I shall find anyone who can measure up after him. But I'll try. I must have someone. I want a grand love affair before I die."

Which was one of the things *Cruze* thought had ruined their marriage. Whenever she reminisced about George Loane Tucker, he would yell: "Get that guy out of your mind — a husband's greatest rival is a dead lover!"

After their break-up Cruze went into bankruptcy, and Miss Compson suddenly found his creditors descending on her. She was forced to sell all her real estate including the big house she owned on Hollywood Boulevard. She let it be known that she was ready to work again, and was dismayed, but only briefly, when she discovered that the major studios regarded her as a has-been. Without a shred of false pride, she made a string of Poverty Row quickies at a big weekly salary, often working only a week per picture. But she worked often and hard; the excess weight came off; and in one year she made $180,000.

"I wasn't quite licked while I could make that much money out of films," Miss Compson remarks. "They say I love money. I do, though it was pretty cold comfort, a pretty poor substitute, for all I'd lost. But, believe me, I wasn't going to pass up that much money for any false pride. Or any hurt I got down there on Poverty Row. I think if I hadn't felt that way, hadn't worked, I would have been done forever. I'd have gone straight to hell, to be frank about it."

Undefeated, and slimmed down, Miss Compson forced the major studios to re-evaluate her talents. Director E. A. Dupont, then at Universal, gave her a juicy second lead to Mary Philbin in *Love Me and the World Is Mine;* Tod Browning, at M-G-M, cast her opposite Lon Chaney in *The Big City;* Joseph von Sternberg, at Paramount, used her to excellent advantage opposite George Bancroft in *The Docks of New York.*

"I came back," says Miss Compson, "by just working." She had overcome other setbacks in her professional career. When she was a Paramount star, she had been promised *Rain,* but Will Hays wouldn't let it be made then. She had wanted to make a movie with John Gilbert when he was at Fox, and had brought him the script of *The Man Who Came Back.* Fox bought it, but it was filmed as a silent with Dorothy Mackaill and George O'Brien. When Gilbert moved over to M-G-M, she had fourth billing with him in *Twelve Miles Out,* but the preview and trial-run engagements revealed that the picture was considered downbeat, and it was hastily withdrawn. Her role was re-written into *two* so-called comedy relief parts — Latin American sailor bait — and Paulette DuVal and Dorothy Sebastian played them. When Garbo was reluctant to make *Flesh and the Devil* without a salary hike, Miss Compson was signed to stand ready to replace her opposite Gilbert. Her tests and wardrobe were all settled — and then the studio and Garbo reached an agreement.

In the course of her comeback via Poverty Row, a South American who lived in New York sent Miss Compson a 1912 Rolls-Royce he had had stored in a Manhattan garage for several years. She says she was annoyed at first, because she already owned a limousine, but she soon discovered she could rent it out to studios for $100 a day. "In a couple of years I'd made nearly $20,000 on it, and I then sold it at a good price. So I decided to buy a new Rolls. I went to their Hollywood agency purposely dressed as a not-too-affluent character. When I pointed to the Rolls in the window and asked what it cost, the saleman said $18,000 and added: 'Do you think you can afford it?'

"I apologised for playing a game, told him who I was, and wrote out a check in full for that lovely Rolls. Doing so, paid off almost at once.

"Two days later, I was being driven down Hollywood Boulevard, and the chauffeur stopped for a red light at La Brea. A car stopping next to my new Rolls contained George Fitzmaurice, the director, with his wife, Diane Kane, Lois Wilson's younger sister. 'Betty Compson!' he exclaimed. 'You look wonderful! Listen — go downtown and see that play, "The Barker," and then phone me.'

Betty Compson with Dorothy Mackaill and Douglas Fairbanks, Jr., in THE BARKER

"I went to see "The Barker" that night, phoned Fitz, and got the marvellous part of the 'carnie gal' in the film version. It was a heavenly cast — Dorothy Mackaill, Milton Sills, and Fairbanks Jr. The studio liked it well enough to re-shoot four main sequences in dialogue, for by then it was clear that talkies were here to stay. My voice recorded all right — all those early years playing in vaudeville stood me in good stead — and I was soon so busy in talking pictures that I had to turn down leading lady to Lon Chaney in his only talkie, his last picture, the re-make of *The Unholy Three*. I suggested to Lon that he get my friend Lila Lee for it, and he did."

Miss Compson was also nominated for an Academy Award for Best Performance by an Actress in *The Barker* — but lost out to Mary Pickford in *Coquette*.

The Barker brought her some other good roles in First National pictures, especially the one opposite Richard Barthelmess in *Weary River,* and the one as a temperamental *prima donna* in *On with the Show,* and it led to her signing a non-exclusive contract with RKO as a full-fledged star.

Her first film for RKO, *Street Girl,* proved she could carry a picture *by herself.* Starring roles at Warners and Universal followed, and Paramount gave her the Cherry Malotte part in the third filming of Rex Beach's *The Spoilers* (the one with Gary Cooper).

These appearances in major studio films were interspersed with acting jobs at Monogram, Chesterfield, PRC, and even fly-by-night outfits. When she was warned that working in Poverty Row would damage her prestige, she replied that she would work in Poverty Row whenever her salary demands were met. But even this work became scarce as the Thirties advanced, and for a year she went out on the road as the star of a vaudeville show called "A Night at the Cocoanut Grove," in which she played her violin, sang, danced, and even did an imitation of Marlene Dietrich singing "Falling in Love again."

On her return to Hollywood, she appeared on the local stage in a play "Privilege Car," in which she had a role similar to the one she had enacted in *The Barker*. And she married again.

Her second husband was Irving Weinberg, a handsome, blue-eyed, self-styled producer she called "Lover Boy." Her divorce from Cruze had still left in its wake unpaid income taxes and other financial problems, and Weinberg guided her through some of the difficulties. She mortgaged the new real estate she had bought, sold her automobiles and fine furniture, and worked up a vaudeville act that Weinberg booked in Hawaii and the Orient.

"I hauled out the violin once more," Miss Compson says, "and the gorgeous gowns that had been designed by Howard Greer for the vaudeville act I'd done on the Fanchon & Marco circuit. By the time we'd played Hawaii and Manila, we were out of hock, and we did very well in Japan and Shanghai. But the poverty, filth and disease of the Orient depressed me, and the Japanese-Sino War was on — we could hear the guns booming all the time we were in Shanghai. So we called it quits and brought our very nice profit back to Hollywood."

She renewed her battle for roles and did not hesitate to steal one from a newcomer, or even from one of her contemporaries who no longer bothered to care. Sometimes, unfortunately, as in M-G-M's *Strange Cargo*, her scenes ended up almost entirely on the cutting-room floor.

She and Weinberg soon separated — they ultimately divorced — and on her own she incorporated a business, called House of Hollywood, for the manufacture of an inexpensive cosmetic line which exploited her name. She made frequent personal appearances in the stores that handled the product. When the returns from this were no longer commensurate with the effort, she took over the management of the House of Suede, on Wilshire Boulevard.

During the Second World War she went on the road in two plays, "This Thing Called Love" and "Smilin' Through," and in San Jose, following a performance for servicemen, she met Silvius Jack Gall, an American-born professional boxer of Romanian descent who had become a Navy athletic specialist.

Eventually they married, and settled down in the luxurious home her mother, who had died, had built near the Glendale foothills. Gall started a remunerative business, Ashtrays Unlimited, which supplies personalised ashtrays to hotels, restaurants, country clubs, etc.

Although Miss Compson had retired from the screen, "the ham in me came out when Walter Lang asked me to play the part of a loud, frowsy, but gutsy gal in *Claudia and David*," as she says.

Then, with Betty Blythe, Clara Kimball Young, and Francis X. Bushman, she was hired for the Pacific Coast edition of Billy Rose's "Diamond Horseshoe Show." She danced and played her violin again. Rose lured her to come to Manhattan and replace Mae Murray, who was having temperamental problems with her dancing partner, George Fontana. Miss Murray had persisted in believing prerogatives would be forthcoming because "once a star, always a star." Miss Compson knew that the reality is much more often otherwise.

She appeared in public once again — as a guest on the programme, of TV's "This Is Your Life." featuring Gilda Gray.

Although Miss Compson was seventy-six, her figure was still trim and her eyes were still that unusually bright blue. She had an inexhaustible fund of amusing stories — about film-making and just living — and she enjoyed telling them.

After her husband's death in 1962, she herself began supervising Ashtrays Unlimited from her home. "I've saved money," she said, and added proudly: "There will never be a benefit performance for Betty Compson."

On April 19, 1974, Betty Compson died. She was buried in the San Fernando Mission Cemetery.

BETTY COMPSON FILMOGRAPHY

(Miss Compson was leading lady in twenty-nine comedies produced by Al E. Christie and released by Nestor-Universal between November 20, 1915 and June 19, 1916. Christie wrote and directed most of them, but a few were directed by Horace Davey. Most of those comedies were two reels in length, but a few were a single long reel. The principal players in Christie's stock company of comedians included Eddie Lyons, Lee Moran, Ethel Lynn, Billie Rhodes, Stella Adams, Ray Gallagher, Harry Rattenberry and Neal Burns.

Miss Compson continued as leading lady for Al Christie when he set up his own studio and releasing organisation. This series of comedies was released between September 25, 1916 and June 8, 1918, and included fifty-five two-reelers. Most of these were also written and directed by Christie, but a few of the earlier ones were directed by Horace Davey. Christie's regular company at his own studio included Neal Burns, Harry Rattenberry, Dave Morris, Eddie Barry, George French, Harry Ham, Jay Belasco, Eddie Gribbon, "Smiling" Billy Mason, Stella Adams, Ethel Lynn, Margaret Gibson and Billie Rhodes. Altogether, Miss Compson made eighty-four comedies for Christie, the first entitled *Wanted – a Leading Lady,* and the last one, *Somebody's Baby.*

She was then leading lady to Roscoe "Fatty" Arbuckle in a single comedy, *The Sheriff,* released in 1918, which he starred in and directed for Paramount release. It, like most of the Christie comedies, was a two-reeler. Miss Compson then graduated to features.)

BORDER RAIDERS (1918). Western romance; as a rancher's daughter almost done out of her inheritance by a scheming woman. *Dir:* Stuart Paton. *Sc:* Paton and Jack Cunningham. *With* George Larkin, Frank Deshon, Horace C. Carpenter, Claire Du Brey, Fred Malatesta. *Prod:* Pathé. 5 reels.

THE TERROR OF THE RANGE (1919). Serial in 7 chapters; as the ranch girl heroine. *Dir:* Stuart Paton. *Sc:* (from a story, "The Wolf-Faced Man," by W. A. S. Douglas and Lucien Hubbard.) *With* George Larkin, Horace C. Carpenter, Fred Malatesta, Ora Carewe. *Prod:* Pathé 15 reels (first chapter 3 reels; all others, 2).

THE PRODIGAL LIAR (1919). Western romance; as a romance-loving heroine who gets kidnapped. *Dir:* Thomas N. Heffron. *With* William Desmond, Louis Morrison, Walter Perry, Frank Lanning. *Prod:* Robertson-Cole. 5 reels.

LIGHT OF VICTORY (1919). Drama of regeneration; as a girl who loves an alcoholic. *Dir:* William Wolbert. *Sc:* Waldemar Young (from a story by George Hull). *With* Monroe Salisbury, Fred Kelsey, Beatrice Dominguez, George Nicholls. *Prod:* Bluebird/Universal. 5 reels.

THE LITTLE DIPLOMAT (1919). Romantic comedy drama; as a girl whose sweetheart is accused of complicity in theft. *Dir:* Stuart Paton. *With* Baby Marie Osborne, Lydia Knott, William Welsh, Jack Connolly, Murdoch MacQuarrie, Al MacQuarrie. *Prod:* Pathé. 5 reels.

THE DEVIL'S TRAIL (1919). Northwest melodrama; as Rose, the daughter of a sergeant in the Northwest Mounted Police. *Dir./Sc:* Stuart Paton. *With* George Larkin, William Quinn, Fred Malatesta, Claire Du Brey. Working title: *Rose of the Border. Prod:* World. 5 reels.

THE MIRACLE MAN (1919). Crook regeneration drama; as the gangster's moll, Rose. *Dir/Sc:* George Loane Tucker (as dramatised by George M. Cohan from a Frank Packard story). *With* Thomas Meighan, Lon Chaney, J. M. Dumont, W. Lawson Butt, Elinor Fair, F. A. Turner, Lucille Hutton, Joseph S. Dowling, (Re-made as talkie, 1932, with Sylvia Sidney in the Compson role.) *Prod:* Paramount-Artcraft. 8 reels. (Compare listing in Lon Chaney filmography.)

PRISONERS OF LOVE (1921). Romantic drama; as Blanche Davis. *Dir:* Arthur Rosson. *Sc:* Catherine Henry. *With* Emory Johnson, Roy Stewart, Ralph Lewis, Claire McDowell, Clara Horton, Kate Toncray. *Prod:* Goldwyn. 6 reels.

AT THE END OF THE WORLD (1921). Romantic drama of Shanghai; as Cherry O'Day, a lure for male patrons in her father's bar, "The Paper Lantern." *Dir:* Penrhyn Stanlaws. *Sc:* Edfrid A. Bingham (adapted by Adelaide Heilbron from a play by Ernest Klein). *With* Milton Sills, Casson Ferguson, Mitchell Lewis, Spottiswoode Aitken, Joseph Kilgour. (Compson's first feature under her long Paramount starring contract.) *Prod:* Paramount. 6 reels.

LADIES MUST LIVE (1921). Romantic drama; as Christine Bleeker. *Dir/Sc:* George Loane Tucker (who died before finishing it), (from a novel by Alice Duer Miller). *With* Robert Ellis, Mahlon Hamilton, Leatrice Joy, John Gilbert, Hardee Kirkland, Gibson Gowland, Cleo Madison, Snitz Edwards, Lucille Hutton, William V. Mong, Marcia Manon. *Prod:* Paramount. 8 reels.

FOR THOSE WE LOVE (1921). Romantic melodrama; as Bernice Arnold. *Dir:* Arthur Rosson. *Sc:* Rosson and Perley Poore Sheehan (from a story by Sheehan). *With* Lon Chaney, Richard Rosson, Camille Astor, Bert Woodruff, Harry Duffield, Walter Moroso, George Cooper, Frank Campeau. *Prod:* Goldwyn. 6 reels. (Compare listing in Lon Chaney filmography.)

THE LITTLE MINISTER (1922). Romantic drama of Scotland; as Lady Babbie, the Barrie heroine created by Maude Adams on Broadway. *Dir:* Penrhyn Stanlaws. *Sc:* Edfrid A. Bingham (from the play by Sir James M. Barrie). *With* George Hackathorne, Edwin Stevens, Nigel Barrie, Will R. Walling, Guy Oliver, Fred Huntley, Robert Brower, Joseph Hazelton, Mary Wilkinson. (A Vitagraph version, based on the Barrie novel, starring Alice Calhoun, was released simultaneously; Vitagraph had made an earlier version starring Clara Kimball Young; Katharine Hepburn starred in the RKO Radio talking version.) *Prod:* Paramount. 6 reels.

THE LAW AND THE WOMAN (1922). Murder melodrama; as Margaret Rolfe. *Dir:* Penrhyn Stanlaws. *Sc:* Albert S. LeVino (from a play, "The Woman in the Case," by Clyde Fitch, previously filmed, 1916, starring Pauline Frederick). *With* William T. Carleton, Cleo Ridgely, Casson Ferguson, Henry Barrows, Helen Dunbar, Clarence Burton, J. S. Stembridge. *Prod:* Paramount. 7 reels.

THE GREEN TEMPTATION (1922). Jewel theft melodrama; in a triple role: as Genelle/Coralyn/ Joan Parker, all masquerades for the girl crook after the emerald known as "The Green Temptation." *Dir:* William Desmond Taylor. *Sc:* Monte M. Katterjohn and Julia Crawford Ivers (from a story, "The Noose," by Constance Lindsay Skinner). *With* Mahlon Hamilton, Thedore Kosloff, Neely Edwards, Edmund Burns, Lymore Lynard, Mary Thurman, M. Van Hardenberg, Betty Brice, Arthur Hull. *Prod:* Paramount. 6 reels.

OVER THE BORDER (1922). Northwest romantic melodrama; as Jen Galbraith. *Dir:* Penrhyn Stanlaws. *Sc:* (from the short story, "She of the Triple Chevron," by Sir Gilbert Parker). *With* Tom Moore, J. Farrell MacDonald, Casson Ferguson, Sidney D'Albrook, L. C. Shumway, Jean de Briac, Edward J. Brady. (Jen was the heroine of several stories and at least two plays by Sir Gilbert Parker; both Elsie Ferguson and Dorothy Dalton played Jen, and in 1942 M-G-M released *Pierre of the Plains*, with Ruth Hussey as Jen.) *Prod:* Paramount. 7 reels.

ALWAYS THE WOMAN (1922). Romantic drama of reincarnation; as Celia Thaxter. *Dir:* Richard Rosson. *Sc:* Perley Poore Sheehan. *With* Emory Johnson, Doris Pawn, Gerald Pring, Richard Rosson, Arthur Delmore, Macey Harlan. *Prod:* Goldwyn. 6 reels.

THE BONDED WOMAN (1922). Romantic melodrama; as Angela Gaskell. *Dir:* Philip E. Rosen. *Sc:* Albert Shelby LeVino (from a story, "The Salving of John Somers," by John Fleming Wilson). *With* Richard Dix, John Bowers, J. Farrell MacDonald, Ethel Wales. *Prod:* Paramount. 6 reels. (Compare listing in Richard Dix filmography.)

TO HAVE AND TO HOLD (1922). Costume drama; as Lady Jocelyn Leigh, who escapes from a hateful marriage in the court of James I, and finds love in Jamestown, Virginia. *Dir:* George Fitzmaurice. *Sc:* Ouida Bergere (from the novel by Mary Johnson). *With* Bert Lytell, Theodore Kosloff, W. J. Ferguson, Raymond Hatton, Claire Du Brey, Walter Long, Anne Cornwall, Fred Huntley, Arthur Rankin, Lucien Littlefield. (Previously filmed, 1916, with Mae Murray and Wallace Reid.) *Prod:* Paramount. 8 reels.

KICK IN (1922). Crook melodrama; as Molly Brandon, the district attorney's daughter. *Dir:* George Fitzmaurice. *Sc:* Ouida Bergere (from the play by Willard Mack). *With* Bert Lytell, May McAvoy, Gareth Hughes, Robet Agnew, John Miltern, Charles Stevenson, Jed Prouty, Charles Ogle, Kathleen Clifford, Maym Kelso, Walter Long. (Previously filmed by Fitzmaurice for Astra-Pathé, 1917, with William Courtenay and Mollie King; re-made by Paramount as a talkie, starring Clara Bow.) *Prod:* Paramount. 7 reels. (Compare listing in May McAvoy filmography.)

THE WHITE FLOWER (1923). Romantic drama, filmed in the Hawaiian Islands; as Konia Markham, half-caste daughter of a rich plantation owner. *Dir./Sc:* Julia Crawford Ivers. *With* Edmund Lowe, Edward Martindale, Arline Pretty, Sylvia Ashton, Arthur Hoyt, Leon Barry, Lily Phillips, Reginald Carter. *Prod:* Paramount. 6 reels.

THE RUSTLE OF SILK (1923). Romantic drama; as Lala De Breeze, a lady's maid, in love with a British statesman. *Dir:* Herbert Brenon. *Sc:* Sada Cowan and Ouida Bergere (from a novel by Cosmo Hamilton). *With* Conway Tearle, Anna Q. Nilsson, Frederick Esmelton, Charles Stevenson, Cyril Chadwick. *Prod:* Paramount. 7 reels.

THE WOMAN WITH FOUR FACES (1923). Melodrama; as Elizabeth West, reformed jewel thief, who helps a district attorney break up a narcotics ring. *Dir:* Herbert Brenon. *Sc:* George Hopkins (from a play by Bayard Veiller). *With* Richard Dix, George Fawcett,

Betty Compson in THE ROYAL OAK

Theodore von Eltz, Joseph Kilgour, James Farley, Guy Oliver, Charles Stevenson, Gladden James, Eulalie Jensen. *Prod:* Paramount. 6 reels. (Compare listing in Richard Dix filmography.)

THE ROYAL OAK (1923). Costume drama; as Lady Mildred Cholmondeley, who disguises herself as Charles II so the king may escape. *Dir:* Maurice Elvey. *Sc:* Lucita Squier (from a Drury Lane melodrama by Henry Hamilton and Sir Augustus Harris). *With* Clive Brook, Henry Victor, Henry Ainley. *Prod:* Stoll (British). 6,170 ft.

WOMAN TO WOMAN (1924) (Filmed in England in 1922). Romantic drama; as Louise Boucher, dancer of the Moulin Rouge, later known as the English dancer, Deloryse. *Dir:* Graham Cutts. *Sc:* Alfred Hitchcock (from a story by Michael Morton). *With* Clive Brook, Josephine Earle, Marie Ault, M. Peter, A. Harding Steerman. (Re-made as a 1929 talkie starring Betty Compson; re-made in England with Adele Dixon, Joyce Howard and Douglass Montgomery.) *Prod:* Lewis J. Selznick (in America). 7,455 ft.

THE STRANGER (1924). Psychological melodrama; as Peggy Bowlin. *Dir:* Joseph Henabery. *Sc:* Edfrid A. Bingham (from a story, "The First and the Last," by John Galsworthy). *With* Richard Dix, Lewis Stone, Tully Marshall, Robert Schable, Frank Nelson. (In 1940 Columbia released a British-made talking version, *21 Days Together,* with Laurence Olivier and Vivien Leigh.) *Prod:* Paramount. 7 reels. (Compare listing in Richard Dix filmography.)

MIAMI (1924). Melodrama; as Joan Bruce. *Dir:* Alan Crosland. *Sc:* John Lynch. *With* Lawford Davidson, Hedda Hopper, J. Barney Sherry, Lucy Fox, Benjamin F. Finney Jr. *Prod:* Hodkinson. 7 reels.

THE ENEMY SEX (1924). Drama of a girl who comes through sex unscathed; as a chorus girl, Dodo Baxter. *Dir:* James Cruze. *Sc:* Walter Woods and Harvey Thew (from à novel, "The Salamander," by Owen Johnson). *With* DeWitt Jennings, Huntley Gordon, Sheldon Lewis, Percy Marmont, Edward Faust, Will H. Turner, Dot Farley. *Prod:* Paramount. 8 reels.

THE WHITE SHADOW (1924). (Filmed and released in England, 1923). Drama; in a dual role: as twin sisters, Nancy and Georgina Brent. *Dir:* Graham Cutts. (Ass't dir. and art director: Alfred Hitchcock). *Sc:* Alfred Hitchcock (from a story by Michael Morton). *With* Clive Brook, A. B. Imeson, Daisy Campbell, Henry Victor. *Prod:* Lewis J. Selznick (in America). 7 reels.

RAMSHACKLE HOUSE (1924). Romantic drama; as Pen Broome. *Dir:* Harmon Weight. *Sc:* Coolidge Streeter (from a novel by Hulbert Footner). *With* Robert Lowing, John Davidson, Henry James, William Black, Duke Pelzer, Josephine Norman. *Prod:* PDC. 5 reels.

THE FEMALE (1924). Romantic drama; as Dalla, a South African girl reputed to have been raised by lions. *Dir:* Sam Wood. *Sc:* Agnes Christine Johnston (from a story, "Dalla, the Lion's Cub," by Cynthia Stockley). *With* Warner Baxter, Noah Beery, Dorothy Cumming, Freeman Wood, Helen Butler, Pauline French, Edgar Norton. *Prod:* Paramount. 7 reels.

THE GARDEN OF WEEDS (1924). Marital drama; as Dorothy Delbridge. *Dir:* James Cruze. *Sc:* Walter Woods and Anthony Coldeway (from a play by Leon Gordon and Doris Marquette). *With* Rockcliffe Fellowes, Warner Baxter, Charles Ogle, King Zany, William Austin, Lucille Thorndyke, William Turner, Lilyan Tashman, Toyo Fujita, Al St. John. *Prod:* Paramount. 6 reels.

THE FAST SET (1924). Fast-living society drama; as Margaret Stone, a neglected wife. *Dir:* William C. de Mille. *Sc:* Clara Beranger (from a play, "Spring Cleaning," by Frederick Lonsdale). *With* Adolphe Menjou, Elliott Dexter, ZaSu Pitts, Dawn O'Day (Anne Shirley), Grace Carlysle, Claire Adams, Rosalind Byrne, Edgar Norton, Louis Natheaux. *Prod:* Paramount. 8 reels.

LOCKED DOORS (1925). Marital drama; as Mary Reed Carter, a young wife married to an old husband. *Dir:* William C. de Mille. *Sc:* Clara Beranger. *With* Theodore Roberts, Kathyln Williams, Theodore von Eltz, Robert Edeson, Elmo Billings. *Prod:* Paramount. 7 reels.

NEW LIVES FOR OLD (1925). Espionage drama; as Olympe, Parisian cabaret dancer, who works for the American Secret Service. *Dir:* Clarence Badger. *Sc:* Adelaide Heilbron. *With* Wallace MacDonald, Theodore Kosloff, Sheldon Lewis, Jack Joyce, Margaret Seddon, Joseph J. Dowling, Helen Dunbar, Gale Henry. *Prod:* Paramount. 7 reels.

EVE'S SECRET (1925). Romantic drama; as Eve, a cobbler's daughter, who becomes a duchess. *Dir:* Clarence Badger. *Sc:* Adelaide Heilbron (from a play, "The Moon-Flower," adapted by Zoë Akins from a Lajos Biros

play). *With* Jack Holt, Lionel Belmore, William Collier Jr., Mario Carillo, Vera Lewis. *Prod:* Paramount. 6 reels.

BEGGAR ON HORSEBACK (1925). Fantasy comedy; as The Princess in the dream pantomime. *Dir:* James Cruze. *Sc:* Walter Woods (from the play by George S. Kaufman and Marc Connelly). *With* Edward Everett Horton, Esther Ralston, Edwin Connelly, Ethel Wales, Gertrude Short, James Mason, Theodore Kosloff, Frederick Sullivan. *Prod:* Paramount. 7,197 ft.

PATHS TO PARADISE (1925). Crook comedy; as Molly, a maid, who is also a jewel thief. *Dir:* Clarence Badger. *Sc:* Keene Thompson (from a play, "Heart of a Thief," by Paul Armstrong). *With* Raymond Griffith, Tom Santschi, Bert Woodruff, Fred Kelsey. *Prod:* Paramount. 7 reels.

THE PONY EXPRESS (1925). Western drama; as Molly Jones. *Dir:* James Cruze. *Sc:* Walter Woods (from a story by Woods and Henry James Forman). *With* Ricardo Cortez, Ernest Torrence, Wallace Beery, George Bancroft, Frank Lackteen, John Fox, William Turner, Al Hart, Charles Gerson, Rose Tapley, Vondell Darr. *Prod:* Paramount. 10 reels.

PALACE OF PLEASURE (1926). Romantic costume drama; as Lola Montez. *Dir:* Emmett G. Flynn. *Sc:* Bradley King (ad. by Benjamin Glazer from a play, "Lola Montez," by Adolf Paul.) *With* Edmund Lowe, Henry Kolker, Harvey Clark, Nina Romano, Francis McDonald. *Prod:* Fox. 6 reels.

COUNSEL FOR THE DEFENSE (1926). Drama of the law courts; as Katherine West, attorney. *Dir:* Burton King. *Sc:* Arthur Hoerl (from a story by Leroy Scott). *With* House Peters, Rockcliffe Fellowes, Jay Hunt. *Prod:* Associated Exhibitors. 7 reels.

THE WISE GUY (1926). Dramatic expose of the evangelist racket; as Hula Kate from a medicine show who becomes a bigtime evangelist. *Dir:* Frank Lloyd. *Sc:* Ada McQuillan (from a story by Jules Furthman). *With* James Kirkwood, Mary Astor, Mary Carr, George Marion Sr., George Cooper. *Prod:* First National, 8 reels.

BELLE OF BROADWAY (AKA, GB, *Darling of Paris*) Backstage drama; as Marie Duval, who poses as a former star. *Dir:* Harry O. Hoyt. *Sc:* J. Grubb Alexander (from a story by Alexander and Jean Perry). *With* Herbert Rawlinson, Edith Yorke, Armand Kaliz, Thomas Ricketts, Wilfred North. *Prod:* Columbia. 6 reels.

TWELVE MILES OUT (1927). Hi-jacking melodrama; Miss Compson had a dramatic second lead in this, but after a few trial runs, the film was recalled as being too sombre, and her role was edited out to be re-played by Dorothy Sebastian and Paulette Du Val for "comedy." *Dir:* Jack Conway. *Sc:* Sada Cowan (from a play by William Anthony McGuire). *With* John Gilbert, Joan Crawford, Ernest Torrence, Bert Roach, Eileen Percy, Edward Earle, Tom O'Brien. *Prod:* M-G-M. 6,379 ft.

THE LADYBIRD (1927). Crook melodrama; as Diane Wyman, society girl, who helps round up a gang of crooks. *Dir:* Walter Lang. *Sc:* John F. Natteford (from a story by William Dudley Pelley). *With* Malcolm McGregor, John Miljan, Leo White, Ruth Stonehouse, Hank Mann, Sheldon Lewis, James Gerard. *Prod:* Chadwick. 7 reels.

SAY IT WITH DIAMONDS (1927). Marital drama; as Betty Howard, who misunderstands her husband. *Dir:* Jack Nelson *With* Earle Williams, Jocelyn Lee, Armand Kaliz, Betty Baker. *Prod:* Chadwick. 7 reels.

TEMPTATIONS OF A SHOP GIRL (1927). Crook melodrama; as Ruth Harrington, who frames a major crook. *Dir:* Tom Terriss. *Sc:* L. V. Jefferson. *With* Armand Kaliz, Pauline Garon, Raymond Glenn, John F. Dillon, Cora Williams, William Humphries. *Prod:* Chadwick. 6 reels.

CHEATING CHEATERS (1927). Romantic crook melodrama; as Nan Carey, fashionable lady crook who is really a detective. *Dir:* Edward Laemmle. *Sc:* James T. O'Donohue (ad. by Charles A. Logue from the play by Max Marcin). *With* Kenneth Harlan, Lucien Littlefield, Eddie Gribbon, Cesare Gravina, Sylvia Ashton, Maude Turner Gordon, E. J. Ratcliffe. (Previously filmed starring Clara Kimball Young; filmed as a talkie, 1935, with Fay Wray.) *Prod:* Universal. 6 reels.

LOVE ME AND THE WORLD IS MINE (1928). Romantic drama of Old Vienna; as Mitzel, a ballet dancer. *Dir:* E. A. Dupont. *Sc:* Paul Kohner & Dupont (ad. by Imre Fazekas from a novel, "Affairs of Hannerl," by Rudolph Hans Bartsch). *With* Mary Philbin, Norman Kerry, Henry B. Walthall, George Seigmann, Albert Conti. *Prod:* Universal. 6 reels.

THE BIG CITY (1928). Crook drama; as a girl of the underworld, Helen, who loves Chaney. *Dir:* Tod Browning. *Sc:* Waldemar Young (from a story by Browning). *With* Lon Chaney, Marceline Day, James Murray, Matthew Betz, John George, Virginia Pearson, *Prod:* M-G-M. 8 reels. (Compare listing in Lon Chaney filmography.)

THE MASKED ANGEL (1928). Romantic drama; as Betty Carlisle, a cabaret girl with a past who marries a blind soldier. *Dir:* Frank O'Connor. *Sc:* Maxine Alton (from a story, "Remorse," by Evelyn Campbell). With Erik

Arnold, Wheeler Oakman, Jocelyn Lee, Grace Cunard, Lincoln Plummer, Robert Homans, Jane Keckley. *Prod:* Chadwick. 6 reels.

THE DESERT BRIDE (1928). Desert espionage drama; as Diane Duval. *Dir:* Walter Lang. *Sc:* Elmer Harris (ad. by Anthony Coldeway from a story, "The Adventuress," by Ewart Adamson). *With* Allan Forrest, Edward Martindel, Otto Matiesen, Roscoe Karns, Frank Austin. *Prod:* Columbia. 6 reels.

LIFE'S MOCKERY (1928). Social drama of heredity vs. environment; in a dual role: as Kit Miller and Isabelle Fullerton. *Dir:* Robert F. Hill. *Sc:* Isadore Bernstein. *With* Theodore von Eltz, Alec B. Francis, Dorothy Cumming, Russell Simpson. *Prod:* Chadwick. 7 reels.

THE DOCKS OF NEW YORK (1928). Romantic drama; as Sadie, a girl who tries to commit suicide and falls in love with the man who saves her. *Dir:* Joseph von Sternberg. *Sc:* Jules Furthman (from a story, "The Dock Walloper," by John Monk Saunders). *With* George Bancroft, Olga Baclanova, Clyde Cook, Mitchell Lewis, Gustav von Seyffertitz, Guy Oliver, May Foster, Lillian Worth. *Prod:* Paramount. 8 reels.

COURT MARTIAL (1928). Civil War Western melodrama; as Belle Starr, leader of a guerilla band. *Dir:* George B. Seitz. *Sc:* Anthony Coldeway (from a story by Elmer Harris). *With* Jack Holt, Doris Hill, Pat Harmon. *Prod:* Columbia. 7 reels.

THE BARKER (1928). Romantic carnival drama; as Carrie, the "carny" girl. *Dir:* George Fitzmaurice. *Sc:* Benjamin Glazer, with dialogue by Joseph Jackson and titles by Herman J. Mankiewicz (from the play by Kenyon Nicholson). Four sequences had spoken dialogue, and this film marks Miss Compson's *début* as a talking film actress; she was nominated for an Academy Award for Best Performance by an Actress, but lost to Mary Pickford for *Coquette*. *With* Milton Sills, Dorothy Mackaill, Douglas Fairbanks Jr., Sylvia Ashton, George Cooper, S. S. Simon. *Prod:* First National. 8 reels. (Re-made by Fox, starring Clara Bow, as *Hoopla!*)

SCARLET SEAS (1928). Romantic sea drama; as Rose, a dance-hall girl in a Singapore dive, who gets shanghaied. *Dir:* John Francis Dillon. *Sc:* Bradley King (from a story by W. Scott Darling). *With* Richard Barthelmess, Loretta Young, James Bradbury Sr., Jack Curtis, Knute Erickson. *Prod:* First National. 7 reels.

WEARY RIVER (1929). Prison regeneration drama; as Alice, who loves a prisoner who wins a pardon. *Dir:* Frank Lloyd. *Sc:* Bradley King; dialogue by Tom J. Geraghty (from a story by Courtney Riley Cooper). *With* Richard Barthelmess, William Holden, Louis

Natheaux, George E. Stone, Raymond Turner, Gladden James. *Prod:* First National. 8 reels.

ON WITH THE SHOW (1929). Backstage drama; as Nita, temperamental prima donna. *Dir:* Alan Crosland. *Sc:* Robert Lord (from a play by Humphrey Pearson). *With* Sally O'Neil, Louise Fazenda, Joe E. Brown, Purnell Pratt, William Bakewell, The Fairbanks Twins, Wheeler Oakman, Sam Hardy, Thomas Jefferson, Lee Moran, Harry Gribbon, Arthur Lake, Josephine Hutton, Henry Fink, Otto Hoffman, Ethel Waters. (This plot, with variations, was later used in *42nd Street,* with Bebe Daniels as the temperamental star; and Glenda Jackson appeared in a parody role of it in Ken Russell's *The Boy Friend.*) *Prod:* Warner Bros./First National. 12 reels.

THE TIME, THE PLACE & GIRL (1929). Romantic comedy drama; as Doris Ward. *Dir:* Howard Bretherton. *Sc:* Robert Lord (from the musical comedy by Frank R. Adams, James E. Howard and Will Haigh). *With* Grant Withers, Gertrude Olmstead, James Kirkwood, Vivian Oakland, Gretchen Hartman, Irene Haisman, John Davidson, Gerald King, Bert Roach. *Prod:* Warner Bros. 7 reels.

STREET GIRL (1929). Romantic drama, with music; as the violinist, Freddie Joyzelle. *Dir:* Wesley Ruggles. *Sc:* Jane Murfin (from a story, "The Viennese Charmer," by W. Carey Wonderly). *With* John Harron, Ned Sparks, Jack Oakie, Guy Buccola, Joseph Cawthorn, Ivan Lebedeff, Eddie Kane, Doris Eaton, Gus Arnheim & his Ambassador Band, Raymond Maurel and his Cimini Male Chorus. (The story formed the basis for Lily Pons in *That Girl from Paris;* and it was re-made in 1941 as *Four Jacks and a Jill.*) *Prod:* RKO. 9 reels.

THE GREAT GABBO (1929). Backstage drama; as Mary, a dancer. *Dir:* James Cruze. *Sc:* Hugh Herbert (from a story by Ben Hecht). *With* Erich von Stroheim, Don Douglas, Margie (Babe) Kane. *Prod:* Sono-Art. 10 reels.

SKIN DEEP (1929). Drama of revenge; as Sadie Rogers. *Dir:* Ray Enright. *Sc:* Gordon Rigby (from a story, "Lucky Damage," by Marc Edmunds Jones). *With* Monte Blue, Davey Lee, Alice Day, John Davidson, John Bowers, George E. Stone, Tully Marshall, Robert Perry. *Prod:* Warner Bros. 6 reels.

WOMAN TO WOMAN (1929). Re-make of the 1924 Selznick romantic drama; this time as the dancer Deloryce who becomes the favourite, Lola. *Dir:* Victor Saville. *Sc:* (from the play by Michael Morton). *With* George Barraud, Juliette Compton, Margaret Chambers, Reginald Sharland, George Billings, Winter Hall. *Prod:* Tiffany. 8 reels. (Re-made in England, 1947.)

THE SHOW OF SHOWS (1929). Variety revue; as "Lady Luck." *Dir:* John Adolfi. Nearly everybody then under contract to Warner Bros./First National played something in this all-dialogue revue, with songs and dances (86%) Technicolor). Although topbilled, Miss Compson appears as the personification of "Lady Luck" in an elaborate show-girl costume for the picture's finale, and she neither says a word nor sings a note. *Prod:* Warner Bros./First National. 15 reels.

BLAZE O' GLORY (1930). Courtroom-war melodrama; as Helen Williams. *Dir:* Renaud Hoffman and George J. Crone. *Sc:* Henry McCarthy (ad. by Renaud Hoffman from a story, "The Long Shot," by Thomas Alexander Boyd). *with* Eddie Dowling, Ferdinand Schuman-Heinck, Frankie Darro, Henry B. Walthall, William Davidson, Eddie Conrad. *Prod:* Sono-Art. 10 reels.

THE CASE OF SERGEANT GRISCHA (1930). First World War drama; as Babka, a Russian peasant who befriends a fellow Russian escaped from a German prison camp. *Dir:* Herbert Brenon. *Sc:* Elizabeth Meehan (from a novel by Arnold Zweig). *With* Chester Morris, Alec B. Francis, Gustav von Seyffertitz, Jean Hersholt, Leyland Hodgson, Paul MacAllister, Frank McCormack. *Prod:* RKO. 10 reels.

ISLE OF ESCAPE (1930). South Seas melodrama; as Stella. *Dir:* Howard Bretherton. *Sc:* Lucien Hubbard and J. Grubb Alexander (from a story by Jack McClaren). *With* Monte Blue, Myrna Loy, Noah Beery, Ivan Simpson, Jack Ackroyd, Nena Quartaro, Duke Kahanamoku, Rose Dione. *Prod:* Warner Bros. 6 reels.

THE MIDNIGHT MYSTERY (1930). Murder mystery; as Sally Wayne. *Dir:* George B. Seitz. *Sc:* Beulah Marie Dix (from the play, "Hawk Island," by Howard Irving Young). *With* Hugh Trevor, Lowell Sherman, Rita LeRoy, Ivan Lebedeff, Raymond Hatton, June Clyde, Sidney D'Albrook, William Bart. *Prod:* RKO. 7 reels.

THE CZAR OF BROADWAY (1930). Drama; as Connie Colton, who helps a reporter bring her ex-lover to justice. *Dir:* William James Craft. *Sc:* Gene Towne. *With* John Wray, John Harron, Claude Allister, Wilbur Mack, King Baggot, Edmund Bresse. *Prod:* Universal. 8 reels.

INSIDE THE LINES (1930). Counterespionage melodrama; as Jane Gershon, a British spy posing as a German agent. *Dir:* Roy J. Pomeroy *Sc:* Ewart Adamson and John Farrow. (from a story, "Behind the Lines," by Earl Derr Biggers). *With* Ralph Forbes, Montagu Love, Mischa Auer, Ivan Simpson, Evan Thomas, Reginald Sharland, William von Brincken. *Prod:* RKO. 8 reels.

THOSE WHO DANCE (1930). Gangster melodrama; as Kitty, a gangster's moll. *Dir:* William Beaudine. *Sc:* Joseph Jackson (from a story by George Kibbe Turner). *With* Monte Blue, Lila Lee, William (Stage) Boyd, William Janney, Wilfred Lucas, Cornelius Keefe, De-Witt Jennings. (Spanish and German versions were shot simultaneously; Thomas Ince had filmed it in 1924 with Blanche Sweet in the Compson role.) *Prod:* Warner Bros. 7 reels.

THE SPOILERS (1930). Melodrama of the Alaskan gold rush; as Cherry Malotte, faro-dealer. *Dir:* Edwin Carewe. *Sc:* Agnes Brand Leahy (ad. with dialogue by Bartlett Cormack from the novel by Rex Beach). *With* Gary Cooper, William (Stage) Boyd, Kay Johnson, Harry Green, Slim Summerville, James Kirkwood, Lloyd Ingraham, Oscar Apfel, George Irving, Knute Erickson. (To date, there have been five screenings of *The Spoilers:* Cherry Malotte has been played by Kathlyn Williams, 1914; Anna Q. Nilsson, 1923; Betty Compson, 1930; Marlene Dietrich, 1942; Anne Baxter, 1955.) *Prod:* Paramount. 11 reels.

SHE GOT WHAT SHE WANTED (1930). Vaudeville vs. society drama; as Mahyna, a hoofer with aspirations. *Dir:* James Cruze. *Sc:* George Rosener. *With* Lee Tracy, Alan Hale, Gaston Glass, Dorothy Christy, Fred Kelsey. *Prod:* Tiffany. 9 reels.

THE BOUDOIR DIPLOMAT (1930). Romantic comedy drama; as Helene, an Ambassador's wife. *Dir:* Mal St. Clair. *Sc:* Benjamin Glazer and Tom Reed (from a German play, "The Command to Love"). *With* Ian Keith, Mary Duncan, Jeanette Loff, Lawrence Grant, André Beranger, Lionel Belmore. *Prod:* Universal. 8 reels.

THE LADY REFUSES (1931). Romantic drama; as June, a girl of the streets. *Dir:* George Archainbaud. *Sc:* Wallace Smith (from a story, "Lady for Hire," by Robert Milton and Guy Bolton). *With* Gilbert Emery, John Darrow, Margaret Livingston, Ivan Lebedeff, Edgar Norton, Daphne Pollard, Reginald Sharland. *Prod:* RKO. 7 reels.

THE VIRTUOUS HUSBAND (AKA, GB, *What Wives Don't Want*) (1931). Romantic comedy drama; as Inez Wakefield. *Dir:* Vin Moore. *Sc:* Dale Van Every, Jerome Horwin, Fred Niblo Jr. (from a play, "Apron Strings" by Dorrance Davis). With Elliott Nugent, Jean Arthur, J. C. Nugent, Alison Skipworth. *Prod:* Universal. 75m.

THREE WHO LOVED 1931). Drama; as Helga, a Swedish girl, loved by two men. *Dir:* George Archainbaud. *Sc:* Martin Flavin. *With* Conrad Nagel, Robert Ames, Robert E. O'Connor, Bodil Rosing, Dickie Moore. *Prod:* RKO 72m.

THE GAY DIPLOMAT (1931). Romantic espionage drama set in Budapest; as the Baroness Corri. *Dir:* Richard Boleslavsky. *Sc:* Doris Anderson (based on a play by Benn W. Levy). *With* Ivan Lebedeff, Genevieve Tobin, Ilka Chase, Purnell Pratt, Rita LeRoy, Colin Campbell, Edward Martindel. Arthur Edmund Carewe. *Prod:* RKO 70m.

THE SILVER LINING (1932). Women's prison drama; as Kate Flynn, a prison-workhouse girl. *Dir:* Alan Crosland. *Sc:* Gertrude Orr & Claire Corvalho (from a story by Hal Conklin). *With* Maureen O'Sullivan, John Warburton, Montagu Love, Mary Doran, Cornelius Keefe, Martha Mattox, Wally Albright, Grace Valentine. *Prod:* Patrician-United Artists. 59m.

GUILTY OR NOT GUILTY (1932). Gangster drama; as Maizie. *Dir:* Albert Ray. *Sc:* Frances Hyland (from a story by Arthur Hoerl). *With* Claudia Dell, Tom Douglas, George Irving, Wheeler Oakman, Luis Alberni, William Davidson. *Prod:* Monogram. 67m.

WEST OF SINGAPORE (1933). Oilfield drama; as Lou, a happy-go-lucky oilfield girl. *Dir:* Albert Ray. *Sc:* Adele Buffington (from a story by Houston Branch). *With* Weldon Hayburn, Margaret Lindsay, Noel Madison, Tom Douglas, Clyde Cook. *Prod:* Monogram. 65m.

DESTINATION UNKNOWN (1933). Melodrama about rum-runners, with spiritual mysticism; as Ruby Smith. *Dir:* Tay Garnett. *Sc:* Tom Buckingham. *With* Pat O'Brien, Ralph Bellamy, Alan Hale, Russell Hopton, Tom Brown, Noel Madison, Stanley Fields, Rollo Lloyd, Willard Robertson, Charles Middleton. *Prod:* Universal. 67m.

NOTORIOUS BUT NICE (1933). Murder drama; as Millie Sprague. *Dir:* Richard Thorpe. *Sc:* M. A. Anderson (from a story by Carol Webster). *With* Marian Marsh, Donald Dillaway. Rochelle Hudson, John Sainpolis, Henry Kolker, J. Carrol Naish, Dewey Robinson, Robert Ellis, Wilfred Lucas, Robert Frazer, Jane Keckley. *Prod:* Chesterfield. 65m.

NO SLEEP ON THE DEEP (1934). Romantic comedy; as a girl on a cruise. *Dir:* Charles Lamont. *With* Don Alvarado. *Prod:* Educational-Mermaid Comedy. 21m.

FALSE PRETENSES (1935). Romantic comedy drama; as Clarissa Stanhope, society girl. *Dir:* Charles Lamont. *Sc:* Ewart Adamson (from a story, "Suicide Bridge," by Betty Burbridge). *With* Irene Ware, Sidney Blackmer, Russell Hopton, Edward Gargan. *Prod:* Chesterfield. 68m.

MANHATTAN BUTTERFLY (AKA, GB, *The Midnight Butterfly*) (1935). New York drama; as a girl who lives too fast. *Dir:* Louis

Collins. *Sc:* F. McGrew Willis (from a story by Lois Buel). *With* Dorothy Grainger, William Bakewell, Kenneth Thomson, Dorothy Burgess, Carmelita Geraghty, Harry Holman, George Meeker, Matty Fain, Alphonse Martel, Edward Keene, William Arnold, Jack Trent. *Prod:* Imperial. 73m.

LAUGHING IRISH EYES (1936). Romantic comedy; as Molly. *Dir:* Joseph Santley. *Sc:* Olive Cooper, Ben Ryan & Stanley Rauh. *With* Phil Regan, Walter C. Kelly, Evalyn Knapp, Ray Walker, Mary Gordon, Warren Hymer, J. M. Kerrigan, Herman Bing, Raymond Hatton, Clarence Muse. *Prod:* Republic. 70m.

THE MILLIONAIRE KID (1936). Teenage melodrama; as Mrs. Neville. *Dir:* Bernard B. Ray. *Sc:* Jack Natteford and Blanche Church. *With* Bryant Washburn, Charles Delaney, Lois Wilde, Creighton Hale, Bradley Metcalfe, Eddie Gribbon, Al St. John, Josef Swickard. *Prod:* Reliable. 59m.

TRUE DRAGNET (1936). Murder drama; as Mollie Cole, who gets murdered. *Dir:* Vin Moore. *Sc:* J. Mulhauser (from a play by Willard Mack). *With* Rod LaRocque, Marian Nixon, Jack Adair, Edward LeSaint, Donald Kerr, Edward Keane, Al K. Hall, Joseph Girard. *Prod:* Burroughs. 61m.

AUGUST WEEKEND (AKA, GB, *Weekend Madness*). (1936) Society drama; as an amoral society woman. *Dir:* Charles Lamont. *Sc:* Paul Perez (from a story by Faith Baldwin). *With* Valerie Hobson, G. P. Huntley Jr., Paul Harvey, Claire McDowell, Frank Melton, Dorothea Kent, Maynard Holmes, Edgar Norton, Gigi Parrish, Howard Hickman, Paul Irving, Paul West. *Prod:* Chesterfield. 62m.

HOLLYWOOD BOULEVARD (1936). Character melodrama of the Hollywood studios; as a star in a sequence being directed by Maurice Costello. *Dir:* Robert Florey. *Sc:* Marguerite Roberts. *With* John Halliday, Marsha Hunt, Robert Cummings, C. Henry Gordon, Esther Ralston, Esther Dale, Frieda Inescort, Albert Conti, Bert Roach, Creighton Hale, Francis X. Bushman, Maurice Costello, Mae Marsh, Charles Ray, Herbert Rawlinson, Bryant Washburn, William Desmond, Jack Mulhall, Frank Mayo. *Prod:* Paramount.

BULLDOG EDITION (1936). Newspaper melodrama; as Billie, sweetheart of a no-good racketeer. *Dir:* Charles Lamont. *Sc:* Richard English and Karen DeWolf (from a story, "Back in Circulation," by Denny Ahearn). *With* Ray Walker, Evalyn Knapp, Regis Toomey, Cy Kendall, Billy Newell, Oscar Apfel, Robert Warwick, George Lloyd, Frank Puglia, Edward LeSaint. *Prod:* Republic. 57m.

KILLER AT LARGE (1936). Murder mystery; as Kate, a shoplifter, one of the victims. *Dir:* Dave Selman. *Sc:* Harold Shumate (from

a story by Carl Clausen). *With* Mary Brian, Russell Hardie, George McKay, Thurston Hall, Henry Brandon, Harry Hayden, Boyd Irwin Sr., Lon Chaney Jr. *Prod:* Columbia. 53m.

CIRCUS GIRL (1937). Circus melodrama; as Carlotta, a tiger trainer. *Dir:* John H. Auer. *Sc:* Adele Buffington and Bradford Ropes (from a story, "Without a Net," by Frank R. Adams). *With* June Travis, Robert Livington, Charlie Murray, Emma Dunn, Donald Cook, Lucille Osborne, John Holland. *Prod:* Republic. 66m.

GOD'S COUNTRY AND THE MAN (AKA, GB, *The Avenging Stranger*) (1937). Western melodrama; as Roxy, who helps the hero find the man who murdered his father. *Dir:* Robert N. Bradbury. *Sc:* Robert Emmett. *With* Tom Keene, Charlotte Henry. *Prod:* Monogram. 5041 ft.

TWO MINUTES TO PLAY (1937). College football drama; as a woman who almost gets the hero kicked off his team. *Dir:* Bob Hill. *Sc:* William Buchanan. *With* Herman Brix (Bruce Bennett), Eddie Nugent, Jeanne Martel, Grady Sutton, Duncan Renaldo, David Sharpe, Sammy Cohen, Forrest Taylor, Richard Tucker. *Prod:* Victory. 74m.

FEDERAL BULLETS (1937). G-Men vs. gangsters; as Sue, a stool pigeon. *Dir:/Sc:* Karl Brown (from a story by Major George F. Elliot). *With* Milburn Stone, Zeffie Tilbury, Terry Walker, William Harrigan, Warner Richmond, Matty Fain, Eddie Phillips, Helen MacKellar. *Prod:* Monogram. 62m.

BLONDES AT WORK (1938). A Torchy Blane comedy murder mystery; as one of the blondes. *Dir:* Frank McDonald. *Sc:* Albert DeMond (from characters created by Frederick Nebel). *With* Glenda Farrell, Barton MacLane, Tom Kennedy, Rosella Towne, Donald Briggs, John Ridgely, Thomas E. Jackson, Frank Shannon, Carole Landis, Suzanne Kaaren, Theodore von Eltz, Charles Richman, Robert Middlemass, Kenneth Harlan. *Prod:* Warner Bros. 64m.

A SLIGHT CASE OF MURDER (1938). Underworld mystery comedy; as Loretta, a gangster's moll. *Dir:* Lloyd Bacon. *Sc:* Earl Baldwin and Joseph Schrank (from a play by Howard Lindsay and Damon Runyon). *With* Edward G. Robinson, Jane Bryan, Willard Parker, Ruth Donnelly, Allen Jenkins, John Litel, Eric Stanley, Harold Huber, Bobby Jordan, Ed Brophy, Paul Harvey, Margaret Hamilton, George E. Stone, George Lloyd, Myrtle Stedman, Joe Downing. *Prod:* Warner Bros./First National. 86m.

THE PORT OF MISSING GIRLS (1938). Melodrama from San Francisco to Shanghai; as "Chicago," a gangster's moll. *Dir:/Sc:* Karl Brown. *With* Judith Allen, Milburn Stone,

Harry Carey, Matty Fain, Jane Jones, George Cleveland. *Prod:* Monogram. 65m.

TORCHY BLANE IN PANAMA (1938). Bank robbery melodrama; as Kitty, friend to Torchy Blane, girl reporter. *Dir:* William Clemens. *Sc:* George Bricker (from a story by Anthony Coldeway, based upon characters created by Frederick Nebel). *With* Lola Lane, Paul Kelly, Tom Kennedy, Larry Williams, Anthony Averill, John Ridgely, Hugh O'Connell. *Prod:* Warner Bros. 59m.

TWO GUN JUSTICE (1938). Western melodrama; as a romantic saloon keeper. *Dir:* Alan James. *Sc:* Fred Myton. *With* Tim McCoy, Joan Barclay, John Merton, Al Bridges, Lane Chandler. *Prod:* Monogram. 57m.

UNDER THE BIG TOP (AKA, GB, *The Circus Comes to Town*) (1938). Romantic drama of a small-time circus; as Marie, a performer. *Dir:* Karl Brown. *Sc:* Marion Orth (from a story by Llewellyn Hughes). *With* Anne Nagel, Marjorie Main, Jack LaRue, Grant Richards, George Cleveland, Herbert Rawlinson, Rolfe Sedan, "Snowflake," Harry Harvey, Charlene Wyatt. *Prod:* Monogram. 64m.

NEWS IS MADE AT NIGHT (1939). Newspaper murder story; as Kitty Truman. *Dir:* Albert Werker. *Sc:* John Larkin. *With* Preston Foster, Lynn Bari, Russell Gleason, George Barbier, Eddie Collins, Minor Watson, Paul Harvey, Richard Lane, Charles Lane, Paul Fix, Paul Guilfoyle. *Prod:* 20th Century-Fox. 72m.

THE MYSTIC CIRCLE MURDER (AKA, *Religious Racketeers*) (1939). Drama of murder among a circle of phony spiritualists; as Ada Barnard, a victim of the phony spiritualist. *Dir:* Frank O'Connor. *Sc:* Charles Condon and Don Gallagher (from a story by Frank O'Connor). *With* Robert Fiske, Helene LeBerthon, Arthur Gardner, Robert Frazer, Mrs. Harry Houdini. *Prod:* Merit.

COWBOYS FROM TEXAS (1939). Western with "The Three Mesquiteers" about reclamation of wastelands; as Belle Starkey. *Dir:* George Sherman. *Sc:* Oliver Drake. *With* Robert Livingston, Raymond Hatton, Duncan Renaldo, Carole Landis, Charles Middleton, Yakima Canutt. *Prod:* Republic. 56m.

STRANGE CARGO (1940). Psychological study of an escape from a penal colony, with mystic overtones; as Suzanne, the pal of Crawford. *Dir:* Frank Borzage. *Sc:* Lawrence Hazard (from a novel, "Not Too Narrow, Not Too Deep," by Richard Sale). *With* Clark Gable, Joan Crawford, Ian Hunter, Peter Lorre, Paul Lukas, Albert Dekker, J. Edward Bromberg, Eduardo Ciannelli, Victor Varconi, John Arledge, Frederic Worlock, Paul Fix, Bernard Nedell, Francis McDonald, Charles Judels, Jack Mulhall, Dewey Robin-

son. *Prod:* M-G-M. 112m.

MAD YOUTH (1940). Mother & daughter in love with the same gigolo drama; as Mrs. Morgan. *Dir:* Willis Kent. *With* Mary Ainslee, Willy Costello, Betty Atkinson. *Prod:* Atlas. 76m.

LAUGHING AT DANGER (1940). Beauty shop melodrama; as Mrs. Van Horn. *Dir:* Howard Bretherton. *Sc:* James West and John Kraft (from a story by West). *With* Frankie Darro, Manton Moreland, Joy Hodges, George Houston, Kay Sutton, Veda Ann Borg, Rolfe Sedan. *Prod:* Monogram. 64m.

MR. AND MRS. SMITH (1941). Marital comedy; as Gertie, a good-time gal. *Dir:* Alfred Hitchcock. *Sc:* Norman Krasna. *With* Carole Lombard, Robert Montgomery, Gene Raymond, Jack Carson, Philip Merivale, Lucile Watson, William Tracy, Charles Halton, Esther Dale, Emma Dunn, Patricia Farr, William Edmunds, *Prod:* RKO. 90m.

THE INVISIBLE GHOST (AKA, *The Phantom Killer*) (1941). Murder melodrama; as Mrs. Kessler, the insane wife of Lugosi. *Dir:* Joseph H. Lewis. *Sc:* Helen and Al Martin. *With* Bela Lugosi, John McGuire, Polly Ann Young, Clarence Muse, Terry Walker, Ottola Nesmith, Jack Mulhall, Fred Kelsey. *Prod:* Monogram. 63m.

THE ROAR OF THE PRESS (1941) Newspaper and fifth column melodrama; as Thelma Tate. *Dir:* Philip E. Rosen. *Sc:* Albert Duffy (from a story by Alfred Block.) *With* Jean Parker, Wallace Ford, Jed Prouty, Suzanne Kaaren, Harland Tucker, Evalyn Knapp, Robert Frazer, Dorothy Lee, John Holland, Maxine Leslie, Paul Fix, Matty Fain, Charles King, Dennis Moore. *Prod:* Monogram. 71m. Working title: *Widows of the Press.*

DANGER! WOMEN AT WORK (1943). A comedy about the trucking business; as a Fortune Teller. *Dir:* Sam Newfield. *Sc:* Martin Mooney (from a story by Gertrude Walker and Edgar G. Ulmer). *With* Patsy Kelly, Mary Brian, Isabel Jewell, Wanda McKay, Cobina Wright Sr., Allan Byron, Warren Hymer, Michael Kirk, Vince Barnett. *Prod:* PRC. 59m.

HER ADVENTUROUS NIGHT (1946). Cops-and-robbers comedy melodrama; as a Schoolteacher. *Dir:* John Rawlins. *Sc:* Jerry Warner. *With* Dennis O'Keefe, Helen Walker, Tom Powers, Fuzzy Knight, Charles Judels, Scotty Beckett. *Prod:* Universal. 76m.

CLAUDIA AND DAVID (1946). Character drama; as a good-natured blonde. *Dir:* Walter Lang. *Sc:* Rose Franken and William B. Meloney (ad. by Vera Caspary from Miss Franken's original stories). *With* Dorothy McGuire, Robert Young, Mary Astor, John

Sutton, Gail Patrick, Rose Hobart, Harry Davenport, Florence Bates, Jerome Cowan, Else Janssen, Henry Mowbray, Pierre Watkins, Clara Blandick. A sequel to *Claudia*. *Prod:* 20th Century-Fox. 78m.

HARD BOILED MAHONEY (1947). Mystery drama; as a woman who claims that her sister is missing. *Dir:* William Beaudine. *Sc:* Cyril Endfield. *With* Leo Gorcey, Hunt Hall, Bobby Jordan, Gabriel Dell, Billy Benedict, David Gorcey, Bernard Gorcey, Patti Brill, Teale Loring, Noble Johnson, Byron Foulger. *Prod:* Monogram. 64m.

SECOND CHANCE (1947). Melodrama of jewel thieves and insurance agents; in a supporting role. *Dir:* James S. Tinling. *Sc:* Arnold Belgard (from a story by Louis Breslow and John Patrick). *With* Kent Taylor, Louise Currie, Dennis Hoey, Larry Blake, Ann Doran, John Eldredge, Paul Guilfoyle, William Newell, Guy Kingsford, Edwin Maxwell.

Prod: 20th Century-Fox. 63m.

HERE COMES TROUBLE (*Laff-Time, Part 1*) (1948). Slapstick murder comedy; as a newspaper publisher's wife who gets mixed up with an ex-GI in a murder. *Dir:* Fred Guiol. *Sc:* George Carleton Brown and Edward E. Seabrook. *With* Bill Tracy, Joe Sawyer, Emory Parnell, Paul Stanton, Beverly Lloyd, Joan Woodbury. *Prod:* United Artists-Roach.

(Miss Compson played cameo bits as herself in the feature directed by her husband, James Cruze, *Hollywood,* in which practically all the Paramount stars were to be seen, at least those working in the Hollywood studio in 1923; she is also to be glimpsed as herself in a two reel featurette, *A Trip to Paramountown,* an exploitation film of 1922 which featured all the stars working on the Hollywood lot of Paramount. She may very possibly also appear as Lady Mary in a 1917 Nestor two-reeler, *Where the Heather Blooms.*)

12
BEBE DANIELS

The actors and actresses who have been most popular among their fellows in Hollywood have not always been those who got to the top of the ladder. Bebe Daniels was one who did.

In the November, 1922 issue of "Photoplay," Adela Rogers St. Johns said that Miss Daniels was the most popular girl in Hollywood, but added: "Betty Compson might perhaps have more close personal friends and admirers." Which may have been irony, since many of those "close friends" later proved to be of the fair-weather variety.

Bebe Daniels was easy-going, fun-loving, open, honest, and friendly. She was also knowledgeable about the utilisation of her beauty and talent, hard-working, and ambitious. And she was versatile: she could portray a madcap, or the girl next door, or a DeMille exotic, with equal ease. Jack Holt once called her his favourite leading lady. "From her Spanish ancestor," said Holt, "she has inherited the fire and sparkle her masculine admirers like. Also that hint of naughtiness which has won her the title of 'the screen's good little bad girl.'"

She was born in Dallas, Texas, on January 14, 1901. Her father, Melville Daniels, was Scottish, and her mother, despite the maiden name of Phyllis Griffin, was of predominantly Spanish descent. The parents were show people, and at the age of ten weeks, Bebe — which in Spanish means "baby," but was pronounced "bee-bee," American style — was carried onstage every night by her mother in a 1901 comedy, "Jane." Aged four, Bebe was touring the country with her parents as one of the little princes in the Tower in Shakespeare's "King Richard III."

In Los Angeles at that time there were two outstanding resident stock companies — the Belasco, managed by Frederic Belasco, and the Burbank, managed by Oliver Morosco. Stars were often interchanged, and Fay Bainter, for example, who was a native of Los Angeles, made her first stage appearance for the Belasco Company, but by the time she left for Broadway in 1912 she was the top leading lady of Pacific Coast stock, playing star roles for every company.

In 1906, five-year-old Bebe Daniels was playing with a cast headed by Lewis Stone in Morosco's production of "The Squaw Man." She had already taken to the life like a duck to water, and Morosco himself said, "Watch little

261

Bebe Daniels!'' At seven, she had the child lead in ''The Common Enemy,''
and then re-created that role for the movie version at Selig-Polyscope, her
screen debut. It was a Civil War story dealing with that common enemy of
both the North and the South — marauding guerilla fighters — and of how a
child, played by young Bebe, escapes through the guerilla lines to bring aid to
her beleaguered family.

Between stage engagements, Bebe played many child roles for Selig,
NYMP, Pathe, Kalem, and 101 Bison, where she was usually cast as the
heroine's younger sister ''invariably kidnapped by Indians and rescued by the
hero,'' as she remembered. Her mother was for a time wardrobe mistress at
Keystone, and Bebe did play for Mack Sennett in a few comedies. She would
have liked to have become a bathing beauty, but both her mother and Sennett
said she was much too young. Her mother thought it all right to pick up extra
money for film work, but as far as making a fulltime profession of it, God
forbid!

But when her mother enrolled her in school at the Sacred Heart Convent in
Los Angeles, Bebe soon discovered she already knew much more than the
other children. ''I didn't like their games or playing with dolls and thought
them stupid because they didn't know about Shakespeare and the great names
of the theatre,'' she said many years later, and added: ''Whatever I missed as
a child I didn't mind missing.''

She left the convent school before she was fourteen and signed a contract
with Hal Roach to appear in one and two-reel comedies with Harold Lloyd
and Snub Pollard. This forsaking of the stage at first distressed her mother,
who said she ''never thought Bebe would sink that low.'' But Mrs. Daniels
was soon reconciled to Bebe's movie success and until Bebe married — in
1930 — she and *her* mother (Grandma Griffin) lived with Bebe in Bebe's big
Hollywood house.

For the next four years Bebe worked at the Rolin-Pathe Studio as Harold
Lloyd's leading lady, first in his *Lonesome Luke* series, and averaged a
comedy a week, for which she was paid $30 weekly. The comedies, for the
most part, were made in the old Bradbury mansion in Los Angeles. It was
wonderful training. ''When you know how to play comedy,'' Miss Daniels has
said, ''you know how to play anything.'' The second year she was with Lloyd,
he abandoned the ''Luke'' character for that of the young man with horn-
rimmed glasses, and his comedies became more popular than ever — and so
did Bebe.

In those days, Hollywood actors often worked from sun-up until after
midnight, and often in a number of pictures at the same time. There was no
Screen Actors' Guild, and Bebe did what the director told her to do, even if it
involved jumping off the Ocean Park Pier.

Hollywood's social life was then centered in the Alexandria Hotel, the
Sunset Inn, at the Ship's Café down in Venice, at Nat Goodwin's on the pier in
Santa Monica, and — on special occasions — at the Vernon Country Club.
Bebe and Harold Lloyd were frequently together and usually walked off with
the dancing prize. In later years, Bebe's son Richard uncovered a lot of those
silver cups in the basement of their Santa Monica home. He dusted them off
and shined them up, remarking, as Harold Lloyd's mother had once done,
that there were so many he didn't see why Bebe hadn't divided them between
Lloyd and herself.

''That honestly never occurred to me,'' Bebe replied.

Bebe Daniels in VOLCANO

She was dining with Lloyd in a Hollywood restaurant one night when she attracted the attention of Cecil B. DeMille, who recounted the incident in his autobiography: "...when I saw her one evening at dinner in a restaurant, it occurred to me that there might be more behind those big dark eyes and cupid's-bow mouth than a steady diet of comedy roles had brought out. Then and there I asked Bebe Daniels if she wanted to work for me. More honorable than some in those cut-throat days, she said that she could not because she was under contract to Mr. Roach. More than a year later, however, she came to see me, all dressed up in her mother's clothes to make her look mature enough for dramatic roles, and I gave her a small part in *Male and Female*."

Thus it was that, aged eighteen, Bebe Daniels entered feature-length films, playing a sultry favourite to Thomas Meighan's Babylonian king in the flashback sequence of DeMille's version of the James M. Barrie play "The Admirable Crichton."

Bebe was quickly put into a second picture by Paramount — a movie version of the modern morality play called *Everywoman,* in which she symbolised Vice. Said "Photoplay's" film critic: "There never has been a Vice, on stage or screen, so gorgeous or glittering as Bebe Daniels."

DeMille then co-starred her with Thomas Meighan and Gloria Swanson in *Why Change Your Wife?*, in which both Swanson and Daniels "were glorious camera subjects wrapped and unwrapped in a million dollars worth of lace and lingerie."

This led to Bebe playing opposite Wallace Reid, Paramount's top male star, in two romantic comedies, *The Dancin' Fool* and *Sick Abed.* After which, DeMille called her back to his set for the sexploiter he was adapting from Arthur Schnitzler's charming Viennese comedy, "Anatol." DeMille at first intended to title it *Five Kisses,* but one of the "Kisses," the one with Dorothy Cumming, was deleted so that it could be padded out as a later full-length release (*Don't Tell Everything*). Four kisses seemed shabby and too even a number, so DeMille retitled his picture *The Affairs of Anatol.* Bebe, as Satan Synne, the wickedest woman in New York, wore an octopus-motif negligee.

Paramount was then forming a subsidiary company, to be known as Realart, to make programmers that would build up the international appeal of Paramount's most promising players. Bebe went over to Realart, along with Alice Brady, Mary Miles Minter, May McAvoy, Wanda Hawley, Constance Binney, Julia Faye, and Justine Johnstone. She was the only one of these ladies to become a full-fledged star for Paramount itself, and remain there for a good many years as one of the stellar lights at her studio. In a popularity contest conducted on behalf of "Motion Picture Magazine" and "Motion Picture Classic" at that time (November, 1920), Bebe finished in sixth place among actresses, a remarkable feat since she had only appeared in supporting roles in five features. Yet her popularity was exceeded only by Mary Pickford, Norma Talmadge, Pearl White, Nazimova, and Constance Talmadge.

Miss Daniels's Realart pictures were undistinguished and it's hard to tell the plots of the ten comedies she made between 1920 and 1922 one from another.

The only one of any note was *The Speed Girl,* which was hastily written to capitalise on her own arrest and jail sentence for speeding. Bebe had a Stutz roadster and was caught driving 56½ miles an hour in Orange County by a motorcycle officer who had been hiding behind a Santa Ana farm windmill. Bebe pleaded guilty, but did remark that lots of people drove faster than she — look at Ralph de Palma.

She was sentenced to ten days in jail.

This may seen to moderns, hardened by the ways of today's ballyhoo, to have been a publicity stunt to get her name on front pages. But Hollywood was still rocking from the notoriety of the Arbuckle case, and Paramount was at first fearful that Bebe's escapade might endanger her screen career.* It was only afterwards, when it all turned into a lark, that Paramount's story department quickly threw a scenario together. Even at that, *The Speed Girl* didn't receive national distribution for almost a year.

Bebe's stay in jail was bizarre. Santa Ana merchants lent her an elegant Persian rug to cover the floor of her cell, and an ivory bedroom set. Her mother and grandmother moved into an inn across the street, from which all her meals were dispatched. Local musicians serenaded her daily, and nearly everybody in Hollywood came to visit her (she kept a guestbook and 792 names were entered in it). Jesse Lasky brought a huge basket of fruit; Mack Sennett came with flowers; as did Jack Pickford and his other sister Lottie; as well as Priscilla Dean and Wheeler Oakman. Sometimes there were as many stars in Bebe's cell as there now are at Chasen's on a gala preview night.

She spent eight full days in the jail, entering before midnight on her first day so that it counted as one day, and being released after midnight, of the ninth day, so that the few minutes of the tenth would count as the final day. She was on the front pages for more than the ten days and on the covers of fan magazines for several months.

From 1922 through 1928 she was one of Paramount's brightest stars and played almost every kind of role — from slapstick comedy, French bedroom farce, Zane Grey westerns, and opulent costume drama, to modern jazz romances. Her most dazzling role was as the Princess Henriette de Bourbon opposite Valentino's Beaucaire, and her most dramatic one was as the Martinique beauty accused of being an octoroon and nearly sold into slavery by a villainous Wally Beery in *Volcano*. Her athletic college comedies endeared her to the young and the sporting world. Charlie Paddock trained her for the track sequences in *The Campus Flirt,* and Gertrude Ederle, fresh from her Channel swimming triumph, coached Bebe for the swimming scenes in *Swim, Girl, Swim.* Both Paddock and Ederle played themselves in these pictures.

Her best comedies for Paramount, however, were two tongue-in-cheek ones. In *Señorita* she played a female Fairbanks-Zorro-Don Q, and in *She's a Sheik* she was a sheik's adopted daughter who abducts a Legionnaire-lover, much as Valentino kidnapped Agnes Ayres in *The Sheik.*

Like Constance Talmadge, who was always getting herself engaged, Bebe had a small army of suitors. In the early days before he wooed and won

---

*Jesse L. Lasky once remarked in despair that Paramount seemed to have been signaled out by the destroying breath of scandal. First, there had been the Roscoe Arbuckle trials after the death of Virginia Rappé, which had ruined Arbuckle's career as a screen comedian; then the unsolved murder of William Desmond Taylor, which ruined the career of Mary Miles Minter; and finally the tragic death of Wallace Reid as a drug addict. Arbuckle, Taylor, and Reid had all been under contract to Paramount. Lasky and Zukor were grooming Miss Minter at Realart to be a rival to Mary Pickford, whom Paramount had lost, but Miss Minter never ascended to the same league as "America's Sweetheart."

Mildred Davis, there had been Harold Lloyd. Then there was Jack Dempsey, until Estelle Taylor caught the champion's eye. Jack Pickford had been a loyal swain until Bebe brought a tethered goat to "Pickfair" as a gag birthday present; Jack thought that was funny, but others at "Pickfair" didn't. And for beaux and dancing, there had been Charlie Paddock, Harold "Red" Grange, Eddie Sutherland, Richard Dix, Bill Tilden, Rod La Rocque, Richard Arlen, and Michael Arlen.

She enjoyed being a movie star, and, like Ruth Roland and Corinne Griffith, invested her money in Wilshire Boulevard real estate and Santa Monica beachfront. She played bridge at Louella Parsons' home on Maple Drive in Beverly Hills, and was a regular guest at Marion Davies's beach home and Hearst's "San Simeon."

But the handwriting was on the wall. Al Jolson had made *The Jazz Singer,* and talking pictures were on their way in. Although Bebe had been a stage actress and wasn't afraid of the microphone, a front-office shake-up brought to the control of Paramount a group of men who were determined to get rid of high-priced "silent" stars and start afresh with stars from the Broadway stage. The acting plums were given to Ruth Chatterton, Jeanne Eagels, Kay Francis, Miriam Hopkins, and Claudette Colbert, while the old contract stars like Bebe, Clara Bow, Richard Dix, and Thomas Meighan begged in vain for a chance to speak their lines.

"Clara Bow and I went to the front-office together and pled in person with them to put us without salary in a talking picture together," Bebe once told me, "but our words fell on deaf ears."

Bebe never made a talking picture for Paramount, which wouldn't even test her voice, and her last two silents, released late in 1928, were sloughed off.

In disgust, Bebe finally bought up the last nine months of her contract and left the studio for which she had worked since 1919. Paramount did let Clara Bow, Dix and Meighan make several talkies, but when their contracts terminated, Paramount did not renew them. Pola Negri and Emil Jannings were sent back to Europe because their English was accented.

It was a wasteful policy, foolhardy and blind. The Kaufman and Hart satire of Hollywood's early frantic talkie days, "Once in a Lifetime," has more reality than parody. Everything that happened was terribly illogical, and sad, and only secondarily funny.

William Le Baron, an erstwhile Paramount producer who had gone to the newly-formed RKO studios and assumed production reins there, offered Bebe a singing role in an all-talking, all-singing, all-dancing movie version of Ziegfeld's extravaganza *Rio Rita.* When it opened late in 1929, all Hollywood was amazed. Nobody had dreamt that Bebe could sing so effectively. A few close friends had heard her strum a ukelele at beach parties and sing a popular song or two, usually harmonising with Bessie Love, who had also startled the public with her skill as the singing-dancing heroine of *The Broadway Melody.* And now Bebe Daniels, whom everybody thought a has-been at twenty-eight, was on the threshold of a brilliant new career as an operetta star!

It can truthfully be said, with the meteoric success of *Rio Rita,* just as it had been said of Theda Bara and the history of the Fox Film Company, that had there been no Bebe Daniels, the entry of RKO into the big league would have been very much delayed.

Bebe Daniels and Rudolph Valentino in MONSIEUR BEAUCAIRE (photo courtesy Valentino Memorial Guild)

Bebe's voice was a pleasant lyric soprano. She recorded her two big numbers from *Rio Rita* for Victor — "When You're in Love, You'll Waltz" and "You're Always in My Arms," and later cut discs of her songs from her other singing roles at RKO. Her voice had some of the lyric quality of the voices of Evelyn Laye, Anna Neagle, and Jessie Matthews. Tito Schipa, the Metropolitan Opera tenor, thought Bebe's "the loveliest feminine voice on the screen." Bebe also sang in her second picture for RKO, *Love Comes Along,* and in her fourth one, *Dixiana,* a big song-and-dance spectacular.

Her leading man for her third talkie, *Alias French Gertie,* was Ben Lyon, with whom she was constantly being seen at the more elegant Mayfair Club dinner dances. Lyon, a handsome Southerner who had played juveniles at Eastern Vitagraph, had distinguished himself on the Broadway stage as a top juvenile leading man before becoming an important film actor, and his romances on and off screen with such big stars as Marilyn Miller, Gloria

Swanson, Pola Negri, Barbara La Marr, and Jean Harlow were the talk of the town. Wiseacres predicted that if Bebe actually married him, of all people, it simply couldn't last. They were married on June 14, 1930, and remained man and wife until the day of her death more than forty years later.

In 1924 Bebe had answered an interviewer's question as to why she'd never married by saying: "I have contemplated marriage, and been on the verge of it. But I would not give up my work for marriage. It seems very difficult to reconcile a career and a husband. It's so difficult for the man. To me, marriage is a sacrament, and, when I marry, I hope it will be 'until death do us part'...I do not believe in divorce, for myself, at least, and so I am going to do my part to be reasonably sure, before I take the sacred vows, that my marriage has the best possible chance of being a successful one."

Bebe made five pictures for RKO, and then went to United Artists to co-star with Douglas Fairbanks in *Reaching for the Moon*. Everybody was sure it would be a smash, for Fairbanks was still an athletic romantic hero and Bebe was a perfect feminine counterpart. But it proved disappointing, probably because it had been conceived originally as a flimsy plot upon which to hang an Irving Berlin score, and then, because screen musicals were temporarily on the wane, almost all the numbers were cut.

Bebe then negotiated a six-picture deal at Warners, where her best role was as Edward G. Robinson's younger second wife, the legendary Baby Doe, in *Silver Dollar,* although she was actually called "Lily Owens" in the script. Her flashiest and most popular Warner picture, however, was *42nd Street,* which brought film musicals back into favour and was the definitive movie musical of the Thirties. Warners had filmed the story several years before as *On with the Show*, with Betty Compson in the role now played by Bebe, and recently Glenda Jackson did a vignette of the characterisation in *The Boy Friend* that was a real show-stopper.

With one exception, Bebe's subsequent pictures are negligible. The exception is the film she made in 1933 at Universal for William Wyler, playing opposite John Barrymore in a movie version of the Elmer Rice stage success, *Counsellor at Law*. Her performance for Wyler had a simple sincerity and subtlety she never again had a chance to equal on the screen.

She returned to the theatre in the early Thirties and starred with success in a Pacific Coast production of Lonsdale's "The Last of Mrs. Cheyney." In 1935 she toured the United States with her husband and Skeets Gallagher in an original comedy, "Hollywood Holiday."

She had made a movie in London in 1933, *The Song You Gave Me,* and in 1936 she and Ben Lyon went to London for what they thought would be a three-week booking at the Palladium.

They opened there on June 29, 1936, with a variety act made up of songs and comedy patter — the kind of man-and-wife act dear to the English music hall. It was an instant hit, and until 1939 they spent most of their time touring the variety theatres of England and the British Commonwealth. Ben became head of talent for the English office of 20th Century-Fox, and Bebe made several pictures, in one of which, *Not Wanted on Voyage,* released in 1938, Ben was her leading man. In December 1939, they opened in London at the Holborn Empire in a revue, "Haw-Haw," and played it for over a year, even though an early Nazi bomb wrecked the theatre — fortunately at two in the morning when the auditorium was empty.

Bebe Daniels and Ben Lyon

Early in the Thirties Bebe had borne a daughter, Barbara, and in 1941 she and Ben adopted a son, Richard, an early war orphan. Hastily, they brought the two children to Hollywood to remain with Bebe's mother, and returned to London for the duration, opening almost at once at the Palladium in a new revue, "Gangway."

The bombing of London was a constant concern, but their work as entertainers kept them busy and helped Londoners to forget. They originated a radio show called "Hi Gang," which lasted twelve years, plus four more on television. Ben got into uniform, became a member of General Ira Eaker's staff, and served in England, North Africa and Italy, becoming by war's end, a lieutenant-colonel. Meanwhile, Bebe interviewed the American wounded in Normandy and Italy for service programmes, "Stars and Stripes in Britain" and "Purple Heart Corner." She was the first woman to land with the troops on D-Day, when the Allies had secured but ten miles of the Normandy coast and had penetrated inland only two and a half miles. For her war work, the United States gave Bebe the Medal of Freedom, which is awarded only for service under fire.

In November,1943, Bebe opened at the London Piccadilly in the musical which Ethel Merman had created on Broadway, "Panama Hattie." It was just what war-weary, escape-hungry London audiences craved, and Bebe, already dear to them because of her personal courage, became London's darling. She toured "Hattie" in the provinces after a year's run in the West End, and re-opened it in London in 1945.

When the war was over, Bebe and Ben returned to Hollywood, where Ben became head of talent in the Hollywood office of 20th Century-Fox, and discovered and gave the name of Marilyn Monroe to Norma Jean Baker. Bebe contracted with Hal Roach to produce feature-length comedies at the same studio where she had begun. There haven't been many female producers, and Bebe joined the ranks then dominated by Harriet Parsons and Joan Harrison and produced a modestly-budgeted feature-length comedy, released by Roach through Eagle-Lion, called *The Fabulous Joe*.

Barbara Lyon, their daughter, had grown up during the war years, and Richard had established himself as a child actor, playing with Irene Dunne in *Anna and the King of Siam*, and in *The Unseen* and *The Green Years*. For a time the Lyons family seemed content in their big house on the Santa Monica beachfront, but they soon realised that they were, at heart, Londoners, and finally announced they would re-establish their home base in England.

I was invited to the farewell party at their beach home, as was everybody they had known and worked with in Hollywood. "All during the war," Bebe told us, "we kept saying, Ben and I, that when it was over, we'd come back to Hollywood. But now we've been here, and we just have to be honest, this is no longer home. Home's back in London, because we went through the bombings with them."

Once back in London, Bebe and Ben wrote and rehearsed a new radio show, "Life with the Lyons." This later became a TV show, and the basis of two movies — *Life with the Lyons* and *The Lyons in Paris*.

Their daughter, a singer for British-Columbia records, married and divorced, and their son became London's leading disc jockey. Then, with Bebe, he opened and ran an interior decorating and antique studio on Kensington High Street, and married a young English actress, by whom he had one child. Divorced, he married again, this time happily; he now works as a special staff photographer for the National Film Theatre.

Bebe had seldom committted herself to public statements about producers, directors, fellow players, or friends. She is grateful to Jesse L. Lasky and Cecil B. DeMille because they "opened another door for me, the one to stardom," and to William Le Baron because he gave her a new start with *Rio Rita*.

In May,1963, Miss Daniels suffered a stroke, and was a long time convalescing in a London hospital. Ben Lyon devoted himself to her care, and when, in several years time, she became well enough to attend a few film and theatre performances, it was he who wheeled her in her chair to various theatres. He chartered a yacht and took her for summer holidays to European watering-places like Majorca.

In November, 1970 she suffered antther stroke, developed pneumonia, and remained in Wimbledon Hospital until early in March, 1971, when she was allowed to return home. There, on March 16, at 5 a.m., she died of a cerebral haemorrhage.

Her death came just a week after that of Harold Lloyd, her first partner in comedy, who died of cancer at his Beverly Hills mansion.

"I am completely shattered and lost," said Ben Lyon at the time of Bebe's death. "She was a wonderful woman who gave me forty years of the greatest happiness any man ever had. She was more than my wife; she was my life."

I myself was visiting London in the fall of 1971, and twice spent evenings with Ben Lyon there. We had drinks at the Dolphin Square apartment he had shared with Bebe, and he took me to dinner at a Piccadilly restaurant; subsequently, he invited me to a Saturday night family dinner at his apartment, when he entertained his children and their children (both Barbara and Richard have married a second time and are very happy with new families of their own). On this occasion, Ben ran a sixteen-millimetre print of the "This Is Your Life" television show honouring Bebe when she was visting once in the United States. I had never seen it, and found it intensely moving. Ben seemed resigned to his loss, but no more than that, for even then, months after Bebe's death, he was, in a way, lost; his mourning had not abated.

It was with pleasure, I think, that the friends of the Lyon family, at home and abroad, learned of the marriage of Ben Lyon and screen actress Marian Nixon in mid-1972. They had known one another in Hollywood years ago, and had even played together once in a film. A few years previously, Miss Nixon had been widowed by the death of her husband, director William A. Seiter, and subsequently, while visiting London, she met again with Ben. He, a widower, and she, a widow, married, and came back to the United States, where they now make their home.

BEBE DANIELS FILMOGRAPHY

(The films Bebe Daniels made as a child actress are well nigh impossible to list by title, because few players had billing at all in those pioneer days. Other than *The Common Enemy* (Selig, 1910), which marked her film *début,* I have only found listings for her by name in *The Savage,* directed by James Young Deer for Norbig-Pathé, and *Anne of the Golden Heart* (Vitagraph, 1914). She worked as a child actress, however, for about six months at Selig and for a good year at 101-Bison. She played a few bits at Keystone, but was much too young to be a Sennett Bathing Beauty. She also played several other roles, unbilled, at Vitagraph.

In 1916 she joined Rolin, and became Harold Lloyd's leading lady when he was making the "Lonesome Luke" comedies, and continued as his leading lady when he changed his image to the be-spectacled one that made him famous. During those four years (1916-19) when she was Lloyd's leading lady, she played in 172 comedies — everything from simple slapstick like *Lonesome Luke's Honeymoon* to her last with Lloyd, *Captain Kidd's Kids* — and she was already much admired as a very pretty and accomplished comedienne when DeMille chose her to groom as one of his more exotic ladies.)

MALE AND FEMALE (AKA, GB, *The Admirable Crichton*) (1919) Drawing-room vs. desert island romantic comedy; as the decorative Babylonian favourite appearing only in the flashback. *Dir:* Cecil B. DeMille. *Sc:* Jeanie Macpherson (from the play, "The Admirable Crichton," by Sir James M. Barrie). *With* Thomas Meighan, Gloria Swanson, Lila Lee, Theodore Roberts, Raymond Hatton, Mildred Reardon, Robert Cain, Julia Faye, Rhy Darby, Maym Kelso, Lucien Littlefield, Edna Mae Cooper, Jane Woolf. *Prod*: Paramount/Artcraft. 7 reels.

EVERYWOMAN (1919). Modern morality drama, as Vice. *Dir:* George Melford. *Sc:* Will M. Ritchey (from the play by Walter Browne). *With* Violet Heming, Irving Cummings, Wanda Hawley, Monte Blue, Margaret Loomis, Theodore Roberts, Clara Horton, James Neill, Edythe Chapman, Raymond Hatton, Tully Marshall. *Prod:* Paramount-Artcraft. 7072 ft.

WHY CHANGE YOUR WIFE? (1920). Domestic comedy drama; as Sally Clark, the other woman. *Dir:* Cecil B. DeMille. *Sc:* Olga Printzlau and Sada Cowan (from a story by William C. de Mille). *With* Thomas Meighan, Gloria Swanson, Theodore Kosloff, Sylvia Ashton, Clarence Geldart, Maym Kelso, Lucien Litlefield, Edna Mae Cooper, Jane Woolf. *Prod:* Paramount-Artcraft. 7 reels.

THE DANCIN' FOOL (1920). Romantic comedy; as June Budd. *Dir:* Sam Wood. *Sc:* Clara Genevieve Kennedy (from a story by Henry Payson Dowst). *With* Wallace Reid, Raymond Hatton, Lillian Leighton, Tully Marshall, Ernest Joy. *Prod:* Paramount-Artcraft. 5 reels. (Compare listing in Wallace Reid filmography.)

SICK ABED (1920). Romantic comedy; as Constance Weems, nurse. *Dir:* Sam Wood. *Sc:* Clara Genevieve Kennedy (from a play by Ethel Watts Mumford). *With* Wallace Reid, Winifred Greenwood, Tully Marshall, Clarence Geldart, Lucien Littlefield. *Prod:* Paramount-Artcraft. 5 reels. (Compare listing in Wallace Reid filmography.)

THE FOURTEENTH MAN (AKA, GB, *The Man from Blankley's*) (1920). Farce comedy; as Marjory Seaton. *Dir:* Joseph Henabery. *Sc:* Walter Woods (from a play by F. Anstey). *With* Robert Warwick, Walter Hiers, Robert Milash, Norman Selby ("Kid McCoy"), James Farley, Sylvia Ashton, Lucien Littlefield. *Prod:* Paramount-Artcraft. 5 reels. Re-made, Warner Bros., 1930, with Loretta Young as the heroine.

OH, LADY, LADY (1920). Romantic comedy; as Mary Barber, who makes a hit as an actress named Rilla Rooke. *Dir:* Major Maurice Campbell. *Sc:* Edith Kennedy (from a play by Guy Bolton and P. G. Wodehouse). *With* Harrison Ford, Walter Hiers, Lillian Langdon, Charlotte Woods. *Prod:* Realart (Paramount). 5 reels.

YOU NEVER CAN TELL (AKA, GB, *Class*) (1920). Romantic comedy, as Rowena Patricia Jones, a hat-check girl who wants to marry a millionaire. *Dir:* Chester Franklin. *Sc:* Tom Geraghty and H. W. Bergman (from two "SatEvePost" stories by Grace Lovell Bryan). *With* Jack Mulhall, Edward Martindel, Helen Dunbar, Harold Goodwin. *Prod:* Realart (Paramount). 5 reels.

THE AFFAIRS OF ANATOL (AKA, GB, *A Prodigal Knight*). (1921). Romantic comedy drama; as Satan Synne, "the wickedest woman in New York." *Dir:* Cecil B. DeMille. *Sc:* Jeanie Macpherson, Beulah Marie Dix, Lorna Moon and Elmer Harris (suggested by the Viennese comedy, "Anatol," by Arthur Schnitzler, and the paraphrase thereof by Granville Barker). *With* Wallace Reid, Gloria Swanson, Elliott Dexter, Monte Blue, Wanda Hawley, Theodore Roberts, Agnes Ayres, Theodore Kosloff, Polly Moran, Raymond Hatton, Julia Faye, Charles Ogle, Winter Hall, Guy Oliver, Ruth Miller, Lucien Littlefield, Zelma Maja, Shannon Day, Elinor Glyn, William Boyd, Maude Wayne, Fred Huntley, Lady Gilbert Parker. *Prod:* Famous Players-Lasky (released as a DeMille Paramount Special). 9 reels. Working title: *Five Kisses*. (Compare listing in Wallace Reid filmography.)

TWO WEEKS WITH PAY (1921). Romantic comedy; in a dual role: as Pansy O'Donnell, a mannequin and as a movie star known as "The Diving Venus" whom the mannequin has to impersonate. *Dir:* Major Maurice Campbell. *Sc:* Alice Eyton (from a "SatEvePost" story by Nina Wilcox Putnam). *With* Jack Mulhall, George Periolat, Polly Moran, Walter Hiers. *Prod:* Realart (Paramount). 5 reels.

SHE COULDN'T HELP IT (1921). Romantic crook comedy; as "Young Nance," a thief who climbs into a bishop's carriage to escape the police, and is reformed. *Dir:* Major Maurice Campbell. *Sc:* Douglas Bronston (from the play, "In the Bishop's Carriage," by Channing Pollock, dramatised from the novel by Miriam Nicholson). *With* Emory Johnson, Wade Boteler, Vera Lewis, Herbert Standing. (Previously filmed by Mary Pickford as *In the Bishop's Carriage*). *Prod:* Realart (Paramount). 5 reels.

DUCKS AND DRAKES (1921). Romantic comedy; as Teddy Simpson, madcap heiress. *Dir:* Major Maurice Campbell. *Sc:* Elmer Harris. *With* Jack Holt, Maym Kelso, Edward Martindel, Wade Boteler. *Prod:* Realart (Paramount). 5 reels.

THE MARCH HARE (1921). Romantic comedy; as Lisbeth Ann Palmer. *Dir:* Major Maurice Campbell. *Sc:* Elmer Harris. *With* Harry Myers, Maym Kelso, Melbourne McDowell, Helen Jerome Eddy. *Prod:* Realart (Paramount). 5 reels.

ONE WILD WEEK (1921). Romantic comedy; as Pauline Hathaway. *Dir:* Major Maurice Campbell. *Sc:* Percy Heath (from a Frances Harmer story). *With* Frank Kingsley, Maym Kelso, Frances Raymond, Edythe Chapman, Herbert Standing. *Prod:* Realart (Paramount). 5 reels.

THE SPEED GIRL (1921). Romantic comedy; as Betty Lee, movie star. *Dir:* Major Maurice Campbell. *Sc:* Douglas Doty (from a story by Elmer Harris based upon an incident in Miss Daniels's life). *With* Theodore von Eltz, Walter Hiers, Frank Elliott, Truly Shattuck. *Prod:* Realart (Paramount). 5 reels.

NANCY FROM NOWHERE (1922). Romantic comedy; as Nancy, a slavey who weds a millionaire. *Dir:* Chester Franklin. *Sc:* Douglas Doty (from a story, "Spring Fever," by Grace Drew Brown and Katherine Pinkerton). *With* Edward Sutherland, Vera Lewis, James Gordon, Myrtle Stedman. *Prod:* Realart (Paramount). 5 reels.

A GAME CHICKEN (1922). Romantic comedy; as Inez Hastings, a Cuban señorita. *Dir:* Chester Franklin. *Sc:* Fred Myton (from a story by Nina Wilcox Putnam). *With* Pat O'Malley, Martha Mattox, James Gordon, Hugh Thompson. *Prod:* Realart (Paramount). 5 reels.

NORTH OF THE RIO GRANDE (1922). Western romance; as Val Hannon. *Dir:* Rollin S. Sturgeon. *Sc:* Will M. Ritchie (from a story, "Val of Paradise," by Vingie E. Roe). *With* Jack Holt, Shannon Day, Charles Ogle, Alec B. Francis. Photographed in the Apache border country. Working title: *The Stampede Madonna. Prod:* Paramount. 5 reels.

NICE PEOPLE (1922). Romantic comedy drama of the jazz age; as a flapper, Theodora (Teddy) Gloucester. *Dir:* William C. de Mille. *Sc:* Clara Beranger (from the play by Rachel Crothers). *With* Wallace Reid, Conrad Nagel, Julia Faye, Claire McDowell, Edward Martindel, Eve Southern, Bertram Johns, William Boyd, Ethel Wales. *Prod:* Paramount. 7 reels. (Compare listing in Wallace Reid filmography.)

PINK GODS (1922). Romantic drama; as Lorraine Temple. *Dir:* Penrhyn Stanlaws. *Sc:* Ewart Adamson (adapted by J. E. Nash and Sonya Levien from a story, "Pink Gods and Blue Demons," by Cynthia Stockley). *With* James Kirkwood, Anna Q. Nilsson, Raymond Hatton, Adolphe Menjou. *Prod:* Paramount. 5 reels.

SINGED WINGS (1922). Romantic drama of the Barbary Coast; as Bonita della Guerda, dancer. *Dir:* Penrhyn Stanlaws. *Sc:* Ewart Adamson and Edfrid A. Bingham (from a novel by Katherine Newlin Burt). *With* Conrad Nagel, Adolphe Menjou, Ernest Torrence, Mabel Trunelle. *Prod:* Paramount. 8 reels.

THE WORLD'S APPLAUSE (1923). Backstage murder drama; as Corinne d'Alys, whose reputation is shattered when she becomes involved in a murder. *Dir:* William C. de Mille. *Sc:* Clara Beranger. *With* Lewis Stone, Kathlyn Williams, Adolphe Menjou, Brandon Hurst. *Prod:* Paramount. 8 reels.

THE GLIMPSES OF THE MOON (1923). Romantic society drama; as Susan Branch. *Dir:* Allan Dwan. *Sc:* E. Lloyd Sheldon and Edfrid A. Bingham (from the novel by Edith Wharton). *With* David Powell, Nita Naldi, Maurice Costello, Rubye de Remer, Charles Gerard, William Quirk, Pearl Sindelar, Dolores Costello. *Prod:* Paramount. 7 reels. Exteriors filmed in Florida. (Compare listing in Dolores Costello filmography.)

THE EXCITERS (1923). Romantic melodrama; as Ronnie Rand. *Dir:* Major Maurice Campbell. *Sc:* John Colton and Sonya Levien (from a play by Martin Brown). *With* Antonio Moreno, Burr McIntosh, Diana Allen, Cyril Ring, Jane Thomas, Ida Darling. *Prod:* Paramount. 6 reels.

HIS CHILDREN'S CHILDREN (1923). Drama of the jazz age; as Diane Kayne. *Dir:* Sam Wood. *Sc:* Monte M. Katterjohn (from a novel by Arthur Chesney Train). *With* James Rennie, Dorothy Mackaill, Hale Hamilton, George Fawcett, Mary Eaton, Mahlon Hamilton, Warner Oland, John Davidson, Lawrence D'Orsay. *Prod:* Paramount. 8 reels.

SINNERS IN HEAVEN (1924). Desert island romantic drama; as Barbara Stockley. *Dir:* Alan Crosland. *Sc:* James Ashmore Creelman (from the novel by Clive Arden). *With* Richard Dix, Montagu Love, Holmes Herbert, Effie Shannon, Florence Billings, Betty Hilburn. *Prod:* Paramount. 7 reels. (Compare listing in Richard Dix filmography.)

UNGUARDED WOMEN (1924). Romantic drama; as Breta Banning, widow of a war hero, who is living dangerously and losing face. *Dir:* Alan Crosland. *Sc:* James Ashmore Creelman (from a story, "Face," by Lucy Stone Terrill). *With* Richard Dix, Mary Astor, Walter McGrail, Frank Losee, Helen Lindroth, Harry Mestayer, Donald Hall, Joe King. *Prod:* Paramount. 6 reels. (compare listing in Richard Dix filmography.)

DARING YOUTH (1924). Marital comedy drama; as Alita Allen. *Dir:* William Beaudine. *Sc:* Alexander Neal (from a story by Dorothy

*Bebe Daniels with Rudolph Valentino in MONSIEUR BEAUCAIRE (photo
courtesy Valentino Memorial Guild)*

Farnum, suggested by Shakespeare's "Taming of the Shrew"). *With* Norman Kerry, Lee
Moran, Arthur Hoyt, Lillian Langdon. (Miss
Daniels's only loan-out on her Paramount contract.) *Prod:* Principal. 6 reels.

HERITAGE OF THE DESERT (1924). Western romance; as Mescal, a Mexican. *Dir:* Irvin
V. Willat. *Sc:* Albert Shelby LeVino (from a
novel by Zane Grey). *With* Lloyd Hughes, Ernest Torrence, Noah Beery. *Prod:* Paramount.
6 reels. (re-made as talkies, 1933 and 1939).

MONSIEUR BEAUCAIRE (1924). Romantic
costume drama; as the Princess Henriette. *Dir:*
Sidney Olcott. *Sc:* Forrest Halsey (from the
play by Booth Tarkington and Evelyn Green-
leaf Sutherland). *With* Rudolph Valentino,
Doris Kenyon, Lois Wilson, Lowell Sherman,
Paulette Du Val, Flora Finch, John Davidson,
Oswald Yorke, Louis Waller, Ian MacLaren,
H. Cooper Cliffe, Downing Clarke, Yvonne
Hughes, Florence O'Denishawn. (Re-filmed in
1946 as a Bob Hope comedy.) *Prod:*
Paramount. 10 reels.

DANGEROUS MONEY (1924). Romantic
melodrama; as Adele Clark, who inherits great
riches — and big problems. *Dir:* Frank Tuttle.
Sc: Julie Herne (ad. by John Russell from a
novel. "Clark's Field," by Robert Herrick).
With Tom Moore, William Powell, Dolores
Cassinelli. *Prod:* Paramount. 6 reels.

ARGENTINE LOVE (1924). Romantic
drama; as Consuelo Garcia. *Dir:* Allan Dwan.
Sc: Gerald Duffy (ad. by John Russell from a
novel by Vincente Blasco Ibáñez). *With*
Ricardo Cortez, James Rennie. *Prod:*
Paramount. 6 reels.

MISS BLUEBEARD (1925). Romantic farce;
as Colette Girard, French actress who sud-
denly finds herself a bigamist. *Dir:* Frank Tut-
tle. *Sc:* Townsend Martin (from a play, "Little
Miss Bluebeard," by Avery Hopwood). *With*
Robert Frazer, Kenneth MacKenna,
Raymond Griffith, Diana Kane. *Prod:*
Paramount. 6 reels.

THE CROWDED HOUR (1925) Backstage
and First World War drama; as Peggy Laurence, actress. *Dir:* E. Mason Hopper. *Sc:* John
Russell (from the play by Channing Pollock
and Edgar Selwyn in which Jane Cowl had
starred on Broadway). *With* Kenneth Harlan,
T. Roy Barnes, Frank Morgan, Warner Richmond, Helen Lee Worthing. *Prod:* Paramount.
7 reels.

THE MANICURE GIRL (1925). Romantic
comedy; as Maria Maretti, gold-digging manicurist who almost loses her real love. *Dir:*
Frank Tuttle. *Sc:* Townsend Martin (from a
story by Frederic and Fanny Hatton). *With*
Edmund Burns, Dorothy Cumming, Hale
Hamilton, Charlotte Walker, Maria Shotwell.

Prod: Paramount. 6 reels.

WILD, WILD SUSAN (1925). Romantic comedy; as Susan Van Dusen, heiress, who falls in love with a cabdriver. *Dir:* Edward Sutherland. *Sc:* Tom J. Geraghty (from a story, "The Wild Wild Child," by Stewart M. Emery). *With* Rod La Rocque, Henry Stephenson, Ivan Simpson. *Prod:* Paramount. 6 reels.

LOVERS IN QUARANTINE (1925). Romantic comedy; as Diana, the role created onstage by Helen Hayes. *Dir:* Frank Tuttle. *Sc:* Townsend Martin and Luther Reed (from a comedy, "Quarantine," by F. Tennyson Jesse). *With* Harrison Ford, Alfred Lunt, Edna May Oliver, Diana Kane, Ivan Simpson, Marie Shotwell. *Prod:* Paramount. 7 reels.

THE SPLENDID CRIME (1925). Romantic crook drama; as Jenny, a society crook who reforms when she falls in love. *Dir:* William C. de Mille. *Sc:* Violet Clark (from a story by William C. de Mille). *With* Neil Hamilton, Anne Cornwall, Anthony Jowitt, Lloyd Corrigan, Josephine Crowell. (Re-make of a 1916 film, *The Ragamuffin,* with Blanche Sweet.) *Prod:* Paramount. 6 reels.

MISS BREWSTER'S MILLIONS (1926). Comedy drama; as Polly Brewster, who bets she can spend a million dollars in one year and have nothing to show for it. *Dir:* Clarence Badger. *Sc:* Lloyd Corrigan and Harold Shumate (ad. by Monte Brice from the novel, "Brewster's Millions," by George Barr McCutcheon, as dramatised by Winchell Smith and Byron Ongley). *With* Warner Baxter, Ford Sterling, André Beranger. (Originally written for a male star and first played on the screen by Edward Abeles for Famous Players-Lasky, *Brewster's Millions* was subsequently re-made many times, but only this once turned successfully into a vehicle for a female star.) *Prod:* Paramount. 7 reels.

VOLCANO (1926) Romantic costume melodrama; as Zabette de Chavvalons. *Dir:* William K. Howard. *Sc:* Bernard McConville (from the play, "Martinique," by Laurence Eyre). *With* Richardo Cortez, Wallace Beery, Arthur Edmund Carewe, Dale Fuller, Eulalie Jensen, Brandon Hurst. *Prod:* Paramount. 6 reels.

THE PALM BEACH GIRL (1926). Romantic comedy; as Emily (Julia) Bennett. *Dir:* Erle Kenton. *Sc:* Forrest Halsey (ad. by Byron Morgan from a farce, "Please Help Emily," by Harold Marsh Harwood). *With* Lawrence Grey, Marguerite Clayton, Josephine Drake, John Patrick. Exteriors filmed at Palm Beach, Florida. *Prod:* Paramount. 7 reels.

THE CAMPUS FLIRT (1926). Romantic college comedy; as Patricia Mansfield. *Dir:* Clarence Badger. *Sc:* Louise Long and Lloyd Corrigan. *With* James Hall, El Brendel, Gilbert Roland, Charlie Paddock. *Prod:* Paramount. 7 reels.

STRANDED IN PARIS (1926). Romantic comedy; as Julie McFadden, shopgirl, who wins a trip to Paris. *Dir:* Arthur Rosson. *Sc:* Ethel Doherty and Louise Long (from a comedy by Hans Backwitz and Fritz Jakobstetter). *With* James Hall, Ford Sterling, Mabel Julienne Scott, Helen Dunbar. *Prod:* Paramount. 7 reels.

A KISS IN A TAXI (1927). Romantic slapstick comedy; as Ginette, a French cafe waitress. *Dir:* Clarence Badger. *Sc:* Doris Anderson (from a play, "Sunny Days," by Maurice Hennequin, Pierre Veber and Clifford Grey). *With* Douglas Gilmore, Chester Conklin, Henry Kolker, Richard Tucker, Eulalie Jensen. *Prod:* Paramount. 7 reels.

SENORITA (1927). Romantic comedy; as Señorita Francesca Hernandez, who,poses as a daring caballero (after the fashion of Fairbanks as Zorro). *Dir:* Clarence Badger. *Sc:* John McDermott and Lloyd Corrigan (from a story by John McDermott). *With* James Hall, William Powell, Josef Swickard. *Prod:* Paramount. 7 reels.

SWIM, GIRL, SWIM (1927). Romantic college comedy; as Alice Smith, ugly duckling who becomes champion swimmer and campus favourite. *Dir:* Clarence Badger. *Sc:* Lloyd Corrigan. *With* James Hall, Gertrude Ederle, Josephine Dunn. *Prod:* Paramount. 7 reels.

SHE'S A SHEIK (1928). Romantic comedy; as Zaida, daughter of an Arab chieftain, who kidnaps a handsome Legionnaire captain (after the fashion of Valentino as The Sheik). *Dir:* Clarence Badger. *Sc:* Lloyd Corrigan and Grover Jones (from a story by John McDermott). *With* Richard Arlen, William Powell, Josephine Dunn. *Prod:* Paramount. 6 reels.

THE FIFTY-FIFTY GIRL (1928). Romantic comedy; as Kathleen O'Hara, who inherits half a gold mine. *Dir:* Clarence Badger. *Sc:* Ethel Doherty (ad. by Lloyd Corrigan from a story by John McDermott). *With* James Hall, Harry T. Morey, William Austin. *Prod:* Paramount. 7 reels.

HOT NEWS (1928). Romantic comedy of rival newsreel cameramen; as Pat Clancy, ace cinematographer. *Dir:* Clarence Badger. *Sc:* Florence Ryerson (ad. by Lloyd Corrigan and Grover Jones from a story by Harlan Thompson and Monte Brice). *With* Neil Hamilton, Paul Lukas, Alfred Allen. *Prod:* Paramount. 7 reels.

FEEL MY PULSE (1928). Romantic comedy melodrama; as Barbara Manning. *Dir:* Gregory La Cava. *Sc:* Keene Thompson and Nick Burrows (from a story by Howard Emmett Rogers). *With* Richard Arlen, William Powell, Melbourne MacDowell, George Irving,

Charles Sellon. *Prod:* Paramount. 6 reels.

TAKE ME HOME (1928). Backstage romantic comedy; as Peggy Lane, chorus girl. *Dir:* Marshall Neilan. *Sc:* Ethel Doherty (from a story by Grover Jones, Tom Crizer, Harlan Thompson). *With* Neil Hamilton, Lilyan Tashman, Doris Hill, Joe E. Brown. *Prod:* Paramount. 6 reels.

WHAT A NIGHT! (1928). Romantic newspaper comedy; as Dorothy Winston, bungling cub reporter who stumbles onto the year's prize story. *Dir:* Edward Sutherland. *Sc:* Louise Long (from a story by Grover Jones and Lloyd Corrigan). *With* Neil Hamilton, William Austin, Wheeler Oakman. (Miss Daniels's last silent film, and the end of her long association with Paramount as one of its top stars.) Working title: *Number Please? Prod:* Paramount. 6 reels.

RIO RITA (1929). Musical romance; as Rita Ferguson. *Dir:* Luther Reed; stage direction by Russell Mack, meaning dialogue director. *Sc:* Luther Reed; with dialogue: Russell Mack. In her first talking feature, Bebe Daniels not only proved that she could handle dialogue like the professional she was, but could sing a musical role as well as any Ziegfeld soprano. *With* John Boles, Don Alvarado, Dorothy Lee, Bert Wheeler, Robert Woolsey. A Technicolor fiesta sequence. *Prod:* RKO Radio. 15 reels.

LOVES COMES ALONG (1930). Romantic drama; with music; as Peggy, a girl in a Mexican port village. *Dir:* Rupert Julian. *Sc:* Wallace Smith (from a play, "Conchita," by Edward Knoblock). *With* Lloyd Hughes, Montagu Love, Ned Sparks, Lionel Belmore, Alma Tell. *Prod:* RKO Radio. 8 reels.

ALIAS FRENCH GERTIE (1930). Crook comedy melodrama; as Marie, a lady's maid, who is really "French Gertie," a jewel thief. *Dir:* George Archainbaud. *Sc:* Wallace Smith (from a play, "The Chatterbox," by Bayard Veiller. *With* Ben Lyon, Robert Emmett O'Connor, John Ince, Daisy Belmore. *Prod:* RKO Radio. 7 reels. Previously filmed, 1925, as *Smooth as Satin*, starring Evelyn Brent; re-made 1936, as *The Chatterbox*, starring Anne Shirley.

DIXIANA (1930). Romantic musical of Old New Orleans and the Mardi Gras; as Dixiana of the Cayetano Circus Theatre. *Dir./Sc:* Luther Reed. *With* Everett Marshall, Dorothy Lee, Bert Wheeler, Robert Woolsey, Joseph Cawthorn, Ralf Harolde, Jobyna Howland, Bill Robinson. *Prod:* RKO Radio. 12 reels.

LAWFUL LARCENY (1930). Marital drama; as Marion Dorsey, a wife who turns tables on the vamp who has stolen her husband. *Dir:* Lowell Sherman. *Sc:* Jane Murfin (from the play by Samuel Shipman). *With* Kenneth

Thomson, Lowell Sherman, Olive Tell, Bert Roach. (Silent film made by Paramount, 1923, with Hope Hampton in the Daniels role.) *Prod:* RKO Radio 7 reels.

REACHING FOR THE MOON (1931). Comedy romance, with music; as Vivian Benton. *Dir./Sc:* Edmund Goulding (with additional dialogue by Elsie Janis, and songs by Irving Berlin). *With* Douglas Fairbanks, Edward Everett Horton, Claude Allister, Jack Mulhall, Bing Crosby, June MacCloy, Helen Jerome Eddy. *Prod:* United Artists. 9 reels. (Compare listing in Douglas Fairbanks filmography.)

MY PAST (1931). Sex drama; as Doree, stage star. *Dir:* Roy Del Ruth. *Sc:* Charles Kenyon (from a novel, "Ex-Mistress," by Dora Macy). *With* Ben Lyon, Lewis Stone, Joan Blondell, Natalie Moorhead, Albert Gran, Virginia Sale, Daisy Belmore. *Prod:* Warner Bros. 8 reels.

THE MALTESE FALCON (1931). Detective murder mystery; as Ruth Wonderly. *Dir:* Roy Del Ruth. *Sc:* Maude Fulton (from the novel by Dashiell Hammett). *With* Ricardo Cortez, Dudley Digges, Una Merkel, Robert Elliott, J. Farrell MacDonald, Otto Matiesen, Walter Long, Thelma Todd. (This was the first picturisation of this most famous adventure of Hammett's hero, Sam Spade; later versions included one with Bette Davis in the Daniels role (*Satan Met a Lady*, 1936), and ultimately the definitive one (1941) with Mary Astor in the feminine lead). *Prod:* Warner Bros. 9 reels.

HONOUR OF THE FAMILY (1931). Drama; as Laura, an adventuress. *Dir:* Lloyd Bacon. *Sc:* James Ashmore Creelman (with continuity by Lenore Coffee and additional dialogue by Roland Pertwee — from a play by Emile Fabre, based upon a novel by Honoré de Balzac). *With* Warren William, Alan Mowbray, Blanche Friderici, Dita Parlo. *Prod:* Warner Bros. 7 reels.

SILVER DOLLAR (1932). Romantic Western drama; as Lily Owens, based on the real and legendary character of "Baby Doe," of the Tabor silver mining days. *Dir:* Alfred E. Green. *Sc:* Carl Erickson and Harvey Thew (from a story by David Karsner). *With* Edward G. Robinson, Aline MacMahon, Harry Holman, Russell Simpson, Jobyna Howland, Robert Warwick, David Durand, Marjorie Gateson. Bonita Granville, DeWitt Jennings. Warner Bros./First National. 8 reels.

42ND STREET (1933). Musical comedy; as Dorothy Brock, temperamental stage star. *Dir:* Lloyd Bacon. *Sc:* Rian James and James Seymour (from a novel by Bradford Ropes). *With* Warner Baxter, George Brent, Ruby Keeler, Dick Powell, Guy Kibbee, George E. Stone, Allen Jenkins, Ginger Rogers, Una Merkel, Eddie Nugent. *Prod:* Warner Bros. First National. 8,145 ft.

COCKTAIL HOUR (1933). Romantic drama; as Cynthia Warren, successful commercial artist. *Dir:* Victor Schertzinger. *Sc:* Gertrude Purcell and Richard Schayer (from a story, "Pearls and Emeralds," by James K. McGuinness). *With* Randolph Scott, Muriel Kirkland, Jessie Ralph, Sidney Blackmer, Barry Norton, Marjorie Gateson. *Prod:* Columbia. 8 reels.

COUNSELLOR AT LAW (1933). Legal drama; as Regina Gordon, private secretary. *Dir:* William Wyler. *Sc:* Elmer Rice (from his play). *With* John Barrymore, Doris Kenyon, Onslow Stevens, Isabel Jewell, Melvyn Douglas, Thelma Todd, Mayo Methot, Vincent Sherman, Richard Quine. *Prod:* Universal. 9 reels. (Compare listing in John Barrymore filmography.)

THE SONG YOU GAVE ME (1934). Romantic drama of a Viennese song charmer and an ex-guardsman; as Mitzi Hansen, singer. *Dir:* Paul Stein. *Sc:* Clifford Grey (from a story, "The Song Is Ended," by Walter Reisch). *With* Victor Varconi, Frederick Lloyd, Claude Hulbert, Lester Matthews, Iris Ashley. *Prod:* British International-Columbia. 7 reels.

REGISTERED NURSE (1934) . Romantic melodrama; as Sylvia Benton, nurse. *Dir:* Robert Florey. *Sc:* Lillie Hayward and Peter Milne (from a play by Florence Johns and Wilton Lackaye Jr.). *With* John Halliday, Lyle Talbot, Gordon Westcott, Sidney Toler, Irene Franklin, Mayo Methot, Beulah Bondi, Philip Reed, Minna Gombell. *Prod:* Warner Bros. 7 reels.

MUSIC IS MAGIC (1935). Backstage drama; as Diane DeValle, temperamental stage and screen star. *Dir:* George Marshall. *Sc:* Edward Eliscu and Lou Breslow (from a play by Gladys Unger and Jesse Lasky Jr.). *With* Alice Faye, Ray Walker, Frank Mitchell, Jack Durant, Thomas Beck, Hattie McDaniel. *Prod:* 20th Century-Fox. 6 reels.

A SOUTHERN MAID (1936). Romantic drama, with music; in a dual role: as Juanita and Dolores. *Dir:* Harry Hudges. *Sc:* Austin Melford, Arthur Woods, Frank Miller, Frank Launder (from a musical play by Dion Clayton Calthorp and Harry Graham). *With* Clifford Mollinson, Lupino Lane, Harry Welchman, Hal Gordon. *Prod:* British Alliance. 83m.

TREACHERY ON THE HIGH SEAS (AKA, GB, *Not Wanted on Voyage*) (1938). Melodrama among jewel thieves aboard a luxury liner; as May Hardy, nightclub singer. *Dir:* Emil Reinert. *Sc:* Harold Simpson and Charles Lincoln (from a play, "Murder in the Stalls," by Maurice Messenger). *With* Ben Lyon, Charles Farrell, Tom Helmore, Hay Petrie, Gordon McLeod. (Re-made, 1956, by Byron Films.) *Prod:* British-Lion (Dela Films). 69m.

THE RETURN OF CAROL DEANE (1939). Mother love drama; as Carol Deane, model with a prison record who silently protects her son from being fleeced at the gambling tables. *Dir:* Arthur Woods, *Sc:* John Meehan Jr., Paul Gangelin, Tom Phipps (from a story, "The House on 56th Street," by Joseph Stanley). *With* Arthur Margetson, Zena Dare, Michael Drake, Wyndham Goldie. *Prod:* Warners-Taddington. 76m. (Previously filmed, 1933, as *The House on 56th Street* by Warner Bros., with Kay Francis.)

HI GANG (1941). (never released in the USA). British radio romantic comedy; with Bebe and Ben as rival radio commentators, Bebe known as "The Victory Girl," *Dir:* Marcel Varnel. *Sc:* Val Guest, Marriott Edgar, J. O. C. Orton, Howard Irving Young. *With* Ben Lyon, Vic Oliver, Moore Marriott, Graham Moffatt, Felix Aylmer. *Prod:* Gainsborough. 100m.

LIFE WITH THE LYONS (Sometimes AKA, USA, *Family Affair*) (1954). Situation comedy, with the Lyons trying to buy a Marble Arch home; as the image of Bebe Daniels she established on her radio and television show. *Dir:* Val Guest. *Sc:* Robert Dunbar and Val Guest (from the long-running radio and television show). *With* Ben Lyon, Barbara Lyon, Richard Lyon, Horace Percival, Molly Weir, Belinda Lee, Hugh Morton, *Prod:* Hammer. 81m.

THE LYONS IN PARIS (1956). Situation comedy, a follow-up to *Life With the Lyons;* in her same role as before, only with the action in Paris. *Dir:* Val Guest. *Sc:* Robert Dunbar and Val Guest (based upon characters established in *Life With the Lyons*). *With* Ben Lyon, Barbara Lyon, Richard Lyon, Reginald Beckwith, Horace Percival, Molly Weir, Hugh Morton. *Prod:* Hammer. 7,345 ft.

Bebe Daniels also worked as producer for:

THE FABULOUS JOE (Part Two: Hal Roach Comedy Carnival). (1947). Comedy about Joe, a shaggy talking dog of uncertain lineage and some of the people whose paths he crosses. *Prod:* Bebe Daniels. *Dir:* Harve Foster. *Sc:* Jack Jeune and Arnold Belgard (from a story by Hal Roach Jr.). *With* Walter Abel, Margot Grahame, Marie Wilson, Donald Meek, Sheldon Leonard, John Eldredge, Howard Petrie, Barbara Bates, Nana Bryant, Johnny Miles, Clarence Kolb. *Prod:* Hal Roach/UA. Cinecolor. 59m.

Miss Daniels also prepared for production MR. WILMER, a comedy to have been directed by Harve Foster, but Hal Roach Productions ran into financial difficulties, and filming was called off.

There is a brief cameo bit of Bebe Daniels as

herself in the exploitation film, *A Trip to Paramountown*, 1922. One of the most successful *This Is Your Life* programmes on television featured her and the people she knew in her private and professional life.

13
DOLORES DEL RIO

Aristotle called beauty "the gift of God," but Socrates described it more accurately when he said it is "a short-lived tyranny."

It is so for most actresses. Furthermore, beauty can be a great handicap to them. It can delude them into thinking they do not have to master the acting craft, and it can so enchant audiences that the public does not realise a beautiful woman may also have acting ability.

Great beauties often retire from stage and screen before their beauty starts to go, as did Billie Dove, Corinne Griffith, Dolores Costello, Florence Vidor, and a few others. Even Garbo retired when she was only thirty-six. But Dolores Del Rio, certainly one of the screen's most beautiful women, still appears on stage, screen, and television — and she is now in her very late sixties.

She is an only child, and was born Lolita Dolores Asunsolo in Durango, Mexico, on August 3, 1905. Close friends call her Lolita, or Lola, which has abetted the error that Dolores Del Rio has a younger sister of that name.

On her father's side, she was the third generation of a Spanish-Basque family to be born in Mexico. Her father was a bank president and semi-feudal landowner. Her mother was descended from the Toltecs.

She was only four when, in the dead of night, her father, mother and she fled to Mexico City from Pancho Villa, who seized their home and the local bank. The Asunsolos never returned to Durango.

She grew up behind the walls of the old French convent of Saint Joseph in Mexico City, and was only fifteen when she attracted the eye of Jaime Martinez del Rio, son of one of the Castilian families longest in Mexico.

Two months later they were married, and after a honeymoon in Madrid, the Pyrenees and Paris, they went to live on a large cattle ranch in northern Mexico that had been owned by the del Rio family for three hundred years.

They soon moved to Mexico City, where Señora del Rio's youth, beauty, and singing and dancing ability were much appreciated. But she herself did not long appreciate "the teas, dinners, dances, and the same people — in winter the opera, in summer the bullfights, the annual trips to Europe." Her husband was also restless, and for a little while they toyed with the idea of living for a year in the Latin Quarter, of Paris where she would study singing with De Reszke and he would write plays. Instead, Señora del Rio went to

Hollywood and became Dolores Del Rio.

It came about through Hollywood director Edwin Carewe's honeymoon visit to Mexico City with a party of friends. The del Rios invited the Carewes to tea, at which Señora del Rio danced a tango, and Carewe was openly dazzled.

She has herself described what transpired that afternoon: ''All the time at the tea-party I saw Mr. Carewe staring at me, and, after a while, he called my husband over, and said. 'Your wife should come to Hollywood and go into the movies.' My husband laughed very loud when he heard that. He thought it was an American joke. When he translated it to me, I laughed too, but maybe not quite so hard, or quite so long! After that we saw Mr. Carewe many times and always he offered me a contract, so I finally decided to accept.''

Her decision to go to Hollywood was not opposed by her husband, but his family, and her own, did fight it. She was adamant, and, when it was pointed out as a disgrace that she should be the first Mexican girl of family to become an actress, her reply was: ''Very well, I will be the first.''

''Jaime thought it was only a whim and that I would soon be bored,'' she explained on her arrival in Hollywood. ''That I, who had never worked in my life, would rebel at having to get up early in the morning and do what I did not wish. And he is right. I shall some day be bored with even the movies. But at present it is a glorious adventure, something new to do, to enjoy, to feel. I wish to succeed, to show my friends back in Mexico City that they were wrong.''

When her first film was released, she was so chagrined that she almost fled from Hollywood. Carewe had introduced her in a minor role in *Joanna,* which he directed and which starred Dorothy Mackaill. Miss Del Rio had invited her Mexican, and also her new Hollywood, friends to witness her screen *début,* and she was mortified when she discovered that most of her scenes had been edited out and only two fleeting moments of her had been retained. Much the same happened with her second screen appearance in Carewe's *High Steppers.* She fared better in her third picture, a routine crook comedy-melodrama called *Pals First,* which Carewe also directed.

She was under personal contract to him, and he then lent her to Universal for a second lead in an Edward Everett Horton comedy entitled *The Whole Town's Talking.*

Carewe was already determined to make her his wife, and realised that to do so he would first have to make her a star. Said Dolores Del Rio at that time: ''Hollywood, what a place it is! It is so far away from the the rest of the world, so narrow. No one thinks of anything but motion pictures or talks of anything else. And I, too, am getting like the rest. I have not read anything for a year. I do not know what is happening in the world or what people are talking about, or even which revue is the favourite in Paris.''

Hollywood had something to talk about when it was learned that Raoul Walsh was borrowing her for the coveted role of Charmaine in his big film production of the Broadway hit, *What Price Glory?*, and that she would receive co-star billing with Edmund Lowe and Victor McLaglen. The rival actresses who enviously hoped she would flounder and be lost amid the hard-boiled, roughneck squabbling of Captain Flagg and Sergeant Quirt were disappointed. Her radiant beauty shone only the more brilliantly in the midst of that film's masculine horseplay. And when Carewe co-starred her with Rod La Rocque in a special production of Tolstoy's *Resurrection,* even her detractors grudgingly admitted that not only was she a great beauty but that she also could act.

Dolores Del Rio did not achieve stardom until a year later, and during the year before *Ramona,* the picture that made her a star, she did three programmers with other directors and turned down a chance to be Douglas Fairbanks's leading lady in *The Gaucho* — a big break for her country-woman, Lupe Velez.

The title role in the third film verison of *Ramona,* Helen Hunt Jackson's historical novel of Spanish and Indian life in old California, exactly suited Miss Del Rio's dark but delicate beauty, and Carewe's direction of her is redolent of his personal devotion; he still had hopes of marrying Miss Del Rio, and his wife, Mary Akin, had by now started divorce proceedings. *Ramona* is an altogether superior film, and Carewe had every right to expect that Miss Del Rio would be grateful. She said in the flush of her triumph: "In two or three years, not longer, I will be finished with Hollywood."

But she diligently began improving her English so she could star in talking pictures. There were other complications, however, of which Carewe was but one.

Her husband, in order to be near her in the studio, had stifled his Latin pride and accepted a job as script clerk on her pictures. Then, in an attempt to establish his own existence, he went to New York, where he collaborated on a play, "From Hell Came a Lady." When it failed, he could not bear returning to Hollywood and resuming the "Husband of Dolores Del Rio" role. Where-upon Miss Del Rio sued for divorce. A chance to go to Germany for the American Play Company was offered him and he accepted. There, suddenly, in a sanitarium, he died. Not a few believed he had no longer wished to live. The official cause of his death was given as "blood poisoning following a minor operation."

There were also those who thought Miss Del Rio was about to consent, finally, to be the new Mrs. Edwin Carewe.

Evangeline, in which she starred for Carewe in 1929, is important on at least two counts: it served as a partial introduction for her to the talking picture; and it is the last film in which Carewe directed her. It had a recorded score and sound effects; she sang two songs in it; her leading man, Roland Drew, sang one; and, at its end, when the ill-fated lovers are finally reunited, she speaks a few lines. They proved her English was understandable, her voice, interest-ing, and that a career for her in talking pictures was feasible.

She then broke with Carewe and signed a contract with Joseph Schenck to star for United Artists. Carewe sued, and the case was settled out of court.

Her first all-talkie, *The Bad One,* presented her as a virtuous, high-spirited heroine in a Marseilles brothel! Reviewers commented favourably on the fiery delivery of her lines, the charm of her singing voice, and the grace with which she danced to Irving Berlin's "To a Tango Melody."

It was at this time that she met Cedric Gibbons, M-G-M's great art director, at a Marion Davies party. He was a shy man, twelve years older than she, but their engagement was announced only a few weeks after they had met, and shortly thereafter they were married in the chapel of the historic Santa Barbara mission. After a honeymoon in Monterey, he brought her to the new, ultra-modern home he had just built in Santa Monica Canyon. For a time they also maintained a house nearer the studio. Gibbons's marriage to one of Hollywood's most beautiful women took many by surprise. A few weeks after their return to Hollywood from their honeymoon, Miss Del Rio fell ill.

She had been scheduled to star in *The Dove* as her second all-talking feature for United Artists. Her contract, which gave her $9000 a week when she

Dolores Del Rio with Victor McLaglen, Edmund Lowe, and director Raoul Walsh (wearing visor) on set of WHAT PRICE GLORY

worked, contained a clause which stipulated that if she were away from the studio for one month for any cause whatever, the contract automatically terminated. When her doctors said it might be many months before she could work again, United Artists enforced that clause. No Del Rio pictures were released in 1931. Rumors said she was finished.

There was, and still is, a mystery about this illness. The commonest guess was that she had had a nervous breakdown, the causes of which were her treatment of her first husband and Carewe. But that is speculation only.

Not until late in 1934 did she offer any kind of public explanation, and her statement at that time creates a new perspective to that turbulent phase of her life: "All of my most frightful troubles came while I was at the height of my career. Jaime was thrilled at first by my success. We both thought that he would achieve success, too, in pictures. But gradually he came to hate me because I had succeeded and he had not. It was terrible for both of us...*Everything* happened to me! Things crashed around me. Tragic, terrifying things. I lived in a hotbed of intrigue, of politics, of lies and malice, of cross currents of human purposes. I was hurt so often, I was afraid to express myself!''

When she recovered, she signed a contract with RKO, which, for her first picture, bought *The Dove* from United Artists, and re-titled it *The Girl of the Rio*. Her second RKO film was *The Bird of Paradise,* which David O. Selznick produced and King Vidor directed, with Joel McCrea as leading man. Its exteriors were shot in Hawaii.

Vidor, in his autobiography, ''A Tree Is a Tree,'' relates amusingly the fact that neither he nor Selznick could get through a full reading of the old play version of *The Bird of Paradise*. ''I want Del Rio and McCrea in a South Seas romance,'' Vidor says Selznick told him. ''Just give me three wonderful love scenes like you had in *The Big Parade* and *Bardelys the Magnificent*. I don't care what story you use so long as we call it *Bird of Paradise* and Del Rio jumps into a flaming volcano at the finish.''

Accompanied by writer Wells Root, Vidor sailed for Honolulu, and, with the help of an efficient script girl, Elizabeth Hill, whom he later married, put together a new story combining the ingredients Selznick demanded. They often shot scenes that had been written only the previous night. Despite all, *The Bird of Paradise* emerged as an extraordinarily beautiful picture, and Del Rio was never more exquisitely photographed than by cameraman Clyde De Vinna, and she and McCrea were one of filmdom's handsomest pairs, in and out of clothes.

But that picture cost more than a million dollars, and, to recoup, RKO then put Miss del Rio into what it regarded as a routine musical. This was *Flying Down to Rio,* which became an overnight success, not because of its principal stars, but because of the songs and dances of a pair of supporting players carrying the secondary romance: Fred Astaire and Ginger Rogers.

After that, Miss Del Rio signed a contract with Warner Bros., and made five features for that company. Three were musicals, in which she sang and danced. In *Madame Dubarry,* in which she played the title role and was lavishly costumed, she showed an unexpected talent for comedy.

After a quick trip to England for a backstage murder mystery, *Accused,* with Douglas Fairbanks Jr., she began studying stage acting privately. This was a revival of an interest dating back to 1932, after she had recovered her health but before she signed her RKO contract. She had then indicated to Oliver Hinsdell, M-G-M's drama coach, that she would like to make a vaudeville tour in a dramatic playlet. He had given her two one-acters to read that I had written, and she had asked to see me about one of them. I had taken it for granted that she would be more interested in the one about an early California real-life murderess who woos her jailer, and was surprised when she preferred the other, in which a female protagonist, a woman of the world, is wooed by both father and son.

I remember I lost my way trying to find the secluded canyon house where the Gibbonses lived, and was late. But Miss Del Rio was gracious, and

Opposite: Dolores Del Rio with Joel McCrea in BIRD OF PARADISE

launched immediately into a discussion of the script she preferred. Her dark beauty was complemented by the stark modernity of the Gibbons home, and I could see at once why she wanted to present herself in a stylish comedy. She felt graduated from the literarily romantic heroines that had brought her fame and considered herself a "very modern" woman.

But she did not go on the stage then, and the film roles she accepted in the next few years, with one exception, were of little interest. She played a taxi-dancer wife in *The Devil's Playground,* with Richard Dix and Chester Morris, and *femme fatale* roles in *Lancer Spy* and *International Settlement.* In *The Man from Dakota,* a Wallace Beery vehicle, she had the only important woman's role.

In 1941 she and Cedric Gibbons divorced, and shortly thereafter she met the then boy-wonder of Hollywood: Orson Welles. They were seen everywhere together, and no one was surprised when she was cast in his third RKO production, *Journey into Fear.*

But the romance was short-lived, for Welles met Rita Hayworth, and that romance flamed into marriage. Furthermore, the new powers-that-be at RKO, in re-editing *Journey into Fear,* made it, some thought purposely, a mess. Miss Del Rio was so disgusted with the way her professional and private lives had turned that she left Hollywood and returned to Mexico City.

Said she to the press: "I wish to chose my own stories, my own director, and cameraman. I can accomplish this better in Mexico." Said Louella O. Parsons several years later to explain why Miss Del Rio hadn't returned to Hollwood: "It must be that remnants of a heartache, even though healed over, still haunt her. Women are that way."

Her first Mexican-produced film, *Flor Silvestre,* established her as her native country's top female star, and the pictures which followed, although they had limited release in the United States, were big money-makers in Latin America and Europe. M-G-M thought so highly of *Maria Candelaria* (1943), a moving tragedy largely filmed in the flower gardens of Xochimilco, that they released it in the United States as *Portrait of Maria.* To date, Miss Del Rio has won four "Arieles," which are the Mexican equivalent of our "Oscar," and one "Quixote," the Spanish equivalent.

One of her Mexican Films, *La otra (The Other One,* released in 1947), is interesting because it gave her an opportunity to play a dual role — twin sisters. Warners purchased the rights to re-make it in English, and eventually filmed it as *Dead Ringer,* starring Bette Davis.

In 1947, Miss Del Rio played the only important female role in an American-financed picture largely filmed in Mexico, John Ford's *The Fugitive.* Widely released in the states, it made American audiences aware of her long absence from our screen. Not a few critics commented on her preservation of her beauty and praised the acting talent she had developed.

She went to Argentina in 1948 to play Mrs. Erlynne in *Historia de una mala mujer,* a South American film version of Oscar Wilde's "Lady Windermere's Fan."

When, early in the Fifties, 20th Century-Fox offered her a good role in *Broken Lance,* she was unable to get a visa because our state department feared her association with Communists in Mexico's film industry had infected her. Miss Del Rio declared that she was "delighted to say I am not a

Communist and have never been a Communist. I love America and regard it as my very own.'' She also pointed out that she was Roman Catholic by faith and so could not possibly be a Communist. The visa *was* granted, but too late, for the studio had already replaced her with Katy Jurado.

Some years thereafter (1960), when Miss Del Rio did return to Hollywood to play Elivis Presley's mother in *Flaming Star,* she told Louella O. Parsons: ''We're fighting Communism with all our strength. We fear Cuba — it's so close to us. Mexico intends to take action against any aggression from Cuba or Russia with all the power we can command. Any group that has any Communist ideas is not received by the better class of people, or by the men in charge of the Mexican government.''

Miss Del Rio has long continued to reign as Mexico's top female star. Whenever a rival appears on the horizon, she does not hesitate to co-star with her. She did this with Miroslava in *La casa chica,* with Esther Fernandez in *Doña Perfecta,* and with Maria Felix in *La cucaracha.*

She never relinquished her desire to act on the stage and has become one of Latin America's most popular stage actresses. In 1956 she appeared in the title role of ''Anastasia'' in Eastern United States summer stock. In 1959 she married Lewis A. Riley Jr., an American who produces stage shows in Latin American countries, and first starred for him in his Buenos Aires stage production of Robert E. Sherwood's ''The Road to Rome.'' She has continued to alternate movie and stage appearances.

Encouraged by her husband, she had also proved herself in television. There are few TV series in which she has not been a guest star, and she was especially notable in a segment of ''I Spy,'' as well as in a US Steel Hour presentation, ''The Public Prosecutor.'' In 1963 she joined an all-star cast for a CBS special, ''Hotel Paradiso,'' and I thought her wholly effective when she co-starred with Cesar Romero in a romantic comedy I wrote for TV, ''The Actress and the Bullfighter'' (also shown in re-runs as ''The Moment of Truth'').

In 1964 she played the ''Spanish Woman'' in John Ford's *Cheyenne Autumn,* performing a difficult role with great dignity. The following year she flew to Spain to star for Rovira Beleta, whose *Los Tarantos* had been enthusiastically received in the United States and was one of the nominees for the Academy's Best Foreign Language Picture Award. The Beleta picture in which Del Rio appeared, *La dama del alba (Lady of the Dawn)* was well-liked in Spain, where it premiered in the summer of 1966. So was a film she made in Mexico, *Casa de mujeres (House of Women).*

She played the mother of Omar Sharif in a Sophia Loren costume comedy, *Once upon a Time,* and looked absolutely stunning photographed in colour. On her return to Mexico, she starred in the big historical and sociological drama called *Rio Blanco.* In more recent years, she has starred on the Mexico City stage in two such disparate theatrical pieces as ''La dame aux camélias'' and Ugo Betti's ''The Queen and the Rebels.''

Miss Del Rio and her husband live in a two hundred-year-old house, surrounded by celebrated gardens, in the fashionable Mexico City suburb of Coyocan. She neither smokes nor drinks, and doesn't believe either in over-exercising or in ''killing diets.'' She says she has always remembered Arthur Brisbane's remark that it takes two weeks of regular sleep to overcome the

Dolores Del Rio with Henry Fonda in John Ford's THE FUGITIVE

effect of one night of incomplete rest, and has always made a point of getting eight hours sleep a night.

She is quite conscious of having lived in two worlds. As she said in 1928, just after becoming a star: "I greatly admire the independence of American women, although when I first met them I thought them rather masculine. Their walk, their self-assurance, their automobile driving, their working, writing, directing, supervising, were in such extreme contrast to the retiring, shy, almost cringing manner in which Mexican girls conduct themselves, not daring to go anywhere unescorted, not daring to be seen looking in shop-windows, always accompanied by other women, that I had to revise my entire philosophy of life."

When, soon after her first marriage, she decided to abandon her life as a Mexico City matron, and her family, opposing her, argued that no Mexican girl of good family had ever worked in Hollywood, she had replied: "Very well, I will be the first." Today, after nearly half a century, she is still the first, but not the last. She paved the way to Hollywood, and although Hollywood is gone, all the world beckons. Because of the determination with which she surmounted every personal and professional obstacle, many talented girls of good Latin American families are still following in her footsteps.

DOLORES DEL RIO FILMOGRAPHY

JOANNA (1925). Jazz age drama; as Carlotta de Silva. *Dir:* Edwin Carewe. *Sc:* Lois Leeson (from a newspaper serial, "Joanna, of the Skirts Too Short and the Lips Too Red and the Tongue Too Pert," by Henry Leyford Gates). *With* Dorothy Mackaill, Jack Mulhall, Paul Nicholson, George Fawcett, Edwards Davis, John T. Murray, Rita Carewe, Lillian Langdon, Bob Hart. *Prod:* First National. 8 reels.

HIGH STEPPERS (1926). Post First World War social drama; as Evelyn Iffield, daughter of an English noblewoman. *Dir:* Edwin Carewe. *Sc:* Lois Leeson (ad. by Finis Fox from a novel, "Heirs Apparent," by Philip Gibbs). *With* Mary Astor, Lloyd Hughes, Emily Fitzroy, Rita Carewe, John T. Murray, Edwards Davis, Alec B. Francis, Clarissa Selwynne, Charles Sellon, John Steppling, Margaret McWade. *Prod:* First National. 7 reels.

PALS FIRST (1926). Crook reformation romance; as Jeanne Lamont. *Dir:* Edwin Carewe. *Sc:* Lois Leeson (ad. by Olga Printzlau from the novel by Francis Perry Elliott and the dramatisation thereof by Lee Wilson Dodd). *With* Lloyd Hughes, Alec B. Francis, George Cooper, Edward Earle, George Reed. *Prod:* First National. 7 reels. (Previously made, 1918, Metro, with Harold Lockwood; re-made as a talkie, with songs 1931, by M-G-M, as *The Southerner,* with Lawrence Tibbett and Esther Ralston.)

THE WHOLE TOWN'S TALKING (1926). Comedy; as Rita Renault. *Dir:* Edward Laemmle. *Sc:* Raymond Cannon (from the play by John Emerson and Anita Loos). *With* Edward Everett Horton, Virginia Lee Corbin, Trixie Friganza, Otis Harlan, Robert Ober, Hayden Stevenson, Margaret Quimby, August Tollaire, Mathilde Comont. (Re-filmed as a talkie called *Ex-Bad Boy.*) *Prod:* Universal. 7 reels.

WHAT PRICE GLORY (1926). First World War drama; as Charmaine. *Dir:* Raoul Walsh. *Sc:* T. O'Donohue (from the play by Laurence Stallings & Maxwell Anderson). *With* Edmund Lowe, Victor McLaglen, Phyllis Haver, Sammy Cohen, Ted McNamara, Leslie Fenton, William V. Mong, Barry Norton, Pat Rooney, Elena Jurado. (Re-filmed as a talkie, 1952.) *Prod:* Fox. 12 reels.

RESURRECTION (1927). Drama of Tsarist Russia; as Katusha Maslova. *Dir:* Edwin Carewe. *Sc:* Finis Fox (ad. by Edwin Carewe, Finis Fox and Count Ilya Tolstoy from the novel by Count Leo Tolstoy). *With* Rod La Rocque, Marc McDermott, Rita Carewe, Eve Southern, Clarissa Selwynne, Lucy Beaumont, Vera Lewis, Count Ilya Tolstoy. (Filmed by Biograph, 1909; by Fox, 1915, as *A Woman's Resurrection;* by Paramount with Pauline Frederick in 1918; as a talkie by Universal with Lupe Velez, 1931; by Goldwyn in 1934 with Anna Sten as *We Live Again;* in Mexico, 1943, with Lupita Tovar; by Artkino in Russia, 1963.) *Prod:* United Artists. 10 reels.

THE LOVES OF CARMEN (1927). Romantic tragedy; as Carmen. *Dir:* Raoul Walsh. *Sc:* Gertrude Orr (from the novel by Prosper Mérimée). *With* Don Alvarado, Victor McLaglen, Nancy Nash, Mathilde Comont, Fred Kohler, Carmen Costello, Jack Baston. (See listing in Theda Bara's *Carmen* for other versions.) *Prod:* Fox. 9 reels.

THE GATEWAY OF THE MOON (1928). Jungle romance; as Chela (Toni), half-caste native girl. *Dir:* John Griffith Wray. *Sc:* Bradley King (from the play, "Upstream," by Clifford Bax). *With* Walter Pidgeon, Anders Randolph, Ted McNamara, Leslie Fenton, Adolph Millar, Noble Johnson, Virginia LaFonde. *Prod:* Fox: 6 reels.

THE TRAIL OF '98 (1928). Romantic Klondike melodrama; as Berna, forced to become a dancehall girl when she is abandoned by her lover. *Dir:* Clarence Brown. *Sc:* Benjamin Glazer and Waldemar Young (ad. by Glazer from a novel, "The Trail of '98: a Northland Romance," by Robert William Service). *With* Ralph Forbes, Harry Carey, Karl Dane, Tully Marshall, George Cooper, Russell Simpson, Emily Fitzroy, Tenen Holtz, Cesare Gravina, Polly Moran, Doris Lloyd, Ray Gallagher, John Down, E. Alyn Warren. Movietone, with Sound Effects; also a silent version. *Prod:* M-G-M. 10 reels.

RAMONA (1928). California romance; as Ramona. *Dir:* Edwin Carewe. *Sc:* Finis Fox (from the novel by Helen Hunt Jackson). *With* Warner Baxter, Roland Drew, Vera Lewis, Michael Visaroff, John T. Prince, Mathilde Comont, Rita Carewe, Jess Cavin, Carlos Amor. (Previously filmed by D. W. Griffith/Biograph, 1910, with Mary Pickford; then in 1916 by W. H. Clune, with Adda Gleason; re-filmed as a Technicolor talkie in 1936, 20th Century-Fox, with Loretta Young; and then re-made, Mexico, 1946, starring Esther Fernández.) *Prod:* United Artists. Movietone, with Sound Effects; also a silent version. 8 reels.

NO OTHER WOMEN (1928). Marital drama; as Carmelita De Granados. *Dir:* Lou Tellegen.

Sc: Jessie Burns and Bernard Vorhaus (from a novel by Polan Banks). *With* Don Alvarado, Ben Bard, Paulette Du Val, Rosita Martini, Andre Laney. *Prod:* Fox. 6 reels.

THE RED DANCE (1928). Romantic drama of the Russian Revolution; as Tasia, peasant girl, who becomes the famous "Red Dancer of the Revolution." *Dir:* Raoul Walsh. *Sc:* James A. Creelman (from an adaptation by Pierre Collings and Philip Klein of a story by Eleanor Browne, taken from a novel, "The Red Dancer of Moscow," by Henry Leyford Gates). *With* Charles Farrell, Ivan Linow, Boris Charsky, Dorothy Revier, Andre Seguorola. *Prod:* Fox, Movietone, with Sound Effects: also a silent version. 10 reels.

REVENGE (1928). Gypsy romance; as Rascha, a fiery gypsy girl. *Dir:* Edwin Carewe. *Sc:* Finis Fox (from a story, "The Bear Tamer's Daughter," by Konrad Bercovici). *With* LeRoy Mason, James Marcus, Rita Carewe, Jose Crespo, Jess Cavin, Marta Golden, Sophia Ortiga. Movietone, with Sound Effects. *Prod:* United Artists. 7 reels.

EVANGELINE (1929). Romance of two lovers separated on their wedding day; as Evangeline, Arcadian maid. *Dir:* Edwin Carewe. *Sc:* Finis Fox (from the narrative poem, "Evangeline" a Tale of Arcadia," by Henry Wadsworth Longfellow). *With* Roland Drew, Alec B. Francis, Donald Reed, Paul McAllister, James Marcus, George Marion, Lou Payne, Lee Shumway. (Previously filmed by Fox, 1919, starring Miriam Cooper.) This marked Miss Del Rio's talking and singing *début,* but it was only a part-talkie; she sang two songs and Roland Drew sang one, and she had one speech to say at the end of the film. Movietone, with Sound, Talking and Singing Sequences; also a silent version. *Prod:* United Artists. 9 reels.

THE BAD ONE (1930). Romantic drama of the waterfront; as Lita, a virtuous bordello señorita. *Dir:* George Fitzmaurice. *Sc:* Carey Wilson and Howard E. Rogers (from a story by John Farrow). *With* Edmund Lowe, Don Alvarado, Blanche Friderici, Adrienne d'Ambricourt, Ulrich Haupt, Mitchell Lewis, Ralph Lewis, Yola d'Avril, John Sainpolis, Henry Kolker, George Fawcett, Victor Potel, Henry Stubbs, Tommy Dugan. Miss Del Rio's first all-talking feature. *Prod:* United Artists. 8 reels.

THE GIRL OF THE RIO (AKA, GB, *The Dove*) (1932). Romance of the Rio Grande; as Dolores, a cantina performer known as "The Dove." *Dir:* Herbert Brenon. *Sc:* Elizabeth Meehan (from the play, "The Dove," by Willard Mack, which was based on a story, "The Blue Ribbon," by Gerald Beaumont). *With* Leo Carrillo, Norman Foster, Ralph Ince, Lucille Gleason, Edna Murphy, Stanley Fields, Frank Campeau. (The play, produced

by David Belasco, had starred Judith Anderson on Broadway; first filmed, 1928, with Norma Talmadge and Gilbert Roland; refilmed as a talkie, 1939, *The Girl and the Gambler.*) *Prod:* RKO-Radio. 65m.

THE BIRD OF PARADISE (1932). Romance of Hawaii, and filmed in the Hawaiian Islands; as Lucana. *Dir:* King Vidor. *Sc:* Wells Root, Leonard Praskins, Wanda Tuchock (from the play by Richard Walton Tully). *With* Joel McCrea, John Halliday, Skeets Gallagher, Lon Chaney Jr., Bert Roach, Wade Boteler. (Re-made by 20th Century-Fox, 1951, with Debra Paget.) *Prod:* RKO-Radio. 10m.

FLYING DOWN TO RIO (1933). Musical romance; as Belinda. *Dir:* Thornton Freeland. *Sc:* Louis Brock. *With* Gene Raymond, Raoul Roulien, Ginger Rogers, Fred Astaire, Blanche Friderici, Walter Walker, Roy D'Arcy, Armand Kaliz, Paul Porcasi, Reginald Barlow, Eric Blore, Alice Gentle, Franklin Pangborn, Luis Alberni. *Prod:* RKO-Radio. 89m.

WONDER BAR (1934). Musical drama; as Inez, a jealous dancer. *Dir:* Lloyd Bacon. *Sc:* Earl Baldwin (from a play by Geza Herczeg, Karl Farkas and Robert Katscher). *With* Al Jolson, Kay Francis, Ricardo Cortez, Dick Powell, Guy Kibbee, Ruth Donnelly, Hugh Herbert, Louise Fazenda, Fifi D'Orsay, Merna Kennedy, Hal LeRoy, Henry O'Neill, Robert Barrat, Henry Kolker, Kathryn Sergava, Emil Chautard, Pauline Garon, Jane Darwell. *Prod:* Warner Bros. 81m.

MADAME DUBARRY (1934). Costume bedroom farce; as DuBarry, mistress of Louis XV. *Dir:* William Dieterle. *Sc:* Edward Chodorov. *With* Reginald Owen, Victor Jory, Osgood Perkins, Veree Teasdale, Henry O'Neill, Anita Louise, Ferdinand Gottschalk, Maynard Holmes, Dorothy Tree, Helen Lowell, Joan Wheeler, Hobart Cavanaugh, Virginia Sale, Halliwell Hobbes, Arthur Treacher, Doris Lloyd, Phillips Smalley, Howard Hickman, Edward Le Saint. *Prod:* Warner Bros. 77m. (See Theda Bara filmography for other outstanding performances of DuBarry.)

IN CALIENTE (1935). Musical romance; as Rita Gomez, a Mexican dancer. *Dir:* Lloyd Bacon. *Sc:* Ralph Block and Warren Dubb (from a story, "Caliente," by Jerry Wald and Julius Epstein). *With* Pat O'Brien, Leo Carrillo, Edward Everett Horton, Glenda Farrell, The DeMarcos, The Canova Family, Phil Regan, Dorothy Dare, Winifred Shaw, Harry Holman, Herman Bing, Luis Alberni, Soledad Jimenez. *Prod:* Warner Bros. 85m.

I LIVE FOR LOVE (AKA, GB, *I Live for You*) (1935). Romance, with music; as Donna Berkeley. *Sc:* Jerry Wald, Julius Epstein and Robert Andrews. *With* Everett Marshall, Guy Kibbee, Allen Jenkins, Hobart Cavanaugh,

Berton Churchill, Don Alvarado, Mary Treen. Working Title: *Romance in a Glass House*. *Prod:* Warner Bros. 64m.

THE WIDOW FROM MONTE CARLO (AKA. GB *A Present from Margate*) (1935). Romantic comedy drama of blackmail: as Inez, duchess of Rye. *Dir:* Arthur Collins. *Sc:* F. Hugh Herbert and Charles Beldon (from a play, "A Present from Margate," by Ian Hunter and A. E. W. Mason). *With* Warren William, Louise Fazenda, Colin Clive, Herbert Mundin, Warren Hymer, Olin Howland, E. E. Clive, Mary Forbes, Eily Malyon, Ann Douglas. Working title: *Meet the Duchess*. *Prod:* Warner Bros. 60m.

ACCUSED (1936). A backstage murder mystery; as Gaby Seymour who is innocent but accused of knifing the star. *Dir:* Thornton Freeland. *Sc:* Zoë Akins, George Barraud and Harold French (from a story by Miss Akins). *With* Douglas Fairbanks Jr., Florence Desmond, Basil Sydney, Cecil Humphries, Esme Percy, Googie Withers, Athole Stewart, Roland Culver. *Prod:* United Artists-Criterion (British). 86m.

THE DEVIL'S PLAYGROUND (1937). Romantic submarine melodrama; as Carmen. *Dir:* Erle C. Kenton. *Sc:* Liam O'Flaherty, Jerome Chodorov and Dalton Trumbo (from a story by Norman Springer). *With* Richard Dix, Chester Morris, George McKay, John Gallaudet, Pierre Watkins, Ward Bond, Don Rowan, Francis McDonald, Stanley Andrews. Working title: *The Depths Below*. *Prod:* Columbia. 72m. (Compare listing in Richard Dix filmography.)

LANCER SPY (1937). Romantic espionage drama; as Fraulein Dolores Daria Sunnell. *Dir:* Gregory Ratoff. *Sc:* Philip Dunne (from a novel by Martha McKenna). *With* George Sanders, Peter Lorre, Joseph Schildkraut, Virginia Field, Sig Rumann, Maurice Moscovich, Lionel Atwill, Luther Adler, Fritz Feld, Holmes E. Herbert, Lester Matthews, Gregory Gaye, Frank Reicher, Leonard Mudie. *Prod:* 20th Century-Fox. 88m.

INTERNATIONAL SETTLEMENT (1938). Romantic melodrama; as Lorne, a French singer. *Dir:* Eugene J. Forde. *Sc:* Lou Breslow and John Patrick (from a story by Lynn Root and Frank Fenton). *With* George Sanders, June Lang, Dick Baldwin, Ruth Terry, John Carradine, Keye Luke, Harold Huber, Leon Ames, Pedro de Cordoba. Working title: *Shanghai Deadline*. *Prod:* 20th Century-Fox. 84m.

THE MAN FROM DAKOTA (AKA, GB, *Arouse and Beware*) (1940). Civil War melodrama; as Jenny, a Russian-born girl. *Dir:* Leslie Fenton. *Sc:* Laurence Stallings (from a novel, "Arouse and Beware," by MacKinlay Kantor). *With* Wallace Beery, John Howard,

Donald Meek, Robert Barrat, Addison Richards, John Wray, Gregory Gaye, Frank M. Thomas, Francis Wade Boteler, Howard Hickman. *Prod:* M-G-M. 74m.

JOURNEY INTO FEAR (1942). Nazi espionage thriller; as Josette. *Dir:* Norman Foster. *Sc:* Orson Welles and Joseph Cotten (from the novel by Eric Ambler). *With* Joseph Cotten, Orson Welles, Ruth Warrick, Agnes Moorehead, Jack Durant, Everett Sloane, Eustace Wyatt, Edgar Barrier, Hans Conried, Richard Bennett. *Prod:* RKO Radio. 71m.

FLOR SILVESTRE (1943). Romantic drama of Mexico; as Esperanza, a labourer's daughter. *Dir:* Emilio Fernandez. *Sc:* Fernandez and Mauricio Magdaleno (from *Sucedio Ayer by Fernando Robles*). *With* Pedro Armendáriz, Emilio Fernandez, Miguel Angel Ferriz, Alfonso Bedoya, Margarita Cortés, "Isunza," Mimi Derba, Alfonso Bedoya, Margarita Cortés, Eduardo Arozamena, "El Chicote." Del Rio's first film produced in her native country made her, actor Pedro Armendáriz, director-actor Emilio Fernandez, and cameraman Gabriel Figueroa known as "The Big Four" of Mexican films. Her performance won her the first of four "Arieles" (Mexico's Oscar). *Prod:* Films Mundiales. 96m.

MARIA CANDELARIA (AKA, *Xochimilco*). (1943). Romantic tragedy; as Maria Candelaría, an outcast Indian girl. *Dir:* Emilio Fernandez. *Sc:* Fernandez and Mauricio Magdaleno (from a story by Fernandez). *With* Pedro Armendáriz, Alberto Galán, Rafaelo Icardo, Beatriz Ramos, Miguel Inclán, Margarita Cortés. Filmed in the flower gardens of Mexico's Xochimilco. (Released by M-G-M in the USA, with English subtitles, as *Portrait of Maria*.) *Prod:* Films Mundiales. 110m.

BUGAMBILIA (1944). Period romance; as Amalita de los Robles, a society girl who falls in love with a gambler. *Dir:/Sc:* Emilio Fernandez. (from a story by Fernandez and Mauricio Magdaleno). *With* Pedro Armendáriz, Julio Villarreal, Alberto Galán, Elba Albarez, Victor Velazquez, Paco Fuentes, Eduardo Aroamena, Robert Cañedo, Francisco Fuentes. *Prod:* Films Mundiales. 98m.

LAS ABANDONADAS (1944). Mother love drama; as Margarita Perez. *Dir:/Sc:* Emilio Fernandez (from a story by Fernandez and Mauricio Magdaleno). *With* Pedro Armendáriz, Victor Junco, Paco Fuentes, Arturo Soto Rangel, Alfonso Bedoya, Fanny Schiller, Tina Romagnoli, Paco Fuentes. Del Rio won her second "Ariel" for her performance in this picture. *Prod:* Films Mundiales. 95m.

LA SELVA DE FUEGO (1945). Passion in a jungle camp among chicle workers; as Estrella, a shipwrecked wealthy girl. *Dir:* Fernando de Fuentes. *Sc:* De Fuentes and Paulino Masip (novel by Antonio M. Bolio). *With* Arturo de Cordova, Miguel Inclan, Gilberto González, Felipe Montoya, Daniel Herrera, Jose Laboriel. *Prod:* Dyana. 100m.

LA OTRA (1946). Melodrama; in a dual role: as twin sisters, one a manicurist, the other a rich widow. *Dir:* Roberto Gavaldón. *Sc:* Gavaldón and Jose Revueltas (from a novel, "Dead Pigeon," by Rian James). *With* Victor Juno, Agostin Irusta, Jose Baviera. (Re-made by Warner Bros., 1964, in Hollywood as *Dead Ringer,* starring Bette Davis.) *Prod:* Mercurio. 98m.

THE FUGITIVE (1947). A modern variation on the Passion Play, filmed by an American company in Mexico; as An Indian Woman. *Dir:* John Ford. *Sc:* Dudley Nichols (from a novel, "The Labyrinthine Ways" (AKA, "The Power and the Glory" by Graham Greene). *With* Henry Fonda, Pedro Armendáriz, J. Carrol Naish, Leo Carrillo, Robert Armstrong, John Qualen, Ward Bond, Fortunio Bonanova, Chris-Pin-Martin, Manuel Inclan. (Subsequently filmed as a television feature, *The Power and the Glory,* starring Laurence Olivier.) *Prod:* RKO Radio. 104m.

HISTORIA DE UNA MALA MUJER (1948). Society drama; as Mrs. Erlynne. *Dir:* Luis Salslavsky. *Sc:* Pedro Miguel Obligado (from the play, "Lady Windermere's Fan," by Oscar Wilde). *With* Fernando Lamas, Maria Duval, Francisco de Paula, Alberto Closas. (Previously filmed under Wilde's title by Triangle in 1919; by Ernst Lubitsch for Warner Bros. in 1925; re-filmed as *The Fan* by 20th Century-Fox. 1949.) *Prod:* Argentine Sono.

LA MALQUERIDA (1949). Marital drama; as Raimunda, a country widow who marries a second time. *Dir/Sc:* Emilio Fernandez (from the play by Jacinto Benavente). *With* Pedro Armendáriz, Columba Dominguez, Roberto Cañedo, Julio Villarreal, Mimi Derba. *Prod:* Cabrera. 83m.

LA CASA CHICA (1949). Romantic tragedy; as Amalia Estrada, aide to a married research scientist. *Dir:* Roberto Gavaldón. *Sc:* Jose Revueltas. *With* Roberto Cañedo, Miroslava, Domingo Soler, Maria Douglas, Julio Villarreal, Jose Elias Moreno. *Prod:* Peliculas Nacionales. 96m.

DONA PERFECTA (1950). Domestic drama; as Doña Perfecta, an arrogant arbiter of Mexican society at the turn of the century. *Dir:* Alejandro Galindo. *Sc:* (from the novel by Benito Perez Galdos). *With* Esther Fernández, Carlos Navarro, Julio Villarreal, Jose Elias Moreno. Del Rio won her third "Ariel" for her performance in this film. *Prod:* Clasa Mohme.

DESEADA (1951). Romantic tragedy; as Deseada. *Dir:* Roberto Gavaldon. *Sc:* Gavaldon

and Eduardo Marquino (from a play "La Ermita, La Fuente y El Rio," by Marquino). *With* Jorge Mistral, Anabella Guiterrez, Arturo Soto Rangel. Filmed among the Mayan ruins in Merida, capital of Yucatan. *Prod:* Sanson.

REPORTAJE (1953). Romantic drama, with songs and dances, in which nearly all the leading lights of the Mexican cinema participated; as Maria Enriqueta. *Dir:* Emilio Fernandez. *Sc:* Mauricio Magdaleno (from a story by Magdaleno and Emilio Fernandez). *With* Jorge Negrete, Maria Felix, Maria Elena Marques, Domingo Soler, Columba Dominguez, Roberto Cañedo, Fernando Soler, Arturo de Córdova, Jorge Mistral, Carmen Sevilla, Pedro Infante, Sarita Montiel, David Silva, Miroslava, Esther Fernández, Carlos Navarro, Julio Villarreal, Silvia Pinal. *Prod:* Periodistas Cinematograficos Mexicanos A.A.Y Asociancion Nacional de Actores.

EL NINO Y LA NIEBLA (1953). Drama of hereditary insanity; as Marta, a mother who knows there has been insanity in her family, and fearing for her child, suffers a breakdown herself. *Dir:* Roberto Gavaldón. *Sc:* Gavaldón and Edmundo Baez (from a play by Rodolfo Usigli). *With* Pedro Lope Lagar, Eduardo Noriega, Alejandro Ciangherotti, Miguel Angel Ferriz, Carlos Riguelme, This film won eight "Arieles," including Del Rio's fourth one. *Prod:* Grovas.

SENORA AMA (1954). Drama; as a Spanish señora — Señora Ama. *Dir:* Julio Bracho. *Sc:* Enrique Llovet and Julio Bracho (from the play, known in translation as "The Lady of the House," by Jacinto Benavente). *With* Jose Suarez, Maria Luz Galicia, Manuel Monroy. Miss Del Rio's first film to be made in Spain. *Prod:* Union films, Spain.

LA CUCARACHA (1958). Drama of the Mexican Revolution; as Chabela, a sedate society widow who loves a peasant general, whose mistress is an earthy female warrior known as "La Cucaracha." *Dir:* Ismael Rodriguez. *Sc:* Ricardo Garibay (from a story by Garibay, Jose Prado and Jose Celis). *With* Maria Felix, Emilio Fernandez, Antonio Aguilar, Pedro Armendáriz. *Prod:* Unifilms-Cimex. 89m. (Eastmancolor).

A DONDE VAN NUESTROS HIJOS (1958). Social domestic drama; as a middle-class mother of four children, the eldest of whom is nineteen. *With* Ana Berta Lepe, Martha Mijares, Tito Junco, Carlos Rivas, Andrea Palma. *Prod:* Cinetomatgrafica Filmex-Azteca.

FLAMING STAR (1960). Dramatic tragedy; as Neddy Burton. *Dir:* Don Siegel. *Sc:* Clair Huffaker and Nunnally Johnson (from a novel by Huffaker). *With* Elvis Presley, Steve Forrest, Barbara Eden, John McIntire, Rudolph Acosta, Karl Swenson, Richard Jaeckel,

Douglas Dick, L. Q. Jones, Virginia Christine. (As the Indian mother of half-breed Presley, who sings only one song over the title and credits, Miss Del Rio gained top notices.) Working titles: *Flaming Lance* and *Flaming Heart. Prod:* 20th Century-Fox. 92m.

EL PECADO DE UNA MADRE (1960). Mother love drama; as a mother who adopts the son born to her husband's mistress. *Dir:* Alfonso Corona Blake. *Sc:* Julio Alejandro (from a story by Fernando Galiana). *With* Libertad Lamarque, Pedro Geraldo, Teresa Velasquez, Enrique Rambal. Peliculas Nacionales. 90m.

CHEYENNE AUTUMN (1964). Shabby treatment given by the government to 960 American Indians, of the Cheyenne tribe; as "Spanish Woman." *Dir:* John Ford. *Sc:* James R. Webb (suggested by a book by Mari Sandoz). *With* Richard Widmark, Carroll Baker, Karl Malden, Sal Mineo, Richard Montalban, Gilbert Roland, Arthur Kennedy, Patrick Wayne, Elizabeth Allen, John Carradine, Victor Jory, Mike Mazurki, George O'Brien, Sean McClory, Ken Curtis, James Stewart, Edward G. Robinson. Working title: *The Long Flight. Prod:* Warner Bros. 161m.

LA DAMA DEL ALBA (1966). Drama; in the title role, "Lady of the Dawn." *Dir:* Rovira Beleta. *Sc:* (from the play by Alejandro Casona). *With* Elena Samarina, Juliette Villars, Daniel Martin. (Miss Del Rio's second Spanish-produced film.)

CASA DE MUJERES (1966). Comedy drama; as the madam of a house which is obviously not a home. *Dir:* Julian Soler. *With* Fernando Soler, Carlos Lopez Moctezuma, Enrique Alvarez Felix (last-named is the son of Maria Felix, who made his film *début* in this picture). *Prod:* Carlos Amador.

C'ERA UNA VOLTA (AKA, *More Than a Miracle, La Belle et le Cavalier, Cinderella--Italian Style, Once Upon a Time,* and *Happily Ever After*) (1966). Romantic comedy drama; a kind of fairy tale Cinderella, Italian style; as The Princess Mother. *Dir:* Francesco Rosi. *With* Sophia Loren, Omar Sharif, Leslie French. (Filmed in Italy.) *Prod:* Ponti-M-G-M.

RIO BLANCO (1967). Social drama of the massacre of unarmed striking textile workers by government troops, which touched off the revolution against Mexico's Diaz; as a pivotal revolutionary character. *Dir:* Roberto Gavaldón. *Sc:* Gavaldón and Tito Davidson. *With* Silvia Pinal, Ignacio Lopez Tarso, David Reynoso. Filmed in and around Vera Cruz, Mexico. *Prod:* Galindo Bros.

(Dolores Rio also made brief cameo appearances as herself in *Ali Baba Goes to Town* (20th Century-Fox, 1937), and in the Mexican-produced *Torero!,* 1956.)

(In addition to her stage appearance in Buenos Aires in Robert E. Sherwood's *The Road to Rome,* Miss Del Rio also made some summer stage appearances in the United States in *Anastasia.* She gained the title of "First Lady of the Mexican Theatre" by appearing in Mexico and other Latin American countries in stage productions of Ibsen's "Ghosts," Lillian Hellman's "The Little Foxes," Wilde's "Lady Windermere's Fan," Roussin's "La Clairvoyante," Turgenev's "A Month in the Country," Dumas *fils'* "Camille", Ugo Betti's "The Queen and the Rebels," and as Mrs. Pat Campbell in "Dear Liar." She has also made several tours in vaudeville, and, in 1961, appeared at the Million Dollar Theatre in Los Angeles in a Spanish-speaking dramatic skit.)

(I wish to express thanks to the late Hector C. Fernandez, director of the Asociacion de Productores y Distribuidores de Peliculas Mexicanas, and to Alfonso Pintó, of Bern, Switzerland, for invaluable aid in compiling this index of Miss Del Rio's feature films, especially those made away from the Hollywood studios.)

14
RICHARD DIX

It was not for nothing that six-foot, 180-pound Richard Dix was facetiously called "The Jaw." Strong, determined, stalwart — he was all of these; in fact, no screen actor ever exemplified the masculine ideal more completely.

Dix was a serious, well-trained actor. Even in his last vehicles, when he was portraying characters in whom he had little interest — alcoholics, egomaniacs, and other kinds of neurotics — he projected a vitality that audiences liked and came to expect.

His real name was Ernest Carlton Brimmer, and he was born in St. Paul, Minnesota, on July 18, 1894. Both his mother and father were of English stock and Dix was proud that the first John Brimmer in this country, and his wife, Elizabeth Manchester, had been early settlers in the Massachusetts Bay Colony in the mid-Seventeenth century.

After graduating from St. Paul's Central High School young Ernest entered the University of Minnesota Medical School, intending to become a surgeon like his much older brother, Archie, who was already well established as a surgeon when his younger brother graduated from high school. But watching several operations decided him against surgery, and he tried working in a bank and then in an architect's office.

He spent his evenings, however, attending the University of Minnesota's drama classes, and when he told his parents that he was bitten by the stage bug, they did everything they could to dissuade him. Only his brother, the successful surgeon, encouraged him, and secretly gave him financial support. "Archie was the greatest single influence in the shaping of my career," Dix once said.

When E. H. Sothern visited St. Paul in repertory, he gave Ernest Brimmer a reading for "Richelieu" and, impressed, offered him $18 a week to play small parts in his company; but at that time the youth lacked the courage to leave his family. Sothern's interest, however, generated some self-confidence, and he soon applied to the James Neill and Edythe Chapman company when they played St. Paul in "The College Widow" and let it be known that they needed a football player for a supporting role. Ernest had played football for the University of Minnesota, and he got the part.

His family saw him in "The College Widow," and, realising he was in earnest about seeking a career in the theatre, they did everything they could to

299

help him become a regular member of a St. Paul stock company, which he finally did under the name of Richard Dix. He had long before decided that "Richard" was a name that suited his stage image, and an aunt suggested that the surname of "Dix" went well with Richard.

Emboldened by a season of stock, he went to New York to try his luck. He was almost down to his last penny when he landed a job in a stock company in Pittsburgh at $35 a week. An engagement with a company in Dallas followed, and that was succeeded by one with a Montreal company. When the United States entered the First World War he enlisted in the Army, but the Armistice was declared before he got overseas. He then tried Broadway again, and this time made it.

His Manhattan *début* was in support of William Faversham in "The Hawk," and thereafter he played on Broadway in "The Song of Songs," "The Little Brother," "The First Is Last," and Maxim Gorky's "A Night's Lodging." Oliver Morosco then engaged him as leading man for his Los Angeles stock company, and Dix spent two and a half years with it.

Lewis Stone, Douglas MacLean, Warner Baxter, David Butler, and Edmund Lowe were only a few of Morosco's leading men who became successful film players. In 1916 Dix had made his screen *début* in Metro's Eastern-made *One of Many,* in which he played a despicably villainous role. He hated the picture and, even more, hated himself in it. He never referred to it in later years, and always hoped that it had been forgotten and all record of it buried in the vault of time. Three years later, Jeanie Macpherson, attracted by his heroic image as a Morosco leading man, arranged a screen test for Dix, but he didn't like himself in that bit of film either, and turned down several subsequent movie offers.

One day he went out to Inceville on the Santa Monica coast where David Butler was acting in a picture. Frederick Butler was Morosco's stage director, and his talented actor-son David later became a good screen director. The Butlers bullied Dix into making a new screen test.

"Dave made me up," Dix said later, "and his father put me through a few scenes. With two old friends helping, there was no danger of nervousness. But there were still a lot of ragged spots. Some of them looked pretty bad when we ran them off in the projection room. But Dave systematically cut them out until all we had left were the good parts — and a practically hundred per cent test!"

Director Sidney Franklin looked at that test and signed Dix for a dual-role lead (twin brothers) in *Not Guilty,* a film he was then casting for First National. When Samuel Goldwyn saw that feature, he induced Dix to sign a contract with him.

Severely self-critical, Dix always groaned when people mentioned what he hoped would be considered his first film. "Between the making of *Not Guilty* and the release of it," he said, "I learned much about screen acting, and had come to recognise all the little faults and exaggerations that I had brought with me from the stage." By the time he made his fifth, and first really important, movie, *The Sin Flood,* he had adjusted to camera technique and was projecting the brave stalwart personality movie audiences, men as well as women, found attractive.

His widowed mother came to Hollywood to live with him. A gracious

woman and an accomplished water colourist, she usually accompanied him to the *premières* he attended. But when fan-magazine writers sentimentalised that she was his "best girl," Dix scoffed: "Bunk! She's my mother."

Later, when he started going to parties with a succession of pretty girls, most of whom were his current leading ladies — Bebe Daniels, May Collins, Mary Brian, Lois Wilson, Marceline Day — and the columns gushed that he was at last engaged, he retorted that much as he admired these ladies, he was not engaged, nor even in love, and that he didn't intend to consider marriage until he fell in love.

His blunt honesty helped to age more than one publicity man. When Goldwyn sent him to England to play the lead in Sir Hall Caine's *The Christian,* a press release asserted that Dix had been selected "over eighty other stars."

"More bunk!" said Dix in a press release of his own. "I was lucky to get the part, and got it because they couldn't find anybody willing to take it. John Barrymore, James Kirkwood, and H. B. Warner all turned it down." When a neophyte reported that Dix had risked life and limb performing a hazardous stunt, Dix at once answered that he always had a well-paid, experienced stuntman who "knows what he's doing. I don't." The shrewder publicity men soon realised they got better copy when they let Dix tell the truth.

The Christian made him the most promising young actor in films. Said the critic for "Picturegoer": "The acting of Richard Dix in the part of John Storm again goes to prove how very wrong Charles Chaplin was when he said that Richard would never become a successful cinema actor."*

Goldwyn was grooming Dix for the title-role in *Ben Hur,* but when Wallace Reid's death early in 1923 forced Paramount to find a replacement, Dix signed a contract with them. He was a good business man and negotiated an agreement that soon sent his weekly salary far beyond that ever paid to Reid.

Dix played some of the parts that had been intended for Reid: in the Byron Morgan auto story, *Racing Hearts;* he was the virtuous hero in the modern story of DeMille's *The Ten Commandments;* and the leads in two Zane Grey Westerns, *To the Last Man* and *Call of the Canyon.* But what he projected was not at all similar to the handsome, insouciant, daredevil image which Reid had created. Dix was light-hearted, wholesome, completely masculine, and very solid and American.

Hollywood never had any lure for Dix, and he was delighted in 1924 when Paramount sent him to New York, where he remained for nearly three years, shooting most of his films on location or at Paramount's Astoria studios on Long Island.

He first received solo star billing in a fast-moving, romantic comedy called *Manhattan,* and Paramount was soon casting as leading lady to Dix all the promising young actresses they wanted seen by a wide public. Jacqueline Logan, Nancy Carroll, Esther Ralston, Jean Arthur, Alyce Mills, Thelma Todd, and Frances Howard (who soon quit to become Mrs. Samuel Goldwyn) all cut their Paramount teeth in Dix films.

*In the early Twenties Chaplin fancied himself as Hollywood's top Lothario, which he was. But every time a girl he was courting also chose to be seen in public with a young actor, and especially with one not yet a star, Chaplin's pique took childish forms. His denigration of Dix occured over May Collins, who, after she became leading lady on the Goldwyn lot, started going out in public with Dix.

When Dix thought some unknown had potentialities, he did everything he could to get that player started. Jeanette MacDonald and Ramon Novarro are only two of many for whom he tried to get a break, only to find that even he could not buck front-office politics. Of his efforts to help Novarro break into films, Dix said: "I was going with a girl named Derelys Perdue, who danced at the Kinema Theatre in Los Angeles. Her dancing partner was a handsome young Mexican named Ramon Samaniegos. I had seen him play a bit in a Mabel Normand picture. And he *played* it! I was so sold on him I tried to induce Paramount to give him a chance. No one seemed especially interested.

So I took it upon myself to have a screen test made of him. Photographed it myself. At that time Colleen Moore and I were being co-featured in *The Wall Flower,* and directed by Rupert Hughes. After the screen test, I tried again to interest Paramount in Ramon. I even tried to persuade Mr. Goldwyn to get him as the hero in *Hungry Hearts* (a role Dix had turned down). I failed.

"About a month later, Ramon got his first good break in *Omar Khayyam,* which was released under another title (*A Lover's Oath*). Then Rex Ingram gave him a chance in *The Prisoner of Zenda,* and Ramon changed his last name to Novarro. Who doesn't know him now?"

Dix was an easy man to work with, and when he liked a co-worker who was both as easy and professional as he, he would request that director, writer, or player to be assigned again to his unit. Even a cursory glance at the index of his films will reveal recurring names, including those of such directors as Gregory LaCava, Paul Sloane, Frank Tuttle, and Mal St. Clair. LaCava started as a gag-writer on Dix pictures, and Dix liked his work so much that he got him assigned as his director for *Womanhandled.* Later, at RKO, he did the same thing for J. Walter Ruben, who had written the scripts for a succession of his starring vehicles. The names of such first-rate supporting players as Edna May Oliver, Noah Beery, Gunboat Smith, Walter Long, Paul Panzer, William Orlamond, George Seigmann, and Charles Beyer reappear in the casts of many Dix films.

Some of Dix's Paramount silents are memorable only because they are outstanding examples of his clean-cut American appeal. William C. de Mille's film version of Owen Davis's Pulitzer prizewinning play, *Icebound,* is especially notable for the way in which it presented Dix as the reluctant hero. Several years ago in London, I saw *The Lucky Devil* again at the National Film Theatre and found Dix, as the happy-go-lucky hero of that old Byron Morgan racing-formula story, still very entertaining. The same may be said for a football comedy, *The Quarterback,* and for *Let's Get Married,* an amusing variation of that perennial farce, *The Man from Mexico.* The hero of those comedies always got himself into such a predicament that it seemed impossible for him to win, and then, by a series of surprise story twists, everything changed in his favour, and he emerged, as he should, triumphant over all odds. This was the basic and well-developed plan in all the big Harold Lloyd comedies, and it worked equally effectively in the Dix romantic comedies.

Whenever Dix disagreed with studio policy, he made no secret of his feelings, and when Paramount closed down its Eastern studios and he was obliged to return to Hollywood, he complained in no uncertain terms. Then, when Paramount bought up the rights to *Quicksands,* a picture he had made in 1923 that had been given only a limited release, and re-released it in 1927, expecting to make a quick profit on his name, he demanded that he be allowed to buy up his contract for a million in cash.

Paramount refused the offer, promised to withdraw the offending re-release and sought to conciliate him by offering a salary hike ($4500 on a straight 52-week yearly contract). They issued a press-release which asserted that he was their biggest moneymaker (followed by Adolphe Menjou and Bebe Daniels) Dix was mollified, but things were never again really amicable between him and Paramount.

In that same year (1927), the talking film brought about a complete re-organisation of Paramount's brass. Dix was impatient to make his talkie *début,* and when his good friend, producer William Le Baron, left Paramount, the studio insisted he continue to turn out routine silent programmers, since they could be profitably exploited in the American hinterlands and abroad, where the talkie was still only talked about. Not until 1929 did Paramount agree to Dix making a talkie, and, aware that they were going to lose him, forced him to complete his contract with them in three unimportant talking films.

Meanwhile, Le Baron had become one of the front-rank producers at the new RKO studios and had already opened the door for a brilliant new career to Bebe Daniels, who had also been given the slough-off treatment, at Paramount. So Le Baron signed Dix to an RKO contract, and supervised Dix's advent there as a talkie star, presenting him first in the sure-fire mystery comedy, *Seven Keys to Baldpate.*

Dix hit the big-time again with his fourth RKO release, as tne colourful Yancey Cravat in *Cimarron.* That film was not only voted by the youthful Academy of Motion Pictures Arts and Sciences as the best picture of the previous year, but gained for its stars, Dix and Irene Dunne, nominations as best actor and actress.

Incidentally, Dix had helped Irene Dunne get the heroine's role. RKO favoured Fay Bainter, and even director Wesley Ruggles, when the name of Irene Dunne was first brought up, said he wanted an actress with more experience. Thanks to make-up man Ernie Westmore and still photographer Ernest Bracken, Miss Dunne spent a Saturday afternoon shooting photographs, in costume and make-up, in order to show how convincingly she could age. Dix was in Le Baron's office on Monday morning when the Dunne pictures were put on Le Baron's desk with a note from Westmore: "This is Irene Dunne, the girl who should play the lead in *Cimarron."* Le Baron was convinced enough to order a screen test, and Dix at once volunteered to make the test with her. He did, and she got the part.

Norbert Lusk, reviewing *Cimarron* in "Picture Play," wrote: "Yancey is so easily Richard Dix's best performance that everything else he has done seems preparation for this triumph. The complex character of the idealistic, rhetorical spellbinder is the most difficult Dix has ever undertaken, and could easily have become a thing of bombast and heroics in hands less adept than Mr. Dix's. But the actor's humour and charm, his good nature and manliness, succeed in making the character understandable and sympathetic."

Dix made twenty-seven films for RKO, and though none of them ever again offered him the scope of *Cimarron,* they were all well-produced and provided him with a good range — from the gangster who inherits an orphan boy and

Richard Dix and William Collier, Jr., in Cimarron

has to reform in Rex Beach's *Young Donovan's Kid* to the devil-may-care father protecting his daughter from her own venal mother in *His Greatest Gamble,* and on to Dix's final film for RKO, Val Lewton's *The Ghost Ship,* in which he played a mentally deranged sea captain finding excuses for murdering members of his crew.

Away from the studio, Dix continued to be regarded as a social enigma. After his mother's death (1924), he maintained a bachelor's apartment and between pictures went fishing or to New York to see the new plays. He was a rich man, with big real estate holdings in the East and on the Pacific Coast. When the 1929 stock market crashed, there were those who gleefully announced that he must be broke. Said Dix: "The only money I have lost was on paper."

He continued to go his independent way, and turned down most invitations. When he appeared at a public function, it was usually with Lois Wilson, his favourite leading lady. And then, just when Hollywood had about conceded he was not the marrying kind, he married Winifred Coe, a San Francisco socialite, on October 20, 1931. They had a daughter, Martha Mary Ellen Brimmer, but two years of marriage ended in their divorce in Mexico.

In 1932 Dix starred in a picture in London — the action-spectacle, *Trans-Atlantic Tunnel*. He was much admired abroad. Michael Orme wrote in the "Illustrated London News": "Mr. Dix is one of those actors who combines the 'grand manner' with keen concentration and an incisiveness that lend to a part of even conventional contours an inwardness the part itself does not possess."

Shortly after his return to Hollywood, Dix bought a 148-acre ranch in the Santa Monica mountains near Topanga. It had a fifteen-room farmhouse that boasted everything except a telephone. Dix's pleasures there were breeding prize dogs and raising turkeys.

And on June 29, 1934, he married, in Jersey City, his secretary of six months, Virginia Webster. She bore him identical-twin sons, Richard Jr. and Robert, and they later adopted a baby daughter, Sara Sue. The marriage was happy, and lasted.

The films Dix made in the last decade of his career included some unusually well-made Westerns. He was excellent as Sam Houston in Republic's *Man of Conquest,* and two of his best-liked vehicles were Universal's *Badlands of*

Richard Dix with C. Henry Gordon in HELL'S HIGHROAD

Dakota, in which he played Wild Bill Hickok, and Paramount's *Tombstone, the Town Too Tough to Die*, in which he was Wyatt Earp.

While he was making *The Ghost Ship*, his last picture at RKO, I was working on a nearby set (as dialogue director for *Curse of the Cat People*, the original screenplay of which I had written). I met Dix and frequently visited him on-set, and lunched with him and Val Lewton. I noticed on one occasion that, while waiting for a camera call, he was reading a book of essays by H. L. Mencken, and he told me that while working at Paramount's Eastern studio, he had known both Mencken and George Jean Nathan, and counted them as friends. Like them, he had frequently dined downtown at Luchow's, and he was full of fond memories of Manhattan. He hadn't liked New York when he was a struggling actor, but during the Paramount years the city had come to mean a great deal to him, particularly the theatre. "I sometimes wish I had the drive to continue in both films and theatre," he told me.

I suspected then that he was not in the best of health, for he was unusually red of face and short of breath. "Blood pressure," he explained. "I've had to cut down on the booze, and no more big action-stuff for yours truly. But the industry's been very good to me, and I'll keep going as long as they want me."

In the next four years he made seven pictures at Columbia — low-budget thrillers suggested by that longtime popular CBS radio programme, *The Whistler*. Well-produced, they were extremely popular, and even the critics thought some of them far from run-of-the-mill.

In October 1948, Dix had a serious heart attack and was in a Monrovia sanitarium. Shortly thereafter, he sold his Santa Monica ranch, and he and his wife sailed for a European vacation. In August 1949, they boarded ship at Cherbourg — and before it sailed, he had another heart attack.

Nevertheless, he remained on board; but on reaching New York, he was briefly hospitalised before being allowed to take the train for California. Then, at Chicago, he was taken off the 20th Century Limited in a practically pulseless state, and was in Chicago's Presbyterian Hospital four weeks, constantly asking to be allowed to return home. At length, he was flown to Los Angeles, and died in the Hollywood Presbyterian Hospital on September 20, 1949. His physician called the cause of death "acute cardiac collapse."

His estate was in the neighbourhood of two and a half million dollars.

His twin sons entered the University of California at Santa Barbara. Richard Dix. Jr, married, and was a father, at sixteen. Two years later he was dead, the victim of a summer logging camp accident at Pondosa, in Northern California. His twin, Robert, has married twice; was once under contract as an actor at M-G-M; and is now head of an independent production company, Dix International Pictures; on occasion he still plays supporting roles in films and television. Nearly seven months after being widowed, Mrs. Dix married Walter Van de Kamp, head of a chain of Southern California bakeries.

At least three of Richard Dix's pictures — *The Christian, The Ten Commandments*, and *Cimarron* — are landmarks in the history of American films. And his acting credo — "Be honest, and you will be believed" — is still the very essence of the acting art.

RICHARD DIX FILMOGRAPHY

ONE OF MANY (1917). Social drama; in a villain's role, as a petty blackmailer. *Dir:/Sc:* W. Christy Cabanné. *With* Frances Nelson, Niles Welch, Harold Entwhistle, Shirley Bryson, Mary Mersch, Caroline Harris, Walter Worden, Adella Baker. *Prod:* Metro. 5 reels.

NOT GUILTY (1921). Melodrama; in a dual role: as identical twin brothers, Paul and Arthur Ellison. *Dir:* Sidney Franklin. *Sc:* J. G. Alexander and E. B. Hesser (from a novel, "Parrot and Co.," by Harold McGrath). *With* Sylvia Breamer, Herbert Prior, Molly Malone. *Prod:* First National. 7 reels.

DANGEROUS CURVE AHEAD (1921). Domestic comedy drama; as Harley Jones. *Dir:* E. Mason Hopper. *Sc:* Julien Josephson (from a story by Rupert Hughes). *With* Helene Chadwick, Maurice B. ("Lefty") Flynn, James Neill, Edythe Chapman, Kate Lester. *Prod:* Goldwyn. 5 reels.

ALL'S FAIR IN LOVE (1921). Romantic comedy; as Bobby Cameron. *Dir:* E. Mason Hopper. *Sc:* Arthur E. Statter (from a story by Thompson Buchanan). *With* May Collins, Marcia Manon, Raymond Hatton, Stuart Holmes. *Prod:* Goldwyn. 5 reels.

POVERTY OF RICHES (1921). Marital drama; as John Colby. *Dir:* Reginald Barker. *Sc:* Arthur E. Statter (from a story by Leroy Scott). *With* Leatrice Joy, John Bowers, Louise Lovely, Irene Rich, DeWitt Jennings, Frankie Lee. *Prod:* Goldwyn. 6 reels.

THE SIN FLOOD (1921). Psychological character drama of a group of people trapped in a basement café during a Mississippi River flood; as Bill Bear. *Dir:* Frank Lloyd. *Sc:* J. G. Hawks (from a play, "Syndafloden," by Henning Berger). *With* Helene Chadwick, James Kirkwood, John Steppling, Ralph Lewis, Howard Davies, Will Walling, William Orlamond, Darwin Karr, Otto Hoffman. (Produced on Broadway as a play translated by Frank Allen, "The Deluge," by Arthur Hopkins, with Pauline Lord; re-made as a talking film, "Way of all Men," 1930, First National, with Douglas Fairbanks Jr. and Loretta Young). *Prod:* Goldwyn. 7 reels.

THE GLORIOUS FOOL (1922). Romantic drama; as Billy Grant. *Dir:* E. Mason Hopper. *Sc:* J. G. Hawks (from two stories, "In the Pavillion" and "Twenty-two," by Mary Roberts Rinehart). *With* Helene Chadwick, Vera Lewis, Theodore von Eltz, Kate Lester, Otto Hoffman, George Cooper, Lillian Langdon, John Ince. *Prod:* Goldwyn. 5 reels.

YELLOW MEN AND GOLD (1922). Melodrama about a treasure hunt for buried gold on a deserted isle; as Parrish. *Dir/Sc:* Irvin V. Willat (from a story by Gouverneur Morris). *With* Helene Chadwick, Rosemary Theby, Henry Burrows, Richard Tucker, Fred Kohler, Henry J. Herbert, Robert Frazer, William Moran, Goro Kino, George King, William A. Carroll. *Prod:* Goldwyn. 6 reels.

THE WALLFLOWER (1922). Romantic drama; as Walt Breen. *Dir/Sc:* Rupert Hughes. *With* Colleen Moore, Laura LaPlante, Rush Hughes, Gertrude Astor, Tom Gallery, Fanny Stockbridge. *Prod:* Goldwyn. 6 reels.

FOOLS FIRST (1922). Romantic melodrama; as Tommy Frazer. *Dir:* Marshall Neilan. *Sc:* Marion Fairfax (from a story by Hugh McNair Kahler). *With* Claire Windsor, Raymond Griffith, George Seigmann, George Dromgold, Helen Lynch, Claude Gillingwater, Robert Brower. *Prod:* First National. 6 reels.

THE BONDED WOMAN (1922). Romantic melodrama; as Lee Marvin. *Dir:* Philip E. Rosen. *Sc:* Albert Shelby LeVino (from a story, "The Salving of John Somers," by John Fleming Wilson). *With* Betty Compson, John Bowers, J. Farrell MacDonald, Ethel Wales. *Prod:* Paramount. 6 reels. (Compare listing in Betty Compson filmography.)

THE CHRISTIAN (1923). Drama; as John Storm, a dedicated man of God. *Dir:* Maurice Tourneur. *Sc:* Paul Bern (from the novel by Sir Hall Caine). *With* Mae Busch, Gareth Hughes, Phyllis Haver, Cyril Chadwick, Mahlon Hamilton, Joseph Dowling, Claude Gillingwater, Beryl Mercer, Aileen Pringle, Harry Northrup, Eric Mayne. Exteriors shot in London. (Previously filmed by Vitagraph, 1914, with Earle Williams and Edith Storey; filmed also in London, 1915, George Loane Tucker director.) *Prod:* Goldwyn. 8 reels.

RACING HEARTS (1923). Automobile racing romantic drama; as Robby Smith, daredevil racer. *Dir:* Paul Powell . *Sc:* Will M. Ritchey (from a story by Byron Morgan). *With* Agnes Ayres, Theodore Roberts, Robert Cain, Warren Rogers, J. Farrell MacDonald. *Prod:* Paramount. 5 reels.

SOULS FOR SALE (1923). Romantic drama about Hollywood; as Frank Claymore, film director. *Dir:/Sc:* Rupert Hughes (from his own novel). *With* Eleanor Boardman, Barbara La Marr, Mae Busch, Frank Mayo, Lew Cody, Aileen Pringle, William Haines, Eve

Southern, Sylvia Ashton, Arthur Hoyt, Rush Hughes, David Imboden, William Orlamond, Jack Richardson, Dale Fuller, Snitz Edwards. *Prod:* Goldwyn. 8 reels.

QUICKSANDS (1923). Melodrama about drug smuggling across the Mexican border; as Lt. Bill, a U.S. cavalry officer. *Dir:* Jack Conway. *Sc:* Howard Hawks. *With* Helene Chadwick, Alan Hale, Noah Beery, J. Farrell MacDonald, George Cooper, Tom Wilson, Dick Sutherland, Hardee Kirkland, Walter Long, Jean Hersholt, Edwin Stevens, Frank Campeau, Lionel Belmore. *Prod:* American. 6 reels. (Re-released by Paramount, 1927.)

THE WOMAN WITH FOUR FACES (1923) Melodrama; as Richard Templer, district attorney. *Dir:* Herbert Brenon. *Sc:* George Hopkins (from play by Bayard Veiller). *With* Betty Compson, George Fawcett, Theodore von Eltz, Joseph Kilgour, James Farley, Guy Oliver, Charles Stevenson, Gladden James, Eulalie Jensen. *Prod:* Paramount. 6 reels. (Compare listing in Betty Compson filmography.)

TO THE LAST MAN (1923). Arizona feudal drama between the Isbels and the Jorths; as Jean Isbel. *Dir:* Victor Fleming. *Sc:* Doris Schroeder (from a novel by Zane Grey). *With* Lois Wilson, Noah Beery, Robert Edeson, Frank Campeau, Fred Huntley, Edward Brady, Eugene Pallette, Guy Oliver, Winifred Greenwood, Leonard Clapham. *Prod:* Paramount. 7 reels. (Re-made, 1933, with Randolph Scott in the Dix role.)

THE TEN COMMANDMENTS (1923). Melodramatic sermon; as John McTavish, the son who keeps the Commandments. *Dir:* Cecil B. DeMille. *Sc:* Jeanie Macpherson (from the Holy Bible, Book of Exodus, the first part; and an original story for the second part). *With* (Part I) Theodore Roberts, Charles de Roche, Estelle Taylor, Julia Faye, Terrence Moore, James Neill, W. Lawson Butt, Clarence Burton, Noble Johnson; (Part II) Leatrice Joy, Rob La Rocque, Edythe Chapman, Nita Naldi, Robert Edeson, Charles Ogle, Agnes Ayres. (Dix is in only Part II, This did not figure in the 1956 re-make, which was devoted entirely to the Moses story.) *Prod:* Paramount. 13 reels.

CALL OF THE CANYON (1923). Romantic drama of the Southwest; as Glenn Kilbourne. *Dir:* Victor Fleming. *Sc:* Doris Schroeder and Edfrid A. Bingham (from the novel by Zane Grey). With Lois Wilson, Marjorie Daw, Noah Beery, Ricardo Cortez, Fred Huntley, Lillian Leighton, Helen Dunbar, Leonard Clapham, Edward Clayton, Dorothy Seastrom, Laura Anson, Charles Richards, Ralph Yearsley, Arthur Rankin, Mervyn LeRoy. *Prod:* Paramount. 7 reels.

THE STRANGER (1924). Psychological melodrama; as Larry Darrant. *Dir:* Joseph Henabery. *Sc:* Edfrid A. Bingham (from a story, "The First and the Last", by John Galsworthy). *With* Betty Compson, Lewis Stone, Tully Marshall, Robert Schable, Frank Nelson. (Re-made in England, 1940, as *21 Days Together*, with Laurence Oliver and Vivien Leigh.) *Prod:* Paramount. 7 reels. (Compare listing in Betty Compson filmography.)

ICEBOUND (1924). Romantic drama of New England; as Ben Jordan. *Dir:* William C. de Mille. *Sc:* Clara Beranger (from the Pulitzer Prize winning play by Owen Davis). *With* Lois Wilson, Vera Reynolds, Edna May Oliver, Helen Dubois, Mary Foy, Ethel Wales, Joseph Depew, Frank Shannon, Alice Chapin, John Daly Murphy. *Prod:* Paramount. 7 reels.

UNGUARDED WOMEN (1924). Romantic drama; as Douglas Allbright. *Dir:* Alan Crosland. *Sc:* James Ashmore Creelman (from a story, "Face," by Lucy Stone Terrill). *With* Bebe Daniels, Mary Astor, Walter McGrail, Frank Losee, Helen Lindroth, Harry Mestayer, Donald Hall, Joe King. *Prod:* Paramount. 6 reels. (Compare listing in Bebe Daniels filmography.)

SINNERS IN HEAVEN (1924). Desert island romantic drama; as Alan Croft. *Dir:* Alan Crosland. *Sc:* James Ashmore Creelman (from the novel by Clive Arden). *With* Bebe Daniels, Montagu Love, Holmes Herbert, Effie Shannon, Florence Billings, Betty Hilburn. *Prod:* Paramount. 7 reels. (Compare listing in Bebe Daniels filmography.)

MANHATTAN (1924). Romantic adventure in Manhattan's Hell's Kitchen; as Peter Minuit, the last of his name. *Dir:* R. H. Burnside. *Sc:* Paul Sloane and Frank Tuttle (from a story, "The Definite Object," by Jeffrey Farnol). *With* Jacqueline Logan, Gregory Kelly, George Seigmann, Edna May Oliver, Gunboat Smith, Oscar Figman, Alice Chapin. Dix's first starring vehicle at Paramount. *Prod:* Paramount. 6,329 ft.

A MAN MUST LIVE (1925). Modern adventure; as Geoffrey Farnell, penniless captain, who becomes a newspaperman. *Dir:* Paul Sloane. *Sc:* James Ashmore Creelman (from a novel, "Jungle Law," by I. A. R. Wylie). *With* Jacqueline Logan, George Nash, Edna Murphy, Charles Beyer, Dorothy Walters, William Ricciardi, Arthur Housman. *Prod:* Paramount. 6 reels.

TOO MANY KISSES (1925). Adventure story of an American traveling in Spain; as Richard Gaylord. *Dir:* Paul Sloane. *Sc:* Gerald Duffy (from a story, "A Maker of Gestures," by John Monk Saunders). *With* Frances Howard, Frank Currier, William Powell, Paul Panzer,

Harpo Marx, Joe Burke, Alyce Mills. *Prod:* Paramount. 6 reels.

MEN AND WOMEN (1925). Romantic triangle drama; as Will Prescott. *Dir:* William C. de Mille. *Sc:* Clara Beranger (from the play by David Belasco and Henry C. DeMille). *With* Claire Adams, Neil Hamilton, Robert Edeson, Henry Stephenson. *Prod:* Paramount. 6 reels. (Filmed by Biograph, 1914.)

THE SHOCK PUNCH (1925). Manhattan adventure; as Randall Lee Savage, who wants to be a prizefighter but becomes a riveter. *Dir:* Paul Sloane. *Sc:* Luther Reed (from a play by John Monk Saunders). *With* Frances Howard, Theodore Babcock, Percy Moore, Charles Beyer, Gunboat Smith, Walter Long, Paul Panzer. *Prod:* Paramount. 6 reels.

THE LUCKY DEVIL (1925). Auto racing drama; as "Randy" Farnum, a drivin' fool. *Dir:* Frank Tuttle. *Sc:* Townsend Martin (from a story by Byron Morgan). *With* Esther Ralston, Edna May Oliver, Tom Findley, Anthony Jowitt, Mary Foy, Gunboat Smith, Charles Sellon. *Prod:* Paramount. 6 reels.

THE VANISHING AMERICAN (AKA, GB, *The Vanishing Race*) (1925). Dramatic propaganda of mistreatment of the Indians; as Nophaie. *Dir:* George B. Seitz. *Sc:* Ethel Doherty (from an adaptation by Lucien Hubbard of a novel by Zane Grey). *With* Lois Wilson, Noah Beery, Malcolm McGregor, Charles Crockett, Bert Woodruff, Guy Oliver, Shannon Day, John Webb Dillon. *Prod:* Paramount. 10 reels.

WOMANHANDLED (1926). Romantic comedy; as Bill Dana. *Dir:* Gregory La Cava. *Sc:* Luther Reed (from a story by Arthur Stringer). *With* Esther Ralston, Cora Williams, Olive Tell, Eli Nadel, Edmund Breese, Margaret Morris, Ivan Simpson, Edgar Nelson, Tammany Young. *Prod:* Paramount. 7 reels.

LET'S GET MARRIED (1926). Romantic farce; as Billy Dexter. *Dir:* Gregory La Cava. *Sc:* Luther Reed (from a farce, "The Man from Mexico," by J. A. DuSouchet). *With* Lois Wilson, Nat Pendleton, Edna May Oliver, Douglas MacPherson, Gunboat Smith, Joseph Kilgour, Tom Findley. *Prod:* Paramount. 7 reels. (Filmed as a silent, 1914, starring John Barrymore.)

SAY IT AGAIN (1926). Mythical kingdom romance; as Bob Howard. *Dir:* Gregory La Cava. *Sc:* Luther Reed and Ray Harris. *With* Alyce Mills, Chester Conklin, Gunboat Smith, Bernard Randall, Paul Porcasi, Ida Waterman, William Ricciardi. *Prod:* Paramount. 8 reels.

THE QUARTERBACK (1926). College football romantic drama; as Jack Stone, quarterback. *Dir:* Fred Newmeyer. *Sc:* Ray Harris

(from a story by W. O. McGeehan and William Slavens McNutt). *With* Esther Ralston, Harry Beresford, David Butler, Robert W. Craig, Mona Palma. *Prod:* Paramount. 8 reels.

PARADISE FOR TWO (1927). Romantic comedy; as Steve Porter. *Dir:* Gregory La Cava. *Sc:* J. Clarkson Miller (ad. by Ray Harris and Tom J. Crizer from a story by Howard E. Rogers). *With* Betty Bronson, Edmund Breese, André Beranger. *Prod:* Paramount. 7 reels.

KNOCKOUT REILLY (1927). Prizefight drama; as Dundee "Knockout" Reilly. *Dir:* Mal St. Clair. *Sc:* Pierre Collins and Kenneth Raisbeck (from a story, "The Hunch," by Albert Payson Terhune). *With* Mary Brian, Jack Renault, Harry Gribbon, Osgood Perkins, Lucia Backus Segar, Larry McGrath. *Prod:* Paramount. 7 reels.

MAN POWER (1927). Romantic drama; as Tom Roberts, a kind of male Cinderella. *Dir:* Clarence Badger. *Sc:* Louise Long (from an adaptation by Ray Harris and Sam Mintz of a story by Byron Morgan). *With* Mary Brian, Philip Strange, Charles H. Mailes, Oscar Smith, George Irving, Charles Clary. *Prod:* Paramount. 6 reels.

SHANGHAI BOUND (1927). Adventure in China; as Jim Bucklin, a domineering sea captain. *Dir:* Luther Reed. *Sc:* John Goodrich and Ray Harris (from a story by E. S. O'Reilly). *With* Mary Brian, Charles Beyer, George Irving, Jocelyn Lee, Tom MacGuire, Arthur Hoyt. *Prod:* Paramount. 6 reels.

THE GAY DEFENDER (1927). Romance of Old California; as Joaquin Murietta, bandit. *Dir:* Gregory La Cava. *Sc:* Ray Harris, Sam Mintz and Kenneth Raisbeck (from a story by Grover Jones). *With* Thelma Todd, Fred Kohler, Robert Brower, Fred Esmelton. *Prod:* Paramount. 7 reels.

SPORTING GOODS (1928). Romantic comedy; as Richard Shelby, a sporting goods salesman. *Dir:* Mal St. Clair. *Sc:* Tom J. Crizer and Ray Harris. *With* Gertrude Olmstead, Ford Sterling, Philip Strange, Myrtle Stedman, Wade Boteler, Claude King, Maude Turner Gordon. *Prod:* Paramount. 6 reels.

EASY COME, EASY GO (1928). Romantic crook drama; as Robert Parker. *Dir:* Frank Tuttle. *Sc:* Florence Ryerson (from a play by Owen Davis). *With* Nancy Carroll, Charles Sellon, Frank Currier, Arnold Kent, Guy Oliver. *Prod:* Paramount. 6 reels. (Re-filmed as a talkie, 1947).

WARMING UP (1928). Baseball romantic comedy; as Bert Tulliver, rube pitcher who finally makes the World Series. *Dir:* Fred Newmeyer. *Sc:* Ray Harris (from a story by

Sam Mintz). *With* Jean Arthur, Claude King, Philo McCullough, Wade Boteler, Roscoe Karns. *Prod:* Paramount. 8 reels.

MORAN OF THE MARINES (1928). Romantic melodrama in China; as Michael Moran. *Dir:* Frank Strayer. *Sc:* Agnes Brand Leahy (from an adaptation by Sam Mintz and Ray Harris of a story by Linton Wells). *With* Ruth Elder, Roscoe Karns, Brooks Benedict, Capt. E. H. Calvert, Duke Martin, Tetsu Komai. *Prod:* Paramount. 7 reels.

REDSKIN (1929). Drama of an outcast Indian; as Wing Foot, a runner. *Dir:* Victor Schertzinger. *Sc:* Elizabeth Pickett. *With* Gladys Belmont, Tully Marshall, Jane Novak, George Rigas, Noble Johnson. Movietone, with Sound. Technicolor sequences. *Prod:* Paramount. 9 reels.

NOTHING BUT THE TRUTH (1929). Romantic farce; as Robert Bennett, who bets that he can tell the absolute truth for twenty-four hours. *Dir:* Victor Schertzinger. *Sc:* John McGowan (from the play by James Montgomery and novel by Frederic S. Isham). *With* Wynne Gibson, Helen Kane, Dorothy Hall, Berton Churchill, Louis John Bartels, Ned Sparks. Richard Dix's *début* in talking films. (Previously filmed in 1921 with Taylor Holmes; again filmed in 1941 with Bob Hope.) *Prod:* Paramount. 8 reels.

THE WHEEL OF LIFE (1929). Romantic melodrama in the Orient; as Captain Leslie Yeullet, who falls in love with his colonel's wife. *Dir:* Victor Schertzinger. *Sc:* John Farrow, with dialogue by Julian Johnson (from the play by James B. Fagan). *With* Esther Ralston, O. P. Heggie, Arthur Hoyt, Myrtle Stedman, Larry Steers, Regis Toomey, Nigel de Brulier. Movietone, both Sound and Silent versions. *Prod:* Paramount. 6 reels.

THE LOVE DOCTOR (1929). Romantic comedy; as Dr. Gerald Summer. *Dir:* Melville Brown. *Sc:* J. Walter Ruben and Guy Bolton (from the play, "The Boomerang," by Winchell Smith and Victor Mapes). *With* June Collyer, Morgan Farley, Miriam Seegar, Winifred Harris, Lawford Davidson, Gale Henry. Dix's last film on his long-term contract at Paramount. (Previously filmed as a silent, 1925, by Schulberg-Preferred.) *Prod:* Paramount. 6 reels.

SEVEN KEYS TO BALDPATE (1929). Mystery comedy; as William Magee, who must turn out a detective thriller in twenty-four hours. *Dir:* Reginald Barker. *Sc:* Jane Murfin (from a story by Earl Derr Biggers and a play by George M. Cohan). *With* Miriam Seegar, Crauford Kent, Margaret Livingston, Joseph Allen, Lucien Littlefield, DeWitt Jennings, Carleton Macy, Nella Walker, Joe Herbert, Allan Roscoe, Harvey Clark, Edith Yorke. (Previously filmed in 1917 with George M.

Cohan, and in 1925 with Douglas MacLean; re-filmed in 1935 with Gene Raymond, and in 1947 with Philip Terry.) *Prod:* RKO-Radio. 8 reels.

LOVIN' THE LADIES (1930). Romantic comedy; as Peter Darby, electrician, who masquerades as a Park Avenue playboy. *Dir:* Melville Brown. *Sc:* J. Walter Ruben (from the play, "I Love You," by William LeBaron). *With* Lois Wilson, Allen Kearns, Rita LeRoy, Virginia Sale, Anthony Bushell, Henry Armetta. Working title: *The Roughneck Lover.* *Prod:* RKO-Radio. 7 reels.

SHOOTING STRAIGHT (1930). Big time gambling and crook melodrama; as Larry Sheldon. *Dir:* George Archainbaud. *Sc:* Wallace Smith, with dialogue by J. Walter Ruben (from a story by Barney Serecky). *With* Mary Lawlor, James Neill, Matthew Betz, George Cooper, William Janney, Robert E. O'Connor. Working title: *Dead Game.* *Prod:* RKO-Radio. 8 reels.

CIMARRON (1931). Romantic Western of the Oklahoma land rush; as Yancey Cravat. *Dir:* Wesley Ruggles. *Sc:* Howard Estabrook (from the novel by Edna Ferber). *With* Irene Dunne, Estelle Taylor, Edna May Oliver, Nance O'Neil, William Collier Jr., Roscoe Ates, George E. Stone, Stanley Fields, Robert McWade, Frank Darrien, Eugene Jackson, Dolores Brown, William Orlamond, Helen Parrish, Donald Dillaway, Nell Craig. (Dix was nominated for Best Performance by an Actor by Academy members.) (Re-made, 1960, M-G-M, with Glenn Ford.) *Prod:* RKO-Radio. 13 reels.

YOUNG DONOVAN'S KID (AKA, GB, *Jim Donovan's Kid*) (1931). Drama; as Jim Donovan, gangster, who adopts an orphan boy and has to reform. *Dir:* Fred Niblo. *Sc:* J. Walter Ruben (from a story, "Big Brother," by Rex Beach). *With* Jackie Cooper, Marion Shilling, Boris Karloff, Frank Sheridan, Dick Rush, Fred Kelsey, Wilfred Lucas. (Filmed as a silent, 1923, with Tom Moore.) *Prod:* RKO-Radio. 9 reels.

PUBLIC DEFENDER (1931). Courtroom-gangster drama; as Pike Winslow, who defends crooks, and is known as "The Reckoner." *Dir:* J. Walter Ruben. *Sc:* Bernard Schubert (from the novel, "The Splendid Crime," by George Goodschild). *With* Shirley Grey, Boris Karloff, Paul Hurst, Nella Walker, Edmund Breese, Purnell Pratt, Alan Roscoe, Ruth Weston, Frank Sheridan, Carl Gerrard. *Prod:* RKO-Radio. 8 reels.

SECRET SERVICE (1931). Civil War romantic melodrama; as Lewis Dumont, Yankee captain. *Dir:* J. Walter Ruben. *Sc:* Bernard Schubert (from the play by William Gillette). *With* Shirley Grey, William Post Jr., Gavin Gordon, Fred Warren, Nance O'Neil, Virginia

Sale,.Florence Lake, Clarence Muse. (Previously filmed in 1919 with Robert Warwick.) *Prod:* RKO-Radio. 7 reels.

THE LOST SQUADRON (1932). Melodrama of the Hollywood stunt flyer; as Captain Gibson. *Dir:* George Archainbaud. *Sc:* Wallace Smith, with dialogue by Herman J. Mankiewicz and Robert Presnell (from a story by Dick Grace). *With* Mary Astor, Erich von Stroheim, Dorothy Jordan, Joel McCrea, Robert Armstrong, Hugh Herbert, Ralph Ince, Dick Grace, Art Goebel, Leo Nomis, Frank Clark. *Prod:* RKO-Radio. 79m.

ROAR OF THE DRAGON (1932). Melodrama in China; as Carson, captain of a Chinese river boat. *Dir:* Wesley Ruggles. *Sc:* Howard Estabrook (from a story by George Kibbe Turner, Merian C. Cooper and Jane Bigelow). *With* Gwili Andre, Edward Everett Horton, Arline Judge, ZaSu Pitts, Dudley Digges, C. Henry Gordon, Arthur Stone, William Orlamond. *Prod:* RKO-Radio. 68m.

HELL'S HIGHWAY (1932). Realistic Southern prison camp drama; as Duke Ellis, prisoner. *Dir:* Rowland Brown. *Sc:* Samuel Ornitz, Robert Tasker and Rowland Brown. *With* Louise Carter, Tom Brown, Rochelle Hudson, C. Henry Gordon, Warner Richmond, Charles Middleton, Clarence Muse, Stanley Fields, Fuzzy Knight. *Prod:* RKO-Radio. 7 reels.

THE CONQUERORS (1932). Drama of an American family weathering the panics of 1870, 1902 and 1913; as Roger Standish. *Dir:* William Wellman. *Sc:* Robert Lord (from a story by Howard Estabrook). *With* Ann Harding, Edna May Oliver, Guy Kibbee, Julie Haydon, Donald Cook, Harry Holman, Jason Robards Sr., Walter Walker, Marilyn Knowlden, Wally Albright. *Prod:* RKO-Radio. 8 reels.

THE GREAT JASPER (1933). Romantic American drama: as Jasper Horn. *Dir:* J. Walter Ruben. *Sc:* Samuel Ornitz and H. W. Hanemann (from a novel by Fulton Oursler). *With* Florence Eldridge, Wera Engels, Edna May Oliver, Walter Walker, David Durand, Bruce Cabot, Betty Furness. *Prod:* RKO-Radio. 85m.

NO MARRIAGE TIES (1933). Marital and success drama; as Bruce Foster. *Dir:* J. Walter Ruben. *Sc:* Arthur Caesar, Sam Mintz & H. W. Hanemann (from a play, "Ad-Man," by Arch Gaffney and Charles Curran). *With* Elisabeth Allan, Alan Dinehart, Doris Kenyon, David Landau, Hilda Vaughn, Hobart Cavanaugh. Working title: *The Public Be Sold.* *Prod:* RKO-Radio. 8 reels.

DAY OF RECKONING (1933). Prison melodrama; as John Day. *Dir:* Charles Brabin. *Sc:* Zelda Sears and Eve Green (from a story by Morris Levine). *With* Madge Evans, Conway

Tearle, Una Merkel, Stuart Erwin, Spanky McFarlane, Isabel Jewell, James Bell, Raymond Hatton, Paul Hurst, Wilfred Lucas, Samuel S. Hinds. *Prod:* M-G-M. 7 reels.

THE ACE OF ACES (1933). First World War flying drama; as Lt. Rex Thorne, sculptor, who becomes a bloodthirsty flying ace. *Dir:* J. Walter Ruben. *Sc:* John Monk Saunders and H. W. Hanemann (from a story by Saunders, "Bird of Prey"). *With* Elizabeth Allan, Ralph Bellamy, Theodore Newton, Bill Cagney, Claude Stroud, Art Jarrett. *Prod:* RKO-Radio. 8 reels.

STINGAREE (1934). Romantic costume drama; as "Stingaree," a music-loving Australian bandit. *Dir:* William Wellman. *Sc:* Lynn Riggs and Leonard Spigelgass (from a story by E. W. Hornung). *With* Irene Dunne, Mary Boland, Conway Tearle, Andy Devine, Henry Stephenson, Una O'Connor, George Barraud, Reginald Owen, Snub Pollard. (Filmed in 1918 by FBO, a fifteen two-episode serial, *The Further Adventures of Stingaree,* starring True Boardman). *Prod:* RKO-Radio. 73m.

HIS GREATEST GAMBLE (1934). Father-daughter story, with the venal mother the real villain; as Philip Eden. *Dir:* John S. Robertson. *Sc:* Sidney Buchman and Harry Hervey (from a story, "Family Man," by Salisbury Field). *With* Dorothy Wilson, Bruce Cabot, Erin O'Brien-Moore, Edith Fellows, Leonard Carey, Eily Malyon. *Prod:* RKO-Radio. 72m.

WEST OF THE PECOS (1934). Western drama in Texas after the Civil War; as Pecos Smith. *Dir:* Phil E. Rosen. *Sc:* Milton Krims and John Twist (from a novel by Zane Grey). *With* Martha Sleeper, Samuel S. Hinds, Fred Kohler, Louise Beavers, Maria Alba. (Previously filmed, 1922; re-filmed, 1945). *Prod:* RKO-Radio. 7 reels.

THE ARIZONIAN (1935). Romantic Western of lawless Silver City; as Clay Tallant, reform marshal. *Dir:* Charles Vidor. *Sc:* Dudley Nichols. *With* Margot Grahame, Preston Foster, Louis Calhern, James Bush, Francis Ford. *Prod:* RKO-Radio. 8 reels.

TRANS-ATLANTIC TUNNEL (AKA, GB, *The Tunnel*). (1935). About the making of a tunnel between England and the U.S.A.; as McAllan. *Dir:* Maurice Elvey. *Sc:* Curt Siodmak, L. du Garde Peach and Clemence Dane (from a novel by B. Kellermann). *With* Madge Evans, Leslie Banks, Helen Vinson, C. Aubrey Smith, Basil Sydney, Henry Oscar, Hilda Trevelyan; and (courtesy players) Walter Huston as President of the U.S.A, and George Arliss as England's Prime Minister. (Previously made in Germany at Ufa as *Der Tunnel.*) *Prod:* Gaumont-British. 10 reels.

YELLOW DUST (1936). Western drama; as Culpepper. *Dir:* Wallace Fix. *Sc:* Cyril Hume and John Twist (from the play, "Mother Lode," by Dan Totheroh and George O'Neil. *With* Leila Hyams, Moroni Olsen, Jessie Ralph, Andy Clyde, Onslow Stevens, Victor Potel. *Prod:* RKO-Radio. 7 reels.

SPECIAL INVESTIGATOR (1936). Western melodrama of vengeance; as William Fenwick, Eastern criminal lawyer. *Dir:* Louis King. *Sc:* Louis Stevens, Thomas Lennon, Ferdinand Reyher (from a novel. "Fugitive Gold," by Erle Stanley Gardner). *With* Margaret Callahan, Erik Rhodes, Harry Jans, Owen Davis Jr., Ray Mayer, Joseph Sawyer, J. Carrol Naish, Sheila Terry, J. M. Kerrigan, Jed Prouty, Russell Hicks. *Prod:* RKO-Radio. 61m.

DEVIL'S SQUADRON (1936). Test pilot thriller; as Paul Redmond, "the man who bails out." *Dir:* Erle C. Kenton. *Sc:* Howard J. Green, Bruce Manning, Lionel Houser (from a story by Dick Grace). *With* Karen Morley, Lloyd Nolan, Shirley Ross, Henry Mollison, Gene Morgan, Gordon Jones, Thurston Hall, Boyd Irwin Sr., Bill Burrud, Cora Sue Collins, Arthur Rankin. *Prod:* Columbia. 8 reels.

THE DEVIL'S PLAYGROUND (1937). Romantic submarine melodrama; as Jack Dorgan, Navy deep sea diver. *Dir:* Erle C. Kenton. *Sc:* Liam O'Flaherty, Jerome Chodorov and Dalton Trumbo (from a story by Norma Springer). *With* Dolores Del Rio, Chester Morris, George McKay, John Gallaudet, Pierre Watkins, Ward Bond, Don Rowan, Francis McDonald, Stanley Andrews. Working Title: *The Depths Below. Prod:* Columbia. 72m. (Compare listing in Dolores Del Rio filmography.)

THE DEVIL IS DRIVING (1937). Dramatic indictment against drunken drivers; as Paul Driscoll, attorney. *Dir:* Harry Lachman. *Sc:* Jo Milward and Richard Blake (from a story by Lee Loeb and Harold Buchman). *With* Joan Perry, Nana Bryant, Elisha Cook Jr., Henry Kolker, Walter Kingsford, Ann Rutherford, Paul Harvey, John Wray. *Prod:* Columbia. 7 reels.

IT HAPPENED IN HOLLYWOOD (AKA, GB, *Once a Hero*) (1937). Drama of a has-been Western movie star who makes it back to the screen; as Tim Bart. *Dir:* Harry Lachman. *Sc:* Ethel Hill, Harvey Fergusson and Sam Fuller (from a story, "Once a Hero", by Myles Connolly). *With* Fay Wray, Victor Kilian, Franklin Pangborn, Charles Arnt, Granville Bates, William B. Davidson, Bill Burrud, Zeffie Tilbury, Harold Goodwin. *Prod:* Columbia. 67m.

BLIND ALIBI (1938). Melodrama of a sculptor who feigns blindness and thwarts a blackmailer; as Paul Dove. *Dir:* Lew Landers. *Sc:* Lionel Houser, Harry Segall and Ron Ferguson (from a story by William Joyce Cowan.) *With* Whitney Bourne, Eduardo Ciannelli, Frances Mercer, Paul Guilfoyle, Richard Lane, Walter Miller, Frank M. Thomas. *Prod:* RKO-Radio. 7 reels.

SKY GIANT (1938). Aviation drama; as "Stag," a flier unfairly grounded. *Dir:* Lew Landers. *Sc:* Lionel Houser. *With* Chester Morris, Joan Fontaine, Harry Carey, Paul Guilfoyle, Robert Strange, Vicki Lester, James Bush. *Prod:* RKO-Radio. 80m.

TWELVE CROWDED HOURS (1939). Melodrama of a star reporter vs. an underworld policy king; as Nick Green. *Dir:* Lew Landers. *Sc:* John Twist (from a story by Garrett Ford and Peter Ruric). *With* Lucille Ball. Allen Lane, Donald McBride, Dorothy Lee, Cy Kendall, Granville Bates, John Arledge, Bradley Page, Addison Richards. *Prod:* RKO-Radio. 64m.

MAN OF CONQUEST (1939). Big-scale Western drama; as Sam Houston. *Dir:* George Nichols Jr. *Sc:* Wells Root, E. E. Paramore Jr. and Jan Fortune (from a story, "Wagons Westward," by Root and Harold Shumate). *With* Gail Patrick, Joan Fontaine, Edward Ellis, George Hayes, C. Henry Gordon, Victor Jory, Robert Barrat, Robert Armstrong, Ralph Morgan, Janet Beecher, Jason Robards Sr., Lane Chandler, Ferris Taylor, Pedro de Cordoba, Leon Ames, Kathleen Lockhart, Sarah Padden. *Prod:* Republic 11 reels.

HERE I AM A STRANGER (1939). Father-son drama of rehabilitation; as Duke Allen. *Dir:* Roy Del Ruth. *Sc:* Milton Sperling and Sam Hellman (from a story by Gordon M. Hillman). *With* Richard Greene, Brenda Joyce, Roland Young, Gladys George, Katherine Aldrich, Russell Gleason, George Zucco, Edward Norris, Henry Kolker, Robert Kellard, Jan Duggan, Minor Watson. *Prod:* 20th Century-Fox. 8 reels.

RENO (1939). Dramatic father-daughter picture of the easy divorce laws in Nevada; as Bill Shear, lawyer. *Dir:* John Farrow. *Sc:* John Twist (from a story by Ellis St. Joseph). *With* Gail Patrick, Anita Louise, Paul Cavanagh, Laura Hope Crews, Louis Jean Heydt, Hobart Cavanaugh, Charles Halton, Astrid Allwyn, Joyce Compton, Frank Faylen. *Prod:* RKO-Radio. 73m.

THE MARINES FLY HIGH (1940). Marine Air Corps drama; as Lt. Darrick. *Dir:* George Nichols Jr. and Ben Stoloff. *Sc:* Jerry Cady and Lt. Commander A. J. Bolton (from a story by A. C. Edington). *With* Chester Morris, Lucille Ball, Steffi Duna, John Eldredge, Paul Harvey, Horace MacMahon, Ann Shoemaker, Nestor Paiva. *Prod:* RKO-Radio. 68m.

MEN AGAINST THE SKY (1940). Aviation drama; as Phil Mercedes, who has become a drunken stunt flier and rehabilitates himself. *Dir:* Leslie Goodwins. *Sc:* Nathaniel West (from a story by John Twist). *With* Kent Taylor, Edmund Lowe, Wendy Barrie, Granville Bates, Grant Withers, Charles Quigley. *Prod:* RKO-Radio. 75m.

CHEROKEE STRIP (1940). Western drama; as Dave Morrell, a new marshal who brings law and order to a killer-town called Goliath in Oklahoma Territory. *Dir:* Lesley Selander. *Sc:* Norman Houston and Bernard McConville (from a story by McConville). *With* Florence Rice, Victor Jory, Andy Clyde, George E. Stone, Morris Ankrum, Douglas Fowley, Addison Richards, William Henry, Tom Tyler, William Haade. *Prod:* Paramount. 9 reels.

THE ROUNDUP (1941). Western romance; as Steve. *Dir:* Lesley Selander. *Sc:* Harold Shumate (from the play by Edmund Day). *With* Patricia Morison, Preston Foster, Don Wilson, Ruth Donnelly, Betty Brewer, Douglas Dumbrille, Jerome Cowan, William Haade, Morris Ankrum, Clara Kimball Young. (Previously filmed, 1920). *Prod:* Paramount. 90m.

BADLANDS OF DAKOTA (1941). Gold Rush days in Dakota's Black Hills; as Will Bill Hickok (with Miss Farmer as Calamity Jane). *Dir:* Alfred E. Green. *Sc:* Gerald Geraghty (from a story by Harold Shumate). *With* Frances Farmer, Robert Stack, Ann Rutherford, Broderick Crawford, Hugh Herbert, Andy Devine, Lon Chaney Jr., Fuzzy Knight, Addison Richards, Samuel S. Hinds, *Prod:* Universal. 8 reels.

TOMBSTONE, THE TOWN TOO TOUGH TO DIE (1942). Western drama of the clean-up of a bad town; as Wyatt Earp, marshal. *Dir:* William McGann. *Sc:* Albert Shelby LeVino and Edward E. Paramore (from the book, "Tombstone," by Walter Noble Burns). *With* Kent Taylor, Edgar Buchanan, Frances Gifford, Don Castle, Clem Bevans, Victor Jory, Rex Bell, Charles Halton, Harvey Stephens, Beryl Wallace. Working title: *Bad Man of Arizona. Prod:* Paramount. 8 reels.

AMERICAN EMPIRE (AKA, GB, *My Son Alone*) (1942). Texas Western; as Dan Taylor, cattle breeder, who builds Texas into an empire during the Reconstruction Period following the Civil War. *Dir:* William McGann. *Sc:* J. Robert Bren, Gladys Atwater and Ben Grauman Kohn. *With* Leo Carrillo, Preston Foster, Frances Gifford, Robert Barrat, Jack La Rue, Guinn Williams, Cliff Edwards, William Farnum, Chris-Pin Martin. *Prod:* United Artists. 7,359 ft.

EYES OF THE UNDERWORLD (1943). Melodrama of the police vs. the underworld; as The Chief, forced to resign when a gangster threatens to expose his former prison record. *Dir:* Roy William Neill. *Sc:* Michael L. Simmons and Arthur Strawn (from a Maxwell Shane story). *With* Wendy Barrie, Lon Chaney Jr., Lloyd Corrigan, Don Porter, Marc

Lawrence, Wade Boteler. *Prod:* Universal. 6 reels.

BUCKSKIN FRONTIER (AKA, GB, *Iron Road*). (1943). Western drama of the battle between the railroad men and the wagon freight-haulers; as Stephen Bent, gunfighter. *Dir:* Lesley Selander. *Sc:* Norman Houston (from a book, "Buckskin Empire," by Sinclair Drago). *With* Jane Wyatt, Albert Dekker, Lee J. Cobb, Victor Jory, Lola Lane, Max Baer, Joseph Sawyer, Francis McDonald. *Prod:* United Artists. 65m.

THE KANSAN (1943). Western drama of the making of a Kansas frontier town; as John Bonniwell, elected marshal after he has routed the James Gang. *Dir:* George Archainbaud. *Sc:* Harold Shumate (from a novel, "Peace Marshal," by Frank Gruber). *With* Jane Wyatt, Albert Dekker, Eugene Pallette, Victor Jory, Robert Armstrong, Beryl Wallace, Clem Bevans, Hobart Cavanaugh, Francis McDonald, Douglas Fowley, Rod Cameron. *Prod:* United Artists. 79m.

TOP MAN (1943). Family drama of Second World War; as Tom, the father, a Navy man. *Dir:* Charles Lamont. *Sc:* Zachary Gold (from a story by Ken Goldsmith). *With* Lillian Gish, Donald O'Connor, Susanna Foster, Anne Gwynne, Peggy Ryan, Noah Beery Jr., Samuel S. Hinds, Louise Beavers, Marcia Mae Jones, David Holt. *Prod:* Universal. 8 reels.

THE GHOST SHIP (1943). Suspense drama, with murder and mystery aboard a ship; as Captain Stone, who not only has a dictator complex, but is a psychopathic killer. *Dir:* Mark Robson. *Sc:* Donald Henderson Clarke (from a story by Leo Mittler). *With* Russell Wade, Edith Barrett, Ben Bard, Edmund Glover, Skelton Knaggs, Tom Barton, Steve Winston, Robert Bice, Lawrence Tierney, Dewey Robinson, Charles Lung, Sir Lancelot. *Prod:* RKO-Radio. 69m.

THE WHISTLER (1944). Mystery suspense drama; as Earl Conrad, who pays to be killed, and then finds he has every reason to live. *Dir:* William Castle. *Sc:* Eric Taylor (from a story by J. Donald Wilson, suggested by the CBS radio programme). *With* J. Carrol Naish, Gloria Stuart, Alan Dinehart, Don Costello, Joan Woodbury, Cy Kendall, Otto Forrest. *Prod:* Columbia. 59m.

THE MARK OF THE WHISTLER (1944). Mystery suspense drama; as Lee Nugent, who establishes a false identity for himself, and finds his new personality had enemies who want him dead. *Dir:* William Castle. *Sc:* George Bricker (from a story by Cornell Woolrich). *With* Janis Carter, Porter Hall, Paul Guilfoyle, John Calvert, Matt Willis. *Prod:* Columbia. 6 reels.

THE POWER OF THE WHISTLER (1945). Murder melodrama; as William Everest, amnesiac who is also a homicidal maniac. *Dir:* Lew Landers. *Sc:* Aubrey Wisberg. *With* Janis Carter, Jeff Donnell, Loren Tindall, Tala Birell, John Abbott, Cy Kendall, Murray Alper. *Prod:* Columbia. 66m.

THE VOICE OF THE WHISTLER (1945). Romantic melodrama; as John Sinclair, who thinks he has only six months to live, and searches desperately for love. *Dir:* William Castle. *Sc:* Castle and Wilfred H. Pettit (from a story by Allan Radar). *With* Lynn Merrick, Rhys Williams, James Cardwell, Tom Kennedy, Donald Woods, Egon Brecher, Gigi Perreau. *Prod:* Columbia. 6 reels.

THE MYSTERIOUS INTRUDER (1946). Mystery and murder touch off the search for two records supposedly made by Jenny Lind; as Don Gale, private detective. *Dir:* William Castle. *Sc:* Eric Taylor. *With* Barton MacLane, Nina Vale, Regis Toomey, Helen Mowery, Mike Mazurki, Pamela Blake, Charles Lane, Edith Evanson, Isabel Withers. *Prod:* Columbia. 6 reels.

THE SECRET OF THE WHISTLER (1946). Murder mystery; as Ralph Harrison, artist, who murders two wives. *Dir:* George Sherman. *Sc:* Raymond L. Schrock (from a story by Richard Landau). *With* Leslie Brooks, Mary Currier, Michael Duane, Mona Barrie, Claire Du Brey, Ray Walker. *Prod:* Columbia. 65m.

THE 13TH HOUR (1947). Murder drama; as Steve Reynolds, who has to track down the real killer when he is accused of killing a policeman. *Dir:* William Clemens. *Sc:* Edward Bock and Raymond L. Schrock (from a story by Leslie Edgley). *With* Karen Morley, John Kellogg, Jim Bannon, Regis Toomey, Bernadene Hayes. *Prod:* Columbia. 65m.

(Richard Dix appeared as himself in a cameo role in Paramount's *Fascinating Youth,* 1926, which starred the graduating students of the only class of film actors. Sam Wood directed, and Charles "Buddy" Rogers and Thelma Todd were the two most important graduate students.)

15
DOUGLAS FAIRBANKS

To be a super-star in films, an image is mandatory. The image Douglas Fairbanks projected from the screen — that of the athletic daredevil hero who not only blithely overcomes but recognises no real adversary — was one that endeared him to the hearts of every boy and young man in his contemporary world.

"Doug is, perhaps, the type par excellence of the modern American — restless, dissatisfied, a little careless and fond of getting-there-quick, but cheerful, persevering, resourceful, and clean," wrote Charles Fuhr Jr. in "Pictures and Picturegoer," for August 30, 1919.

But youth has changed since the days when Fairbanks ruled as an ace star, and today the pictures he made are treasured only by young film buffs who seem to like anything as long as it's on film or by authentic historians seeking to discover the manners and mores of a time gone by.

One of the latter, Gavin Lambert, writing on Fairbanks and Valentino as "The Last Heroes" in the magazine "Sequence" (summer, 1949), had this to say of "Doug"; "In the Twenties, Fairbanks, a modern Robin Hood, astounded a great many people by re-affirming the most simple, naive qualities of the hero — gallantry, physical courage, 'going through life with a smile' — and performed with such energy and conviction that he made a considerable impression in a cynical, disillusioned period. The silent film ideally suited this gesture and made its exaggerations natural: it must, at the time, have been an act of daring effrontery, and however tiresome Fairbanks appears today he will be remembered as the only figure of his time to attempt a revival of the heroic spirit in popular terms. What was overlooked, perhaps, in the excitement of the moment, was that Fairbanks had to create an old-fashioned world to contain the antics."

The features that Fairbanks starred in for Triangle, Artcraft, and the first ones for United Artists, remain rollicking, good-humoured comedies that point up the indomitable and agreeable victories of the American hero overcoming all odds. With *The Mark of Zorro* in 1920, the pattern changes, and after the August 1921 release of *The Three Musketeers*, the new pattern is definitely set. The subsequent films are big roadshows, superbly mounted and costumed adventure tales, and with the exception of only a few, they are — when viewed today in their entirety — over-length and astonishingly slow in

319

movement. They didn't seem that long and laboured when seen in their day, but they do now — and what is more distressing, the fun is no longer existent. *The Mark of Zorro, The Black Pirate,* much of *Don Q,* and some of *The Gaucho* represent the costumed Fairbanks at his best. On the other hand, *The Three Musketeers, Robin Hood, The Thief of Bagdad,* and *The Iron Mask,* in spite of much photographic beauty (particularly in the middle two films), are museum pieces. I myself always preferred Fairbanks in his earlier vehicles, and today these still have a tongue-in-cheek bravura and zest for life that were not often captured in the later, more pretentious United Artists releases.

It is these later films that fit Gavin Lambert's comments: "A mature, not a youthful hero, Fairbanks' agility, cocksuredness and versatile strength make for a detached emotional level. One never feels him to be in danger, since he himself does not (he tricks his opponents like fools) — and the heroines are lifeless even at moments of predicament. Should the heavy lay hands on one of them when she is defenceless, Zorro or D'Artagnan is bound to leap from his horse through an open window before anything serious has happened. Admirers of Fairbanks...make much of his animal grace and spirits: Fairbanks had the exuberance of the virtuoso, but there is no poetry in his movements, agility and vigour rather than grace. *The Thief of Bagdad* showed his feelings for the exotic to be ludicrously undeveloped."

Fairbanks himself was not always the happy-go-lucky, breezy hero he portrayed on the screen. His black moods have often been remarked on by those who knew and worked with him: the eternal practical jokes wore thin, and then thinner. It has been said that he had humour, but little wit. And the audacious, daredevil mask frequently slipped and revealed the unhappy Harlequin beneath with all his human frailties plainly marked: jealousy, snobbery, resentment, and then — worst of all — fear of advancing old age, those damnable black oxen forever encroaching upon and threatening his supremacy as a hero.

There is a poignant anecdote dating from his United Artists days, when he ruefully commented that his three partners — Griffith, Pickford, and Chaplin — were geniuses, and their work would survive. "But I am not a genius," he admitted sadly. He knew even then that the day would come when he would not be accorded the respect and admiration given the Titans.

He was born Douglas Elton Ulman on May 23, 1883, in Denver, Colorado. His mother had been a Southern belle, Ella Adelaide Marsh, and his father, H. (Hezekiah) Charles Ulman, was one of the several sons of upper middle class Jewish parents. Ulman had organised and served as first president of the United States Law Association, and was titular head of a New York legal firm. One of his closest friends and a good client was wealthy John Fairbanks, owner of sugar mills and plantations around New Orleans. Fairbanks died of tuberculosis shortly after the birth of a son (John Jr.) and Mrs. Fairbanks married a second time to an Edward Wilcox, by whom she had one son (Norris E.). Too late, Ella Fairbanks learned that her new husband drank to excess, and she separated from him and asked her old friend, H. Charles Ulman, to secure a legal divorce for her.

By the time that was finalised, Ulman and Ella Fairbanks had fallen in love. They married and in the spring of 1881 they settled in Denver, where Ulman had mining interests to look after. Their first son, Robert was born in Denver

in 1882, and the following year Douglas Elton was born at their house on 61 South 14th Street.

Douglas related details of his early life to Charles Fuhr in the article quoted earlier. "I was the blackest baby in captivity. Friends of the family were all anxious to see the new baby. My mother would say:'Oh, I don't want to disturb him now — he's asleep and I'd rather not.' She hated to show such a dark baby. I never smiled until I was about two. That is, they tell me so. I learned how then and that smile has smoothed many a hard road. I can't remember much of my pre-school days. I did my first stunt when I was about three and a half years old. It had disastrous results. We were at a mining camp in Jamestown, Colorado, where father had interests. There was a barn — a big barn it seemed to me. I thought I ought to climb it. I shinned up, crawled out upon the ridgepole, and fell, striking on a rock below. I still have the scar. When I became old enough, I was sent to the Wyman and Corona public schools in Denver. They tell me I spent most of my time getting out of scrapes that I started. Old Daddy Long, the principal of Wyman school, had to walk home with me nearly every other night to carry a tale of wickedness to my parents. Mother wanted us to be real boys. We had the best of bringing up, and had to conform to all conventions, but our parents never forgot that we were just boys and we enjoyed our youthful days."

It was bright lights other than show business that first fired Doug's ambitions. "One night, at the old St. James, in Denver, we were up pretty late. Father had just sent me to bed, but somehow I wasn't sleepy. I looked out of the window and there was a tailor shop opposite, lights still burning brightly. The poor tailor had to finish up his work, I suppose. I'd like to be a tailor when I grow up, I informed my father, and then I can stay up all night if I want to. I was then five years old."

Soon after, his father left for political work in New York and by Christmas of that year (1888) his mother realised that she was deserted, left virtually penniless with three sons to raise. She saw that her three sons were baptised into her own faith, the Roman Catholic church, secured a divorce, opened a boarding-house, and placed her sons in good schools. She abandoned the name of Ulman, returning to the surname of her deceased first husband. Thus both Robert and Douglas became, like their half-brother John, a Fairbanks, and their mother was henceforth always Mrs. Ella Fairbanks.

However, Douglas's father had stayed long enough to introduce him to the drama. "Early in life father taught me the beauties of Shakespeare. I could spout Shakespeare by the yard, and it never bothered me that I was a good deal in doubt as to what it all meant." Stories told him by an older boy next door also encouraged young Douglas to re-enact them in impromptu shows with his friends for other kids to see. They were long on action, short on dialogue.

Fairbanks also used to amuse himself with daring exploits. In the Fuhr interview, he recounts how, at the age of twelve, he and Robert climbed the highest building in Denver. "We got upon the roof and there was a very tempting cornice. I had nothing else to do but to crawl out upon that cornice and see how it would feel to hang from it by my toes. Robert nearly died of fright."

On Saturday afternoons they went to the Tabor Grand Opera House:

"They played all the good old melodramas, and I enjoyed them immensely. Even when I was about ten, I would watch at the stage doors for the actors, and follow them to their hotels and try to get acquainted with them. My first theatrical engagement was at the age of twelve — my mother learned about it weeks later. I had just seen Steve Brodie in "On the Bowery." I hung around the stage door that night until Steve came out. I informed him that I could speak a piece in Italian dialect. Steve heard me, which resulted in a job. I was to be a newsboy on the Bowery and speak the piece. I did it for a whole week, and I got a great reception, too. But while it was very pleasant to go with mother on Saturday matinees, it was much better fun to climb up the fire escapes of the Broadway Theatre, to clamber over the roof trusses above the stage, and then perch atop of one of the upper tier boxes and see the show free of charge."

Douglas followed up his first stage appearance by playing Icilius in "Virginius" for the veteran touring classic actor Frederick Warde who, more to get rid of him than anything else, said that Fairbanks might look him up if he ever came to New York to continue his acting career.

It was my own good fortune to know Effie Shannon well during the Thirties, and Miss Shannon once told me of how, when she was appearing with Herbert Kelcey in Denver in "The Charity Ball," Mr. Kelcey one night came to her dressing-room after a performance and asked her to hear a young Denver boy he had just auditioned. She went out into the auditorium quietly, and there onstage was an eager youth, who promptly on cue delivered Marc Antony's funeral oration from "Julius Caesar."

"Mr. Kelcey asked me later what I thought of the boy," Miss Shannon told me. "I told him that while the young man obviously had a flair for the theatrical, he needed good coaching. I also said that I didn't really see him as an actor of classical drama, but he was certainly engaging and had an eager American personality that might shine with special brightness were he to play a juvenile role in a contemporary American play. Mr. Kelcey smiled and said that was exactly his opinion and he had suggested that the boy look him up should he come to New York when we were there. The boy, of course, was Douglas Fairbanks, then about sixteen years old."

In the spring of 1900, when Douglas Fairbanks was still not yet seventeen, his mother moved her family from Denver to New York. Young Fairbanks first looked up Frederick Warde, who was then gathering together a new touring company, and he was accepted. From September on of that year he made several appearances with Warde's company, including the Shakespearean roles of Cassio and Laertes. In later life, he would enjoy recalling a Duluth critic's comment: "Mr. Warde's supporting company was bad, but worst of all was Douglas Fairbanks as Laertes."

When the tour was disbanded, Fairbanks, recognising his lack of training, enrolled as a special student at Harvard for a few months in 1901 before he and two friends took off as hay stewards on a cattle-freighter to Liverpool, where they spent the summer on a gay-hearted, if penny-pinched, tour of England, France, and Belgium.

Returning to New York, Fairbanks worked as a clerk in a hardware store and then served nearly six months as an order clerk with the Wall Street stocks and bonds firm of De Coppett and Doremus. He resigned in a sudden panic, fearful that his superiors would discover his total ignorance of high finance.

He also knew that Herbert Kelcey and Effie Shannon were back in town and found they were casting a play. He was accepted for it, and on Febuary 24, 1902, he made his Broadway acting *début* at the old Manhattan Theatre as Glen Masters in "Her Lord and Master." That engagement lasted into the summer. He next played Philippe de la Noye in "A Rose o' Plymouth Town," in which Minnie Dupree starred and told Fairbanks that "I, as an actor, was about the nicest case of St. Vitus' dance that ever came under her notice."

In 1903 Fairbanks took over from Edward Abeles in a play, "Mrs. Jack," starring Alice Fisher, and he toured the United States with it. That summer, after a brief interval studying law, he blithely set off on the longest route to the Orient, but ran into a friend in England and stayed there a while.

Back in America, William A. Brady, attracted by his effervescent personality, gave him a bit part on Broadway in "The Pit." Fairbanks was literally outstanding, because for the first time he displayed his athletic prowess by leaping over the actors in a crowd scene and making himself noticed. Brady also noticed him anew, and had him featured in "Two Little Sailor Boys" and the only musical Fairbanks ever appeared in on stage, an operetta called "Fantana." Brady then signed him to a five-year exclusive contract, and starred him in "Frenzied Finance," in which he was able to utilise much of the knowledge and background he had come to know on Wall Street, because it was a typical comedy of the American financial world. He played the romantic juvenile in a play "Clothes," which starred Brady's wife Grace George, and the lead in a drama "As Ye Sow," before hitting the jackpot as the lead in George Broadhurst's new play, "The Man of the Hour," which ran for 479 performances on Broadway.

It was at this time that he also fell in love. The girl was Anna Beth Sully, eldest daughter of Daniel J. (Cotton King) Sully, who demanded that his prospective son-in-law should abandon the "degrading profession" of actor and work in a respectable business. Fairbanks, in spite of Brady's advice, agreed to give up his newly established stardom and Sully put him to work for a soap company. On July 11, 1907, Beth Sully became the bride of Douglas Fairbanks, and two years later — on December 9, 1909 — it was recorded that their only son, Douglas Fairbanks Jr., was born.

Sully lost his fortune in the cotton crash, however, and the soap company also went out of business. So Fairbanks returned to Broadway as the star of Rupert Hughes's "All for a Girl," which opened at the old Bijou Theatre on August 22, 1908. Several other roles followed for Brady, and then George M. Cohan approached Fairbanks, advising that he wanted to write a play to star him, to be produced by the firm of Cohan and Harris. William Brady agreed to release him, and he signed a three-year contract with the new outfit.

While waiting for Cohan to write him the promised play, Fairbanks embarked on one of his typical athletic holidays: he hiked across the island of Cuba and then made a walking tour in Yucatan. When he returned to New York, the Cohan play still wasn't completed, so Fairbanks made a vaudeville tour in a one-acter, "A Regular Business Man," and then played Chicago in "Officer 666." The Cohan play was even then unfinished and playright Lewis Waller suggested that Fairbanks star in his romantic comedy, "Hawthorne of the U.S.A." It allowed Fairbanks a wide exhibition of his athletic prowess, and became another long-running hit, so that when Cohan's "Broaday Jones" was finally ready, Fairbanks couldn't play it, and Cohan had to open in it himself.

After two more plays, Fairbanks opened on New Year's Eve of 1914 in what was to be his last theatre engagement, starring in James Forbes's "The Show Shop."

Early in 1915, Harry Aitken of Triangle Pictures came to Fairbanks with the offer of a $2,000-a-week contract to star for D. W. Griffith in Hollywood films. Although Fairbanks was not keen on the movies, the money was irresistible and he signed for three years with Triangle, arranging $500 raises every six months after the first year. In the early summer of 1915, he took the train for Los Angeles. His stage career proves that Fairbanks was no novice or pretender to acting fame. Still in his early thirties, he was an established theatrical star with a national reputation, seen as a Richard Harding Davis type of American hero, the kind of man whom every young American would like to be, the kind boys worshipped as an ideal, the kind every romantic woman dreamed of as a lover — the kind she almost never got.

That image carried into his film career. His first picture, *The Lamb,* was directed by W. Christy Cabanné; its author was D. W. Griffith, who also supervised the production. Fairbanks said this of his *début,* in typically breezy style: "*The Lamb,* they called it. I meant to be the lion — wrestled with a real one, in fact, during the picture. Also let a rattlesnake crawl over me, ju-jitsued a bunch of Yaqui Indians, and had a few fights without fake." But the Fairbanks image almost finished him: his athletic prowess dismayed and then irked set-workers, who resented Broadway actors anyway, and the make-up man deliberately did a bad job. The "monkey antics" that Fairbanks genially displayed in contrast to the thoughtful, painstaking atmosphere customary to a Griffith picture even appalled the great director himself. Fairbanks recalled: "D. W. didn't like my athletic tendencies. Or my spontaneous habit of jumping a fence or scaling a church at unexpected moments which were not in the script. Griffith told me to go into Keystone comedies."

Triangle was so named because three producers — Griffith, Thomas H. Ince, and Mack Sennett — had each signed to contribute films to a weekly release calendar of a three-hour programme. The first Triangle offering consisted of the Griffith-supervised *The Lamb,* Ince's *The Iron Strain* starring Dustin Farnum, and two from Sennett — *The Valet* with Raymond Hitchcock, Mabel Normand, and Sennett, and *A Game Old Knight* with Charles Murray and Louise Fazenda.

The films opened nationally on September 23, 1915, and *The Lamb* was received with genuine enthusiasm. Griffith was pleasantly astonished when the reviewer for a Manhattan paper commented of *The Lamb's* climax (when Fairbanks and Seena Owen, fighting off the Mexican border insurrectionists, are rescued by the the cavalry at the last moment) that the "dash of the mounted troops to his aid was reminiscent of the Ku-Klux-Klan raid in *The Birth of a Nation.*"

Fairbanks himself was flabbergasted by the good reviews; he had liked *The Lamb* no better than the Triangle executives had, and he had even begun to think that his film career might end as a one-shot and that he would be paid off.

Douglas Fairbanks with Charles Chaplin and Mary Pickford on the set of her film, POLLYANNA

He was back in Manhattan for the *première,* staying at his Algonquin Hotel residence with his wife and son, and delighted in his new fame.

He had met Mary Pickford and her husband, Owen Moore, the previous year at Elise Janis's Tarrytown home, Phillipse Manor. Miss Pickford has confessed that she did not care much for Fairbanks on a first meeting. Naturally shy and withdrawn, she was not impressed by his ever-smiling, eager-beaver personality, and thought him overly brash. But she began to change her mind when, out on a walk with a party and unable to cross a stream, she was suddenly swept up in his arms as he gallantly carried her to the other side.

After the success of *The Lamb,* Frank Case, manager of the Algonquin, hosted a dinner dance at the hotel, and it was there, when they danced together, that "America's Sweetheart" and "America's Hero" fell in love. Miss Pickford was already having domestic problems with her husband; Owen Moore was jealous of the idolatry his wife was tended, and he openly belittled her work as an actress. A dark, Irish gloom had settled upon him, and excessive drinking was already a personal problem. Fairbanks did not drink at all, except for wine with dinner; he had promised his mother, who had had her problems with men who drank, that he would never touch the stuff — and he never broke that pledge. It was an abstinence Miss Pickford admired in a man.

They met in secret and their romance blossomed. Then Fairbanks returned to Hollywood with his friend Frank Case. They hiked, rode horseback, and raced through Hollywood with Fairbanks at the wheel of his yellow Stutz bearcat. He soon started filming another Triangle feature, *Double Trouble*. "In my second picture I ran a car over a cliff, had six rounds with a 'pro' pugilist, jumped off an Atlantic liner, fought six gunmen at once and leapt off a speeding train," he later recalled.

There was even less communication between Griffith and the star. Griffith asked Harry Aitken to take "the monkey" off his back. Aitken put Frank Woods in unofficial charge of Fairbanks's career, and it was Woods who, sensing what was right for the actor, introduced him to the writing-directing team of John Emerson and Anita Loos. "There were two other people in the Triangle concern with whom 'D. W.' did not see eye to eye," Fairbanks once said. "One was Anita Loos. She was writing film scripts for him. Used to put in snappy captions — which 'D.W.' used to knock out. Anita made sub-title writing an art, and was really the originator of what we now know as 'wise-cracking.' John Emerson, actor and director, agreed with Anita. The three of us had ideas of our own to develop..."

Emerson and Loos wrote the best of the subsequent Fairbanks scenarios; Miss Loos's jaunty sub-titles gained wide approval while Emerson, along with Allan Dwan and Joseph Henabery, became one of the directors who hit it off best with Fairbanks.

In 1916, Fairbanks was planning to spend the Christmas holidays with his mother, but she died of pneumonia while he was on his way to her. It was the first great personal loss he had ever sustained; he had always adored his mother, an emotion he had not accorded the father who had deserted her and him. Stunned by the tragedy, Fairbanks could not even weep until one afternoon when he was alone with Mary Pickford. They were both deeply in love by then, and Fairbanks, like the heroes he played, was resolutely determined that all odds would be faced and overcome and that they would marry.

It has been remarked that those who idly doodle while telephoning often reveal their secret natures, and Frank Case has noted that the telephone pad in the Fairbanks suite was scribbled with repetitions of the one word — "Success, success, success" — and then "Great Success."

Triangle was suffering its first financial reverses, and it was easy for Fairbanks to secure his release. While he was in Manhattan in that last month of 1916, he set up the Douglas Fairbanks Film Corporation, with an Artcraft-Paramount release. He would be the star and would supervise writing, direction and production; his brother Robert would be production manager, in charge of all set construction; and his half-brother John would be business manager.

It was a giant step into the big time, and *In Again, Out Again,* the first release of his corporation, demonstrated as much. His new releases were to be specials that shone with a smooth gloss. In no time, he was personally worth over a million dollars.

He, Mary Pickford, and Charles Chaplin went on a Liberty Bond tour which was enormously successful, and ended in a big reception for the stars in Washington, D. C., where Fairbanks had his first close touch with top-brass society. He loved every minute of it. Admittedly touched by snobbery, he loved mingling with political bigwigs, foreign diplomats, and titled guests.

He left for New York with the intention of joining his wife and son for Christmas, but he never arrived. He checked in at a hotel and set about arranging a settlement with his wife. Over half a million dollars was brought in cash to her, and on November 30, 1918, she filed for divorce, seeking sole custody of their only son, Fairbanks Jr.

Meanwhile, Fairbanks's film career had reached a new phase. "I made a whole string of films one after the other...But I was making films for other people. So were Charlie and Mary. We were making a lot of money, but were depending on other people for the distribution of our pictures. That did not mean independence — and it was independence we wanted." At Miss Pickford's initial suggestion, she, Fairbanks, Chaplin, and D. W. Griffith met and set up a new corporation called United Artists, formed to distribute all future productions of "The Big Four." Announcemant of its incorporation and intentions was made on February 5, 1919. "The film colony thought we were mad in making such a stand for independence. The news created a sensation. Hearing that we had founded our own 'business,' the head of one prominent film company was terse. 'So,' said he, 'the lunatics have taken charge of the asylum.'"

But United Artists flourished and moved at once into top playing time. The scene was set for the next step. Miss Pickford and Owen Moore had separated. An undisclosed amount of money was reportedly settled on him, and on March 3, 1920, Mary Pickford divorced her husband in Minden, Nevada. Returning to Hollywood, she announced with annoyance and some anger that she had no intention of any immediate second marriage. On March 28, however, she and Douglas Fairbanks were married quietly, and for a few days the wedding was not made public, because their license had been obtained under their legal names of Gladys Smith and Douglas Ulman.

Then banner headlines blazed the news of the marriage. The Pickford-Fairbanks fans at once rallied to their idols' cause. Few Americans worshipped their President and his First Lady, but almost everybody acknowledged "Mary" and "Doug" as the undeclared King and Queen of America. They were received like royalty when in 1921 they sailed for a delayed honeymoon abroad. For the first time, "America's Sweetheart," who had travelled only in America, her native Canada, and briefly in Cuba, was far away from home. In Fairbanks's gregarious company, she blossomed, and in the company of her new husband, she did more for American diplomatic relations in Europe and England than the whole Washington battery of official ambassadors. Victoriously, they returned to Hollywood to resume residence in their new home, which some anonymous newsman with a flair for the apt phrase had christened "Pickfair." The name caught on, and they adopted it as theirs. During the Twenties, when the White House under Harding teemed with scandal and then under Coolidge lapsed into the dreariest of social routines, the affairs at "Pickfair" were noted as if it were the American Buckingham Palace. Lord and Lady Mountbatten, the Duchess of Sutherland, the Duke and Duchess of Alba, the King and Queen of Siam were only some of the titled

Douglas Fairbanks as Mercutio in THE TAMING OF THE SHREW

guests of Mary and Doug, and they shared the list democratically with such personages as Otto Kahn, Charles Schwab, and "Babe" Ruth.

During the Twenties also, the Pickford-Fairbanks pictures were at their peak of popularity, enjoying every critical and financial acclaim. The films they produced between 1920-27 amassed a fortune for them, even though not all those films are to be reckoned as their most endearing and endurable. When the Academy of Motion Picture Arts and Sciences was formed, Fairbanks served as its first president. In 1929, when it was obvious that the talking film was here to stay, Fairbanks added sound effects and music to *The Iron Mask* (the sequel he had made to *The Three Musketeers),* and for the first time addressed the mike for his talkie *début* in spoken prologues to the two parts of the picture. His stage experience backed him well, and his voice registered pleasantly with a dash and authority becoming to his screen personality.

Mary Pickford successfully made her talking *début* in *Coquette,* for which she received the Academy's coveted Oscar for best performance by an actress; she and her husband thereupon announced that they would film Shakespeare's *The Taming of the Shrew* as their first feature together. It turned out to be the only one they made as a co-starring venture. She was not comfortable working with her husband, and he did nothing to put her at ease. When she, unhappy with a scene, requested a re-take, he often refused it. He had become wilful, sulky, and moody.

Booth Tarkington has said of him: "Fairbanks is a faun who has been to Sunday school. He has a pagan body which yields instantly to any heathen or gypsy impulse...but he has a mind reliably furnished with a full set of morals and proprieties. He would be a sympathetic companion for anybody's aunt. I don't know his age; I think he hasn't any."

By 1930, however, Fairbanks was well aware of his age. At forty-seven, he was still blessed with a slim, trim body, but the face was strained, the eyes restless and worried, the hairline receding. He departed in December 1930, with director Victor Fleming, sailing from San Francisco on a world tour.

His attitude toward his son had been strange but explicable. Deserted by his own father when he was but five, he denied himself any personal paternal emotion. When his son made a screen *début* in the Twenties as a teen-aged actor, Fairbanks scowled and declared with annoyance that there was only *one* Fairbanks. He confessed unhappily to Frank Case: "You know, I have no more paternal feeling than a tiger in the jungle for his cub." A revealing statement, in a sense, because of the chosen figure of speech: a tiger's feeling for its cub is actually fiercely protective. Fairbanks ignored both the seventeenth and eighteenth birthdays of his son and gave him no Christmas present for those years. Yet on his nineteenth birthday, young Douglas received a beautiful and expensive automobile from his father, the first he had ever owned. Fairbanks attended a stage production of "Young Woodley," in which his son starred on the Pacific Coast, and for the first time glowed in reflected glory. Father and son became close, and then closer, friends.

When Fairbanks returned to Hollywood from his world tour, he co-starred with Bebe Daniels in an Edmund Goulding feature, *Reaching for the Moon,* with story and music by Goulding and Irving Berlin. It should have been gay and charming, because Fairbanks and Miss Daniels were an amiable, athletic pair of players. When it was released early in 1931, however, almost all the score was eliminated because musical films were temporaily out of vogue. What audiences saw was a smart but brief and rather unfunny musical comedy book.

Mary Pickford, who was having her own professional problem in trying to find the right vehicle for herself, was disturbed by her husband's vagaries. His temper was short, his *mien* scowling. He had already destroyed the confidence she had gained with *Coquette* by his attitude during the making of *The Shrew,* and now his sullen moods of indifference and fears for his future continued to distress her as she tried to revive his spirits.

Her words had just the kind of cheerful optimism he had once sponsored. He long ago had authored a series of slim books filled with just such Rotarian aphorisms as would have done credit to Edgar Guest or Mary Baker Eddy. "Laugh and Live," "Making Life Worthwhile," and "Youth Points the Way" are titles of three, and they are highlighted with such optimistically titled chapters as "Taking Stock of Ourselves," "Wedlock in Time," and "Whistle and Hoe — Sing as We Go." He thought of them now glumly as "Words, words, words."

Late in 1931, *Around the World in 80 Minutes,* the feature comedy travelogue Victor Fleming and he had filmed during their cruise, was released. Scarely three months later, Edward Sutherland and Fairbanks sailed for Tahiti to make *Mr. Robinson Crusoe,* a similar and even more enjoyable film.

Fairbanks now found little pleasure playing host at "Pickfair;" he was more often away than at home. In the winter of 1933, he left for an extended visit to England and Europe. Brash and cheerful in his public farewells, he privately told one of his favourite directors, Raoul Walsh, that there was nothing as humiliating as being a has-been.

He started making a film in England, *The Private Life of Don Juan.* Rumours of amorous indiscretions off-set drifted back to his home country, and the name most frequently associated with his was that of Lady Sylvia Ashley, an ex-chorus girl who had wed into nobility, but who, during her marriages with Fairbanks and then with Clark Gable, was always known to Hollywood as "that Ashley woman."

Fairbanks returned to Hollywood, filled with remorse, yet an attempt to effect a reconciliation by telegram with Mary Pickford went astray. His telegram never reached her, and Fairbanks equated her silence with a pretence of indifference, sailed back to Europe and made Lady Sylvia a marriage proposal.

Miss Pickford filed suit for divorce, receiving her final papers on January 10, 1936. On March 7 of that year, Fairbanks and the former Lady Ashley were married in Paris, and a week later he made a public statement announcing that he had retired from acting.

He was like a tired man who has been everywhere, met everybody, seen and done everythhg. Only one thing still gave him any real appetite: film production. Late in 1938, he announced from London the formation of his own producing company, Fairbanks-International.

He remained in London until the oncoming Second World War led to his return to Hollywood. There he took a beach house, from where in the autumn of 1939 he announced his new company's first production — *The Californian,* to star his son, Douglas Fairbanks Jr.

But the heart of Fairbanks was too tired. By December, he had been forced to take to his bed, and a male nurse attended him. On the evening of December 11, 1939, he asked his nurse to open the window and let him hear the sea. Somewhat later, the nurse entered the room to find his patient awake and unusually quiet, insisting that he had never felt better.

At 12:45, Douglas Fairbanks was dead, aged fifty-six.

Shortly afterwards, further along the beach, Norma Shearer, widow of Irving Thalberg, received a telephone call. She was entertaining with a midnight supper. She blanched slightly on hearing the news, then spoke quietly to her butler, who had just as quietly removed the place setting at the table for the Fairbankes, who had been invited guests. Not until hours later did Miss Shearer confide to Hedda Hopper that she had received word from a household servant of Douglas Fairbanks's death. She had not announced it to her guests, not wanting to cast a pall over the evening's entertainment.

Douglas Fairbanks Jr. was shooting night scenes on the film *Safari,* the night his father died. On set he received word of his father's weakening condition and with his wife raced to the beach home. His father had died by the time he arrived.

Frank Nugent, then motion picture editor for the New York "Times," wrote in the December 17, 1939 issue a moving eulogy: "Doug Fairbanks was make-believe at its best, a game we youngsters never tired of playing, a game — we are convinced — our fathers secretly shared. He was a complete fantasy, not like Disney's which has an overlayer of whimsy and sophistication, but unashamed and joyous. Balustrades were made to be vaulted, draperies to be a giant slide, chandeliers to swing from, citadels to be scaled.There wasn't a small boy in the neighborhood who did not, in a Fairbanks picture, see himself triumphing over the local bully, winning the soft-eyed adoration of whatever ten-year-old blonde he had been courting, and wreaking vengeance on the teacher who made him stand in the corner that afternoon."

DOUGLAS FAIRBANKS FILMOGRAPHY

THE LAMB (1915). Mexican border romantic melodrama; as Gerald, the lamb. *Dir:* W. Christy Cabanné (*Sup:* D. W. Griffith). *Sc:* Cabanné (from the story, "The Man and the Test," by D. W. Griffith). *With* Seena Owen, Lillian Langdon, Monroe Salisbury, Kate Toncray, Alfred Paget. *Prod:* Triangle/Fine Arts. 5 reels.

DOUBLE TROUBLE (1915). Romantic comedy about a dual personality; as Mr. Amidon, a banker, and as Mr. Brassfield, a man who doesn't need money. *Dir:* W. Christy Cabanné (*Sup:* D. W. Griffith). *Sc:* D. W. Griffith (adaptation of a novel by Herbert Quick). *With* Margery Wilson, Tom Kennedy, Gladys Brockwell, Olga Grey, Kate Toncray, Monroe Salisbury. *Prod:* Triangle/Fine Arts. 5 reels.

HIS PICTURE IN THE PAPERS (1916). Satire on American publicity and those who crave it; as Pete Prindle, a go-getter. *Dir:* John Emerson (*Sup:* D. W. Griffith). *Sc:* John Emerson and Anita Loos. *With* Loretta Blake, Clarence Handysides, *Prod:* Triangle/Fine Arts. 5 reels.

THE HABIT OF HAPPINESS (1916). Comedy; as "Sunny" Wiggins, a do-gooder. *Dir:* Allan Dwan. (*Sup:* D. W. Griffith). *Sc:* Shannon Fife, Douglas Fairbanks and Allan Dwan (from an idea by D. W. Griffith). *With* Dorothy West, George Fawcett, George Backens, William Jefferson, Margery Wilson. *Prod:* Triangle/Fine Arts. 5 reels.

THE GOOD BAD MAN (1916). Romance about a Robin Hood of the Old West; as "Pas-

sin' Thru," an outlaw. *Dir:* Allan Dwan. (*Sup:* D. W. Griffith) *Sc:* Douglas Fairbanks. *With* Bessie Love, Sam de Grasse, Joe Singleton, Mary Alden. *Prod:* Triangle/Mutual. 5 reels.

REGGIE MIXES IN (AKA, GB, *Facing the Music*) (1916). Romantic comedy; as Reginald Morton (AKA Van Deusen). *Dir:* W. Christy Cabanné (*Sup:* D. W. Griffith). *Sc:* Roy Somerville. *With* Bessie Love, Frank Bennett, Joseph Singleton, W. E. Lowery, Alma Rubens. *Prod:* Triangle/Fine Arts. 5 reels.

THE MYSTERY OF THE LEAPING FISH (1916). Slapstick farce; as Coke Ennyday, who is a human submarine and outwits Japanese opium-runners. *Dir:* John Emerson (*Sup:* D. W. Griffith). *Sc:* ("The Triangle," weekly exhibitors' magazine, lists Granville Warwick, which is a pseudonym for D. W. Griffith; another creditable source lists Tod Browning as writer.) *With* Bessie Love, A. D. Sears, Alma Rubens, Charles Stevens, George Hall, Tom Wilson. *Prod:* Triangle/Keystone. 2 reels.

FLIRTING WITH FATE (1916). Romantic comedy; as "Augy" Holliday. *Dir:* W. Christy Cabanné (*Sup:* D. W. Griffith). *Sc:* W. Christy Cabanné (from a story by Robert M. Baker). *With* Jewel Carmen, Howard Gaye, Lillian Langdon, W. E. Lawrence. *Prod:* Triangle / Fine Arts. 5 reels.

THE HALF BREED (1916). Love story of a half-breed American Indian in love with a white girl; as Lo Dorman, the half-breed. *Dir:* Allan Dwan (*Sup:* D. W. Griffith). *Sc:* Anita Loos (from a story, "In the Carquinez

Woods," by Bret Harte). *With* Alma Rubens, Jewel Carmen, Sam de Grasse, Jack Brownlee, Tom Wilkerson, André Beranger. *Prod:* Triangle/Fine Arts. (An abridged version, reissued years later, was called *Flames of '49*, and left the half-breed with Jewel Carmen rather than Alma Rubens.) *Prod:* Triangle/Fine Arts. 5 reels.

MANHATTAN MADNESS (AKA, GB, *Mysteries of New York*) (1916). Romantic comedy; as Steve O'Dare, a bored Westerner who comes East. *Dir:* Allan Dwan (*Sup:* D. W. Griffith). *Sc:* E. V. Durling, with Anita Loos and Frank M. Dazey. *With* Jewel Carmen, George (André) Beranger, Warner P. Richmond, Albert MacQuarrie, Norman Kerry, Ruth Darling, John Richmond, Eugenie Armonde, Macey Harlan. *Prod:* Triangle/Fine Arts. 5 reels.

AMERICAN ARISTOCRACY (1916). Romantic comedy; as Cassius Lee, a Southerner who outwits munitions smugglers. *Dir:* Lloyd Ingraham (*Sup:* D. W. Griffith). *Sc:* Anita Loos. *With* Jewel Carmen, Albert Parker, Lillian Langdon, Douglas Fairbanks Jr., Charles Stevens, Arthur Ortega. *Prod:* Triangle/Fine Arts.

THE MATRIMANIAC (1916). Romantic comedy about the difficulty of getting married; as Jimmy Conroy. *Dir:* Paul Powell (*Sup:* D. W. Griffith). *Sc:* Anita Loos (from a story by Octavus Roy Cohen and J. V. Giesey). *With* Constance Talmadge, Winifred Westover, Fred Warren, William Higby, Clyde Hopkins, Monte Blue, Charles Stevens, Mildred Harris, Carmel Myers. *Prod:* Triangle/Fine Arts. 5 reels.

THE AMERICANO (1916). Romantic adventure, set in a mythical kingdom; as Blaze Derringer, "The Americano." *Dir:* John Emerson (*Sup:* D. W. Griffith). *Sc:* Anita Loos and John Emerson (from a novel, "Blaze Derringer," by Eugene P. Lyle Jr.). *With* Alma Rubens, Spottiswoode Aitken, Lillian Langdon, Carl Stockdale, Tom Wilson. *Prod:* Triangle/Fine Arts. 5 reels.

IN AGAIN, OUT AGAIN (1917). Comedy of preparedness vs. pacifism; as Teddy Rotherford, a pacifist who is always prepared. *Dir:* John Emerson. *Sc:* Anita Loos. *With* Arline Pretty, Bull Montana, Albert Parker. *Prod:* F Fairbanks/Artcraft-Paramount. 5 reels.

WILD AND WOOLLY (1917). A romantic comedy of the real vs. the imaginary Wild West; as Jeff Hillington. *Dir:* John Emerson. *Sc:* Anita Loos (from a story by Horace B. Carpenter). *With* Eileen Percy, Sam de Grasse, Joseph Singleton, Charles Stevens, Monte Blue, Tom Wilson, Bull Montana, Adolphe Menjou. *Prod:* Fairbanks / Artcraft-Paramount. 5 reels.

DOWN TO EARTH (1917). Romantic comedy of the trials and tribulations of hypochondria; as Bill Gaynor. *Dir:* John Emerson. *Sc:* Anita Loos (from a story by Douglas Fairbanks). *With* Eileen Percy, Gustav von Seyffertitz, Charles Gerrard, Bull Montana. *Prod:* Fairbanks/Artcraft-Paramount. 5 reels.

THE MAN FROM PAINTED POST (1917). Romantic comedy melodrama about the Far West; as Fancy Jim Sherwood. *Dir:* Joseph Henabery. *Sc:* Douglas Fairbanks (from a story by Jackson Gregory). *With* Eileen Percy, Frank Campeau, Herbert Standing, Monte Blue. *Prod:* Fairbanks/Artcraft-Paramount. 5 reels.

REACHING FOR THE MOON (1917). Romantic fantasy-comedy; as Alexis Caesar Napoleon Brown, who discovers he's really of royal blood. *Dir:* John Emerson. *Sc:* Anita Loos and John Emerson. *With* Eileen Percy, Eugene Ormonde, Richard Cummings, Frank Campeau, Bull Montana, Charles Stevens, Erich von Stroheim, Millard Webb. *Prod:* Fairbanks/Artcraft-Paramount. 5 reels.

A MODERN MUSKETEER (1918). Romantic fantasy-comedy, largely set in Arizona's Grand Canyon; as Ned Thacker, who dreams of being D'Artagnan. *Dir:/Sc:* Allan Dwan (from a story, "D'Artagnan of Kansas," by F. R. Lyle Jr.). *With* Marjorie Daw, Kathleen Kirkham, Tully Marshall, Frank Campeau, ZaSu Pitts. *Prod:* Fairbanks / Artcraft-Paramount. 5 reels.

HEADIN' SOUTH (1918). Romantic comedy about the Far West; As "Headin' South," an outlaw who is really a member of the Canadian Mounted Police. *Dir:* Arthur Rosson (*Sup:* Allan Dwan). *Sc:* Allan Dwan. *With* Katherine MacDonald, Frank Campeau, Jack Holt, Hoot Gibson, Art Acord. Fairbanks / Artcraft-Paramount. 5 reels.

MR. FIX-IT (1918). Romantic comedy of Manhattan; as the young man known as "Mr. Fix-It," who nearly messes up his own life. *Dir:/Sc:* Allan Dwan and Joseph Henabery (from a story suggested by Ernest Butterworth). *With* Wanda Hawley, Marjorie Daw, Katherine MacDonald, Frank Campeau, Jack Pickford, Fred Mace, Pauline Curley. *Prod:* Fairbanks/Artcraft-Paramount. 5 reels.

SAY! YOUNG FELLOW (1918). Romantic comedy; as "Young Fellow," a Manhattan newspaper reporter who is sent to a small town. *Dir:/Sc:* Joseph Henabery. *With* Marjorie Daw, Frank Campeau, Edythe Chapman, James Neill. *Prod:* Fairbanks / Artcraft-Paramount. 5 reels.

BOUND IN MOROCCO (1918). Romantic action comedy of American tourists in Morocco; as "The Boy." *Dir./Sc:* Allan Dwan. *With* Pauline Curley, Edythe Chapman, Frank Campeau, Tully Marshall. *Prod:* Fairbanks /Artcraft-Paramount. 64m.

HE COMES UP SMILING (1918). Romantic comedy about a young man who finds happiness when he becomes a hobo; as Jerry Martin ("The Watermelon"). *Dir:* Allan Dwan. *Sc:* Frances Marion (from a novel by Charles Sherman and the play dramatised therefrom by Byron Ongley and Emil Mytray, in which Fairbanks had starred on Broadway). *With* Marjorie Daw, Herbert Standing, Bull Montana, Albert MacQuarrie, Frank Campeau. Jay Dwiggins, Kathleen Kirkham. *Prod:* Fairbanks/Artcraft-Paramount. 5 reels.

ARIZONA (1918). Romantic drama of the early West; as Lt. Danton, of an Arizona outpost. *Dir./Sc:* Douglas Fairbanks and Albert Parker (from the play by Augustus Thomas, adapted by Allan Dwan). *With* Marjorie Daw, Marguerite de la Motte, Theodore Roberts, Kate Price, Frank Campeau, Raymond Hatton, Kathleen Kirkham. (Some sources list Allan Dwan as writer and Albert Parker as director, for this picture). *Prod:* Fairbanks/Artcraft-Paramount. 5 reels. (Remade as a talkie, 1930, by Columbia.)

THE KNICKERBOCKER BUCKAROO (1919). Romantic comedy of a New Yorker in the Southwest; as Teddy Drake. *Dir:* Albert Parker. *Sc:* Douglas Fairbanks. *With* Marjorie Daw, William Wellman, Edythe Chapman, Frank Campeau, Albert MacQuarrie. *Prod:* Fairbanks/Artcraft-Paramount. 5 reels.

HIS MAJESTY, THE AMERICAN (AKA, GB, *One of the Blood*) (1919). Romantic comedy set in Manhattan, Mexico, and Europe; as William Brooks, an American. *Dir:* Joseph Henabery. *Sc:* Henabery and Elton Banks (Douglas Fairbanks). *With* Marjorie Daw, Lillian Langdon, Frank Campeau. *Prod:* Fairbanks/United Artists (the initial UA release). 8 reels.

WHEN THE CLOUDS ROLL BY (1919). Action romance, climaxed by a big flood; as Daniel Boone Brown. *Dir:* Victor Fleming. *Sc:* Douglas Fairbanks, Lewis Weadon, Tom J. Geraghty. *With* Kathleen Clifford, Frank Campeau, Ralph Lewis, Daisy Robinson, Bull Montana, Herbert Grimwood, Albert MacQuarrie. *Prod:* Fairbanks/United Artists. 6 reels.

THE MOLLYCODDLE (1920). Romantic comedy of Monte Carlo and Arizona; as Richard Marshall, the darling of Europe who becomes the audacious daredevil of Arizona. *Dir:* Victor Fleming. *Sc:* Tom J. Geraghty and Douglas Fairbanks (from a story by Harold McGrath). *With* Ruth Rennick, Betty Boulton, Wallace Beery, George Stewart, Albert Mac-Quarrie, Charles Stevens. *Prod:* Fairbanks / United Artists. 6 reels.

THE MARK OF ZORRO (1920). Romantic comedy of Old California; in a dual role: as Señor Zorro and Don Diego Vega. *Dir:* Fred Niblo. *Sc:* Elton Thomas [Douglas Fairbanks] (from a novel, "The Curse of Capistrano," by Johnston McCulley. *With* Marguerite de la Motte, Noah Beery, Charles Hill Mailes, Claire McDowell, Robert McKim, George Periolat. (Various re-makes, the most important being with Tyrone Power at 20th Century-Fox.) Prod: Fairbanks/United Artists. 7 reels.

THE NUT (1921). Romantic farce set in New York's Greenwich Village; as Charlie Jackson. *Dir:* Ted Reed. *Sc:* Elton Thomas [Douglas Fairbanks], with Lotta Wood and William Parker. (from a story by Kenneth Davenport). *With* Marguerite de la Motte, Barbara La Marr, Charles Chaplin (guest appearance as himself). William Lowery, Gerald Pring, Morris Hughes, Charles Stevens, Frank Campeau. *Prod:* Fairbanks/United Artists. 6 reels.

THE THREE MUSKETEERS (1921). Romantic adventure of Old France; as D'Artagnan. *Dir:* Fred Niblo. *Sc:* Edward Knoblock, Kenneth Davenport, and Elton Thomas [Douglas Fairbanks] (script editor: Lotta Woods) (from the novel by Alexandre Dumas). *With* Marguerite de la Motte, Barbara La Marr, Adolphe Menjou, Leon Barry, George Seigmann, Eugene Pallette, Mary MacLaren, Nigel de Brulier, Lon Poff, Boyd Irwin, Thomas Holding, Sidney Franklin, Charles Belcher, Charles Stevens, Walt Whitman. *Prod:* Fairbanks/United Artists. 10 reels. (Triangle presented one of the best *Three Musketeers* first with an all-star cast; and there have been many re-makes, the best-known being that by M-G-M, with Gene Kelly as D'Artagnan; France has produced several, including the ambitious English-speaking version in 1973, by Richard Lester, with Michael York as D'Artagnan, and Oliver Reed, Richard Chamberlain, Frank Finlay, Faye Dunaway, Christopher Lee, Geraldine Chaplin, and Charlton Heston in the cast.)

ROBIN HOOD (1922). Swashbucking romance of Old England; as The Earl of Huntingdon, afterwards Robin Hood. *Dir:* Allan Dwan. *Sc:* Elton Thomas [Douglas Fairbanks], Edward Knoblock, Kenneth Davenport, (script editor: Lotta Woods). *With* Enid Bennett, Wallace Beery, Sam de Grasse, Willard Louis, Alan Hale, Paul Dickey, William Lowery, Lloyd Talman, Kay Coulson, Billie Bennett, Merrill McCormick, Wilson Benge, Maine Geary. *Prod:* Fairbanks/United Artists. 12 reels. (There have been many movie versions, before and after the Fairbanks treatment, the most memorable being the one at Warner Bros., in Technicolor, with Errol Flynn and Olivia de Havilland.)

THE THIEF OF BAGDAD (1924). Arabian Nights romantic fantasy; as "The Thief of Bagdad." *Dir:* Raoul Walsh. *Sc:* Elton Thomas [Douglas Fairbanks] (script editor: Lotta Woods). *With* Julanne Johnston, Anna May Wong, Snitz Edwards, Charles Belcher, Sojin, Brandon Hurst. *Prod:* Fairbanks / United Artists. 140m. (Re-made as a talkie in Technicolor by Alexander Korda.)

DON Q, SON OF ZORRO (1925). Adventure romance of Old California, a sequel to *The Mark of Zorro;* in a dual role: as Don Cesar de Vega and as Zorro, his father. *Dir:* Donald Crisp. *Sc:* Jack Cunningham and Lotta Woods (from the novel, *Don Q's Love Story,* by K. and Esketh Prichard). *With* Mary Astor, Jack McDonald, Donald Crisp, Warner Oland, Jean Hersholt, Lottie Pickford Forrest, Albert MacQuarrie, Stella De Lanti, Charles Stevens, Martha Franklin, Ray Coulson, Enrique Acosta, Tote Du Crow. *Prod:* Fairbanks / United Artist. 11,000 ft.

THE BLACK PIRATE (1926). Romantic melodrama of buried treasure and piracy on the high seas; as "The Black Pirate". *Dir:* Albert Parker. *Sc:* Jack Cunningham (from a story by Elton Thomas [Douglas Fairbanks]. Script editor: Lotta Woods. (Technicolor). *With* Billie Dove, Donald Crisp, Sam de Grasse, Tempe Piggott, Anders Randolph, Charles Stevens, John Wallace, Fred Belcher, Charles Belcher, E. J. Ratcliffe. *Prod:* Fairbanks/United Artists. 88m.

THE GAUCHO (1927). Romantic drama of South America; as "The Gaucho." *Dir:* F.

Douglas Fairbanks as Mercutio in THE TAMING OF THE SHREW

Richards Jones. *Sc:* Elton Thomas [Douglas Fairbanks] and Lotta Woods (from a story by Fairbanks). (One sequence in Technicolor). *With* Lupe Velez, Eve Southern, Gustav von Seyffertitz, Michael Vavitch, Nigel de Brulier, Mary Pickford (in a special cameo performance as "The Virgin"). *Prod:* Fairbanks/United Artists 102m.

THE IRON MASK (1929). Romantic costume melodrama of Old France, a sequel to *The Three Musketeers*. *Dir:* Allan Dwan. *Sc:* Elton Thomas [Douglas Fairbanks] with Lotta Woods and Jack Cunningham, (from "The Three Musketeers" and "The Iron Mask", by Alexandre Dumas, and the Memoirs of D'Artagnan, Richelieu, and de Rochefort). Sound: Western Electric, on discs (prologue to both parts spoken by Douglas Fairbanks). *With* Marguerite de la Motte, Stanley Sandford, Leon Barry, Gino Corrado, Dorothy Revier, Belle Bennett, William Bakewell (in a dual role), Nigel de Brulier, Rolfe Sedan, Vera Lewis, Ulrich Haupt, Lon Poff, Charles Stevens, Henry Otto, Gordon Thorpe. *Prod:* Fairbanks/United Arists. 95m.

THE TAMING OF THE SHREW (1929). Classic Shakepearean comedy; as Petruchio. *Dir:* Sam Taylor. *Sc:* (play by William Shakespeare, with additional dialogue by Sam Taylor). *With* Mary Pickford, Edwin Maxwell, Joseph Cawthorn, Clyde Cook, Dorothy Jordan, Geoffrey Wardwell. *Prod:* Fairbanks / United Artists. 65m. (Re-made by Zeffirelli in Technicolor, with Richard Burton and Elizabeth Taylor.)

REACHING FOR THE MOON (1931). Modern romantic comedy, with music; as Larry Dacy. *Dir./Sc:* Edmund Goulding (from a story and with music by Irving Berlin; additional dialogue by Elsie Janis). *With* Bebe Daniels, Edward Everett Horton, June MacCloy, Bing Crosby, Claude Allister, Jack Mulhall, Helen Jerome Eddy, Larry Steers, Dennis O'Keefe, Bill Elliot. *Prod:* United Artists. 9 reels. (Compare listing in Bebe Daniels filmography).

AROUND THE WORLD IN 80 MINUTES (1931). Modern comedy travelogue; as himself. *Dir:* Victor Fleming and Douglas Fairbanks. *Sc:* Douglas Fairbanks (with dialogue by Robert E. Sherwood). *With* Victor Fleming and the crew as themselves and various celebrities in foreign lands also as themselves. *Prod:* Fairbanks/United Artists. 80m.

MR. ROBINSON CRUSOE (1932). Romantic comedy melodrama; as Steve Drexel. *Dir:* Edward Sutherland. *Sc:* Tom J. Geraghty (with story by Elton Thomas [Douglas Fairbanks]. *With* Maria Alba, William Farnum, Earle Browne. *Prod:* Fairbanks/United Artists. 72m.

THE PRIVATE LIFE OF DON JUAN (1934). Costume drama of a man who falls in love with his own wife; as Don Juan. *Dir:* Alexander Korda. *Sc:* Frederick Lonsdale, Lajos Biro. *With* Merle Oberon, Benita Hume, Binnie Barnes, Heather Thatcher, Melville Cooper, Owen Nares, Gibson Gowland. *Prod:* London Films. 80m. (Shot in London).

ADDENDA

Fairbanks is supposed to have played a bit as an extra in *Intolerance* (1916), as did almost all the other Triangle players of the period — Sir Herbert Beerbohm Tree, DeWolf Hopper, etc. He would only have done it as a gag. As many times as I've seen the film, I've never been able to identify him; if he is in it, he's probably one of the warriors in armour and behind a beard, or he's one of the real mob up on a platform at the base of the elephants (there is publicity on the pleasure he took in riding up there in the elevator).

During the first World War, Fairbanks (like almost all film stars of the era) made short subject films for every Liberty Loan issue, as well as going on personal bond-selling tours, which the newsreel cameras photographed extensively. A still has appeared in numerous anthologies (including Daniel Blum's "Pictorial History of the Silent Screen," p. 158) for one such Liberty Loan issue film supposedly called *War Relief,* showing Fairbanks, Mary Pickford, William S. Hart, Theodore Roberts and Julian Eltinge; it's the only still that ever shows up, and I sometimes wonder if the film itself is non-existent and it is just a propaganda still. Fairbanks made a short for the 4th Liberty Loan called *Fire the Kaiser* just before he made *Arizona,* and at the same time he made one for the Canadian 5th Victory Loan. The only one of these shorts for which credits are known at this date (via the Copyright Catalogue) is:

SIC 'EM SAM (1918). *Dir:* Albert Parker. *Sc:* (story by Tom Reed). *With* Fairbanks and G. Butler Clonebaugh (Gustav von Seyffertitz). Copyrighted September 14. These shorts were made at the Lasky studio on Vine Street in Hollywood, and released to U.S. theatres across the nation as an "added attraction."

Footage of Fairbanks, with Mary Pickford, Charlie Chaplin, and Teddy Rosevelt selling Liberty Bonds, with Jack Dempsey and Chaplin entertaining the troops, and concerning the formation of United Artists, appears in Vernon Becker's compilation about Chaplin, *The Funniest Man in the* World (1967).

Fairbanks appears as himself as the camera pans around a table in the M-G-M commissary, and he is one of a number of stars seen in King Vidor's film with Marion Davies, *Show People* (1928).

In 1954 a new version of *The Iron Mask* was released with Douglas Fairbanks Jr. speaking a narration especially written by Richard Llewellyn replacing the original titles, and with a new music score by Allan Gray, recorded by the London Philharmonic Orchestra.

In 1966 a revised version of *The Taming of The Shrew* was re-issued for wide-screen, using Todd-AO sound, supervised by Matty Kemp. Released with it was a documentary:

BIRTH OF A LEGEND (1966). 27-minute account of the Fairbanks-Pickford careers, also with D. W. Griffith and Charlie Chaplin. *Dir./Prod:* Matty Kemp. *Sc:* Leslie Gargan (story and research by Matty Kemp.) Narration: Paul Frees. Release: Cinema Classics.

Fairbanks's work has also been featured in several screen documentaries. One such was Robert Youngson's *Day of Thrills and Laughter* (1961), which included highlights from *Wild and Woolly* (1917).

NOTES ON FILMOGRAPHIES

Before 1915, directorial, writing, and acting credits were not always listed as a matter of form or of contemporary interest. As much information as is now available from the film libraries at the Academy of Motion Picture Arts and Sciences and the British Film Institute is listed in the following filmographies relative to the fifteen personality stories which precede. With the release of D. W. Griffith's *The Birth of a Nation* in 1915, credits were listed on programmes, in reviews and publicity releases, and on the film itself. By 1916, audiences *wanted* to know the credits, and they were usually given them. The early features, it must be remembered, were only one or two reels in length, and occasionally three reels. By 1916, the standard length for a programme feature was five or six reels, and special exploitation features were double that and more. Titles are listed in order of American release.

The form for each entry is as follows: picture's title is in CAPS; if there is a second title, that is given in parentheses as AKA; if the title has been changed for British release, the new title is given, wherever possible, after AKA, GB. The date that follows in parentheses indicates the year when the picture was first released in the United States. A brief description of the type or *genre* of the picture follows; and after a semi-colon, the name of the character the actor plays is given, or a description of the part noted. After *Dir:*, the director's name appears; and after *Sc:*, the scenarist or screenplay writer's name or names is noted, followed by, in parentheses, the acknowledged basis for the story. If none is so indicated, it is presumed that the scenario or screenplay is either an original one, or the derivative basis is unknown. The names following are those of the leading actors in the cast; these are not complete cast lists, but they credit the leading players, at least. Wherever possible, previous and subsequent filmings of the property are then noted. The releasing company's name then appears and, after it, the running time of the picture — indicated either numerically in footage, or number of reels, or minutes — however listed at the time of original release in America.

In the early years of the silents, many players did not play a character to whom an actual name had been given. If a name was not indicated on the subtitles, the character was simply noted, as in the Griffith films, as The Girl, The Blonde, The Boy, or by some pet name as Brown Eyes, The Dear One, or The Princess Beloved. In the early Wallace Reid films, the characters he played were simply named "Wallace," or "Wally", or "Reid." The image was established as the actor's own, and the player merely fitted his own personality to the action — and very often the stories did not much vary.

A number of supporting players changed the spelling of their names for one reason or another; an attempt has been made here to standardise the spelling (thus, it is consistently "W. Chrystie Miller" and not "Walter C. Miller," as he was sometimes also listed; "Montagu" and not "Montague Love" as he became toward the end of his career; "Anders Randolph," not "Randolf," as he likewise was listed toward the end of his acting days). This is not limited to actors, for actresses are even more erratic (witness "Jeanie Macpherson," whose name was spelled nearly a dozen different ways until she became established as writer for Cecil B. DeMille, or "Paulette Du Val," or "Claire Du Brey," whose names suffered every variant possible in spelling).

It has not always been possible to ascertain certain credits for every picture from acceptable source material. This is especially true in the early silent era, when there are sometimes no acknowledgements for directorial, writing, or supporting player credit, and often the running time or footage of a feature at the time of its original release is not traceable from accepted sources. In these cases, listing in these categories is, regrettably, left blank.

Younger movie enthusiasts must be warned that certain actors of the silent era possessed the same names as latter-day actors do. They are not the same person. Robert Walker, Robert Cummings, William Holden, and James Mason, for instance, were all well-established character actors of their time, and have no relation to the contemporary players bearing those names. Nor is the actor George Stevens of the silent era the same as the George Stevens, director, of today. There were also two William Boyds of the period; the younger had a long reign in talkies, after previously establishing himself as a star, in the "Hopalong Cassidy" Western series; the other William Boyd came from the theatre, and, to avoid confusion, was often billed as William (Stage) Boyd. And, of course, the Mary Martin of the silent film era is not the same as the stage and screen star of today.

INDEX